COMPILATION OF SELECTED

UNITED STATES COAST GUARD AND

MARITIME TRANSPORTATION RELATED

LAWS

VOLUME 2

TITLE 46 UNITED STATES CODE — SHIPPING

SUBTITLES II THROUGH VIII

As amended through Public Law 118-233, enacted January 4, 2025; except for

Public Law 118-159.

Prepared By M. TWINCHEK

2025

Forward

This Compilation of Selected United States Coast Guard Laws is a resource for those interested in U.S. laws governing the Coast Guard. This compilation includes laws governing United States Coast Guard and its establishment; the Coast Guard Academy; water pollution; lifesaving; ports and waterways; merchant marines; and other aspects of the United States Coast Guard.

The materials included comes from publicly available, open source information, prepared for the public by the Office of the Legislative Counsel of the U.S. House of Representatives and the Office of the Law Revision Counsel.

Items listed as a Statute Compilation do not appear in the U.S. Code or that have been classified to a title of the U.S. Code that has not been enacted into positive law. Each Statute Compilation incorporates the amendments made to the underlying statute since it was originally enacted and are current as of the date noted.

This compilation is not an official document and should not be cited as evidence of any law. The official version of Federal law is found in the United States Statutes at Large and in the U.S. Code, the legal effect of which is established in sections 112 and 204, respectively, of title 1, United States Code.

A special thanks is extended to the Office of Law Revision Counsel and the House Office of the Legislative Counsel for providing the U.S. Code and statute compilations; and to the Government Publications Office for hosting and making these available for use to the public. An additional thank you is offered to the staff of the House and Senate Committees who were gracious in responding to inquiries and providing background information on the legislation included.

Questions and comments may be directed to:
M. Twinchek
Email: mtwinchek@outlook.com

Contents

SELECTED PROVISIONS OF

TITLE 46 U.S.C. — SHIPPING

CURRENT THROUGH PUBLIC LAW 118-233, EXCEPT FOR
PUBLIC LAW 118-159

SUBTITLE III
MARITIME LIABILITY

Subtitle III—Maritime Liability

CHAPTER 301—GENERAL LIABILITY PROVISIONS

§30101. EXTENSION OF JURISDICTION TO CASES OF DAMAGE OR INJURY ON LAND

(a) IN GENERAL.—The admiralty and maritime jurisdiction of the United States extends to and includes cases of injury or damage, to person or property, caused by a vessel on navigable waters, even though the injury or damage is done or consummated on land.

(b) PROCEDURE.—A civil action in a case under subsection (a) may be brought in rem or in personam according to the principles of law and the rules of practice applicable in cases where the injury or damage has been done and consummated on navigable waters.

(c) ACTIONS AGAINST UNITED STATES.—

(1) EXCLUSIVE REMEDY.—In a civil action against the United States for injury or damage done or consummated on land by a vessel on navigable waters, chapter 309 or 311 of this title, as appropriate, provides the exclusive remedy.

(2) ADMINISTRATIVE CLAIM.—A civil action described in paragraph (1) may not be brought until the expiration of the 6-month period after the claim has been presented in writing to the agency owning or operating the vessel causing the injury or damage.

(Pub. L. 109–304, §6(c), Oct. 6, 2006, 120 Stat. 1509.)

§30102. LIABILITY TO PASSENGERS

(a) LIABILITY.—The owner and master of a vessel, and the vessel, are liable for personal injury to a passenger or damage to a passenger's baggage caused by—

(1) a neglect or failure to comply with part B or F of subtitle II of this title; or

(2) a known defect in the steaming apparatus or hull of the vessel.

(b) NOT SUBJECT TO LIMITATION.—A liability imposed under this section is not subject to limitation under chapter 305 of this title.

(Pub. L. 109–304, §6(c), Oct. 6, 2006, 120 Stat. 1509.)

§30103. LIABILITY OF MASTER, MATE, ENGINEER, AND PILOT

A person may bring a civil action against a master, mate, engineer, or pilot of a vessel, and recover damages, for personal injury or loss caused by the master's, mate's, engineer's, or pilot's—

(1) negligence or willful misconduct; or

(2) neglect or refusal to obey the laws governing the navigation of vessels.

(Pub. L. 109–304, §6(c), Oct. 6, 2006, 120 Stat. 1510.)

§30104. PERSONAL INJURY TO OR DEATH OF SEAMEN

(a) IN GENERAL.—A seaman injured in the course of employment or, if the seaman dies from the injury, the personal representative of the seaman may elect to bring a civil action at law, with the right of trial by jury, against the employer. Laws of the United States regulating recovery for personal injury to, or death of, a railway employee apply to an action under this section.

(b) LIMITATION ON RECOVERY BY AQUACULTURE WORKERS.—

(1) IN GENERAL.—For purposes of subsection (a), the term "seaman" does not include an individual who—

(A) is an aquaculture worker if State workers' compensation is available to such individual; and

(B) was, at the time of injury, engaged in aquaculture in a place where such individual had lawful access.

(2) AQUACULTURE WORKER DEFINED.—In this subsection, the term "aquaculture worker" means an individual who—

(A) is employed by a commercial enterprise that is involved in the controlled cultivation and harvest of aquatic plants and animals, including—

(i) the cleaning, processing, or canning of fish and fish products;

(ii) the cultivation and harvesting of shellfish; and

(iii) the controlled growing and harvesting of other aquatic species;

(B) does not hold a license issued under section 7101(c); and

(C) is not required to hold a merchant mariner credential under part F of subtitle II.

(Pub. L. 109–304, §6(c), Oct. 6, 2006, 120 Stat. 1510; Pub. L. 110–181, div. C, title XXXV, §3521(a), Jan. 28, 2008, 122 Stat. 596; Pub. L. 117–263, div. K, title CXV, §11520(a), Dec. 23, 2022, 136 Stat. 4142.)

§30105. RESTRICTION ON RECOVERY BY NON-CITIZENS AND NON-RESIDENT ALIENS FOR INCIDENTS IN WATERS OF OTHER COUNTRIES

(a) DEFINITION.—In this section, the term "continental shelf" has the meaning given that term in article I of the 1958 Convention on the Continental Shelf.

(b) RESTRICTION.—Except as provided in subsection (c), a civil action for maintenance and cure or for damages for personal injury or death may not be brought under a maritime law of the United States if—

(1) the individual suffering the injury or death was not a citizen or permanent resident alien of the United States at the time of the incident giving rise to the action;

(2) the incident occurred in the territorial waters or waters overlaying the continental shelf of a country other than the United States; and

(3) the individual suffering the injury or death was employed at the time of the incident by a person engaged in the exploration, development, or production of offshore mineral or energy resources, including drilling, mapping, surveying, diving, pipelaying,

maintaining, repairing, constructing, or transporting supplies, equipment, or personnel, but not including transporting those resources by a vessel constructed or adapted primarily to carry oil in bulk in the cargo spaces.

(c) NONAPPLICATION.—Subsection (b) does not apply if the individual bringing the action establishes that a remedy is not available under the laws of—
(1) the country asserting jurisdiction over the area in which the incident occurred; or
(2) the country in which the individual suffering the injury or death maintained citizenship or residency at the time of the incident.

(Pub. L. 109–304, §6(c), Oct. 6, 2006, 120 Stat. 1510.)

§30106. TIME LIMIT ON BRINGING MARITIME ACTION FOR PERSONAL INJURY OR DEATH

Except as otherwise provided by law, a civil action for damages for personal injury or death arising out of a maritime tort must be brought within 3 years after the cause of action arose.

(Pub. L. 109–304, §6(c), Oct. 6, 2006, 120 Stat. 1511.)

CHAPTER 303—DEATH ON THE HIGH SEAS

§30301. SHORT TITLE

This chapter may be cited as the "Death on the High Seas Act".

(Pub. L. 109–304, §6(c), Oct. 6, 2006, 120 Stat. 1511.)

§30302. CAUSE OF ACTION

When the death of an individual is caused by wrongful act, neglect, or default occurring on the high seas beyond 3 nautical miles from the shore of the United States, the personal representative of the decedent may bring a civil action in admiralty against the person or vessel responsible. The action shall be for the exclusive benefit of the decedent's spouse, parent, child, or dependent relative.

(Pub. L. 109–304, §6(c), Oct. 6, 2006, 120 Stat. 1511.)

§30303. AMOUNT AND APPORTIONMENT OF RECOVERY

The recovery in an action under this chapter shall be a fair compensation for the pecuniary loss sustained by the individuals for whose benefit the action is brought. The court shall apportion the recovery among those individuals in proportion to the loss each has sustained.

(Pub. L. 109–304, §6(c), Oct. 6, 2006, 120 Stat. 1511.)

§30304. CONTRIBUTORY NEGLIGENCE

In an action under this chapter, contributory negligence of the decedent is not a bar to recovery. The court shall consider the degree of negligence of the decedent and reduce the recovery accordingly.

(Pub. L. 109–304, §6(c), Oct. 6, 2006, 120 Stat. 1511.)

§30305. DEATH OF PLAINTIFF IN PENDING ACTION

If a civil action in admiralty is pending in a court of the United States to recover for personal injury caused by wrongful act, neglect, or default described in section 30302 of this title, and the individual dies during the action as a result of the wrongful act, neglect, or default, the personal representative of the decedent may be substituted as the plaintiff and the action may proceed under this chapter for the recovery authorized by this chapter.

(Pub. L. 109–304, §6(c), Oct. 6, 2006, 120 Stat. 1511.)

§30306. FOREIGN CAUSE OF ACTION

When a cause of action exists under the law of a foreign country for death by wrongful act, neglect, or default on the high seas, a civil action in admiralty may be brought in a court of the United States based on the foreign cause of action, without abatement of the amount for which recovery is authorized.

(Pub. L. 109–304, §6(c), Oct. 6, 2006, 120 Stat. 1511.)

§30307. COMMERCIAL AVIATION ACCIDENTS

(a) DEFINITION.—In this section, the term "nonpecuniary damages" means damages for loss of care, comfort, and companionship.

(b) BEYOND 12 NAUTICAL MILES.—In an action under this chapter, if the death resulted from a commercial aviation accident occurring on the high seas beyond 12 nautical miles from the shore of the United States, additional compensation is recoverable for nonpecuniary damages, but punitive damages are not recoverable.

(c) WITHIN 12 NAUTICAL MILES.—This chapter does not apply if the death resulted from a commercial aviation accident occurring on the high seas 12 nautical miles or less from the shore of the United States.

(Pub. L. 109–304, §6(c), Oct. 6, 2006, 120 Stat. 1512.)

§30308. NONAPPLICATION

(a) STATE LAW.—This chapter does not affect the law of a State regulating the right to recover for death.

(b) INTERNAL WATERS.—This chapter does not apply to the Great Lakes or waters within the territorial limits of a State.

(Pub. L. 109–304, §6(c), Oct. 6, 2006, 120 Stat. 1512.)

CHAPTER 305—EXONERATION AND LIMITATION OF LIABILITY

SUBCHAPTER I—GENERAL PROVISIONS

SUBCHAPTER II—EXONERATION AND LIMITATION OF LIABILITY

SUBCHAPTER I—GENERAL PROVISIONS

§30501. DEFINITIONS

In this chapter:

(1) COVERED SMALL PASSENGER VESSEL.—The term "covered small passenger vessel"—

(A) means a small passenger vessel, as defined in section 2101, that is—

(i) not a wing-in-ground craft; and

(ii) carrying—

(I) not more than 49 passengers on an overnight domestic voyage; and

(II) not more than 150 passengers on any voyage that is not an overnight domestic voyage; and

(B) includes any wooden vessel constructed prior to March 11, 1996, carrying at least 1 passenger for hire.

(2) OWNER.—The term "owner" includes a charterer that mans, supplies, and navigates a vessel at the charterer's own expense or by the charterer's own procurement.

(Pub. L. 109–304, §6(c), Oct. 6, 2006, 120 Stat. 1512; Pub. L. 117–263, div. K, title CXV, §11503(b), Dec. 23, 2022, 136 Stat. 4130.)

§30502. APPLICATION

(a) IN GENERAL.—Except as otherwise provided, this chapter (except section 30521) applies to seagoing vessels and vessels used on lakes or rivers or in inland navigation, including canal boats, barges, and lighters.

(b) EXCEPTION.—This chapter (except for section 30526) shall not apply to covered small passenger vessels.

(Pub. L. 109–304, §6(c), Oct. 6, 2006, 120 Stat. 1512; Pub. L. 117–263, div. K, title CXV, §11503(c), Dec. 23, 2022, 136 Stat. 4130.)

SUBCHAPTER II—EXONERATION AND LIMITATION OF LIABILITY

§30521. DECLARATION OF NATURE AND VALUE OF GOODS

(a) IN GENERAL.—If a shipper of an item named in subsection (b), contained in a parcel, package, or trunk, loads the item as freight or baggage on a vessel, without at the time of loading giving to the person receiving the item a written notice of the true character and value of the item and having that information entered on the bill of lading, the owner and master of the vessel are not liable as carriers. The owner and master are not liable beyond the value entered on the bill of lading.

(b) ITEMS.—The items referred to in subsection (a) are precious metals, gold or silver plated articles, precious stones, jewelry, trinkets, watches, clocks, glass, china, coins, bills, securities, printings, engravings, pictures, stamps, maps, papers, silks, furs, lace, and similar items of high value and small size.

(Pub. L. 109–304, §6(c), Oct. 6, 2006, 120 Stat. 1512, §30503; renumbered §30521, Pub. L. 117–263, div. K, title CXV, §11503(a)(3), Dec. 23, 2022, 136 Stat. 4130.)

§30522. LOSS BY FIRE

The owner of a vessel is not liable for loss or damage to merchandise on the vessel caused by a fire on the vessel unless the fire resulted from the design or neglect of the owner.

(Pub. L. 109–304, §6(c), Oct. 6, 2006, 120 Stat. 1513, §30504; renumbered §30522, Pub. L. 117–263, div. K, title CXV, §11503(a)(3), Dec. 23, 2022, 136 Stat. 4130.)

§30523. GENERAL LIMIT OF LIABILITY

(a) IN GENERAL.—Except as provided in section 30524 of this title, the liability of the owner of a vessel for any claim, debt, or liability described in subsection (b) shall not exceed the value of the vessel and pending freight. If the vessel has more than one owner, the proportionate share of the liability of any one owner shall not exceed that owner's proportionate interest in the vessel and pending freight.

(b) CLAIMS SUBJECT TO LIMITATION.—Unless otherwise excluded by law, claims, debts, and liabilities subject to limitation under subsection (a) are those arising from any embezzlement, loss, or destruction of any property, goods, or merchandise shipped or put on board the vessel, any loss, damage, or injury by collision, or any act, matter, or thing, loss, damage, or forfeiture, done, occasioned, or incurred, without the privity or knowledge of the owner.

(c) WAGES.—Subsection (a) does not apply to a claim for wages.

(Pub. L. 109–304, §6(c), Oct. 6, 2006, 120 Stat. 1513, §30505; renumbered §30523 and amended Pub. L. 117–263, div. K, title CXV, §11503(a)(3), (f)(2), Dec. 23, 2022, 136 Stat. 4130, 4131.)

§30524. LIMIT OF LIABILITY FOR PERSONAL INJURY OR DEATH

(a) APPLICATION.—This section applies only to seagoing vessels, but does not apply to pleasure yachts, tugs, towboats, towing vessels, tank vessels, fishing vessels, fish tender vessels, canal boats, scows, car floats, barges, lighters, or nondescript vessels.

(b) MINIMUM LIABILITY.—If the amount of the vessel owner's liability determined under section 30523 of this title is insufficient to pay all losses in full, and the portion available to pay claims for personal injury or death is less than $420 times the tonnage of the vessel, that portion shall be increased to $420 times the tonnage of the vessel. That portion may be used only to pay claims for personal injury or death.

(c) CALCULATION OF TONNAGE.—Under subsection (b), the tonnage of a self-propelled vessel is the gross tonnage without deduction for engine room, and the tonnage of a sailing vessel is the tonnage for documentation. However, space for the use of seamen is excluded.

(d) CLAIMS ARISING ON DISTINCT OCCASIONS.—Separate limits of liability apply to claims for personal injury or death arising on distinct occasions.

(e) PRIVITY OR KNOWLEDGE.—In a claim for personal injury or death, the privity or knowledge of the master or the owner's superintendent or managing agent, at or before the beginning of each voyage, is imputed to the owner.

(Pub. L. 109–304, §6(c), Oct. 6, 2006, 120 Stat. 1513, §30506; renumbered §30524 and amended Pub. L. 117–263, div. K, title CXV, §11503(a)(3), (f)(3), Dec. 23, 2022, 136 Stat. 4130, 4131.)

§30525. APPORTIONMENT OF LOSSES

If the amounts determined under sections 30523 and 30524 of this title are insufficient to pay all claims—

(1) all claimants shall be paid in proportion to their respective losses out of the amount determined under section 30523 of this title; and

(2) personal injury and death claimants, if any, shall be paid an additional amount in proportion to their respective losses out of the additional amount determined under section 30524(b) of this title.

(Pub. L. 109–304, §6(c), Oct. 6, 2006, 120 Stat. 1513, §30507; renumbered §30525 and amended Pub. L. 117–263, div. K, title CXV, §11503(a)(3), (f)(4), Dec. 23, 2022, 136 Stat. 4130, 4131.)

§30526. PROVISIONS REQUIRING NOTICE OF CLAIM OR LIMITING TIME FOR BRINGING ACTION

(a) APPLICATION.—This section applies only to seagoing vessels, but does not apply to pleasure yachts, tugs, towboats, towing vessels, tank vessels, fishing vessels, fish tender vessels, canal boats, scows, car floats, barges, lighters, or nondescript vessels.

(b) MINIMUM TIME LIMITS.—The owner, master, manager, or agent of a vessel transporting passengers or property between ports in the United States, or between a port in the United States and a port in a foreign country, may not limit by regulation, contract, or otherwise the period for—

(1) giving notice of, or filing a claim for, personal injury or death, in the case of seagoing vessels, to less than 6 months after the date of the injury or death, or in the case of covered small passenger vessels, to less than two years after the date of the injury or death; or

(2) bringing a civil action for personal injury or death, in the case of seagoing vessels, to less than one year after the date of the injury or death, or in the case of covered small passenger vessels, to less than two years after the date of the injury or death.

(c) EFFECT OF FAILURE TO GIVE NOTICE.—When notice of a claim for personal injury or death is required by a contract, the failure to give the notice is not a bar to recovery if—

(1) the court finds that the owner, master, or agent of the vessel had knowledge of the injury or death and the owner has not been prejudiced by the failure;

(2) the court finds there was a satisfactory reason why the notice could not have been given; or

(3) the owner of the vessel fails to object to the failure to give the notice.

(d) TOLLING OF PERIOD TO GIVE NOTICE.—If a claimant is a minor or mental incompetent, or if a claim is for wrongful death, any period provided by a contract for giving notice of the claim is tolled until the earlier of—

(1) the date a legal representative is appointed for the minor, incompetent, or decedent's estate; or

(2) 3 years after the injury or death.

(Pub. L. 109–304, §6(c), Oct. 6, 2006, 120 Stat. 1514, §30508; renumbered §30526 and amended Pub. L. 117–263, div. K, title CXV, §11503(a)(3), (d), Dec. 23, 2022, 136 Stat. 4130, 4131.)

§30527. PROVISIONS LIMITING LIABILITY FOR PERSONAL INJURY OR DEATH

(a) PROHIBITION.—

(1) IN GENERAL.—The owner, master, manager, or agent of a vessel transporting passengers between ports in the United States, or between a port in the United States and a port in a foreign country, may not include in a regulation or contract a provision limiting—

(A) the liability of the owner, master, or agent for personal injury or death caused by the negligence or fault of the owner or the owner's employees or agents; or

(B) the right of a claimant for personal injury or death to a trial by court of competent jurisdiction.

(2) VOIDNESS.—A provision described in paragraph (1) is void.

(b) EMOTIONAL DISTRESS, MENTAL SUFFERING, AND PSYCHOLOGICAL INJURY.—

(1) IN GENERAL.—Subsection (a) does not prohibit a provision in a contract or in ticket conditions of carriage with a passenger that relieves an owner, master, manager, agent, operator, or crewmember of a vessel from liability for infliction of emotional distress, mental suffering, or psychological injury so long as the provision does not limit such liability when the emotional distress, mental suffering, or psychological injury is—

(A) the result of physical injury to the claimant caused by the negligence or fault of a crewmember or the owner, master, manager, agent, or operator;

(B) the result of the claimant having been at actual risk of physical injury, and the risk was caused by the negligence or fault of a crewmember or the owner, master, manager, agent, or operator; or

(C) intentionally inflicted by a crewmember or the owner, master, manager, agent, or operator.

(2) SEXUAL OFFENSES.—This subsection does not limit the liability of a crewmember

or the owner, master, manager, agent, or operator of a vessel in a case involving sexual
harassment, sexual assault, or rape.

(Pub. L. 109–304, §6(c), Oct. 6, 2006, 120 Stat. 1514, §30509; renumbered §30527, Pub. L. 117–263, div.
K, title CXV, §11503(a)(3), Dec. 23, 2022, 136 Stat. 4130.)

§30528. VICARIOUS LIABILITY FOR MEDICAL MALPRACTICE WITH REGARD TO CREW

In a civil action by any person in which the owner or operator of a vessel or employer of
a crewmember is claimed to have vicarious liability for medical malpractice with regard to
a crewmember occurring at a shoreside facility, and to the extent the damages resulted from
the conduct of any shoreside doctor, hospital, medical facility, or other health care provider,
the owner, operator, or employer is entitled to rely on any statutory limitations of liability
applicable to the doctor, hospital, medical facility, or other health care provider in the State
of the United States in which the shoreside medical care was provided.

(Pub. L. 109–304, §6(c), Oct. 6, 2006, 120 Stat. 1515, §30510; renumbered §30528, Pub. L. 117–263, div.
K, title CXV, §11503(a)(3), Dec. 23, 2022, 136 Stat. 4130.)

§30529. ACTION BY OWNER FOR LIMITATION

(a) IN GENERAL.—The owner of a vessel may bring a civil action in a district court of
the United States for limitation of liability under this chapter. The action must be brought
within 6 months after a claimant gives the owner written notice of a claim.

(b) CREATION OF FUND.—When the action is brought, the owner (at the owner's option)
shall—

(1) deposit with the court, for the benefit of claimants—

(A) an amount equal to the value of the owner's interest in the vessel and pending
freight, or approved security; and

(B) an amount, or approved security, that the court may fix from time to time as
necessary to carry out this chapter; or

(2) transfer to a trustee appointed by the court, for the benefit of claimants—

(A) the owner's interest in the vessel and pending freight; and

(B) an amount, or approved security, that the court may fix from time to time as
necessary to carry out this chapter.

(c) CESSATION OF OTHER ACTIONS.—When an action has been brought under this section
and the owner has complied with subsection (b), all claims and proceedings against the
owner related to the matter in question shall cease.

(Pub. L. 109–304, §6(c), Oct. 6, 2006, 120 Stat. 1515, §30511; renumbered §30529, Pub. L. 117–263, div.
K, title CXV, §11503(a)(3), Dec. 23, 2022, 136 Stat. 4130.)

§30530. LIABILITY AS MASTER, OFFICER, OR SEAMAN NOT AFFECTED

This chapter does not affect the liability of an individual as a master, officer, or seaman,
even though the individual is also an owner of the vessel.

(Pub. L. 109–304, §6(c), Oct. 6, 2006, 120 Stat. 1516, §30512; renumbered §30530, Pub. L. 117–263, div.

K, title CXV, §11503(a)(3), Dec. 23, 2022, 136 Stat. 4130.)

CHAPTER 307—LIABILITY OF WATER CARRIERS

§30701. DEFINITION

In this chapter, the term "carrier" means the owner, manager, charterer, agent, or master of a vessel.

(Pub. L. 109–304, §6(c), Oct. 6, 2006, 120 Stat. 1516.)

§30702. APPLICATION

(a) IN GENERAL.—Except as otherwise provided, this chapter applies to a carrier engaged in the carriage of goods to or from any port in the United States.

(b) LIVE ANIMALS.—Sections 30703 and 30704 of this title do not apply to the carriage of live animals.

(Pub. L. 109–304, §6(c), Oct. 6, 2006, 120 Stat. 1516.)

§30703. BILLS OF LADING

(a) ISSUANCE.—On demand of a shipper, the carrier shall issue a bill of lading or shipping document.

(b) CONTENTS.—The bill of lading or shipping document shall include a statement of—

(1) the marks necessary to identify the goods;

(2) the number of packages, or the quantity or weight, and whether it is carrier's or shipper's weight; and

(3) the apparent condition of the goods.

(c) PRIMA FACIE EVIDENCE OF RECEIPT.—A bill of lading or shipping document issued under this section is prima facie evidence of receipt of the goods described.

(Pub. L. 109–304, §6(c), Oct. 6, 2006, 120 Stat. 1516.)

§30704. LOADING, STOWAGE, CUSTODY, CARE, AND DELIVERY

A carrier may not insert in a bill of lading or shipping document a provision avoiding its liability for loss or damage arising from negligence or fault in loading, stowage, custody, care, or proper delivery. Any such provision is void.

(Pub. L. 109–304, §6(c), Oct. 6, 2006, 120 Stat. 1516.)

§30705. Seaworthiness

(a) Prohibition.—A carrier may not insert in a bill of lading or shipping document a provision lessening or avoiding its obligation to exercise due diligence to—

(1) make the vessel seaworthy; and

(2) properly man, equip, and supply the vessel.

(b) Voidness.—A provision described in subsection (a) is void.

(Pub. L. 109–304, §6(c), Oct. 6, 2006, 120 Stat. 1516.)

§30706. Defenses

(a) Due Diligence.—If a carrier has exercised due diligence to make the vessel in all respects seaworthy and to properly man, equip, and supply the vessel, the carrier and the vessel are not liable for loss or damage arising from an error in the navigation or management of the vessel.

(b) Other Defenses.—A carrier and the vessel are not liable for loss or damage arising from—

(1) dangers of the sea or other navigable waters;

(2) acts of God;

(3) public enemies;

(4) seizure under legal process;

(5) inherent defect, quality, or vice of the goods;

(6) insufficiency of package;

(7) act or omission of the shipper or owner of the goods or their agent; or

(8) saving or attempting to save life or property at sea, including a deviation in rendering such a service.

(Pub. L. 109–304, §6(c), Oct. 6, 2006, 120 Stat. 1517.)

§30707. Criminal penalty

(a) In General.—A carrier that violates this chapter shall be fined under title 18.

(b) Lien.—The amount of the fine and costs for the violation constitute a lien on the vessel engaged in the carriage. A civil action in rem to enforce the lien may be brought in the district court of the United States for any district in which the vessel is found.

(c) Disposition of Fine.—Half of the fine shall go to the person injured by the violation and half to the United States Government.

(Pub. L. 109–304, §6(c), Oct. 6, 2006, 120 Stat. 1517.)

CHAPTER 309—SUITS IN ADMIRALTY AGAINST THE UNITED STATES

§30901. Short title

This chapter may be cited as the "Suits in Admiralty Act".

(Pub. L. 109–304, §6(c), Oct. 6, 2006, 120 Stat. 1517.)

§30902. Definition

In this chapter, the term "federally-owned corporation" means a corporation in which the United States owns all the outstanding capital stock.

(Pub. L. 109–304, §6(c), Oct. 6, 2006, 120 Stat. 1517.)

§30903. Waiver of immunity

(a) In General.—In a case in which, if a vessel were privately owned or operated, or if cargo were privately owned or possessed, or if a private person or property were involved, a civil action in admiralty could be maintained, a civil action in admiralty in personam may be brought against the United States or a federally-owned corporation. In a civil action in admiralty brought by the United States or a federally-owned corporation, an admiralty claim in personam may be filed or a setoff claimed against the United States or corporation.

(b) Non-Jury.—A claim against the United States or a federally-owned corporation under this section shall be tried without a jury.

(Pub. L. 109–304, §6(c), Oct. 6, 2006, 120 Stat. 1518.)

§30904. Exclusive remedy

If a remedy is provided by this chapter, it shall be exclusive of any other action arising out of the same subject matter against the officer, employee, or agent of the United States or the federally-owned corporation whose act or omission gave rise to the claim.

(Pub. L. 109–304, §6(c), Oct. 6, 2006, 120 Stat. 1518.)

§30905. Period for bringing action

A civil action under this chapter must be brought within 2 years after the cause of action arose.

(Pub. L. 109–304, §6(c), Oct. 6, 2006, 120 Stat. 1518.)

§30906. Venue

(a) In General.—A civil action under this chapter shall be brought in the district court of the United States for the district in which—

(1) any plaintiff resides or has its principal place of business; or

(2) the vessel or cargo is found.

(b) Transfer.—On a motion by a party, the court may transfer the action to any other district court of the United States.

(Pub. L. 109–304, §6(c), Oct. 6, 2006, 120 Stat. 1518.)

§30907. Procedure for hearing and determination

(a) In General.—A civil action under this chapter shall proceed and be heard and determined according to the principles of law and the rules of practice applicable in like cases between private parties.

(b) In Rem.—

(1) Requirements.—The action may proceed according to the principles of an action in rem if—

(A) the plaintiff elects in the complaint; and

(B) it appears that an action in rem could have been maintained had the vessel or cargo been privately owned and possessed.

(2) Effect on relief in personam.—An election under paragraph (1) does not prevent the plaintiff from seeking relief in personam in the same action.

(Pub. L. 109–304, §6(c), Oct. 6, 2006, 120 Stat. 1518.)

§30908. Exemption from arrest or seizure

The following are not subject to arrest or seizure by judicial process in the United States:

(1) A vessel owned by, possessed by, or operated by or for the United States or a federally-owned corporation.

(2) Cargo owned or possessed by the United States or a federally-owned corporation.

(Pub. L. 109–304, §6(c), Oct. 6, 2006, 120 Stat. 1518.)

§30909. Security

Neither the United States nor a federally-owned corporation may be required to give a bond or admiralty stipulation in a civil action under this chapter.

(Pub. L. 109–304, §6(c), Oct. 6, 2006, 120 Stat. 1519.)

§30910. Exoneration and limitation

The United States is entitled to the exemptions from and limitations of liability provided by law to an owner, charterer, operator, or agent of a vessel.

(Pub. L. 109–304, §6(c), Oct. 6, 2006, 120 Stat. 1519.)

§30911. Costs and interest

(a) In General.—A judgment against the United States or a federally-owned corporation under this chapter may include costs and interest at the rate of 4 percent per year until satisfied. Interest shall run as ordered by the court, except that interest is not allowable for the period before the action is filed.

(b) Contract Providing for Interest.—Notwithstanding subsection (a), if the claim is based on a contract providing for interest, interest may be awarded at the rate and for the period provided in the contract.

(Pub. L. 109–304, §6(c), Oct. 6, 2006, 120 Stat. 1519.)

§30912. Arbitration, compromise, or settlement

The Secretary of a department of the United States Government, or the board of trustees of a federally-owned corporation, may arbitrate, compromise, or settle a claim under this chapter.

(Pub. L. 109–304, §6(c), Oct. 6, 2006, 120 Stat. 1519.)

§30913. Payment of judgment or settlement

(a) In General.—The proper accounting officer of the United States shall pay a final judgment, arbitration award, or settlement under this chapter on presentation of an authenticated copy.

(b) Source of Payment.—Payment shall be made from an appropriation or fund available specifically for the purpose. If no appropriation or fund is specifically available, there is hereby appropriated, out of money in the Treasury not otherwise appropriated, an amount sufficient to pay the judgment, award, or settlement.

(Pub. L. 109–304, §6(c), Oct. 6, 2006, 120 Stat. 1519.)

§30914. Release of privately owned vessel after arrest or attachment

If a privately owned vessel not in the possession of the United States or a federally-owned corporation is arrested or attached in a civil action arising or alleged to have arisen from prior ownership, possession, or operation by the United States or corporation, the vessel shall be released without bond or stipulation on a statement by the United States, through the Attorney General or other authorized law officer, that the United States

27

is interested in the action, desires release of the vessel, and assumes liability for the satisfaction of any judgment obtained by the plaintiff. After the vessel is released, the action shall proceed against the United States in accordance with this chapter.

(Pub. L. 109–304, §6(c), Oct. 6, 2006, 120 Stat. 1519.)

§30915. SEIZURES AND OTHER PROCEEDINGS IN FOREIGN JURISDICTIONS

(a) IN GENERAL.—If a vessel or cargo described in section 30908 or 30914 of this title is arrested, attached, or otherwise seized by judicial process in a foreign country, or if an action is brought in a court of a foreign country against the master of such a vessel for a claim arising from the ownership, possession, or operation of the vessel, or the ownership, possession, or carriage of such cargo, the Secretary of State, on request of the Attorney General or another officer authorized by the Attorney General, may direct the United States consul residing at or nearest the place at which the action was brought—

(1) to claim the vessel or cargo as immune from arrest, attachment, or other seizure, and to execute an agreement, stipulation, bond, or undertaking, for the United States or federally-owned corporation, for the release of the vessel or cargo and the prosecution of any appeal; or

(2) if an action has been brought against the master of such a vessel, to enter the appearance of the United States or corporation and to pledge the credit of the United States or corporation to the payment of any judgment and costs in the action.

(b) ARRANGING BOND OR STIPULATION.—The Attorney General may—

(1) arrange with a bank, surety company, or other person, whether in the United States or a foreign country, to execute a bond or stipulation; and

(2) pledge the credit of the United States to secure the bond or stipulation.

(c) PAYMENT OF JUDGMENT.—The appropriate accounting officer of the United States or corporation may pay a judgment in an action described in subsection (a) on presentation of a copy of the judgment if certified by the clerk of the court and authenticated by—

(1) the certificate and seal of the United States consul claiming the vessel or cargo, or by the consul's successor; and

(2) the certificate of the Secretary as to the official capacity of the consul.

(d) RIGHT TO CLAIM IMMUNITY NOT AFFECTED.—This section does not affect the right of the United States to claim immunity of a vessel or cargo from foreign jurisdiction.

(Pub. L. 109–304, §6(c), Oct. 6, 2006, 120 Stat. 1519.)

§30916. RECOVERY BY THE UNITED STATES FOR SALVAGE SERVICES

(a) CIVIL ACTION.—The United States, and the crew of a merchant vessel owned or operated by the United States, or a federally-owned corporation, may bring a civil action to recover for salvage services provided by the vessel and crew.

(b) DEPOSIT OF AMOUNTS RECOVERED.—Any amount recovered under this section by the United States for its own benefit, and not for the benefit of the crew, shall be deposited in the Treasury to the credit of the department of the United States Government, or the corporation, having control of the possession or operation of the vessel.

(Pub. L. 109–304, §6(c), Oct. 6, 2006, 120 Stat. 1520.)

§30917. DISPOSITION OF AMOUNTS RECOVERED BY THE UNITED STATES

Amounts recovered in a civil action brought by the United States on a claim arising from the ownership, possession, or operation of a merchant vessel, or the ownership, possession, or carriage of cargo, shall be deposited in the Treasury to the credit of the department of the United States Government, or the federally-owned corporation, having control of the vessel or cargo, for reimbursement of the appropriation, insurance fund, or other fund from which the compensation for which the judgment was recovered was or will be paid.

(Pub. L. 109–304, §6(c), Oct. 6, 2006, 120 Stat. 1520.)

§30918. REPORTS

The Secretary of each department of the United States Government, and the board of trustees of each federally-owned corporation, shall report to Congress at each session thereof all arbitration awards and settlements agreed to under this chapter since the previous session, for which the time to appeal has expired or been waived.

(Pub. L. 109–304, §6(c), Oct. 6, 2006, 120 Stat. 1521.)

CHAPTER 311—SUITS INVOLVING PUBLIC VESSELS

§31101. SHORT TITLE

This chapter may be cited as the "Public Vessels Act".

(Pub. L. 109–304, §6(c), Oct. 6, 2006, 120 Stat. 1521.)

§31102. WAIVER OF IMMUNITY

(a) IN GENERAL.—A civil action in personam in admiralty may be brought, or an impleader filed, against the United States for—

(1) damages caused by a public vessel of the United States; or

(2) compensation for towage and salvage services, including contract salvage, rendered to a public vessel of the United States.

(b) COUNTERCLAIM OR SETOFF.—If the United States brings a civil action in admiralty for damages caused by a privately owned vessel, the owner of the vessel, or the successor in interest, may file a counterclaim in personam, or claim a setoff, against the United States for damages arising out of the same subject matter.

(Pub. L. 109–304, §6(c), Oct. 6, 2006, 120 Stat. 1521.)

§31103. APPLICABLE PROCEDURE

A civil action under this chapter is subject to the provisions of chapter 309 of this title except to the extent inconsistent with this chapter.

(Pub. L. 109–304, §6(c), Oct. 6, 2006, 120 Stat. 1521.)

§31104. VENUE

(a) IN GENERAL.—A civil action under this chapter shall be brought in the district court of the United States for the district in which the vessel or cargo is found within the United States.

(b) VESSEL OR CARGO OUTSIDE TERRITORIAL WATERS.—If the vessel or cargo is outside the territorial waters of the United States—

(1) the action shall be brought in the district court of the United States for any district in which any plaintiff resides or has an office for the transaction of business; or

(2) if no plaintiff resides or has an office for the transaction of business in the United States, the action may be brought in the district court of the United States for any district.

(Pub. L. 109–304, §6(c), Oct. 6, 2006, 120 Stat. 1521.)

§31105. SECURITY WHEN COUNTERCLAIM FILED

If a counterclaim is filed for a cause of action for which the original action is filed under this chapter, the respondent to the counterclaim shall give security in the usual amount and form to respond to the counterclaim, unless the court for cause shown orders otherwise. The proceedings in the original action shall be stayed until the security is given.

(Pub. L. 109–304, §6(c), Oct. 6, 2006, 120 Stat. 1522.)

§31106. EXONERATION AND LIMITATION

The United States is entitled to the exemptions from and limitations of liability provided by law to an owner, charterer, operator, or agent of a vessel.

(Pub. L. 109–304, §6(c), Oct. 6, 2006, 120 Stat. 1522.)

§31107. INTEREST

A judgment in a civil action under this chapter may not include interest for the period before the judgment is issued unless the claim is based on a contract providing for interest.

(Pub. L. 109–304, §6(c), Oct. 6, 2006, 120 Stat. 1522.)

§31108. ARBITRATION, COMPROMISE, OR SETTLEMENT

The Attorney General may arbitrate, compromise, or settle a claim under this chapter if a civil action based on the claim has been commenced.

(Pub. L. 109–304, §6(c), Oct. 6, 2006, 120 Stat. 1522.)

§31109. PAYMENT OF JUDGMENT OR SETTLEMENT

The proper accounting officer of the United States shall pay a final judgment, arbitration award, or settlement under this chapter on presentation of an authenticated copy. Payment shall be made from any money in the Treasury appropriated for the purpose.

(Pub. L. 109–304, §6(c), Oct. 6, 2006, 120 Stat. 1522.)

§31110. SUBPOENAS TO OFFICERS OR MEMBERS OF CREW

An officer or member of the crew of a public vessel may not be subpoenaed in a civil action under this chapter without the consent of—

(1) the Secretary of the department or the head of the independent establishment having control of the vessel at the time the cause of action arose; or

(2) the master or commanding officer of the vessel at the time the subpoena is issued.

(Pub. L. 109–304, §6(c), Oct. 6, 2006, 120 Stat. 1522.)

§31111. CLAIMS BY NATIONALS OF FOREIGN COUNTRIES

A national of a foreign country may not maintain a civil action under this chapter unless it appears to the satisfaction of the court in which the action is brought that the government of that country, in similar circumstances, allows nationals of the United States to sue in its courts.

(Pub. L. 109–304, §6(c), Oct. 6, 2006, 120 Stat. 1522.)

§31112. LIEN NOT RECOGNIZED OR CREATED

This chapter shall not be construed as recognizing the existence of or as creating a lien against a public vessel of the United States.

(Pub. L. 109–304, §6(c), Oct. 6, 2006, 120 Stat. 1522.)

§31113. REPORTS

The Attorney General shall report to Congress at each session thereof all claims settled under this chapter.

(Pub. L. 109–304, §6(c), Oct. 6, 2006, 120 Stat. 1523.)

CHAPTER 313—COMMERCIAL INSTRUMENTS AND MARITIME LIENS

SUBCHAPTER I—GENERAL

SUBCHAPTER II—COMMERCIAL INSTRUMENTS

SUBCHAPTER III—MARITIME LIENS

SUBCHAPTER I—GENERAL

§31301. DEFINITIONS

In this chapter—

(1) "acknowledge" means making—

(A) an acknowledgment or notarization before a notary public or other official authorized by a law of the United States or a State to take acknowledgments of deeds; or

(B) a certificate issued under the Hague Convention Abolishing the Requirement of Legalisation for Foreign Public Documents, 1961;

(2) "district court" means—

(A) a district court of the United States (as defined in section 451 of title 28);

(B) the District Court of Guam;

(C) the District Court of the Virgin Islands;

(D) the District Court for the Northern Mariana Islands;

(E) the High Court of American Samoa; and

(F) any other court of original jurisdiction of a territory or possession of the United States;

(3) "mortgagee" means—

(A) a person to whom property is mortgaged; or

(B) when a mortgage on a vessel involves a trust, the trustee that is designated in the trust agreement;

(4) "necessaries" includes repairs, supplies, towage, and the use of a dry dock or marine railway;

(5) "preferred maritime lien" means a maritime lien on a vessel—

(A) arising before a preferred mortgage was filed under section 31321 of this title;

(B) for damage arising out of maritime tort;

(C) for wages of a stevedore when employed directly by a person listed in section 31341 of this title;

(D) for wages of the crew of the vessel;

(E) for general average; or

(F) for salvage, including contract salvage;

(6) "preferred mortgage"—

(A) means a mortgage that is a preferred mortgage under section 31322 of this title; and

(B) also means in sections 31325 and 31326 of this title, a mortgage, hypothecation, or similar charge that is established as a security on a foreign vessel if the mortgage, hypothecation, or similar charge was executed under the laws of the foreign country under whose laws the ownership of the vessel is documented and has been registered under those laws in a public register at the port of registry of the vessel or at a central

§31302. Availability of instruments, copies, and information

CHAPTER 313—COMMERCIAL INSTRUMENTS AND MARITIME LIENS

office; and

(7) "Secretary" means the Secretary of the Department of Homeland Security, unless otherwise noted.

(Pub. L. 100–710, title I, §102(c), Nov. 23, 1988, 102 Stat. 4739; Pub. L. 111–281, title IX, §913(a)(2)–(4), Oct. 15, 2010, 124 Stat. 3017.)

§31302. AVAILABILITY OF INSTRUMENTS, COPIES, AND INFORMATION

The Secretary shall—

(1) make any instrument filed or recorded with the Secretary under this chapter available for public inspection;

(2) on request, provide a copy, including a certified copy, of any instrument made available for public inspection under this chapter; and

(3) on request, provide a certificate containing information included in an instrument filed or recorded under this chapter.

(Pub. L. 100–710, title I, §102(c), Nov. 23, 1988, 102 Stat. 4740; Pub. L. 111–281, title IX, §913(a)(1), Oct. 15, 2010, 124 Stat. 3017.)

§31303. CERTAIN CIVIL ACTIONS NOT AUTHORIZED

If a mortgage covers a vessel and additional property that is not a vessel, this chapter does not authorize a civil action in rem to enforce the rights of the mortgagee under the mortgage against the additional property.

(Pub. L. 100–710, title I, §102(c), Nov. 23, 1988, 102 Stat. 4740.)

§31304. LIABILITY FOR NONCOMPLIANCE

(a) If a person makes a contract secured by, or on the credit of, a vessel covered by a mortgage filed or recorded under this chapter and sustains a monetary loss because the mortgagor or the master or other individual in charge of the vessel does not comply with a requirement imposed on the mortgagor, master, or individual under this chapter, the mortgagor is liable for the loss.

(b) A civil action may be brought to recover for losses referred to in subsection (a) of this section. The district courts have original jurisdiction of the action, regardless of the amount in controversy or the citizenship of the parties. If the plaintiff prevails, the court shall award costs and attorney fees to the plaintiff.

(Pub. L. 100–710, title I, §102(c), Nov. 23, 1988, 102 Stat. 4740.)

§31305. WAIVER OF LIEN RIGHTS

This chapter does not prevent a mortgagee or other lien holder from waiving or subordinating at any time by agreement or otherwise the lien holder's right to a lien, the priority or, if a preferred mortgage lien, the preferred status of the lien.

(Pub. L. 100–710, title I, §102(c), Nov. 23, 1988, 102 Stat. 4741.)

§31306. DECLARATION OF CITIZENSHIP

(a) Except as provided by the Secretary, when an instrument transferring an interest in a vessel is presented to the Secretary for filing or recording, the transferee shall file with the instrument a declaration, in the form the Secretary may prescribe by regulation, stating information about citizenship and other information the Secretary may require to show the transaction involved does not violate section 56102 or 56103 of this title.

(b) A declaration under this section filed by a corporation must be signed by its president, secretary, treasurer, or other official authorized by the corporation to execute the declaration.

(c) Except as provided by the Secretary, an instrument transferring an interest in a vessel is not valid against any person until the declaration required by this section has been filed.

(d) A person knowingly making a false statement of a material fact in a declaration filed under this section shall be fined under title 18, imprisoned for not more than 5 years, or both.

(Pub. L. 100–710, title I, §102(c), Nov. 23, 1988, 102 Stat. 4741; Pub. L. 101–225, title III, §303(1), Dec. 12, 1989, 103 Stat. 1923; Pub. L. 109–304, §15(27), Oct. 6, 2006, 120 Stat. 1704; Pub. L. 111–281, title IX, §913(a)(1), Oct. 15, 2010, 124 Stat. 3017.)

§31307. State statutes superseded

This chapter supersedes any State statute conferring a lien on a vessel to the extent the statute establishes a claim to be enforced by a civil action in rem against the vessel for necessaries.

(Pub. L. 100–710, title I, §102(c), Nov. 23, 1988, 102 Stat. 4741.)

§31308. Secretary of Commerce or Transportation as mortgagee

The Secretary of Commerce or Transportation, as a mortgagee under this chapter, may foreclose on a lien arising from a right established under a mortgage under chapter 537 of this title, subject to section 362(b) of title 11.

(Pub. L. 100–710, title I, §102(c), Nov. 23, 1988, 102 Stat. 4741; Pub. L. 101–595, title VI, §603(13), Nov. 16, 1990, 104 Stat. 2993; Pub. L. 109–304, §15(28), Oct. 6, 2006, 120 Stat. 1704; Pub. L. 111–281, title IX, §913(b), Oct. 15, 2010, 124 Stat. 3017.)

§31309. General civil penalty

Except as otherwise provided in this chapter, a person violating this chapter or a regulation prescribed under this chapter is liable to the United States Government for a civil penalty of not more than $10,000.

(Pub. L. 100–710, title I, §102(c), Nov. 23, 1988, 102 Stat. 4741.)

SUBCHAPTER II—COMMERCIAL INSTRUMENTS

§31321. FILING, RECORDING, AND DISCHARGE

(a)(1) A bill of sale, conveyance, mortgage, assignment, or related instrument, whenever made, that includes any part of a documented vessel or a vessel for which an application for documentation is filed, must be filed with the Secretary to be valid, to the extent the vessel is involved, against any person except—

(A) the grantor, mortgagor, or assignor;

(B) the heir or devisee of the grantor, mortgagor, or assignor; and

(C) a person having actual notice of the sale, conveyance, mortgage, assignment, or related instrument.

(2) Each bill of sale, conveyance, mortgage, assignment, or related instrument that is filed in substantial compliance with this section is valid against any person from the time it is filed with the Secretary.

(3) The parties to an instrument or an application for documentation shall use diligence to ensure that the parts of the instrument or application for which they are responsible are in substantial compliance with the filing and documentation requirements.

(4) A bill of sale, conveyance, mortgage, assignment, or related instrument may be filed electronically under regulations prescribed by the Secretary.

(b) To be filed, a bill of sale, conveyance, mortgage, assignment, or related instrument must—

(1) identify the vessel;

(2) state the name and address of each party to the instrument;

(3) state, if a mortgage, the amount of the direct or contingent obligations (in one or more units of account as agreed to by the parties) that is or may become secured by the mortgage, excluding interest, expenses, and fees;

(4) state the interest of the grantor, mortgagor, or assignor in the vessel;

(5) state the interest sold, conveyed, mortgaged, or assigned; and

(6) be signed and acknowledged.

(c) If a bill of sale, conveyance, mortgage, assignment, or related document is filed that involves a vessel for which an application for documentation is filed, and the Secretary decides that the vessel cannot be documented by an applicant—

(1) the Secretary shall send notice of the Secretary's decision, including reasons for the decision, to each interested party to the instrument filed for recording; and

(2) 90 days after sending the notice as provided under clause (1) of this subsection, the Secretary—

(A) may terminate the filing; and

(B) may return the instrument filed without recording it under subsection (e) of this section.

(d) A person may withdraw an application for documentation of a vessel for which a mortgage has been filed under this section only if the mortgagee consents.

41

(e) The Secretary shall—

(1) record the bills of sale, conveyances, mortgages, assignments, and related instruments of a documented vessel complying with subsection (b) of this section in the order they are filed; and

(2) maintain appropriate indexes, for use by the public, of instruments filed or recorded, or both.

(f) On full and final discharge of the indebtedness under a mortgage recorded under subsection (e)(1) of this section, a mortgagee, on request of the Secretary or mortgagor, shall provide the Secretary with an acknowledged certificate of discharge of the indebtedness in a form prescribed by the Secretary. The Secretary shall record the certificate.

(g) The mortgage or related instrument of a vessel covered by a preferred mortgage under section 31322(d) of this title, that is later filed under this section at the time an application for documentation is filed, is valid under this section from the time the mortgage or instrument representing financing became a preferred mortgage under section 31322(d).

(h) On full and final discharge of the indebtedness under a mortgage deemed to be a preferred mortgage under section 31322(d) of this title, a mortgagee, on request of the Secretary, a State, or mortgagor, shall provide the Secretary or the State, as appropriate, with an acknowledged certificate of discharge of the indebtedness in a form prescribed by the Secretary or the State, as applicable. If filed with the Secretary, the Secretary shall enter that information in the vessel identification system under chapter 125 of this title.

(Pub. L. 100–710, title I, §102(c), Nov. 23, 1988, 102 Stat. 4741; Pub. L. 101–225, title III, §303(2), Dec. 12, 1989, 103 Stat. 1923; Pub. L. 104–324, title III, §305, Oct. 19, 1996, 110 Stat. 3918; Pub. L. 107–295, title IV, §420, Nov. 25, 2002, 116 Stat. 2124; Pub. L. 111–281, title IX, §913(a)(1), Oct. 15, 2010, 124 Stat. 3017.)

§31322. PREFERRED MORTGAGES

(a) A preferred mortgage is a mortgage, whenever made, that—

(1) includes the whole of the vessel;

(2) is filed in substantial compliance with section 31321 of this title;

(3)(A) covers a documented vessel; or

(B) covers a vessel for which an application for documentation is filed that is in substantial compliance with the requirements of chapter 121 of this title and the regulations prescribed under that chapter; and

(4) with respect to a vessel with a fishery endorsement that is 100 feet or greater in registered length, has as the mortgagee—

(A) a person eligible to own a vessel with a fishery endorsement under section 12113(c) of this title;

(B) a State or federally chartered financial institution that is insured by the Federal Deposit Insurance Corporation;

(C) a farm credit lender established under title 12, chapter 23 of the United States Code;

(D) a commercial fishing and agriculture bank established pursuant to State law;

(E) a commercial lender organized under the laws of the United States or of a State and eligible to own a vessel for purposes of documentation under section 12103 of this title; or

(F) a mortgage trustee under subsection (f) of this section.

(b) Any indebtedness secured by a preferred mortgage that is filed or recorded under this chapter, or that is subject to a mortgage, security agreement, or instruments granting a security interest that is deemed to be a preferred mortgage under subsection (d) of this section, may have any rate of interest to which the parties agree.

(c)(1) If a preferred mortgage includes more than one vessel or property that is not a vessel, the mortgage may provide for the separate discharge of each vessel and all property not a vessel by the payment of a part of the mortgage indebtedness.

(2) If a vessel covered by a preferred mortgage that includes more than one vessel or property that is not a vessel is to be sold on the order of a district court in a civil action in rem, and the mortgage does not provide for separate discharge as provided under paragraph (1) of this subsection—

(A) the mortgage constitutes a lien on that vessel in the full amount of the outstanding mortgage indebtedness; and

(B) an allocation of mortgage indebtedness for purposes of separate discharge may not be made among the vessel and other property covered by the mortgage.

(d)(1) A mortgage, security agreement, or instrument granting a security interest perfected under State law covering the whole of a vessel titled in a State is deemed to be a preferred mortgage if—

(A) the Secretary certifies that the State titling system complies with the Secretary's guidelines for a titling system under section 13107(b)(8) of this title; and

(B) information on the vessel covered by the mortgage, security agreement, or instrument is made available to the Secretary under chapter 125 of this title.

(2) This subsection applies to mortgages, security agreements, or instruments covering vessels titled in a State after—

(A) the Secretary's certification under paragraph (1)(A) of this subsection; and

(B) the State begins making information available to the Secretary under chapter 125 of this title.

(3) A preferred mortgage under this subsection continues to be a preferred mortgage even if the vessel is no longer titled in the State where the mortgage, security agreement, or instrument granting a security interest became a preferred mortgage under this subsection.

(e) If a vessel is already covered by a preferred mortgage when an application for titling or documentation is filed—

(1) the status of the preferred mortgage covering the vessel to be titled in the State is determined by the law of the jurisdiction where the vessel is currently titled or documented; and

(2) the status of the preferred mortgage covering the vessel to be documented under chapter 121 is determined by subsection (a) of this section.

(f)(1) A mortgage trustee may hold in trust, for an individual or entity, an instrument or evidence of indebtedness, secured by a mortgage of the vessel to the mortgage trustee, provided that the mortgage trustee—

(A) is eligible to be a preferred mortgagee under subsection (a)(4), subparagraphs (A)–(E) of this section;

(B) is organized as a corporation, and is doing business, under the laws of the United States or of a State;

(C) is authorized under those laws to exercise corporate trust powers;

(D) is subject to supervision or examination by an official of the United States Government or a State;

(E) has a combined capital and surplus (as stated in its most recent published report of condition) of at least $3,000,000; and

(F) meets any other requirements prescribed by the Secretary.

(2) If the beneficiary under the trust arrangement is not a commercial lender, a lender syndicate or eligible to be a preferred mortgagee under subsection (a)(4), subparagraphs (A)–(E) of this section, the Secretary must determine that the issuance, assignment, transfer, or trust arrangement does not result in an impermissible transfer of control of the vessel to a person not eligible to own a vessel with a fishery endorsement under section 12113(c) of this title.

(3) A vessel with a fishery endorsement may be operated by a mortgage trustee only with the approval of the Secretary.

(4) A right under a mortgage of a vessel with a fishery endorsement may be issued, assigned, or transferred to a person not eligible to be a mortgagee of that vessel under this section only with the approval of the Secretary.

(5) The issuance, assignment, or transfer of an instrument or evidence of indebtedness contrary to this subsection is voidable by the Secretary.

(g) For purposes of this section a "commercial lender" means an entity primarily engaged in the business of lending and other financing transactions with a loan portfolio in excess of $100,000,000, of which not more than 50 per centum in dollar amount consists of loans to borrowers in the commercial fishing industry, as certified to the Secretary by such lender.

(h) For purposes of this section a "lender syndicate" means an arrangement established for the combined extension of credit of not less than $20,000,000 made up of four or more entities that each have a beneficial interest, held through an agent, under a trust arrangement established pursuant to subsection (f), no one of which may exercise powers thereunder without the concurrence of at least one other unaffiliated beneficiary.

(Pub. L. 100–710, title I, §102(c), Nov. 23, 1988, 102 Stat. 4743; Pub. L. 101–225, title III, §303(3), Dec. 12, 1989, 103 Stat. 1923; Pub. L. 104–324, title XI, §1113(a), Oct. 19, 1996, 110 Stat. 3970; Pub. L. 105–277, div. C, title II, §202(b), Oct. 21, 1998, 112 Stat. 2681–618; Pub. L. 105–383, title IV, §401(c)(1)–(4), Nov. 13, 1998, 112 Stat. 3425; Pub. L. 106–31, title III, §3027(a)(1), May 21, 1999, 113 Stat. 101; Pub. L. 107–20, title II, §2202(b), (c), July 24, 2001, 115 Stat. 168, 169; Pub. L. 109–304, §§15(29), 16(c)(7), Oct. 6, 2006, 120 Stat. 1704, 1706; Pub. L. 115–232, div. C, title XXXV, §3546(l), Aug. 13, 2018, 132 Stat. 2327.)

§31323. DISCLOSING AND INCURRING OBLIGATIONS BEFORE EXECUTING PREFERRED MORTGAGES

(a) On request of the mortgagee and before executing a preferred mortgage, the mortgagor shall disclose in writing to the mortgagee the existence of any obligation known to the mortgagor on the vessel to be mortgaged.

(b) After executing a preferred mortgage and before the mortgagee has had a reasonable time to file the mortgage, the mortgagor may not incur, without the consent of the mortgagee, any contractual obligation establishing a lien on the vessel except a lien for—

(1) wages of a stevedore when employed directly by a person listed in section 31341 of this title;

(2) wages for the crew of the vessel;

(3) general average; or

(4) salvage, including contract salvage.

(c) On conviction of a mortgagor under section 31330(a)(1)(A) or (B) of this title for violating this section, the mortgage indebtedness, at the option of the mortgagee, is payable immediately.

(Pub. L. 100–710, title I, §102(c), Nov. 23, 1988, 102 Stat. 4744.)

§31324. RETENTION AND EXAMINATION OF MORTGAGES OF VESSELS COVERED BY PREFERRED MORTGAGES

(a) On request, the owner, master, or individual in charge of a vessel covered by a preferred mortgage shall permit a person to examine the mortgage if the person has business with the vessel that may give rise to a maritime lien or the sale, conveyance, mortgage, or assignment of a mortgage of the vessel.

(b) A mortgagor of a preferred mortgage covering a self-propelled vessel shall use diligence in keeping a certified copy of the mortgage on the vessel.

(Pub. L. 100–710, title I, §102(c), Nov. 23, 1988, 102 Stat. 4744.)

§31325. PREFERRED MORTGAGE LIENS AND ENFORCEMENT

(a) A preferred mortgage is a lien on the mortgaged vessel in the amount of the outstanding mortgage indebtedness secured by the vessel.

(b) On default of any term of the preferred mortgage, the mortgagee may—

(1) enforce the preferred mortgage lien in a civil action in rem for a documented vessel, a vessel to be documented under chapter 121 of this title, a vessel titled in a State, or a foreign vessel;

(2) enforce a claim for the outstanding indebtedness secured by the mortgaged vessel in—

(A) a civil action in personam in admiralty against the mortgagor, maker, comaker, or guarantor for the amount of the outstanding indebtedness or any deficiency in full payment of that indebtedness; and

(B) a civil action against the mortgagor, maker, comaker, or guarantor for the amount of the outstanding indebtedness or any deficiency in full payment of that indebtedness; and

(3) enforce the preferred mortgage lien or a claim for the outstanding indebtedness secured by the mortgaged vessel, or both, by exercising any other remedy (including an extrajudicial remedy) against a documented vessel, a vessel for which an application for documentation is filed under chapter 121 of this title, a vessel titled in a State, a foreign vessel, or a mortgagor, maker, comaker, or guarantor for the amount of the outstanding indebtedness or any deficiency in full payment of that indebtedness, if—

(A) the remedy is allowed under applicable law; and

(B) the exercise of the remedy will not result in a violation of section 56101 or 56102 of this title.

(c) The district courts have original jurisdiction of a civil action brought under subsection (b)(1) or (2) of this section. However, for a documented vessel, a vessel to be documented under chapter 121 of this title, a vessel titled in a State, or a foreign vessel, this jurisdiction is exclusive of the courts of the States for a civil action brought under subsection (b)(1) of this section.

(d)(1) Actual notice of a civil action brought under subsection (b)(1) of this section, or to enforce a maritime lien, must be given in the manner directed by the court to—

(A) the master or individual in charge of the vessel;

(B) any person that recorded under section 31343(a) or (d) of this title an unexpired notice of a claim of an undischarged lien on the vessel; and

(C) a mortgagee of a mortgage filed or recorded under section 31321 of this title that is an undischarged mortgage on the vessel.

(2) Notice under paragraph (1) of this subsection is not required if, after search satisfactory to the court, the person entitled to the notice has not been found in the United States.

(3) Failure to give notice required by this subsection does not affect the jurisdiction of the court in which the civil action is brought. However, unless notice is not required under paragraph (2) of this subsection, the party required to give notice is liable to the person not notified for damages in the amount of that person's interest in the vessel terminated by the action brought under subsection (b)(1) of this section. A civil action may be brought to recover the amount of the terminated interest. The district courts have original jurisdiction of the action, regardless of the amount in controversy or the citizenship of the parties. If the plaintiff prevails, the court may award costs and attorney fees to the plaintiff.

(e) In a civil action brought under subsection (b)(1) of this section—

(1) the court may appoint a receiver and authorize the receiver to operate the mortgaged vessel and shall retain in rem jurisdiction over the vessel even if the receiver operates the vessel outside the district in which the court is located; and

(2) when directed by the court, a United States marshal may take possession of a mortgaged vessel even if the vessel is in the possession or under the control of a person claiming a possessory common law lien.

(f)(1) Before title to the documented vessel or vessel for which an application for documentation is filed under chapter 121 is transferred by an extrajudicial remedy, the person exercising the remedy shall give notice of the proposed transfer to the Secretary, to the mortgagee of any mortgage on the vessel filed in substantial compliance with section 31321 of this title before notice of the proposed transfer is given to the Secretary, and to any person that recorded an unexpired notice of a claim of an undischarged lien on the vessel under section 31343(a) or (d) of this title before notice of the proposed transfer is given to the Secretary.

(2) Failure to give notice as required by this subsection shall not affect the transfer of title to a vessel. However, the rights of any holder of a maritime lien or a preferred mortgage on the vessel shall not be affected by a transfer of title by an extrajudicial remedy exercised under this section, regardless of whether notice is required by this subsection or given.

(3) The Secretary shall prescribe regulations establishing the time and manner for providing notice under this subsection.

(Pub. L. 100–710, title I, §102(c), Nov. 23, 1988, 102 Stat. 4745; Pub. L. 101–225, title III, §303(4), Dec. 12, 1989, 103 Stat. 1923; Pub. L. 104–324, title XI, §1124(a), (b), Oct. 19, 1996, 110 Stat. 3980; Pub. L. 105–383, title IV, §401(c)(5)–(7), Nov. 13, 1998, 112 Stat. 3425; Pub. L. 107–295, title II, §205(b), Nov. 25, 2002, 116 Stat. 2096; Pub. L. 109–304, §15(30), Oct. 6, 2006, 120 Stat. 1704; Pub. L. 110–181, div. C, title XXXV, §3529(b)(1)(B), Jan. 28, 2008, 122 Stat. 603.)

§31326. COURT SALES TO ENFORCE PREFERRED MORTGAGE LIENS AND MARITIME LIENS AND PRIORITY OF CLAIMS

(a) When a vessel is sold by order of a district court in a civil action in rem brought to enforce a preferred mortgage lien or a maritime lien, any claim in the vessel existing on the date of sale is terminated, including a possessory common law lien of which a person is deprived under section 31325(e)(2) of this title, and the vessel is sold free of all those claims.

(b) Each of the claims terminated under subsection (a) of this section attaches, in the same amount and in accordance with their priorities to the proceeds of the sale, except that—

(1) the preferred mortgage lien, including a preferred mortgage lien on a foreign vessel whose mortgage has been guaranteed under chapter 537 of this title, has priority over all claims against the vessel (except for expenses and fees allowed by the court, costs imposed by the court, and preferred maritime liens); and

(2) for a foreign vessel whose mortgage has not been guaranteed under chapter 537 of this title, the preferred mortgage lien is subordinate to a maritime lien for necessaries provided in the United States.

(Pub. L. 100–710, title I, §102(c), Nov. 23, 1988, 102 Stat. 4746; Pub. L. 103–160, div. A, title XIII, §1360, Nov. 30, 1993, 107 Stat. 1816; Pub. L. 109–304, §15(31), Oct. 6, 2006, 120 Stat. 1704.)

§31327. FORFEITURE OF MORTGAGEE INTEREST

The interest of a mortgagee in a documented vessel or a vessel covered by a preferred mortgage under section 31322(d) of this title may be terminated by a forfeiture of the vessel for a violation of a law of the United States only if the mortgagee authorized, consented, or conspired to do the act, failure, or omission that is the basis of the violation.

(Pub. L. 100–710, title I, §102(c), Nov. 23, 1988, 102 Stat. 4746.)

[§31328. Repealed. Pub. L. 104–324, title XI, §1113(b)(1), Oct. 19, 1996, 110 Stat. 3970]

CHAPTER 313—COMMERCIAL
INSTRUMENTS AND MARITIME LIENS

[§31328. Repealed. Pub. L. 104–324, title XI, §1113(b)(1), Oct. 19, 1996, 110 Stat. 3970]

Section, Pub. L. 100–710, title I, §102(c), Nov. 23, 1988, 102 Stat. 4746, related to limitations on parties serving as trustees of mortgaged vessel interests.

§31329. Court sales of documented vessels

(a) A documented vessel may be sold by order of a district court only to—

(1) a person eligible to own a documented vessel under section 12103 of this title; or

(2) a mortgagee of that vessel.

(b) When a vessel is sold to a mortgagee not eligible to own a documented vessel—

(1) the vessel must be held by the mortgagee for resale;

(2) the vessel held by the mortgagee is subject to chapter 563 of this title; and

(3) the sale of the vessel to the mortgagee is not a sale to a person not a citizen of the United States under section 12132 of this title.

(c) Unless waived by the Secretary of Transportation, a person purchasing a vessel by court order under subsection (a)(1) of this section or from a mortgagee under subsection (a)(2) of this section must document the vessel under chapter 121 of this title.

(d) The vessel may be operated by the mortgagee not eligible to own a documented vessel only with the approval of the Secretary of Transportation.

(e) A sale of a vessel contrary to this section is void.

(f) This section does not apply to a documented vessel that has been operated only for pleasure.

(Pub. L. 100–710, title I, §102(c), Nov. 23, 1988, 102 Stat. 4747; Pub. L. 104–324, title XI, §1118, Oct. 19, 1996, 110 Stat. 3973; Pub. L. 109–304, §15(32), Oct. 6, 2006, 120 Stat. 1704; Pub. L. 111–281, title IX, §913(c), Oct. 15, 2010, 124 Stat. 3017.)

§31330. Penalties

(a)(1) A mortgagor shall be fined under title 18, imprisoned for not more than 2 years, or both, if the mortgagor—

(A) with intent to defraud, does not disclose an obligation on a vessel as required by section 31323(a) of this title;

(B) with intent to defraud, incurs a contractual obligation in violation of section 31323(b) of this title; or

(C) with intent to hinder or defraud an existing or future creditor of the mortgagor or a lienor of the vessel, files a mortgage with the Secretary.

(2) A mortgagor is liable to the United States Government for a civil penalty of not more than $10,000 if the mortgagor—

(A) does not disclose an obligation on a vessel as required by section 31323(a) of this title;

(B) incurs a contractual obligation in violation of section 31323(b) of this title; or

(C) files with the Secretary a mortgage made not in good faith.

(b)(1) A person that knowingly violates section 31329 of this title shall be fined under title 18, imprisoned for not more than 3 years, or both.

(2) A person violating section 31329 of this title is liable to the Government for a civil penalty of not more than $25,000.

(3) A vessel involved in a violation under section 31329 of this title and its equipment may be seized by, and forfeited to, the Government.

(c) If a person not an individual violates this section, the president or chief executive of the person also is subject to any penalty provided under this section.

(Pub. L. 100–710, title I, §102(c), Nov. 23, 1988, 102 Stat. 4747; Pub. L. 104–324, title XI, §1113(b)(2), Oct. 19, 1996, 110 Stat. 3970; Pub. L. 111–281, title IX, §913(a)(1), (d), Oct. 15, 2010, 124 Stat. 3017.)

SUBCHAPTER III—MARITIME LIENS

§31341. Persons presumed to have authority to procure necessaries

(a) The following persons are presumed to have authority to procure necessaries for a vessel:

(1) the owner;

(2) the master;

(3) a person entrusted with the management of the vessel at the port of supply; or

(4) an officer or agent appointed by—

(A) the owner;

(B) a charterer;

(C) an owner pro hac vice; or

(D) an agreed buyer in possession of the vessel.

(b) A person tortiously or unlawfully in possession or charge of a vessel has no authority to procure necessaries for the vessel.

(Pub. L. 100–710, title I, §102(c), Nov. 23, 1988, 102 Stat. 4748; Pub. L. 101–225, title III, §303(5), Dec. 12, 1989, 103 Stat. 1924.)

§31342. Establishing maritime liens

(a) Except as provided in subsection (b) of this section, a person providing necessaries to a vessel on the order of the owner or a person authorized by the owner—

(1) has a maritime lien on the vessel;

(2) may bring a civil action in rem to enforce the lien; and

(3) is not required to allege or prove in the action that credit was given to the vessel.

(b) This section does not apply to a public vessel.

(Pub. L. 100–710, title I, §102(c), Nov. 23, 1988, 102 Stat. 4748; Pub. L. 101–225, title III, §303(6), Dec. 12, 1989, 103 Stat. 1924.)

§31343. Recording and discharging notices of claim of maritime lien

(a) Except as provided under subsection (d) of this section, a person claiming a lien on a vessel documented, or for which an application for documentation has been filed, under chapter 121 may record with the Secretary a notice of that person's lien claim on the vessel. To be recordable, the notice must—

(1) state the nature of the lien;

(2) state the date the lien was established;

(3) state the amount of the lien;

(4) state the name and address of the person; and

(5) be signed and acknowledged.

(b)(1) The Secretary shall record a notice complying with subsection (a) of this section if, when the notice is presented to the Secretary for recording, the person having the claim files with the notice a declaration stating the following:

(A) The information in the notice is true and correct to the best of the knowledge, information, and belief of the individual who signed it.

(B) A copy of the notice, as presented for recordation, has been sent to each of the following:

(i) The owner of the vessel.

(ii) Each person that recorded under subsection (a) of this section an unexpired notice of a claim of an undischarged lien on the vessel.

(iii) The mortgagee of each mortgage filed or recorded under section 31321 of this title that is an undischarged mortgage on the vessel.

(2) A declaration under this subsection filed by a person that is not an individual must be signed by the president, member, partner, trustee, or other individual authorized to execute the declaration on behalf of the person.

(c)(1) On full and final discharge of the indebtedness that is the basis for a notice of claim of lien recorded under subsection (b) of this section, the person having the claim shall provide the Secretary with an acknowledged certificate of discharge of the indebtedness. The Secretary shall record the certificate.

(2) The district courts of the United States shall have jurisdiction over a civil action in Admiralty to declare that a vessel is not subject to a lien claimed under subsection (b) of this section, or that the vessel is not subject to the notice of claim of lien, or both, regardless of the amount in controversy or the citizenship of the parties. Venue in such an action shall be in the district where the vessel is found or where the claimant resides or where the notice of claim of lien is recorded. The court may award costs and attorneys fees to the prevailing party, unless the court finds that the position of the other party was substantially justified or other circumstances make an award of costs and attorneys fees unjust. The Secretary shall record any such declaratory order.

(d) A person claiming a lien on a vessel covered by a preferred mortgage under section 31322(d) of this title must record and discharge the lien as provided by the law of the State in which the vessel is titled.

(e)(1) A notice of claim of lien recorded under subsection (b) of this section shall expire 3 years after the date the lien was established, as such date is stated in the notice under subsection (a) of this section.

(2) On expiration of a notice of claim of lien under paragraph (1), and after a request by the vessel owner, the Secretary shall annotate the abstract of title to reflect the expiration of the lien.

(f) This section does not alter in any respect the law pertaining to the establishment of a maritime lien, the remedy provided by such a lien, or the defenses thereto, including any defense under the doctrine of laches.

(Pub. L. 100–710, title I, §102(c), Nov. 23, 1988, 102 Stat. 4748; Pub. L. 107–295, title II, §205(a)(1), Nov. 25, 2002, 116 Stat. 2095; Pub. L. 111–281, title IX, §913(a)(1), Oct. 15, 2010, 124 Stat. 3017; Pub. L. 116–283, div. G, title LVXXXIII [LXXXIII], §8333, Jan. 1, 2021, 134 Stat. 4705.)

SUBTITLE IV
REGULATION OF OCEAN SHIPPING

Subtitle IV—Regulation of Ocean Shipping

[1] *Section number editorially supplied.*

PART A—OCEAN SHIPPING

CHAPTER 401—GENERAL

§40101. Purposes

The purposes of this part are to—

(1) establish a nondiscriminatory regulatory process for the common carriage of goods by water in the foreign commerce of the United States with a minimum of government intervention and regulatory costs;

(2) ensure an efficient, competitive, and economical transportation system in the ocean commerce of the United States;

(3) encourage the development of an economically sound and efficient liner fleet of vessels of the United States capable of meeting national security needs and supporting commerce; and

(4) promote the growth and development of United States exports through a competitive and efficient system for the carriage of goods by water in the foreign commerce of the United States, and by placing a greater reliance on the marketplace.

(Pub. L. 109–304, §7, Oct. 6, 2006, 120 Stat. 1523; Pub. L. 117–146, §2, June 16, 2022, 136 Stat. 1272.)

§40102. Definitions

In this part:

(1) AGREEMENT.—The term "agreement"—

(A) means a written or oral understanding, arrangement, or association, and any modification or cancellation thereof; but

(B) does not include a maritime labor agreement.

(2) ANTITRUST LAWS.—The term "antitrust laws" means—

(A) the Sherman Act (15 U.S.C. 1 et seq.);

(B) sections 73 and 74 of the Wilson Tariff Act (15 U.S.C. 8, 9);

(C) the Clayton Act (15 U.S.C. 12 et seq.);

(D) the Act of June 19, 1936 (15 U.S.C. 13, 13a, 13b, 21a);

(E) the Federal Trade Commission Act (15 U.S.C. 41 et seq.);

(F) the Antitrust Civil Process Act (15 U.S.C. 1311 et seq.); and

(G) Acts supplementary to those Acts.

(3) ASSESSMENT AGREEMENT.—The term "assessment agreement" means an agreement, whether part of a collective bargaining agreement or negotiated separately, to the extent the agreement provides for the funding of collectively bargained fringe-benefit obligations on other than a uniform worker-hour basis, regardless of the cargo handled

or type of vessel or equipment used.

(4) BULK CARGO.—The term "bulk cargo" means cargo that is loaded and carried in bulk without mark or count.

(5) CERTAIN COVERED SERVICES.—For purposes of sections 41105 and 41307, the term "certain covered services" means, with respect to a vessel—

(A) the berthing or bunkering of the vessel;

(B) the loading or unloading of cargo to or from the vessel to or from a point on a wharf or terminal;

(C) the positioning, removal, or replacement of buoys related to the movement of the vessel; and

(D) with respect to injunctive relief under section 41307, towing vessel services provided to such a vessel.

(6) CHEMICAL PARCEL-TANKER.—The term "chemical parcel-tanker" means a vessel that has—

(A) a cargo-carrying capability consisting of individual cargo tanks for bulk chemicals that—

(i) are a permanent part of the vessel; and

(ii) have segregation capability with piping systems to permit simultaneous carriage of several bulk chemical cargoes with minimum risk of cross-contamination; and

(B) a valid certificate of fitness under the International Maritime Organization Code for the Construction and Equipment of Ships Carrying Dangerous Chemicals in Bulk.

(7) COMMON CARRIER.—The term "common carrier"—

(A) means a person that—

(i) holds itself out to the general public to provide transportation by water of passengers or cargo between the United States and a foreign country for compensation;

(ii) assumes responsibility for the transportation from the port or point of receipt to the port or point of destination; and

(iii) uses, for all or part of that transportation, a vessel operating on the high seas or the Great Lakes between a port in the United States and a port in a foreign country; but

(B) does not include a carrier engaged in ocean transportation by ferry boat, ocean tramp, or chemical parcel-tanker, or by vessel when primarily engaged in the carriage of perishable agricultural commodities—

(i) if the carrier and the owner of those commodities are wholly-owned, directly or indirectly, by a person primarily engaged in the marketing and distribution of those commodities; and

(ii) only with respect to the carriage of those commodities.

(8) CONFERENCE.—The term "conference"—

(A) means an association of ocean common carriers permitted, pursuant to an approved or effective agreement, to engage in concerted activity and to use a common tariff; but

(B) does not include a joint service, consortium, pooling, sailing, or transshipment agreement.

(9) CONTROLLED CARRIER.—The term "controlled carrier" means an ocean common carrier that is, or whose operating assets are, directly or indirectly, owned or controlled by a government, with ownership or control by a government being deemed to exist for a carrier if—

(A) a majority of the interest in the carrier is owned or controlled in any manner by that government, an agency of that government, or a public or private person controlled by that government; or

(B) that government has the right to appoint or disapprove the appointment of a majority of the directors, the chief operating officer, or the chief executive officer of the carrier.

(10) DEFERRED REBATE.—The term "deferred rebate" means a return by a common carrier of any freight money to a shipper, where the return is—

(A) consideration for the shipper giving all or any portion of its shipments to that or any other common carrier over a fixed period of time;

(B) deferred beyond the completion of the service for which it was paid; and

(C) made only if the shipper has agreed to make a further shipment with that or any other common carrier.

(11) FOREST PRODUCTS.—The term "forest products" includes lumber in bundles, rough timber, ties, poles, piling, laminated beams, bundled siding, bundled plywood, bundled core stock or veneers, bundled particle or fiber boards, bundled hardwood, wood pulp in rolls, wood pulp in unitized bales, and paper and paper board in rolls or in pallet or skid-sized sheets.

(12) INLAND DIVISION.—The term "inland division" means the amount paid by a common carrier to an inland carrier for the inland portion of through transportation offered to the public by the common carrier.

(13) INLAND PORTION.—The term "inland portion" means the charge to the public by a common carrier for the non-ocean portion of through transportation.

(14) LOYALTY CONTRACT.—The term "loyalty contract" means a contract with an ocean common carrier or agreement providing for—

(A) a shipper to obtain lower rates by committing all or a fixed portion of its cargo to that carrier or agreement; and

(B) a deferred rebate arrangement.

(15) MARINE TERMINAL OPERATOR.—The term "marine terminal operator" means a person engaged in the United States in the business of providing wharfage, dock, warehouse, or other terminal facilities in connection with a common carrier, or in connection with a common carrier and a water carrier subject to subchapter II of chapter

135 of title 49.

(16) MARITIME LABOR AGREEMENT.—The term "maritime labor agreement"—

(A) means—

(i) a collective bargaining agreement between an employer subject to this part, or a group of such employers, and a labor organization representing employees in the maritime or stevedoring industry;

(ii) an agreement preparatory to such a collective bargaining agreement among members of a multi-employer bargaining group; or

(iii) an agreement specifically implementing provisions of such a collective bargaining agreement or providing for the formation, financing, or administration of a multi-employer bargaining group; but

(B) does not include an assessment agreement.

(17) NON-VESSEL-OPERATING COMMON CARRIER.—The term "non-vessel-operating common carrier" means a common carrier that—

(A) does not operate the vessels by which the ocean transportation is provided; and

(B) is a shipper in its relationship with an ocean common carrier.

(18) OCEAN COMMON CARRIER.—The term "ocean common carrier" means a vessel-operating common carrier.

(19) OCEAN FREIGHT FORWARDER.—The term "ocean freight forwarder" means a person that—

(A) in the United States, dispatches shipments from the United States via a common carrier and books or otherwise arranges space for those shipments on behalf of shippers; and

(B) processes the documentation or performs related activities incident to those shipments.

(20) OCEAN TRANSPORTATION INTERMEDIARY.—The term "ocean transportation intermediary" means an ocean freight forwarder or a non-vessel-operating common carrier.

(21) SERVICE CONTRACT.—The term "service contract" means a written contract, other than a bill of lading or receipt, between one or more shippers, on the one hand, and an individual ocean common carrier or an agreement between or among ocean common carriers, on the other, in which—

(A) the shipper or shippers commit to providing a certain volume or portion of cargo over a fixed time period; and

(B) the ocean common carrier or the agreement commits to a certain rate or rate schedule and a defined service level, such as assured space, transit time, port rotation, or similar service features.

(22) SHIPMENT.—The term "shipment" means all of the cargo carried under the terms of a single bill of lading.

(23) SHIPPER.—The term "shipper" means—

(A) a cargo owner;

(B) the person for whose account the ocean transportation of cargo is provided;

(C) the person to whom delivery is to be made;

(D) a shippers' association; or

(E) a non-vessel-operating common carrier that accepts responsibility for payment of all charges applicable under the tariff or service contract.

(24) SHIPPERS' ASSOCIATION.—The term "shippers' association" means a group of shippers that consolidates or distributes freight on a nonprofit basis for the members of the group to obtain carload, truckload, or other volume rates or service contracts.

(25) THROUGH RATE.—The term "through rate" means the single amount charged by a common carrier in connection with through transportation.

(26) THROUGH TRANSPORTATION.—The term "through transportation" means continuous transportation between origin and destination for which a through rate is assessed and which is offered or performed by one or more carriers, at least one of which is a common carrier, between a United States port or point and a foreign port or point.

(Pub. L. 109–304, §7, Oct. 6, 2006, 120 Stat. 1523; Pub. L. 115–282, title VII, §704, Dec. 4, 2018, 132 Stat. 4294.)

§40103. ADMINISTRATIVE EXEMPTIONS

(a) IN GENERAL.—The Federal Maritime Commission, on application or its own motion, may by order or regulation exempt for the future any class of agreements between persons subject to this part or any specified activity of those persons from any requirement of this part if the Commission finds that the exemption will not result in substantial reduction in competition or be detrimental to commerce. The Commission may attach conditions to an exemption and may, by order, revoke an exemption.

(b) OPPORTUNITY FOR HEARING.—An order or regulation of exemption or revocation of an exemption may be issued only if the Commission has provided an opportunity for a hearing to interested persons and departments and agencies of the United States Government.

(Pub. L. 109–304, §7, Oct. 6, 2006, 120 Stat. 1527.)

§40104. REPORTS FILED WITH THE COMMISSION

(a) REPORTS.—

(1) IN GENERAL.—The Federal Maritime Commission may require a common carrier or marine terminal operator, or an officer, receiver, trustee, lessee, agent, or employee of the common carrier or marine terminal operator to file with the Commission a periodical or special report, an account, record, rate, or charge, or a memorandum of facts and transactions related to the business of the common carrier or marine terminal operator, as applicable.

(2) REQUIREMENTS.—Any report, account, record, rate, charge, or memorandum required to be filed under paragraph (1) shall—

(A) be made under oath if the Commission requires; and

(B) be filed in the form and within the time prescribed by the Commission.

(3) LIMITATION.—The Commission shall—

(A) limit the scope of any filing ordered under this section to fulfill the objective of the order; and

(B) provide a reasonable period of time for respondents to respond based upon their capabilities and the scope of the order.

(b) CONFERENCE MINUTES.—Conference minutes required to be filed with the Commission under this section may not be released to third parties or published by the Commission.

(Pub. L. 109–304, §7, Oct. 6, 2006, 120 Stat. 1527; Pub. L. 115–282, title VII, §705, Dec. 4, 2018, 132 Stat. 4294.)

CHAPTER 403—AGREEMENTS

§40301. APPLICATION

(a) OCEAN COMMON CARRIER AGREEMENTS.—This part applies to an agreement between or among ocean common carriers to—

(1) discuss, fix, or regulate transportation rates, including through rates, cargo space accommodations, and other conditions of service;

(2) pool or apportion traffic, revenues, earnings, or losses;

(3) allot ports or regulate the number and character of voyages between ports;

(4) regulate the volume or character of cargo or passenger traffic to be carried;

(5) engage in an exclusive, preferential, or cooperative working arrangement between themselves or with a marine terminal operator;

(6) control, regulate, or prevent competition in international ocean transportation; or

(7) discuss and agree on any matter related to a service contract.

(b) MARINE TERMINAL OPERATOR AGREEMENTS.—This part applies to an agreement between or among marine terminal operators, or between or among one or more marine terminal operators and one or more ocean common carriers, to—

(1) discuss, fix, or regulate rates or other conditions of service; or

(2) engage in exclusive, preferential, or cooperative working arrangements, to the extent the agreement involves ocean transportation in the foreign commerce of the United States.

(c) ACQUISITIONS.—This part does not apply to an acquisition by any person, directly or indirectly, of any voting security or assets of any other person.

(d) MARITIME LABOR AGREEMENTS.—This part does not apply to a maritime labor agreement. However, this subsection does not exempt from this part any rate, charge, regulation, or practice of a common carrier that is required to be set forth in a tariff or is an essential term of a service contract, whether or not the rate, charge, regulation, or practice arises out of, or is otherwise related to, a maritime labor agreement.

(e) ASSESSMENT AGREEMENTS.—This part (except sections 40305 and 40307(a)) does not apply to an assessment agreement.

(Pub. L. 109–304, §7, Oct. 6, 2006, 120 Stat. 1528.)

§40302. Filing requirements

(a) In General.—A true copy of every agreement referred to in section 40301(a) or (b) of this title shall be filed with the Federal Maritime Commission. If the agreement is oral, a complete memorandum specifying in detail the substance of the agreement shall be filed.

(b) Exceptions.—Subsection (a) does not apply to—

(1) an agreement related to transportation to be performed within or between foreign countries; or

(2) an agreement among common carriers to establish, operate, or maintain a marine terminal in the United States.

(c) Regulations.—The Commission may by regulation prescribe the form and manner in which an agreement shall be filed and any additional information and documents necessary to evaluate the agreement.

(Pub. L. 109–304, §7, Oct. 6, 2006, 120 Stat. 1528.)

§40303. Content requirements

(a) Ocean Common Carrier Agreements.—

(1) Restrictions.—An ocean common carrier agreement may not—

(A) prohibit or restrict a member of the agreement from engaging in negotiations for a service contract with a shipper;

(B) require a member of the agreement to disclose a negotiation on a service contract, or the terms of a service contract, other than those terms required to be published under section 40502(d) of this title; or

(C) adopt mandatory rules or requirements affecting the right of an agreement member to negotiate and enter into a service contract.

(2) Voluntary guidelines.—An ocean common carrier agreement may provide authority to adopt voluntary guidelines relating to the terms and procedures of an agreement member's service contracts if the guidelines explicitly state the right of members of the agreement not to follow the guidelines. Any guidelines adopted shall be submitted confidentially to the Federal Maritime Commission.

(b) Conference Agreements.—Each conference agreement must—

(1) state its purpose;

(2) provide reasonable and equal terms for admission and readmission to conference membership for any ocean common carrier willing to serve the particular trade or route;

(3) permit any member to withdraw from conference membership on reasonable notice without penalty;

(4) at the request of any member, require an independent neutral body to police fully the obligations of the conference and its members;

(5) prohibit the conference from engaging in conduct prohibited by section 41105(1) or (3) of this title;

(6) provide for a consultation process designed to promote—

(A) commercial resolution of disputes; and

(B) cooperation with shippers in preventing and eliminating malpractices;

(7) establish procedures for promptly and fairly considering requests and complaints of shippers; and

(8) provide that—

(A) any member of the conference may take independent action on a rate or service item on not more than 5 days' notice to the conference; and

(B) except for an exempt commodity not published in the conference tariff, the conference will include the new rate or service item in its tariff for use by that member, effective no later than 5 days after receipt of the notice, and by any other member that notifies the conference that it elects to adopt the independent rate or service item on or after its effective date, in lieu of the existing conference tariff provision for that rate or service item.

(c) INTERCONFERENCE AGREEMENTS.—Each agreement between carriers not members of the same conference must provide the right of independent action for each carrier. Each agreement between conferences must provide the right of independent action for each conference.

(d) VESSEL SHARING AGREEMENTS.—

(1) IN GENERAL.—An ocean common carrier that is the owner, operator, or bareboat, time, or slot charterer of a liner vessel documented under section 12103 or 12111(c) of this title may agree with an ocean common carrier described in paragraph (2) to which it charters or subcharters the vessel or space on the vessel that the charterer or subcharterer may not use or make available space on the vessel for the carriage of cargo reserved by law for vessels of the United States.

(2) CARRIER DESCRIBED.—An ocean common carrier described in this paragraph is one that is not the owner, operator, or bareboat charterer for at least one year of liner vessels of the United States that are eligible to be included in the Maritime Security Fleet Program and are enrolled in an Emergency Preparedness Program under chapter 531 of this title.

(Pub. L. 109–304, §7, Oct. 6, 2006, 120 Stat. 1529.)

§40304. COMMISSION ACTION

(a) NOTICE OF FILING.—Not later than 7 days after the date an agreement is filed, the Federal Maritime Commission shall—

(1) transmit a notice of the filing to the Federal Register for publication; and

(2) request interested persons to submit relevant information and documents.

(b) PRELIMINARY REVIEW AND REJECTION.—After preliminary review, the Commission shall reject an agreement that it finds does not meet the requirements of sections 40302 and 40303 of this title. The Commission shall notify in writing the person filing the agreement of the reason for rejection.

(c) REVIEW AND EFFECTIVE DATE.—Unless rejected under subsection (b), an agreement (other than an assessment agreement) is effective—

(1) on the 45th day after filing, or on the 30th day after notice of the filing is published

in the Federal Register, whichever is later; or

(2) if additional information or documents are requested under subsection (d)—

(A) on the 45th day after the Commission receives all the additional information and documents; or

(B) if the request is not fully complied with, on the 45th day after the Commission receives the information and documents submitted and a statement of the reasons for noncompliance with the request.

(d) REQUEST FOR ADDITIONAL INFORMATION.—Before the expiration of the period specified in subsection (c)(1), the Commission may request from the person filing the agreement any additional information and documents the Commission considers necessary to make the determinations required by this part.

(e) MODIFICATION OF REVIEW PERIOD.—

(1) SHORTENING.—On request of the party filing an agreement, the Commission may shorten a period specified in subsection (c), but not to a date that is less than 14 days after notice of the filing of the agreement is published in the Federal Register.

(2) EXTENSION.—The period specified in subsection (c)(2) may be extended only by the United States District Court for the District of Columbia in a civil action brought by the Commission under section 41307(c) of this title.

(f) FIXED TERMS.—The Commission may not limit the effectiveness of an agreement to a fixed term.

(Pub. L. 109–304, §7, Oct. 6, 2006, 120 Stat. 1530; Pub. L. 115–282, title VII, §706(a), (b), Dec. 4, 2018, 132 Stat. 4295.)

§40305. ASSESSMENT AGREEMENTS

(a) FILING REQUIREMENT.—An assessment agreement shall be filed with the Federal Maritime Commission and is effective on filing.

(b) COMPLAINTS.—If a complaint is filed with the Commission within 2 years after the date of an assessment agreement, the Commission shall disapprove, cancel, or modify the agreement, or an assessment or charge pursuant to the agreement, that the Commission finds, after notice and opportunity for a hearing, to be unjustly discriminatory or unfair as between carriers, shippers, or ports. The Commission shall issue its final decision in the proceeding within one year after the date the complaint is filed.

(c) ADJUSTMENTS OF ASSESSMENTS AND CHARGES.—To the extent that the Commission finds under subsection (b) that an assessment or charge is unjustly discriminatory or unfair as between carriers, shippers, or ports, the Commission shall adjust the assessment or charge for the period between the filing of the complaint and the final decision by awarding prospective credits or debits to future assessments and charges. However, if the complainant has ceased activities subject to the assessment or charge, the Commission may award reparations.

(Pub. L. 109–304, §7, Oct. 6, 2006, 120 Stat. 1531.)

§40306. NONDISCLOSURE OF INFORMATION

Information and documents (other than an agreement) filed with the Federal Maritime

Commission under this chapter are exempt from disclosure under section 552 of title 5 and may not be made public except as may be relevant to an administrative or judicial proceeding. This section does not prevent disclosure to either House of Congress or to a duly authorized committee or subcommittee of Congress.

(Pub. L. 109–304, §7, Oct. 6, 2006, 120 Stat. 1531.)

§40307. EXEMPTION FROM ANTITRUST LAWS

(a) IN GENERAL.—The antitrust laws do not apply to—

(1) an agreement (including an assessment agreement) that has been filed and is effective under this chapter;

(2) an agreement that is exempt under section 40103 of this title from any requirement of this part;

(3) an agreement or activity within the scope of this part, whether permitted under or prohibited by this part, undertaken or entered into with a reasonable basis to conclude that it is—

(A) pursuant to an agreement on file with the Federal Maritime Commission and in effect when the activity takes place; or

(B) exempt under section 40103 of this title from any filing or publication requirement of this part;

(4) an agreement or activity relating to transportation services within or between foreign countries, whether or not via the United States, unless the agreement or activity has a direct, substantial, and reasonably foreseeable effect on the commerce of the United States;

(5) an agreement or activity relating to the foreign inland segment of through transportation that is part of transportation provided in a United States import or export trade;

(6) an agreement or activity to provide wharfage, dock, warehouse, or other terminal facilities outside the United States; or

(7) an agreement, modification, or cancellation approved before June 18, 1984, by the Commission under section 15 of the Shipping Act, 1916, or permitted under section 14b of that Act, and any properly published tariff, rate, fare, or charge, or classification, rule, or regulation explanatory thereof implementing that agreement, modification, or cancellation.

(b) EXCEPTIONS.—This part does not extend antitrust immunity to—

(1) an agreement with or among air carriers, rail carriers, motor carriers, tug operators, or common carriers by water not subject to this part relating to transportation within the United States;

(2) a discussion or agreement among common carriers subject to this part relating to the inland divisions (as opposed to the inland portions) of through rates within the United States;

(3) an agreement among common carriers subject to this part to establish, operate, or maintain a marine terminal in the United States; or

(4) a loyalty contract.

(c) RETROACTIVE EFFECT OF DETERMINATIONS.—A determination by an agency or court that results in the denial or removal of the immunity to the antitrust laws under subsection (a) does not remove or alter the antitrust immunity for the period before the determination.

(d) RELIEF UNDER CLAYTON ACT.—A person may not recover damages under section 4 of the Clayton Act (15 U.S.C. 15), or obtain injunctive relief under section 16 of that Act (15 U.S.C. 26), for conduct prohibited by this part.

(Pub. L. 109–304, §7, Oct. 6, 2006, 120 Stat. 1531; Pub. L. 115–282, title VII, §709(c), Dec. 4, 2018, 132 Stat. 4297.)

CHAPTER 405—TARIFFS, SERVICE CONTRACTS, REFUNDS, AND WAIVERS

§40501. GENERAL RATE AND TARIFF REQUIREMENTS

(a) AUTOMATED TARIFF SYSTEM.—

(1) IN GENERAL.—Each common carrier and conference shall keep open to public inspection in an automated tariff system, tariffs showing all its rates, charges, classifications, rules, and practices between all points or ports on its own route and on any through transportation route that has been established. However, a common carrier is not required to state separately or otherwise reveal in tariffs the inland divisions of a through rate.

(2) EXCEPTIONS.—Paragraph (1) does not apply with respect to bulk cargo, forest products, recycled metal scrap, new assembled motor vehicles, waste paper, or paper waste.

(b) CONTENTS OF TARIFFS.—A tariff under subsection (a) shall—

(1) state the places between which cargo will be carried;

(2) list each classification of cargo in use;

(3) state the level of compensation, if any, of any ocean freight forwarder by a carrier or conference;

(4) state separately each terminal or other charge, privilege, or facility under the control of the carrier or conference and any rules that in any way change, affect, or determine any part or the total of the rates or charges;

(5) include sample copies of any bill of lading, contract of affreightment, or other document evidencing the transportation agreement; and

(6) include copies of any loyalty contract, omitting the shipper's name.

(c) ELECTRONIC ACCESS.—A tariff under subsection (a) shall be made available electronically to any person, without time, quantity, or other limitation, through appropriate access from remote locations. A reasonable fee may be charged for such access, except that no fee may be charged for access by a Federal agency.

(d) TIME-VOLUME RATES.—A rate contained in a tariff under subsection (a) may vary with the volume of cargo offered over a specified period of time.

(e) EFFECTIVE DATES.—

(1) INCREASES.—A new or initial rate or change in an existing rate that results in an increased cost to a shipper may not become effective earlier than 30 days after publication. However, for good cause, the Federal Maritime Commission may allow the rate to become effective sooner.

(2) DECREASES.—A change in an existing rate that results in a decreased cost to a shipper may become effective on publication.

(f) MARINE TERMINAL OPERATOR SCHEDULES.—A marine terminal operator may make available to the public a schedule of rates, regulations, and practices, including limitations of liability for cargo loss or damage, pertaining to receiving, delivering, handling, or storing property at its marine terminal. Any such schedule made available to the public is enforceable by an appropriate court as an implied contract without proof of actual knowledge of its provisions.

(g) REGULATIONS.—

(1) IN GENERAL.—The Commission shall by regulation prescribe the requirements for the accessibility and accuracy of automated tariff systems established under this section. The Commission, after periodic review, may prohibit the use of any automated tariff system that fails to meet the requirements established under this section.

(2) REMOTE TERMINALS.—The Commission may not require a common carrier to provide a remote terminal for electronic access under subsection (c).

(3) MARINE TERMINAL OPERATOR SCHEDULES.—The Commission shall by regulation prescribe the form and manner in which marine terminal operator schedules authorized by this section shall be published.

(Pub. L. 109–304, §7, Oct. 6, 2006, 120 Stat. 1532.)

§40502. SERVICE CONTRACTS

(a) IN GENERAL.—An individual ocean common carrier or an agreement between or among ocean common carriers may enter into a service contract with one or more shippers subject to the requirements of this part.

(b) FILING REQUIREMENTS.—

(1) IN GENERAL.—Each service contract entered into under this section by an individual ocean common carrier or an agreement shall be filed confidentially with the Federal Maritime Commission.

(2) EXCEPTIONS.—Paragraph (1) does not apply to contracts regarding bulk cargo, forest products, recycled metal scrap, new assembled motor vehicles, waste paper, or paper waste.

(c) ESSENTIAL TERMS.—Each service contract shall include—

(1) the origin and destination port ranges;

(2) the origin and destination geographic areas in the case of through intermodal movements;

(3) the commodities involved;

(4) the minimum volume or portion;

(5) the line-haul rate;

(6) the duration;

(7) service commitments;

(8) the liquidated damages for nonperformance, if any; and

(9) any other essential terms that the Federal Maritime Commission determines necessary or appropriate through a rulemaking process.

(d) PUBLICATION OF CERTAIN TERMS.—When a service contract is filed confidentially with the Commission, a concise statement of the essential terms specified in paragraphs (1), (3), (4), and (6) of subsection (c) shall be published and made available to the general public in tariff format.

(e) DISCLOSURE OF CERTAIN TERMS.—

(1) DEFINITIONS.—In this subsection, the terms "dock area" and "within the port area" have the same meaning and scope as in the applicable collective bargaining agreement between the requesting labor organization and the carrier.

(2) DISCLOSURE.—An ocean common carrier that is a party to or is otherwise subject to a collective bargaining agreement with a labor organization shall, in response to a written request by the labor organization, state whether it is responsible for the following work at a dock area or within a port area in the United States with respect to cargo transportation under a service contract:

(A) The movement of the shipper's cargo on a dock area or within the port area or to or from railroad cars on a dock area or within the port area.

(B) The assignment of intraport carriage of the shipper's cargo between areas on a dock or within the port area.

(C) The assignment of the carriage of the shipper's cargo between a container yard on a dock area or within the port area and a rail yard adjacent to the container yard.

(D) The assignment of container freight station work and container maintenance and repair work performed at a dock area or within the port area.

(3) WITHIN REASONABLE TIME.—The common carrier shall provide the information described in paragraph (2) to the requesting labor organization within a reasonable period of time.

(4) EXISTENCE OF COLLECTIVE BARGAINING AGREEMENT.—This subsection does not require the disclosure of information by an ocean common carrier unless there exists an applicable and otherwise lawful collective bargaining agreement pertaining to that carrier. A disclosure by an ocean common carrier may not be deemed an admission or an agreement that any work is covered by a collective bargaining agreement. A dispute about whether any work is covered by a collective bargaining agreement and the responsibility of an ocean common carrier under a collective bargaining agreement shall be resolved solely in accordance with the dispute resolution procedures contained in the collective bargaining agreement and the National Labor Relations Act (29 U.S.C. 151 et seq.), and without reference to this subsection.

(5) EFFECT UNDER OTHER LAWS.—This subsection does not affect the lawfulness or unlawfulness under this part or any other Federal or State law of any collective bargaining agreement or element thereof, including any element that constitutes an essential term of a service contract.

(f) REMEDY FOR BREACH.—Unless the parties agree otherwise, the exclusive remedy for a breach of a service contract is an action in an appropriate court. The contract dispute resolution forum may not be controlled by or in any way affiliated with a controlled carrier or by the government that owns or controls the carrier.

(Pub. L. 109–304, §7, Oct. 6, 2006, 120 Stat. 1533; Pub. L. 117–146, §3, June 16, 2022, 136 Stat. 1272.)

§40503. Refunds and waivers

The Federal Maritime Commission, on application of a carrier or shipper, may permit a common carrier or conference to refund a portion of the freight charges collected from a shipper, or to waive collection of a portion of the charges from a shipper, if—

(1) there is an error in a tariff, a failure to publish a new tariff, or an error in quoting a tariff, and the refund or waiver will not result in discrimination among shippers, ports, or carriers;

(2) the common carrier or conference, before filing an application for authority to refund or waive any charges for an error in a tariff or a failure to publish a tariff, has published a new tariff setting forth the rate on which the refund or waiver would be based; and

(3) the application for the refund or waiver is filed with the Commission within 180 days from the date of shipment.

(Pub. L. 109–304, §7, Oct. 6, 2006, 120 Stat. 1535.)

§40504. Shipping exchange registry

(a) In General.—No person may operate a shipping exchange involving ocean transportation in the foreign commerce of the United States unless the shipping exchange is registered as a national shipping exchange under the terms and conditions provided in this section and the regulations issued pursuant to this section.

(b) Registration.—A person shall register a shipping exchange by filing with the Federal Maritime Commission an application for registration in such form as the Commission, by rule, may prescribe, containing the rules of the exchange and such other information and documents as the Commission, by rule, may prescribe as necessary or appropriate to complete a shipping exchange's registration.

(c) Exemption.—The Commission may exempt, conditionally or unconditionally, a shipping exchange from registration under this section if the Commission finds that the shipping exchange is subject to comparable, comprehensive supervision and regulation by the appropriate governmental authorities in a foreign country where the shipping exchange is headquartered.

(d) Regulations.—Not later than 3 years after the date of enactment of the Ocean Shipping Reform Act of 2022, the Commission shall issue regulations pursuant to subsection (a), which shall set standards necessary to carry out subtitle IV of this title for registered national shipping exchanges. For consideration of a service contract entered into by a shipping exchange, the Commission shall be limited to the minimum essential terms for service contracts established under section 40502 of this title.

(e) Definition of Shipping Exchange.—In this section, the term "shipping exchange" means a platform (digital, over-the-counter, or otherwise) that connects shippers with common carriers for the purpose of entering into underlying agreements or contracts for the transport of cargo, by vessel or other modes of transportation.

(Added Pub. L. 117–146, §4(a), June 16, 2022, 136 Stat. 1272.)

CHAPTER 407—CONTROLLED CARRIERS

§40701. RATES

(a) IN GENERAL.—A controlled carrier may not—

(1) maintain a rate or charge in a tariff or service contract, or charge or assess a rate, that is below a just and reasonable level; or

(2) establish, maintain, or enforce in a tariff or service contract a classification, rule, or regulation that results, or is likely to result, in the carriage or handling of cargo at a rate or charge that is below a just and reasonable level.

(b) COMMISSION PROHIBITION.—The Federal Maritime Commission, at any time after notice and opportunity for a hearing, may prohibit the publication or use of a rate, charge, classification, rule, or regulation that a controlled carrier has failed to demonstrate is just and reasonable.

(c) BURDEN OF PROOF.—In a proceeding under this section, the burden of proof is on the controlled carrier to demonstrate that its rate, charge, classification, rule, or regulation is just and reasonable.

(d) VOIDNESS.—A rate, charge, classification, rule, or regulation that has been suspended or prohibited by the Commission is void and its use is unlawful.

(Pub. L. 109–304, §7, Oct. 6, 2006, 120 Stat. 1535.)

§40702. RATE STANDARDS

(a) DEFINITION.—In this section, the term "constructive costs" means the costs of another carrier, other than a controlled carrier, operating similar vessels and equipment in the same or a similar trade.

(b) STANDARDS.—In determining whether a rate, charge, classification, rule, or regulation of a controlled carrier is just and reasonable, the Federal Maritime Commission—

(1) shall take into account whether the rate or charge that has been published or assessed, or that would result from the pertinent classification, rule, or regulation, is below a level that is fully compensatory to the controlled carrier based on the carrier's actual costs or constructive costs; and

(2) may take into account other appropriate factors, including whether the rate, charge, classification, rule, or regulation is—

(A) the same as, or similar to, those published or assessed by other carriers in the same trade;

(B) required to ensure movement of particular cargo in the same trade; or

(C) required to maintain acceptable continuity, level, or quality of common carrier service to or from affected ports.

(Pub. L. 109–304, §7, Oct. 6, 2006, 120 Stat. 1536.)

§40703. Effective date of rates

Notwithstanding section 40501(e) of this title and except for service contracts, a rate, charge, classification, rule, or regulation of a controlled carrier may not become effective, without special permission of the Federal Maritime Commission, until the 30th day after publication.

(Pub. L. 109–304, §7, Oct. 6, 2006, 120 Stat. 1536.)

§40704. Commission review

(a) Request for Justification.—On request of the Federal Maritime Commission, a controlled carrier shall file with the Commission, within 20 days of the request, a statement of justification that sufficiently details the carrier's need and purpose for an existing or proposed rate, charge, classification, rule, or regulation and upon which the Commission may reasonably base a determination of its lawfulness.

(b) Determination.—Within 120 days after receipt of information requested under subsection (a), the Commission shall determine whether the rate, charge, classification, rule, or regulation may be unjust and unreasonable.

(c) Show Cause Order.—Whenever the Commission is of the opinion that a rate, charge, classification, rule, or regulation published or assessed by a controlled carrier may be unjust and unreasonable, the Commission shall issue an order to the controlled carrier to show cause why the rate, charge, classification, rule, or regulation should not be prohibited.

(d) Suspension Pending Determination.—

(1) Not yet effective.—Pending a determination of the lawfulness of a rate, charge, classification, rule, or regulation in a proceeding under subsection (c), the Commission may suspend the rate, charge, classification, rule, or regulation at any time before its effective date.

(2) Already effective.—If a rate, charge, classification, rule, or regulation has already become effective, the Commission, on issuance of an order to show cause, may suspend the rate, charge, classification, rule, or regulation on at least 30 days' notice to the controlled carrier.

(3) Maximum suspension.—A period of suspension under this subsection may not exceed 180 days.

(e) Replacement During Suspension.—Whenever the Commission has suspended a rate, charge, classification, rule, or regulation under this section, the controlled carrier may publish a new rate, charge, classification, rule, or regulation to take effect immediately during the suspension in lieu of the suspended rate, charge, classification, rule, or regulation. However, the Commission may reject the new rate, charge, classification, rule, or regulation if the Commission believes it is unjust and unreasonable.

(Pub. L. 109–304, §7, Oct. 6, 2006, 120 Stat. 1536.)

§40705. PRESIDENTIAL REVIEW OF COMMISSION ORDERS

(a) TRANSMISSION TO PRESIDENT.—The Federal Maritime Commission shall transmit to the President, concurrently with publication thereof, each order of suspension or final order of prohibition issued under section 40704 of this title.

(b) PRESIDENTIAL REQUEST AND COMMISSION ACTION.—Within 10 days after receipt or the effective date of a Commission order referred to in subsection (a), the President, in writing, may request the Commission to stay the effect of the order if the President finds that the stay is required for reasons of national defense or foreign policy. The reasons shall be specified in the request. The Commission shall immediately grant the request by issuing an order in which the President's request shall be described. During a stay, the President shall, whenever practicable, attempt to resolve the matter by negotiating with representatives of the applicable foreign governments.

(Pub. L. 109–304, §7, Oct. 6, 2006, 120 Stat. 1537.)

§40706. EXCEPTIONS

This chapter does not apply to—

(1) a controlled carrier of a foreign country whose vessels are entitled by a treaty of the United States to receive national or most-favored-nation treatment; or

(2) a trade served only by controlled carriers.

(Pub. L. 109–304, §7, Oct. 6, 2006, 120 Stat. 1537.)

CHAPTER 409—OCEAN TRANSPORTATION INTERMEDIARIES

Sec.
40901. License requirement.
40902. Financial responsibility.
40903. Suspension or revocation of license.
40904. Compensation by common carriers.

§40901. LICENSE REQUIREMENT

(a) IN GENERAL.—A person in the United States may not advertise, hold oneself out, or act as an ocean transportation intermediary unless the person holds an ocean transportation intermediary's license issued by the Federal Maritime Commission. The Commission shall issue a license to a person that the Commission determines to be qualified by experience and character to act as an ocean transportation intermediary.

(b) EXCEPTION.—A person whose primary business is the sale of merchandise may forward shipments of the merchandise for its own account without an ocean transportation intermediary's license.

(c) APPLICABILITY.—Subsection (a) and section 40902 do not apply to a person that performs ocean transportation intermediary services on behalf of an ocean transportation intermediary for which it is a disclosed agent.

(Pub. L. 109–304, §7, Oct. 6, 2006, 120 Stat. 1538; Pub. L. 115–282, title VII, §707(a), (b), Dec. 4, 2018, 132 Stat. 4295.)

§40902. FINANCIAL RESPONSIBILITY

(a) IN GENERAL.—A person may not advertise, hold oneself out, or act as an ocean transportation intermediary unless the person furnishes a bond, proof of insurance, or other surety—

(1) in a form and amount determined by the Federal Maritime Commission to insure financial responsibility; and

(2) issued by a surety company found acceptable by the Secretary of the Treasury.

(b) SCOPE OF FINANCIAL RESPONSIBILITY.—A bond, insurance, or other surety obtained under this section—

(1) shall be available to pay any penalty assessed under section 41109 of this title or any order for reparation issued under section 41305 of this title;

(2) may be available to pay any claim against an ocean transportation intermediary arising from its transportation-related activities—

(A) with the consent of the insured ocean transportation intermediary and subject to review by the surety company; or

(B) when the claim is deemed valid by the surety company after the ocean transportation intermediary has failed to respond to adequate notice to address the validity of the claim; and

(3) shall be available to pay any judgment for damages against an ocean transportation

intermediary arising from its transportation-related activities, if the claimant has first attempted to resolve the claim under paragraph (2) and the claim has not been resolved within a reasonable period of time.

(c) REGULATIONS ON COURT JUDGMENTS.—The Commission shall prescribe regulations for the purpose of protecting the interests of claimants, ocean transportation intermediaries, and surety companies with respect to the process of pursuing claims against ocean transportation intermediary bonds, insurance, or sureties through court judgments. The regulations shall provide that a judgment for monetary damages may not be enforced except to the extent that the damages claimed arise from the transportation-related activities of the insured ocean transportation intermediary, as defined by the Commission.

(d) RESIDENT AGENT.—An ocean transportation intermediary not domiciled in the United States shall designate a resident agent in the United States for receipt of service of judicial and administrative process, including subpoenas.

(Pub. L. 109–304, §7, Oct. 6, 2006, 120 Stat. 1538; Pub. L. 115–282, title VII, §707(c), Dec. 4, 2018, 132 Stat. 4295.)

§40903. SUSPENSION OR REVOCATION OF LICENSE

(a) FAILURE TO MAINTAIN QUALIFICATIONS OR TO COMPLY.—The Federal Maritime Commission, after notice and opportunity for a hearing, shall suspend or revoke an ocean transportation intermediary's license if the Commission finds that the ocean transportation intermediary—

(1) is not qualified to provide intermediary services; or

(2) willfully failed to comply with a provision of this part or with an order or regulation of the Commission.

(b) FAILURE TO MAINTAIN BOND, PROOF OF INSURANCE, OR OTHER SURETY.—The Commission may revoke an ocean transportation intermediary's license for failure to maintain a bond, proof of insurance, or other surety as required by section 40902(a) of this title.

(Pub. L. 109–304, §7, Oct. 6, 2006, 120 Stat. 1539.)

§40904. COMPENSATION BY COMMON CARRIERS

(a) CERTIFICATION OF LICENSE AND SERVICES.—A common carrier may compensate an ocean freight forwarder for a shipment dispatched for others only when the ocean freight forwarder has certified in writing that it holds an ocean transportation intermediary's license (if required under section 40901 of this title) and has—

(1) engaged, booked, secured, reserved, or contracted directly with the carrier or its agent for space aboard a vessel or confirmed the availability of the space; and

(2) prepared and processed the ocean bill of lading, dock receipt, or other similar document for the shipment.

(b) DUAL COMPENSATION.—A common carrier may not pay compensation for services described in subsection (a) more than once on the same shipment.

(c) BENEFICIAL INTEREST SHIPMENTS.—An ocean freight forwarder may not receive compensation from a common carrier for a shipment in which the ocean freight forwarder has a direct or indirect beneficial interest. A common carrier may not knowingly pay compensation on that shipment.

(d) LIMITS ON AUTHORITY OF CONFERENCE OR GROUP.—A conference or group of two or more ocean common carriers in the foreign commerce of the United States that is authorized to agree on the level of compensation paid to an ocean freight forwarder may not—

(1) deny a member of the conference or group the right, upon notice of not more than 5 days, to take independent action on any level of compensation paid to an ocean freight forwarder; or

(2) agree to limit the payment of compensation to an ocean freight forwarder to less than 1.25 percent of the aggregate of all rates and charges applicable under a tariff and assessed against the cargo on which the services of the ocean freight forwarder are provided.

(Pub. L. 109–304, §7, Oct. 6, 2006, 120 Stat. 1539.)

CHAPTER 411—PROHIBITIONS AND PENALTIES

[1] *Section catchline amended by Pub. L. 117–146 without corresponding amendment of chapter analysis.*

§41101. JOINT VENTURES AND CONSORTIUMS

In this chapter, a joint venture or consortium of two or more common carriers operating as a single entity is deemed to be a single common carrier.

(Pub. L. 109–304, §7, Oct. 6, 2006, 120 Stat. 1540.)

§41102. GENERAL PROHIBITIONS

(a) OBTAINING TRANSPORTATION AT LESS THAN APPLICABLE RATES.—A person may not knowingly and willfully, directly or indirectly, by means of false billing, false classification, false weighing, false report of weight, false measurement, or any other unjust or unfair device or means, obtain or attempt to obtain ocean transportation for property at less than the rates or charges that would otherwise apply.

(b) OPERATING CONTRARY TO AGREEMENT.—A person may not operate under an agreement required to be filed under section 40302 or 40305 of this title if—

(1) the agreement has not become effective under section 40304 of this title or has been rejected, disapproved, or canceled; or

(2) the operation is not in accordance with the terms of the agreement or any modifications to the agreement made by the Federal Maritime Commission.

(c) PRACTICES IN HANDLING PROPERTY.—A common carrier, marine terminal operator, or ocean transportation intermediary may not fail to establish, observe, and enforce just and reasonable regulations and practices relating to or connected with receiving, handling, storing, or delivering property.

(d) RETALIATION AND OTHER DISCRIMINATORY ACTIONS.—A common carrier, marine terminal operator, or ocean transportation intermediary, acting alone or in conjunction with any other person, directly or indirectly, may not—

(1) retaliate against a shipper, an agent of a shipper, an ocean transportation

intermediary, or a motor carrier by refusing, or threatening to refuse, an otherwise-available cargo space accommodation; or

(2) resort to any other unfair or unjustly discriminatory action for—

(A) the reason that a shipper, an agent of a shipper, an ocean transportation intermediary, or motor carrier has—

(i) patronized another carrier; or

(ii) filed a complaint against the common carrier, marine terminal operator, or ocean transportation intermediary; or

(B) any other reason.

(Pub. L. 109–304, §7, Oct. 6, 2006, 120 Stat. 1540; Pub. L. 117–146, §5, June 16, 2022, 136 Stat. 1273.)

§41103. DISCLOSURE OF INFORMATION

(a) PROHIBITION.—A common carrier, marine terminal operator, or ocean freight forwarder, either alone or in conjunction with any other person, directly or indirectly, may not knowingly disclose, offer, solicit, or receive any information concerning the nature, kind, quantity, destination, consignee, or routing of any property tendered or delivered to a common carrier, without the consent of the shipper or consignee, if the information—

(1) may be used to the detriment or prejudice of the shipper, the consignee, or any common carrier; or

(2) may improperly disclose its business transaction to a competitor.

(b) EXCEPTIONS.—Subsection (a) does not prevent providing the information—

(1) in response to legal process;

(2) to the Federal Maritime Commission or an agency of the United States Government; or

(3) to an independent neutral body operating within the scope of its authority to fulfill the policing obligations of the parties to an agreement effective under this part.

(c) DISCLOSURE FOR DETERMINING BREACH OR COMPILING STATISTICS.—An ocean common carrier that is a party to a conference agreement approved under this part, a receiver, trustee, lessee, agent, or employee of the carrier, or any other person authorized by the carrier to receive information—

(1) may give information to the conference or any person or agency designated by the conference, for the purpose of—

(A) determining whether a shipper or consignee has breached an agreement with the conference or its member lines;

(B) determining whether a member of the conference has breached the conference agreement; or

(C) compiling statistics of cargo movement; and

(2) may not prevent the conference or its designee from soliciting or receiving information for any of those purposes.

(Pub. L. 109–304, §7, Oct. 6, 2006, 120 Stat. 1540.)

§41104. Common carriers

(a) In General.—A common carrier, either alone or in conjunction with any other person, directly or indirectly, shall not—

(1) allow a person to obtain transportation for property at less than the rates or charges established by the carrier in its tariff or service contract by means of false billing, false classification, false weighing, false measurement, or any other unjust or unfair device or means;

(2) provide service in the liner trade that is—

(A) not in accordance with the rates, charges, classifications, rules, and practices contained in a tariff published or a service contract entered into under chapter 405 of this title, unless excepted or exempted under section 40103 or 40501(a)(2) of this title; or

(B) under a tariff or service contract that has been suspended or prohibited by the Federal Maritime Commission under chapter 407 or 423 of this title;

(3) unreasonably refuse cargo space accommodations when available, or resort to other unfair or unjustly discriminatory methods;

(4) for service pursuant to a tariff, engage in any unfair or unjustly discriminatory practice in the matter of—

(A) rates or charges;

(B) cargo classifications;

(C) cargo space accommodations or other facilities, with due regard being given to the proper loading of the vessel and the available tonnage;

(D) loading and landing of freight; or

(E) adjustment and settlement of claims;

(5) for service pursuant to a service contract, engage in any unfair or unjustly discriminatory practice against any commodity group or type of shipment or in the matter of rates or charges with respect to any port;

(6) use a vessel in a particular trade for the purpose of excluding, preventing, or reducing competition by driving another ocean common carrier out of that trade;

(7) offer or pay any deferred rebates;

(8) for service pursuant to a tariff, give any undue or unreasonable preference or advantage or impose any undue or unreasonable prejudice or disadvantage;

(9) for service pursuant to a service contract, give any undue or unreasonable preference or advantage or impose any undue or unreasonable prejudice or disadvantage with respect to any port;

(10) unreasonably refuse to deal or negotiate, including with respect to vessel space accommodations provided by an ocean common carrier;

(11) knowingly and willfully accept cargo from or transport cargo for the account of a non-vessel-operating common carrier that does not have a tariff as required by section 40501 of this title, or an ocean transportation intermediary that does not have a bond, insurance, or other surety as required by section 40902 of this title;

(12) knowingly and willfully enter into a service contract with an ocean transportation intermediary that does not have a tariff as required by section 40501 of this title and

a bond, insurance, or other surety as required by section 40902 of this title, or with an affiliate of such an ocean transportation intermediary;

(13) continue to participate simultaneously in a rate discussion agreement and an agreement to share vessels, in the same trade, if the interplay of the authorities exercised by the specified agreements is likely, by a reduction in competition, to produce an unreasonable reduction in transportation service or an unreasonable increase in transportation cost;

(14) assess any party for a charge that is inconsistent or does not comply with all applicable provisions and regulations, including subsection (c) of section 41102 or part 545 of title 46, Code of Federal Regulations (or successor regulations);

(15) invoice any party for demurrage or detention charges unless the invoice includes information as described in subsection (d) showing that such charges comply with—

(A) all provisions of part 545 of title 46, Code of Federal Regulations (or successor regulations); and

(B) applicable provisions and regulations, including the principles of the final rule published on May 18, 2020, entitled "Interpretive Rule on Demurrage and Detention Under the Shipping Act" (or successor rule); or

(16) for service pursuant to a service contract, give any undue or unreasonable preference or advantage or impose any undue or unreasonable prejudice or disadvantage against any commodity group or type of shipment.

(b) RULE OF CONSTRUCTION.—Notwithstanding any other provision of law, there is no private right of action to enforce the prohibition under subsection (a)(13).

(c) AGREEMENT VIOLATION.—Participants in an agreement found by the Commission to violate subsection (a)(13) shall have 90 days from the date of such Commission finding to withdraw from the agreement as necessary to comply with that subsection.

(d) DETENTION AND DEMURRAGE INVOICE INFORMATION.—

(1) INACCURATE INVOICE.—If the Commission determines, after an investigation in response to a submission under section 41310, that an invoice under subsection (a)(15) was inaccurate or false, penalties or refunds under section 41107 shall be applied.

(2) CONTENTS OF INVOICE.—An invoice under subsection (a)(15), unless otherwise determined by subsequent Commission rulemaking, shall include accurate information on each of the following, as well as minimum information as determined by the Commission:

(A) Date that container is made available.

(B) The port of discharge.

(C) The container number or numbers.

(D) For exported shipments, the earliest return date.

(E) The allowed free time in days.

(F) The start date of free time.

(G) The end date of free time.

(H) The applicable detention or demurrage rule on which the daily rate is based.

(I) The applicable rate or rates per the applicable rule.

(J) The total amount due.

(K) The email, telephone number, or other appropriate contact information for questions or requests for mitigation of fees.

(L) A statement that the charges are consistent with any of Federal Maritime Commission rules with respect to detention and demurrage.

(M) A statement that the common carrier's performance did not cause or contribute to the underlying invoiced charges.

(e) SAFE HARBOR.—If a non-vessel operating common carrier passes through to the relevant shipper an invoice made by the ocean common carrier, and the Commission finds that the non-vessel operating common carrier is not otherwise responsible for the charge, then the ocean common carrier shall be subject to refunds or penalties pursuant to subsection (d)(1).

(f) ELIMINATION OF CHARGE OBLIGATION.—Failure to include the information required under subsection (d) on an invoice with any demurrage or detention charge shall eliminate any obligation of the charged party to pay the applicable charge.

(Pub. L. 109–304, §7, Oct. 6, 2006, 120 Stat. 1541; Pub. L. 115–282, title VII, §708(a), Dec. 4, 2018, 132 Stat. 4295; Pub. L. 117–146, §7(a), June 16, 2022, 136 Stat. 1274.)

§41105. CONCERTED ACTION

A conference or group of two or more common carriers may not—

(1) boycott or take any other concerted action resulting in an unreasonable refusal to deal;

(2) engage in conduct that unreasonably restricts the use of intermodal services or technological innovations;

(3) engage in any predatory practice designed to eliminate the participation, or deny the entry, in a particular trade of a common carrier not a member of the conference, a group of common carriers, an ocean tramp, or a bulk carrier;

(4) negotiate with a non-ocean carrier or group of non-ocean carriers (such as truck, rail, or air operators) on any matter relating to rates or services provided to ocean common carriers within the United States by those non-ocean carriers, unless the negotiations and any resulting agreements are not in violation of the antitrust laws and are consistent with the purposes of this part, except that this paragraph does not prohibit the setting and publishing of a joint through rate by a conference, joint venture, or association of ocean common carriers;

(5) negotiate with a tug or towing vessel service provider on any matter relating to rates or services provided within the United States by those tugs or towing vessels;

(6) with respect to a vessel operated by an ocean common carrier within the United States, negotiate for the purchase of certain covered services, unless the negotiations and any resulting agreements are not in violation of the antitrust laws and are consistent with the purposes of this part, except that this paragraph does not prohibit the setting and publishing of a joint through rate by a conference, joint venture, or association of ocean common carriers;

(7) deny in the export foreign commerce of the United States compensation to an ocean freight forwarder or limit that compensation to less than a reasonable amount;

(8) allocate shippers among specific carriers that are parties to the agreement or

prohibit a carrier that is a party to the agreement from soliciting cargo from a particular shipper, except as—

    (A) authorized by section 40303(d) of this title;

    (B) required by the law of the United States or the importing or exporting country; or

    (C) agreed to by a shipper in a service contract;

    (9) for service pursuant to a service contract, engage in any unjustly discriminatory practice in the matter of rates or charges with respect to any locality, port, or person due to the person's status as a shippers' association or ocean transportation intermediary; or

    (10) for service pursuant to a service contract, give any undue or unreasonable preference or advantage or impose any undue or unreasonable prejudice or disadvantage with respect to any locality, port, or person due to the person's status as a shippers' association or ocean transportation intermediary.

(Pub. L. 109–304, §7, Oct. 6, 2006, 120 Stat. 1542; Pub. L. 115–282, title VII, §709(a), Dec. 4, 2018, 132 Stat. 4296.)

§41105A. AUTHORITY

Nothing in section 41105, as amended by the Federal Maritime Commission Authorization Act of 2017, shall be construed to limit the authority of the Department of Justice regarding antitrust matters.

(Added Pub. L. 115–282, title VII, §709(b)(1), Dec. 4, 2018, 132 Stat. 4296.)

§41106. MARINE TERMINAL OPERATORS

A marine terminal operator may not—

    (1) agree with another marine terminal operator or with a common carrier to boycott, or unreasonably discriminate in the provision of terminal services to, a common carrier or ocean tramp;

    (2) give any undue or unreasonable preference or advantage or impose any undue or unreasonable prejudice or disadvantage with respect to any person; or

    (3) unreasonably refuse to deal or negotiate.

(Pub. L. 109–304, §7, Oct. 6, 2006, 120 Stat. 1543.)

§41107. MONETARY PENALTIES OR REFUNDS

(a) IN GENERAL.—A person that violates this part or a regulation or order of the Federal Maritime Commission issued under this part is liable to the United States Government for a civil penalty or, in addition to or in lieu of a civil penalty, is liable for the refund of a charge. Unless otherwise provided in this part, the amount of the penalty may not exceed $5,000 for each violation or, if the violation was willfully and knowingly committed, $25,000 for each violation. Each day of a continuing violation is a separate violation.

(b) LIEN ON CARRIER'S VESSELS.—The amount of a civil penalty or, in addition to or in lieu of a civil penalty, the refund of a charge, imposed on a common carrier under this section constitutes a lien on the vessels operated by the carrier. Any such vessel is subject to an action in rem to enforce the lien in the district court of the United States for the district in which it is found.

(Pub. L. 109–304, §7, Oct. 6, 2006, 120 Stat. 1543; Pub. L. 117–146, §8(a)(1), June 16, 2022, 136 Stat. 1276.)

§41108. ADDITIONAL PENALTIES

(a) SUSPENSION OF TARIFFS.—For a violation of paragraph (1), (2), or (7) of section 41104(a) of this title, the Federal Maritime Commission may suspend any or all tariffs of the common carrier, or that common carrier's right to use any or all tariffs of conferences of which it is a member, for a period not to exceed 12 months.

(b) OPERATING UNDER SUSPENDED TARIFF.—A common carrier that accepts or handles cargo for carriage under a tariff that has been suspended, or after its right to use that tariff has been suspended, is liable to the United States Government for a civil penalty of not more than $50,000 for each shipment.

(c) FAILURE TO PROVIDE INFORMATION.—

(1) PENALTIES.—If the Commission finds, after notice and opportunity for a hearing, that a common carrier has failed to supply information ordered to be produced or compelled by subpoena under section 41303 of this title, the Commission may—

(A) suspend any or all tariffs of the carrier or the carrier's right to use any or all tariffs of conferences of which it is a member; and

(B) request the Secretary of Homeland Security to refuse or revoke any clearance required for a vessel operated by the carrier, and when so requested, the Secretary shall refuse or revoke the clearance.

(2) DEFENSE BASED ON FOREIGN LAW.—If, in defense of its failure to comply with a subpoena or discovery order, a common carrier alleges that information or documents located in a foreign country cannot be produced because of the laws of that country, the Commission shall immediately notify the Secretary of State of the failure to comply and of the allegation relating to foreign laws. On receiving the notification, the Secretary of State shall promptly consult with the government of the nation within which the information or documents are alleged to be located for the purpose of assisting the Commission in obtaining the information or documents.

(d) IMPAIRING ACCESS TO FOREIGN TRADE.—If the Commission finds, after notice and opportunity for a hearing, that the action of a common carrier, acting alone or in concert with another person, or a foreign government has unduly impaired access of a vessel documented under the laws of the United States to ocean trade between foreign ports, the Commission shall take action that it finds appropriate, including imposing any of the penalties authorized by this section. The Commission also may take any of the actions authorized by sections 42304 and 42305 of this title.

(e) SUBMISSION OF ORDER TO PRESIDENT.—Before an order under this section becomes effective, it shall be submitted immediately to the President. The President, within 10 days after receiving it, may disapprove it if the President finds that disapproval is required for reasons of national defense or foreign policy.

(Pub. L. 109–304, §7, Oct. 6, 2006, 120 Stat. 1543; Pub. L. 117–146, §15(a), June 16, 2022, 136 Stat. 1279.)

§41109. ASSESSMENT OF PENALTIES

(a) GENERAL AUTHORITY.—Until a matter is referred to the Attorney General, the Federal Maritime Commission may—

(1) after notice and opportunity for a hearing, in accordance with this part—

(A) assess a civil penalty; or

(B) in addition to, or in lieu of, assessing a civil penalty under subparagraph (A), order a refund of money (including additional amounts in accordance with section 41305(c)), subject to subsection (b)(2); and

(2) compromise, modify, or remit, with or without conditions, a civil penalty or refund imposed under paragraph (1).

(b) DETERMINATION OF AMOUNT.—

(1) FACTORS FOR CONSIDERATION.—In determining the amount of a civil penalty assessed or refund of money ordered pursuant to subsection (a), the Federal Maritime Commission shall take into consideration—

(A) the nature, circumstances, extent, and gravity of the violation committed;

(B) with respect to the violator—

(i) the degree of culpability;

(ii) any history of prior offenses;

(iii) the ability to pay; and

(iv) such other matters as justice may require; and

(C) the amount of any refund of money ordered pursuant to subsection (a)(1)(B).

(2) COMMENSURATE REDUCTION IN CIVIL PENALTY.—

(A) IN GENERAL.—In any case in which the Federal Maritime Commission orders a refund of money pursuant to subsection (a)(1)(B) in addition to assessing a civil penalty pursuant to subsection (a)(1)(A), the amount of the civil penalty assessed shall be decreased by any additional amounts included in the refund of money in excess of the actual injury (as defined in section 41305(a)).

(B) TREATMENT OF REFUNDS.—A refund of money ordered pursuant to subsection (a)(1)(B) shall be—

(i) considered to be compensation paid to the applicable claimant; and

(ii) deducted from the total amount of damages awarded to that claimant in a civil action against the violator relating to the applicable violation.

(c) EXCEPTION.—A civil penalty or refund of money under subparagraph (A) or (B), respectively, of subsection (a)(1) may not be imposed for conspiracy to violate subsection (a) or (d) of section 41102 or paragraph (1) or (2) of section 41104(a) or to defraud the Commission by concealing such a violation.

(d) PROHIBITED BASIS OF PENALTY.—The Commission or a court may not order a person to pay the difference between the amount billed and agreed upon in writing with a common carrier or its agent and the amount set forth in a tariff or service contract by that common carrier for the transportation service provided.

(e) TIME LIMIT.—A proceeding to assess a civil penalty or order a refund of money under this section must be commenced within 5 years after the date of the violation.

(f) REVIEW OF CIVIL PENALTY.—A person against whom a civil penalty is assessed, or that is ordered to refund money, under this section may obtain review under chapter 158 of title 28.

(g) CIVIL ACTIONS TO COLLECT.—If a person does not pay an assessment of a civil penalty or a refund required under this section after it has become final or after the appropriate court has entered final judgment in favor of the Commission, the Attorney General at the request of the Commission may seek to collect the amount assessed in an appropriate district court of the United States. The court shall enforce the order of the Commission unless it finds that the order was not regularly made and duly issued.

(Pub. L. 109–304, §7, Oct. 6, 2006, 120 Stat. 1544; Pub. L. 117–146, §§8(a)(2), 15(b), June 16, 2022, 136 Stat. 1276, 1279.)

§41110. DATA COLLECTION

The Federal Maritime Commission shall publish on its website a calendar quarterly report that describes the total import and export tonnage and the total loaded and empty 20-foot equivalent units per vessel (making port in the United States, including any territory or possession of the United States) operated by each ocean common carrier covered under this chapter. Ocean common carriers under this chapter shall provide to the Commission all necessary information, as determined by the Commission, for completion of this report.

(Added Pub. L. 117–146, §9(a), June 16, 2022, 136 Stat. 1277.)

CHAPTER 413—ENFORCEMENT

§41301. COMPLAINTS

(a) IN GENERAL.—A person may file with the Federal Maritime Commission a sworn complaint alleging a violation of this part, except section 41307(b)(1). If the complaint is filed within 3 years after the claim accrues, the complainant may seek reparations for an injury to the complainant caused by the violation.

(b) NOTICE AND RESPONSE.—The Commission shall provide a copy of the complaint to the person named in the complaint. Within a reasonable time specified by the Commission, the person shall satisfy the complaint or answer it in writing.

(c) IF COMPLAINT NOT SATISFIED.—If the complaint is not satisfied, the Commission shall investigate the complaint in an appropriate manner and make an appropriate order.

(Pub. L. 109–304, §7, Oct. 6, 2006, 120 Stat. 1545.)

§41302. INVESTIGATIONS

(a) IN GENERAL.—The Federal Maritime Commission, on complaint or its own motion, may investigate any conduct [1] agreement, fee, or charge that the Commission believes may be in violation of this part. The Commission may by order disapprove, cancel, or modify any agreement that operates in violation of this part.

(b) EFFECTIVENESS OF AGREEMENT, FEE, OR CHARGE DURING INVESTIGATION.—Unless an injunction is issued under section 41306 or 41307 of this title, an agreement, fee, or charge under investigation by the Commission remains in effect until the Commission issues its order.

(c) DATE FOR DECISION.—Within 10 days after the initiation of a proceeding under this section or section 41301 of this title, the Commission shall set a date by which it will issue its final decision. The Commission by order may extend the date for good cause.

(d) SANCTIONS FOR DELAY.—If, within the period for final decision under subsection (c), the Commission determines that it is unable to issue a final decision because of undue delay caused by a party to the proceeding, the Commission may impose sanctions, including issuing a decision adverse to the delaying party.

(e) REPORT.—The Commission shall make a written report of every investigation under this part in which a hearing was held, stating its conclusions, decisions, findings of fact, and order. The Commission shall provide a copy of the report to all parties and publish the report for public information. A published report is competent evidence in a court of the United States.

(Pub. L. 109–304, §7, Oct. 6, 2006, 120 Stat. 1545; Pub. L. 117–146, §11(a), June 16, 2022, 136 Stat. 1278.)

[1] *So in original. Probably should be followed by a comma.*

§41303. DISCOVERY AND SUBPOENAS

(a) IN GENERAL.—In an investigation or adjudicatory proceeding under this part—
(1) the Federal Maritime Commission may subpoena witnesses and evidence; and
(2) a party may use depositions, written interrogatories, and discovery procedures under regulations prescribed by the Commission that, to the extent practicable, shall conform to the Federal Rules of Civil Procedure (28 App. U.S.C.).

(b) WITNESS FEES.—Unless otherwise prohibited by law, a witness is entitled to the same fees and mileage as in the courts of the United States.

(Pub. L. 109–304, §7, Oct. 6, 2006, 120 Stat. 1545.)

§41304. HEARINGS AND ORDERS

(a) OPPORTUNITY FOR HEARING.—The Federal Maritime Commission shall provide an opportunity for a hearing before issuing an order relating to a violation of this part or a regulation prescribed under this part.

(b) MODIFICATION OF ORDER.—The Commission may reverse, suspend, or modify any of its orders.

(c) REHEARING.—On application of a party to a proceeding, the Commission may grant a rehearing of the same or any matter determined in the proceeding. Except by order of the Commission, a rehearing does not operate as a stay of an order.

(d) PERIOD OF EFFECTIVENESS.—An order of the Commission remains in effect for the period specified in the order or until suspended, modified, or set aside by the Commission or a court of competent jurisdiction.

(Pub. L. 109–304, §7, Oct. 6, 2006, 120 Stat. 1546.)

§41305. AWARD OF REPARATIONS

(a) DEFINITION.—In this section, the term "actual injury" includes the loss of interest at commercial rates compounded from the date of injury.

(b) BASIC AMOUNT.—If the complaint was filed within the period specified in section 41301(a) of this title, the Federal Maritime Commission shall direct the payment of reparations to the complainant for actual injury caused by a violation of this part.

(c) ADDITIONAL AMOUNTS.—On a showing that the injury was caused by an activity prohibited by section subsection [1] (b) or (c) of section 41102, paragraph (3) or (6) of section 41104(a), or paragraph (1) or (3) of section 41105, the Commission may order the payment of additional amounts, but the total recovery of a complainant may not exceed twice the amount of the actual injury.

(d) Difference Between Rates.—If the injury was caused by an activity prohibited by subparagraph (A) or (B) of section 41104(a)(4), the amount of the injury shall be the difference between the rate paid by the injured shipper and the most favorable rate paid by another shipper.

(e) Attorney Fees.—In any action brought under section 41301, the prevailing party may be awarded reasonable attorney fees.

(Pub. L. 109–304, §7, Oct. 6, 2006, 120 Stat. 1546; Pub. L. 113–281, title IV, §402, Dec. 18, 2014, 128 Stat. 3056; Pub. L. 117–146, §§12, 15(c), June 16, 2022, 136 Stat. 1279.)

¹ *So in original.*

§41306. Injunctive relief sought by complainants

(a) In General.—After filing a complaint with the Federal Maritime Commission under section 41301 of this title, the complainant may bring a civil action in a district court of the United States to enjoin conduct in violation of this part.

(b) Venue.—The action must be brought in the judicial district in which—

(1) the Commission has brought a civil action against the defendant under section 41307(a) of this title; or

(2) the defendant resides or transacts business, if the Commission has not brought such an action.

(c) Remedies by Court.—After notice to the defendant, and a showing that the standards for granting injunctive relief by courts of equity are met, the court may grant a temporary restraining order or preliminary injunction for a period not to exceed 10 days after the Commission has issued an order disposing of the complaint.

(d) Attorney Fees.—A defendant prevailing in a civil action under this section shall be allowed reasonable attorney fees to be assessed and collected as part of the costs of the action.

(Pub. L. 109–304, §7, Oct. 6, 2006, 120 Stat. 1546.)

§41307. Injunctive relief sought by the Commission

(a) General Violations.—In connection with an investigation under section 41301 or 41302 of this title, the Federal Maritime Commission may bring a civil action to enjoin conduct in violation of this part. The action must be brought in the district court of the United States for any judicial district in which the defendant resides or transacts business. After notice to the defendant, and a showing that the standards for granting injunctive relief by courts of equity are met, the court may grant a temporary restraining order or preliminary injunction for a period not to exceed 10 days after the Commission has issued an order disposing of the issues under investigation.

(b) Reduction in Competition.—

(1) Action by commission.—If, at any time after the filing or effective date of an agreement under chapter 403 of this title, the Commission determines that the agreement is likely, by a reduction in competition, to produce an unreasonable reduction in transportation service or an unreasonable increase in transportation cost or to substantially lessen competition in the purchasing of certain covered services, the

Commission, after notice to the person filing the agreement, may bring a civil action in the United States District Court for the District of Columbia to enjoin the operation of the agreement. The Commission's sole remedy with respect to an agreement likely to have such an effect is an action under this subsection.

(2) REMEDIES BY COURT.—In an action under this subsection, the court may issue—

(A) a temporary restraining order or a preliminary injunction; and

(B) a permanent injunction after a showing that the agreement is likely to have the effect described in paragraph (1).

(3) BURDEN OF PROOF AND THIRD PARTIES.—In an action under this subsection, the burden of proof is on the Commission. The court may not allow a third party to intervene.

(4) COMPETITION FACTORS.—In making a determination under this subsection regarding whether an agreement is likely to substantially lessen competition in the purchasing of certain covered services, the Commission may consider any relevant competition factors in affected markets, including, without limitation, the competitive effect of agreements other than the agreement under review.

(c) FAILURE TO PROVIDE INFORMATION.—If a person filing an agreement, or an officer, director, partner, agent, or employee of the person, fails substantially to comply with a request for the submission of additional information or documents within the period provided in section 40304(c) of this title, the Commission may bring a civil action in the United States District Court for the District of Columbia. At the request of the Commission, the Court—

(1) may order compliance;

(2) shall extend the period specified in section 40304(c)(2) of this title until there has been substantial compliance; and

(3) may grant other equitable relief that the court decides is appropriate.

(d) REPRESENTATION.—The Commission may represent itself in a proceeding under this section in—

(1) a district court of the United States, on notice to the Attorney General; and

(2) a court of appeals of the United States, with the approval of the Attorney General.

(Pub. L. 109–304, §7, Oct. 6, 2006, 120 Stat. 1547; Pub. L. 115–282, title VII, §710(a), Dec. 4, 2018, 132 Stat. 4297.)

§41308. ENFORCEMENT OF SUBPOENAS AND ORDERS

(a) CIVIL ACTION.—If a person does not comply with a subpoena or order of the Federal Maritime Commission, the Attorney General, at the request of the Commission, or an injured party, may seek enforcement in a district court of the United States having jurisdiction over the parties. If, after hearing, the court determines that the subpoena or order was regularly made and duly issued, the court shall enforce the subpoena or order.

(b) TIME LIMIT ON BRINGING ACTIONS.—An action under this section to enforce an order of the Commission must be brought within 3 years after the date the order was violated.

(Pub. L. 109–304, §7, Oct. 6, 2006, 120 Stat. 1548.)

§41309. ENFORCEMENT OF REPARATION ORDERS

(a) CIVIL ACTION.—If a person does not comply with an order of the Federal Maritime Commission for the payment of a refund of money or reparation, the person to which the refund or reparation was awarded may seek enforcement of the order in a district court of the United States having jurisdiction over the parties.

(b) PARTIES AND SERVICE OF PROCESS.—All parties in whose favor the Commission has ordered a refund of money or any other award of reparation by a single order may be joined as plaintiffs, and all other parties in the order (except for the Commission or any component of the Commission) may be joined as defendants, in a single action in a judicial district in which any one plaintiff could maintain an action against any one defendant. Service of process against a defendant not found in that district may be made in a district in which any office of that defendant is located or in which any port of call on a regular route operated by that defendant is located. Judgment may be entered for any plaintiff against the defendant liable to that plaintiff.

(c) NATURE OF REVIEW.—In an action under this section, the findings and order of the Commission are prima facie evidence of the facts stated in the findings and order.

(d) COSTS AND ATTORNEY FEES.—The plaintiff is not liable for costs of the action or for costs of any subsequent stage of the proceedings unless they accrue on the plaintiff's appeal. A prevailing plaintiff shall be allowed reasonable attorney fees to be assessed and collected as part of the costs of the action.

(e) TIME LIMIT ON BRINGING ACTIONS.—An action under this section to enforce an order of the Commission must be brought within 3 years after the date the order was violated.

(Pub. L. 109–304, §7, Oct. 6, 2006, 120 Stat. 1548; Pub. L. 117–146, §13, June 16, 2022, 136 Stat. 1279.)

§41310. CHARGE COMPLAINTS

(a) IN GENERAL.—A person may submit to the Federal Maritime Commission, and the Commission shall accept, information concerning complaints about charges assessed by a common carrier. The information submitted to the Commission shall include the bill of lading numbers and invoices, and may include any other relevant information.

(b) INVESTIGATION.—Upon receipt of a submission under subsection (a), with respect to a charge assessed by a common carrier, the Commission shall promptly investigate the charge with regard to compliance with section 41104(a) and section 41102. The common carrier shall—

(1) be provided an opportunity to submit additional information related to the charge in question; and

(2) bear the burden of establishing the reasonableness of any demurrage or detention charges pursuant to section 545.5 of title 46, Code of Federal Regulations (or successor regulations).

(c) REFUND.—Upon receipt of submissions under subsection (a), if the Commission determines that a charge does not comply with section 41104(a) or 41102, the Commission shall promptly order the refund of charges paid.

(d) PENALTIES.—In the event of a finding that a charge does not comply with section 41104(a) or 41102 after submission under subsection (a), a civil penalty under section

41107 shall be applied to the common carrier making such charge.

(e) CONSIDERATIONS.—If the common carrier assessing the charge is acting in the capacity of a non-vessel-operating common carrier, the Commission shall, while conducting an investigation under subsection (b), consider—

(1) whether the non-vessel-operating common carrier is responsible for the noncompliant assessment of the charge, in whole or in part; and

(2) whether another party is ultimately responsible in whole or in part and potentially subject to action under subsections (c) and (d).

(Added Pub. L. 117–146, §10(a), June 16, 2022, 136 Stat. 1278.)

PART B—ACTIONS TO ADDRESS FOREIGN PRACTICES

CHAPTER 421—REGULATIONS AFFECTING SHIPPING IN FOREIGN TRADE

§42101. REGULATIONS OF THE COMMISSION

(a) UNFAVORABLE CONDITIONS.—To further the objectives and policy set forth in section 50101 of this title, the Federal Maritime Commission shall prescribe regulations affecting shipping in foreign trade, not in conflict with law, to adjust or meet general or special conditions unfavorable to shipping in foreign trade, whether in a particular trade or on a particular route or in commerce generally, including intermodal movements, terminal operations, cargo solicitation, agency services, ocean transportation intermediary services and operations, and other activities and services integral to transportation systems, and which arise out of or result from laws or regulations of a foreign country or competitive methods, pricing practices, or other practices employed by owners, operators, agents, or masters of vessels of a foreign country.

(b) INITIATION OF REGULATION.—A regulation under subsection (a) may be initiated by the Commission on its own motion or on the petition of any person, including another component of the United States Government.

(Pub. L. 109–304, §7, Oct. 6, 2006, 120 Stat. 1548.)

§42102. REGULATIONS OF OTHER AGENCIES

(a) REQUEST TO AGENCY.—To further the objectives and policy set forth in section 50101 of this title, the Federal Maritime Commission shall request the head of a department, agency, or instrumentality of the United States Government to suspend, modify, or annul any existing regulations, or to make new regulations, affecting shipping in the foreign trade, except regulations relating to the Public Health Service, the Consular Service, or the inspection of vessels.

(b) PRIOR REVIEW AND APPROVAL.—A department, agency, or instrumentality of the Government may not prescribe a regulation affecting shipping in the foreign trade (except a regulation affecting the Public Health Service, the Consular Service, or the inspection of vessels) until the regulation has been submitted to the Commission for its approval and final action has been taken by the Commission or the President.

(c) SUBMISSION TO PRESIDENT.—If the head of a department, agency, or instrumentality of the Government refuses to comply with a request under subsection (a) or objects to a decision of the Commission under subsection (b), the Commission or the head of the department, agency, or instrumentality may submit the facts to the President. The President may establish, suspend, modify, or annul the regulation.

(Pub. L. 109–304, §7, Oct. 6, 2006, 120 Stat. 1549.)

§42103. NO PREFERENCE TO GOVERNMENT-OWNED VESSELS

A regulation may not give a vessel owned by the United States Government a preference over a vessel owned by citizens of the United States and documented under the laws of the United States.

(Pub. L. 109–304, §7, Oct. 6, 2006, 120 Stat. 1549.)

§42104. INFORMATION, WITNESSES, AND EVIDENCE

(a) ORDER TO SUPPLY INFORMATION.—In carrying out section 42101 of this title, the Federal Maritime Commission may order any person (including a common carrier, tramp operator, bulk operator, shipper, shippers' association, ocean transportation intermediary, or marine terminal operator, or an officer, receiver, trustee, lessee, agent, or employee thereof) to file with the Commission a report, answers to questions, documentary material, or other information the Commission considers necessary or appropriate. The Commission may require the response to any such order to be made under oath. The response shall be provided in the form and within the time specified by the Commission.

(b) SUBPOENAS AND DISCOVERY.—In carrying out section 42101 of this title, the Commission may—

(1) subpoena witnesses and evidence; and

(2) authorize a party to use depositions, written interrogatories, and discovery procedures that, to the extent practicable, conform to the Federal Rules of Civil Procedure (28 App. U.S.C.).

(c) WITNESS FEES.—Unless otherwise prohibited by law, and subject to funds being appropriated, a witness in a proceeding under section 42101 of this title is entitled to the same fees and mileage as in the courts of the United States.

(d) PENALTIES.—For failure to supply information ordered to be produced or compelled by subpoena under this section, the Commission may—

(1) after notice and opportunity for a hearing, suspend tariffs and service contracts of a common carrier or the common carrier's right to use tariffs of conferences and service contracts of agreements of which it is a member; or

(2) assess a civil penalty of not more than $5,000 for each day that the information is not provided.

(e) ENFORCEMENT.—If a person does not comply with an order or subpoena of the Commission under this section, the Commission may seek enforcement in a district court of the United States having jurisdiction over the parties. If, after hearing, the court determines that the order or subpoena was regularly made and duly issued, the court shall enforce the order or subpoena.

(Pub. L. 109–304, §7, Oct. 6, 2006, 120 Stat. 1549.)

§42105. DISCLOSURE TO PUBLIC

Notwithstanding any other provision of law, the Federal Maritime Commission may refuse to disclose to the public a response or other information submitted to it under this chapter.

(Pub. L. 109–304, §7, Oct. 6, 2006, 120 Stat. 1550.)

§42106. OTHER ACTIONS TO REMEDY UNFAVORABLE CONDITIONS

If the Federal Maritime Commission finds that conditions unfavorable to shipping in foreign trade as described in section 42101 of this title exist, the Commission may—

(1) limit voyages to and from United States ports or the amount or type of cargo carried;

(2) suspend, in whole or in part, tariffs and service contracts for carriage to or from United States ports, including a common carrier's right to use tariffs of conferences and service contracts of agreements in United States trades of which it is a member for any period the Commission specifies;

(3) suspend, in whole or in part, an ocean common carrier's right to operate under any agreement filed with the Commission, including any agreement authorizing preferential treatment at terminals, preferential terminal leases, space chartering, or pooling of cargo or revenue with other ocean common carriers;

(4) impose a fee not to exceed $1,000,000 per voyage; or

(5) take any other action the Commission finds necessary and appropriate to adjust or meet any condition unfavorable to shipping in the foreign trade of the United States.

(Pub. L. 109–304, §7, Oct. 6, 2006, 120 Stat. 1550.)

§42107. REFUSAL OF CLEARANCE AND ENTRY

At the request of the Federal Maritime Commission—

(1) the Secretary of Homeland Security shall—

(A) refuse the clearance required by section 60105 of this title to a vessel of a country that is named in a regulation prescribed by the Commission under section 42101 of this title; and

(B) collect any fees imposed by the Commission under section 42106(4) of this title; and

(2) the Secretary of the department in which the Coast Guard is operating shall—

(A) deny entry, for purposes of oceanborne trade, of a vessel of a country that is named in a regulation prescribed by the Commission under section 42101 of this title, to a port or place in the United States or the navigable waters of the United States; or

(B) detain the vessel at the port or place in the United States from which it is about to depart for another port or place in the United States.

(Pub. L. 109–304, §7, Oct. 6, 2006, 120 Stat. 1551.)

§42108. PENALTY FOR OPERATING UNDER SUSPENDED TARIFF OR SERVICE CONTRACT

A common carrier that accepts or handles cargo for carriage under a tariff or service contract that has been suspended under section 42104(d)(1) or 42106(2) of this title, or after its right to use another tariff or service contract has been suspended under those provisions, is liable to the United States Government for a civil penalty of not more than $50,000 for each day that it is found to be operating under a suspended tariff or service contract.

(Pub. L. 109–304, §7, Oct. 6, 2006, 120 Stat. 1551.)

§42109. CONSULTATION WITH OTHER AGENCIES

The Federal Maritime Commission may consult with, seek the cooperation of, or make recommendations to other appropriate agencies of the United States Government prior to taking any action under this chapter.

(Pub. L. 109–304, §7, Oct. 6, 2006, 120 Stat. 1551.)

CHAPTER 423—FOREIGN SHIPPING PRACTICES

§42301. DEFINITIONS

(a) DEFINED IN PART A.—In this chapter, the terms "common carrier", "marine terminal operator", "ocean common carrier", "ocean transportation intermediary", "shipper", and "shippers' association" have the meaning given those terms in section 40102 of this title.

(b) OTHER DEFINITIONS.—In this chapter:

(1) FOREIGN CARRIER.—The term "foreign carrier" means an ocean common carrier a majority of whose vessels are documented under the laws of a foreign country.

(2) MARITIME SERVICES.—The term "maritime services" means port-to-port transportation of cargo by vessels operated by an ocean common carrier.

(3) MARITIME-RELATED SERVICES.—The term "maritime-related services" means intermodal operations, terminal operations, cargo solicitation, agency services, ocean transportation intermediary services and operations, and all other activities and services integral to total transportation systems of ocean common carriers and their foreign domiciled affiliates for themselves and others.

(4) UNITED STATES CARRIER.—The term "United States carrier" means an ocean common carrier operating vessels documented under the laws of the United States.

(5) UNITED STATES OCEANBORNE TRADE.—The term "United States oceanborne trade" means the carriage of cargo between the United States and a foreign country, whether directly or indirectly, by an ocean common carrier.

(Pub. L. 109–304, §7, Oct. 6, 2006, 120 Stat. 1551.)

§42302. INVESTIGATIONS

(a) IN GENERAL.—The Federal Maritime Commission shall investigate whether any laws, rules, regulations, policies, or practices of a foreign government, or any practices of a foreign carrier or other person providing maritime or maritime-related services in a foreign country, result in the existence of conditions that—

(1) adversely affect the operations of United States carriers in United States oceanborne trade; and

(2) do not exist for foreign carriers of that country in the United States under the laws of the United States or as a result of acts of United States carriers or other persons providing maritime or maritime-related services in the United States.

(b) INITIATION OF INVESTIGATION.—An investigation under subsection (a) may be initiated by the Commission on its own motion or on the petition of any person, including another component of the United States Government.

(c) TIME FOR DECISION.—The Commission shall complete an investigation under this section and render a decision within 120 days after it is initiated. However, the Commission may extend this 120-day period for an additional 90 days if the Commission is unable to obtain sufficient information to determine whether a condition specified in subsection (a) exists. A notice providing an extension shall state clearly the reasons for the extension.

(Pub. L. 109–304, §7, Oct. 6, 2006, 120 Stat. 1552.)

§42303. INFORMATION REQUESTS

(a) IN GENERAL.—To further the purposes of section 42302(a) of this title, the Federal Maritime Commission may order any person (including a common carrier, shipper, shippers' association, ocean transportation intermediary, or marine terminal operator, or an officer, receiver, trustee, lessee, agent or employee thereof) to file with the Commission any periodic or special report, answers to questions, documentary material, or other information the Commission considers necessary or appropriate. The Commission may require the response to any such order to be made under oath. The response shall be provided in the form and within the time specified by the Commission.

(b) SUBPOENAS.—In an investigation under section 42302 of this title, the Commission may subpoena witnesses and evidence.

(c) NONDISCLOSURE.—Notwithstanding any other provision of law, the Commission may determine that any information submitted to it in response to a request under this section, or otherwise, shall not be disclosed to the public.

(Pub. L. 109–304, §7, Oct. 6, 2006, 120 Stat. 1552.)

§42304. ACTION AGAINST FOREIGN CARRIERS

(a) IN GENERAL.—Subject to section 42306 of this title, whenever the Federal Maritime Commission, after notice and opportunity for comment or hearing, determines that the conditions specified in section 42302(a) of this title exist, the Commission shall take such action to offset those conditions as it considers necessary and appropriate against any foreign carrier that is a contributing cause, or whose government is a contributing cause, to those conditions. The action may include—

(1) limitations on voyages to and from United States ports or on the amount or type of cargo carried;

(2) suspension, in whole or in part, of any or all tariffs and service contracts, including an ocean common carrier's right to use any or all tariffs and service contracts of conferences in United States trades of which it is a member for any period the Commission specifies;

(3) suspension, in whole or in part, of an ocean common carrier's right to operate under any agreement filed with the Commission, including any agreement authorizing preferential treatment at terminals, preferential terminal leases, space chartering, or pooling of cargo or revenue with other ocean common carriers; and

(4) a fee not to exceed $1,000,000 per voyage.

(b) CONSULTATION.—The Commission may consult with, seek the cooperation of, or make recommendations to other appropriate agencies of the United States Government prior to taking any action under subsection (a).

(Pub. L. 109–304, §7, Oct. 6, 2006, 120 Stat. 1553.)

§42305. REFUSAL OF CLEARANCE AND ENTRY

Subject to section 42306 of this title, whenever the Federal Maritime Commission determines that the conditions specified in section 42302(a) of this title exist, then at the request of the Commission—

(1) the Secretary of Homeland Security shall refuse the clearance required by section 60105 of this title to a vessel of a foreign carrier that is identified by the Commission under section 42304 of this title; and

(2) the Secretary of the department in which the Coast Guard is operating shall—

(A) deny entry, for purposes of oceanborne trade, of a vessel of a foreign carrier that is identified by the Commission under section 42304 of this title, to a port or place in the United States or the navigable waters of the United States; or

(B) detain the vessel at the port or place in the United States from which it is about to depart for another port or place in the United States.

(Pub. L. 109–304, §7, Oct. 6, 2006, 120 Stat. 1553.)

§42306. SUBMISSION OF DETERMINATIONS TO PRESIDENT

Before a determination under section 42304 of this title becomes effective or a request is made under section 42305 of this title, the determination shall be submitted immediately to the President. The President, within 10 days after receiving it, may disapprove it in writing, setting forth the reasons for the disapproval, if the President finds that disapproval is required for reasons of national defense or foreign policy.

(Pub. L. 109–304, §7, Oct. 6, 2006, 120 Stat. 1553.)

§42307. REVIEW OF REGULATIONS AND ORDERS

A regulation or final order of the Federal Maritime Commission under this chapter is reviewable exclusively in the same forum and in the same manner as provided in section 2342(3)(B) of title 28.

(Pub. L. 109–304, §7, Oct. 6, 2006, 120 Stat. 1554.)

CHAPTER 425—NATIONAL SHIPPER ADVISORY COMMITTEE

Sec.[1]

[1] *Editorially supplied.*

§42501. DEFINITIONS

In this chapter:
(1) COMMISSION.—The term "Commission" means the Federal Maritime Commission.
(2) COMMITTEE.—The term "Committee" means the National Shipper Advisory Committee established under section 42502.

(Added Pub. L. 116–283, div. G, title LVXXXVI [LXXXVI], §8604(a), Jan. 1, 2021, 134 Stat. 4762.)

§42502. NATIONAL SHIPPER ADVISORY COMMITTEE

(a) ESTABLISHMENT.—There is established a National Shipper Advisory Committee.
(b) FUNCTION.—The Committee shall advise the Federal Maritime Commission on policies relating to the competitiveness, reliability, integrity, and fairness of the international ocean freight delivery system.
(c) MEMBERSHIP.—
(1) IN GENERAL.—The Committee shall consist of 24 members appointed by the Commission in accordance with this section.
(2) EXPERTISE.—Each member of the Committee shall have particular expertise, knowledge, and experience in matters relating to the function of the Committee.
(3) REPRESENTATION.—REPRESENTATION.— [1] Members of the Committee shall be appointed as follows: — [1]
(A) Twelve members shall represent entities who import cargo to the United States using ocean common carriers.
(B) Twelve members shall represent entities who export cargo from the United States using ocean common carriers.

(Added Pub. L. 116–283, div. G, title LVXXXVI [LXXXVI], §8604(a), Jan. 1, 2021, 134 Stat. 4762.)

[1] *So in original.*

§42503. ADMINISTRATION

(a) MEETINGS.—The Committee shall, not less than once each year, meet at the call of the Commission or a majority of the members of the Committee.
(b) EMPLOYEE STATUS.—A member of the Committee shall not be considered an employee of the Federal Government by reason of service on such Committee, except for the purposes of the following:

(1) Chapter 81 of title 5.

(2) Chapter 171 of title 28 and any other Federal law relating to tort liability.

(c) VOLUNTEER SERVICES AND COMPENSATION.—

(1) Notwithstanding any other provision of law, a member of the Committee may serve on such committee on a voluntary basis without pay.

(2) No member of the Committee shall receive compensation for service on the Committee.

(d) STATUS OF MEMBERS.—

(1) IN GENERAL.—Except as provided in paragraph (2), with respect to a member of the Committee whom the Commission appoints to represent an entity or group—

(A) the member is authorized to represent the interests of the applicable entity or group; and

(B) requirements under Federal law that would interfere with such representation and that apply to a special Government employee (as defined in section 202(a) of title 18), including requirements relating to employee conduct, political activities, ethics, conflicts of interest, and corruption, do not apply to the member.

(2) EXCEPTION.—Notwithstanding subsection (b), a member of the Committee shall be treated as a special Government employee for purposes of the committee service of the member if the member, without regard to service on the Committee, is a special Government employee.

(e) SERVICE ON COMMITTEE.—

(1) SOLICITATION OF NOMINATIONS.—Before appointing an individual as a member of the Committee, the Commission shall publish a timely notice in the Federal Register soliciting nominations for membership on such Committee.

(2) APPOINTMENTS.—

(A) IN GENERAL.—After considering nominations received pursuant to a notice published under paragraph (1), the Commission may appoint a member to the Committee.

(B) PROHIBITION.—The Commission shall not seek, consider, or otherwise use information concerning the political affiliation of a nominee in making an appointment to the Committee.

(3) SERVICE AT PLEASURE OF COMMISSION.—Each member of the Committee shall serve at the pleasure of the Commission.

(4) SECURITY BACKGROUND EXAMINATIONS.—The Commission may require an individual to have passed an appropriate security background examination before appointment to the Committee.

(5) PROHIBITION.—A Federal employee may not be appointed as a member of the Committee.

(6) TERMS.—

(A) IN GENERAL.—The term of each member of the Committee shall expire on

December 31 of the third full year after the effective date of the appointment.

(B) Continued service after term.—When the term of a member of the Committee ends, the member, for a period not to exceed 1 year, may continue to serve as a member until a successor is appointed.

(7) Vacancies.—A vacancy on the Committee shall be filled in the same manner as the original appointment.

(8) Special rule for reappointments.—Notwithstanding paragraphs (1) and (2), the Commission may reappoint a member of a committee for any term, other than the first term of the member, without soliciting, receiving, or considering nominations for such appointment.

(f) Staff Services.—The Commission shall furnish to the Committee any staff and services considered by the Commission to be necessary for the conduct of the Committee's functions.

(g) Chair; Vice Chair.—

(1) In general.—The Committee shall elect a Chair and Vice Chair from among the committee's members.

(2) Vice chairman acting as chairman.—The Vice Chair shall act as Chair in the absence or incapacity of, or in the event of a vacancy in the office of, the Chair.

(h) Subcommittees and Working Groups.—

(1) In general.—The Chair of the Committee may establish and disestablish subcommittees and working groups for any purpose consistent with the function of the Committee.

(2) Participants.—Subject to conditions imposed by the Chair, members of the Committee may be assigned to subcommittees and working groups established under paragraph (1).

(i) Consultation, Advice, Reports, and Recommendations.—

(1) Consultation.—Before taking any significant action, the Commission shall consult with, and consider the information, advice, and recommendations of, the Committee if the function of the Committee is to advise the Commission on matters related to the significant action.

(2) Advice, reports, and recommendations.—The Committee shall submit, in writing, to the Commission its advice, reports, and recommendations, in a form and at a frequency determined appropriate by the Committee.

(3) Explanation of actions taken.—Not later than 60 days after the date on which the Commission receives recommendations from the Committee under paragraph (2), the Commission shall—

(A) publish the recommendations on a public website; and

(B) respond, in writing, to the Committee regarding the recommendations, including by providing an explanation of actions taken regarding the recommendations.

(4) SUBMISSION TO CONGRESS.—The Commission shall submit to the Committee on Transportation and Infrastructure of the House of Representatives and the Committee on Commerce, Science, and Transportation of the Senate the advice, reports, and recommendations received from the Committee under paragraph (2).

(j) OBSERVERS.—The Commission may designate a representative to—
(1) attend any meeting of the Committee; and
(2) participate as an observer at such meeting.

(k) TERMINATION.—The Committee shall terminate on September 30, 2029.

(Added Pub. L. 116–283, div. G, title LVXXXVI [LXXXVI], §8604(a), Jan. 1, 2021, 134 Stat. 4762.)

PART C—MISCELLANEOUS

CHAPTER 441—EVIDENCE OF FINANCIAL RESPONSIBILITY FOR PASSENGER TRANSPORTATION

Sec.
44101.   Application.
44102.   Financial responsibility to indemnify passengers for nonperformance of transportation.
44103.   Financial responsibility to pay liability for death or injury.
44104.   Civil penalty.
44105.   Refusal of clearance.
44106.   Conduct of proceedings.

§44101. APPLICATION

This chapter applies to a vessel that—
   (1) has berth or stateroom accommodations for at least 50 passengers; and
   (2) boards passengers at a port in the United States.

(Pub. L. 109–304, §7, Oct. 6, 2006, 120 Stat. 1554.)

§44102. FINANCIAL RESPONSIBILITY TO INDEMNIFY PASSENGERS FOR NONPERFORMANCE OF TRANSPORTATION

(a) FILING REQUIREMENT.—A person in the United States may not arrange, offer, advertise, or provide transportation on a vessel to which this chapter applies unless the person has filed with the Federal Maritime Commission evidence of financial responsibility to indemnify passengers for nonperformance of the transportation.

(b) SATISFACTORY EVIDENCE.—To satisfy subsection (a), a person must file—
   (1) information the Commission considers necessary; or
   (2) a copy of a bond or other security, in such form as the Commission by regulation may require.

(c) AUTHORIZED ISSUER OF BOND.—If a bond is filed, it must be issued by a bonding company authorized to do business in the United States.

(Pub. L. 109–304, §7, Oct. 6, 2006, 120 Stat. 1554.)

§44103. FINANCIAL RESPONSIBILITY TO PAY LIABILITY FOR DEATH OR INJURY

(a) GENERAL REQUIREMENT.—The owner or charterer of a vessel to which this chapter applies shall establish, under regulations prescribed by the Federal Maritime Commission, financial responsibility to meet liability for death or injury to passengers or other individuals on a voyage to or from a port in the United States.

(b) AMOUNTS.—
   (1) IN GENERAL.—The amount of financial responsibility required under subsection (a) shall be based on the number of passenger accommodations as follows:

(A) $20,000 for each of the first 500 passenger accommodations.

(B) $15,000 for each additional passenger accommodation between 501 and 1,000.

(C) $10,000 for each additional passenger accommodation between 1,001 and 1,500.

(D) $5,000 for each additional passenger accommodation over 1,500.

(2) MULTIPLE VESSELS.—If the owner or charterer is operating more than one vessel subject to this chapter, the amount of financial responsibility shall be based on the number of passenger accommodations on the vessel with the largest number of passenger accommodations.

(c) AVAILABILITY TO PAY JUDGMENT.—The amount determined under subsection (b) shall be available to pay a judgment for damages (whether less than or more than $20,000) for death or injury to a passenger or other individual on a voyage to or from a port in the United States.

(d) MEANS OF ESTABLISHING.—Financial responsibility under this section may be established by one or more of the following if acceptable to the Commission:

(1) Insurance.

(2) Surety bond issued by a bonding company authorized to do business in the United States.

(3) Qualification as a self-insurer.

(4) Other evidence of financial responsibility.

(Pub. L. 109–304, §7, Oct. 6, 2006, 120 Stat. 1554.)

§44104. CIVIL PENALTY

A person that violates section 44102 or 44103 of this title is liable to the United States Government for a civil penalty of not more than $5,000, plus $200 for each passage sold, to be assessed by the Federal Maritime Commission. The Commission may remit or mitigate the penalty on terms the Commission considers proper.

(Pub. L. 109–304, §7, Oct. 6, 2006, 120 Stat. 1555.)

§44105. REFUSAL OF CLEARANCE

The Secretary of Homeland Security shall refuse the clearance required by section 60105 of this title, at the port or place of departure from the United States, of a vessel that is subject to this chapter and does not have evidence issued by the Federal Maritime Commission of compliance with sections 44102 and 44103 of this title.

(Pub. L. 109–304, §7, Oct. 6, 2006, 120 Stat. 1555.)

§44106. CONDUCT OF PROCEEDINGS

Part A of this subtitle applies to proceedings conducted by the Federal Maritime Commission under this chapter.

(Pub. L. 109–304, §7, Oct. 6, 2006, 120 Stat. 1555.)

PART D—FEDERAL MARITIME COMMISSION

CHAPTER 461—FEDERAL MARITIME COMMISSION

§46101. GENERAL ORGANIZATION

(a) ORGANIZATION.—The Federal Maritime Commission is an independent establishment of the United States Government.

(b) COMMISSIONERS.—

(1) COMPOSITION.—The Commission is composed of 5 Commissioners, appointed by the President by and with the advice and consent of the Senate. Not more than 3 Commissioners may be appointed from the same political party.

(2) TERMS.—The term of each Commissioner is 5 years. When the term of a Commissioner ends, the Commissioner may continue to serve until a successor is appointed and qualified, but for a period not to exceed 2 years. Except as provided in paragraph (3), no individual may serve more than 3 terms.

(3) VACANCIES.—A vacancy shall be filled in the same manner as the original appointment. An individual appointed to fill a vacancy is appointed only for the unexpired term to which such individual is appointed. An individual appointed to fill a vacancy may serve 3 terms in addition to the remainder of the term for which such individual was appointed.

(4) CONFLICTS OF INTEREST.—

(A) LIMITATION ON RELATIONSHIPS WITH REGULATED ENTITIES.—A Commissioner may not have a pecuniary interest in, hold an official relation to, or own stocks or bonds of any entity the Commission regulates under chapter 401 of this title.

(B) LIMITATION ON OTHER ACTIVITIES.—A Commissioner may not engage in another business, vocation, or employment.

(5) REMOVAL.—The President may remove a Commissioner for inefficiency, neglect of duty, or malfeasance in office.

(c) CHAIRMAN.—

(1) DESIGNATION.—The President shall designate one of the Commissioners as Chairman.

(2) GENERAL AUTHORITY.—The Chairman is the chief executive and administrative

officer of the Commission. In carrying out the duties and powers of the Commission (other than under paragraph (3)), the Chairman is subject to the policies, regulatory decisions, findings, and determinations of the Commission.

(3) PARTICULAR DUTIES.—

(A) IN GENERAL.—The Chairman shall—

(i) appoint and supervise officers and employees of the Commission;

(ii) appoint the heads of major organizational units (with such appointments subject to the approval of the Commission);

(iii) distribute the business of the Commission among personnel and organizational units;

(iv) supervise the expenditure of money for administrative purposes;

(v) assign Commission personnel, including Commissioners, to perform duties and powers delegated by the Commission under section 46104 of this title; and

(vi) prepare and submit to the President and the Congress requests for appropriations for the Commission (with such requests subject to the approval of the Commission).

(B) NONAPPLICATION.—Subparagraph (A) (other than clause (v)) does not apply to personnel employed regularly and full-time in the offices of Commissioners other than the Chairman.

(4) DELEGATION.—The Chairman may designate officers and employees under the Chairman's jurisdiction to perform duties and powers of the Chairman, subject to the Chairman's supervision and direction.

(d) SEAL.—The Commission shall have a seal which shall be judicially recognized.

(Pub. L. 109–304, §4, Oct. 6, 2006, 120 Stat. 1488, §301; Pub. L. 113–281, title IV, §403(a), Dec. 18, 2014, 128 Stat. 3056; Pub. L. 114–120, title IV, §402, Feb. 8, 2016, 130 Stat. 67; renumbered §46101 and amended Pub. L. 116–283, div. G, title LVXXXVI [LXXXVI], §8605(a)(3), (b)(1), Jan. 1, 2021, 134 Stat. 4765; Pub. L. 117–263, div. K, title CXVIII, §11801(a), Dec. 23, 2022, 136 Stat. 4163.)

§46102. QUORUM

A vacancy or vacancies in the membership of the Federal Maritime Commission do not impair the power of the Commission to execute its functions. The affirmative vote of a majority of the Commissioners serving on the Commission is required to dispose of any matter before the Commission.

(Pub. L. 109–304, §4, Oct. 6, 2006, 120 Stat. 1489, §302; renumbered §46102, Pub. L. 116–283, div. G, title LVXXXVI [LXXXVI], §8605(a)(3), Jan. 1, 2021, 134 Stat. 4765.)

§46103. MEETINGS

(a) IN GENERAL.—The Federal Maritime Commission shall be deemed to be an agency for purposes of section 552b of title 5.

(b) RECORD.—The Commission, through its secretary, shall keep a record of its meetings and the votes taken on any action, order, contract, or financial transaction of the Commission.

(c) Nonpublic Collaborative Discussions.—

(1) In general.—Notwithstanding section 552b of title 5, a majority of the Commissioners may hold a meeting that is not open to public observation to discuss official agency business if—

(A) no formal or informal vote or other official agency action is taken at the meeting;

(B) each individual present at the meeting is a Commissioner or an employee of the Commission;

(C) at least 1 Commissioner from each political party is present at the meeting, if applicable; and

(D) the General Counsel of the Commission is present at the meeting.

(2) Disclosure of nonpublic collaborative discussions.—Except as provided under paragraph (3), not later than 2 business days after the conclusion of a meeting under paragraph (1), the Commission shall make available to the public, in a place easily accessible to the public—

(A) a list of the individuals present at the meeting; and

(B) a summary of the matters discussed at the meeting, except for any matters the Commission properly determines may be withheld from the public under section 552b(c) of title 5.

(3) Exception.—If the Commission properly determines matters may be withheld from the public under section 552b(c) of title 5, the Commission shall provide a summary with as much general information as possible on those matters withheld from the public.

(4) Ongoing proceedings.—If a meeting under paragraph (1) directly relates to an ongoing proceeding before the Commission, the Commission shall make the disclosure under paragraph (2) on the date of the final Commission decision.

(5) Preservation of open meetings requirements for agency action.—Nothing in this subsection may be construed to limit the applicability of section 552b of title 5 with respect to a meeting of the Commissioners other than that described in this subsection.

(6) Statutory construction.—Nothing in this subsection may be construed—

(A) to limit the applicability of section 552b of title 5 with respect to any information which is proposed to be withheld from the public under paragraph (2)(B) of this subsection; or

(B) to authorize the Commission to withhold from any individual any record that is accessible to that individual under section 552a of title 5.

(Pub. L. 109–304, §4, Oct. 6, 2006, 120 Stat. 1489, §303; Pub. L. 115–282, title VII, §711(a), Dec. 4, 2018, 132 Stat. 4297; renumbered §46103 and amended Pub. L. 116–283, div. G, title LVXXXVI [LXXXVI], §8605(a)(3), (c), Jan. 1, 2021, 134 Stat. 4765.)

§46104. Delegation of authority

(a) Delegation.—The Federal Maritime Commission, by published order or regulation, may delegate to a division of the Commission, an individual Commissioner, an employee board, or an officer or employee of the Commission, any of its duties or powers, including those relating to hearing, determining, ordering, certifying, reporting, or otherwise acting on any matter. This subsection does not affect section 556(b) of title 5.

(b) REVIEW.—The Commission may review any action taken under a delegation of authority under subsection (a). The review may be taken on the Commission's own initiative or on the petition of a party to or an intervenor in the action, within the time and in the manner prescribed by the Commission. The vote of a majority of the Commission, less one member, is sufficient to bring an action before the Commission for review.

(c) DEEMED ACTION OF COMMISSION.—If the Commission declines review, or if review is not sought, within the time prescribed under subsection (b), the action taken under the delegation of authority is deemed to be the action of the Commission.

(Pub. L. 109–304, §4, Oct. 6, 2006, 120 Stat. 1489, §304; renumbered §46104, Pub. L. 116–283, div. G, title LVXXXVI [LXXXVI], §8605(a)(3), Jan. 1, 2021, 134 Stat. 4765.)

§46105. REGULATIONS

(a) IN GENERAL.—The Federal Maritime Commission may prescribe regulations to carry out its duties and powers.

(b) TRANSPARENCY.—

(1) IN GENERAL.—In conjunction with the transmittal by the President to the Congress of the Budget of the United States for fiscal year 2021 and biennially thereafter, the Federal Maritime Commission shall submit to the Committee on Commerce, Science, and Transportation of the Senate and the Committee on Transportation and Infrastructure of the House of Representatives reports that describe the Commission's progress toward addressing the issues raised in each unfinished regulatory proceeding, regardless of whether the proceeding is subject to a statutory or regulatory deadline.

(2) FORMAT OF REPORTS.—Each report under paragraph (1) shall, among other things, clearly identify for each unfinished regulatory proceeding—

(A) the popular title;

(B) the current stage of the proceeding;

(C) an abstract of the proceeding;

(D) what prompted the action in question;

(E) any applicable statutory, regulatory, or judicial deadline;

(F) the associated docket number;

(G) the date the rulemaking was initiated;

(H) a date for the next action; and

(I) if a date for the next action identified in the previous report is not met, the reason for the delay.

(Pub. L. 109–304, §4, Oct. 6, 2006, 120 Stat. 1489, §305; renumbered §46105 and amended Pub. L. 116–283, div. G, title LVXXXVI [LXXXVI], §§8603, 8605(a)(3), Jan. 1, 2021, 134 Stat. 4761, 4765.)

§46106. ANNUAL REPORT

(a) IN GENERAL.—Not later than April 1 of each year, the Federal Maritime Commission shall submit a report to Congress. The report shall include the results of its investigations, a summary of its transactions, the purposes for which all of its expenditures were made, and any recommendations for legislation.

(b) REPORT ON FOREIGN LAWS AND PRACTICES.—The Commission shall include in its annual report to Congress—

(1) a list of the 20 foreign countries that generated the largest volume of oceanborne liner cargo for the most recent calendar year in bilateral trade with the United States;

(2) an analysis of conditions described in section 42302(a) of this title being investigated or found to exist in foreign countries;

(3) any actions being taken by the Commission to offset those conditions;

(4) any recommendations for additional legislation to offset those conditions;

(5) a list of petitions filed under section 42302(b) of this title that the Commission rejected and the reasons for each rejection;

(6) an analysis of the impacts on competition for the purchase of certain covered services by alliances of ocean common carriers acting pursuant to an agreement under this part [1] between or among ocean common carriers, including a summary of actions, including corrective actions, taken by the Commission to promote such competition; and

(7) an identification of any otherwise concerning practices by ocean common carriers, particularly such carriers that are controlled carriers, that are—

(A) State-owned or State-controlled enterprises; or

(B) owned or controlled by, a subsidiary of, or otherwise related legally or financially (other than a minority relationship or investment) to a corporation based in a country—

(i) identified as a nonmarket economy country (as defined in section 771(18) of the Tariff Act of 1930 (19 U.S.C. 1677(18))) as of the date of enactment of this paragraph;

(ii) identified by the United States Trade Representative in the most recent report required by section 182 of the Trade Act of 1974 (19 U.S.C. 2242) as a priority foreign country under subsection (a)(2) of that section; or

(iii) subject to monitoring by the United States Trade Representative under section 306 of the Trade Act of 1974 (19 U.S.C. 2416).

(c) DEFINITION OF CERTAIN COVERED SERVICES.—In this section, the term "certain covered services" has the meaning given the term in section 40102.

(d) PUBLIC DISCLOSURES.—The Federal Maritime Commission shall publish, and annually update, on the website of the Commission—

(1) all findings by the Commission of false detention and demurrage invoice information by common carriers under section 41104(a)(15) of this title; and

(2) all penalties imposed or assessed against common carriers, as applicable, under sections 41107, 41108, and 41109, listed by each common carrier.

(Pub. L. 109–304, §4, Oct. 6, 2006, 120 Stat. 1489, §306; Pub. L. 115–282, title VII, §703, Dec. 4, 2018, 132 Stat. 4294; renumbered §46106, Pub. L. 116–283, div. G, title LVXXXVI [LXXXVI], §8605(a)(3), Jan. 1, 2021, 134 Stat. 4765; Pub. L. 117–146, §§6, 14, June 16, 2022, 136 Stat. 1274, 1279.)

[1] See References in Text note below.

§46107. EXPENDITURES

(a) IN GENERAL.—The Federal Maritime Commission may make such expenditures as are necessary in the performance of its functions from funds appropriated or otherwise made available to it, which appropriations are authorized.

(b) PROHIBITION.—Notwithstanding subsection (a), the Federal Maritime Commission may not expend any funds appropriated or otherwise made available to it to a non-Federal entity to issue an award, prize, commendation, or other honor that is not related to the purposes set forth in section 40101.

(Pub. L. 109–304, §4, Oct. 6, 2006, 120 Stat. 1490, §307; Pub. L. 114–120, title IV, §403, Feb. 8, 2016, 130 Stat. 67; renumbered §46107, Pub. L. 116–283, div. G, title LVXXXVI [LXXXVI], §8605(a)(3), Jan. 1, 2021, 134 Stat. 4765.)

§46108. AUTHORIZATION OF APPROPRIATIONS

There is authorized to be appropriated to the Federal Maritime Commission $32,869,000 for fiscal year 2022, $38,260,000 for fiscal year 2023, $43,720,000 for fiscal year 2024, and $49,200,000 for fiscal year 2025 for the activities of the Commission authorized under this chapter and subtitle IV.

(Added Pub. L. 114–120, title IV, §401(a), Feb. 8, 2016, 130 Stat. 67, §308; amended Pub. L. 115–282, title VII, §702, Dec. 4, 2018, 132 Stat. 4294; renumbered §46108 and amended Pub. L. 116–283, div. G, title LVXXXVI [LXXXVI], §§8602, 8605(a)(3), Jan. 1, 2021, 134 Stat. 4761, 4765; Pub. L. 117–146, §26, June 16, 2022, 136 Stat. 1286.)

SUBTITLE V
MERCHANT MARINE

Subtitle V—Merchant Marine

PART A—GENERAL

CHAPTER 501—POLICY, STUDIES, AND REPORTS

§50101. OBJECTIVES AND POLICY

(a) OBJECTIVES.—It is necessary for the national defense and the development of the domestic and foreign commerce of the United States that the United States have a merchant marine—

(1) sufficient to carry the waterborne domestic commerce and a substantial part of the waterborne export and import foreign commerce of the United States and to provide shipping service essential for maintaining the flow of the waterborne domestic and foreign commerce at all times;

(2) capable of serving as a naval and military auxiliary in time of war or national emergency;

(3) owned and operated as vessels of the United States by citizens of the United States;

(4) composed of the best-equipped, safest, and most suitable types of vessels constructed in the United States and manned with a trained and efficient citizen personnel; and

(5) supplemented by efficient facilities for building and repairing vessels.

(b) POLICY.—It is the policy of the United States to encourage and aid the development and maintenance of a merchant marine satisfying the objectives described in subsection (a).

(Pub. L. 109–304, §8(b), Oct. 6, 2006, 120 Stat. 1556; Pub. L. 111–84, div. C, title XXXV, §3511, Oct. 28, 2009, 123 Stat. 2722.)

§50102. SURVEY OF MERCHANT MARINE

(a) IN GENERAL.—The Secretary of Transportation shall survey the merchant marine of the United States to determine whether replacements and additions are required to carry out the objectives and policy of section 50101 of this title. The Secretary shall study, perfect, and adopt a long-range program for replacements and additions that will result, as soon as practicable, in—

(1) an adequate and well-balanced merchant fleet, including vessels of all types, that will provide shipping service essential for maintaining the flow of foreign commerce by vessels designed to be readily and quickly convertible into transport and supply vessels in a time of national emergency;

(2) ownership and operation of the fleet by citizens of the United States insofar as practicable;

(3) vessels designed to afford the best and most complete protection for passengers and crew against fire and all marine perils; and

(4) an efficient capacity for building and repairing vessels in the United States with an adequate number of skilled personnel to provide an adequate mobilization base.

(b) COOPERATION WITH SECRETARY OF NAVY.—In carrying out subsection (a)(1), the Secretary of Transportation shall cooperate closely with the Secretary of the Navy as to national defense requirements.

(Pub. L. 109–304, §8(b), Oct. 6, 2006, 120 Stat. 1557.)

§50103. DETERMINATIONS OF ESSENTIAL SERVICES

(a) ESSENTIAL SERVICES, ROUTES, AND LINES.—

(1) IN GENERAL.—The Secretary of Transportation shall investigate, determine, and keep current records of the ocean services, routes, and lines from ports in the United States, or in the territories and possessions of the United States, to foreign markets, which the Secretary determines to be essential for the promotion, development, expansion, and maintenance of the foreign commerce of the United States. In making such a determination, the Secretary shall consider and give due weight to—

(A) the cost of maintaining each line;

(B) the probability that a line cannot be maintained except at a heavy loss disproportionate to the benefit to foreign trade;

(C) the number of voyages and types of vessels that should be employed in a line;

(D) the intangible benefit of maintaining a line to the foreign commerce of the United States, the national defense, and other national requirements; and

(E) any other facts and conditions a prudent business person would consider when dealing with the person's own business.

(2) SAINT LAWRENCE SEAWAY.—For purposes of paragraph (1), the Secretary shall establish services, routes, and lines that reflect the seasonal closing of the Saint Lawrence Seaway and provide for alternate routing of vessels through a different range of ports during that closing to maintain continuity of service on a year-round basis.

(b) BULK CARGO CARRYING SERVICES.—The Secretary shall investigate, determine, and keep current records of the bulk cargo carrying services that should be provided by vessels of the United States (whether or not operating on particular services, routes, or lines) for the promotion, development, expansion, and maintenance of the foreign commerce of the

United States and the national defense or other national requirements.

(c) TYPES OF VESSELS.—The Secretary shall investigate, determine, and keep current records of the type, size, speed, method of propulsion, and other requirements of the vessels, including express-liner or super-liner vessels, that should be employed in—

(1) the services, routes, or lines described in subsection (a), and the frequency and regularity of the voyages of the vessels, with a view to furnishing adequate, regular, certain, and permanent service; and

(2) the bulk cargo carrying services described in subsection (b).

(Pub. L. 109–304, §8(b), Oct. 6, 2006, 120 Stat. 1557.)

§50104. STUDIES OF GENERAL MARITIME PROBLEMS

The Secretary of Transportation shall study all maritime problems arising in carrying out the policy in section 50101 of this title.

(Pub. L. 109–304, §8(b), Oct. 6, 2006, 120 Stat. 1558.)

§50105. STUDIES AND COOPERATION RELATING TO THE CONSTRUCTION OF VESSELS

(a) RELATIVE COSTS AND NEW DESIGNS.—The Secretary of Transportation shall investigate, determine, and keep current records of—

(1) the relative cost of construction of comparable vessels in the United States and in foreign countries; and

(2) new designs, new methods of construction, and new types of equipment for vessels.

(b) RULES, CLASSIFICATIONS, AND RATINGS.—The Secretary shall examine the rules under which vessels are constructed abroad and in the United States and the methods of classifying and rating the vessels.

(c) COLLABORATION WITH OWNERS AND BUILDERS.—The Secretary shall collaborate with vessel owners and shipbuilders in developing plans for the economical construction of vessels and their propelling machinery, of most modern economical types, giving thorough consideration to all well-recognized means of propulsion and taking into account the benefits from standardized production where practicable and desirable.

(d) EXPRESS-LINER AND SUPER-LINER VESSELS.—The Secretary shall study and cooperate with vessel owners in devising means by which there may be constructed, by or with the aid of the United States Government, express-liner or super-liner vessels comparable to those of other nations, especially with a view to their use in a national emergency, and the use of transoceanic aircraft service in connection with or in lieu of those vessels.

(Pub. L. 109–304, §8(b), Oct. 6, 2006, 120 Stat. 1558.)

§50106. STUDIES ON THE OPERATION OF VESSELS

(a) RELATIVE COSTS.—The Secretary of Transportation shall investigate, determine, and keep current records of the relative cost of marine insurance, maintenance, repairs, wages and subsistence of officers and crews, and all other items of expense, in the operation of comparable vessels under the laws and regulations of the United States and those of the foreign countries whose vessels are substantial competitors of American vessels.

(b) SHIPYARDS.—The Secretary shall investigate, determine, and keep current records of the number, location, and efficiency of shipyards in the United States.

(c) NAVIGATION LAWS.—The Secretary shall examine the navigation laws and regulations of the United States and make such recommendations to Congress as the Secretary considers proper for the amendment, improvement, and revision of those laws and for the development of the merchant marine of the United States.

(Pub. L. 109–304, §8(b), Oct. 6, 2006, 120 Stat. 1559.)

§50107. STUDIES ON MARINE INSURANCE

The Secretary of Transportation shall—

(1) examine into the subject of marine insurance, the number of companies in the United States, domestic and foreign, engaging in marine insurance, the extent of the insurance on hulls and cargoes placed or written in the United States, and the extent of reinsurance of American maritime risks in foreign companies; and

(2) ascertain what steps may be necessary to develop an ample marine insurance system as an aid in the development of the merchant marine of the United States.

(Pub. L. 109–304, §8(b), Oct. 6, 2006, 120 Stat. 1559.)

§50108. STUDIES ON CARGO CARRIAGE AND CARGO CONTAINERS

(a) STUDIES.—The Secretary of Transportation shall study—

(1) the methods of encouraging the development and implementation of new concepts for the carriage of cargo in the domestic and foreign commerce of the United States; and

(2) the economic and technological aspects of the use of cargo containers as a method of carrying out the policy in section 50101 of this title.

(b) RESTRICTION.—In carrying out subsection (a) and the policy in section 50101 of this title, the United States Government may not give preference as between carriers based on the length, height, or width of cargo containers or the length, height, or width of cargo container cells. This restriction applies to all existing container vessels and any container vessel to be constructed or rebuilt.

(Pub. L. 109–304, §8(b), Oct. 6, 2006, 120 Stat. 1559.)

§50109. MISCELLANEOUS STUDIES

(a) FOREIGN SUBSIDIES.—The Secretary of Transportation shall investigate, determine, and keep current records of the extent and character of the governmental aid and subsidies granted by foreign governments to their merchant marine.

(b) LAWS APPLICABLE TO AIRCRAFT.—The Secretary shall investigate, determine, and keep current records of the provisions of law relating to shipping that should be made applicable to aircraft engaged in foreign commerce to further the policy in section 50101 of this title, and any appropriate legislation in this regard.

(c) AID FOR COTTON, COAL, LUMBER, AND CEMENT.—The Secretary shall investigate, determine, and keep current records of the advisability of enactment of suitable legislation authorizing the Secretary, in an economic or commercial emergency, to aid farmers and producers of cotton, coal, lumber, and cement in any section of the United States in the transportation and landing of their products in any foreign port, which products can be carried in dry-cargo vessels by reducing rates, by supplying additional tonnage to any American operator, or by operation of vessels directly by the Secretary, until the Secretary considers the special rate reduction and operation unnecessary for the benefit of those farmers and producers.

(d) INTERCOASTAL AND INLAND WATER TRANSPORTATION.—The Secretary shall investigate, determine, and keep current records of intercoastal and inland water transportation, including their relation to transportation by land and air.

(e) OBSOLETE TONNAGE AND TRAMP SERVICE.—The Secretary shall make studies and reports to Congress on—

(1) the scrapping or removal from service of old or obsolete merchant tonnage owned by the United States Government or in use in the merchant marine; and

(2) tramp shipping service and the advisability of citizens of the United States participating in that service with vessels under United States registry.

(f) MORTGAGE LOANS.—The Secretary shall investigate the legal status of mortgage loans on vessel property, with a view to the means of improving the security of those loans and of encouraging investment in American shipping.

(Pub. L. 109–304, §8(b), Oct. 6, 2006, 120 Stat. 1559.)

§50110. SECURING PREFERENCE TO VESSELS OF THE UNITED STATES

(a) POSSIBILITIES OF PROMOTING CARRIAGE.—The Secretary of Transportation shall investigate, determine, and keep current records of the possibilities of promoting the carriage of United States foreign trade in vessels of the United States.

(b) INDUCEMENTS TO IMPORTERS AND EXPORTERS.—The Secretary shall study and cooperate with vessel owners in devising means by which the importers and exporters of the United States can be induced to give preference to vessels of the United States.

(c) LIAISON WITH AGENCIES AND ORGANIZATIONS.—The Secretary shall establish and maintain liaison with such other agencies of the United States Government, and with such representative trade organizations throughout the United States, as may be concerned, directly or indirectly, with any movement of commodities in the waterborne export and import foreign commerce of the United States, for the purpose of securing preference to vessels of the United States in the shipment of those commodities.

(Pub. L. 109–304, §8(b), Oct. 6, 2006, 120 Stat. 1560.)

§50111. SUBMISSION OF ANNUAL MARAD AUTHORIZATION REQUEST

(a) SUBMISSION OF LEGISLATIVE PROPOSAL.—Not later than 30 days after the date on which the President submits to Congress a budget for a fiscal year pursuant to section 1105 of title 31, the Secretary of Transportation shall submit to the Committee on Armed Services and the Committee on Transportation and Infrastructure of the House of Representatives and the Committee on Commerce, Science, and Transportation of the Senate the Maritime Administration authorization request for that fiscal year.

(b) MARITIME ADMINISTRATION REQUEST DEFINED.—In this section, the term "Maritime

Administration authorization request" means a proposal for legislation that, for a fiscal year—

(1) recommends authorizations of appropriations for the Maritime Administration for that fiscal year, including with respect to matters described in subsection [1] 109(j) of title 49 or authorized in subtitle V of this title; and

(2) addresses any other matter with respect to the Maritime Administration that the Secretary determines is appropriate.

(Pub. L. 109–304, §8(b), Oct. 6, 2006, 120 Stat. 1560; Pub. L. 114–92, div. A, title X, §1074(c)(1), Nov. 25, 2015, 129 Stat. 996.)

[1] So in original. Probably should be "section".

§50112. NATIONAL MARITIME ENHANCEMENT INSTITUTES

(a) DESIGNATION.—The Secretary of Transportation may designate National Maritime Enhancement Institutes.

(b) ACTIVITIES.—Activities undertaken by an institute may include—

(1) conducting research about methods to improve the performance of maritime industries;

(2) enhancing the competitiveness of domestic maritime industries in international trade;

(3) forecasting trends in maritime trade;

(4) assessing technological advancements;

(5) developing management initiatives and training;

(6) analyzing economic and operational impacts of regulatory policies and international negotiations or agreements pending before international bodies;

(7) assessing the compatibility of domestic maritime infrastructure systems with overseas transport systems;

(8) fostering innovations in maritime transportation pricing; and

(9) improving maritime economics and finance.

(c) APPLICATION FOR DESIGNATION.—An institution seeking designation as a National Maritime Enhancement Institute shall submit an application under regulations prescribed by the Secretary.

(d) CRITERIA FOR DESIGNATION.—The Secretary shall designate an institute under this section on the basis of the following criteria:

(1) The demonstrated research and extension resources available to the applicant for carrying out the activities specified in subsection (b).

(2) The ability of the applicant to provide leadership in making national and regional contributions to the solution of both long-range and immediate problems of the domestic maritime industry.

(3) The existence of an established program of the applicant encompassing research and training directed to enhancing maritime industries.

(4) The demonstrated ability of the applicant to assemble and evaluate pertinent information from national and international sources and to disseminate results of maritime industry research and educational programs through a continuing education

program.

(5) The qualification of the applicant as a nonprofit institution of higher learning.

(e) FINANCIAL AWARDS.—The Secretary may make awards on an equal matching basis to an institute designated under subsection (a) from amounts appropriated. The aggregate annual amount of the Federal share of the awards by the Secretary may not exceed $500,000.

(f) UNIVERSITY TRANSPORTATION RESEARCH FUNDS.—The Secretary may make a grant under section 5505 of title 49 to an institute designated under subsection (a) for maritime and maritime intermodal research under that section as if the institute were a university transportation center. In making a grant, the Secretary, through the Office of the Assistant Secretary for Research and Technology of the Department of Transportation, shall advise the Maritime Administration on the availability of funds for the grants and consult with the Administration on making the grants.

(Pub. L. 109–304, §8(b), Oct. 6, 2006, 120 Stat. 1561; Pub. L. 113–76, div. L, title I, Jan. 17, 2014, 128 Stat. 574.)

§50113. USE AND PERFORMANCE REPORTS BY OPERATORS OF VESSELS

(a) FILING REQUIREMENT.—The Secretary of Transportation by regulation may require the operator of a vessel in the waterborne foreign commerce of the United States to file such report, account, record, or memorandum on the use and performance of the vessel as the Secretary considers desirable to assist in carrying out this subtitle. The report, account, record, or memorandum shall be signed and verified, and be filed at the times and in the manner, as provided by regulation.

(b) CIVIL PENALTY.—An operator not filing a report, account, record, or memorandum required by the Secretary under this section is liable to the United States Government for a civil penalty of $50 for each day of the violation. A penalty imposed under this section on the operator of a vessel constitutes a lien on the vessel involved in the violation. A civil action in rem to enforce the lien may be brought in the district court of the United States for any district in which the vessel is found. The Secretary may remit or mitigate any penalty imposed under this section.

(Pub. L. 109–304, §8(b), Oct. 6, 2006, 120 Stat. 1562.)

§50114. NATIONAL MARITIME STRATEGY

(a) IN GENERAL.—The Secretary of Transportation, in consultation with the Secretary of the department in which the Coast Guard is operating and the Commander of United States Transportation Command, shall submit to the Committee on Transportation and Infrastructure of the House of Representatives and the Committee on Commerce, Science, and Transportation of the Senate—

(1) a national maritime strategy; and

(2) not less often than once every five years after the submission of such strategy, an update to the strategy.

(b) CONTENTS.—The strategy required under subsection (a) shall include each of the following:

(1) An identification of—

(A) international policies and Federal regulations and policies that reduce the competitiveness of United States-documented vessels with foreign vessels in domestic and international transportation markets; and

(B) the impact of reduced cargo flow due to reductions in the number of members of the United States Armed Forces stationed or deployed outside of the United States.

(2) Recommendations to—

(A) make United States-documented vessels more competitive in shipping routes between United States and foreign ports;

(B) increase the use of United States-documented vessels to carry cargo imported to and exported from the United States;

(C) ensure compliance by Federal agencies with chapter 553;

(D) increase the use of short sea transportation routes, including routes designated under section 55601(b), to enhance intermodal freight movements;

(E) enhance United States shipbuilding capability;

(F) invest in, and identify gaps in, infrastructure needed to facilitate the movement of goods at ports and throughout the transportation system, including innovative physical and information technologies;

(G) enhance workforce training and recruitment for the maritime workforce, including training on innovative physical and information technologies;

(H) increase the resilience of ports and the marine transportation system;

(I) increase the carriage of government-impelled cargo on United States-documented vessels pursuant to chapter 553 of title 46, section 2631 of title 10, or otherwise; and

(J) maximize the cost effectiveness of Federal funding for carriage of non-defense government impelled cargo for the purposes of maintaining a United States flag fleet for national and economic security.

(c) UPDATE.—Upon the release of a strategy or update under subsection (a), the Secretary of Transportation shall make such strategy or update publicly available on the website of the Department of Transportation.

(d) IMPLEMENTATION PLAN.—Not later than six months after the submission of a strategy or update under subsection (a), the Secretary of Transportation, in consultation with the Secretary of the department in which the Coast Guard is operating and the Secretary of Defense, shall make publicly available on an appropriate website an implementation plan for such strategy or update.

(Added Pub. L. 117–263, div. C, title XXXV, §3542(b)(1), Dec. 23, 2022, 136 Stat. 3096.)

CHAPTER 503—ADMINISTRATIVE

Sec.

§50301. Vessel Operations Revolving Fund

(a) IN GENERAL.—There is a "Vessel Operations Revolving Fund" for use by the Secretary of Transportation in carrying out duties and powers related to vessel operations, including charter, operation, maintenance, repair, reconditioning, and improvement of merchant vessels under the jurisdiction of the Secretary. The Fund has a working capital of $20,000,000, to remain available until expended.

(b) RELATIONSHIP TO OTHER LAWS.—Notwithstanding any other law, rates for shipping services provided under the Fund shall be prescribed by the Secretary and the Fund shall be credited with receipts from vessel operations conducted under the Fund. Sections 1(a) and (c), 3(c), and 4 of the Act of March 24, 1943 (50 U.S.C. 4701(a), (c), 4703(c), 4704), apply to those operations and to seamen employed through general agents as employees of the United States Government. Notwithstanding any other law on the employment of persons by the Government, the seamen may be employed in accordance with customary commercial practices in the maritime industry.

(c) ADVANCEMENTS.—With the approval of the Director of the Office of Management and Budget, the Secretary may advance amounts the Secretary considers necessary, but not more than 2 percent of vessel operating expenses, from the Fund to the appropriation "Salaries and Expenses" in carrying out duties and powers related to vessel operations, without regard to the limitations on amounts stated in that appropriation.

(d) TRANSFERS.—The unexpended balances of working funds or of allocation accounts established after January 1, 1951, for the activities provided for in subsection (a), and receipts received from those activities, may be transferred to the Fund, which shall be available for the purposes of those working funds or allocation accounts.

(e) LIMITATION.—

(1) IN GENERAL.—Amounts made available to the Secretary for maritime activities by this section or any other law may not be used to pay for a vessel described in paragraph (2) unless the compensation to be paid is computed under section 56303 of this title as that section is interpreted by the Comptroller General.

(2) APPLICABLE VESSELS.—Paragraph (1) applies to a vessel—

(A) the title to which is acquired by the Government by requisition or purchase;

(B) the use of which is taken by requisition or agreement; or

(C) lost while insured by the Government.

(3) NONAPPLICABLE VESSELS.—Paragraph (1) does not apply to a vessel under a construction-differential subsidy contract.

(f) AVAILABILITY FOR ADDITIONAL PURPOSES.—The Fund is available for—

(1) necessary expenses incurred in the protection, preservation, maintenance, acquisition, or use of vessels involved in mortgage foreclosure or forfeiture proceedings instituted by the Government, including payment of prior claims and liens, expenses of sale, or other related charges;

(2) necessary expenses incident to the redelivery and lay-up, in the United States, of vessels chartered as of June 20, 1956, under agreements not calling for their return to the Government;

(3) the activation, repair, and deactivation of merchant vessels chartered for limited emergency purposes during fiscal year 1957 under the jurisdiction of the Secretary; and

(4) payment of expenses of custody and maintenance of Government-owned vessels not in the National Defense Reserve Fleet.

(g) EXPENSES AND RECEIPTS RELATED TO CHARTER OPERATIONS.—The Fund is available for expenses incurred in activating, repairing, and deactivating merchant vessels chartered under the jurisdiction of the Secretary. Receipts from charter operations of Government-owned vessels under the jurisdiction of the Secretary shall be credited to the Fund.

(Pub. L. 109–304, §8(b), Oct. 6, 2006, 120 Stat. 1562; Pub. L. 118–31, div. C, title XXXV, §3514(d), Dec. 22, 2023, 137 Stat. 810.)

§50302. PORT DEVELOPMENT

(a) GENERAL REQUIREMENTS.—With the objective of promoting, encouraging, and developing ports and transportation facilities in connection with water commerce over which the Secretary of Transportation has jurisdiction, the Secretary, in cooperation with the Secretary of the Army, shall—

(1) investigate territorial regions and zones tributary to ports, taking into consideration the economies of transportation by rail, water, and highway and the natural direction of the flow of commerce;

(2) investigate the causes of congestion of commerce at ports and applicable remedies;

(3) investigate the subject of water terminals, including the necessary docks, warehouses, and equipment, to devise and suggest the types most appropriate for different locations and for the most expeditious and economical transfer or interchange of passengers or property between water carriers and rail carriers;

(4) consult with communities on the appropriate location and plan of construction of wharves, piers, and water terminals;

(5) investigate the practicability and advantages of harbor, river, and port improvements in connection with foreign and coastwise trade; and

(6) investigate any other matter that may tend to promote and encourage the use by vessels of ports adequate to care for the freight that naturally would pass through those ports.

(b) SUBMISSION OF FINDINGS TO SURFACE TRANSPORTATION BOARD.—After an investigation under subsection (a), if the Secretary of Transportation believes that the rates or practices of a rail carrier subject to the jurisdiction of the Surface Transportation Board are detrimental to the objective specified in subsection (a), or that new rates or practices, new or additional port terminal facilities, or affirmative action by a rail carrier is necessary to promote that objective, the Secretary may submit findings to the Board for action the Board considers appropriate under existing law.

(Pub. L. 109–304, §8(b), Oct. 6, 2006, 120 Stat. 1564; Pub. L. 111–84, div. C, title XXXV, §3512, Oct. 28, 2009, 123 Stat. 2722; Pub. L. 113–66, div. C, title XXXV, §3505(b), Dec. 26, 2013, 127 Stat. 1086; Pub. L. 116–92, div. C, title XXXV, §3514(b), Dec. 20, 2019, 133 Stat. 1980; Pub. L. 116–283, div. C, title XXXV, §3504, Jan. 1, 2021, 134 Stat. 4399; Pub. L. 117–81, div. C, title XXXV, §3513(a)(2), Dec. 27, 2021, 135 Stat. 2240.)

§50303. OPERATING PROPERTY AND EXTENDING TERM OF NOTES

(a) GENERAL AUTHORITY.—The Secretary of Transportation may—

(1) operate or lease docks, wharves, piers, vessels, or real property under the Secretary's control, except that the prior consent of the Secretary of Defense for such use shall be required with respect to any vessel in the Ready Reserve Force or in the National Defense Reserve Fleet which is maintained in a retention status for the Department of Defense; and

(2) make extensions and accept renewals of—

(A) promissory notes and other evidences of indebtedness on property; and

(B) mortgages and other contracts securing the property.

(b) TERMS OF TRANSACTIONS.—A transaction under subsection (a) shall be on terms the Secretary considers necessary to carry out the purposes of this subtitle, but consistent with sound business practice.

(c) AVAILABILITY OF AMOUNTS.—Amounts received by the Secretary from a transaction under this section are available for expenditure by the Secretary as provided in this subtitle.

(Pub. L. 109–304, §8(b), Oct. 6, 2006, 120 Stat. 1564; Pub. L. 110–181, div. C, title XXXV, §3512, Jan. 28, 2008, 122 Stat. 594.)

§50304. SALE AND TRANSFER OF PROPERTY

(a) AUTHORITY TO SELL.—The Secretary of Transportation may sell property (other than vessels transferred under section 4 of the Merchant Marine Act, 1920 (ch. 250, 41 Stat. 990)) on terms the Secretary considers appropriate.

(b) TRANSFERS FROM MILITARY TO CIVILIAN CONTROL.—When the President considers it in the interest of the United States, the President may transfer to the Secretary of Transportation possession and control of property described in the second paragraph of section 17 of the Merchant Marine Act, 1920 (ch. 250, 41 Stat. 994), as originally enacted, that is possessed and controlled by the Secretary of a military department.

(c) TRANSFERS FROM CIVILIAN TO MILITARY CONTROL.—When the President considers it necessary, the President by executive order may transfer to the Secretary of a military department possession and control of property described in section 17 of the Merchant

Marine Act, 1920 (ch. 250, 41 Stat. 994), as originally enacted, that is possessed and controlled by the Secretary of Transportation. The President's order shall state the need for the transfer and the period of the need. When the President decides that the need has ended, the possession and control shall revert to the Secretary of Transportation. The property may not be sold except as provided by law.

(d) VESSEL CHARTERS TO OTHER DEPARTMENTS.—On a reimbursable or nonreimbursable basis, as determined by the Secretary of Transportation, the Secretary may charter or otherwise make available a vessel under the jurisdiction of the Secretary to any other department, upon the request by the Secretary of the Department that receives the vessel. The prior consent of the Secretary of Defense for such use shall be required with respect to any vessel in the Ready Reserve Force or in the National Defense Reserve Fleet which is maintained in a retention status for the Department of Defense.

(Pub. L. 109–304, §8(b), Oct. 6, 2006, 120 Stat. 1565; Pub. L. 110–181, div. C, title XXXV, §3515, Jan. 28, 2008, 122 Stat. 595.)

§50305. APPOINTMENT OF TRUSTEE OR RECEIVER AND OPERATION OF VESSELS

(a) APPOINTMENT OF TRUSTEES AND RECEIVERS.—

(1) APPOINTMENT OF SECRETARY.—In a proceeding in a court of the United States in which a trustee or receiver may be appointed for a corporation operating a vessel of United States registry between the United States and a foreign country, on which the United States Government holds a mortgage, the court may appoint the Secretary of Transportation as the sole trustee or receiver (subject to the direction of the court) if—

(A) the court finds that the appointment will—

(i) inure to the advantage of the estate and the parties in interest; and

(ii) tend to carry out the purposes of this subtitle; and

(B) the Secretary expressly consents to the appointment.

(2) APPOINTMENT OF OTHER PERSON.—The appointment of another person as trustee or receiver without a hearing becomes effective when ratified by the Secretary, but the Secretary may demand a hearing.

(b) OPERATION OF VESSELS.—

(1) IN GENERAL.—If the court is unwilling to allow the trustee or receiver to operate the vessel in foreign commerce without financial aid from the Government pending termination of the proceeding, and the Secretary certifies to the court that the continued operation of the vessel is essential to the foreign commerce of the United States and is reasonably calculated to carry out the purposes of this subtitle, the court may allow the Secretary to operate the vessel, either directly or through a managing agent or operator employed by the Secretary. The Secretary must agree to comply with terms imposed by the court sufficient to protect the parties in interest. The Secretary also must agree to pay all operating losses resulting from the operation. The operation shall be for the account of the trustee or receiver.

(2) PAYMENT OF OPERATING LOSSES AND OTHER AMOUNTS.—The Secretary has no claim

against the corporation, its estate, or its assets for operating losses paid by the Secretary, but the Secretary may pay amounts for depreciation the Secretary considers reasonable and other amounts the court considers just. The payment of operating losses and the other amounts and compliance with terms imposed by the court shall be in satisfaction of any claim against the Secretary resulting from the operation of the vessel.

(3) DEEMED OPERATION BY GOVERNMENT.—A vessel operated by the Secretary under this subsection is deemed to be a vessel operated by the United States under chapter 309 of this title.

(Pub. L. 109–304, §8(b), Oct. 6, 2006, 120 Stat. 1565.)

§50306. REQUIRING TESTIMONY AND RECORDS IN INVESTIGATIONS

(a) IN GENERAL.—In conducting an investigation that the Secretary of Transportation considers necessary and proper to carry out this subtitle, the Secretary may administer oaths, take evidence, and subpoena persons to testify and produce documents relevant to the matter under investigation. Persons may be required to attend or produce documents from any place in the United States at any designated place of hearing.

(b) FEES AND MILEAGE.—Persons subpoenaed by the Secretary under subsection (a) shall be paid the same fees and mileage paid to witnesses in the courts of the United States.

(c) ENFORCEMENT OF SUBPOENAS.—If a person disobeys a subpoena issued under subsection (a), the Secretary may seek an order enforcing the subpoena from the district court of the United States for the district in which the person resides or does business. Process may be served in the judicial district in which the person resides or is found. The court may issue an order to obey the subpoena and punish a refusal to obey as a contempt of court.

(Pub. L. 109–304, §8(b), Oct. 6, 2006, 120 Stat. 1566.)

§50307. MARITIME ENVIRONMENTAL AND TECHNICAL ASSISTANCE PROGRAM

(a) EMERGING MARINE TECHNOLOGIES AND PRACTICES.—

(1) IN GENERAL.—The Secretary of Transportation, acting through the Maritime Administrator, shall engage in or support the study, research, development, assessment, and deployment of emerging marine technologies and practices related to the maritime transportation system through eligible entities.

(2) COMPONENTS.—Under this subsection, the Secretary of Transportation shall identify, study, evaluate, test, demonstrate, improve, or support efforts related to, emerging marine technologies and practices to improve—

(A) environmental performance to meet United States Federal and international standards and guidelines, including—

(i) reducing air emissions, water emissions, or other ship discharges;

(ii) increasing fuel economy or the use of alternative fuels and alternative energy (including the use of shore power); or

(iii) controlling aquatic invasive species; or

(iv) reducing incidental vessel-generated underwater noise, such as noise from propeller cavitation or hydrodynamic flow; and

(B) the efficiency and safety of domestic maritime industries.

(3) COORDINATION.—Coordination with other Federal agencies or with State, local, or Tribal governments, as appropriate, under paragraph (2)(B) may include—
  (A) activities that are associated with the development or approval of validation and testing regimes; and
  (B) certification or validation of emerging technologies or practices that demonstrate significant environmental or other benefits to domestic maritime industries.

(4) ASSISTANCE.—The Secretary of Transportation may accept gifts, or enter into cooperative agreements, contracts, or other agreements with eligible entities to carry out the activities authorized under this subsection.

(5) GRANTS.—Subject to the availability of appropriations, the Maritime Administrator, may establish and carry out a competitive grant program to award grants to eligible entities for projects in the United States consistent with the goals of this subsection to study, evaluate, test, demonstrate, or apply technologies and practices to improve environmental performance.

(b) USES.—The results of activities conducted under this section shall be used to inform—
  (1) the policy decisions of the United States related to domestic regulations; and
  (2) the position of the United States on matters before the International Maritime Organization.

(c) VESSELS.—Activities carried out under a grant or cooperative agreement made under this section may be conducted on public vessels under the control of the Maritime Administration, upon approval of the Maritime Administrator.

(d) ELIGIBLE ENTITY DEFINED.—In this section, the term "eligible entity" means—
  (1) a private entity, including a nonprofit organization;
  (2) a State, regional, or local government or entity, including special districts;
  (3) an Indian Tribe (as defined in section 4 of the Indian Self-Determination and Education Assistance Act (25 U.S.C. 5304)) or a consortium of Indian Tribes;
  (4) an institution of higher education as defined under section 102 of the Higher Education Act of 1965 (20 U.S.C. 1002); or
  (5) a partnership or collaboration of entities described in paragraphs (1) through (4).

(e) CENTER FOR MARITIME INNOVATION.—
  (1) IN GENERAL.—The Secretary of Transportation shall, through a cooperative agreement, establish a United States Center for Maritime Innovation (referred to in this subsection as the "Center") to support the study, research, development, assessment, and deployment of emerging marine technologies and practices related to the maritime transportation system.
  (2) SELECTION.—The Center shall be—
    (A) selected through a competitive process of eligible entities, and if a private entity,

a domestic entity;

(B) based in the United States with technical expertise in emerging marine technologies and practices related to the maritime transportation system; and

(C) located in close proximity to eligible entities with expertise in United States emerging marine technologies and practices, including the use of alternative fuels and the development of both vessel and shoreside infrastructure.

(3) COORDINATION.—The Secretary of Transportation shall coordinate with other agencies critical for science, research, and regulation of emerging marine technologies for the maritime sector, including the Department of Energy, the Environmental Protection Agency, the National Science Foundation, and the Coast Guard, when establishing the Center.

(4) FUNCTIONS.—The Center shall—

(A) support eligible entities regarding the development and use of clean energy and necessary infrastructure to support the deployment of clean energy on vessels of the United States;

(B) monitor and assess, on an ongoing basis, the current state of knowledge regarding emerging marine technologies in the United States;

(C) identify any significant gaps in emerging marine technologies research specific to the United States maritime industry, and seek to fill those gaps;

(D) conduct research, development, testing, and evaluation for equipment, technologies, and techniques to address the components under subsection (a)(2);

(E) provide—

(i) guidance on best available technologies;

(ii) technical analysis;

(iii) assistance with understanding complex regulatory requirements; and

(iv) documentation of best practices in the maritime industry, including training and informational webinars on solutions for the maritime industry; and

(F) work with academic and private sector response training centers and Domestic Maritime Workforce Training and Education Centers of Excellence to develop maritime strategies applicable to various segments of the United States maritime industry, including the inland, deep water, and coastal fleets.

(Added Pub. L. 112–213, title IV, §403(a), Dec. 20, 2012, 126 Stat. 1569; amended Pub. L. 116–92, div. C, title XXXV, §3503, Dec. 20, 2019, 133 Stat. 1969; Pub. L. 116–283, div. G, title LVXXXV [LXXXV], §8504(b), Jan. 1, 2021, 134 Stat. 4747; Pub. L. 117–81, div. C, title XXXV, §3514, Dec. 27, 2021, 135 Stat. 2243; Pub. L. 117–263, div. C, title XXXV, §3543(a), Dec. 23, 2022, 136 Stat. 3098.)

§50308. MARITIME TRANSPORTATION SYSTEM EMERGENCY RELIEF PROGRAM

(a) GENERAL AUTHORITY.—The Maritime Administrator may make grants to, and enter into contracts and agreement with, eligible State and Tribal entities and eligible entities for—

(1) the costs of capital projects to protect, repair, reconstruct, or replace equipment and facilities of the United States maritime transportation system that the Maritime

Administrator determines is in danger of suffering serious physical damage, or has suffered serious physical damage, as a result of an emergency; and

(2) eligible operating costs of United States maritime transportation equipment and facilities in an area directly affected by an emergency during—

(A) the one-year period beginning on the date of a declaration of an emergency referred to in subparagraph (A) or (B) of subsection (j)(4); and

(B) an additional one-year period beginning one year after the date of an emergency referred to in subparagraph (A) or (B) of subsection (j)(4), if the Maritime Administrator, in consultation with the Administrator of the Federal Emergency Management Agency, determines there is a compelling need arising out of the emergency for which the declaration is made.

(b) ALLOCATION.—

(1) IN GENERAL.—The Maritime Administrator shall determine an appropriate method for the equitable allocation and distribution of funds under this section to eligible State and Tribal entities and eligible entities.

(2) PRIORITY.—To the extent practicable, in allocating and distributing funds under this section, the Maritime Administrator shall give priority to applications submitted by eligible State or Tribal entities.

(c) APPLICATIONS.—An applicant for assistance under this section shall submit an application for such assistance to the Maritime Administrator at such time, in such manner, and containing such information and assurances as the Maritime Administrator may require.

(d) COORDINATION OF EMERGENCY FUNDS.—

(1) USE OF FUNDS.—Funds appropriated to carry out this section shall be in addition to any other funds available under this chapter.

(2) NO EFFECT ON OTHER GOVERNMENT ACTIVITY.—The provision of funds under this section shall not affect the ability of any other agency of the Government, including the Federal Emergency Management Agency, or a State agency, a local governmental entity, organization, or person, to provide any other funds otherwise authorized by law.

(e) GRANT REQUIREMENTS.—A grant awarded under this section that is made to address an emergency referred to in subsection (j)(4)(B) shall be—

(1) subject to the terms and conditions the Maritime Administrator determines are necessary;

(2) made only for expenses that are not reimbursed under the Robert T. Stafford Disaster Relief and Emergency Assistance Act (42 U.S.C. 5121 et seq.) or any Federal, State, or local assistance program; and

(3) made only for expenses that are not reimbursed under any type of marine insurance.

(f) FEDERAL SHARE OF COSTS.—The Federal share payable of the costs for which a grant is made under this section shall be 100 percent.

(g) ADMINISTRATIVE COSTS.—Of the amounts available to carry out this section, not more than two percent may be used for administration of this section.

(h) QUALITY ASSURANCE.—The Maritime Administrator shall institute adequate policies, procedures, and internal controls to prevent waste, fraud, abuse, and program mismanagement for the distribution of funds under this section.

(i) REPORTS.—On an annual basis, the Maritime Administrator shall submit to the Committee on Commerce, Science, and Transportation of the Senate and the Committee on Transportation and Infrastructure of the House of Representatives a report on the financial assistance provided under this section during the year covered by the report. Each such report shall include, for such year, a description of such assistance provided and of how such assistance—

(1) affected the United States maritime transportation system;

(2) mitigated the financial impact of the emergency on the recipient of the assistance; and

(3) protected critical infrastructure in the United States.

(j) DEFINITIONS.—In this section:

(1) ELIGIBLE STATE OR TRIBAL ENTITY.—The term "eligible State or Tribal entity" means—

(A) a port authority; or

(B) a vessel owned and operated by a State or Tribal government and facilities associated with the operation of such vessel.

(2) ELIGIBLE ENTITY.—The term "eligible entity" means a public or private entity that is created or organized in the United States or under the laws of the United States, with significant operations in and a majority of its employees based in the United States, that is engaged in—

(A) vessel construction, transportation by water, or support activities for transportation by water with an assigned North American Industry Classification System code beginning with 3366, 483, 4883, or 6113, or in the case of such construction, transportation, or support activities conducted by a fish processing vessel, such an assigned code beginning with 3117; or

(B) as determined by the Secretary of Transportation—

(i) construction or water transportation related to activities described in subparagraph (A); or

(ii) maritime education and training.

(3) ELIGIBLE OPERATING COSTS.—The term "eligible operating costs" means costs relating to—

(A) emergency response;

(B) cleaning;

(C) sanitization;

(D) janitorial services;

(E) staffing;

(F) workforce retention;

(G) paid leave;

(H) procurement and use of protective health equipment, testing, and training for employees and contractors;

(I) debt service payments;

(J) infrastructure repair projects;

(K) fuel; and

(L) other maritime transportation system operations, as determined by the Secretary of Transportation;

(4) EMERGENCY.—The term "emergency" means a natural disaster affecting a wide area (such as a flood, hurricane, tidal wave, earthquake, severe storm, or landslide) or a catastrophic failure from any external cause, that impacts the United States maritime transportation system and as a result of which—

(A) the Governor of a State has declared an emergency and the Maritime Administrator, in consultation with the Administrator of the Federal Emergency Management Agency, has concurred in the declaration;

(B) the President has declared a major disaster under section 401 of the Robert T. Stafford Disaster Relief and Emergency Assistance Act (42 U.S.C. 5170);

(C) national emergency declared by the President under the National Emergencies Act (50 U.S.C. 1601 et seq.) is in effect; or

(D) a public health emergency declared pursuant to section 319 of the Public Health Service Act (42 U.S.C. 247d) is in effect.

(Added Pub. L. 116–283, div. C, title XXXV, §3505(a), Jan. 1, 2021, 134 Stat. 4402; amended Pub. L. 118–31, div. C, title XXXV, §3514(e), Dec. 22, 2023, 137 Stat. 811.)

§50309. SECURING LOGISTICS INFORMATION DATA OF THE UNITED STATES

(a) IN GENERAL.—

(1) PROHIBITION.—A covered entity shall not use a covered logistics platform.

(2) ELIGIBILITY.—A covered entity that is found to use a covered logistics platform shall not be eligible to receive any Federal grant funding as long as the covered entity uses a covered logistics platform.

(b) GUIDANCE.—The Secretary of Transportation shall—

(1) notify covered entities of the prohibition in subsection (a) as soon as practicable, including notice of funding opportunities for grant programs; and

(2) publish on a website of the Department of Transportation, and update regularly, a list of covered logistics platforms subject to the prohibition in subsection (a).

(c) CONSULTATION.—In carrying out this section, the Secretary shall consult with—

(1) the Secretary of Defense;

(2) the Secretary of the Department in which the Coast Guard is operating;

(3) the Secretary of State; and

(4) the Secretary of Commerce.

(d) WAIVER.—The Secretary of Transportation, in consultation with the Secretary of

Defense, may waive the provisions of this section for a specific contract if the Secretary of Transportation—

(1) makes a determination that such waiver is vital to the national security of the United States; and

(2) submits to Congress a report justifying the use of such waiver and the importance of such waiver to the national security of the United States.

(e) DEFINITIONS.—In this section:

(1) COVERED LOGISTICS PLATFORM.—The term "covered logistics platform" means a data exchange platform that utilizes or provides, in part or whole—

(A) the national transportation logistics public information platform (commonly referred to as "LOGINK") provided by the People's Republic of China, or departments, ministries, centers, agencies, or instrumentalities of the Government of the People's Republic of China;

(B) any national transportation logistics information platform provided by or sponsored by the People's Republic of China, or a controlled commercial entity; or

(C) a similar system provided by Chinese state-affiliated entities.

(2) COVERED ENTITY.—The term "covered entity" means—

(A) a port authority that receives funding after the date of the enactment of this section under—

(i) the port infrastructure development program under section 54301;

(ii) the maritime transportation system emergency relief program under section 50308; or

(iii) any Federal grant funding program;

(B) any marine terminal operator located on property owned by a port authority as described in subparagraph (A) or at a seaport described in subparagraph (D);

(C) any agency or instrumentality of the United States Government or that of a State; or

(D) a commercial strategic seaport within the National Port Readiness Network.

(Added Pub. L. 118–31, div. A, title VIII, §825(b)(1), Dec. 22, 2023, 137 Stat. 332.)

CHAPTER 504—COMMITTEES

§50401. UNITED STATES COMMITTEE ON THE MARINE TRANSPORTATION SYSTEM

(a) ESTABLISHMENT.—There is established a United States Committee on the Marine Transportation System (in this section referred to as the "Committee").

(b) PURPOSE.—The Committee shall serve as a Federal interagency coordinating committee for the purpose of—

(1) assessing the adequacy of the marine transportation system (including ports, waterways, channels, and their intermodal connections);

(2) promoting the integration of the marine transportation system with other modes of transportation and other uses of the marine environment; and

(3) coordinating, improving the coordination of, and making recommendations with regard to Federal policies that impact the marine transportation system.

(c) MEMBERSHIP.—

(1) IN GENERAL.—The Committee shall consist of—

(A) the Secretary of Transportation;

(B) the Secretary of Defense;

(C) the Secretary of Homeland Security;

(D) the Secretary of Commerce;

(E) the Secretary of the Treasury;

(F) the Secretary of State;

(G) the Secretary of the Interior;

(H) the Secretary of Agriculture;

(I) the Attorney General;

(J) the Secretary of Labor;

(K) the Secretary of Energy;

(L) the Administrator of the Environmental Protection Agency;

(M) the Chairman of the Federal Maritime Commission;

(N) the Chairman of the Joint Chiefs of Staff; and

(O) the head of any other Federal agency who a majority of the voting members of the Committee determines can further the purpose and activities of the Committee.

(2) NONVOTING MEMBERS.—The Committee may include as many nonvoting members as a majority of the voting members of the Committee determines is appropriate to further the purpose and activities of the Committee.

(d) SUPPORT.—

(1) COORDINATING BOARD.—

141

(A) IN GENERAL.—There is hereby established, within the Committee, a Coordinating Board. Each member of the Committee may select a senior level representative to serve on such Board. The Board shall assist the Committee in carrying out its purpose and activities.

(B) CHAIR.—There shall be a Chair of the Coordinating Board. The Chair of the Coordinating Board shall rotate each year among the Secretary of Transportation, the Secretary of Defense, the Secretary of Homeland Security, and the Secretary of Commerce. The order of rotation shall be determined by a majority of the voting members of the Committee.

(2) EXECUTIVE DIRECTOR.—The Secretary of Transportation, in consultation with the Secretary of Defense, the Secretary of Homeland Security, and the Secretary of Commerce, shall appoint an Executive Director of the Committee.

(3) TRANSFERS.—Notwithstanding any other provision of law, the head of a Federal department or agency who is a member of the Committee may—

(A) provide, on a reimbursable or nonreimbursable basis, facilities, equipment, services, personnel, and other support services to carry out the activities of the Committee; and

(B) transfer funds to another Federal department or agency in order to carry out the activities of the Committee.

(e) MARINE TRANSPORTATION SYSTEM ASSESSMENT AND STRATEGY.—Not later than one year after the date of enactment of this Act and every 5 years thereafter, the Committee shall provide to the Committee on Commerce, Science, and Transportation and the Committee on Environment and Public Works of the Senate and the Committee on Transportation and Infrastructure of the House of Representatives a report that includes—

(1) steps taken to implement actions recommended in the document titled "National Strategy for the Marine Transportation System: A Framework for Action" and dated July 2008;

(2) a conditions and performance analysis of the marine transportation system;

(3) a discussion of the challenges the marine transportation system faces in meeting user demand, including estimates of investment levels required to ensure system infrastructure meets such demand;

(4) a plan, with recommended actions, for improving the marine transportation system to meet current and future challenges;

(5) steps taken to implement actions recommended in previous reports required under this subsection; and

(6) a compendium of the Federal programs engaged in the maritime transportation system.

(f) CONSULTATION.—In carrying out its purpose and activities, the Committee may consult with marine transportation system-related advisory committees, interested parties, and the public.

(Added Pub. L. 112–213, title III, §310(a), Dec. 20, 2012, 126 Stat. 1567, §55502; renumbered §55501, Pub. L. 113–281, title III, §301(2), Dec. 18, 2014, 128 Stat. 3042; amended Pub. L. 116–283, div. G, title

LVXXXIII [LXXXIII], §8315, Jan. 1, 2021, 134 Stat. 4699; renumbered §50401 and amended, Pub. L. 117–81, div. C, title XXXV, §3512(a)(3), (4), Dec. 27, 2021, 135 Stat. 2239.)

§50402. Maritime Transportation System National Advisory Committee

(a) ESTABLISHMENT.—There is established a Maritime Transportation System National Advisory Committee (in this section referred to as the "Committee").

(b) FUNCTION.—The Committee shall advise the Secretary of Transportation on matters relating to the United States maritime transportation system and its seamless integration with other segments of the transportation system, including the viability of the United States Merchant Marine.

(c) MEMBERSHIP.—

(1) IN GENERAL.—The Committee shall consist of 27 members appointed by the Secretary of Transportation in accordance with this section and section 15109.

(2) EXPERTISE.—Each member of the Committee shall have particular expertise, knowledge, and experience in matters relating to the function of the Committee.

(3) REPRESENTATION.—Members of the Committee shall be appointed as follows:

(A) At least one member shall represent the Environmental Protection Agency.

(B) At least one member shall represent the Department of Commerce.

(C) At least one member shall represent the Corps of Engineers.

(D) At least one member shall represent the Coast Guard.

(E) At least one member shall represent Customs and Border Protection.

(F) At least one member shall represent State and local governmental entities.

(G) Additional members shall represent private sector entities that reflect a cross-section of maritime industries, including port and water stakeholders, academia, and labor.

(H) The Secretary may appoint additional representatives from other Federal agencies as the Secretary considers appropriate.

(4) RESTRICTIONS ON MEMBERS REPRESENTING FEDERAL AGENCIES.—Members of the Committee that represent Federal agencies shall not—

(A) comprise more than one-third of the total membership of the Committee or of any subcommittee therein; or

(B) serve as the chair or co-chair of the Committee or of any subcommittee therein.

(5) ADMINISTRATION.—For purposes of section 15109—

(A) the Committee shall be treated as a committee established under chapter 151; and

(B) the Secretary of Transportation shall fulfill all duties and responsibilities and have all authorities of the Secretary of Homeland Security with regard to the Committee.

(Added Pub. L. 116–283, div. G, title LVXXXIII [LXXXIII], §8332(a), Jan. 1, 2021, 134 Stat. 4703, §55502; renumbered §50402, Pub. L. 117–81, div. C, title XXXV, §3512(a)(3), Dec. 27, 2021, 135 Stat. 2239.)

CHAPTER 505—OTHER GENERAL PROVISIONS

§50501. Entities deemed citizens of the United States

(a) In General.—In this subtitle, a corporation, partnership, or association is deemed to be a citizen of the United States only if the controlling interest is owned by citizens of the United States. However, if the corporation, partnership, or association is operating a vessel in the coastwise trade, at least 75 percent of the interest must be owned by citizens of the United States.

(b) Additional Requirements for Corporations.—In this subtitle, a corporation is deemed to be a citizen of the United States only if, in addition to satisfying the requirements in subsection (a)—

(1) it is incorporated under the laws of the United States or a State;

(2) its chief executive officer, by whatever title, and the chairman of its board of directors are citizens of the United States; and

(3) no more of its directors are noncitizens than a minority of the number necessary to constitute a quorum.

(c) Determination of Controlling Corporate Interest.—The controlling interest in a corporation is owned by citizens of the United States under subsection (a) only if—

(1) title to the majority of the stock in the corporation is vested in citizens of the United States free from any trust or fiduciary obligation in favor of a person not a citizen of the United States;

(2) the majority of the voting power in the corporation is vested in citizens of the United States;

(3) there is no contract or understanding by which the majority of the voting power in the corporation may be exercised, directly or indirectly, in behalf of a person not a citizen of the United States; and

(4) there is no other means by which control of the corporation is given to or permitted to be exercised by a person not a citizen of the United States.

(d) Determination of 75 Percent Corporate Interest.—At least 75 percent of the interest in a corporation is owned by citizens of the United States under subsection (a) only if—

(1) title to at least 75 percent of the stock in the corporation is vested in citizens of the United States free from any trust or fiduciary obligation in favor of a person not a citizen of the United States;

(2) at least 75 percent of the voting power in the corporation is vested in citizens of the United States;

(3) there is no contract or understanding by which more than 25 percent of the voting power in the corporation may be exercised, directly or indirectly, in behalf of a person not a citizen of the United States; and

(4) there is no other means by which control of more than 25 percent of any interest in the corporation is given to or permitted to be exercised by a person not a citizen of the United States.

(Pub. L. 109–304, §8(b), Oct. 6, 2006, 120 Stat. 1566.)

§50502. APPLICABILITY TO RECEIVERS, TRUSTEES, SUCCESSORS, AND ASSIGNS

This subtitle applies to receivers, trustees, successors, and assigns of any person to whom this subtitle applies.

(Pub. L. 109–304, §8(b), Oct. 6, 2006, 120 Stat. 1567.)

§50503. OCEANOGRAPHIC RESEARCH VESSELS

An oceanographic research vessel (as defined in section 2101 of this title) is deemed not to be engaged in trade or commerce.

(Pub. L. 109–304, §8(b), Oct. 6, 2006, 120 Stat. 1567.)

§50504. SAILING SCHOOL VESSELS

(a) DEFINITIONS.—In this section, the terms "sailing school instructor", "sailing school student", and "sailing school vessel" have the meaning given those terms in section 2101 of this title.

(b) NOT SEAMEN.—A sailing school student or sailing school instructor is deemed not to be a seaman under—

(1) parts B, F, and G of subtitle II of this title; or

(2) the maritime law doctrines of maintenance and cure or warranty of seaworthiness.

(c) NOT MERCHANT VESSEL OR ENGAGED IN TRADE OR COMMERCE.—A sailing school vessel is deemed not to be—

(1) a merchant vessel under section 11101(a)–(c) of this title; or

(2) a vessel engaged in trade or commerce.

(d) EVIDENCE OF FINANCIAL RESPONSIBILITY.—The owner or charterer of a sailing school vessel shall maintain evidence of financial responsibility to meet liability for death or injury to sailing school students and sailing school instructors on a voyage on the vessel. The amount of financial responsibility shall be at least $50,000 for each student and instructor. Financial responsibility under this subsection may be evidenced by insurance or other adequate financial resources.

(Pub. L. 109–304, §8(b), Oct. 6, 2006, 120 Stat. 1568.)

PART B—MERCHANT MARINE SERVICE

CHAPTER 511—GENERAL

§51101. POLICY

It is the policy of the United States that merchant marine vessels of the United States should be operated by highly trained and efficient citizens of the United States and that the United States Navy and the merchant marine of the United States should work closely together to promote the maximum integration of the total seapower forces of the United States.

(Pub. L. 109–304, §8(b), Oct. 6, 2006, 120 Stat. 1568.)

§51102. DEFINITIONS

In this part:

(1) ACADEMY.—The term "Academy" means the United States Merchant Marine Academy located at Kings Point, New York, and maintained under chapter 513 of this title.

(2) COST OF EDUCATION PROVIDED.—The term "cost of education provided" means the financial costs incurred by the United States Government for providing training or financial assistance to students at the Academy and the State maritime academies, including direct financial assistance, room, board, classroom academics, and other training activities.

(3) MERCHANT MARINE OFFICER.—The term "merchant marine officer" means an individual issued a license by the Coast Guard authorizing service as—

(A) a master, mate, or pilot on a documented vessel that—

(i) is of at least 1,000 gross tons as measured under section 14502 of this title or an alternate tonnage measured under section 14302 of this title as prescribed by the Secretary under section 14104 of this title; and

(ii) operates on the oceans or the Great Lakes; or

(B) an engineer officer on a documented vessel propelled by machinery of at least 4,000 horsepower.

(4) STATE MARITIME ACADEMY.—The term "State maritime academy" means—

(A) a State maritime academy or college sponsored by a State and assisted under chapter 515 of this title; and

(B) a regional maritime academy or college sponsored by a group of States and assisted under chapter 515 of this title.

(Pub. L. 109–304, §8(b), Oct. 6, 2006, 120 Stat. 1568.)

§51103. GENERAL AUTHORITY OF SECRETARY OF TRANSPORTATION

(a) EDUCATION AND TRAINING.—The Secretary of Transportation may provide for the education and training of citizens of the United States for the safe and efficient operation of the merchant marine of the United States at all times, including operation as a naval and military auxiliary in time of war or national emergency.

(b) PROPERTY FOR INSTRUCTIONAL PURPOSES.—

(1) IN GENERAL.—The Secretary may cooperate with and assist the institutions named in paragraph (2) by making vessels, fuel, shipboard equipment, and other marine equipment, owned by the United States Government and determined by the entity having custody and control of such property to be excess or surplus, available to those institutions for instructional purposes, by gift, loan, sale, lease, or charter on terms and conditions the Secretary considers appropriate. The consent of the Secretary of the Navy shall be obtained with respect to any property from National Defense Reserve Fleet vessels, if such vessels are either Ready Reserve Force vessels or other National Defense Reserve Fleet vessels determined to be of sufficient value to the Navy to warrant their further preservation and retention.

(2) INSTITUTIONS.—The institutions referred to in paragraph (1) are—

(A) the United States Merchant Marine Academy;

(B) a State maritime academy; and

(C) a nonprofit training institution or a training institution that is an instrumentality of a State, the District of Columbia, a territory or possession of the United States, or a unit of local government thereof jointly approved by the Secretary of Transportation and the Secretary of the department in which the Coast Guard is operating as offering training courses that meet Federal regulations for maritime training.

(c) ASSISTANCE FROM OTHER AGENCIES.—

(1) IN GENERAL.—The Secretary of Transportation may secure directly from an agency, on a reimbursable basis, information, facilities, and equipment necessary to carry out this part.

(2) DETAILING PERSONNEL.—At the request of the Secretary, the head of an agency (including a military department) may detail, on a reimbursable basis, personnel from the agency to the Secretary to assist in carrying out this part.

(d) ACADEMY PERSONNEL.—To carry out this part, the Secretary may—

(1) employ an individual as a professor, lecturer, or instructor at the Academy, without regard to the provisions of title 5 governing appointments in the competitive service; and

(2) pay the individual without regard to chapter 51 and subchapter III of chapter 53 of title 5.

(e) DONATION FOR HISTORICAL PURPOSES.—

(1) IN GENERAL.—The Secretary may convey the right, title, and interest of the United States Government in any property administered by the Maritime Administration, except

real estate or vessels, if—

(A) the Secretary determines that such property is not needed by the Maritime Administration; and

(B) the recipient—

(i) is a nonprofit organization, a State, or a political subdivision of a State;

(ii) agrees to hold the Government harmless for any claims arising from exposure to hazardous materials, including asbestos, polychlorinated biphenyls, or lead paint, after conveyance of the property;

(iii) provides a description and explanation of the intended use of the property to the Secretary for approval;

(iv) has provided to the Secretary proof, as determined by the Secretary, of resources sufficient to accomplish the intended use provided under clause (iii) and to maintain the property;

(v) agrees that when the recipient no longer requires the property, the recipient shall—

(I) return the property to the Secretary, at the recipient's expense and in the same condition as received except for ordinary wear and tear; or

(II) subject to the approval of the Secretary, retain, sell, or otherwise dispose of the property in a manner consistent with applicable law; and

(vi) agrees to any additional terms the Secretary considers appropriate.

(2) REVERSION.—The Secretary shall include in any conveyance under this subsection terms under which all right, title, and interest conveyed by the Secretary shall revert to the Government if the Secretary determines the property has been used other than as approved by the Secretary under paragraph (1)(B)(iii).

(Pub. L. 109–304, §8(b), Oct. 6, 2006, 120 Stat. 1569; Pub. L. 112–213, title IV, §404, Dec. 20, 2012, 126 Stat. 1570; Pub. L. 113–281, title III, §302, Dec. 18, 2014, 128 Stat. 3042.)

§51104. GENERAL AUTHORITY OF SECRETARY OF THE NAVY

The Secretary of the Navy, in cooperation with the Maritime Administrator and the head of each State maritime academy, shall ensure that—

(1) the training of future merchant marine officers at the United States Merchant Marine Academy and at State maritime academies includes programs for naval science training in the operation of merchant vessels as a naval and military auxiliary; and

(2) naval officer training programs for future officers, insofar as possible, are maintained at designated maritime academies consistent with Navy standards and needs.

(Pub. L. 109–304, §8(b), Oct. 6, 2006, 120 Stat. 1570.)

CHAPTER 513—UNITED STATES MERCHANT MARINE ACADEMY

§51301. MAINTENANCE OF THE ACADEMY

(a) IN GENERAL.—The Secretary of Transportation shall maintain the United States Merchant Marine Academy as an institution of higher education to provide instruction to individuals to prepare them for service in the merchant marine of the United States, to conduct research with respect to maritime-related matters, and to provide such other appropriate academic support, assistance, training, and activities in accordance with the provisions of this chapter as the Secretary may authorize.

(b) RECRUITMENT.—The Secretary of Transportation may, subject to the availability of appropriations, expend funds available for United States Merchant Marine Academy operating expenses for recruiting activities, including advertising, in order to obtain recruits for the Academy and cadet applicants.

(c) SUPERINTENDENT.—

(1) IN GENERAL.—The immediate command of the United States Merchant Marine Academy shall be in the Superintendent of the Academy, subject to the direction of the Maritime Administrator under the general supervision of the Secretary of Transportation.

(2) APPOINTMENT.—The Secretary of Transportation shall appoint as the Superintendent—

(A) an individual who has—

(i) attained the rank of Captain, Chief Mate, or Chief Engineer in the merchant marine of the United States, or a general or flag officer rank in the Navy, Army, Air Force, Marine Corps, Coast Guard, or National Oceanic and Atmospheric Administration; and

(ii) served at sea in any rank;

(B) an individual who has—

(i)(I) served at sea in the merchant marine, Navy, Army, Air Force, Marine Corps, Coast Guard, or National Oceanic and Atmospheric Administration; or

(II) held a valid Coast Guard merchant mariner credential; and

(ii) demonstrated exemplary leadership in the education of individuals in the Armed Forces or United States merchant marine; or

(C) if a qualified individual described in subparagraph (A) or (B) does not apply for the position, an individual who has—

(i) attained the grade of captain or above in the merchant marine, Navy, Coast Guard, or National Oceanic and Atmospheric Administration or colonel or above in the Army, Air Force, or Marine Corps; and

(ii) served at sea in any grade.

(3) RULE OF CONSTRUCTION.—Notwithstanding paragraph (2), the Secretary of Transportation may appoint an individual who is the best qualified candidate, even if such individual does not fully meet the criteria described in paragraph (2).

(Pub. L. 109–304, §8(b), Oct. 6, 2006, 120 Stat. 1570; Pub. L. 111–383, div. C, title XXXV, §3504, Jan. 7, 2011, 124 Stat. 4518; Pub. L. 112–81, div. C, title XXXV, §3503, Dec. 31, 2011, 125 Stat. 1716; Pub. L. 112–239, div. A, title X, §1076(i), Jan. 2, 2013, 126 Stat. 1955; Pub. L. 114–328, div. C, title XXXV, §3506(a), Dec. 23, 2016, 130 Stat. 2777; Pub. L. 116–283, div. C, title XXXV, §3503(b), Jan. 1, 2021, 134 Stat. 4399.)

§51302. NOMINATION AND COMPETITIVE APPOINTMENT OF CADETS

(a) REQUIREMENTS.—An individual may be nominated for a competitive appointment as a cadet at the United States Merchant Marine Academy only if the individual—

(1) is a citizen or national of the United States; and

(2) meets the minimum requirements that the Secretary of Transportation shall establish.

(b) NOMINATORS.—Nominations for competitive appointments for the positions allocated under subsection (c) may be made as follows:

(1) A Senator may nominate residents of the State represented by that Senator.

(2) A Member of the House of Representatives may nominate residents of the State in which the congressional district represented by that Member is located.

(3) A Delegate to the House of Representatives from the District of Columbia, the Virgin Islands, Guam, the Northern Mariana Islands, or American Samoa may nominate residents of the jurisdiction represented by that Delegate.

(4) The Resident Commissioner to the United States from Puerto Rico may nominate residents of Puerto Rico.

(5) The Panama Canal Commission may nominate—

(A) residents, or sons or daughters of residents, of an area or installation in Panama and made available to the United States under the Panama Canal Treaty of 1977, the agreements relating to and implementing that Treaty, signed September 7, 1977, and the Agreement Between the United States of America and the Republic of Panama Concerning Air Traffic Control and Related Services, concluded January 8, 1979; and

(B) sons or daughters of personnel of the United States Government and the Panama Canal Commission residing in Panama.

(c) ALLOCATION OF POSITIONS.—Positions for competitive appointments shall be allocated each year as follows:

(1) Positions shall be allocated for residents of each State nominated by the Members of Congress from that State in proportion to the representation in Congress from that State.

(2) Four positions shall be allocated for residents of the District of Columbia nominated by the Delegate to the House of Representatives from the District of Columbia.

(3) One position each shall be allocated for residents of the Virgin Islands, Guam, and American Samoa nominated by the Delegates to the House of Representatives from the Virgin Islands, Guam, and American Samoa, respectively.

(4) One position shall be allocated for a resident of Puerto Rico nominated by the Resident Commissioner to the United States from Puerto Rico.

(5) One position shall be allocated for a resident of the Northern Mariana Islands nominated by the Governor of the Northern Mariana Islands.

(6) Two positions shall be allocated for individuals nominated by the Panama Canal Commission.

(d) COMPETITIVE SYSTEM FOR APPOINTMENT.—

(1) ESTABLISHMENT OF SYSTEM.—The Secretary shall establish a competitive system for selecting individuals nominated under subsection (b) to fill the positions allocated under subsection (c). The system must determine the relative merit of each individual based on competitive examinations, an assessment of the individual's academic background, and other effective indicators of motivation and probability of successful completion of training at the Academy.

(2) APPOINTMENTS BY JURISDICTION.—The Secretary shall appoint individuals to fill

the positions allocated under subsection (c) for each jurisdiction in the order of merit of the individuals nominated from that jurisdiction.

(3) REMAINING UNFILLED POSITIONS.—If positions remain unfilled after the appointments are made under paragraph (2), the Secretary shall appoint individuals to fill the positions in the order of merit of the remaining individuals nominated from all jurisdictions.

(e) CONGRESSIONAL NOTIFICATION IN ADVANCE OF APPOINTMENTS.—When a nominee of a Senator, Representative, or Delegate is selected for appointment as a cadet, the Senator, Representative, or Delegate shall be notified at least 48 hours before the official notification or announcement of the appointment is made.

(Pub. L. 109–304, §8(b), Oct. 6, 2006, 120 Stat. 1570; Pub. L. 111–383, div. C, title XXXV, §3503, Jan. 7, 2011, 124 Stat. 4518; Pub. L. 114–328, div. A, title V, §566(d), Dec. 23, 2016, 130 Stat. 2139.)

§51303. NON-COMPETITIVE APPOINTMENTS

(a) IN GENERAL.—The Secretary of Transportation may appoint each year without competition as cadets at the United States Merchant Marine Academy not more than 50 qualified individuals with qualities the Secretary considers to be of special value to the Academy. In making these appointments, the Secretary shall try to achieve a national demographic balance at the Academy.

(b) APPOINTMENT OF CANDIDATES SELECTED FOR PREPARATORY SCHOOL SPONSORSHIP.—The Secretary of Transportation may appoint each year as cadets at the United States Merchant Marine Academy not more than 40 qualified individuals sponsored by the Academy to attend preparatory school during the academic year prior to entrance in the Academy, and who have successfully met the terms and conditions of sponsorship set by the Academy.

(Pub. L. 109–304, §8(b), Oct. 6, 2006, 120 Stat. 1572; Pub. L. 114–328, div. C, title XXXV, §3516(a), Dec. 23, 2016, 130 Stat. 2789; Pub. L. 116–92, div. C, title XXXV, §3504, Dec. 20, 2019, 133 Stat. 1970.)

§51304. ADDITIONAL APPOINTMENTS FROM PARTICULAR AREAS

(a) OTHER COUNTRIES IN WESTERN HEMISPHERE.—The President may appoint individuals from countries in the Western Hemisphere other than the United States to receive instruction at the United States Merchant Marine Academy. Not more than 12 individuals may receive instruction under this subsection at the same time, and not more than 2 individuals from the same country may receive instruction under this subsection at the same time.

(b) OTHER COUNTRIES GENERALLY.—

(1) APPOINTMENT.—The Secretary of Transportation, with the approval of the Secretary of State, may appoint individuals from countries other than the United States to receive instruction at the Academy. Not more than 30 individuals may receive instruction under this subsection at the same time.

(2) REIMBURSEMENT.—The Secretary of Transportation shall ensure that the country from which an individual comes under this subsection will reimburse the Secretary for the cost (as determined by the Secretary) of the instruction and allowances received by the individual.

(c) PANAMA.—

(1) APPOINTMENT.—The Secretary of Transportation, with the approval of the Secretary of State, may appoint individuals from Panama to receive instruction at the Academy. Individuals appointed under this subsection are in addition to those appointed under any other provision of this chapter.

(2) REIMBURSEMENT.—The Secretary of Transportation shall be reimbursed for the cost (as determined by the Secretary) of the instruction and allowances received by an individual appointed under this subsection.

(d) ALLOWANCES AND REGULATIONS.—Individuals receiving instruction under this section are entitled to the same allowances and are subject to the same regulations on admission, attendance, discipline, resignation, discharge, dismissal, and graduation, as cadets at the Academy appointed from the United States.

(Pub. L. 109–304, §8(b), Oct. 6, 2006, 120 Stat. 1572.)

§51305. PROHIBITED BASIS FOR APPOINTMENT

Preference may not be given to an individual for appointment as a cadet at the United States Merchant Marine Academy because one or more members of the individual's immediate family are alumni of the Academy.

(Pub. L. 109–304, §8(b), Oct. 6, 2006, 120 Stat. 1572.)

§51306. CADET COMMITMENT AGREEMENTS

(a) AGREEMENT REQUIREMENTS.—A citizen of the United States appointed as a cadet at the United States Merchant Marine Academy shall sign, as a condition of the appointment, an agreement to—

(1) complete the course of instruction at the Academy;

(2) obtain a merchant mariner license, unlimited as to horsepower or tonnage, issued by the Coast Guard as an officer in the merchant marine of the United States, accompanied by the appropriate national and international endorsements and certifications required by the Coast Guard for service aboard vessels on domestic and international voyages, without limitation, before graduation from the Academy;

(3) for at least 6 years after graduation from the Academy, maintain—

(A) a valid merchant mariner license, unlimited as to horsepower or tonnage, issued by the Coast Guard as an officer in the merchant marine of the United States, accompanied by the appropriate national and international endorsements and certifications required by the Coast Guard for service aboard vessels on domestic and international voyages, without limitation;

(B) a valid transportation worker identification credential; and

(C) a Coast Guard medical certificate;

(4) apply for, and accept if tendered, an appointment as a commissioned officer in the Navy Reserve (including the Strategic Sealift Officer Program, Navy Reserve), the Coast Guard Reserve, or any other reserve component of an armed force of the United

States, and, if tendered the appointment, to serve, meet the participation requirements, and maintain active status in good standing, as determined by the program manager of the appropriate military service, for at least 8 years after the date of commissioning;

(5) serve the foreign and domestic commerce and the national defense of the United States for at least 5 years after graduation from the Academy—

(A) as a merchant marine officer on a documented vessel or a vessel owned and operated by the United States Government or by a State;

(B) as an employee in a United States maritime-related industry, profession, or marine science (as determined by the Secretary of Transportation), if the Secretary determines that service under subparagraph (A) is not available to the individual;

(C) as a commissioned officer on active duty in an armed force of the United States, as a commissioned officer in the National Oceanic and Atmospheric Administration, or in other maritime-related Federal employment which serves the national security interests of the United States, as determined by the Secretary; or

(D) by a combination of the service alternatives referred to in subparagraphs (A)–(C); and

(6) report to the Secretary on compliance with this subsection.

(b) FAILURE TO COMPLETE COURSE OF INSTRUCTION.—

(1) ACTIVE DUTY.—If the Secretary of Transportation determines that an individual who has attended the Academy for at least 2 years has failed to fulfill the part of the agreement described in subsection (a)(1), the individual may be ordered by the Secretary of Defense to serve on active duty in one of the armed forces of the United States for a period of not more than 2 years. In cases of hardship as determined by the Secretary of Transportation, the Secretary of Transportation may waive this paragraph in whole or in part.

(2) RECOVERY OF COST.—If the Secretary of Defense is unable or unwilling to order an individual to serve on active duty under paragraph (1), or if the Secretary of Transportation determines that reimbursement of the cost of education provided would better serve the interests of the United States, the Secretary of Transportation may recover from the individual the cost of education provided by the Government.

(c) FAILURE TO CARRY OUT OTHER REQUIREMENTS.—

(1) ACTIVE DUTY.—If the Secretary of Transportation determines that an individual has failed to fulfill any part of the agreement described in subsection (a)(2)–(6), the individual may be ordered to serve on active duty for a period of at least 3 years but not more than the unexpired period (as determined by the Secretary) of the service required by subsection (a)(5). The Secretary of Transportation, in consultation with the Secretary of Defense, shall determine in which service the individual shall serve. In cases of hardship as determined by the Secretary of Transportation, the Secretary of Transportation may waive this paragraph in whole or in part.

(2) RECOVERY OF COST.—If the Secretary of Defense is unable or unwilling to order an individual to serve on active duty under paragraph (1), or if the Secretary of Transportation determines that reimbursement of the cost of education provided would

better serve the interests of the United States, the Secretary of Transportation may recover from the individual the cost of education provided. The Secretary may reduce the amount to be recovered to reflect partial performance of service obligations and other factors the Secretary determines merit a reduction.

(d) ACTIONS TO RECOVER COST.—To aid in the recovery of the cost of education provided by the Government under a commitment agreement under this section, the Secretary of Transportation may—

(1) request the Attorney General to bring a civil action against the individual; and

(2) make use of the Federal debt collection procedures in chapter 176 of title 28 or other applicable administrative remedies.

(e) ALTERNATIVE SERVICE.—

(1) SERVICE AS COMMISSIONED OFFICER.—An individual who, for the 5-year period following graduation from the Academy, serves as a commissioned officer on active duty in an armed force of the United States or as a commissioned officer of the National Oceanic and Atmospheric Administration or the Public Health Service shall be excused from the requirements of paragraphs (3) through (5) of subsection (a).

(2) MODIFICATION OR WAIVER.—The Secretary may modify or waive any of the terms and conditions set forth in subsection (a) through the imposition of alternative service requirements.

(f) SERVICE OBLIGATION PERFORMANCE REPORTING REQUIREMENT.—

(1) IN GENERAL.—Subject to any otherwise applicable restrictions on disclosure in section 552a of title 5, the Secretary of Defense, the Secretary of the department in which the Coast Guard is operating, the Administrator of the National Oceanic and Atmospheric Administration, and the Surgeon General of the Public Health Service—

(A) shall report the status of obligated service of an individual graduate of the Academy upon request of the Secretary; and

(B) may, in their discretion, notify the Secretary of any failure of the graduate to perform the graduate's duties, either on active duty or in the Ready Reserve component of their respective service, or as a commissioned officer of the National Oceanic and Atmospheric Administration or the Public Health Service, respectively.

(2) INFORMATION TO BE PROVIDED.—A report or notice under paragraph (1) shall identify any graduate determined to have failed to comply with service obligation requirements and provide all required information as to why such graduate failed to comply.

(3) CONSIDERED AS IN DEFAULT.—Upon receipt of such a report or notice, such graduate may be considered to be in default of the graduate's service obligations by the Secretary, and subject to all remedies the Secretary may have with respect to such a default.

(Pub. L. 109–304, §8(b), Oct. 6, 2006, 120 Stat. 1572; Pub. L. 109–163, div. A, title V, §515(g)(2)(A), Jan. 6, 2006, 119 Stat. 3236; Pub. L. 109–364, div. C, title XXXV, §§3505(a), 3506(a), Oct. 17, 2006, 120 Stat. 2516, 2517; Pub. L. 110–181, div. C, title XXXV, §§3523(a)(1), (b), 3526(b)(1), (c)(1), (g), Jan. 28, 2008,

122 Stat. 598, 600–602; Pub. L. 114–92, div. C, title XXXV, §3506, Nov. 25, 2015, 129 Stat. 1220.)

§51307. PLACES OF TRAINING

(a) IN GENERAL.—The Secretary of Transportation may provide for the training of cadets at the United States Merchant Marine Academy—

(1) on vessels owned, subsidized by, or contracted with the United States Government;

(2) on other documented vessels, with the permission of the owner;

(3) in shipyards or plants and with industrial or educational organizations; and

(4) on any other vessel considered by the Secretary to be necessary or appropriate or in the national interest.

(b) SEA YEAR CADETS ON CERTAIN VESSELS.—

(1) REQUIREMENTS.—The Secretary shall require an operator of a vessel participating in the Maritime Security Program under chapter 531 of this title, the Cable Security Fleet under chapter 532 of this title, or the Tanker Security Fleet under chapter 534 of this title to—

(A) carry on each Maritime Security Program vessel, Cable Security Fleet vessel, or Tanker Security Fleet vessel 2 United States Merchant Marine Academy cadets, if available, on each voyage; and

(B) implement and adhere to policies, programs, criteria, and requirements established pursuant to section 51322 of this title.

(2) FAILURE TO IMPLEMENT OR ADHERE TO REQUIREMENTS.—Failure to implement or adhere to the policies, programs, criteria, and requirements referred to in paragraph (1) may, as determined by the Maritime Administrator, constitute a violation of an operating agreement entered into under chapter 531, 532, or 534 of this title and the Maritime Administrator may—

(A) require the operator to take corrective actions; or

(B) withhold payment due to the operator until the violation, as determined by the Maritime Administrator, has been remedied.

(3) WITHHELD PAYMENTS.—Any payment withheld pursuant to paragraph (2)(B) may be paid, upon a determination by the Maritime Administrator that the operator is in compliance with the policies, programs, criteria, and requirements referred to in paragraph (1).

(c) MILITARY SEALIFT COMMAND VESSELS.—

(1) IN GENERAL.—Except as provided in paragraph (2), the Commander of the Military Sealift Command shall require an operator of a vessel in the United States Navy's Military Sealift Command to carry on each such vessel 2 United States Merchant Marine Academy cadets, if available, on each voyage, if the vessel—

(A) is flagged in the United States; and

(B) is rated at 10,000 gross tons or higher.

(2) WAIVER.—The Commander of the Military Sealift Command may waive the requirement under paragraph (1) at any time if the Commander determines that carrying

a cadet from the United States Merchant Marine Academy would place an undue burden on the vessel or the operator of the vessel.

(d) DEFINITION OF OPERATOR.—In this section, the term "operator" includes a government operator and a non-government operator.

(e) SAVINGS CLAUSE.—Nothing in this section may be construed as affecting—

(1) the discretion of the Secretary to determine whether to place a United States Merchant Marine Academy cadet on a vessel;

(2) the authority of the Coast Guard regarding a vessel security plan approved under section 70103; or

(3) the discretion of the master of the vessel to ensure the safety of all crew members.

(Pub. L. 109–304, §8(b), Oct. 6, 2006, 120 Stat. 1574; Pub. L. 109–241, title III, §307, July 11, 2006, 120 Stat. 528; Pub. L. 110–181, div. C, title XXXV, §3525(a)(3), (b), Jan. 28, 2008, 122 Stat. 600, 601; Pub. L. 115–232, div. C, title XXXV, §3512, Aug. 13, 2018, 132 Stat. 2311; Pub. L. 116–283, div. C, title XXXV, §3506, Jan. 1, 2021, 134 Stat. 4405; Pub. L. 117–263, div. C, title XXXV, §3517(a)(1), Dec. 23, 2022, 136 Stat. 3073.)

§51308. UNIFORMS, TEXTBOOKS, AND TRANSPORTATION ALLOWANCES

The Secretary of Transportation shall provide cadets at the United States Merchant Marine Academy—

(1) all required uniforms and textbooks; and

(2) allowances for transportation (including reimbursement of traveling expenses) when traveling under orders as a cadet.

(Pub. L. 109–304, §8(b), Oct. 6, 2006, 120 Stat. 1574.)

§51309. ACADEMIC DEGREE

(a) BACHELOR'S DEGREE.—

(1) IN GENERAL.—The Superintendent of the United States Merchant Marine Academy may confer the degree of bachelor of science on an individual who—

(A) has met the conditions prescribed by the Secretary of Transportation; and

(B) if a citizen of the United States, has passed the examination for a merchant marine officer's license.

(2) EFFECT OF PHYSICAL OR PSYCHOLOGICAL DISQUALIFICATION.—An individual not able or allowed to take the examination for a merchant marine officer's license solely due to a documented medical or psychological condition shall not be denied a degree for not taking the examination.

(b) MASTER'S DEGREE.—The Superintendent of the Academy may confer a master's degree on an individual who has met the conditions prescribed by the Secretary. A master's degree program may be funded through non-appropriated funds. To maintain the appropriate academic standards, the program shall be accredited by the appropriate accreditation body. Nonappropriated funds received for this purpose shall be credited to the Maritime Administration's Operations and Training appropriation, to remain available until expended, for those expenses directly related to the purpose of such receipts. The

Superintendent shall maintain a separate and detailed accounting of nonappropriated fund receipts and all associated expenses. The Secretary may prescribe regulations necessary to administer such a program.

(c) GRADUATION NOT ENTITLEMENT TO HOLD LICENSE.—Graduation from the Academy does not entitle an individual to hold a license authorizing service on a merchant vessel.

(d) DEFINITION OF DOCUMENTED MEDICAL OR PSYCHOLOGICAL CONDITION.—In this section the term "documented medical or psychological condition" means, with respect to an individual, a physical disqualification or psychological condition, including a mental health condition arising from sexual assault or sexual harassment, for which the individual has been treated or is being treated by a medical or psychological provider.

(Pub. L. 109–304, §8(b), Oct. 6, 2006, 120 Stat. 1574; Pub. L. 111–84, div. C, title XXXV, §3514, Oct. 28, 2009, 123 Stat. 2724; Pub. L. 117–263, div. C, title XXXV, §3511, Dec. 23, 2022, 136 Stat. 3065.)

§51310. DEFERMENT OF SERVICE OBLIGATION UNDER CADET COMMITMENT AGREEMENTS

The Secretary of Transportation may defer the service commitment of an individual under section 51306(a)(5) of this title (as specified in the cadet commitment agreement) for not more than 2 years if the individual is engaged in a graduate course of study approved by the Secretary. However, deferment of service as a commissioned officer under section 51306(a)(5) must be approved by the Secretary of the military department that has jurisdiction over the service or by the Secretary of Commerce for service with the National Oceanic and Atmospheric Administration.

(Pub. L. 109–304, §8(b), Oct. 6, 2006, 120 Stat. 1575.)

§51311. MIDSHIPMAN STATUS IN THE NAVY RESERVE

(a) APPLICATION REQUIREMENT.—Before being appointed as a cadet at the United States Merchant Marine Academy, a citizen of the United States must agree to apply for midshipman status in the Navy Reserve (including the Merchant Marine Reserve, Navy Reserve).

(b) APPOINTMENT.—

(1) IN GENERAL.—A citizen of the United States appointed as a cadet at the Academy shall be appointed by the Secretary of the Navy as a midshipman in the Navy Reserve (including the Merchant Marine Reserve, Navy Reserve).

(2) RIGHTS AND PRIVILEGES.—The Secretary of the Navy shall provide for cadets of the Academy who are midshipmen in the United States Navy Reserve to be—

(A) issued an identification card (referred to as a "military ID card"); and

(B) entitled to all rights and privileges in accordance with the same eligibility criteria as apply to other members of the Ready Reserve of the reserve components of the armed forces.

(3) COORDINATION.—The Secretary of the Navy shall carry out paragraphs (1) and (2) in coordination with the Secretary of Transportation.

(Pub. L. 109–304, §8(b), Oct. 6, 2006, 120 Stat. 1575; Pub. L. 109–163, div. A, title V, §515(g)(2), Jan. 6, 2006, 119 Stat. 3236; Pub. L. 110–181, div. C, title XXXV, §3523(a)(1), (b), Jan. 28, 2008, 122 Stat. 598, 600.)

§51312. BOARD OF VISITORS

(a) IN GENERAL.—There shall be a Board of Visitors to the United States Merchant Marine Academy (referred to in this section as the "Board" and the "Academy", respectively) to provide independent advice and recommendations on matters relating to the United States Merchant Marine Academy.

(b) MEMBERSHIP.—

(1) IN GENERAL.—The Board shall be composed of—

(A) 2 Senators appointed by the Chairman of the Committee on Commerce, Science, and Transportation of the Senate in consultation with the ranking member of such Committee;

(B) 3 Members of the House of Representatives appointed by the Chairman of the Committee on Armed Services of the House of Representatives in consultation with the ranking member of such Committee;

(C) 1 Senator appointed by the Vice President, who shall be a member of the Committee on Appropriations of the Senate;

(D) 2 Members of the House of Representatives appointed by the Speaker of the House of Representatives, in consultation with the Minority Leader, at least 1 of whom shall be a member of the Committee on Appropriations of the House of Representatives;

(E) 5 individuals appointed by the President; and

(F) as ex officio members—

(i) the Commander of the Military Sealift Command;

(ii) the Deputy Commandant for Operations of the Coast Guard;

(iii) the chairman of the Committee on Commerce, Science, and Transportation of the Senate;

(iv) the chairman of the Committee on Armed Services of the House of Representatives;

(v) the chairman of the Advisory Board to the Academy established under section 51313; and

(vi) the Member of the House of Representatives for the congressional district in which the Academy is located, as a nonvoting member, unless such Member of the House of Representatives is appointed as a voting member of the Board under subparagraph (B) or (D).

(2) PRESIDENTIAL APPOINTEES.—Of the individuals appointed by the President under paragraph (1)(E)—

(A) at least 2 shall be graduates of the Academy;

(B) at least 1 shall be a senior corporate officer from a United States maritime shipping company that participates in the Maritime Security Program, or in any Maritime Administration program providing incentives for companies to register their vessels in the United States, and this appointment shall rotate biennially among such companies;

(C) at least 1 shall be a representative of a maritime labor organization; and

(D) 1 or more may be a Senate-confirmed Presidential appointee, a member of the Senior Executive Service, or an officer of flag-rank from the Coast Guard, the

National Oceanic and Atmospheric Administration, or any of the military services that commission graduates of the Academy, other than the individuals who are members of the Board under clauses (i) and (ii) of paragraph (1)(F).

(3) TERM OF SERVICE.—

(A) IN GENERAL.—Except as provided in subparagraph (B), each member of the Board, other than an ex officio member under paragraph (1)(F), shall serve for a term of 2 years commencing at the beginning of each Congress.

(B) CONTINUATION OF SERVICE.—Any member described in subparagraph (A) whose term on the Board has expired, other than a member appointed under any of subparagraphs (A) through (D) of paragraph (1) who is no longer a Member of Congress, shall continue to serve until a successor is appointed.

(C) REPLACEMENT.—If a member of the Board is replaced, not later than 60 days after the date of the replacement, the Designated Federal Officer selected under subsection (g)(2) shall notify that member.

(4) VACANCIES.—If a member of the Board is no longer able to serve on the Board or resigns, the Designated Federal Officer selected under subsection (g)(2) shall immediately notify the person who appointed such member. Not later than 60 days after that notification, such person shall designate a replacement to serve the remainder of such member's term.

(5) DESIGNATION AND RESPONSIBILITY OF SUBSTITUTE BOARD MEMBERS.—

(A) AUTHORITY TO DESIGNATE.—A member of the Board under clause (i) or (ii) of paragraph (1)(F) or appointed under subparagraph (B) or (C) of paragraph (2) may, if unable to attend or participate in an activity described in subsection (d), (e), or (f), designate another individual to serve as a substitute member of the Board, on a temporary basis, to attend or participate in such activity.

(B) REQUIREMENTS.—A substitute member of the Board designated under subparagraph (A) shall be—

(i) an individual serving in a position for which the individual was appointed by the President and confirmed by the Senate;

(ii) a member of the Senior Executive Service; or

(iii) an officer of flag-rank who is employed by—

(I) the Coast Guard; or

(II) the Military Sealift Command.

(C) PARTICIPATION.—A substitute member of the Board designated under subparagraph (A)—

(i) shall be permitted by the Board to fully participate in the proceedings and activities of the Board;

(ii) shall report to the member that designated the substitute member on the Board's activities not later than 15 days following the substitute member's participation in such activities; and

(iii) shall be permitted by the Board to participate in the preparation of reports described in paragraph [1] (j) related to any proceedings or activities of the Board in which such substitute member participates.

(c) CHAIRPERSON.—

(1) IN GENERAL.—On a biennial basis and subject to paragraph (2), the Board shall select from among its members a Member of the House of Representatives or a Senator to serve as the Chairperson.

(2) ROTATION.—A Member of the House of Representatives and a Member of the Senate shall alternately be selected as the Chairperson of the Board.

(3) TERM.—An individual may not serve as Chairperson for consecutive terms.

(d) MEETINGS.—

(1) IN GENERAL.—The Board shall meet as provided for in the Charter adopted under paragraph (2)(B), including at least 1 meeting held at the Academy and 2 additional meetings, which may be held in person or virtually.

(2) CHAIRPERSON AND CHARTER.—The Designated Federal Officer selected under subsection (g)(2) shall organize a meeting of the Board for the purposes of—

(A) selecting a Chairperson under subsection (c); and

(B) adopting an official Charter for the Board, which shall establish the schedule of meetings of the Board.

(3) SCHEDULING; NOTIFICATION.—When scheduling a meeting of the Board, the Designated Federal Officer shall coordinate, to the greatest extent practicable, with the members of the Board to determine the date and time of the meeting. Members of the Board shall be notified of the date of each meeting not less than 30 days prior to the meeting date.

(e) VISITING THE ACADEMY.—

(1) ANNUAL VISIT.—The Board shall visit the Academy annually on a date selected by the Board, in consultation with the Secretary of Transportation and the Superintendent of the Academy.

(2) OTHER VISITS.—In cooperation with the Superintendent, the Board or its members may make other visits to the Academy in connection with the duties of the Board.

(3) ACCESS.—While visiting the Academy under this subsection, members of the Board shall have reasonable access to the grounds, facilities, midshipmen, faculty, staff, and other personnel of the Academy for the purpose of carrying out the duties of the Board.

(4) STAFF.—One or more staff of each member of the Board may accompany them on Academy visits.

(5) SCHEDULING; NOTIFICATION.—When scheduling a visit to the Academy, the Designated Federal Officer shall coordinate, to the greatest extent practicable, with the members of the Board to determine the date and time of the visit. Members of the Board shall be notified of the date of each visit not less than 30 days prior to the visit date.

(f) RESPONSIBILITY.—The Board shall inquire into the state of morale and discipline, the curriculum, instruction, physical equipment, fiscal affairs, and academic methods of the Academy, and other matters relating to the Academy that the Board decides to consider.

(g) DEPARTMENT OF TRANSPORTATION SUPPORT.—The Secretary of Transportation shall—

(1) provide support as deemed necessary by the Board for the performance of the Board's functions;

(2) select a Designated Federal Officer to support the performance of the Board's functions; and

(3) in cooperation with the Maritime Administrator and the Superintendent of the Academy, advise the Board of any institutional issues, consistent with applicable laws concerning the disclosure of information.

(h) STAFF.—Each of the chairman and ranking member of the Committee on Commerce, Science, and Transportation of the Senate and the chairman and ranking member of the Committee on Armed Services of the House of Representatives may designate staff members of such Committee to serve, without additional reimbursement (except as provided in subsection (i)), as staff for the Board. Such staff may attend meetings and may visit the Academy.

(i) TRAVEL EXPENSES.—While serving away from his or her home or regular place of business, a member of the Board or a staff member designated under subsection (h) shall be allowed travel expenses, including per diem in lieu of subsistence, as authorized under section 5703 of title 5, United States Code.

(j) REPORTS.—

(1) ANNUAL REPORT.—Not later than 60 days after each annual visit required under subsection (e)(1), the Board shall submit to the President a written report of its actions, views, and recommendations pertaining to the Academy.

(2) OTHER REPORTS.—If the members of the Board visit the Academy under subsection (e)(2), the Board may—

(A) prepare a report on such visit; and

(B) if approved by a majority of the members of the Board, submit such report to the President not later than 60 days after the date of the approval.

(3) ADVISORS.—The Board may call in advisers—

(A) for consultation regarding the execution of the Board's responsibility under subsection (f); or

(B) to assist in the preparation of a report described in paragraph (1) or (2).

(4) SUBMISSION.—A report submitted to the President under paragraph (1) or (2) shall be concurrently submitted to—

(A) the Secretary of Transportation;

(B) the Committee on Commerce, Science, and Transportation of the Senate; and

(C) the Committee on Armed Services of the House of Representatives.

(Pub. L. 109–304, §8(b), Oct. 6, 2006, 120 Stat. 1575; Pub. L. 113–291, div. C, title XXXV, §3504(a), Dec. 19, 2014, 128 Stat. 3905; Pub. L. 117–263, div. C, title XXXV, §3512, Dec. 23, 2022, 136 Stat. 3065.)

[1] So in original. Probably should be "subsection".

§51313. ADVISORY BOARD

(a) IN GENERAL.—An Advisory Board to the United States Merchant Marine Academy shall be established to visit the Academy at least once during each academic year, for the purpose of examining the course of instruction and management of the Academy and advising the Maritime Administrator and the Superintendent of the Academy.

(b) APPOINTMENT AND TERMS.—The Board shall be composed of not more than 7 individuals appointed by the Secretary of Transportation. The individuals must be distinguished in education and other fields related to the Academy. Members of the Board shall be appointed for terms of not more than 3 years and may be reappointed. The Secretary shall designate one of the members as chairman.

(c) TRAVEL EXPENSES.—When serving away from home or regular place of business, a member of the Board shall be allowed travel expenses, including per diem in lieu of subsistence, as authorized by section 5703 of title 5.

(d) RELATIONSHIP TO OTHER LAW.—Chapter 10 of title 5 does not apply to the Board.

(Pub. L. 109–304, §8(b), Oct. 6, 2006, 120 Stat. 1576; Pub. L. 117–286, §4(a)(292), Dec. 27, 2022, 136 Stat. 4338.)

§51314. LIMITATION ON CHARGES AND FEES FOR ATTENDANCE

(a) PROHIBITION.—Except as provided in subsection (b), no charge or fee for tuition, room, or board for attendance at the United States Merchant Marine Academy may be imposed unless the charge or fee is specifically authorized by a law enacted after October 5, 1994.

(b) EXCEPTION.—The prohibition specified in subsection (a) does not apply with respect to any item or service provided to cadets for which a charge or fee is imposed as of October 5, 1994, or for calculators, computers, personal and academic supplies, midshipman services such as barber, tailor, or laundry services, and Coast Guard license fees. The Secretary of Transportation shall present at the next meeting of the Board of Visitors, and post on a publicly available website, any change made by the Academy in the amount of a charge or fee authorized under this subsection. Such fees shall be credited to the Maritime Administration's Operations and Training appropriation, to remain available until expended, for those expenses directly related to the purposes of the fees. Fees collected in excess of actual expenses may be refunded to the Midshipmen through a mechanism approved by the Secretary. The Academy shall maintain a separate and detailed accounting of fee revenue and all associated expenses.

(Pub. L. 109–304, §8(b), Oct. 6, 2006, 120 Stat. 1576; Pub. L. 111–84, div. C, title XXXV, §3510, Oct. 28, 2009, 123 Stat. 2722; Pub. L. 111–117, div. A, title I, §176, Dec. 16, 2009, 123 Stat. 3068; Pub. L. 115–420, §2, Jan. 3, 2019, 132 Stat. 5444.)

§51315. GIFTS TO THE MERCHANT MARINE ACADEMY

(a) IN GENERAL.—The Maritime Administrator may accept and use conditional or unconditional gifts of money or property for the benefit of the United States Merchant Marine Academy, including acceptance and use for non-appropriated fund instrumentalities of the Merchant Marine Academy. The Maritime Administrator may accept a gift of services in carrying out the Administrator's duties and powers. Property accepted under this section and proceeds from that property must be used, as nearly as possible, in accordance with the terms of the gift.

(b) ESTABLISHMENT OF ACADEMY GIFT FUND.—There is established in the Treasury a fund, to be known as the "Academy Gift Fund". Disbursements from the Fund shall be made on order of the Maritime Administrator. Unless otherwise specified by the terms of the gift, the Maritime Administrator may use monies in the Fund for appropriated or non-appropriated purposes at the Academy. The Fund consists of—

(1) gifts of money;

(2) income from donated property accepted under this section;

(3) proceeds from the sale of donated property; and

(4) income from securities under subsection (c) of this section.

(c) INVESTMENT OF FUND BALANCES.—On request of the Maritime Administrator, the Secretary of the Treasury may invest and reinvest amounts in the Fund in securities of, or in securities the principal and interest of which is guaranteed by, the United States Government.

(d) DISBURSEMENT AUTHORITY.—There are hereby authorized to be disbursed from the Fund such sums as may be on deposit, to remain available until expended.

(e) DEDUCTIBILITY OF GIFTS.—Gifts accepted under this section are a gift to or for the use of the Government under the Internal Revenue Code of 1986.

(f) PAYMENT OF EXPENSES.—The Maritime Administrator may pay all necessary expenses in connection with the conveyance or transfer of a gift, devise, or bequest accepted under this section.

(Added Pub. L. 110–417, div. C, title XXXV, §3506(g)(1), Oct. 14, 2008, 122 Stat. 4764; amended Pub. L. 115–91, div. C, title XXXV, §3511, Dec. 12, 2017, 131 Stat. 1918.)

§51316. TEMPORARY APPOINTMENTS TO THE ACADEMY

Notwithstanding any other provision of law, the Maritime Administrator may appoint any present employee of the United States Merchant Marine Academy non-appropriated fund instrumentality to a position on the General Schedule of comparable pay. Eligible personnel shall be engaged in work permissibly funded by annual appropriations, and such appointments to the Civil Service shall be without regard to competition, for a term not to exceed 2 years.

(Added Pub. L. 110–417, div. C, title XXXV, §3506(h)(1), Oct. 14, 2008, 122 Stat. 4765.)

§51317. ADJUNCT PROFESSORS

(a) IN GENERAL.—The Maritime Administrator may establish a program for the purpose of contracting with individuals as personal services contractors to provide services as adjunct professors at the Academy, if the Maritime Administrator determines that there is a need for adjunct professors and the need is not of permanent duration.

(b) CONTRACT REQUIREMENTS.—Each contract under the program—

(1) must be approved by the Maritime Administrator;

(2) shall be for a duration, including options, of not to exceed one year unless the Maritime Administrator finds that exceptional circumstances justify an extension of up

to one additional year; and

(3) shall be subject to the availability of appropriations.

(Added Pub. L. 111–84, div. C, title XXXV, §3503(a), Oct. 28, 2009, 123 Stat. 2719; amended Pub. L. 115–91, div. C, title XXXV, §3509, Dec. 12, 2017, 131 Stat. 1916.)

§51318. POLICY ON SEXUAL HARASSMENT, DATING VIOLENCE, DOMESTIC VIOLENCE, SEXUAL ASSAULT, AND STALKING

(a) REQUIRED POLICY.—

(1) IN GENERAL.—The Secretary of Transportation shall direct the Superintendent of the United States Merchant Marine Academy to prescribe a policy on sexual harassment, dating violence, domestic violence, sexual assault, and stalking applicable to the cadets and other personnel of the Academy.

(2) MATTERS TO BE SPECIFIED IN POLICY.—The policy on sexual harassment, dating violence, domestic violence, sexual assault, and stalking prescribed under this subsection shall include—

(A) a program to promote awareness and prevention of the incidence of rape, acquaintance rape, domestic violence, dating violence, stalking, and other sexual offenses of a criminal nature that involve cadets or other Academy personnel;

(B) procedures for documenting, tracking, and maintaining the data required to conduct the annual assessments to determine the effectiveness of the policies, procedures, and training program of the Academy with respect to sexual harassment, dating violence, domestic violence, sexual assault, and stalking involving cadets or other Academy personnel, as required by subsection (c);

(C) procedures that a cadet or other Academy personnel should follow in the case of an occurrence of sexual harassment, dating violence, domestic violence, sexual assault, or stalking, including—

(i) specifying the person or persons to whom an alleged occurrence of sexual harassment, dating violence, domestic violence, sexual assault, or stalking should be reported by the victim and the options for confidential reporting;

(ii) specifying any other person whom the victim should contact; and

(iii) procedures on the preservation of evidence potentially necessary for proof of a criminal sexual offense;

(D) procedures for investigating sexual harassment, dating violence, domestic violence, sexual assault, or stalking involving a cadet or other Academy personnel to determine whether disciplinary action is necessary;

(E) a procedure for disciplinary action in cases of alleged criminal sexual assault involving a cadet or other Academy personnel;

(F) any other sanction authorized to be imposed in a substantiated case of sexual harassment, dating violence, domestic violence, sexual assault, or stalking involving a cadet or other Academy personnel in rape, acquaintance rape, or any other criminal sexual offense, whether forcible or nonforcible;

(G) procedures through which—

(i) questions regarding sexual harassment, dating violence, domestic violence, sexual assault, or stalking can be confidentially asked and confidentially answered;

(ii) victims can report incidents of sexual harassment, dating violence, domestic violence, sexual assault, or stalking confidentially; and

(iii) the privacy of victims of sexual harassment, dating violence, domestic violence, sexual assault, or stalking will be protected; and

(H) required training on the policy for all cadets and other Academy personnel, including the specific training required for personnel who process allegations of sexual harassment, dating violence, domestic violence, sexual assault, or stalking involving Academy personnel.

(3) MINIMUM TRAINING REQUIREMENTS FOR CERTAIN INDIVIDUALS REGARDING SEXUAL HARASSMENT, DATING VIOLENCE, DOMESTIC VIOLENCE, SEXUAL ASSAULT, AND STALKING.—

(A) REQUIREMENT.—The Maritime Administrator shall direct the Superintendent of the United States Merchant Marine Academy to develop a mandatory training program at the Academy for each individual who is involved in implementing the Academy's student disciplinary grievance procedures, including each individual who is responsible for—

(i) resolving complaints of reported sexual harassment, dating violence, domestic violence, sexual assault, and stalking;

(ii) resolving complaints of reported violations of the sexual misconduct policy of the Academy; or

(iii) conducting an interview with a victim of sexual harassment, dating violence, domestic violence, sexual assault, or stalking.

(B) CONSULTATION.—The Superintendent shall develop the training program described in subparagraph (A) in consultation with national, State, or local sexual assault, dating violence, domestic violence, or stalking victim advocacy, victim services, or prevention organizations.

(C) ELEMENTS.—The training required by subparagraph (A) shall include the following:

(i) Information on working with and interviewing persons subjected to sexual harassment, dating violence, domestic violence, sexual assault, or stalking.

(ii) Information on particular types of conduct that would constitute sexual harassment, dating violence, domestic violence, sexual assault, or stalking, regardless of gender, including same-sex sexual harassment, dating violence, domestic violence, sexual assault, or stalking.

(iii) Information on consent and the effect that drugs or alcohol may have on an individual's ability to consent.

(iv) Information on the effects of trauma, including the neurobiology of trauma.

(v) Training regarding the use of trauma-informed interview techniques, which means asking questions of an individual who has been a victim of sexual harassment, dating violence, domestic violence, sexual assault, or stalking in a manner that is focused on the experience of the victim, does not judge or blame the victim, and is informed by evidence-based research on the neurobiology of trauma.

(vi) Training on cultural awareness regarding how dating violence, domestic violence, sexual assault, or stalking may impact midshipmen differently depending on their cultural background.

(vii) Information on sexual assault dynamics, sexual assault perpetrator behavior, and barriers to reporting.

(D) IMPLEMENTATION.—

(i) DEVELOPMENT AND APPROVAL SCHEDULE.—The training program required by subparagraph (A) shall be developed not later than 90 days after the date of the enactment of the National Defense Authorization Act for Fiscal Year 2018.

(ii) COMPLETION OF TRAINING.—Each individual who is required to complete the training described in subparagraph (A) shall complete such training not later than—

(I) 270 days after the date of the enactment of the National Defense Authorization Act for Fiscal Year 2018; or

(II) 180 days after starting a position with responsibilities that include the activities described in clause (i), (ii), or (iii) of subparagraph (A).

(4) AVAILABILITY OF POLICY.—The Secretary shall ensure that the policy developed under this subsection is available to—

(A) all cadets and employees of the Academy; and

(B) the public.

(5) CONSULTATION AND ASSISTANCE.—In developing the policy under this subsection, the Secretary may consult with or receive assistance from such Federal, State, local, and national organizations and subject matter experts as the Secretary considers appropriate.

(6) CONSISTENCY WITH THE HIGHER EDUCATION ACT OF 1965.—The Secretary shall ensure that the policy developed under this subsection meets the requirements set out in section 485(f)(8) of the Higher Education Act of 1965 (20 U.S.C. 1092(f)(8)).

(b) DEVELOPMENT PROGRAM.—

(1) IN GENERAL.—The Maritime Administrator shall ensure that the development program of the Academy includes a section that—

(A) describes the relationship between honor, respect, and character development and the prevention of sexual harassment, dating violence, domestic violence, sexual assault, and stalking at the Academy;

(B) includes a brief history of the problem of sexual harassment, dating violence, domestic violence, sexual assault, and stalking in the merchant marine, in the Armed Forces, and at the Academy; and

(C) includes information relating to reporting sexual harassment, dating violence, domestic violence, sexual assault, and stalking, victims' rights, and dismissal for offenders.

(2) MINIMUM REQUIREMENTS TO COMBAT RETALIATION.—

(A) REQUIREMENT FOR PLAN.—Not later than 90 days after the date of the enactment of the National Defense Authorization Act for Fiscal Year 2018, the Maritime

Administrator shall direct the Superintendent of the United States Merchant Marine Academy to implement and maintain a plan to combat retaliation against cadets at the Academy and other Academy personnel who report sexual harassment, dating violence, domestic violence, sexual assault, or stalking.

(B) VIOLATION OF CODE OF CONDUCT.—The Superintendent shall consider an act of retaliation against a cadet at the Academy who reports sexual harassment, dating violence, domestic violence, sexual assault, or stalking as a Class I violation of the Midshipman Regulations of the Academy or equivalent code of conduct.

(C) RETALIATION DEFINITION.—The Superintendent shall work with the sexual assault prevention and response staff of the Academy to define "retaliation" for purposes of this subsection.

(3) MINIMUM RESOURCE REQUIREMENTS.—

(A) IN GENERAL.—The Maritime Administrator shall ensure the staff at the Academy are provided adequate and appropriate sexual harassment, dating violence, domestic violence, sexual assault, and stalking prevention and response training materials and resources. Such resources shall include staff as follows:

(i) Sexual assault response coordinator.
(ii) Prevention educator.
(iii) Civil rights officer.
(iv) Staff member to oversee Sea Year.

(B) COMMUNICATION.—The Director of the Office of Civil Rights of the Maritime Administration shall create and maintain a direct line of communication to the sexual assault response staff of the Academy that is outside of the chain of command of the Academy.

(4) MINIMUM TRAINING REQUIREMENTS.—The Superintendent shall ensure that all cadets receive training on the sexual harassment, dating violence, domestic violence, sexual assault, and stalking prevention and response sections of the development program of the Academy, as described in paragraph (1), as follows:

(A) An initial training session, which shall occur not later than 7 days after a cadet's initial arrival at the Academy.

(B) Additional training sessions, which shall occur biannually following the cadet's initial training session until the cadet graduates or leaves the Academy.

(c) ANNUAL ASSESSMENT.—

(1) IN GENERAL.—The Secretary, in cooperation with the Superintendent, shall conduct an assessment at the Academy, during each Academy program year, to determine the effectiveness of the policies, procedures, and training program of the Academy with respect to sexual harassment and sexual assault involving cadets or other Academy personnel.

(2) BIENNIAL SURVEY.—For each assessment of the Academy under paragraph (1) during an Academy program year that begins in an odd-numbered calendar year, the Secretary shall conduct a survey of cadets and other Academy personnel—

(A) to measure—

(i) the incidence, during that program year, of sexual harassment and sexual assault events involving cadets or other Academy personnel, on or off the Academy campus, that have been reported to officials of the Academy; and

(ii) the incidence, during that program year, of sexual harassment and sexual assault events involving cadets or other Academy personnel, on or off the Academy campus, that have not been reported to officials of the Academy; and

(B) to assess the perceptions of cadets and other Academy personnel on—

(i) the policies, procedures, and training programs of the Academy on sexual harassment and sexual assault involving cadets or other Academy personnel;

(ii) the enforcement of the policies described in clause (i);

(iii) the incidence of sexual harassment and sexual assault involving cadets or other Academy personnel; and

(iv) any other issues relating to sexual harassment and sexual assault involving cadets or other Academy personnel.

(3) FOCUS GROUPS FOR YEARS WHEN SURVEY NOT REQUIRED.—In any year in which the Secretary is not required to conduct the survey described in paragraph (2), the Secretary shall conduct focus groups at the Academy for the purposes of ascertaining information relating to sexual assault and sexual harassment issues at the Academy.

(d) ANNUAL REPORT.—

(1) IN GENERAL.—For each Academy program year, the Superintendent shall submit to the Secretary a report that provides information about sexual harassment and sexual assault involving cadets or other Academy personnel.

(2) CONTENTS.—Each report submitted under paragraph (1) shall include, for the Academy program year covered by the report—

(A) the number of sexual assaults, rapes, and other sexual offenses, including sexual harassment, involving cadets or other Academy personnel that have been reported to Academy officials;

(B) the number of the reported cases described in subparagraph (A) that have been substantiated;

(C) the policies, procedures, and training implemented by the Superintendent and the leadership of the Academy in response to incidents of sexual harassment and sexual assault involving cadets and other Academy personnel; and

(D) a plan for the actions that will be taken in the following Academy program year regarding prevention of, and response to, incidents of sexual harassment and sexual assault involving cadets and other Academy personnel.

(3) SURVEY AND FOCUS GROUP RESULTS.—

(A) SURVEY RESULTS.—Each report under paragraph (1) for an Academy program year that begins in an odd-numbered calendar year shall include the results of the survey conducted in that program year under subsection (c)(2).

(B) FOCUS GROUP RESULTS.—Each report under paragraph (1) for an Academy program year in which the Secretary is not required to conduct the survey described in subsection (c)(2) shall include the results of the focus group conducted in that program year under subsection (c)(3).

(4) REPORTING REQUIREMENT.—

(A) BY THE SUPERINTENDENT.—For each incident of sexual harassment or sexual assault reported to the Superintendent, the Superintendent shall provide to the Secretary and the Board of Visitors of the Academy a report that includes—

(i) the facts surrounding the incident, except for any details that would reveal the identities of the people involved; and

(ii) the Academy's response to the incident.

(B) BY THE SECRETARY.—Not later than January 15 of each year, the Secretary shall submit a copy of each report received under subparagraph (A) and the Secretary's comments on the report to the Committee on Commerce, Science, and Transportation of the Senate and the Committee on Transportation and Infrastructure of the House of Representatives.

(e) DATA FOR AGGREGATE REPORTING.—

(1) IN GENERAL.—No requirement related to confidentiality in this section or section 51319 of this title may be construed to prevent a sexual assault response coordinator from providing information for any report required by law regarding sexual harassment, dating violence, domestic violence, sexual assault, or stalking.

(2) IDENTITY PROTECTION.—Any information provided for a report referred to in paragraph (1) shall be provided in a manner that protects the identity of the victim or witness.

(f) DEFINITIONS.—In this section and section 51319 of this title:

(1) DATING VIOLENCE; DOMESTIC VIOLENCE; STALKING.—The terms "dating violence", "domestic violence", and "stalking" have the meanings given those terms is [1] section 40002(a) of the Violence Against Women Act of 1994 (42 U.S.C. 13925(a)).[2]

(2) SEXUAL ASSAULT.—The term "sexual assault" means an offense classified as a forcible or nonforcible sex offense under the uniform crime reporting system of the Federal Bureau of Investigation.

(Added Pub. L. 114–328, div. C, title XXXV, §3510(a), Dec. 23, 2016, 130 Stat. 2782; amended Pub. L. 115–91, div. C, title XXXV, §3514(a)–(d)(1), Dec. 12, 2017, 131 Stat. 1920–1923; Pub. L. 115–232, div. C, title XXXV, §3507(a), Aug. 13, 2018, 132 Stat. 2309.)

[1] So in original. Probably should be "in".

[2] See References in Text note below.

§51319. SEXUAL ASSAULT RESPONSE COORDINATORS AND SEXUAL ASSAULT VICTIM ADVOCATES

(a) SEXUAL ASSAULT RESPONSE COORDINATORS.—

(1) REQUIREMENT FOR COORDINATORS.—The United States Merchant Marine Academy shall employ or contract with at least 1 full-time sexual assault response coordinator who shall reside at or near the Academy. The Secretary of Transportation may assign additional full-time or part-time sexual assault response coordinators at the Academy as necessary.

(2) SELECTION CRITERIA.—Each sexual assault response coordinator shall be selected based on—

(A) experience and a demonstrated ability to effectively provide victim services related to sexual harassment, dating violence, domestic violence, sexual assault, and stalking; and

(B) protection of the individual under applicable law to provide privileged communication.

(3) CONFIDENTIALITY.—A sexual assault response coordinator shall, to the extent authorized under applicable law, provide confidential services to a cadet at the Academy who reports being a victim of, or witness to, sexual harassment, dating violence, domestic violence, sexual assault, or stalking.

(4) TRAINING.—

(A) VERIFICATION.—Not later than 90 days after the date of the enactment of the National Defense Authorization Act for Fiscal Year 2018, the Maritime Administrator, in consultation with the Director of the Maritime Administration Office of Civil Rights, shall develop a process to verify that each sexual assault response coordinator has completed proper training.

(B) TRAINING REQUIREMENTS.—The training referred to in subparagraph (A) shall include training in—

(i) working with victims of sexual harassment, dating violence, domestic violence, sexual assault, and stalking;

(ii) the policies, procedures, and resources of the Academy related to responding to sexual harassment, dating violence, domestic violence, sexual assault, and stalking; and

(iii) national, State, and local victim services and resources available to victims of sexual harassment, dating violence, domestic violence, sexual assault, and stalking.

(C) COMPLETION OF TRAINING.—A sexual assault response coordinator shall complete the training referred to in subparagraphs (A) and (B) not later than—

(i) 270 days after enactment of the National Defense Authorization Act for Fiscal Year 2018; or

(ii) 180 days after starting in the role of sexual assault response coordinator.

(5) DUTIES.—A sexual assault response coordinator shall—

(A) confidentially receive a report from a victim of sexual harassment, dating violence, domestic violence, sexual assault, or stalking;

(B) inform the victim of—

(i) the victim's rights under applicable law;

(ii) options for reporting an incident of sexual harassment, dating violence, domestic violence, sexual assault, or stalking to the Academy and law enforcement;

(iii) how to access available services, including emergency medical care, medical forensic or evidentiary examinations, legal services, services provided by rape crisis centers and other victim service providers, services provided by the volunteer sexual assault victim advocates at the Academy, and crisis intervention counseling and ongoing counseling;

(iv) such coordinator's ability to assist in arranging access to such services, with the consent of the victim;

(v) available accommodations, such as allowing the victim to change living arrangements and obtain accessibility services;

(vi) such coordinator's ability to assist in arranging such accommodations, with the consent of the victim;

(vii) the victim's rights and the Academy's responsibilities regarding orders of protection, no contact orders, restraining orders, or similar lawful orders issued by the Academy or a criminal, civil, or tribal court; and

(viii) privacy limitations under applicable law;

(C) represent the interests of any cadet at the Academy who reports being a victim of sexual harassment, dating violence, domestic violence, sexual assault, or stalking, even if such interests are in conflict with the interests of the Academy;

(D) advise the victim of, and provide written materials regarding, the information described in subparagraph (B);

(E) liaise with appropriate staff at the Academy, with the victim's consent, to arrange reasonable accommodations through the Academy to allow the victim to change living arrangements, obtain accessibility services, or access other accommodations;

(F) maintain the privacy and confidentiality of the victim, and shall not notify the Academy or any other authority of the identity of the victim or the alleged circumstances surrounding the reported incident unless—

(i) otherwise required by applicable law;

(ii) requested to do so by the victim who has been fully and accurately informed about what procedures shall occur if the information is shared; or

(iii) notwithstanding clause (i) or clause (ii), there is risk of imminent harm to other individuals;

(G) assist the victim in contacting and reporting an incident of sexual harassment, dating violence, domestic violence, sexual assault, or stalking to the Academy or law enforcement, if requested to do so by the victim who has been fully and accurately informed about what procedures shall occur if information is shared; and

(H) submit to the Director of the Maritime Administration Office of Civil Rights an annual report summarizing how the resources supplied to the coordinator were used during the prior year, including the number of victims assisted by the coordinator.

(b) OVERSIGHT.—
(1) IN GENERAL.—
(A) REPORTING.—Each sexual assault response coordinator shall—
(i) report directly to the Superintendent; and
(ii) have concurrent reporting responsibility to the Executive Director of the Maritime Administration on matters related to the Maritime Administration and the Department of Transportation and upon belief that the Academy leadership is acting inappropriately regarding sexual assault prevention and response matters.

(B) SUPPORT.—The Maritime Administration Office of Civil Rights shall provide support to the sexual assault response coordinator at the Academy on all sexual harassment, dating violence, domestic violence, sexual assault, or stalking prevention matters.

(2) PROHIBITION ON INVESTIGATION BY THE ACADEMY.—Any request by a victim for an accommodation, as described in subsection (a)(5)(E), made by a sexual assault response coordinator shall not trigger an investigation by the Academy, even if such coordinator deals only with matters relating to sexual harassment, dating violence, domestic violence, sexual assault, or stalking.

(3) PROHIBITION ON RETALIATION.—A sexual assault response coordinator, victim advocate, or companion may not be disciplined, penalized, or otherwise retaliated against by the Academy for representing the interests of the victim, even if such interests are in conflict with the interests of the Academy.

(c) SPECIAL VICTIMS ADVISOR.—
(1) IN GENERAL.—The Secretary shall designate an attorney (to be known as the "Special Victims Advisor") for the purpose of providing legal assistance to any cadet of the Academy who is the victim of an alleged sex-related offense regarding administrative and criminal proceedings related to such offense, regardless of whether the report of that offense is restricted or unrestricted.
(2) SPECIAL VICTIMS ADVISORY.—The Secretary shall ensure that the attorney designated as the Special Victims Advisor has knowledge of the Uniform Code of Military Justice, as well as criminal and civil law.
(3) PRIVILEGED COMMUNICATIONS.—Any communications between a victim of an alleged sex-related offense and the Special Victim Advisor, when acting in their capacity as such, shall have the same protection that applicable law provides for confidential attorney-client communications.

(d) VOLUNTEER SEXUAL ASSAULT VICTIM ADVOCATES.—
(1) IN GENERAL.—The Secretary, acting through the Superintendent of the Academy, shall designate from among volunteers 1 or more permanent employees of the Academy to serve as advocates for victims of sexual assaults involving cadets of the Academy or other Academy personnel.
(2) TRAINING; OTHER DUTIES.—Each victim advocate designated under this subsection

shall—

(A) have or receive training in matters relating to sexual assault and the comprehensive policy developed under section 51318; and

(B) serve as a victim advocate voluntarily, in addition to the individual's other duties as an employee of the Academy.

(3) PRIMARY DUTIES.—While performing the duties of a victim advocate under this subsection, a designated employee shall—

(A) support victims of sexual assault by informing them of the rights and resources available to them as victims;

(B) identify additional resources to ensure the safety of victims of sexual assault; and

(C) connect victims of sexual assault to companions, as described in paragraph (4).

(4) COMPANIONS.—

(A) IN GENERAL.—At least 1 victim advocate designated under this subsection, or a sexual assault response coordinator designated under subsection (a), while performing the duties of a victim advocate, shall act as a companion to a victim described in paragraph (1) in navigating investigative, medical, mental, and emotional health, and recovery processes relating to sexual assault.

(B) ALTERNATE VICTIM ADVOCATES.—If requested by the victim, an alternate victim advocate shall be designated under this subsection to act as a companion to the victim, as described in subparagraph (A).

(5) FORMAL RELATIONSHIPS WITH OTHER ENTITIES.—The Secretary may enter into formal relationships with other entities to make available additional victim advocates or to implement paragraphs (3) and (4).

(e) UNFILLED VACANCIES.—The Administrator of the Maritime Administration may appoint qualified candidates to positions under subsections (a) and (d) of this section without regard to sections 3309 through 3319 of title 5.

(Added Pub. L. 114–328, div. C, title XXXV, §3511(a), Dec. 23, 2016, 130 Stat. 2785; amended Pub. L. 115–91, div. C, title XXXV, §3515(a), (b) (formerly §3515(c)), Dec. 12, 2017, 131 Stat. 1924, 1927, §3515(b) renumbered §3515(c), Pub. L. 117–263, div. C, title XXXV, §3513(c)(2), Dec. 22, 2022, 136 Stat. 3068; Pub. L. 117–263, div. C, title XXXV, §3531(e), Dec. 23, 2022, 136 Stat. 3088.)

§51320. ACCEPTANCE OF GUARANTEES WITH GIFTS FOR MAJOR PROJECTS

(a) DEFINITIONS.—In this section:

(1) MAJOR PROJECT.—The term "major project" means a project estimated to cost at least $1,000,000 for—

(A) the purchase or other procurement of real or personal property; or

(B) the construction, renovation, or repair of real or personal property.

(2) MAJOR UNITED STATES COMMERCIAL BANK.—The term "major United States commercial bank" means a commercial bank that—

(A) is an insured bank (as defined in section 3(h) of the Federal Deposit Insurance Act (12 U.S.C. 1813(h)));

(B) is headquartered in the United States; and

(C) has total net assets of an amount considered by the Maritime Administrator to qualify the bank as a major bank.

(3) MAJOR UNITED STATES INVESTMENT MANAGEMENT FIRM.—The term "major United States investment management firm" means—

(A) any broker or dealer (as such terms are defined in section 3 of the Securities Exchange Act of 1934 (15 U.S.C. 78c));

(B) any investment adviser or provider of investment supervisory services (as such terms are defined in section 202 of the Investment Advisers Act of 1940 (15 U.S.C. 80b–2)); or

(C) a major United States commercial bank that—

(i) is headquartered in the United States; and

(ii) holds for the account of others investment assets in a total amount considered by the Maritime Administrator to qualify the bank as a major investment management firm.

(4) QUALIFIED GUARANTEE.—The term "qualified guarantee", with respect to a major project, means a guarantee that—

(A) is made by 1 or more persons in connection with a donation for the project of a total amount in cash or securities that the Maritime Administrator determines is sufficient to defray a substantial portion of the total cost of the project;

(B) is made to facilitate or expedite the completion of the project in reasonable anticipation that other donors will contribute sufficient funds or other resources in amounts sufficient to pay for completion of the project;

(C) is set forth as a written agreement providing that the donor will furnish in cash or securities, in addition to the donor's other gift or gifts for the project, any additional amount that may become necessary for paying the cost of completing the project by reason of a failure to obtain from other donors or sources funds or other resources in amounts sufficient to pay the cost of completing the project; and

(D) is accompanied by—

(i) an irrevocable and unconditional standby letter of credit for the benefit of the United States Merchant Marine Academy that is in the amount of the guarantee and is issued by a major United States commercial bank; or

(ii) a qualified account control agreement.

(5) QUALIFIED ACCOUNT CONTROL AGREEMENT.—The term "qualified account control agreement", with respect to a guarantee of a donor, means an agreement among the donor, the Maritime Administrator, and a major United States investment management firm that—

(A) ensures the availability of sufficient funds or other financial resources to pay the amount guaranteed during the period of the guarantee;

(B) provides for the perfection of a security interest in the assets of the account for the United States for the benefit of the United States Merchant Marine Academy with the highest priority available for liens and security interests under applicable law;

(C) requires the donor to maintain in an account with the investment management firm assets having a total value that is not less than 130 percent of the amount guaranteed; and

(D) requires the investment management firm, whenever the value of the account is less than the value required to be maintained under subparagraph (C), to liquidate any noncash assets in the account and reinvest the proceeds in Treasury bills issued under section 3104 of title 31.

(b) ACCEPTANCE AUTHORITY.—Subject to subsection (d), the Maritime Administrator may accept a qualified guarantee from a donor or donors for the completion of a major project for the benefit of the United States Merchant Marine Academy.

(c) OBLIGATION AUTHORITY.—The amount of a qualified guarantee accepted under this section shall be considered as contract authority to provide obligation authority for purposes of Federal fiscal and contractual requirements. Funds available for a project for which such a guarantee has been accepted may be obligated and expended for the project without regard to whether the total amount of funds and other resources available for the project (not taking into account the amount of the guarantee) is sufficient to pay for completion of the project.

(d) NOTICE.—The Maritime Administrator may not accept a qualified guarantee under this section for the completion of a major project until 30 days after the date on which a report of the facts concerning the proposed guarantee is submitted to Congress.

(e) PROHIBITION ON COMMINGLING FUNDS.—The Maritime Administrator may not enter into any contract or other transaction involving the use of a qualified guarantee and appropriated funds in the same contract or transaction.

(Added Pub. L. 115–91, div. C, title XXXV, §3510(a), Dec. 12, 2017, 131 Stat. 1916.)

§51321. GRANTS FOR SCIENTIFIC AND EDUCATIONAL RESEARCH

(a) DEFINED TERM.—In this section, the term "qualifying research grant" is a grant that—

(1) is awarded on a competitive basis by the Federal Government (except for the Department of Transportation), a State, a corporation, a fund, a foundation, an educational institution, or a similar entity that is organized and operated primarily for scientific or educational purposes; and

(2) is to be used to carry out a research project with a scientific or educational purpose.

(b) ACCEPTANCE OF QUALIFYING RESEARCH GRANTS.—The United States Merchant Marine Academy may compete for and accept qualifying research grants if the work under the grant is to be carried out by a professor or instructor of the United States Merchant Marine Academy.

(c) ADMINISTRATION OF GRANT FUNDS.—

(1) ESTABLISHMENT OF ACCOUNT.—The Maritime Administrator shall establish a separate account for administering funds received from research grants under this section.

(2) USE OF GRANT FUNDS.—The Superintendent shall use grant funds deposited into

the account established pursuant to paragraph (1) in accordance with applicable regulations and the terms and conditions of the respective grants.

(d) RELATED EXPENSES.—Subject to such limitations as may be provided in appropriations Acts, appropriations available for the United States Merchant Marine Academy may be used to pay expenses incurred by the Academy in applying for, and otherwise pursuing, a qualifying research grant.

(Added Pub. L. 115–91, div. C, title XXXV, §3512(a), Dec. 12, 2017, 131 Stat. 1918.)

§51322. PROTECTION OF CADETS FROM SEXUAL ASSAULT ONBOARD VESSELS

(a) SAFETY CRITERIA.—The Maritime Administrator, after consulting with the Commandant of the Coast Guard, shall establish—

(1) criteria, to which an owner or operator of a vessel engaged in commercial service shall adhere prior to carrying a cadet performing their Sea Year service from the United States Merchant Marine Academy, that addresses prevention of, and response to, sexual harassment, dating violence, domestic violence, sexual assault, and stalking; and

(2) a process for collecting pertinent information from such owners or operators and verifying their compliance with the criteria.

(3) TRAINING.—

(A) IN GENERAL.—As part of training that shall be provided not less than semiannually to all midshipmen of the Academy, pursuant to section 51318, the Maritime Administrator shall develop and implement comprehensive in-person sexual assault risk-reduction and response training that, to the extent practicable, conforms to best practices in the sexual assault prevention and response field and includes appropriate scenario-based training.

(B) DEVELOPMENT AND CONSULTATION WITH EXPERTS.—In developing the sexual assault risk-reduction and response training under subparagraph (A), the Maritime Administrator shall consult with and incorporate, as appropriate, the recommendations and views of experts in the sexual assault field.

(b) MINIMUM STANDARDS.—At a minimum, the criteria established under subsection (a) shall require the vessel owners or operators to have policies that address—

(1) communication between a cadet and an individual ashore who is trained in responding to incidents of sexual harassment, dating violence, domestic violence, sexual assault, and stalking;

(2) the safety and security of cadet staterooms while a cadet is onboard the vessel;

(3) requirements for crew to report complaints or incidents of sexual assault, sexual harassment, dating violence, domestic violence, and stalking consistent with the requirements in section 10104;

(4) the maintenance of records of reports of sexual harassment, dating violence, domestic violence, sexual assault, and stalking onboard a vessel carrying a cadet;

(5) the maintenance of records of sexual harassment, dating violence, domestic violence, sexual assault, and stalking training as required under subsection (f);

(6) a requirement for the owner or operator provide each cadet a copy of the policies and procedures related to sexual harassment, dating violence, domestic violence, sexual

assault, and stalking policies that pertain to the vessel on which they will be employed; and

(7) any other issues the Maritime Administrator determines necessary to ensure the safety of cadets during Sea Year training.

(c) SELF-CERTIFICATION BY OWNERS OR OPERATORS.—The Maritime Administrator shall require the owner or operator of any commercial vessel that is carrying a cadet from the United States Merchant Marine Academy to annually certify that—

(1) the vessel owner or operator is in compliance with the criteria established under subsection (a); and

(2) the vessel is in compliance with the International Convention of Safety of Life at Sea, 1974 (32 UST 47) and sections 8106 and 70103(c).

(d) INFORMATION, TRAINING, AND RESOURCES.—The Maritime Administrator shall ensure that a cadet participating in Sea Year—

(1) receives training specific to vessel safety, including sexual harassment, dating violence, domestic violence, sexual assault, and stalking prevention and response training, prior to the cadet boarding a vessel for Sea Year training;

(2) is equipped with an appropriate means of communication and has been trained on its use;

(3) has access to a helpline to report incidents of sexual harassment, dating violence, domestic violence, sexual assault, or stalking that is monitored by trained personnel; and

(4) is informed of the legal requirements for vessel owners and operators to provide for the security of individuals onboard, including requirements under section 70103(c) and chapter 81.

(e) CHECKS OF COMMERCIAL VESSELS.—

(1) REQUIREMENT.—Not less frequently than biennially, staff of the Academy or staff of the Maritime Administration shall conduct both random and targeted unannounced checks of not less than 10 percent of the commercial vessels that host a cadet from the Academy.

(2) ACCESS TO INFORMATION.—The vessel operator shall make available to staff conducting a vessel check such information as the Maritime Administrator determines is necessary to determine whether the vessel is being operated in compliance with the criteria established under subsection (a).

(3) REMOVAL OF STUDENTS.—If staff of the Academy or staff of the Maritime Administration determine that a commercial vessel is not in compliance with the criteria established under subsection (a), the staff—

(A) may remove a cadet of the Academy from the vessel; and

(B) shall report such determination of non-compliance to the owner or operator of the vessel.

(f) MAINTENANCE OF SEXUAL ASSAULT TRAINING RECORDS.—The Maritime Administrator shall require the owner or operator of a commercial vessel, and the seafarer union for a commercial vessel, to maintain records of sexual assault training for any person required to have such training.

(g) SEA YEAR SURVEY.—

(1) REQUIREMENT.—The Maritime Administrator shall require each cadet from the Academy, upon completion of the cadet's Sea Year, to complete a survey regarding the environment and conditions during the Sea Year of the vessel to which the cadet was assigned.

(2) AVAILABILITY.—The Maritime Administrator shall make available to the public for each year—

(A) the questions used in the survey required by paragraph (1); and

(B) the aggregated data received from such surveys.

(h) NONCOMMERCIAL VESSELS.—

(1) IN GENERAL.—A public vessel (as defined in section 2101) shall not be subject to the requirements of this section.

(2) REQUIREMENTS FOR PARTICIPATION.—The Maritime Administrator may establish criteria and requirements that the operators of public vessels shall meet to participate in the Sea Year program of the United States Merchant Marine Academy that addresses prevention of, and response to, sexual harassment, dating violence, domestic violence, sexual assault, and stalking.

(i) SHARING OF BEST PRACTICES.—The Maritime Administrator shall share with State maritime academies best practices for, and lessons learned with respect to, the prevention of, and response to, sexual harassment, dating violence, domestic violence, sexual assault, and stalking.

(Added Pub. L. 115–91, div. C, title XXXV, §3516(a), Dec. 12, 2017, 131 Stat. 1927; amended Pub. L. 115–232, div. C, title XXXV, §3515(b), Aug. 13, 2018, 132 Stat. 2312; Pub. L. 117–263, div. C, title XXXV, §§3513(a), 3531(g), Dec. 23, 2022, 136 Stat. 3066, 3088.)

§51323. UNITED STATES MERCHANT MARINE ACADEMY ADVISORY COUNCIL

(a) ESTABLISHMENT.—The Secretary of Transportation shall establish an advisory council, to be known as the "United States Merchant Marine Academy Advisory Council" (in this section referred to as the "Council").

(b) MEMBERSHIP.—

(1) IN GENERAL.—The Secretary shall select not fewer than 8 and not more than 14 individuals to serve as members of the Council. Such individuals shall have such expertise as the Secretary determines necessary and appropriate for providing advice and guidance on improving the Academy.

(2) GOVERNMENTAL EXPERTS.—The number of members of the Council who are employees of the Federal Government may not exceed the number of members of the Council who are not employees of the Federal Government.

(3) EMPLOYEE STATUS.—Members of the Council shall not be considered employees of the United States Government by reason of their membership on the Council for any purpose and shall not receive compensation other than reimbursement of travel expenses and per diem allowance in accordance with section 5703 of title 5.

(c) RESPONSIBILITIES.—The Council shall provide advice to the Secretary at the time and in the manner requested by the Secretary.

(d) PERSONALLY IDENTIFIABLE INFORMATION.—In carrying out its responsibilities under this subsection, the Council shall comply with the obligations of the Department of Transportation to protect personally identifiable information.

(Added Pub. L. 117–81, div. C, title XXXV, §3501(c)(1), Dec. 27, 2021, 135 Stat. 2238.)

§51324. UNFILLED VACANCIES

(a) IN GENERAL.—In the event of an unfilled vacancy for any critical position at the United States Merchant Marine Academy, the Secretary of Transportation may appoint, without regard to the provisions of subchapter I of chapter 33 of title 5, other than sections 3303 and 3328 of that title, a qualified candidate for the purposes of filling up to 20 of such positions.

(b) CRITICAL POSITION DEFINED.—In this section, the term "critical position" means a position that contributes to the improvement of—

(1) the culture or infrastructure of the Academy;

(2) student health and well being;

(3) Academy governance; or

(4) any other priority areas identified by the Council.

(Added Pub. L. 117–81, div. C, title XXXV, §3501(c)(1), Dec. 27, 2021, 135 Stat. 2238.)

§51325. SEXUAL ASSAULT AND SEXUAL HARASSMENT PREVENTION INFORMATION MANAGEMENT SYSTEM

(a) INFORMATION MANAGEMENT SYSTEM.—

(1) IN GENERAL.—Not later than January 1, 2023, the Maritime Administrator shall establish within the United States Merchant Marine Academy Sexual Assault prevention and Response Program, an information management system to track and maintain, in such a manner that patterns can be reasonably identified, information regarding claims and incidents involving cadets that are reportable pursuant to subsection (d) of section 51318 of this chapter.

(2) INFORMATION MAINTAINED IN THE SYSTEM.—Information maintained in the system established under paragraph (1) shall include the following information, to the extent that information is available:

(A) The overall number of sexual assault or sexual harassment incidents per fiscal year.

(B) The location of each such incident, including vessel name and the name of the company operating the vessel, if applicable.

(C) The standardized job title or position of the individuals involved in each such incident.

(D) The general nature of each such incident, to include copies of any associated reports completed on the incidents.

(E) The type of inquiry made into each such incident.

(F) A record of whether each such incident was substantiated by the relevant investigative process.

(3) PAST INFORMATION INCLUDED.—The information management system under this section shall include the relevant data listed in this subsection related to sexual assault and sexual harassment that the Maritime Administrator possesses, and shall not be limited to data collected after January 1, 2023.

(4) PRIVACY PROTECTIONS.—The Maritime Administrator and the Chief Information Officer of the Department of Transportation shall coordinate to ensure that the information management system under this section shall—

(A) be established and maintained in a secure fashion to ensure the protection of the privacy of any individuals whose information is entered in such system; and

(B) be free of personally identifiable information and maintain only the data required to satisfy the statistical purpose of such system.

(5) CYBERSECURITY AUDIT.—Ninety days after the implementation of the information management system, the Office of Inspector General of the Department of Transportation shall commence an audit of the cybersecurity of the system and shall submit a report containing the results of that audit to the Committee on Commerce, Science, and Transportation of the Senate and the Committee on Transportation and Infrastructure of the House of Representatives.

(6) CORRECTING RECORDS.—In establishing the information management system, the Maritime Administrator shall create a process to ensure that if any incident report results in a final agency action or final judgement that acquits an individual of wrongdoing, all personally identifiable information about the acquitted individual is removed from that incident report in the system.

(b) SEA YEAR PROGRAM.—The Maritime Administrator shall provide for the establishment of in-person and virtual confidential exit interviews, to be conducted by personnel who are not involved in the assignment of the midshipmen to a Sea Year vessel, for midshipmen from the Academy upon completion of Sea Year and following completion by the midshipmen of the survey under section 51322(d).[1]

(c) DATA-INFORMED DECISIONMAKING.—The data maintained in the data management system under subsection (a) and through the exit interviews under subsection (b) shall be affirmatively referenced and used to inform the creation of new policy or regulation, or changes to any existing policy or regulation, in the areas of sexual harassment, dating violence, domestic violence, sexual assault, and stalking.

(Added Pub. L. 117–263, div. C, title XXXV, §3531(a), Dec. 23, 2022, 136 Stat. 3083.)

[1] See References in Text note below.

§51326. STUDENT ADVISORY BOARD AT THE UNITED STATES MERCHANT MARINE ACADEMY

(a) IN GENERAL.—The Maritime Administrator shall establish at the United States Merchant Marine Academy an advisory board to be known as the Advisory Board to the

Secretary of Transportation (referred to in this section as the "Advisory Board").

(b) MEMBERSHIP.—The Advisory Board shall be composed of not fewer than 12 midshipmen of the Merchant Marine Academy who are enrolled at the Merchant Marine Academy at the time of the appointment, including not fewer than 3 cadets from each class.

(c) APPOINTMENT; TERM.—Midshipmen shall serve on the Advisory Board pursuant to appointment by the Maritime Administrator. Appointments shall be made not later than 60 days after the date of the swearing in of a new class of midshipmen at the Academy. The term of membership of a midshipmen on the Advisory Board shall be 1 academic year.

(d) REAPPOINTMENT.—The Maritime Administrator may reappoint not more than 6 cadets from the previous term to serve on the Advisory Board for an additional academic year if the Maritime Administrator determines such reappointment to be in the best interests of the Merchant Marine Academy.

(e) MEETINGS.—The Advisory Board shall meet with the Secretary of Transportation not less than once each academic year to discuss the activities of the Advisory Board. The Advisory Board shall meet in person with the Maritime Administrator not less than 2 times each academic year to discuss the activities of the Advisory Board.

(f) DUTIES.—The Advisory Board shall—

(1) identify health and wellbeing, diversity, and sexual assault and harassment challenges and other topics considered important by the Advisory Board facing midshipmen at the Merchant Marine Academy, off campus, and while aboard ships during Sea Year or other training opportunities;

(2) discuss and propose possible solutions, including improvements to culture and leadership development at the Merchant Marine Academy; and

(3) periodically review the efficacy of the program in section 51325(b), as appropriate, and provide recommendations to the Maritime Administrator for improvement.

(g) WORKING GROUPS.—The Advisory Board may establish one or more working groups to assist the Advisory Board in carrying out its duties, including working groups composed in part of midshipmen at the Merchant Marine Academy who are not current members of the Advisory Board.

(h) REPORTS AND BRIEFINGS.—The Advisory Board shall regularly provide the Secretary of Transportation and the Maritime Administrator reports and briefings on the results of its duties, including recommendations for actions to be taken in light of such results. Such reports and briefings may be provided in writing, in person, or both.

(Added Pub. L. 117–263, div. C, title XXXV, §3531(a), Dec. 23, 2022, 136 Stat. 3085.)

§51327. SEXUAL ASSAULT ADVISORY COUNCIL

(a) ESTABLISHMENT.—The Secretary of Transportation shall establish a Sexual Assault Advisory Council (in this section referred to as the "Council").

(b) MEMBERSHIP.—

(1) IN GENERAL.—The Council shall be composed of not fewer than 8 and not more than 14 individuals selected by the Secretary of Transportation who are alumni that have graduated within the last 4 years or current midshipmen of the United States Merchant Marine Academy (including midshipmen or alumni who were victims of sexual assault, to the maximum extent practicable, and midshipmen or alumni who were not victims of

sexual assault) and governmental and nongovernmental experts and professionals in the sexual assault field.

(2) EXPERTS INCLUDED.—The Council shall include—

(A) not less than 1 member who is licensed in the field of mental health and has prior experience working as a counselor or therapist providing mental health care to survivors of sexual assault in a victim services agency or organization; and

(B) not less than 1 member who has prior experience developing or implementing sexual assault or sexual harassment prevention and response policies in an academic setting.

(3) RULES REGARDING MEMBERSHIP.—No employee of the Department of Transportation shall be a member of the Council. The number of governmental experts appointed to the Council shall not exceed the number of nongovernmental experts.

(c) DUTIES; AUTHORIZED ACTIVITIES.—

(1) IN GENERAL.—The Council shall meet not less often than semiannually to—

(A) review—

(i) the policies on sexual harassment, dating violence, domestic violence, sexual assault, and stalking under section 51318 of this title;

(ii) the trends and patterns of data contained in the system described under section 51325 of this title; and

(iii) related matters the Council views as appropriate; and

(B) develop recommendations designed to ensure that such policies and such matters conform, to the extent practicable, to best practices in the field of sexual assault and sexual harassment response and prevention.

(2) AUTHORIZED ACTIVITIES.—To carry out this subsection, the Council may—

(A) interview current and former midshipmen of the United States Merchant Marine Academy (to the extent that such midshipmen provide the Department of Transportation express consent to be interviewed by the Council); and

(B) review surveys under section 51322(d).[1]

(3) PERSONALLY IDENTIFIABLE INFORMATION.—In carrying out this subsection, the Council shall comply with the obligations of the Department of Transportation to protect personally identifiable information.

(d) REPORTS.—On an annual basis for each of the 5 years after the date of enactment of this section, and at the discretion of the Council thereafter, the Council shall submit, to the President and the Committee on Commerce, Science, and Transportation and the Committee on Appropriations of the Senate and the Committee on Transportation and Infrastructure and the Committee on Appropriations of the House of Representatives, a report on the Council's findings based on the reviews conducted pursuant to subsection (c) and related recommendations.

(e) EMPLOYEE STATUS.—Members of the Council shall not be considered employees of the United States Government for any purpose and shall not receive compensation other than reimbursement of travel expenses and per diem allowance in accordance with section 5703 of title 5.

(f) NONAPPLICABILITY OF FACA.—The Federal Advisory Committee Act (5 U.S.C. App.) [1] shall not apply to the Council.

(Added Pub. L. 117–263, div. C, title XXXV, §3531(a), Dec. 23, 2022, 136 Stat. 3086.)

[1] *See References in Text note below.*

§51328. STUDENT SUPPORT

The Maritime Administrator shall—

(1) require a biannual survey of midshipmen, faculty, and staff of the Academy assessing the environment of the Academy; and

(2) require an annual survey of faculty and staff of the Academy assessing the Sea Year program.

(Added Pub. L. 117–263, div. C, title XXXV, §3531(a), Dec. 23, 2022, 136 Stat. 3087.)

CHAPTER 515—STATE MARITIME ACADEMY SUPPORT PROGRAM

§51501. GENERAL SUPPORT PROGRAM

(a) ASSISTANCE TO STATE MARITIME ACADEMIES.—The Secretary of Transportation shall cooperate with and assist State maritime academies in providing instruction to individuals to prepare them for service in the merchant marine of the United States.

(b) COURSE DEVELOPMENT.—The Secretary shall provide to each State maritime academy guidance and assistance in developing courses on the operation and maintenance of new vessels, on equipment, and on innovations being introduced to the merchant marine of the United States.

(c) AMERICAN MARITIME CENTERS OF EXCELLENCE.—The Secretary shall designate each State maritime academy as an American Maritime Center of Excellence.

(Pub. L. 109–304, §8(b), Oct. 6, 2006, 120 Stat. 1577; Pub. L. 116–92, div. C, title XXXV, §3505, Dec. 20, 2019, 133 Stat. 1970.)

§51502. DETAILING OF PERSONNEL

At the request of the Governor of a State, the President may detail, without reimbursement, personnel of the Navy, the Coast Guard, and the Maritime Service to a State maritime academy to serve as a superintendent, professor, lecturer, or instructor at the academy.

(Pub. L. 109–304, §8(b), Oct. 6, 2006, 120 Stat. 1577.)

§51503. REGIONAL MARITIME ACADEMIES

The Governors of the States cooperating to sponsor a regional maritime academy shall designate in writing one of those States to conduct the affairs of that academy. A regional maritime academy is eligible for assistance from the United States Government on the same basis as a State maritime academy sponsored by a single State.

(Pub. L. 109–304, §8(b), Oct. 6, 2006, 120 Stat. 1577.)

§51504. USE OF TRAINING VESSELS

(a) APPLICATIONS TO USE VESSELS.—The Governor of a State sponsoring a State maritime academy (or the Governor of the State designated to conduct the affairs of a regional maritime academy) may apply in writing to the Secretary of Transportation to obtain the use of a training vessel for the academy. A vessel provided under this section remains the property of the United States Government.

(b) GENERAL AUTHORITY.—Subject to subsection (c), the Secretary may provide to a State maritime academy, for use as a training vessel, a suitable vessel under the control of the Secretary or made available to the Secretary under subsection (e). If a suitable vessel is not available, the Secretary may build and provide a suitable vessel.

(c) APPROVAL REQUIREMENTS.—The Secretary may provide a vessel under this section only if—

(1) an application has been made under subsection (a);

(2) the State maritime academy satisfies section 51506(a) of this title; and

(3) a suitable port will be available for the safe mooring of the vessel while the academy is using the vessel.

(d) PREPARATION AND MAINTENANCE.—A vessel provided under this section shall be—

(1) repaired, reconditioned, and equipped (with all apparel, charts, books, and instruments of navigation) as necessary for use as a training vessel; and

(2) maintained in good repair by the Secretary.

(e) AGENCY VESSELS.—An agency may provide to the Secretary, for use by a State maritime academy, a vessel (including equipment) that—

(1) is suitable for training purposes; and

(2) can be provided without detriment to the service to which the vessel is assigned.

(f) FUEL COSTS.—

(1) IN GENERAL.—Subject to the availability of appropriations, the Secretary shall pay to each State maritime academy the costs of fuel used by a vessel provided under this section while used for training.

(2) MAXIMUM AMOUNTS.—The amount of the payment to a State maritime academy under paragraph (1) may not exceed—

(A) $100,000 for fiscal year 2006;

(B) $200,000 for fiscal year 2007; and

(C) $300,000 for fiscal year 2008 and each fiscal year thereafter.

(g) VESSEL SHARING.—

(1) IN GENERAL.—Not later than 90 days after the date of enactment of the National Defense Authorization Act for Fiscal Year 2019, the Secretary, acting through the Maritime Administrator, shall upon consultation with the maritime academies, and to the extent feasible with the consent of the maritime academies, implement a program of training vessel sharing, requiring maritime academies to share training vessel [1] provided by the Secretary among maritime academies, as necessary to ensure that training needs of each academy are met.

(2) PROGRAM OF VESSEL SHARING.—For purposes of this subsection, a program of vessel sharing shall include—

(A) ways to maximize the available underway training available in the fleet of training vessels;

(B) coordinating the dates and duration of training cruises with the academic calendars of maritime academies;

(C) coordinating academic programs designed to be implemented aboard training vessels among maritime academies; and

(D) identifying ways to minimize costs.

(3) ADDITIONAL FUNDING.—Subject to the availability of appropriations, the Maritime Administrator may provide additional funding to State maritime academies during periods of limited training vessel capacity, for costs associated with training vessel sharing.

(4) EVALUATION.—Not later than 30 days after the beginning of each fiscal year, the Secretary, acting through the Maritime Administrator, shall evaluate the vessel sharing program under this subsection to determine the optimal utilization of State maritime training vessels, and modify the program as necessary to improve utilization.

(Pub. L. 109–304, §8(b), Oct. 6, 2006, 120 Stat. 1577; Pub. L. 109–163, div. C, title XXXV, §3502(b), Jan. 6, 2006, 119 Stat. 3548; Pub. L. 110–181, div. C, title XXXV, §3523(a)(2), (b), Jan. 28, 2008, 122 Stat. 599, 600; Pub. L. 115–232, div. C, title XXXV, §3505, Aug. 13, 2018, 132 Stat. 2308.)

[1] So in original. Probably should be "vessels".

§51505. ANNUAL PAYMENTS FOR MAINTENANCE AND SUPPORT

(a) PAYMENT AGREEMENTS.—The Secretary of Transportation may make an agreement (effective for not more than 4 years) with the following academies to provide annual payments to those academies for their maintenance and support:

(1) One State maritime academy in each State that satisfies section 51506(a) of this title.

(2) Each regional maritime academy that satisfies section 51506(a) of this title.

(b) PAYMENTS.—

(1) IN GENERAL.—Subject to paragraph (2), an annual payment to an academy under subsection (a) shall be at least equal to the amount given to the academy for its maintenance and support by the State in which it is located, or, for a regional maritime academy, by all States cooperating to sponsor the academy.

(2) MAXIMUM.—The amount under paragraph (1) may not be more than $25,000, unless the academy satisfies section 51506(b) of this title.

(Pub. L. 109–304, §8(b), Oct. 6, 2006, 120 Stat. 1578; Pub. L. 109–163, div. C, title XXXV, §3502(a), Jan. 6, 2006, 119 Stat. 3547; Pub. L. 110–181, div. C, title XXXV, §3523(a)(3), (b), Jan. 28, 2008, 122 Stat. 599, 600; Pub. L. 115–232, div. C, title XXXV, §3515(d), Aug. 13, 2018, 132 Stat. 2313.)

§51506. CONDITIONS TO RECEIVING PAYMENTS AND USE OF VESSELS

(a) GENERAL CONDITIONS.—As conditions of receiving an annual payment or the use of a vessel under this chapter, a State maritime academy shall—

(1) provide courses of instruction on navigation, marine engineering (including steam and diesel propulsion), the operation and maintenance of new vessels and equipment, and innovations being introduced to the merchant marine of the United States;

(2) agree in writing to conform to the standards for courses, training facilities, admissions, and instruction that the Secretary of Transportation may establish after consultation with the superintendents of State maritime academies;

(3) agree in writing to require, as a condition for graduation, that each individual who is a citizen of the United States and who is attending the academy in a merchant marine officer preparation program pass the examination required for the issuance of a license under section 7101 of this title; and

(4) agree that any individual enrolled at such State maritime academy in a merchant marine officer preparation program—

(A) shall, not later than 9 months after such individual's date of enrollment, pass an examination in form and substance satisfactory to the Secretary that demonstrates that such individual meets the medical and physical requirements—

(i) required for the issuance of an original license under section 7101; or

(ii) set by the Coast Guard for issuing merchant mariners' documentation under section 7302, with no limit to the individual's operational authority;

(B) following passage of the examination under subparagraph (A), shall continue to meet the requirements described in subparagraph (A) throughout the remainder of the individual's enrollment at the State maritime academy; and

(C) if the individual has a medical or physical condition that disqualifies the individual from meeting the requirements referred to in subparagraph (A), shall be transferred to a program other than a merchant marine officer preparation program, or otherwise appropriately disenrolled from such State maritime academy, until the individual demonstrates to the Secretary that the individual meets such requirements.

(b) ADDITIONAL CONDITION TO PAYMENTS OF MORE THAN $25,000.—As a condition of receiving an annual payment of more than $25,000 under section 51505 of this title, a State maritime academy also must agree to admit each year a number of citizens of the United States who meet its admission requirements and reside in a State not supporting that academy. The Secretary shall determine the number of individuals to be admitted by each academy under this subsection. The number may not be more than one-third of the total number of individuals attending the academy at any time.

(c) SECRETARIAL WAIVER AUTHORITY.—The Secretary may modify or waive any of the terms set forth in subsection (a)(4) with respect to any individual or State maritime academy.

(Pub. L. 109–304, §8(b), Oct. 6, 2006, 120 Stat. 1579; Pub. L. 114–328, div. C, title XXXV, §3515, Dec. 23, 2016, 130 Stat. 2788.)

§51507. PLACES OF TRAINING

The Secretary of Transportation may provide for the training of students attending a State maritime academy—

(1) on vessels owned or subsidized by the United States Government;

(2) on other documented vessels, with the permission of the owner; and

(3) in shipyards or plants and with industrial or educational organizations.

(Pub. L. 109–304, §8(b), Oct. 6, 2006, 120 Stat. 1579.)

§51508. ALLOWANCES FOR STUDENTS

Under regulations prescribed by the Secretary of Transportation, a student at a State maritime academy shall receive from the Secretary allowances for transportation (including reimbursement of traveling expenses) when traveling under orders to receive training under section 51507 of this title.

(Pub. L. 109–304, §8(b), Oct. 6, 2006, 120 Stat. 1579.)

§51509. STUDENT INCENTIVE PAYMENT AGREEMENTS

(a) GENERAL AUTHORITY.—If a State maritime academy has an agreement with the Secretary of Transportation under section 51505 of this title, the Secretary may make an agreement with a student at the academy who is a citizen of the United States to make student incentive payments to the individual. An agreement with a student may not be effective for more than 4 academic years. The Secretary shall allocate payments under this section among the various State maritime academies in an equitable manner.

(b) PAYMENTS.—

(1) IN GENERAL.—Except as provided in paragraph (2), payments under an agreement under this section shall be equal to $16,000 each academic year and be paid in such installments as the Secretary shall determine while the individual is attending the academy, as prescribed by the Secretary.

(2) EXCEPTION.—The Secretary may modify the payments made to an individual under paragraph (1), but the total amount of payments to that individual may not exceed $64,000.

(3) AUTHORIZED USES.—The payments shall be used for uniforms, tuition, books, and subsistence.

(c) ENLISTED RESERVE STATUS.—An agreement under this section shall require the student to accept enlisted reserve status in the Navy Reserve (including the Strategic Sealift Officer Program, Navy Reserve) or the Coast Guard Reserve before receiving any payments under the agreement.

(d) AGREEMENT REQUIREMENTS.—An agreement under this section shall require the student to—

(1) complete the course of instruction at the academy the individual is attending;

(2) obtain a merchant mariner license, without limitation as to tonnage or horsepower, from the Coast Guard as an officer in the merchant marine of the United States, accompanied by the appropriate national and international endorsements and certification required by the Coast Guard for service aboard vessels on domestic and international voyages, without limitation, within three months of completion of the course of instruction at the academy the individual is attending;

(3) for at least 6 years after graduation from the academy, maintain—

(A) a valid merchant mariner license, unlimited as to horsepower or tonnage, issued by the Coast Guard as an officer in the merchant marine of the United States, accompanied by the appropriate national and international endorsements and certifications required by the Coast Guard for service aboard vessels on domestic and international voyages, without limitation;

(B) a valid transportation worker identification credential; and

(C) a Coast Guard medical certificate;

(4) apply for, and accept, if tendered, an appointment as a commissioned officer in the Navy Reserve (including the Strategic Sealift Officer Program, Navy Reserve), the Coast Guard Reserve, or any other reserve component of an armed force of the United States, and, if tendered the appointment, to serve and meet the participation requirements and to maintain active status in good standing, as determined by the program manager of the appropriate military service, for at least 8 years after the date of commissioning;

(5) serve the foreign and domestic commerce and the national defense of the United States for at least 3 years after graduation from the academy—

(A) as a merchant marine officer on a documented vessel or a vessel owned and operated by the United States Government or by a State;

(B) as an employee in a United States maritime-related industry, profession, or marine science (as determined by the Secretary), if the Secretary determines that service under subparagraph (A) is not available to the individual;

(C) as a commissioned officer on active duty in an armed force of the United States, as a commissioned officer in the National Oceanic and Atmospheric Administration, or in other maritime-related Federal employment which serves the national security interests of the United States, as determined by the Secretary; or

(D) by a combination of the service alternatives referred to in subparagraphs (A)–(C); and

(6) report to the Secretary on compliance with this subsection.

(e) FAILURE TO COMPLETE COURSE OF INSTRUCTION.—

(1) ACTIVE DUTY.—

(A) IN GENERAL.—The Secretary of Defense may order an individual to serve on active duty in the armed forces of the United States for a period of not more than 2 years if—

(i) the individual has attended an academy under this section for more than 2 academic years, but less than 3 academic years;

(ii) the individual has accepted the payments described in subsection (b) in an amount totaling at least $8,000; and

(iii) the Secretary of Transportation has determined that the individual has failed to fulfill the part of the agreement described in subsection (d)(1).

(B) 3 OR MORE YEARS.—The Secretary of Defense may order an individual to serve on active duty in the armed forces of the United States for a period of not more than 3 years if—

(i) the individual has attended an academy under this section for 3 or more academic years;

(ii) the individual has accepted the payments described in subsection (b) in an amount totaling at least $16,000; and

(iii) the Secretary of Transportation has determined that the individual has failed to fulfill the part of the agreement described in subsection (d)(1).

(C) HARDSHIP WAIVER.—In cases of hardship as determined by the Secretary of Transportation, the Secretary of Transportation may waive this paragraph in whole or in part.

(2) RECOVERY OF COST.—If the Secretary of Defense is unable or unwilling to order an individual to serve on active duty under paragraph (1), or if the Secretary of Transportation determines that reimbursement of the cost of education provided would better serve the interests of the United States, the Secretary of Transportation may recover from the individual the amount of student incentive payments, plus interest and attorney fees. The Secretary may reduce the amount to be recovered to reflect partial performance of service obligations and other factors the Secretary determines merit a reduction.

(f) FAILURE TO CARRY OUT OTHER REQUIREMENTS.—

(1) ACTIVE DUTY.—If the Secretary of Transportation determines that an individual has failed to fulfill any part of the agreement described in subsection (d)(2)–(6), the individual may be ordered to serve on active duty for a period of at least 2 years but not more than the unexpired period (as determined by the Secretary) of the service required by subsection (d)(5). The Secretary of Transportation, in consultation with the Secretary of Defense, shall determine in which service the individual shall serve. In cases of hardship as determined by the Secretary of Transportation, the Secretary of Transportation may waive this paragraph in whole or in part.

(2) RECOVERY OF COST.—If the Secretary of Defense is unable or unwilling to order an individual to serve on active duty under paragraph (1), or if the Secretary of Transportation determines that reimbursement of the cost of education provided would better serve the interests of the United States, the Secretary of Transportation may recover from the individual the amount of student incentive payments, plus interest and attorney fees. The Secretary may reduce the amount to be recovered to reflect partial performance of service obligations and other factors the Secretary determines merit a reduction.

(g) ACTIONS TO RECOVER COST.—To aid in the recovery of the cost of education provided by the Government under a commitment agreement under this section, the Secretary of Transportation may—

(1) request the Attorney General to bring a civil action against the individual; and

(2) make use of the Federal debt collection procedures in chapter 176 of title 28 or other applicable administrative remedies.

(h) ALTERNATIVE SERVICE.—

(1) SERVICE AS COMMISSIONED OFFICER.—An individual who, for the 5-year period following graduation from an academy, serves as a commissioned officer on active duty in an armed force of the United States or as a commissioned officer of the National Oceanic and Atmospheric Administration or the Public Health Service shall be excused from the requirements of paragraphs (3) through (5) of subsection (d).

(2) MODIFICATION OR WAIVER.—The Secretary may modify or waive any of the terms and conditions set forth in subsection (d) through the imposition of alternative service requirements.

(i) AGE REQUIREMENT.—The Secretary may make an agreement under this section only with a qualified student who will meet the age requirement for enlistment or commission in the Navy Reserve at the time of graduation from the academy.

(Pub. L. 109–304, §8(b), Oct. 6, 2006, 120 Stat. 1579; Pub. L. 109–163, div. A, title V, §515(g)(2)(A), Jan. 6, 2006, 119 Stat. 3236; Pub. L. 109–364, div. C, title XXXV, §3508, Oct. 17, 2006, 120 Stat. 2517; Pub. L. 110–181, div. C, title XXXV, §§3523(a)(1), (b), 3526(d), (g), Jan. 28, 2008, 122 Stat. 598, 600, 602; Pub. L. 110–417, div. C, title XXXV, §3503, Oct. 14, 2008, 122 Stat. 4762; Pub. L. 111–8, div. I, title I, §177, Mar. 11, 2009, 123 Stat. 944; Pub. L. 111–84, div. C, title XXXV, §3507, Oct. 28, 2009, 123 Stat. 2721; Pub. L. 114–92, div. C, title XXXV, §3507, Nov. 25, 2015, 129 Stat. 1221; Pub. L. 118–7, §2, June 30, 2023, 137 Stat. 52; Pub. L. 118–31, div. C, title XXXV, §3501(b), Dec. 22, 2023, 137 Stat. 808.)

§51510. DEFERMENT OF SERVICE OBLIGATION UNDER STUDENT INCENTIVE PAYMENT AGREEMENTS

The Secretary of Transportation may defer the service commitment of an individual under section 51509(d)(5) of this title (as specified in the agreement under section 51509) for not more than 2 years if the individual is engaged in a graduate course of study approved by the Secretary. However, deferment of service as a commissioned officer on active duty must be approved by the Secretary of the affected military department (or the Secretary of Commerce, for service with the National Oceanic and Atmospheric Administration).

(Pub. L. 109–304, §8(b), Oct. 6, 2006, 120 Stat. 1581.)

§51511. MIDSHIPMAN STATUS IN THE NAVY RESERVE

A citizen of the United States attending a State maritime academy may be appointed by the Secretary of the Navy as a midshipman in the Navy Reserve (including the Merchant Marine Reserve, Navy Reserve).

(Pub. L. 109–304, §8(b), Oct. 6, 2006, 120 Stat. 1582; Pub. L. 109–163, div. A, title V, §515(g)(2), Jan. 6, 2006, 119 Stat. 3236; Pub. L. 110–181, div. C, title XXXV, §3523(a)(1), (b), Jan. 28, 2008, 122 Stat. 598, 600.)

CHAPTER 517—OTHER SUPPORT FOR MERCHANT MARINE TRAINING

§51701. UNITED STATES MARITIME SERVICE

(a) GENERAL AUTHORITY.—The Secretary of Transportation may establish and maintain a voluntary organization, to be known as the United States Maritime Service, for the training of citizens of the United States to serve on merchant vessels of the United States and to perform functions to assist the United States merchant marine, as determined necessary by the Secretary.

(b) SPECIFIC AUTHORITY.—The Secretary may—

(1) determine the number of individuals to be enrolled for training and reserve purposes in the Service;

(2) fix the rates of pay and allowances of the individuals without regard to chapter 51 or subchapter III of chapter 53 of title 5;

(3) prescribe the course of study and the periods of training for the Service; and

(4) prescribe the uniform of the Service and the rules on providing and wearing the uniform.

(c) RANKS, GRADES, AND RATINGS.—The ranks, grades, and ratings for personnel of the Service shall be the same as those prescribed for personnel of the Coast Guard.

(d) MEDALS AND AWARDS.—The Secretary may establish and maintain a medals and awards program to recognize distinguished service, superior achievement, professional performance, and other commendable achievement by personnel of the Service.

(Pub. L. 109–304, §8(b), Oct. 6, 2006, 120 Stat. 1582; Pub. L. 109–163, div. C, title XXXV, §3509, Jan. 6, 2006, 119 Stat. 3557; Pub. L. 109–364, div. C, title XXXV, §3510(d)(1), Oct. 17, 2006, 120 Stat. 2520; Pub. L. 110–181, div. C, title XXXV, §3523(a)(4), (b), Jan. 28, 2008, 122 Stat. 599, 600.)

§51702. CIVILIAN NAUTICAL SCHOOLS

(a) DEFINITION.—In this section, the term "civilian nautical school" means a school operated in the United States (except the United States Merchant Marine Academy, a State maritime academy, or another school operated by the United States Government) that offers instruction to individuals quartered on a vessel primarily to train them for service in the merchant marine.

(b) INSPECTION.—Each civilian nautical school is subject to inspection by the Secretary of Transportation.

(c) RATING AND CERTIFICATION.—The Secretary may, under regulations the Secretary may prescribe, provide for the rating and certification of civilian nautical schools as to the adequacy of their course of instruction, the competence of their instructors, and the suitability of the equipment used in their course of instruction.

(Pub. L. 109–304, §8(b), Oct. 6, 2006, 120 Stat. 1582.)

§51703. ADDITIONAL TRAINING

(a) GENERAL AUTHORITY.—The Secretary of Transportation may provide additional training on maritime subjects to supplement other training opportunities and make the training available to the personnel of the merchant marine of the United States and individuals preparing for a career in the merchant marine of the United States.

(b) EQUIPMENT, SUPPLIES, AND CONTRACTS.—The Secretary may—

(1) prepare or buy equipment or supplies required for the additional training; and

(2) without regard to section 6101(b) to (d) of title 41, make contracts for services the Secretary considers necessary to prepare the equipment and supplies and to supervise and administer the additional training.

(Pub. L. 109–304, §8(b), Oct. 6, 2006, 120 Stat. 1583; Pub. L. 111–350, §5(n), Jan. 4, 2011, 124 Stat. 3853.)

§51704. TRAINING FOR MARITIME OIL POLLUTION PREVENTION, RESPONSE, AND CLEAN-UP

(a) ASSISTANCE IN ESTABLISHING PROGRAM.—The Secretary of Transportation shall assist maritime training institutions approved by the Secretary in establishing a training program for maritime oil pollution prevention, response, and clean-up.

(b) PROVIDING TRAINING VESSELS.—Subject to subsection (c), the Secretary may provide, with title free of all liens, to maritime training institutions that have a program established under subsection (a), offshore supply vessels and tug/supply vessels that were built in the United States and are in the possession of the Maritime Administration because of a default on a loan guaranteed under chapter 537 of this title.

(c) REQUIREMENTS.—In addition to any other requirements the Secretary considers appropriate, the following requirements apply to vessels provided under this section:

(1) The vessel shall be offered to the institution at a location selected by the Secretary.

(2) The institution shall use the vessel to train students and appropriate maritime industry personnel in oil spill prevention, response, clean-up, and related skills.

(3) The institution shall make the vessel and qualified students available to appropriate Federal, State, and local oil spill response authorities when there is a maritime oil spill.

(4) The institution may not sell, trade, charter, donate, scrap, or in any way alter or dispose of the vessel without prior approval of the Secretary.

(5) The institution may not use the vessel in competition with a privately-owned vessel documented under chapter 121 of this title or titled under the law of a State, unless necessary to carry out this section.

(6) When the institution can no longer use the vessel for its training program, the institution shall return the vessel to the Secretary. The Secretary shall take possession at the institution and thereafter may provide the vessel to another institution under this section or dispose of the vessel.

(Pub. L. 109–304, §8(b), Oct. 6, 2006, 120 Stat. 1583.)

§51705. TRAINING FOR USE OF FORCE AGAINST PIRACY

The Secretary of Transportation, in consultation with the Secretary of Defense and the Secretary of the department in which the Coast Guard is operating, shall certify a training curriculum for United States mariners on the use of force against pirates. The curriculum shall include—

(1) information on waters designated as high-risk waters by the Commandant of the Coast Guard;

(2) information on current threats and patterns of attack by pirates;

(3) tactics for defense of a vessel, including instruction on the types, use, and limitations of security equipment;

(4) standard rules for the use of force for self-defense as developed by the Secretary of the department in which the Coast Guard is operating under section 912(c) of the Coast Guard Authorization Act of 2010 (Public Law 111–281; 46 U.S.C. 8107 note), including instruction on firearm safety for crewmembers of vessels carrying cargo under section 55305 of this title; and

(5) procedures to follow to improve crewmember survivability if captured and taken hostage by pirates.

(Added Pub. L. 112–213, title V, §502(a), Dec. 20, 2012, 126 Stat. 1574.)

§51706. CENTERS OF EXCELLENCE FOR DOMESTIC MARITIME WORKFORCE TRAINING AND EDUCATION

(a) DESIGNATION.—

(1) IN GENERAL.—The Secretary of Transportation, after consultation with the Coast Guard, may designate, for a 5-year period, as a center of excellence for domestic maritime workforce training and education an entity which is a covered training entity.

(2) WITHDRAWAL OF DESIGNATION.—The Secretary of Transportation may withdraw a designation as a center of excellence for domestic maritime workforce training and education of a covered training entity upon discovery of adverse information, including discovery of information that the covered training entity has engaged in fraudulent or unlawful activities, or has been subjected to disciplinary or adverse administrative action by Federal, State, or other regulatory bodies.

(b) GRANT PROGRAM.—

(1) IN GENERAL.—The Secretary may award a maritime career training grant to a center of excellence designated under subsection (a) for the purpose of developing, offering, or improving career and technical education or training programs related to the United States maritime industry for United States workers.

(2) GRANT PROPOSAL.—To be eligible to receive a grant under this subsection, a center of excellence designated under subsection (a) shall submit to the Secretary a grant proposal that includes a detailed description of—

(A) the specific project proposed to be funded by the grant, including a description of the manner in which the grant will be used to develop, offer, or improve a career and technical education or training program that is suited to United States maritime industry workers;

(B) the extent to which the project for which the grant proposal is submitted will meet the educational or career training needs of United States maritime industry workers;

(C) any previous experience of the center of excellence in providing United States maritime industry career and technical education or training programs;

(D) how the project proposed to be funded by the grant would address shortcomings in existing educational or career training opportunities available to United States maritime industry workers; and

(E) the extent to which employers, including small and medium-sized firms, have demonstrated a commitment to employing United States maritime industry workers who would benefit from the project for which the grant proposal is submitted.

(3) CRITERIA FOR AWARD OF GRANTS.—Subject to the appropriation of funds to carry out this section, the Secretary shall award grants under this subsection to centers of excellence based on—

(A) an determination of the merits of a grant proposal submitted under paragraph (2) to develop, offer, or improve career and technical education or training programs to be made available to United States maritime industry workers;

(B) an evaluation of the likely employment opportunities available to United States maritime industry workers who complete a maritime career and technical education or training program that a center proposes to develop, offer, or improve; and

(C) an evaluation of prior demand for training programs by workers served by centers of excellence designated under subsection (a), as well as the availability and capacity of existing maritime training programs to meet future demand for training programs.

(4) COMPETITIVE AWARDS.—

(A) IN GENERAL.—The Secretary shall award grants under this subsection to centers of excellence designated under subsection (a) on a competitive basis.

(B) TIMING OF GRANT NOTICE.—The Secretary shall post a Notice of Funding Opportunity regarding grants awarded under this subsection not more than 90 days after the date of the enactment of the appropriations Act for the fiscal year concerned.

(C) TIMING OF GRANTS.—The Secretary shall award grants under this subsection not later than 270 days after the date of the enactment of the appropriations Act for the fiscal year concerned.

(D) REUSE OF UNEXPENDED GRANT FUNDS.—Notwithstanding subparagraph (C), amounts awarded as a grant under this subsection that are not expended by the grantee shall remain available to the Secretary for use for grants under this subsection.

(E) ADMINISTRATIVE COSTS.—Not more than 3 percent of amounts made available to carry out this subsection may be used for the necessary costs of grant administration.

(F) PROHIBITED USE.—A center of excellence designated under subsection (a) that has received funds awarded under section 54101(a)(2) for training purposes for a fiscal year shall not be eligible for grants under this subsection during the same fiscal year.

(5) ELIGIBLE USES OF GRANT FUNDS.—A center of excellence receiving a grant under this subsection shall—

(A) carry out activities that are identified as priorities for the purpose of developing, offering, or improving educational or career training programs for the United States maritime industry workforce; and

(B) provide training to upgrade the skills of the United States maritime industry workforce, including training to acquire covered requirements as well as technical skills training for jobs in the United States maritime industry.

(c) DEFINITIONS.—In this section,

(1) COVERED TRAINING ENTITY.—The term "covered training entity" means an entity that—

(A) is located in a State that borders on the—

(i) Gulf of Mexico;
(ii) Atlantic Ocean;
(iii) Long Island Sound;
(iv) Pacific Ocean;
(v) Great Lakes; or
(vi) Mississippi River System;

(B) is—

(i) a postsecondary educational institution (as such term is defined in section 3(39) of the Carl D. Perkins Career and Technical Education Act of 2006 (20 U.S.C. 2302));

(ii) a postsecondary vocational institution (as such term is defined in section 102(c) of the Higher Education Act of 1965 (20 U.S.C. 1002(c)); [1]

(iii) a public or private nonprofit entity that offers one or more other structured experiential learning training programs for United States workers in the United States maritime industry, including a program that is offered by a labor organization or conducted in partnership with a nonprofit organization or one or more employers in the United States maritime industry;

(iv) an entity sponsoring an apprenticeship program registered with the Office of Apprenticeship of the Employment and Training Administration of the Department of Labor or a State apprenticeship agency recognized by the Office of Apprenticeship pursuant to the Act of August 16, 1937 (commonly known as the 'National Apprenticeship Act'; 50 Stat. 664, chapter 663; 29 U.S.C. 50 et seq.); or

(v) a maritime training center designated prior to the date of enactment of the National Defense Authorization Act for Fiscal Year 2023;

(C) has a demonstrated record of success in maritime workforce training and education; and

(D) has—

(i) not been subject to a disciplinary or adverse administrative action by Federal, State, or other regulatory bodies;

(ii) no unresolved nonconformities from administrative audits by regulatory bodies; and

(iii) not been subject to any adverse criminal action by a Federal, State, or local law enforcement authority.

(2) ARCTIC.—The term "Arctic" has the meaning that term has under section 112 of the Arctic Research and Policy Act of 1984 (15 U.S.C. 4111).

(3) CAREER AND TECHNICAL EDUCATION.—The term "career and technical education" has the meaning given such term in section 3(5) of the Carl D. Perkins Career and Technical Education Act [2] (20 U.S.C. 2302).

(4) SECRETARY.—The term "Secretary" means the Secretary of Transportation.

(5) TRAINING PROGRAM.—The term "training program" means a program that provides training services, as described in section 134(c)(3)(D) of the Workforce Innovation and Opportunity Act (Public Law 113–128; 29 U.S.C. 3174).

(6) UNITED STATES MARITIME INDUSTRY.—The term "United States maritime industry" means the design, construction, repair, operation, manning, and supply of vessels in all segments of the maritime transportation system of the United States, including—

(A) the domestic and foreign trade;

(B) the coastal, offshore, and inland trade;

(C) non-commercial maritime activities, including—

(i) recreational boating; and

(ii) oceanographic and limnological research as described in section 2101(24).

(Added Pub. L. 115–91, div. C, title XXXV, §3507(a), Dec. 12, 2017, 131 Stat. 1914, §54102; renumbered §51706, Pub. L. 116–283, div. C, title XXXV, §3507(a), Jan. 1, 2021, 134 Stat. 4405; amended Pub. L. 117–263, div. C, title XXXV, §3532(a), Dec. 23, 2022, 136 Stat. 3089; Pub. L. 118–31, div. C, title XXXV, §3534(k), Dec. 22, 2023, 137 Stat. 834.)

---

[1] *So in original. Another closing parenthesis probably should precede the semicolon.*

[2] *The words "of 2006" probably should appear. See subsec. (c)(1)(B)(i).*

§51707. MERCHANT MARINER RECRUITMENT, TRAINING, AND RETENTION STRATEGIC PLAN

(a) [1] STRATEGIC PLAN.—

(1) IN GENERAL.—Not later than one year after the date of the enactment of this section, and at least once every five years thereafter until the termination date under paragraph (6), the Secretary of Transportation, acting through the Administrator of the Maritime Administration, shall publish in the Federal Register a plan to recruit, train, and retain merchant mariners for the five-year period following the date of publication of the most recently published plan under this paragraph.

(2) CONTENTS.—A plan published under paragraph (1) shall contain—

(A) a strategy to address merchant mariner recruitment, training, and retention issues in the United States; and

(B) demonstration and research priorities concerning merchant mariner recruitment, training, and retention.

(3) FACTORS.—In developing a plan under paragraph (1), the Secretary shall take into account, at a minimum—
    (A) the availability of existing research (as of the date of publication of the plan); and
    (B) the need to ensure results that have broad applicability for the United States merchant marine workforce development.

(4) CONSULTATION.—In developing a plan under paragraph (1), the Secretary shall consult with representatives of the maritime industry, labor organizations, including the Commander of the Transportation Command and the Commander of the Military Sealift Command, and other governmental entities and stakeholders in the maritime industry.

(5) TRANSMITTAL TO CONGRESS.—The Secretary shall transmit copies of any plan published under paragraph (1) to the Committee on Transportation and Infrastructure of the House of Representatives and the Committee on Commerce, Science, and Transportation of the Senate.

(6) TERMINATION DATE.—The requirement to publish a plan under this paragraph shall terminate on the date that the Administrator of the Maritime Administration determines that there is an adequate number of United States mariners for sustained strategic sealift.

(Added Pub. L. 116–283, div. C, title XXXV, §3508(a), Jan. 1, 2021, 134 Stat. 4405.)

---

[1] So in original. No subsec. (b) has been enacted.

CHAPTER 519—MERCHANT MARINE AWARDS

[1] So in original. Probably should be followed by a period.

§51901. AWARDS FOR INDIVIDUAL ACTS OR SERVICE

(a) GENERAL AUTHORITY.—The Secretary of Transportation may award decorations and medals of appropriate design (including ribbons, ribbon bars, emblems, rosettes, miniature facsimiles, plaques, citations, or other suitable devices or insignia) for individual acts or service in the merchant marine of the United States. The design may be similar to the design of a decoration or medal authorized for members of the armed forces for similar acts or service.

(b) SPECIFIC AUTHORITY.—The Secretary may award—

(1) a Merchant Marine Distinguished Service Medal to an individual for outstanding acts, conduct, or valor beyond the line of duty;

(2) a Merchant Marine Meritorious Service Medal to an individual for meritorious acts, conduct, or valor in the line of duty, but not of the outstanding character that would warrant the award of the Merchant Marine Distinguished Service Medal;

(3) a decoration or medal to an individual for service during a war, national emergency proclaimed by the President or Congress, or operations by the armed forces outside the continental United States under conditions of danger to life and property; and

(4) a decoration or medal to an individual for other acts or service of conspicuous gallantry, intrepidity, and extraordinary heroism under conditions of danger to life and property that would warrant a similar decoration or medal for a member of the armed forces.

(Pub. L. 109–304, §8(b), Oct. 6, 2006, 120 Stat. 1584.)

§51902. GALLANT SHIP AWARD

(a) AWARDS TO VESSELS.—The Secretary of Transportation may award a Gallant Ship Award and a citation to a vessel (including a foreign vessel) participating in outstanding or gallant action in a marine disaster or other emergency to save life or property at sea. The Secretary may award a plaque to the vessel, and a replica of the plaque may be preserved as a permanent historical record.

(b) AWARDS TO CREWS.—The Secretary of Transportation may award an appropriate citation ribbon bar to the master and each individual serving, at the time of the action, on a vessel issued an award under subsection (a).

(c) CONSULTATION.—The Secretary of Transportation shall consult with the Secretary of State before awarding an award or citation to a foreign vessel or its crew under this section.

(Pub. L. 109–304, §8(b), Oct. 6, 2006, 120 Stat. 1584.)

§51903. MULTIPLE AWARDS

An individual may not be awarded more than one of any type of decoration or medal under this chapter. For each succeeding act or service justifying the same decoration or medal, a suitable device may be awarded to be worn with the decoration or medal.

(Pub. L. 109–304, §8(b), Oct. 6, 2006, 120 Stat. 1585.)

§51904. PRESENTATION TO REPRESENTATIVES

If an individual to be issued an award under this chapter is unable to accept the award personally, the Secretary of Transportation may present the award to an appropriate representative.

(Pub. L. 109–304, §8(b), Oct. 6, 2006, 120 Stat. 1585.)

§51905. FLAGS AND GRAVE MARKERS

Except as authorized under another law, the Secretary of Transportation may issue, at no cost, a flag of the United States and a grave marker to the family or personal representative of a deceased individual who served in the merchant marine of the United States in support of the armed forces of the United States or its allies during a war or national emergency.

(Pub. L. 109–304, §8(b), Oct. 6, 2006, 120 Stat. 1585.)

§51906. SPECIAL CERTIFICATES FOR CIVILIAN SERVICE TO ARMED FORCES

(a) GENERAL AUTHORITY.—The Maritime Administrator may issue a special certificate to an individual, or the personal representative of an individual, in recognition of service of that individual in the merchant marine of the United States, if the service has been determined to be active duty under section 401 of the GI Bill Improvement Act of 1977 (Public Law 95–202; 38 U.S.C. 106 note).

(b) RELATIONSHIP TO OTHER LAWS.—Issuance of a certificate under subsection (a) does not entitle an individual to any rights, privileges, or benefits under a law of the United States.

(Pub. L. 109–304, §8(b), Oct. 6, 2006, 120 Stat. 1585.)

§51907. PROVISION OF DECORATIONS, MEDALS, AND REPLACEMENTS

The Secretary of Transportation may provide—

(1) the decorations and medals authorized by this chapter and replacements for those decorations and medals; and

(2) replacements for decorations and medals issued under a prior law.

(Pub. L. 109–304, §8(b), Oct. 6, 2006, 120 Stat. 1585; Pub. L. 109–163, div. C, title XXXV, §3510, Jan. 6,

2006, 119 Stat. 3557; Pub. L. 110–181, div. C, title XXXV, §3523(a)(5)(A), (b), Jan. 28, 2008, 122 Stat. 599, 600.)

§51908. PROHIBITION AGAINST UNAUTHORIZED MANUFACTURE, SALE, POSSESSION, OR DISPLAY OF AWARDS

(a) PROHIBITION.—Except as authorized by this chapter or the Secretary of Transportation, a person may not manufacture, sell, possess, or display a decoration or medal provided for in this chapter.

(b) CIVIL PENALTY.—A person violating this section is liable to the United States Government for a civil penalty of not more than $2,000.

(Pub. L. 109–304, §8(b), Oct. 6, 2006, 120 Stat. 1585; Pub. L. 109–364, div. C, title XXXV, §3510(b), Oct. 17, 2006, 120 Stat. 2520; Pub. L. 110–181, div. C, title XXXV, §3526(e), (g), Jan. 28, 2008, 122 Stat. 602.)

CHAPTER 521—MISCELLANEOUS

Sec.
52101.   Reemployment rights for certain merchant seamen.

§52101. REEMPLOYMENT RIGHTS FOR CERTAIN MERCHANT SEAMEN

(a) IN GENERAL.—An individual who is certified by the Secretary of Transportation under subsection (c) shall be entitled to reemployment rights and other benefits substantially equivalent to the rights and benefits provided for by chapter 43 of title 38 for any member of a reserve component of the armed forces of the United States who is ordered to active duty.

(b) TIME FOR APPLICATION.—An individual may submit an application for certification under subsection (c) to the Secretary not later than 45 days after the date the individual completes a period of employment described in subsection (c)(1)(A) with respect to which the application is submitted.

(c) CERTIFICATION DETERMINATION.—Not later than 20 days after the date the Secretary receives from an individual an application for certification under this subsection, the Secretary shall—

(1) determine whether the individual—

(A) was employed in the activation or operation of a vessel—

(i) in the National Defense Reserve Fleet maintained under section 57100 in a period in which the vessel was in use or being activated for use under subsection (b) of that section;

(ii) requisitioned or purchased under chapter 563 of this title; or

(iii) owned, chartered, or controlled by the United States Government and used by the Government for a war, armed conflict, national emergency, or maritime mobilization need (including for training purposes or testing for readiness and suitability for mission performance); and

(B) during the period of that employment, possessed a valid license, certificate of registry, or merchant mariner's document issued under chapter 71 or 73 of this title; and

(2) if the Secretary makes affirmative determinations under subparagraphs (A) and (B) of paragraph (1), certify that individual under this subsection.

(d) EQUIVALENCE TO MILITARY SELECTIVE SERVICE ACT CERTIFICATE.—For purposes of reemployment rights and benefits provided by this section, a certification under subsection (c) shall be considered to be the equivalent of a certificate described in section 9(a) of the Military Selective Service Act (50 U.S.C. 3808(a)).

(Pub. L. 109–304, §8(b), Oct. 6, 2006, 120 Stat. 1585; Pub. L. 115–91, div. C, title XXXV, §3502(b)(4), Dec. 12, 2017, 131 Stat. 1910; Pub. L. 115–232, div. C, title XXXV, §3546(m), Aug. 13, 2018, 132 Stat. 2327.)

PART C—FINANCIAL ASSISTANCE PROGRAMS

CHAPTER 531—MARITIME SECURITY FLEET

§53101. DEFINITIONS

In this chapter:

(1) BULK CARGO.—The term "bulk cargo" means cargo that is loaded and carried in bulk without mark or count.

(2) CONTRACTOR.—The term "contractor" means an owner or operator of a vessel that enters into an operating agreement for the vessel with the Secretary under section 53103.

(3) FLEET.—The term "Fleet" means the Maritime Security Fleet established under section 53102(a).

(4) FOREIGN COMMERCE.—The term "foreign commerce" means—

(A) commerce or trade between the United States, its territories or possessions, or the District of Columbia, and a foreign country; and

(B) commerce or trade between foreign countries.

(5) PARTICIPATING FLEET VESSEL.—The term "participating fleet vessel" means any vessel that—

(A) on October 1, 2015—

(i) meets the requirements of paragraph (1), (2), (3), or (4) of section 53102(c); and

(ii) is less than 20 years of age if the vessel is a tank vessel, or is less than 25 years of age for all other vessel types; and

(B) on December 31, 2014, is covered by an operating agreement under this chapter.

(6) PERSON.—The term "person" includes corporations, partnerships, and associations existing under or authorized by the laws of the United States, or any State, Territory, District, or possession thereof, or of any foreign country.

(7) PRODUCT TANK VESSEL.—The term "product tank vessel" means a double hulled tank vessel capable of carrying simultaneously more than 2 separated grades of refined petroleum products.

(8) SECRETARY.—The term "Secretary" means the Secretary of Transportation.

(9) TANK VESSEL.—The term "tank vessel" has the meaning that term has under section 2101 of this title.

(10) UNITED STATES.—The term "United States" includes the District of Columbia, the Commonwealth of Puerto Rico, the Northern Mariana Islands, Guam, American Samoa, the Virgin Islands.

(11) UNITED STATES CITIZEN TRUST.—(A) Subject to subparagraph (C), the term "United States citizen trust" means a trust that is qualified under this paragraph.

(B) A trust is qualified under this paragraph with respect to a vessel only if—

(i) each of the trustees is a citizen of the United States; and

(ii) the application for documentation of the vessel under chapter 121 of this title includes the affidavit of each trustee stating that the trustee is not aware of any reason involving a beneficiary of the trust that is not a citizen of the United States, or involving any other person that is not a citizen of the United States, as a result of which the beneficiary or other person would hold more than 25 percent of the aggregate power to influence or limit the exercise of the authority of the trustee with respect to matters involving any ownership or operation of the vessel that may adversely affect the interests of the United States.

(C) If any person that is not a citizen of the United States has authority to direct or participate in directing a trustee for a trust in matters involving any ownership or operation of the vessel that may adversely affect the interests of the United States or in removing a trustee for a trust without cause, either directly or indirectly through the control of another person, the trust is not qualified under this paragraph unless the trust instrument provides that persons who are not citizens of the United States may not hold more than 25 percent of the aggregate authority to so direct or remove a trustee.

(D) This paragraph shall not be considered to prohibit a person who is not a citizen of the United States from holding more than 25 percent of the beneficial interest in a trust.

(12) UNITED STATES-DOCUMENTED VESSEL.—The term "United States-documented vessel" means a vessel documented under chapter 121 of this title.

(Added Pub. L. 108–136, div. C, title XXXV, §3531(a), Nov. 24, 2003, 117 Stat. 1803; amended Pub. L. 112–239, div. C, title XXXV, §3508(a), Jan. 2, 2013, 126 Stat. 2223.)

§53102. ESTABLISHMENT OF MARITIME SECURITY FLEET

(a) IN GENERAL.—The Secretary of Transportation, in consultation with the Secretary of Defense, shall establish a fleet of active, commercially viable, militarily useful, privately owned vessels to meet national defense and other security requirements and maintain a United States presence in international commercial shipping. The Fleet shall consist of privately owned, United States-documented vessels for which there are in effect operating agreements under this chapter, and shall be known as the Maritime Security Fleet.

(b) VESSEL ELIGIBILITY.—A vessel is eligible to be included in the Fleet if—

(1) the vessel meets the requirements of paragraph (1), (2), (3), or (4) of subsection (c);

(2) the vessel is operated (or in the case of a vessel to be constructed, will be operated) in providing transportation in foreign commerce;

(3) the vessel is self-propelled and—

(A) is a tank vessel that is 10 years of age or less on the date the vessel is included in the Fleet; or

(B) is any other type of vessel that is 15 years of age or less on the date the vessel is included in the Fleet;

(4) the vessel—

(A) is suitable for use by the United States for national defense or military purposes in time of war or national emergency, as determined by the Secretary of Defense; and

(B) is commercially viable, as determined by the Secretary; and

(5) the vessel—

(A) is a United States-documented vessel; or

(B) is not a United States-documented vessel, but—

(i) the owner of the vessel has demonstrated an intent to have the vessel documented under chapter 121 of this title if it is included in the Fleet; and

(ii) at the time an operating agreement for the vessel is entered into under this chapter, the vessel is eligible for documentation under chapter 121 of this title.

(c) REQUIREMENTS REGARDING CITIZENSHIP OF OWNERS, CHARTERERS, AND OPERATORS.—

(1) VESSEL OWNED AND OPERATED BY SECTION 50501 CITIZENS.—A vessel meets the requirements of this paragraph if, during the period of an operating agreement under this chapter that applies to the vessel, the vessel will be owned and operated by one or more persons that are citizens of the United States under section 50501 of this title.

(2) VESSEL OWNED BY SECTION 50501 CITIZEN OR UNITED STATES CITIZEN TRUST, AND CHARTERED TO DOCUMENTATION CITIZEN.—A vessel meets the requirements of this paragraph if—

(A) during the period of an operating agreement under this chapter that applies to the vessel, the vessel will be—

(i) owned by a person that is a citizen of the United States under section 50501 of this title or that is a United States citizen trust; and

(ii) demise chartered to a person—

(I) that is eligible to document the vessel under chapter 121 of this title;

(II) the chairman of the board of directors, chief executive officer, and a majority of the members of the board of directors of which are citizens of the United States under section 50501 of this title, and are appointed and subjected to removal only upon approval by the Secretary; and

(III) that certifies to the Secretary that there are no treaties, statutes, regulations, or other laws that would prohibit the contractor for the vessel from performing its obligations under an operating agreement under this chapter;

(B) in the case of a vessel that will be demise chartered to a person that is owned or controlled by another person that is not a citizen of the United States under section 50501 of this title, the other person enters into an agreement with the Secretary not to influence the operation of the vessel in a manner that will adversely affect the interests of the United States; and

(C) the Secretary and the Secretary of Defense notify the Committee on Armed Services and the Committee on Commerce, Science, and Transportation of the Senate and the Committee on Armed Services of the House of Representatives that they concur with the certification required under subparagraph (A)(ii)(III), and have reviewed and agree that there are no other legal, operational, or other impediments that would prohibit the contractor for the vessel from performing its obligations under an operating agreement under this chapter.

(3) VESSEL OWNED AND OPERATED BY DEFENSE CONTRACTOR.—A vessel meets the requirements of this paragraph if—

(A) during the period of an operating agreement under this chapter that applies to the vessel, the vessel will be owned and operated by a person that—

(i) is eligible to document a vessel under chapter 121 of this title;

(ii) operates or manages other United States-documented vessels for the Secretary of Defense, or charters other vessels to the Secretary of Defense;

(iii) has entered into a special security agreement for purposes of this paragraph with the Secretary of Defense;

(iv) makes the certification described in paragraph (2)(A)(ii)(III); and

(v) in the case of a vessel described in paragraph (2)(B), enters into an agreement referred to in that paragraph; and

(B) the Secretary and the Secretary of Defense notify the Committee on Armed Services and the Committee on Commerce, Science, and Transportation of the Senate and the Committee on Armed Services of the House of Representatives that they concur with the certification required under subparagraph (A)(iv), and have reviewed and agree that there are no other legal, operational, or other impediments that would prohibit the contractor for the vessel from performing its obligations under an operating agreement under this chapter.

(4) VESSEL OWNED BY DOCUMENTATION CITIZEN AND CHARTERED TO SECTION 50501 CITIZEN.—A vessel meets the requirements of this paragraph if, during the period of an operating agreement under this chapter that applies to the vessel, the vessel will be—

(A) owned by a person that is eligible to document a vessel under chapter 121 of this title; and

(B) demise chartered to a person that is a citizen of the United States under section 50501 of this title.

(d) REQUEST BY SECRETARY OF DEFENSE.—The Secretary of Defense shall request the Secretary of Homeland Security to issue any waiver under section 501 of this title that is necessary for purposes of this chapter.

(e) VESSEL STANDARDS.—

(1) CERTIFICATE OF INSPECTION.—A vessel used to provide oceangoing transportation which the Secretary of the department in which the Coast Guard is operating determines meets the criteria of subsection (b) of this section but which, on the date of enactment of the Maritime Security Act of 2003, is not documented under chapter 121 of this title, shall be eligible for a certificate of inspection if the Secretary determines that—

(A) the vessel is classed by and designed in accordance with the rules of the American Bureau of Shipping, or another classification society accepted by the Secretary;

(B) the vessel complies with applicable international agreements and associated guidelines, as determined by the country in which the vessel was documented immediately before becoming documented under chapter 121; and

(C) that country has not been identified by the Secretary as inadequately enforcing international vessel regulations as to that vessel.

(2) CONTINUED ELIGIBILITY FOR CERTIFICATE.—Paragraph (1) does not apply to a vessel after any date on which the vessel fails to comply with the applicable international agreements and associated guidelines referred to in paragraph (1)(B).

(3) RELIANCE ON CLASSIFICATION SOCIETY.—

(A) IN GENERAL.—The Secretary may rely on a certification from the American Bureau of Shipping or, subject to subparagraph (B), another classification society accepted by the Secretary to establish that a vessel is in compliance with the requirements of paragraphs (1) and (2).

(B) FOREIGN CLASSIFICATION SOCIETY.—The Secretary may accept certification from a foreign classification society under subparagraph (A) only—

(i) to the extent that the government of the foreign country in which the society is headquartered provides access on a reciprocal basis to the American Bureau of Shipping; and

(ii) if the foreign classification society has offices and maintains records in the United States.

(f) AUTHORITY TO WAIVE AGE RESTRICTION FOR ELIGIBILITY OF A VESSEL TO BE INCLUDED IN FLEET.—The Secretary of Defense, in conjunction with the Secretary of Transportation, may waive the application of an age restriction under subsection (b)(3) if the Secretaries jointly determine that the waiver—

(1) is in the national interest;

(2) is appropriate to allow the maintenance of the economic viability of the vessel and any associated operating network; and

(3) is necessary due to the lack of availability of other vessels and operators that comply with the requirements of this chapter.

(g) AUTHORITY TO EXTEND MAXIMUM SERVICE AGE FOR VESSEL.—The Secretary of Defense, in conjunction with the Secretary of Transportation, may, for a particular participating fleet vessel, treat the ages specified in section 53101(5)(A)(ii) and section

53106(c)(3) as increased by up to 5 years if the Secretaries jointly determine that it is in the national interest to do so.

(Added Pub. L. 108–136, div. C, title XXXV, §3531(a), Nov. 24, 2003, 117 Stat. 1805; amended Pub. L. 109–304, §13(a)(1), Oct. 6, 2006, 120 Stat. 1700; Pub. L. 112–239, div. C, title XXXV, §3508(b), Jan. 2, 2013, 126 Stat. 2223; Pub. L. 114–328, div. C, title XXXV, §3502(a), Dec. 23, 2016, 130 Stat. 2774.)

§53103. AWARD OF OPERATING AGREEMENTS

(a) IN GENERAL.—The Secretary shall require, as a condition of including any vessel in the Fleet, that the person that is the owner or operator of the vessel for purposes of section 53102(c) enter into an operating agreement with the Secretary under this section.

(b) EXTENSION OF EXISTING OPERATING AGREEMENTS.—

(1) OFFER TO EXTEND.—Not later than 60 days after the date of enactment of this paragraph, the Secretary shall offer, to an existing contractor, to extend, through September 30, 2035, an operating agreement that is in existence on the date of enactment of this paragraph. The terms and conditions of the extended operating agreement shall include terms and conditions authorized under this chapter, as amended from time to time.

(2) TIME LIMIT.—An existing contractor shall have not later than 120 days after the date the Secretary offers to extend an operating agreement to agree to the extended operating agreement.

(3) SUBSEQUENT AWARD.—The Secretary may award an operating agreement to an applicant that is eligible to enter into an operating agreement for fiscal years 2016 through 2035 if the existing contractor does not agree to the extended operating agreement under paragraph (2).

(c) PROCEDURE FOR AWARDING NEW OPERATING AGREEMENTS.—The Secretary may enter into a new operating agreement with an applicant that meets the requirements of section 53102(c) (for vessels that meet the qualifications of section 53102(b)) on the basis of priority for vessel type established by military requirements of the Secretary of Defense. The Secretary shall allow an applicant at least 30 days to submit an application for a new operating agreement. After consideration of military requirements, priority shall be given to an applicant that is a United States citizen under section 50501 of this title. The Secretary may not approve an application without the consent of the Secretary of Defense. The Secretary shall enter into an operating agreement with the applicant or provide a written reason for denying the application.

(d) LIMITATION.—The Secretary may not award operating agreements under this chapter that require payments under section 53106 for a fiscal year for more than 60 vessels.

(Added Pub. L. 108–136, div. C, title XXXV, §3531(a), Nov. 24, 2003, 117 Stat. 1808; amended Pub. L. 109–304, §13(a)(2), Oct. 6, 2006, 120 Stat. 1700; Pub. L. 109–364, div. C, title XXXV, §3502(b)(1), Oct. 17, 2006, 120 Stat. 2515; Pub. L. 112–239, div. C, title XXXV, §3508(c), Jan. 2, 2013, 126 Stat. 2224; Pub. L. 116–92, div. C, title XXXV, §3502(a), Dec. 20, 2019, 133 Stat. 1969.)

§53104. EFFECTIVENESS OF OPERATING AGREEMENTS

(a) EFFECTIVENESS, GENERALLY.—The Secretary may enter into an operating agreement under this chapter for fiscal year 2006. Except as provided in subsection (b), the agreement shall be effective only for 1 fiscal year, but shall be renewable, subject to the availability of appropriations, for each subsequent fiscal year through the end of fiscal year 2035.

(b) VESSELS UNDER CHARTER TO UNITED STATES.—Unless an earlier date is requested by the applicant, the effective date for an operating agreement with respect to a vessel that is, on the date of entry into an operating agreement, on charter to the United States Government, other than a charter pursuant to an Emergency Preparedness Agreement under section 53107, shall be the expiration or termination date of the Government charter covering the vessel, or any earlier date the vessel is withdrawn from that charter.

(c) TERMINATION.—

(1) TERMINATION BY SECRETARY.—If the contractor with respect to an operating agreement materially fails to comply with the terms of the agreement—

(A) the Secretary shall notify the contractor and provide a reasonable opportunity to comply with the operating agreement;

(B) the Secretary shall terminate the operating agreement if the contractor fails to achieve such compliance; and

(C) upon such termination, any funds obligated by the agreement shall be available to the Secretary to carry out this chapter.

(2) EARLY TERMINATION BY CONTRACTOR, GENERALLY.—An operating agreement under this chapter shall terminate on a date specified by the contractor if the contractor notifies the Secretary, by not later than 60 days before the effective date of the termination, that the contractor intends to terminate the agreement.

(d) NONRENEWAL FOR LACK OF FUNDS.—If, by the first day of a fiscal year, sufficient funds have not been appropriated under the authority provided by this chapter for that fiscal year, then the Secretary shall notify the Committee on Armed Services and the Committee on Commerce, Science, and Transportation of the Senate and the Committee on Armed Services of the House of Representatives that operating agreements authorized under this chapter for which sufficient funds are not available will not be renewed for that fiscal year if sufficient funds are not appropriated by the 60th day of that fiscal year.

(e) RELEASE OF VESSELS FROM OBLIGATIONS.—If funds are not appropriated for payments under an operating agreement under this chapter for any fiscal year by the 60th day of that fiscal year, then—

(1) each vessel covered by the operating agreement is thereby released from any further obligation under the operating agreement;

(2) the owner or operator of the vessel may transfer and register such vessel under a foreign registry that is acceptable to the Secretary of Transportation and the Secretary of Defense, notwithstanding section 56101 of this title; and

(3) if chapter 563 of this title is applicable to such vessel after registration of the vessel under such a registry, then the vessel is available to be requisitioned by the Secretary of Transportation pursuant to chapter 563.

(Added Pub. L. 108–136, div. C, title XXXV, §3531(a), Nov. 24, 2003, 117 Stat. 1810; amended Pub. L.

109–304, §13(a)(3), Oct. 6, 2006, 120 Stat. 1701; Pub. L. 111–383, div. C, title XXXV, §3502(1), Jan. 7, 2011, 124 Stat. 4518; Pub. L. 112–239, div. C, title XXXV, §3508(d), Jan. 2, 2013, 126 Stat. 2224; Pub. L. 116–92, div. C, title XXXV, §3502(b), Dec. 20, 2019, 133 Stat. 1969.)

§53105. OBLIGATIONS AND RIGHTS UNDER OPERATING AGREEMENTS

(a) OPERATION OF VESSEL.—An operating agreement under this chapter shall require that, during the period a vessel is operating under the agreement—

(1) the vessel—

(A) shall be operated exclusively in the foreign commerce or, except as provided in paragraph (2), in mixed foreign commerce and domestic trade allowed under a registry endorsement issued under section 12111 of this title; and

(B) shall not otherwise be operated in the coastwise trade;

(2) in the case of a vessel, other than a replacement vessel under subsection (f), first covered by an operating agreement after the date of the enactment of the National Defense Authorization Act for Fiscal Year 2018, the vessel shall not be operated in the transportation of cargo between points in the United States and its territories either directly or via a foreign port; and

(3) the vessel shall be documented under chapter 121 of this title.

(b) ANNUAL PAYMENTS BY SECRETARY.—

(1) IN GENERAL.—An operating agreement under this chapter shall require, subject to the availability of appropriations, that the Secretary make a payment each fiscal year to the contractor in accordance with section 53106.

(2) OPERATING AGREEMENT IS OBLIGATION OF UNITED STATES GOVERNMENT.—An operating agreement under this chapter constitutes a contractual obligation of the United States Government to pay the amounts provided for in the agreement to the extent of actual appropriations.

(c) DOCUMENTATION REQUIREMENT.—Each vessel covered by an operating agreement (including an agreement terminated under section 53104(c)(2)) shall remain documented under chapter 121 of this title, until the date the operating agreement would terminate according to its terms.

(d) NATIONAL SECURITY REQUIREMENTS.—

(1) IN GENERAL.—A contractor with respect to an operating agreement (including an agreement terminated under section 53104(c)(2)) shall continue to be bound by the provisions of section 53107 until the date the operating agreement would terminate according to its terms.

(2) EMERGENCY PREPAREDNESS AGREEMENT.—All terms and conditions of an Emergency Preparedness Agreement entered into under section 53107 shall remain in effect until the date the operating agreement would terminate according to its terms, except that the terms of such Emergency Preparedness Agreement may be modified by the mutual consent of the contractor, the Secretary of Transportation, and the Secretary of Defense.

(e) TRANSFER OF OPERATING AGREEMENTS.—A contractor under an operating agreement may transfer the agreement (including all rights and obligations under the operating agreement) to any person that is eligible to enter into the operating agreement under this chapter if the Secretary and the Secretary of Defense determine that the transfer is in the best interests of the United States. A transaction shall not be considered a transfer of an operating agreement if the same legal entity with the same vessels remains the contracting party under the operating agreement.

(f) REPLACEMENT VESSELS.—A contractor may replace a vessel under an operating agreement with another vessel that is eligible to be included in the Fleet under section 53102(b), if the Secretary, in conjunction with the Secretary of Defense, approves the replacement of the vessel.

(Added Pub. L. 108–136, div. C, title XXXV, §3531(a), Nov. 24, 2003, 117 Stat. 1812; amended Pub. L. 109–304, §13(a)(4), Oct. 6, 2006, 120 Stat. 1701; Pub. L. 109–364, div. C, title XXXV, §3502(a), Oct. 17, 2006, 120 Stat. 2514; Pub. L. 110–181, div. C, title XXXV, §3526(f), Jan. 28, 2008, 122 Stat. 602; Pub. L. 112–239, div. C, title XXXV, §3508(e), Jan. 2, 2013, 126 Stat. 2225; Pub. L. 115–91, div. C, title XXXV, §3503(a), Dec. 12, 2017, 131 Stat. 1911.)

§53106. PAYMENTS

(a) ANNUAL PAYMENT.—

(1) IN GENERAL.—The Secretary, subject to the availability of appropriations and the other provisions of this section, shall pay to the contractor for an operating agreement, for each vessel that is covered by the operating agreement, an amount equal to—

(A) $5,000,000 for each of fiscal years 2018, 2019, and 2020;

(B) $8,233,463 for fiscal year 2021;

(C) $5,300,000 for each of fiscal years 2022, 2023, 2024, and 2025;

(D) $5,800,000 for each of fiscal years 2026, 2027, and 2028;

(E) $6,300,000 for each of fiscal years 2029, 2030, and 2031; and

(F) $6,800,000 for each of fiscal years 2032, 2033, 2034, and 2035.

(2) TIMING.—The amount shall be paid in equal monthly installments at the end of each month. The amount shall not be reduced except as provided by this section or section 51307(b).

(b) CERTIFICATION REQUIRED FOR PAYMENT.—As a condition of receiving payment under this section for a fiscal year for a vessel, the contractor for the vessel shall certify, in accordance with regulations issued by the Secretary, that the vessel has been and will be operated in accordance with paragraph (1) and (2) of section 53105(a), as otherwise applicable with respect to such vessel, for at least 320 days in the fiscal year. Days during which the vessel is drydocked, surveyed, inspected, or repaired shall be considered days of operation for purposes of this subsection.

(c) GENERAL LIMITATIONS.—The Secretary of Transportation shall not make any payment under this chapter for a vessel with respect to any days for which the vessel is—

(1) under a charter to the United States Government, other than a charter pursuant to

an Emergency Preparedness Agreement under section 53107;

(2) not operated or maintained in accordance with an operating agreement under this chapter; or

(3) more than—

(A) 25 years of age, except as provided in subparagraph (B); or

(B) 20 years of age, in the case of a tank vessel.

(d) REDUCTIONS IN PAYMENTS.—With respect to payments under this chapter for a vessel covered by an operating agreement, the Secretary—

(1) except as provided in paragraph (2), shall not reduce any payment for the operation of the vessel to carry military or other preference cargoes under section 55302(a), 55304, 55305, or 55314 of this title, section 2631 of title 10, or any other cargo preference law of the United States;

(2) shall not make any payment for any day that the vessel is engaged in transporting more than 7,500 tons of civilian bulk preference cargoes pursuant to section 55302(a), 55305, or 55314 of this title that is bulk cargo; and

(3) shall make a pro rata reduction in payment for each day less than 320 in a fiscal year that the vessel is not operated in accordance with paragraph (1) and (2) of section 53105(a), as otherwise applicable with respect to such vessel, with days during which the vessel is drydocked or undergoing survey, inspection, or repair considered to be days on which the vessel is operated.

(e) LIMITATION REGARDING NONCONTIGUOUS DOMESTIC TRADE.—

(1) IN GENERAL.—No contractor shall receive payments pursuant to this chapter during a period in which it participates in noncontiguous domestic trade.

(2) LIMITATION ON APPLICATION.—Paragraph (1) shall not apply to any person that is a citizen of the United States within the meaning of section 50501 of this title, applying the 75 percent ownership requirement of that section.

(3) PARTICIPATES IN A NONCONTIGUOUS DOMESTIC TRADE DEFINED.—In this subsection the term "participates in a noncontiguous domestic trade" means directly or indirectly owns, charters, or operates a vessel engaged in transportation of cargo between a point in the contiguous 48 States and a point in Alaska, Hawaii, or Puerto Rico, other than a point in Alaska north of the Arctic Circle.

(Added Pub. L. 108–136, div. C, title XXXV, §3531(a), Nov. 24, 2003, 117 Stat. 1813; amended Pub. L. 109–304, §13(a)(5), Oct. 6, 2006, 120 Stat. 1701; Pub. L. 109–364, div. C, title XXXV, §3502(c), Oct. 17, 2006, 120 Stat. 2516; Pub. L. 111–383, div. C, title XXXV, §3502(2), Jan. 7, 2011, 124 Stat. 4518; Pub. L. 112–239, div. C, title XXXV, §3508(f), Jan. 2, 2013, 126 Stat. 2225; Pub. L. 114–113, div. O, title I, §101(e)(1), Dec. 18, 2015, 129 Stat. 2988; Pub. L. 114–328, div. C, title XXXV, §3502(b), Dec. 23, 2016, 130 Stat. 2775; Pub. L. 115–91, div. C, title XXXV, §3503(b), Dec. 12, 2017, 131 Stat. 1911; Pub. L. 115–232, div. C, title XXXV, §3546(o), Aug. 13, 2018, 132 Stat. 2327; Pub. L. 116–92, div. C, title XXXV, §3502(c), Dec. 20, 2019, 133 Stat. 1969; Pub. L. 116–283, div. C, title XXXV, §3501(b), Jan. 1, 2021, 134 Stat. 4397; Pub. L. 117–263, div. C, title XXXV, §3517(b)(1), Dec. 23, 2022, 136 Stat. 3074.)

§53107. NATIONAL SECURITY REQUIREMENTS

(a) EMERGENCY PREPAREDNESS AGREEMENT REQUIRED.—The Secretary shall establish an

Emergency Preparedness Program under this section that is approved by the Secretary of Defense. Under the program, the Secretary, in conjunction with the Secretary of Defense, shall include in each operating agreement under this chapter a requirement that the contractor enter into an Emergency Preparedness Agreement under this section with the Secretary. The Secretary shall negotiate and enter into an Emergency Preparedness Agreement with each contractor as promptly as practicable after the contractor has entered into an operating agreement under this chapter.

(b) TERMS OF AGREEMENT.—

(1) IN GENERAL.—An Emergency Preparedness Agreement under this section shall require that a contractor for a vessel covered by an operating agreement under this chapter shall make commercial transportation resources (including services) available, upon request by the Secretary of Defense during a time of war or national emergency, or whenever the Secretary of Defense determines that it is necessary for national security or contingency operation (as that term is defined in section 101 of title 10, United States Code).

(2) BASIC TERMS.—(A) The basic terms of the Emergency Preparedness Agreement shall be established (subject to subparagraph (B)) by the Secretary and the Secretary of Defense.

(B) In any Emergency Preparedness Agreement, the Secretary and a contractor may agree to additional or modifying terms appropriate to the contractor's circumstances if those terms have been approved by the Secretary of Defense.

(3) DEFENSE MEASURES AGAINST UNAUTHORIZED SEIZURES.—(A) The Emergency Preparedness Agreement for any operating agreement that first takes effect or is renewed after the date of enactment of the National Defense Authorization Act for Fiscal Year 2010 shall require that any vessel operating under the agreement in the carriage of cargo for the Department of Defense in an area that is designated by the Coast Guard as an area of high risk of piracy shall be equipped with, at a minimum, appropriate non-lethal defense measures to protect the vessel, crew, and cargo from unauthorized seizure at sea.

(B) The Secretary of Defense and the Secretary of the department in which the Coast Guard is operating shall jointly prescribe the non-lethal defense measures that are required under this paragraph.

(c) PARTICIPATION AFTER EXPIRATION OF OPERATING AGREEMENT.—Except as provided by section 53105(d), the Secretary may not require, through an Emergency Preparedness Agreement or operating agreement, that a contractor continue to participate in an Emergency Preparedness Agreement after the operating agreement with the contractor has expired according to its terms or is otherwise no longer in effect. After expiration of an Emergency Preparedness Agreement, a contractor may volunteer to continue to participate in such an agreement.

(d) RESOURCES MADE AVAILABLE.—The commercial transportation resources to be made available under an Emergency Preparedness Agreement shall include vessels or capacity in vessels, intermodal systems and equipment, terminal facilities, intermodal and management services, and other related services, or any agreed portion of such nonvessel resources for activation as the Secretary of Defense may determine to be necessary, seeking to minimize disruption of the contractor's service to commercial shippers.

(e) COMPENSATION.—

(1) IN GENERAL.—The Secretary shall include in each Emergency Preparedness Agreement provisions approved by the Secretary of Defense under which the Secretary of Defense shall pay fair and reasonable compensation for all commercial transportation resources provided pursuant to this section.

(2) SPECIFIC REQUIREMENTS.—Compensation under this subsection—

(A) shall not be less than the contractor's commercial market charges for like transportation resources;

(B) shall be fair and reasonable considering all circumstances;

(C) shall be provided from the time that a vessel or resource is required by the Secretary of Defense until the time that it is redelivered to the contractor and is available to reenter commercial service; and

(D) shall be in addition to and shall not in any way reflect amounts payable under section 53106.

(f) TEMPORARY REPLACEMENT VESSELS.—Notwithstanding section 55302(a), 55304, 55305, or 55314 of this title, section 2631 of title 10, or any other cargo preference law of the United States—

(1) a contractor may operate or employ in foreign commerce a foreign-flag vessel or foreign-flag vessel capacity as a temporary replacement for a United States-documented vessel or United States-documented vessel capacity that is activated by the Secretary of Defense under an Emergency Preparedness Agreement or under a primary Department of Defense-approved sealift readiness program; and

(2) such replacement vessel or vessel capacity shall be eligible during the replacement period to transport preference cargoes subject to sections 55302(a), 55304, 55305, and 55314 of this title and section 2631 of title 10 to the same extent as the eligibility of the vessel or vessel capacity replaced.

(g) REDELIVERY AND LIABILITY OF UNITED STATES FOR DAMAGES.—

(1) IN GENERAL.—All commercial transportation resources activated under an Emergency Preparedness Agreement shall, upon termination of the period of activation, be redelivered to the contractor in the same good order and condition as when received, less ordinary wear and tear, or the Secretary of Defense shall fully compensate the contractor for any necessary repair or replacement.

(2) LIMITATION ON LIABILITY OF U.S.—Except as may be expressly agreed to in an Emergency Preparedness Agreement, or as otherwise provided by law, the Government shall not be liable for disruption of a contractor's commercial business or other consequential damages to a contractor arising from activation of commercial transportation resources under an Emergency Preparedness Agreement.

(Added Pub. L. 108–136, div. C, title XXXV, §3531(a), Nov. 24, 2003, 117 Stat. 1814; amended Pub. L. 109–304, §13(a)(6), Oct. 6, 2006, 120 Stat. 1701; Pub. L. 111–84, div. C, title XXXV, §3505, Oct. 28, 2009, 123 Stat. 2720; Pub. L. 112–239, div. C, title XXXV, §3508(g), Jan. 2, 2013, 126 Stat. 2225.)

§53108. REGULATORY RELIEF

(a) OPERATION IN FOREIGN COMMERCE.—A contractor for a vessel included in an operating agreement under this chapter may operate the vessel in the foreign commerce of the United States without restriction.

(b) OTHER RESTRICTIONS.—The restrictions of section 55305(a) of this title concerning the building, rebuilding, or documentation of a vessel in a foreign country shall not apply to a vessel for any day the operator of that vessel is receiving payments for operation of that vessel under an operating agreement under this chapter.

(c) TELECOMMUNICATIONS EQUIPMENT.—The telecommunications and other electronic equipment on an existing vessel that is redocumented under the laws of the United States for operation under an operating agreement under this chapter shall be deemed to satisfy all Federal Communications Commission equipment certification requirements, if—

(1) such equipment complies with all applicable international agreements and associated guidelines as determined by the country in which the vessel was documented immediately before becoming documented under the laws of the United States;

(2) that country has not been identified by the Secretary as inadequately enforcing international regulations as to that vessel; and

(3) at the end of its useful life, such equipment will be replaced with equipment that meets Federal Communications Commission equipment certification standards.

(Added Pub. L. 108–136, div. C, title XXXV, §3531(a), Nov. 24, 2003, 117 Stat. 1816; amended Pub. L. 109–304, §13(a)(7), Oct. 6, 2006, 120 Stat. 1701.)

[§53109. REPEALED. PUB. L. 112–239, DIV. C, TITLE XXXV, §3508(H), JAN. 2, 2013, 126 STAT. 2225]

Section, Pub. L. 108–136, div. C, title XXXV, §3531(a), Nov. 24, 2003, 117 Stat. 1817, related to special rule regarding age of participating fleet vessel.

§53110. REGULATIONS

The Secretary and the Secretary of Defense may each prescribe rules as necessary to carry out their respective responsibilities under this chapter.

(Added Pub. L. 108–136, div. C, title XXXV, §3531(a), Nov. 24, 2003, 117 Stat. 1817.)

§53111. AUTHORIZATION OF APPROPRIATIONS

There are authorized to be appropriated for payments under section 53106, to remain available until expended—

(1) $300,000,000 for each of fiscal years 2018, 2019, and 2020;
(2) $494,008,000 for fiscal year 2021;
(3) $318,000,000 for each of fiscal years 2022, 2023, 2024, and 2025;
(4) $348,000,000 for each of fiscal years 2026, 2027, and 2028;
(5) $378,000,000 for each of fiscal years 2029, 2030, and 2031; and
(6) $408,000,000 for each of fiscal years 2032, 2033, 2034, and 2035.

(Added Pub. L. 108–136, div. C, title XXXV, §3531(a), Nov. 24, 2003, 117 Stat. 1817; amended Pub. L.

111–383, div. C, title XXXV, §3502(3), Jan. 7, 2011, 124 Stat. 4518; Pub. L. 112–239, div. C, title XXXV, §3508(i), Jan. 2, 2013, 126 Stat. 2225; Pub. L. 114–92, div. C, title XXXV, §3504(b), Nov. 25, 2015, 129 Stat. 1219; Pub. L. 114–113, div. O, title I, §101(e)(2), Dec. 18, 2015, 129 Stat. 2988; Pub. L. 115–232, div. C, title XXXV, §3546(p), Aug. 13, 2018, 132 Stat. 2327; Pub. L. 116–92, div. C, title XXXV, §3502(d), Dec. 20, 2019, 133 Stat. 1969; Pub. L. 116–283, div. C, title XXXV, §3501(c)(1), Jan. 1, 2021, 134 Stat. 4397.)

CHAPTER 532—CABLE SECURITY FLEET

§53201. DEFINITIONS

In this chapter:

(1) CABLE SERVICES.—The term "cable services" means the installation, maintenance, or repair of submarine cables and related equipment, and related cable vessel operations.

(2) CABLE VESSEL.—The term "cable vessel" means a vessel—

(A) classed as a cable ship or cable vessel by, and designed in accordance with the rules of, the American Bureau of Shipping, or another classification society accepted by the Secretary; and

(B) capable of installing, maintaining, and repairing submarine cables.

(3) CABLE FLEET.—The term "Cable Fleet" means the Cable Security Fleet established under section 53202(a).

(4) CONTINGENCY AGREEMENT.—The term "Contingency Agreement" means the agreement required by section 53207.

(5) CONTRACTOR.—The term "Contractor" means an owner or operator of a vessel that enters into an Operating Agreement for a cable vessel with the Secretary under section 53203.

(6) FISCAL YEAR.—The term "fiscal year" means any annual period beginning on October 1 and ending on September 30.

(7) OPERATING AGENCY.—The term "Operating Agency" means that agency or component of the Department of Defense so designated by the Secretary of Defense under this chapter.

(8) OPERATING AGREEMENT OR AGREEMENT.—The terms "Operating Agreement" or "Agreement" mean the agreement required by section 53203.

(9) PERSON.—The term "person" includes corporations, partnerships, and associations existing under or authorized by the laws of the United States, or any State, Territory, District, or possession thereof, or of any foreign country.

(10) SECRETARY.—The term "Secretary" means the Secretary of Transportation.

(11) UNITED STATES.—The term "United States" includes the States, the District of Columbia, the Commonwealth of Puerto Rico, the Northern Mariana Islands, Guam, American Samoa, and the Virgin Islands.

(12) UNITED STATES CITIZEN TRUST.—

(A) Subject to paragraph (C), the term "United States citizen trust" means a trust that is qualified under this paragraph.

(B) A trust is qualified under this paragraph with respect to a vessel only if—

(i) it was created under the laws of a state of the United States;

(ii) each of the trustees is a citizen of the United States; and

(iii) the application for documentation of the vessel under chapter 121 of this title includes the affidavit of each trustee stating that the trustee is not aware of any reason involving a beneficiary of the trust that is not a citizen of the United States, or involving any other person that is not a citizen of the United States, as a result of which the beneficiary or other person would hold more than 25 percent of the aggregate power to influence, or limit the exercise of the authority of, the trustee with respect to matters involving any ownership or operation of the vessel that may adversely affect the interests of the United States.

(C) If any person that is not a citizen of the United States has authority to direct, or participate in directing, the trustee for a trust in matters involving any ownership or operation of the vessel that may adversely affect the interests of the United States or in removing a trustee for a trust without cause, either directly or indirectly through the control of another person, the trust is not qualified under this paragraph unless the trust instrument provides that persons who are not citizens of the United States may not hold more than 25 percent of the aggregate authority to direct or remove a trustee.

(D) This paragraph shall not be considered to prohibit a person who is not a citizen of the United States from holding more than 25 percent of the beneficial interest in a trust.

(Added Pub. L. 116–92, div. C, title XXXV, §3521(a), Dec. 20, 2019, 133 Stat. 1988.)

§53202. ESTABLISHMENT OF THE CABLE SECURITY FLEET

(a) IN GENERAL.—(1) The Secretary, in consultation with the Operating Agency, shall establish a fleet of active, commercially viable, cable vessels to meet national security requirements. The fleet shall consist of privately owned, United States-documented cable vessels for which there are in effect Operating Agreements under this chapter, and shall be known as the Cable Security Fleet.

(2) The Fleet described under this section shall include two vessels.

(b) VESSEL ELIGIBILITY.—A cable vessel is eligible to be included in the Fleet if—

(1) the vessel meets the requirements of paragraph (1), (2), (3), or (4) of subsection (c);

(2) the vessel is operated (or in the case of a vessel to be constructed, will be operated) in commercial service providing cable services;

(3) the vessel is 40 years of age or less on the date the vessel is included in the Fleet;

(4) the vessel is—

(A) determined by the Operating Agency to be suitable for engaging in cable services by the United States in the interest of national security; and

(B) determined by the Secretary to be commercially viable, whether independently or taking any payments which are the consequence of participation in the Cable Fleet into account; and

(5) the vessel—
(A) is a United States-documented vessel; or
(B) is not a United States-documented vessel, but—
(i) the owner of the vessel has demonstrated an intent to have the vessel documented under chapter 121 of this title if it is included in the Cable Fleet; and
(ii) at the time an Operating Agreement is entered into under this chapter, the vessel is eligible for documentation under chapter 121 of this title.

(c) REQUIREMENTS REGARDING CITIZENSHIP OF OWNERS AND OPERATORS.—

(1) VESSELS OWNED AND OPERATED BY SECTION 50501 CITIZENS.—A vessel meets the requirements of this paragraph if, during the period of an Operating Agreement under this chapter that applies to the vessel, the vessel will be owned and operated by one or more persons that are citizens of the United states [1] under section 50501 of this title.

(2) VESSELS OWNED BY A SECTION 50501 CITIZEN, OR UNITED STATES CITIZEN TRUST, AND CHARTERED TO A DOCUMENTATION CITIZEN.—A vessel meets the requirements of this paragraph if—
(A) during the period of an Operating Agreement under this chapter that applies to the vessel, the vessel will be—
(i) owned by a person that is a citizen of the United States under section 50501 of this title or that is a United States citizen trust; and
(ii) demise chartered to and operated by a person—
(I) that is eligible to document the vessel under chapter 121 of this title;
(II) the chairman of the board of directors, chief executive officer, and a majority of the members of the board of directors of which are citizens of the United States under section 50501 of this title, and are appointed and subject to removal only upon approval by the Secretary; and
(III) that certifies to the Secretary that there are no treaties, statutes, regulations, or other laws that would prohibit the Contractor for the vessel from performing its obligations under an Operating Agreement under this chapter;

(B) in the case of a vessel that will be demise chartered to a person that is owned or controlled by another person that is not a citizen of the United States under section 50501 of this title, the other person enters into an agreement with the Secretary not to influence the operation of the vessel in a manner that will adversely affect the interests of the United States; and
(C) the Secretary and the Operating Agency notify the Committee on Armed Services and the Committee on Commerce, Science and Transportation of the Senate, and the Committee on Armed Services of the House of Representatives that they concur, and have reviewed the certification required under subparagraph (A)(ii)(III) and determined that there are no legal, operational, or other impediments that would prohibit the Contractor for the vessel from performing its obligations under an Operating Agreement under this chapter.

(3) VESSEL OWNED AND OPERATED BY A DEFENSE CONTRACTOR.—A vessel meets the requirements of this paragraph if—

(A) during the period of an Operating Agreement under this chapter that applies to the vessel, the vessel will be owned and operated by a person that—

(i) is eligible to document a vessel under chapter 121 of this title;

(ii) operates or manages other United States-documented vessels for the Secretary of Defense, or charters other vessels to the Secretary of Defense;

(iii) has entered into a special security agreement for purposes of this paragraph with the Secretary of Defense;

(iv) makes the certification described in paragraph (2)(A)(ii)(III); and

(v) in the case of a vessel described in paragraph (2)(B), enters into an agreement referred to in that paragraph; and

(B) the Secretary and the Secretary of Defense notify the Committee on Armed Services and Committee on Commerce, Science, and Transportation of the Senate and the Committee on Armed Services of the House of Representatives that they have reviewed the certification required by subparagraph (A)(iv) and determined that there are no other legal, operational, or other impediments that would prohibit the Contractor for the vessel from performing its obligations under an Operating Agreement under this chapter.

(4) VESSEL OWNED BY A DOCUMENTATION CITIZEN AND CHARTERED TO A SECTION 50501 CITIZEN.—A vessel meets the requirements of this paragraph if, during the period of an Operating Agreement under this chapter that applies to the vessel, the vessel will be—

(A) owned by a person that is eligible to document a vessel under chapter 121 of this title; and

(B) demise chartered to a person that is a citizen of the United States under section 50501 of this title.

(d) VESSEL STANDARDS.—

(1) CERTIFICATE OF INSPECTION.—A cable vessel which the Secretary of the Department in which the Coast Guard is operating determines meets the criteria of subsection (b) of this section but which, on the date of enactment of the Act, is not documented under chapter 121 of this title, shall be eligible for a certificate of inspection if that Secretary determines that—

(A) the vessel is classed by, and designed in accordance with the rules of, the American Bureau of Shipping, or another classification society accepted by that Secretary;

(B) the vessel complies with applicable international agreements and associated guidelines, as determined by the country in which the vessel was documented immediately before becoming documented under chapter 121; and

(C) that country has not been identified by that Secretary as inadequately enforcing international vessel regulations as to that vessel.

(2) CONTINUED ELIGIBILITY FOR CERTIFICATE.—Paragraph (1) does not apply to a

vessel after any date on which the vessel fails to comply with the applicable international agreements and associated guidelines referred to in paragraph (1)(B).

(3) RELIANCE ON CLASSIFICATION SOCIETY.—

(A) IN GENERAL.—The Secretary of the Department in which the Coast Guard is operating may rely on a certification from the American Bureau of Shipping or, subject to subparagraph (B), another classification society accepted by that Secretary to establish that a vessel is in compliance with the requirements of paragraphs (1) and (2).

(B) FOREIGN CLASSIFICATION SOCIETY.—The Secretary of the Department in which the Coast Guard is operating may accept certification from a foreign classification society under subparagraph (A) only—

(i) to the extent that the government of the foreign country in which the society is headquartered provides access on a reciprocal basis to the American Bureau of Shipping; and

(ii) if the foreign classification society has offices and maintains records in the United States.

(e) WAIVER OF AGE REGISTRATION.—The Secretary, in conjunction with the Operating Agency, may waive the application of the age restriction under subsection (b)(3) if they jointly determine that the waiver—

(1) is in the national interest;

(2) the subject cable vessel and any associated operating network is and will continue to be economically viable; and

(3) is necessary due to the lack of availability of other vessels and operators that comply with the requirements of this chapter.

(Added Pub. L. 116–92, div. C, title XXXV, §3521(a), Dec. 20, 2019, 133 Stat. 1989.)

---

[1] So in original. Probably should be capitalized.

§53203. AWARD OF OPERATING AGREEMENTS

(a) IN GENERAL.—The Secretary shall require, as a condition of including any vessel in the Cable Fleet, that the person that is the owner or operator of the vessel for purposes of section 53202(c) enter into an Operating Agreement with the Secretary under this section.

(b) PROCEDURE FOR APPLICATIONS.—

(1) ACCEPTANCE OF APPLICATIONS.—Beginning no later than 60 days after the effective date of this chapter, the Secretary shall accept applications for enrollment of vessels in the Cable Fleet.

(2) ACTION ON APPLICATIONS.—Within 120 days after receipt of an application for enrollment of a vessel in the Cable Fleet, the Secretary shall approve the application in conjunction with the Operating Agency, and shall enter into an Operating Agreement with the applicant, or provide in writing the reason for denial of that application.

(c) Priority for Awarding Agreements.—Subject to the availability of appropriations, the Secretary shall enter into Operating Agreements with those vessels determined by the

Operating Agency, in its sole discretion, to best meet the national security requirements of the United States. After consideration of national security requirements, priority shall be given to an applicant that is a United States citizen under section 50501 of this title.

(Added Pub. L. 116–92, div. C, title XXXV, §3521(a), Dec. 20, 2019, 133 Stat. 1992.)

§53204. Effectiveness of operating agreements

(a) EFFECTIVENESS GENERALLY.—The Secretary may enter into an Operating Agreement under this chapter for fiscal year 2021. Except as provided in subsection (d), the agreement shall be effective only for one fiscal year, but shall be renewable, subject to available appropriations, for each subsequent year.

(b) VESSELS UNDER CHARTER TO THE UNITED STATES.—Vessels under charter to the United States are eligible to receive payments pursuant to their Operating Agreements.

(c) TERMINATION.—

(1) TERMINATION BY THE SECRETARY.—If the Contractor with respect to an Operating Agreement materially fails to comply with the terms of the Agreement—

(A) the Secretary shall notify the Contractor and provide a reasonable opportunity for it to comply with the Operating Agreement;

(B) the Secretary shall terminate the Operating Agreement if the Contractor fails to achieve such compliance; and

(C) upon such termination, any funds obligated by the Agreement shall be available to the Secretary to carry out this chapter.

(2) EARLY TERMINATION BY A CONTRACTOR.—An Operating Agreement under this chapter shall terminate on a date specified by the Contractor if the Contractor notifies the Secretary, not fewer than 60 days prior to the effective date of the termination, that the Contractor intends to terminate the Agreement.

(d) NONRENEWAL FOR LACK OF FUNDS.—If, by the first day of a fiscal year, sufficient funds have not been appropriated under the authority provided by this chapter for that fiscal year for all Operating Agreements, then the Secretary shall notify the Committee on Armed Services and the Committee on Commerce, Science, and Transportation of the Senate and the Committee on Armed Services of the House of Representatives that Operating Agreements authorized under this chapter for which sufficient funds are not available will not be renewed for that fiscal year if sufficient funds are not appropriated by the 60th day of that fiscal year. If only partial funding is appropriated by the 60th day of such fiscal year, then the Secretary, in consultation with the Operating Agency, shall select the vessels to retain under Operating Agreements, based on their determinations of which vessels are most useful for national security. In the event that no funds are appropriated, then no Operating Agreements shall be renewed and each Contractor shall be released from its obligations under the Operating Agreement. Final payments under an Operating Agreement that is not renewed shall be made in accordance with section 53206. To the extent that sufficient funds are appropriated in a subsequent fiscal year, an Operating Agreement that has not been renewed pursuant to this subsection may be reinstated if mutually acceptable to the Secretary, in consultation with the Operating Agency, and the Contractor, provided the vessel remains eligible for participation pursuant to section 53202, without regard to subsection 53202 (b)(3).

(e) RELEASE OF VESSELS FROM OBLIGATIONS.—If funds are not appropriated for payments under an Operating Agreement under this chapter for any fiscal year by the 60th day of a fiscal year, and the Secretary, in consultation with the Operating Agency determines to not renew a Contractor's Operating Agreement for a vessel, then—

(1) each vessel covered by the Operating Agreement that is not renewed is thereby released from any further obligation under the Operating Agreement;

(2) the owner or operator of the vessel whose Operating Agreement was not renewed may transfer and register such vessel under a foreign registry that is acceptable to the Secretary and the Operating Agency, notwithstanding section 56101 of this title; and

(3) if chapter 563 of this title is applicable to such vessel after registration, then the vessel is available to be requisitioned by the Secretary pursuant to chapter 563.

(Added Pub. L. 116–92, div. C, title XXXV, §3521(a), Dec. 20, 2019, 133 Stat. 1993.)

§53205. OBLIGATIONS AND RIGHTS UNDER OPERATING AGREEMENTS

(a) OPERATION OF VESSEL.—An Operating Agreement under this chapter shall require that, during the period the vessel is operating under the Agreement, the vessel—

(1) shall be operated in the trade for Cable Services, or under a charter to the United States; and

(2) shall be documented under chapter 121 of this title.

(b) ANNUAL PAYMENTS BY THE SECRETARY.—

(1) IN GENERAL.—An Operating Agreement under this chapter shall require, subject to the availability of appropriations, that the Secretary make payment to the Contractor in accordance with section 53206.

(2) OPERATING AGREEMENT IS AN OBLIGATION OF THE UNITED STATES GOVERNMENT.—An Operating Agreement under this chapter constitutes a contractual obligation of the United States Government to pay the amounts provided for in the Operating Agreement to the extent of actual appropriations.

(c) DOCUMENTATION REQUIREMENT.—Each vessel covered by an Operating Agreement (including an Agreement terminated under section 53204(c)(2)) shall remain documented under chapter 121 of this title, until the date the Operating Agreement would terminate according to its own terms.

(d) NATIONAL SECURITY REQUIREMENTS.—

(1) IN GENERAL.—A Contractor with respect to an Operating Agreement (including an Agreement terminated under section 53204(c)(2)) shall continue to be bound by the provisions of section 53207 until the date the Operating Agreement would terminate according to its terms.

(2) CONTINGENCY AGREEMENT WITH OPERATING AGENCY.—All terms and conditions of a Contingency Agreement entered into under section 53207 shall remain in effect until a date the Operating Agreement would terminate according to its terms, except that the terms of such Contingency Agreement may be modified by the mutual consent of the Contractor, and the Operating Agency.

(e) TRANSFER OF OPERATING AGREEMENTS.—Operating Agreements shall not be transferrable by the Contractor.

(f) REPLACEMENT VESSEL.—A Contractor may replace a vessel under an Operating Agreement with another vessel that is eligible to be included in the Fleet under section 53202(b), if the Secretary and the Operating Agency jointly determine that the replacement vessel meets national security requirements and approve the replacement.

(Added Pub. L. 116–92, div. C, title XXXV, §3521(a), Dec. 20, 2019, 133 Stat. 1994.)

§53206. PAYMENTS

(a) ANNUAL PAYMENT.—

(1) IN GENERAL.—The Secretary, subject to availability of appropriations and other provisions of this section, shall pay to the Contractor for an operating agreement, for each vessel that is covered by the operating agreement, an amount equal to $5,000,000 for each fiscal year 2021 through 2035.

(2) TIMING.—This amount shall be paid in equal monthly installments at the end of each month. The amount shall not be reduced except as provided by this section or section 51307(b).

(b) CERTIFICATION REQUIRED FOR PAYMENT.—As a condition of receiving payment under this section for a fiscal year for a vessel, the Contractor for the vessel shall certify that the vessel has been and will be operated in accordance with section 53205(a)(1) for 365 days in each fiscal year. Up to thirty (30) days during which the vessel is drydocked, surveyed, inspected, or repaired shall be considered days of operation for purposes of this subsection.

(c) GENERAL LIMITATIONS.—The Secretary shall not make any payment under this chapter for a vessel with respect to any days for which the vessel is—

(1) not operated or maintained in accordance with an Operating Agreement under this chapter; or

(2) more than 40 years of age.

(d) REDUCTIONS IN PAYMENTS.—With respect to payments under this chapter for a vessel covered by an Operating Agreement, the Secretary shall make a pro rata reduction for each day less than 365 in a fiscal year that the vessel is not operated in accordance with section 53205(a)(1), with days during which the vessel is drydocked or undergoing survey, inspection or repair to be considered days on which the vessel is operated as provided in subsection (b).

(Added Pub. L. 116–92, div. C, title XXXV, §3521(a), Dec. 20, 2019, 133 Stat. 1995; amended Pub. L. 117–263, div. C, title XXXV, §3517(b)(2), Dec. 23, 2022, 136 Stat. 3074.)

§53207. NATIONAL SECURITY REQUIREMENTS

(a) CONTINGENCY AGREEMENT REQUIRED.—The Secretary shall include in each Operating Agreement under this chapter a requirement that the Contractor enter into a Contingency Agreement with the Operating Agency. The Operating Agency shall negotiate and enter into a Contingency Agreement with each Contractor as promptly as practicable after the Contractor has entered into an Operating Agreement under this chapter.

(b) TERMS OF CONTINGENCY AGREEMENT.—

(1) IN GENERAL.—A Contingency Agreement under this section shall require that a Contractor for a vessel covered by an Operating Agreement under this chapter make the vessel, including all necessary resources to engage in Cable Services required by the Operating Agency, available upon request by the Operating Agency.

(2) TERMS.—

(A) IN GENERAL.—The basic terms of a Contingency Agreement shall be established (subject to subparagraph (B)) by the Operating Agency.

(B) ADDITIONAL TERMS.—The Operating Agency and a Contractor may agree to additional or modifying terms appropriate to the Contractor's circumstances.

(c) DEFENSE MEASURES AGAINST UNAUTHORIZED SEIZURES.—(1) The Contingency Agreement shall require that any vessel operating under the direction of the Operating Agency operating in area that is designated by the Coast Guard as an area of high risk of piracy shall be equipped with, at a minimum, appropriate non-lethal defense measures to protect the vessel and crew from unauthorized seizure at sea.

(2) The Secretary of Defense and the Secretary of the department in which the Coast Guard is operating shall jointly prescribe the non-lethal defense measures that are required under this paragraph.

(d) PARTICIPATION AFTER EXPIRATION OF OPERATING AGREEMENT.—Except as provided by section 53205(d), the Operating Agency may not require, through a Contingency Agreement or an Operating Agreement, that a Contractor continue to participate in a Contingency Agreement after the Operating Agreement with the Contractor has expired according to its terms or is otherwise no longer in effect.

(e) RESOURCES MADE AVAILABLE.—The resources to be made available in addition to the vessel under a Contingency Agreement shall include all equipment, personnel, supplies, management services, and other related services as the Operating Agency may determine to be necessary to provide the Cable Services required by the Operating Agency.

(f) COMPENSATION.—

(1) IN GENERAL.—The Operating Agency shall include in each Contingency Agreement provisions under which the Operating Agency shall pay fair and reasonable compensation for use of the vessel and all Cable Services provided pursuant to this section and the Contingency Agreement.

(2) SPECIFIC REQUIREMENTS.—Compensation under this subsection—

(A) shall be at the rate specified in the Contingency Agreement;

(B) shall be provided from the time that a vessel is required by the Operating Agency under the Contingency Agreement until the time it is made available by the Operating Agency available to reenter commercial service; and

(C) shall be in addition to and shall not in any way reflect amounts payable under section 53206.

(g) LIABILITY OF THE UNITED STATES FOR DAMAGES.—

(1) LIMITATION ON THE LIABILITY OF THE U.S.—Except as otherwise provided by law, the Government shall not be liable for disruption of a Contractor's commercial

business or other consequential damages to a Contractor arising from the activation of the Contingency Agreement.

(2) AFFIRMATIVE DEFENSE.—In any action in any Federal or State court for breach of third-party contract, there shall be available as an affirmative defense that the alleged breach of contract was caused predominantly by action taken to carry out a Contingent Agreement. Such defense shall not release the party asserting it from any obligation under applicable law to mitigate damages to the greatest extent possible.

(Added Pub. L. 116–92, div. C, title XXXV, §3521(a), Dec. 20, 2019, 133 Stat. 1995.)

§53208. REGULATORY RELIEF

The telecommunications and other electronic equipment on an existing vessel that is redocumented under the laws of the United States for operation under an Operating Agreement under this chapter shall be deemed to satisfy all Federal Communication Commission equipment certification requirements, if—

(1) such equipment complies with all applicable international agreements and associated guidelines as determined by the country in which the vessel was documented immediately before becoming documented under the laws of the United States;

(2) that country has not been identified by the Secretary of the Department in which the Coast Guard is operating as inadequately enforcing international regulations as to that vessel; and

(3) at the end of its useful life, such equipment shall be replaced with equipment that meets Federal Communication Commission equipment certification standards.

(Added Pub. L. 116–92, div. C, title XXXV, §3521(a), Dec. 20, 2019, 133 Stat. 1997.)

§53209. AUTHORIZATION OF APPROPRIATIONS

There are authorized to be appropriated for payments under section 53206, $10,000,000 for each of the fiscal years 2021 through 2035.

(Added Pub. L. 116–92, div. C, title XXXV, §3521(a), Dec. 20, 2019, 133 Stat. 1997.)

CHAPTER 533—CONSTRUCTION RESERVE FUNDS

§53301. Definitions

(a) In General.—In this chapter:

(1) Construction contract.—The term "construction contract" includes, for a taxpayer constructing a new vessel in a shipyard owned by that taxpayer, an agreement between the taxpayer and the Secretary of Transportation for that construction containing provisions the Secretary considers advisable to carry out this chapter.

(2) New vessel.—The term "new vessel" means—

(A) a vessel—

(i) constructed in the United States after December 31, 1939, constructed with a construction-differential subsidy under title V of the Merchant Marine Act, 1936, or constructed with financing or a financing guarantee under chapter 537 or 575 of this title;

(ii) documented or agreed with the Secretary to be documented under the laws of the United States; and

(iii)(I) of a type, size, and speed that the Secretary determines is suitable for use on the high seas or Great Lakes in carrying out this subtitle, but not less than 2,000 gross tons or less than 12 knots speed unless the Secretary certifies in each case that a vessel of lesser tonnage or speed is desirable for use by the United States Government in case of war or national emergency; or

(II) constructed to replace a vessel bought or requisitioned by the Government; and

(B) a vessel reconstructed or reconditioned for use only on the Great Lakes, including the Saint Lawrence River and Gulf, if the Secretary finds that the reconstruction or reconditioning will promote the objectives of this subtitle.

(b) Additional Tax-Related Terms.—Other terms used in this chapter have the same meaning as in chapter 1 of the Internal Revenue Code of 1986 (26 U.S.C. ch. 1).

(Pub. L. 109–304, §8(c), Oct. 6, 2006, 120 Stat. 1587.)

§53302. AUTHORITY FOR CONSTRUCTION RESERVE FUNDS

(a) GENERAL AUTHORITY.—An eligible person under section 53303 of this title may establish a construction reserve fund for the construction, reconstruction, reconditioning, or acquisition of a new vessel or for other purposes authorized by this chapter.

(b) APPLICATION OF CERTAIN LAWS AND REGULATIONS.—The fund shall be established, maintained, expended, and used as provided by this chapter and regulations prescribed jointly by the Secretary of Transportation and the Secretary of the Treasury.

(Pub. L. 109–304, §8(c), Oct. 6, 2006, 120 Stat. 1587.)

§53303. PERSONS ELIGIBLE TO ESTABLISH FUNDS

A construction reserve fund may be established by a citizen of the United States that—

(1) is operating a vessel in the foreign or domestic commerce of the United States or in the fisheries;

(2) owns, in whole or in part, a vessel being operated in the foreign or domestic commerce of the United States or in the fisheries;

(3) was operating a vessel in the foreign or domestic commerce of the United States or in the fisheries when it was bought or requisitioned by the United States Government;

(4) owned, in whole or in part, a vessel being operated in the foreign or domestic commerce of the United States or in the fisheries when it was bought or requisitioned by the Government; or

(5) had acquired or was having constructed a vessel to operate in the foreign or domestic commerce of the United States or in the fisheries when it was bought or requisitioned by the Government.

(Pub. L. 109–304, §8(c), Oct. 6, 2006, 120 Stat. 1587.)

§53304. VESSEL OWNERSHIP

In this chapter, a vessel is deemed to be constructed or acquired by a taxpayer if constructed or acquired by a corporation when the taxpayer owns at least 95 percent of each class of stock of the corporation.

(Pub. L. 109–304, §8(c), Oct. 6, 2006, 120 Stat. 1588.)

§53305. ELIGIBLE FUND DEPOSITS

A construction reserve fund may include deposits of—

(1) the proceeds from the sale of a vessel;

(2) indemnities for the loss of a vessel;

(3) earnings from the operation of a documented vessel and from services incident to the operation; and

(4) interest or other amounts accrued on deposits in the fund.

(Pub. L. 109–304, §8(c), Oct. 6, 2006, 120 Stat. 1588.)

§53306. RECOGNITION OF GAIN FOR TAX PURPOSES

(a) DEFINITIONS.—In this section, the terms "net proceeds" and "net indemnity" mean the

sum of—
> (1) the adjusted basis of the vessel; and
> (2) the amount of gain the taxpayer would recognize without regard to this section.

(b) RECOGNITION OF GAIN.—In computing net income under the income or excess profits tax laws of the United States, a taxpayer does not recognize a gain on the sale or the actual or constructive total loss of a vessel if the taxpayer—
> (1) deposits an amount equal to the net proceeds of the sale or the net indemnity for the loss in a construction reserve fund within 60 days after receiving the payment of proceeds or indemnity; and
> (2) elects under this section not to recognize the gain.

(c) WHEN ELECTION MUST BE MADE.—
> (1) IN GENERAL.—Except as provided in paragraph (2), the taxpayer must make the election referred to in subsection (b) in the taxpayer's income tax return for the taxable year in which the gain was realized.
> (2) RECEIPT AFTER TAXABLE YEAR.—If the vessel is bought or requisitioned by the United States Government, or is lost, and the taxpayer receives payment for the vessel or indemnity for the loss from the Government after the end of the taxable year in which it was bought, requisitioned, or lost, the taxpayer must make the election referred to in subsection (b) within 60 days after receiving the payment or indemnity, on a form prescribed by the Secretary of the Treasury.

(d) EFFECT OF STATUTE OF LIMITATION.—If the taxpayer makes an election under subsection (c)(2), and computation or recomputation under this section is otherwise allowable but is prevented by a statute of limitation on the date the election is made or within 6 months thereafter, the computation or recomputation nevertheless shall be made notwithstanding the statute if the taxpayer files a claim for the computation or recomputation within 6 months after the date of making the election.

(Pub. L. 109–304, §8(c), Oct. 6, 2006, 120 Stat. 1588.)

§53307. BASIS FOR DETERMINING GAIN OR LOSS AND FOR DEPRECIATING NEW VESSELS

Under the income or excess profits tax laws of the United States, the basis for determining a gain or loss and for depreciation of a new vessel constructed, reconstructed, reconditioned, or acquired by the taxpayer, or for which purchase-money indebtedness is liquidated as provided in section 53310 of this title, with amounts from a construction reserve fund, shall be reduced by that part of the deposits in the fund expended in the construction, reconstruction, reconditioning, acquisition, or liquidation of purchase-money indebtedness of the new vessel that represents a gain not recognized for tax purposes under section 53306 of this title.

(Pub. L. 109–304, §8(c), Oct. 6, 2006, 120 Stat. 1589.)

§53308. ORDER AND PROPORTIONS OF DEPOSITS AND WITHDRAWALS

In this chapter—

(1) if the net proceeds of a sale or the net indemnity for a loss is deposited in more than one deposit, the amount consisting of the gain shall be deemed to be deposited first;

(2) amounts expended, obligated, or otherwise withdrawn shall be applied against the amounts deposited in the fund in the order of deposit; and

(3) if a deposit consists in part of a gain not recognized under section 53306 of this title, any expenditure, obligation, or withdrawal applied against that deposit shall be deemed to be a gain in the proportion that the part of the deposit consisting of a gain bears to the total amount of the deposit.

(Pub. L. 109–304, §8(c), Oct. 6, 2006, 120 Stat. 1589.)

§53309. ACCUMULATION OF DEPOSITS

For any taxable year, amounts on deposit in a construction reserve fund on the last day of the taxable year, for which the requirements of section 53310 of this title have been satisfied (to the extent they apply on the last day of the taxable year), are deemed to have been retained for the reasonable needs of the business within the meaning of section 537(a) of the Internal Revenue Code of 1986 (26 U.S.C. 537(a)).

(Pub. L. 109–304, §8(c), Oct. 6, 2006, 120 Stat. 1589.)

§53310. OBLIGATION OF DEPOSITS AND PERIOD FOR CONSTRUCTION OF CERTAIN VESSELS

(a) APPLICATION OF SECTIONS 53306 AND 53309.—Sections 53306 and 53309 of this title apply to a deposit in a construction reserve fund only if, within 3 years after the date of the deposit (and any extension under subsection (c))—

(1)(A) a contract is made for the construction or acquisition of a new vessel or, with the approval of the Secretary of Transportation, for a part interest in a new vessel or for the reconstruction or reconditioning of a new vessel;

(B) the deposit is expended or obligated for expenditure under that contract;

(C) at least 12.5 percent of the construction or contract price of the vessel is paid or irrevocably committed for payment; and

(D) the plans and specifications for the vessel are approved by the Secretary to the extent the Secretary considers necessary; or

(2) the deposit is expended or obligated for expenditure for the liquidation of existing or subsequently incurred purchase-money indebtedness to a person not a parent company of, or a company affiliated or associated with, the mortgagor on a new vessel.

(b) ADDITIONAL REQUIREMENTS FOR CERTAIN VESSELS.—In addition to the requirements of subsection (a)(1), for a vessel not constructed under a construction-differential subsidy contract or not bought from the Secretary of Transportation—

(1) at least 5 percent of the construction (or, if the contract covers more than one vessel, at least 5 percent of the construction of the first vessel) must be completed within 6 months after the date of the construction contract (or within the period of an extension under subsection (c)), as estimated by the Secretary and certified by the Secretary to the

Secretary of the Treasury; and

(2) construction under the contract must be completed with reasonable dispatch thereafter.

(c) EXTENSIONS.—The Secretary of Transportation may grant extensions of the period within which the deposits must be expended or obligated or within which the construction must have progressed to the extent of 5 percent completion under this section. However, the extensions may not be for a total of more than 2 years for the expenditure or obligation of deposits or one year for the progress of construction.

(Pub. L. 109–304, §8(c), Oct. 6, 2006, 120 Stat. 1589.)

§53311. TAXATION OF DEPOSITS ON FAILURE OF CONDITIONS

A deposited gain, if otherwise taxable income under the law applicable to the taxable year in which the gain was realized, shall be included in gross income for that taxable year, except for purposes of the declared value excess profits tax and the capital stock tax, if—

(1) the deposited gain is not expended or obligated within the appropriate period under section 53310 of this title;

(2) the deposited gain is withdrawn before the end of that period;

(3) the construction related to that deposited gain has not progressed to the extent of 5 percent of completion within the appropriate period under section 53310 of this title; or

(4) the Secretary of Transportation finds and certifies to the Secretary of the Treasury that, for causes within the control of the taxpayer, the entire construction related to that deposited gain is not completed with reasonable dispatch.

(Pub. L. 109–304, §8(c), Oct. 6, 2006, 120 Stat. 1590.)

§53312. ASSESSMENT AND COLLECTION OF DEFICIENCY TAX

Notwithstanding any other provision of law, a deficiency in tax for a taxable year resulting from the inclusion of an amount in gross income as provided by section 53311 of this title, and the amount to be treated as a deficiency under section 53311 instead of as an adjustment for the declared value excess profits tax, may be assessed or a civil action may be brought to collect the deficiency without assessment, at any time. Interest on a deficiency or amount to be treated as a deficiency does not begin until the date the deposited gain or part of the deposited gain in question is required to be included in gross income under section 51111.

(Pub. L. 109–304, §8(c), Oct. 6, 2006, 120 Stat. 1590.)

CHAPTER 534—TANKER SECURITY FLEET

Sec.[1]

[1] *Editorially supplied.*

§53401. DEFINITIONS

In this chapter:

(1) FOREIGN COMMERCE.—The term "foreign commerce" means—

(A) commerce or trade between the United States, its territories or possessions, or the District of Columbia, and a foreign country; and

(B) commerce or trade between foreign countries.

(2) PARTICIPATING FLEET VESSEL.—The term "participating Fleet vessel" means any product tank vessel covered by an operating agreement under this chapter on or after January 1, 2022, that—

(A) meets the requirements of one of paragraphs (1) through (4) of section 53402(b) of this title; and

(B) is no more than 20 years of age.

(3) PERSON.—The term "person" includes corporations, partnerships, and associations existing under, or authorized by, laws of the United States, or any State, territory, district, or possession thereof, or any foreign country.

(4) PRODUCT TANK VESSEL.—The term "product tank vessel" means a double-hulled tank vessel capable of carrying simultaneously more than 2 separated grades of refined petroleum products.

(5) PROGRAM PARTICIPANT.—The term "program participant" means an owner or operator of a vessel that enters into an operating agreement covering a participating fleet vessel with the Secretary under section 53403.

(6) SECRETARY.—The term "Secretary" means the Secretary of Transportation, unless the context indicates otherwise.

(7) UNITED STATES CITIZEN TRUST.—The term "United States citizen trust"—
   (A) means a trust for which—
      (i) each of the trustees is a citizen of the United States; and
      (ii) the application for documentation of the vessel under chapter 121 of this title includes an affidavit of each trustee stating that the trustee is not aware of any reason involving a beneficiary of the trust that is not a citizen of the United States, or involving any other person who is not a citizen of the United States, as a result of which the beneficiary or other person would hold more than 25 percent of the aggregate power to influence or limit the exercise of the authority of the trustee with respect to matters involving any ownership or operation of the vessel that may adversely affect the interests of the United States;

   (B) does not include a trust for which any person that is not a citizen of the United States has authority to direct, or participate in directing, a trustee for a trust in matters involving any ownership or operation of the vessel that may adversely affect the interests of the United States or in removing a trustee without cause, either directly or indirectly through the control of another person, unless the trust instrument provides that persons who are not citizens of the United States may not hold more than 25 percent of the aggregate authority to so direct or remove a trustee; and

   (C) may include a trust for which a person who is not a citizen of the United States holds more than 25 percent of the beneficial interest in the trust.

(8) LONG TERM CHARTER.—The term "long term charter" means any time charter of a product tank vessel to the United States Government that, together with options, occurs for a continuous period of more than 180 days.

(Added Pub. L. 116–283, div. C, title XXXV, §3511(a), Jan. 1, 2021, 134 Stat. 4408; amended Pub. L. 117–81, div. C, title XXXV, §3515(a), Dec. 27, 2021, 135 Stat. 2243.)

§53402. ESTABLISHMENT OF THE TANKER SECURITY FLEET

(a) IN GENERAL.—The Secretary of Transportation, in consultation with the Secretary of Defense, shall establish a fleet of active, commercially viable, militarily useful, privately owned product tank vessels to meet national defense and other security requirements and maintain a United States presence in international commercial shipping. The fleet shall consist of privately owned vessels of the United States for which there are in effect operating agreements under this chapter, and shall be known as the "Tanker Security Fleet" (hereafter in this chapter referred to as the "Fleet").

(b) VESSEL ELIGIBILITY.—A vessel is eligible to be included in the Fleet if the vessel—
   (1) meets the requirements under paragraph (1), (2), (3), or (4) of subsection (c);
   (2) is operated (or in the case of a vessel to be constructed, will be operated) in providing transportation in United States foreign commerce;
   (3) is self-propelled;
   (4) is not more than 10 years of age on the date the vessel is first included in the Fleet;
   (5) is determined by the Secretary of Defense to be suitable for use by the United States for national defense or military purposes in time of war or national emergency;

(6) is commercially viable, as determined by the Secretary of Transportation; and

(7) is—

(A) a vessel of the United States; or

(B) not a vessel of the United States, but—

(i) the owner of the vessel has demonstrated an intent to have the vessel documented under chapter 121 of this title if it is included in the Fleet; and

(ii) at the time an operating agreement is entered into under this chapter, the vessel is eligible for documentation under chapter 121 of this title.

(c) REQUIREMENTS REGARDING CITIZENSHIP OF OWNERS, CHARTERERS, AND OPERATORS.—

(1) VESSELS OWNED AND OPERATED BY SECTION 50501 CITIZENS.—A vessel meets the requirements of this paragraph if, during the period of an operating agreement under this chapter that applies to the vessel, the vessel will be owned and operated by one or more persons that are citizens of the United States under section 50501 of this title.

(2) VESSELS OWNED BY A SECTION 50501 CITIZEN, OR UNITED STATES CITIZEN TRUST, AND CHARTERED TO A DOCUMENTATION CITIZEN.—A vessel meets the requirements of this paragraph if—

(A) during the period of an operating agreement under this chapter that applies to the vessel, the vessel will be—

(i) owned by a person that is a citizen of the United States under section 50501 of this title or that is a United States citizen trust; and

(ii) demise chartered to a person—

(I) that is eligible to document the vessel under chapter 121 of this title;

(II) the chairman of the board of directors, chief executive officer, and a majority of the members of the board of directors of which are citizens of the United States under section 50501 of this title, and are appointed and subjected to removal only upon approval by the Secretary of Transportation; and

(III) that certifies to the Secretary of Transportation that there are no treaties, statutes, regulations, or other laws that would prohibit the program participant for the vessel from performing its obligations under an operating agreement under this chapter;

(B) in the case of a vessel that will be demise chartered to a person that is owned or controlled by another person that is not a citizen of the United States under section 50501 of this title, the other person enters into an agreement with the Secretary of Transportation not to influence the operation of the vessel in a manner that will adversely affect the interests of the United States; and

(C) the Secretary of Transportation and the Secretary of Defense notify the Committee on Armed Services and the Committee on Commerce, Science, and Transportation of the Senate and the Committee on Armed Services and the Committee on Transportation and Infrastructure of the House of Representatives that the Secretaries concur with the certification required under subparagraph (A)(ii)(III), and have reviewed and agree that there are no legal, operational, or other impediments that would prohibit the owner or operator for the vessel from performing its obligations under an operating agreement under this chapter.

(3) VESSELS OWNED AND OPERATED BY A DEFENSE CONTRACTOR.—A vessel meets the requirements of this paragraph if—

(A) during the period of an operating agreement under this chapter that applies to the vessel, the vessel will be owned and operated by a person that—

(i) is eligible to document a vessel under chapter 121 of this title;

(ii) operates or manages other vessels of the United States for the Secretary of Defense, or charters other vessels to the Secretary of Defense;

(iii) has entered into a special security agreement for the purpose of this paragraph with the Secretary of Defense;

(iv) makes the certification described in paragraph (2)(A)(ii)(III); and

(v) in the case of a vessel described in paragraph (2)(B), enters into an agreement referred to in that paragraph; and

(B) the Secretary of Transportation and the Secretary of Defense notify the Committee on Armed Services and the Committee on Commerce, Science, and Transportation of the Senate and the Committee on Armed Services and the Committee on Transportation and Infrastructure of the House of Representatives that they concur with the certification required under subparagraph (A)(iv), and have reviewed and agree that there are no legal, operational, or other impediments that would prohibit the program participant for the vessel from performing its obligations under an operating agreement under this chapter.

(4) VESSELS OWNED BY DOCUMENTATION CITIZENS AND CHARTERED TO SECTION 50501 CITIZENS.—A vessel meets the requirements of this paragraph if, during the period of an operating agreement under this chapter, the vessel will be—

(A) owned by a person who is eligible to document a vessel under chapter 121 of this title; and

(B) demise chartered to a person that is a citizen of the United States under section 50501 of this title.

(d) REQUEST BY SECRETARY OF DEFENSE.—The Secretary of Defense shall request that the Secretary of Homeland Security issue any waiver under section 501 of this title that the Secretary of Defense determines is necessary for purposes of this chapter.

(e) VESSEL STANDARDS.—

(1) CERTIFICATE OF INSPECTION.—A vessel used to provide oceangoing transportation the Secretary of the department in which the Coast Guard is operating determines meets the criteria of subsection (b) but which, on the date of enactment of this section, is not documented under chapter 121, shall be eligible for a certificate of inspection if the Secretary of the department in which the Coast Guard is operating determines that—

(A) the vessel is classed by and designed in accordance with the rules of the American Bureau of Shipping, or another classification society accepted by the Commandant of the Coast Guard;

(B) the vessel complies with applicable international agreements and associated guidelines, as determined by the country in which the vessel was documented immediately before becoming documented under chapter 121 of this title; and

(C) the country has not been identified by the Commandant of the Coast Guard as inadequately enforcing international vessel regulations as to that vessel.

(2) CONTINUED ELIGIBILITY FOR CERTIFICATE.—Subsection (a) shall not apply to any vessel that has failed to comply with the applicable international agreements and associated guidelines referred to in paragraph (1)(B).

(3) RELIANCE ON CLASSIFICATION SOCIETY.—

(A) IN GENERAL.—The Commandant of the Coast Guard may rely on a certification from the American Bureau of Shipping or, subject to subparagraph (B), another classification society accepted by the Commandant of the Coast Guard, to establish that a vessel is in compliance with the requirements of paragraph (1).

(B) FOREIGN CLASSIFICATION SOCIETY.—The Commandant of the Coast Guard may accept certification from a foreign classification society under subparagraph (A) only—

(i) to the extent that the government of the foreign country in which the society is headquartered provides access on a reciprocal basis to the American Bureau of Shipping; and

(ii) if the foreign classification society has offices and maintains records in the United States.

(Added Pub. L. 116–283, div. C, title XXXV, §3511(a), Jan. 1, 2021, 134 Stat. 4409.)

§53403. AWARD OF OPERATING AGREEMENTS

(a) IN GENERAL.—The Secretary of Transportation shall require, as a condition of including any vessel in the Fleet, that the program participant of the vessel enter into an operating agreement with the Secretary under this section.

(b) PROCEDURE FOR APPLICATIONS.—

(1) ELIGIBLE VESSELS.—The Secretary of Transportation shall accept an application for an operating agreement for an eligible product tank vessel under the priority under paragraph (2) only from a person that has authority to enter into an operating agreement under this chapter.

(2) ESTABLISHMENT OF PRIORITY.—The Secretary of Transportation may enter into a new operating agreement with an applicant that meets the requirements of section 53402(c) for a vessel that meets the qualifications of section 53402(b), and shall give priority to applications based on—

(A) vessel capabilities, as established by the Secretary of Defense; then

(B) after consideration of vessel type, according to an applicant's record of owning and operating vessels; then

(C) after consideration of ownership and operation, according to such additional priorities as the Secretary of Transportation may consider appropriate.

(3) CONCURRENCE OF AWARD.—The Secretary of Transportation may not approve an application for an operating agreement without the concurrence of the Secretary of

Defense.

(c) LIMITATION.—The Secretary of Transportation may not award operating agreements under this chapter that require payments under section 53406 of this title for more than—.[1]

(1) for each of fiscal years 2022 and 2023, 10 vessels; and

(2) for any subsequent fiscal year, 20 vessels.

(d) JUDICIAL REVIEW.—No court shall have jurisdiction to review the Secretary's decision with respect to the award or non-award of an operating agreement issued under this chapter.

(Added Pub. L. 116–283, div. C, title XXXV, §3511(a), Jan. 1, 2021, 134 Stat. 4412; amended Pub. L. 117–263, div. C, title XXXV, §3501(b)(2), Dec. 23, 2022, 136 Stat. 3064.)

[1] So in original. The period probably should not appear.

§53404. EFFECTIVENESS OF OPERATING AGREEMENTS

(a) IN GENERAL.—Subject to the availability of appropriations for such purpose, the Secretary may enter into an operating agreement under this chapter for fiscal year 2022 and any subsequent fiscal year. The agreement shall be effective only for 1 fiscal year, but shall be renewable, subject to the availability of appropriations, for each fiscal year through the end of fiscal year 2035.

(b) VESSELS UNDER CHARTER TO THE UNITED STATES.—Any vessel under long term charter to the United States is not eligible to participate in the Fleet.

(c) TERMINATION.—

(1) TERMINATION BY SECRETARY FOR LACK OF PROGRAM PARTICIPANT COMPLIANCE.—If the program participant with respect to an operating agreement materially fails to comply with the terms of the agreement—

(A) the Secretary shall notify the program participant and provide a reasonable opportunity to comply with the operating agreement; and

(B) the Secretary shall terminate the operating agreement if the program participant fails to achieve such compliance.

(2) TERMINATION BY PROGRAM PARTICIPANT.—If a program participant provides notice of the intent to terminate an operating agreement under this chapter on a date specified by not later than 60 days prior to the date specified by the program participant for such termination, such agreement shall terminate on the date specified by the program participant.

(d) NONRENEWAL FOR LACK OF FUNDS.—If, by the first day of a fiscal year, sufficient funds have not been appropriated under the authority provided by this chapter for that fiscal year, then the Secretary shall notify the Committee on Armed Services and the Committee on Commerce, Science, and Transportation of the Senate and the Committee on Armed Services and the Committee on Transportation and Infrastructure of the House of Representatives that operating agreements authorized under this chapter for which sufficient funds are not available will not be renewed for that fiscal year if sufficient funds are not appropriated by the 60th day of that fiscal year.

(e) RELEASE OF VESSELS FROM OBLIGATIONS.—If funds are not appropriated for payments under an operating agreement under this chapter for any fiscal year by the 60th day of that fiscal year, then—

(1) each vessel covered by the operating agreement is thereby released from any further obligation under the operating agreement;

(2) the program participant for the vessel may transfer and register such vessel under a foreign registry that is acceptable to the Secretary of Transportation and the Secretary of Defense, notwithstanding section 56101 of this title; and

(3) if chapter 563 of this title is applicable to the vessel after registration, then the vessel is available to be requisitioned by the Secretary pursuant to chapter 563 of this title.

(Added Pub. L. 116–283, div. C, title XXXV, §3511(a), Jan. 1, 2021, 134 Stat. 4413; amended Pub. L. 117–81, div. C, title XXXV, §3515(b), Dec. 27, 2021, 135 Stat. 2243.)

§53405. OBLIGATIONS AND RIGHTS UNDER OPERATING AGREEMENTS

(a) OPERATION OF VESSEL.—An operating agreement under this chapter shall require that, during the period the vessel covered by the agreement is operating under the agreement the vessel shall—

(1) be operated in the United States foreign commerce, mixed United States foreign commerce and domestic trade allowed under a registry endorsement issued under section 12111 of this title, in foreign-to-foreign commerce, or under a charter to the United States;

(2) not be operated in the coastwise trade except as described in paragraph (1); and

(3) be documented under chapter 121 of this title.

(b) ANNUAL PAYMENTS BY THE SECRETARY.—

(1) IN GENERAL.—An operating agreement under this chapter shall require, subject to the availability of appropriations, that the Secretary make a payment to the program participant in accordance with section 53406.

(2) OPERATING AGREEMENT IS AN OBLIGATION OF THE UNITED STATES GOVERNMENT.—An operating agreement under this chapter constitutes a contractual obligation of the United States Government to pay the amounts provided for in the agreement to the extent of actual appropriations.

(c) DOCUMENTATION REQUIREMENT.—Each vessel covered by the operating agreement, including an agreement terminated under section 53404(c)(2), shall remain documented under chapter 121 of this title until the date the operating agreement would terminate according to its terms.

(d) NATIONAL SECURITY REQUIREMENTS.—

(1) IN GENERAL.—A program participant with respect to an operating agreement, including an agreement terminated under section 53404(c)(2), shall continue to be bound by the provisions of section 53407 until the date the operating agreement would

terminate according to its terms.

(2) EMERGENCY PREPAREDNESS AGREEMENT.—All terms and conditions of an Emergency Preparedness Agreement entered into under section 53407 shall remain in effect until the date the operating agreement would terminate according to its terms, except that the terms of such Emergency Preparedness Agreement may be modified by the mutual consent of the program participant, the Secretary of Transportation, and the Secretary of Defense.

(e) TRANSFER OF OPERATING AGREEMENTS.—A program participant may transfer an operating agreement (including all rights and obligations under the agreement) to any person that is eligible to enter into that operating agreement under this chapter, if the Secretary of Transportation and the Secretary of Defense determine that the transfer is in the best interests of the United States.

(f) REPLACEMENT OF VESSELS COVERED BY AGREEMENTS.—A program participant may replace the vessel with another vessel that is eligible to be included in the Fleet under section 53402(b), if the Secretary of Transportation, in coordination with the Secretary of Defense, approves the replacement of the vessel. No court shall have jurisdiction to review a decision by the Secretary of Transportation or the Secretary of Defense pertaining to the replacement of a vessel under this section.

(Added Pub. L. 116–283, div. C, title XXXV, §3511(a), Jan. 1, 2021, 134 Stat. 4414.)

§53406. PAYMENTS

(a) ANNUAL PAYMENT.—Subject to the availability of appropriations for such purpose and the other provisions of this chapter, the Secretary shall pay to program participant for an operating agreement under this chapter an amount equal to $6,000,000 for each vessel covered by the agreement for each fiscal year that the vessel is covered by the agreement. Such amount shall be paid in equal monthly installments on the last day of each month. The amount payable under this subsection may not be reduced except as provided by this section or section 51307(b).

(b) CERTIFICATION REQUIRED FOR PAYMENT.—As a condition of receiving payment under this section for a fiscal year for a vessel, the program participant shall certify, in accordance with regulations issued by the Secretary, that the vessel has been and will be operated in accordance with section 53405(a) of this title for at least 320 days during the fiscal year. Days during which the vessel is drydocked, surveyed, inspected, or repaired shall be considered days of operation for purposes of this subsection.

(c) GENERAL LIMITATIONS.—The Secretary may not make any payment under this chapter for a vessel with respect to any days for which the vessel is—

(1) not operated or maintained in accordance with an operating agreement under this chapter;

(2) more than 20 years of age; or

(3) simultaneously operating under an agreement pursuant to chapter 531 of this title.

(d) REDUCTIONS IN PAYMENTS.—With respect to payments under this chapter for a vessel covered by an operating agreement, the Secretary—

(1) except as provided in paragraph (2), may not reduce such a payment for—

(A) the operation of the vessel to carry military or other preference cargoes under section 55302(a), 55304, 55305, or 55314 of this title, section 2631 of title 10, or any other cargo preference law of the United States; or

(B) any days in which the vessel is operated under charter to the United States Government;

(2) may not make such a payment for any day that the vessel is engaged in transporting more than 7,500 tons of civilian bulk preference cargoes pursuant to section 55302(a), 55305, or 55314 of this title; and

(3) shall make a pro rata reduction for each day less than 320 in a fiscal year that the vessel is not operated in accordance with section 53405 of this title.

(e) LIMITATIONS REGARDING NONCONTIGUOUS DOMESTIC TRADE.—

(1) IN GENERAL.—No program participant shall receive payments pursuant to this chapter during a period in which it participates in noncontiguous domestic trade.

(2) LIMITATION ON APPLICATION.—Paragraph (1) shall not apply to a program participant that is a citizen of the United States within the meaning of section 50501 of this title, applying the 75 percent ownership requirement of that section.

(3) PARTICIPATES IN A NONCONTIGUOUS TRADE DEFINED.—In this subsection the term "participates in a noncontiguous domestic trade" means directly or indirectly owns, charters, or operates a vessel engaged in transportation of cargo between a point in the contiguous 48 States and a point in Alaska, Hawaii, or Puerto Rico, other than a point in Alaska north of the Arctic Circle.

(Added Pub. L. 116–283, div. C, title XXXV, §3511(a), Jan. 1, 2021, 134 Stat. 4415; amended Pub. L. 117–263, div. C, title XXXV, §3517(b)(3), Dec. 23, 2022, 136 Stat. 3074.)

§53407. NATIONAL SECURITY REQUIREMENTS

(a) EMERGENCY PREPAREDNESS AGREEMENT REQUIRED.—The Secretary of Transportation, in coordination with the Secretary of Defense, shall establish an emergency preparedness program under this section under which the program participant for an operating agreement under this chapter shall agree, as a condition of the operating agreement, to enter into an emergency preparedness agreement with the Secretary. The Secretary shall negotiate and enter into an Emergency Preparedness Agreement with each program participant as promptly as practicable after the program participant has entered into the operating agreement.

(b) TERMS OF AGREEMENT.—The terms of an agreement under this section—

(1) shall provide that upon request by the Secretary of Defense during time of war or national emergency, or whenever determined by the Secretary of Defense to be necessary for national security or contingency operation (as that term is defined in section 101 of title 10), the program participant shall make available commercial transportation resources (including services) described in subsection (d) to the Secretary of Defense;

(2) shall include such additional terms as may be established by the Secretary of Transportation and the Secretary of Defense; and

(3) shall allow for the modification or addition of terms upon agreement by the

Secretary of Transportation and the program participant and the approval by the Secretary of Defense.

(c) PARTICIPATION AFTER EXPIRATION OF OPERATING AGREEMENT.—Except as provided by section 53406, the Secretary of Transportation may not require, through an emergency preparedness agreement or an operating agreement, that a program participant covered by an operating agreement continue to participate in an emergency preparedness agreement after the operating agreement has expired according to its terms or is otherwise no longer in effect. After the expiration of an emergency preparedness agreement, a program participant may voluntarily continue to participate in the agreement.

(d) RESOURCES MADE AVAILABLE.—The commercial transportation resources to be made available under an emergency preparedness agreement shall include vessels or capacity in vessels, terminal facilities, management services, and other related services, or any agreed portion of such nonvessel resources for activation as the Secretary of Defense may determine to be necessary, seeking to minimize disruption of the program participant's service to commercial customers.

(e) COMPENSATION.—

(1) IN GENERAL.—The Secretary of Transportation shall include in each Emergency Preparedness Agreement provisions approved by the Secretary of Defense under which the Secretary of Defense shall pay fair and reasonable compensation for all commercial transportation resources provided pursuant to this section.

(2) SPECIFIC REQUIREMENTS.—Compensation under this subsection—

(A) shall not be less than the program participant's commercial market charges for like transportation resources;

(B) shall be fair and reasonable considering all circumstances;

(C) shall be provided from the time that a vessel or resource is required by the Secretary of Defense until the time it is redelivered to the program participant and is available to reenter commercial service; and

(D) shall be in addition to and shall not in any way reflect amounts payable under section 53406 of this title.

(f) TEMPORARY REPLACEMENT VESSELS.—Notwithstanding section 55302(a), 55304, 55305, or 55314 of this title, section 2631 of title 10, or any other cargo preference law of the United States—

(1) a program participant may operate or employ in foreign commerce a foreign-flag vessel or foreign-flag vessel capacity as a temporary replacement for a vessel of the United States or vessel of the United States capacity that is activated by the Secretary of Defense under an emergency preparedness agreement or a primary Department of Defense sealift-approved readiness program; and

(2) such replacement vessel or vessel capacity shall be eligible during the replacement period to transport preference cargoes subject to sections 55302(a), 55304, 55305, and 55314 of this title and section 2631 of title 10, United States Code, to the same extent as the eligibility of the vessel or vessel capacity replaced.

(g) REDELIVERY AND LIABILITY OF THE UNITED STATES FOR DAMAGES.—

(1) IN GENERAL.—All commercial transportation resources activated under an emergency preparedness agreement shall, upon termination of the period of activation, be redelivered to the program participant in the same good order and condition as when received, less ordinary wear and tear, or the Secretary of Defense shall fully compensate the program participant for any necessary repair or replacement.

(2) LIMITATION ON UNITED STATES LIABILITY.—Except as may be expressly agreed in an emergency preparedness agreement, or as otherwise provided by law, the Government shall not be liable for disruption of a program participant's commercial business or other consequential damages to the program participant arising from the activation of commercial transportation resources under an emergency preparedness agreement.

(Added Pub. L. 116–283, div. C, title XXXV, §3511(a), Jan. 1, 2021, 134 Stat. 4416.)

§53408. REGULATORY RELIEF

(a) OPERATION IN FOREIGN COMMERCE.—A program participant for a vessel included in an operating agreement under this chapter may operate the vessel in the foreign commerce of the United States without restriction.

(b) OTHER RESTRICTIONS.—The restrictions of section 55305(a) of this title concerning the building, rebuilding, or documentation of a vessel in a foreign country shall not apply to a vessel for any day the operator of the vessel is receiving payments for the operation of that vessel under an operating agreement under this chapter.

(c) TELECOMMUNICATIONS EQUIPMENT.—The telecommunications and other electronic equipment on an existing vessel that is redocumented under the laws of the United States for operation under an operating agreement under this chapter shall be deemed to satisfy all Federal Communications Commission equipment approval requirements, if—

(1) such equipment complies with all applicable international agreements and associated guidelines as determined by the country in which the vessel was documented immediately before becoming documented under the laws of the United States;

(2) that country has not been identified by the Secretary as inadequately enforcing international regulations as to that vessel; and

(3) at the end of its useful life, such equipment shall be replaced with equipment that meets Federal Communications Commission equipment approval standards.

(Added Pub. L. 116–283, div. C, title XXXV, §3511(a), Jan. 1, 2021, 134 Stat. 4417.)

§53409. SPECIAL RULE REGARDING AGE OF PARTICIPATING FLEET VESSELS

Any age restriction under section 53402(b)(4) of this title shall not apply to a participating Fleet vessel during the 30-month period beginning on the date the vessel begins operating under an operating agreement under this chapter, if the Secretary determines that the program participant for the vessel has entered into an arrangement to obtain and operate under the operating agreement for the participating Fleet vessel a replacement vessel that, upon commencement of such operation, will be eligible to be included in the Fleet under section 53402(b) of this title.

(Added Pub. L. 116–283, div. C, title XXXV, §3511(a), Jan. 1, 2021, 134 Stat. 4418.)

§53410. REGULATIONS

The Secretary of Transportation and the Secretary of Defense may each prescribe rules as necessary to carry out their respective responsibilities under this chapter.

(Added Pub. L. 116–283, div. C, title XXXV, §3511(a), Jan. 1, 2021, 134 Stat. 4418.)

§53411. AUTHORIZATION OF APPROPRIATIONS

There is authorized to be appropriated for payments under section 53406, $60,000,000 for each of fiscal years 2022 and 2023, and $120,000,000 for fiscal years 2024 through 2035, to remain available until expended.

(Added Pub. L. 116–283, div. C, title XXXV, §3511(a), Jan. 1, 2021, 134 Stat. 4418; amended Pub. L. 117–263, div. C, title XXXV, §3501(b)(1), Dec. 23, 2022, 136 Stat. 3064.)

§53412. ACQUISITION OF FLEET VESSELS

(a) IN GENERAL.—Upon replacement of a Fleet vessel under an operating agreement under this chapter, and subject to agreement by the program participant of the vessel, the Secretary of Transportation is authorized, subject to the concurrence of the Secretary of Defense, acquire the vessel being replaced for inclusion in the National Defense Reserve Fleet.

(b) REQUIREMENTS.—To be eligible for acquisition by the Secretary of Transportation under this section a vessel shall—

(1) have been covered by an operating agreement under this chapter for not less than 3 years; and

(2) meet recapitalization requirements for the Ready Reserve Force.

(c) FAIR MARKET VALUE.—A fair market value shall be established by the Maritime Administration for acquisition of an eligible vessel under this section.

(d) APPROPRIATIONS.—Vessel acquisitions under this section shall be subject to the availability of appropriations. Amounts made available to carry out this section shall be derived from amounts authorized to be appropriated for the National Defense Reserve Fleet. Amounts authorized to be appropriated to carry out the Maritime Security Program may not be use to carry out this section.

(Added Pub. L. 116–283, div. C, title XXXV, §3511(a), Jan. 1, 2021, 134 Stat. 4418.)

CHAPTER 535—CAPITAL CONSTRUCTION FUNDS

§53501. Definitions

In this chapter:

(1) AGREEMENT VESSEL.—The term "agreement vessel" means—

(A) an eligible vessel or a qualified vessel that is subject to an agreement under this chapter; and

(B) a barge or container that is part of the complement of a vessel described in subparagraph (A) if provided for in the agreement.

(2) ELIGIBLE VESSEL.—The term "eligible vessel" means—

(A) a vessel—

(i) constructed in the United States (and, if reconstructed, reconstructed in the United States), constructed outside the United States but documented under the laws of the United States on April 15, 1970, or constructed outside the United States for use in the United States foreign trade pursuant to a contract made before April 15, 1970;

(ii) documented under the laws of the United States; and

(iii) operated in the foreign or domestic trade of the United States or in the fisheries of the United States; and

(B) a commercial fishing vessel—

(i) constructed in the United States and, if reconstructed, reconstructed in the United States;

(ii) of at least 2 net tons but less than 5 net tons;

(iii) owned by a citizen of the United States;

(iv) having its home port in the United States; and

(v) operated in the commercial fisheries of the United States.

(3) JOINT REGULATIONS.—The term "joint regulations" means regulations prescribed jointly by the Secretary and the Secretary of the Treasury under section 53502(b) of this title.

(4) NONCONTIGUOUS TRADE.—The term "noncontiguous trade" means—

(A) trade between—

(i) one of the contiguous 48 States; and

(ii) Alaska, Hawaii, Puerto Rico, or an insular territory or possession of the United States; and

(B) trade between—

(i) a place in Alaska, Hawaii, Puerto Rico, or an insular territory or possession of the United States; and

(ii) another place in Alaska, Hawaii, Puerto Rico, or an insular territory or possession of the United States.

(5) QUALIFIED VESSEL.—The term "qualified vessel" means—

(A) a vessel—

(i) constructed in the United States (and, if reconstructed, reconstructed in the United States), constructed outside the United States but documented under the laws of the United States on April 15, 1970, or constructed outside the United States for use in the United States foreign trade pursuant to a contract made before April 15, 1970;

(ii) documented under the laws of the United States; and

(iii) agreed, between the Secretary and the person maintaining the capital construction fund established under section 53503 of this title, to be operated in the foreign or domestic trade of the United States or in the fisheries of the United States; and

(B) a commercial fishing vessel—

(i) constructed in the United States and, if reconstructed, reconstructed in the United States;

(ii) of at least 2 net tons but less than 5 net tons;

(iii) owned by a citizen of the United States;

(iv) having its home port in the United States; and

(v) operated in the commercial fisheries of the United States.

(6) SECRETARY.—The term "Secretary" means—

(A) the Secretary of Commerce with respect to an eligible vessel or a qualified vessel operated or to be operated in the fisheries of the United States; and

(B) the Secretary of Transportation with respect to other vessels.

(7) SHORT SEA TRANSPORTATION TRADE.—The term "short sea transportation trade" means the carriage by vessel of cargo—

(A) that is—

(i) contained in intermodal cargo containers and loaded by crane on the vessel; or

(ii) loaded on the vessel by means of wheeled technology; and

(B) that is—

(i) loaded at a port in the United States and unloaded either at another port in the United States or at a port in Canada located in the Great Lakes Saint Lawrence Seaway System; or

(ii) loaded at a port in Canada located in the Great Lakes Saint Lawrence Seaway System and unloaded at a port in the United States.

(8) UNITED STATES FOREIGN TRADE.—The term "United States foreign trade" includes those areas in domestic trade in which a vessel built with a construction-differential subsidy is allowed to operate under the first sentence of section 506 of the Merchant Marine Act, 1936.

(9) VESSEL.—The term "vessel" includes—

(A) cargo handling equipment that the Secretary determines is intended for use primarily on the vessel; and

(B) an ocean-going towing vessel, an ocean-going barge, or a comparable towing vessel or barge operated on the Great Lakes.

(Pub. L. 109–304, §8(c), Oct. 6, 2006, 120 Stat. 1591; Pub. L. 110–140, title XI, §1122(a), Dec. 19, 2007, 121 Stat. 1762; Pub. L. 115–232, div. C, title XXXV, §3546(q), Aug. 13, 2018, 132 Stat. 2327; Pub. L. 117–263, div. C, title XXXV, §3544, Dec. 23, 2022, 136 Stat. 3100.)

§53502. REGULATIONS

(a) IN GENERAL.—Except as provided in subsection (b), the Secretary shall prescribe regulations to carry out this chapter.

(b) TAX LIABILITY.—The Secretary and the Secretary of the Treasury shall prescribe joint regulations for the determination of tax liability under this chapter.

(Pub. L. 109–304, §8(c), Oct. 6, 2006, 120 Stat. 1593.)

§53503. ESTABLISHING A CAPITAL CONSTRUCTION FUND

(a) IN GENERAL.—A citizen of the United States owning or leasing an eligible vessel may make an agreement with the Secretary under this chapter to establish a capital construction fund for the vessel.

(b) ALLOWABLE PURPOSE.—The purpose of the agreement shall be to provide replacement vessels, additional vessels, or reconstructed vessels, built in the United States and documented under the laws of the United States, for operation in the foreign or domestic trade of the United States or in the fisheries of the United States.

(Pub. L. 109–304, §8(c), Oct. 6, 2006, 120 Stat. 1593; Pub. L. 110–140, title XI, §1122(b), Dec. 19, 2007, 121 Stat. 1762; Pub. L. 117–263, div. C, title XXXV, §3545, Dec. 23, 2022, 136 Stat. 3100.)

§53504. DEPOSITS AND WITHDRAWALS

(a) REQUIRED DEPOSITS.—An agreement to establish a capital construction fund shall provide for the deposit in the fund of the amounts agreed to be appropriate to provide for qualified withdrawals under section 53509 of this title.

(b) APPLICABLE REQUIREMENTS.—Deposits in and withdrawals from the fund are subject to the requirements included in the agreement or prescribed by the Secretary by regulation. However, the Secretary may not require a person to deposit in the fund for a taxable year more than 50 percent of that portion of the person's taxable income for that year (as determined under section 53505(a)(1) of this title) that is attributable to the operation of an agreement vessel.

(Pub. L. 109–304, §8(c), Oct. 6, 2006, 120 Stat. 1593.)

§53505. CEILING ON DEPOSITS

(a) MAXIMUM DEPOSITS.—The amount deposited in a capital construction fund for a taxable year may not exceed the sum of—

(1) that portion of the taxable income of the owner or lessee for the taxable year (computed under chapter 1 of the Internal Revenue Code of 1986 (26 U.S.C. ch. 1) but without regard to the carryback of net operating loss or net capital loss or this chapter) that is attributable to the operation of agreement vessels in the foreign or domestic trade of the United States or in the fisheries of the United States;

(2) the amount allowable as a deduction under section 167 of such Code (26 U.S.C. 167) for the taxable year for agreement vessels;

(3) if the transaction is not taken into account for purposes of paragraph (1), the net proceeds (as defined in joint regulations) from the disposition of an agreement vessel or from insurance or indemnity attributable to an agreement vessel; and

(4) the receipts from the investment or reinvestment of amounts held in the fund.

(b) REDUCTIONS FOR LESSEES.—For a lessee, the maximum amount that may be deposited for an agreement vessel under subsection (a)(2) for any period shall be reduced by any amount the owner is required or permitted, under the capital construction fund agreement, to deposit for that period for the vessel under subsection (a)(2).

(Pub. L. 109–304, §8(c), Oct. 6, 2006, 120 Stat. 1593.)

§53506. INVESTMENT AND FIDUCIARY REQUIREMENTS

(a) IN GENERAL.—Amounts in a capital construction fund shall be kept in the depository specified in the agreement and shall be subject to trustee and other fiduciary requirements prescribed by the Secretary. Except as provided in subsection (b), amounts in the fund may be invested only in interest-bearing securities approved by the Secretary.

(b) STOCK INVESTMENTS.—

(1) IN GENERAL.—With the approval of the Secretary, an agreed percentage (but not more than 60 percent) of the assets of the fund may be invested in the stock of domestic corporations that—

(A) is fully listed and registered on an exchange registered with the Securities and Exchange Commission as a national securities exchange; and

(B) would be acquired by a prudent investor seeking a reasonable income and the preservation of capital.

(2) PREFERRED STOCK.—The preferred stock of a corporation is deemed to satisfy the requirements of this subsection, even though it may not be registered and listed because it is nonvoting stock, if the common stock of the corporation satisfies the requirements and the preferred stock otherwise would satisfy the requirements.

(c) MAINTAINING AGREED PERCENTAGE.—If at any time the fair market value of the stock in the fund is more than the agreed percentage of the assets in the fund, any subsequent investment of amounts deposited in the fund, and any subsequent withdrawal from the fund, shall be made in a way that tends to restore the fair market value of the stock to not more than the agreed percentage.

(Pub. L. 109–304, §8(c), Oct. 6, 2006, 120 Stat. 1594.)

§53507. NONTAXATION OF DEPOSITS

(a) TAX TREATMENT.—Subject to subsection (b), under the Internal Revenue Code of 1986 (26 U.S.C. 1 et seq.)—
(1) taxable income (determined without regard to this chapter and section 7518 of such Code (26 U.S.C. 7518)) for the taxable year shall be reduced by the amount deposited for the taxable year out of amounts referred to in section 53505(a)(1) of this title;
(2) a gain from a transaction referred to in section 53505(a)(3) of this title shall not be taken into account if an amount equal to the net proceeds (as defined in joint regulations) from the transaction is deposited in the fund;
(3) the earnings (including gains and losses) from the investment and reinvestment of amounts held in the fund shall not be taken into account;
(4) the earnings and profits of a corporation (within the meaning of section 316 of such Code (26 U.S.C. 316)) shall be determined without regard to this chapter and section 7518 of such Code (26 U.S.C. 7518); and
(5) in applying the tax imposed by section 531 of such Code (26 U.S.C. 531), amounts held in the fund shall not be taken into account.

(b) CONDITION.—This section applies to an amount only if the amount is deposited in the fund under the agreement within the time provided in joint regulations.

(Pub. L. 109–304, §8(c), Oct. 6, 2006, 120 Stat. 1594.)

§53508. SEPARATE ACCOUNTS WITHIN A FUND

(a) IN GENERAL.—A capital construction fund shall have three accounts:
(1) The capital account.
(2) The capital gain account.
(3) The ordinary income account.

(b) CAPITAL ACCOUNT.—The capital account shall consist of—
(1) amounts referred to in section 53505(a)(2) of this title;

(2) amounts referred to in section 53505(a)(3) of this title, except that portion representing a gain not taken into account because of section 53507(a)(2) of this title;

(3) the percentage applicable under section 243(a)(1) of the Internal Revenue Code of 1986 (26 U.S.C. 243(a)(1)) of any dividend received by the fund for which the person maintaining the fund would be allowed (were it not for section 53507(a)(3) of this title) a deduction under section 243 of such Code (26 U.S.C. 243); and

(4) interest income exempt from taxation under section 103 of such Code (26 U.S.C. 103).

(c) CAPITAL GAIN ACCOUNT.—The capital gain account shall consist of—

(1) amounts representing capital gains on assets held for more than 6 months and referred to in section 53505(a)(3) or (4) of this title; minus

(2) amounts representing capital losses on assets held in the fund for more than 6 months.

(d) ORDINARY INCOME ACCOUNT.—The ordinary income account shall consist of—

(1) amounts referred to in section 53505(a)(1) of this title;

(2)(A) amounts representing capital gains on assets held for not more than 6 months and referred to in section 53505(a)(3) or (4) of this title; minus

(B) amounts representing capital losses on assets held in the fund for not more than 6 months;

(3) interest (except tax-exempt interest referred to in subsection (b)(4)) and other ordinary income (except any dividend referred to in paragraph (5)) received on assets held in the fund;

(4) ordinary income from a transaction described in section 53505(a)(3) of this title; and

(5) that portion of any dividend referred to in subsection (b)(3) not taken into account under subsection (b)(3).

(e) WHEN LOSSES ALLOWED.—Except on termination of a fund, capital losses referred to in subsection (c) or (d)(2) shall be allowed only as an offset to gains referred to in subsection (c) or (d)(2), respectively.

(Pub. L. 109–304, §8(c), Oct. 6, 2006, 120 Stat. 1595.)

§53509. QUALIFIED WITHDRAWALS

(a) IN GENERAL.—Subject to subsection (b), a withdrawal from a capital construction fund is a qualified withdrawal if it is made under the terms of the agreement and is for—

(1) the acquisition, construction, or reconstruction of a qualified vessel or a barge or container that is part of the complement of a qualified vessel; or

(2) the payment of the principal on indebtedness incurred in the acquisition, construction, or reconstruction of a qualified vessel or a barge or container that is part of the complement of a qualified vessel.

(b) BARGES AND CONTAINERS.—Except as provided in regulations prescribed by the Secretary, subsection (a) applies to a barge or container only if it is constructed in the

United States.

(c) TREATMENT AS NONQUALIFIED WITHDRAWAL.—Under joint regulations, if the Secretary determines that a substantial obligation under an agreement is not being fulfilled, the Secretary, after notice and opportunity for a hearing to the person maintaining the fund, may treat any amount in the fund as an amount withdrawn from the fund in a nonqualified withdrawal.

(Pub. L. 109–304, §8(c), Oct. 6, 2006, 120 Stat. 1596.)

§53510. TAX TREATMENT OF QUALIFIED WITHDRAWALS AND BASIS OF PROPERTY

(a) ORDER OF WITHDRAWALS.—A qualified withdrawal from a capital construction fund shall be treated as made—

(1) first from the capital account;

(2) second from the capital gain account; and

(3) third from the ordinary income account.

(b) ORDINARY INCOME ACCOUNT WITHDRAWALS.—If a portion of a qualified withdrawal for a vessel, barge, or container is made from the ordinary income account, the basis of the vessel, barge, or container shall be reduced by an amount equal to that portion.

(c) CAPITAL GAIN ACCOUNT WITHDRAWALS.—If a portion of a qualified withdrawal for a vessel, barge, or container is made from the capital gain account, the basis of the vessel, barge, or container shall be reduced by an amount equal to that portion.

(d) WITHDRAWALS TO PAY PRINCIPAL.—If a portion of a qualified withdrawal to pay the principal on indebtedness is made from the ordinary income account or the capital gain account, an amount equal to the total reduction that would be required by subsections (b) and (c) if the withdrawal were a qualified withdrawal for a purpose described in those subsections shall be applied, in the order provided in joint regulations, to reduce the basis of vessels, barges, and containers owned by the person maintaining the fund. The remaining amount of the withdrawal shall be treated as a nonqualified withdrawal.

(e) GAIN ON PROPERTY WITH REDUCED BASIS.—If property, the basis of which was reduced under subsection (b), (c), or (d), is disposed of, any gain realized on the disposition, to the extent it does not exceed the total reduction in the basis of the property under those subsections, shall be treated as an amount referred to in section 53511(c)(1) of this title withdrawn on the date of disposition of the property. Subject to conditions prescribed in joint regulations, this subsection does not apply to a disposition if there is a redeposit, in an amount determined under joint regulations, that restores the fund as far as practicable to the position it was in before the withdrawal.

(Pub. L. 109–304, §8(c), Oct. 6, 2006, 120 Stat. 1596.)

§53511. TAX TREATMENT OF NONQUALIFIED WITHDRAWALS

(a) IN GENERAL.—Except as provided in section 53513 of this title, a withdrawal from a fund that is not a qualified withdrawal shall be treated as a nonqualified withdrawal.

(b) ORDER OF WITHDRAWALS.—A nonqualified withdrawal shall be treated as made—

(1) first from the ordinary income account;

(2) second from the capital gain account; and

(3) third from the capital account.

(c) TAX TREATMENT.—For purposes of the Internal Revenue Code of 1986 (26 U.S.C. 1 et seq.)—

(1) a nonqualified withdrawal from the ordinary income account shall be included in income as an item of ordinary income for the taxable year in which the withdrawal is made;

(2) a nonqualified withdrawal from the capital gain account shall be included in income for the taxable year in which the withdrawal is made as an item of gain realized during that year from the disposition of an asset held for more than 6 months; and

(3) for the period through the last date prescribed for payment of tax for the taxable year in which the withdrawal is made—

(A) no interest shall be payable under section 6601 of such Code (26 U.S.C. 6601) and no addition to the tax shall be payable under section 6651 of such Code (26 U.S.C. 6651);

(B) interest on the amount of the additional tax attributable to an amount treated as a nonqualified withdrawal from the ordinary income account or the capital gain account shall be paid at the rate determined under subsection (d) from the last date prescribed for payment of the tax for the taxable year for which the amount was deposited in the fund; and

(C) no interest shall be payable on amounts treated as withdrawn on a last-in-first-out basis under section 53512 of this title.

(d) INTEREST RATE.—The rate of interest under subsection (c)(3)(B) for a nonqualified withdrawal made in a taxable year beginning after 1971 shall be determined and published jointly by the Secretary and the Secretary of the Treasury. The rate shall be such that its relationship to 8 percent is comparable, as determined by the Secretaries under joint regulations, to the relationship between—

(1) the money rates and investment yields for the calendar year immediately before the beginning of the taxable year; and

(2) the money rates and investment yields for the calendar year 1970.

(e) NONQUALIFIED WITHDRAWALS.—

(1) IN GENERAL.—The following applicable percentage of any amount that remains in a capital construction fund at the close of the following specified taxable year following the taxable year for which the amount was deposited shall be treated as a nonqualified withdrawal:

If the amount remains in the fund at the close of the—	The applicable percent:
26th taxable year	20 percent
27th taxable year	40 percent
28th taxable year	60 percent

29th taxable year	80 percent
30th taxable year	100 percent.

(2) EARNINGS.—The earnings of a capital construction fund for any taxable year (except net gains) shall be treated under this subsection as an amount deposited for the taxable year.

(3) CONTRACT FOR QUALIFIED WITHDRAWAL.—Under paragraph (1), an amount shall not be treated as remaining in a capital construction fund at the close of a taxable year to the extent there is a binding contract at the close of the taxable year for a qualified withdrawal of the amount for an identified item for which the withdrawal may be made.

(4) EXCESS EARNINGS.—If the Secretary determines that the balance in a capital construction fund exceeds the amount appropriate to meet the vessel construction program objectives of the person that established the fund, the amount of the excess shall be treated as a nonqualified withdrawal under paragraph (1) unless the person develops appropriate program objectives within 3 years to dissipate the excess.

(5) AMOUNTS IN FUND ON JANUARY 1, 1987.—Under this subsection, amounts in a capital construction fund on January 1, 1987, shall be treated as having been deposited in that fund on that date.

(f) TAX DETERMINATIONS.—

(1) IN GENERAL.—For a taxable year for which there is a nonqualified withdrawal (including an amount treated as a nonqualified withdrawal under subsection (e)), the tax imposed by chapter 1 of the Internal Revenue Code of 1986 (26 U.S.C. ch. 1) shall be determined by—

(A) excluding the withdrawal from gross income; and

(B) increasing the tax imposed by chapter 1 of such Code by the product of the amount of the withdrawal and the highest tax rate specified in section 1 (or section 11 for a corporation) of such Code (26 U.S.C. 1, 11).

(2) MAXIMUM TAX RATE.—For that portion of a nonqualified withdrawal made from the capital gain account during a taxable year to which section 1(h) or 1201(a) [1] of such Code (26 U.S.C. 1(h), 1201(a)) applies, the tax rate used under paragraph (1)(B) may not exceed 20 percent (or 34 percent for a corporation).

(3) TAX BENEFIT RULE.—If any portion of a nonqualified withdrawal is properly attributable to deposits (except earnings on deposits) made by the taxpayer in a taxable year that did not reduce the taxpayer's liability for tax under chapter 1 of such Code (26 U.S.C. ch. 1) for a taxable year before the taxable year in which the withdrawal occurs—

(A) that portion shall not be taken into account under paragraph (1); and

(B) an amount equal to that portion shall be allowed as a deduction under section 172 of such Code (26 U.S.C. 172) for the taxable year in which the withdrawal occurs.

(4) COORDINATION WITH DEDUCTION FOR NET OPERATING LOSSES.—A nonqualified withdrawal excluded from gross income under paragraph (1) shall be excluded in determining taxable income under section 172(b)(2) of such Code (26 U.S.C. 172(b)(2)).

(Pub. L. 109–304, §8(c), Oct. 6, 2006, 120 Stat. 1597; Pub. L. 112–240, title I, §102(c)(1)(E), Jan. 2, 2013, 126 Stat. 2319.)

[1] *See References in Text note below.*

§53512. FIFO AND LIFO WITHDRAWALS

(a) FIFO.—Except as provided in subsection (b), an amount withdrawn from an account under this chapter shall be treated as withdrawn on a first-in-first-out basis.

(b) LIFO.—An amount withdrawn from an account under this chapter shall be treated as withdrawn on a last-in-first-out basis if it is—

(1) a nonqualified withdrawal for research, development, and design expenses incident to new and advanced vessel design, machinery, and equipment; or

(2) an amount treated as a nonqualified withdrawal under section 53510(d) of this title.

(Pub. L. 109–304, §8(c), Oct. 6, 2006, 120 Stat. 1599.)

§53513. CORPORATE REORGANIZATIONS AND PARTNERSHIP CHANGES

Under joint regulations—

(1) a transfer of a capital construction fund from one person to another person in a transaction to which section 381 of the Internal Revenue Code of 1986 (26 U.S.C. 381) applies may be treated as if the transaction is not a nonqualified withdrawal; and

(2) a similar rule shall be applied to a continuation of a partnership (within the meaning of subchapter K of chapter 1 of such Code (26 U.S.C. 701 et seq.)).

(Pub. L. 109–304, §8(c), Oct. 6, 2006, 120 Stat. 1599.)

§53514. RELATIONSHIP OF OLD FUND TO NEW FUND

(a) DEFINITION.—In this section, the term "old fund" means a capital construction fund maintained before October 21, 1970.

(b) ELECTION TO MAINTAIN OLD FUND.—A person maintaining an old fund may elect to continue the old fund, but may not—

(1) hold amounts in the old fund beyond the expiration date provided in the agreement under which the old fund is maintained (determined without regard to an extension or renewal made after April 14, 1970); or

(2) maintain simultaneously the old fund and a new fund established under this chapter.

(c) APPLICATION OF NEW FUND AGREEMENT TO OLD FUND AMOUNTS.—If a person makes an agreement under this chapter to establish a new fund, the person may agree to extend the agreement to some or all of the amounts in an old fund. Each item in the old fund to be transferred shall be transferred in a nontaxable transaction to the appropriate account in the new fund. For purposes of section 53511(c)(3) of this title, the date of the deposit of an item so transferred shall be July 1, 1971, or the date of the deposit in the old fund, whichever is later.

(Pub. L. 109–304, §8(c), Oct. 6, 2006, 120 Stat. 1599.)

§53515. Records and reports

A person maintaining a fund under this chapter shall keep records and make reports as required by the Secretary or the Secretary of the Treasury.

(Pub. L. 109–304, §8(c), Oct. 6, 2006, 120 Stat. 1599.)

§53516. Termination of agreement after change in regulations

If, after an agreement has been made under this chapter, a change is made either in the joint regulations or in the regulations prescribed by the Secretary under this chapter that could have a substantial effect on the rights or duties of a person maintaining a fund under this chapter, that person may terminate the agreement.

(Pub. L. 109–304, §8(c), Oct. 6, 2006, 120 Stat. 1600.)

§53517. Reports

(a) In General.—Within 120 days after the close of each calendar year, the Secretary of Transportation and the Secretary of Commerce each shall provide the Secretary of the Treasury a written report on the capital construction funds under the particular Secretary's jurisdiction for the calendar year.

(b) Contents.—The report shall state the name and taxpayer identification number of each person—

(1) establishing a capital construction fund during the calendar year;

(2) maintaining a capital construction fund on the last day of the calendar year;

(3) terminating a capital construction fund during the calendar year;

(4) making a deposit to or withdrawal from a capital construction fund during the calendar year, and the amount of the deposit or withdrawal; or

(5) having been determined during the calendar year to have failed to fulfill a substantial obligation under a capital construction fund agreement to which the person is a party.

(Pub. L. 109–304, §8(c), Oct. 6, 2006, 120 Stat. 1600.)

CHAPTER 537—LOANS AND GUARANTEES

SUBCHAPTER I—GENERAL

SUBCHAPTER II—DEFAULT PROVISIONS

SUBCHAPTER III—PARTICULAR PROJECTS

SUBCHAPTER I—GENERAL

§53701. Definitions

In this chapter:

(1) Actual cost.—The term "actual cost" means the sum of—

(A) all amounts paid by or for the account of the obligor as of the date on which a determination is made under section 53715(d)(1) of this title; and

(B) all amounts that the Secretary or Administrator reasonably estimates the obligor will become obligated to pay from time to time thereafter, for the construction, reconstruction, or reconditioning of the vessel, including guarantee fees that will become payable under section 53714 of this title in connection with all obligations issued for construction, reconstruction, or reconditioning of the vessel or equipment to be delivered, and all obligations issued for the delivered vessel or equipment.

(2) Administrator.—The term "Administrator" means the Administrator of the Maritime Administration.

(3) Construction, reconstruction, and reconditioning.—The terms "construction", "reconstruction", and "reconditioning" include designing, inspecting, outfitting, and equipping.

(4) Depreciated actual cost.—The term "depreciated actual cost" of a vessel means—

(A) if the vessel was not reconstructed or reconditioned, the actual cost of the vessel depreciated on a straight line basis over the useful life of the vessel as determined by the Secretary or Administrator, not to exceed 25 years from the date of delivery by the builder; or

(B) if the vessel was reconstructed or reconditioned, the sum of—

(i) the actual cost of the vessel depreciated on a straight line basis from the date of delivery by the builder to the date of the reconstruction or reconditioning, using the original useful life of the vessel, and from the date of the reconstruction or reconditioning, using a useful life of the vessel determined by the Secretary or Administrator; and

(ii) any amount paid or obligated to be paid for the reconstruction or reconditioning, depreciated on a straight line basis using a useful life of the vessel determined by the Secretary or Administrator.

(5) Fishery facility.—

(A) In general.—Subject to subparagraph (B), the term "fishery facility" means—

(i) for operations on land—

(I) a structure or appurtenance thereto designed for the unloading and receiving from vessels, the processing, the holding pending processing, the distribution after processing, or the holding pending distribution, of fish from a fishery;

(II) the land necessary for the structure or appurtenance; and

(III) equipment that is for use with the structure or appurtenance and that is necessary for performing a function referred to in subclause (I);

(ii) for operations not on land, a vessel built in the United States and used for, equipped to be used for, or of a type normally used for, the processing of fish; or

(iii) for aquaculture, including operations on land or elsewhere—

(I) a structure or appurtenance thereto designed for aquaculture;

(II) the land necessary for the structure or appurtenance;

(III) equipment that is for use with the structure or appurtenance and that is necessary for performing a function referred to in subclause (I); and

(IV) a vessel built in the United States and used for, equipped to be used for, or of a type normally used for, aquaculture.

(B) REQUIRED OWNERSHIP.—Under subparagraph (A), the structure, appurtenance, land, equipment, or vessel must be owned by—

(i) an individual who is a citizen of the United States; or

(ii) an entity that is a citizen of the United States under section 50501 of this title and that is at least 75 percent owned (as determined under that section) by citizens of the United States.

(6) FISHING VESSEL.—The term "fishing vessel" has the meaning given that term in section 3 of the Magnuson-Stevens Fishery Conservation and Management Act (16 U.S.C. 1802), and any reference in this chapter to a vessel designed principally for commercial use in the fishing trade or industry is deemed to be a reference to a fishing vessel.

(7) HISTORICAL USES.—The term "historical uses" includes—

(A) refurbishing, repairing, rebuilding, or replacing equipment on a fishing vessel, without materially increasing harvesting capacity;

(B) purchasing a used fishing vessel;

(C) purchasing, constructing, expanding, or reconditioning a fishery facility;

(D) refinancing existing debt;

(E) reducing fishing capacity; and

(F) making upgrades to a fishing vessel, including upgrades in technology, gear, or equipment, that improve—

(i) collection and reporting of fishery-dependent data;

(ii) bycatch reduction or avoidance;

(iii) gear selectivity;

(iv) adverse impacts caused by fishing gear; or

(v) safety.

(8) MORTGAGE.—The term "mortgage" includes—

(A) a preferred mortgage as defined in section 31301 of this title; and

(B) a mortgage on a vessel that will become a preferred mortgage when filed or recorded under chapter 313 of this title.

(9) OBLIGATION.—The term "obligation" means an instrument of indebtedness issued for a purpose described in section 53706 of this title, except—

(A) an obligation issued by the Secretary or Administrator under section 53723 of this title; and

(B) an obligation eligible for investment of funds under section 53715(f) or 53717 of this title.

(10) OBLIGEE.—The term "obligee" means the holder of an obligation.

(11) OBLIGOR.—The term "obligor" means a party primarily liable for payment of the principal of or interest on an obligation.

(12) OCEAN THERMAL ENERGY CONVERSION FACILITY OR PLANTSHIP.—The term "ocean thermal energy conversion facility or plantship" means an at-sea facility or vessel, whether mobile, floating unmoored, moored, or standing on the seabed, that uses temperature differences in ocean water to produce electricity or another form of energy capable of being used directly to perform work, and includes—

(A) equipment installed on the facility or vessel to use the electricity or other form of energy to produce, process, refine, or manufacture a product;

(B) a cable or pipeline used to deliver the electricity, freshwater, or product to shore; and

(C) other associated equipment and appurtenances of the facility or vessel to the extent they are located seaward of the high water mark.

(13) SECRETARY.—The term "Secretary" means the Secretary of Commerce with respect to fishing vessels and fishery facilities.

(14) VESSEL.—The term "vessel" means any type of vessel, whether in existence or under construction, including—

(A) a cargo vessel;

(B) a passenger vessel;

(C) a combination cargo and passenger vessel;

(D) a tanker;

(E) a tug or towboat;

(F) a barge;

(G) a dredge;

(H) a floating drydock with a capacity of at least 35,000 lifting tons and a beam of at least 125 feet between the wing walls;

(I) an oceanographic research vessel;

(J) an instruction vessel;

(K) a pollution treatment, abatement, or control vessel;

(L) a fishing vessel whose ownership meets the citizenship requirements under section 50501 of this title for documenting vessels to operate in the coastwise trade; and

(M) an ocean thermal energy conversion facility or plantship that is or will be documented under the laws of the United States.

(15) VESSEL OF NATIONAL INTEREST.—The term "Vessel of National Interest" means a vessel deemed to be of national interest that meets characteristics determined by the Administrator, in consultation with the Secretary of Defense, the Secretary of the Department in which the Coast Guard is operating when it is not operating as a service

in the Department of the Navy, or the heads of other Federal agencies, as described in section 53703(d).

(Pub. L. 109–304, §8(c), Oct. 6, 2006, 120 Stat. 1601; Pub. L. 109–163, div. C, title XXXV, §3507(a)(1)(A), (b)(1), Jan. 6, 2006, 119 Stat. 3555; Pub. L. 110–181, div. C, title XXXV, §3522(a)(1), (10)(B), (b), Jan. 28, 2008, 122 Stat. 596, 598; Pub. L. 114–120, title III, §302(a)(1), Feb. 8, 2016, 130 Stat. 51; Pub. L. 116–92, div. C, title XXXV, §3506(a), Dec. 20, 2019, 133 Stat. 1970.)

§53702. GENERAL AUTHORITY

(a) IN GENERAL.—

(1) GUARANTEE OF PAYMENTS.—The Secretary or Administrator, on terms the Secretary or Administrator may prescribe, may guarantee or make a commitment to guarantee the payment of the principal of and interest on an obligation eligible to be guaranteed under this chapter. A guarantee or commitment to guarantee shall cover 100 percent of the principal and interest.

(2) PREFERRED ELIGIBLE LENDER.—The Federal Financing Bank shall be the preferred eligible lender of the principal and interest of the guaranteed obligations issued under this chapter.

(b) DIRECT LOANS FOR FISHERIES.—

(1) IN GENERAL.—Notwithstanding any other provision of this chapter, any obligation involving a fishing vessel, fishery facility, aquaculture facility, individual fishing quota, or fishing capacity reduction program issued under this chapter after October 11, 1996, shall be a direct loan obligation for which the Secretary shall be the obligee, rather than an obligation issued to an obligee other than the Secretary and guaranteed by the Secretary. A direct loan obligation under this subsection shall be treated in the same manner and to the same extent as an obligation guaranteed under this chapter except with respect to provisions of this chapter that by their nature can only be applied to obligations guaranteed under this chapter.

(2) INTEREST RATE.—Notwithstanding any other provision of this chapter, the annual rate of interest an obligor shall pay on a direct loan obligation under this subsection is 2 percent plus the additional percent the Secretary must pay as interest to borrow from the Treasury the funds to make the loan.

(3) MINIMUM OBLIGATIONS AVAILABLE FOR HISTORIC USES.—Of the direct loan obligations issued by the Secretary under this chapter, the Secretary shall make a minimum of $59,000,000 available each fiscal year for historic uses.

(4) USE OF OBLIGATIONS IN LIMITED ACCESS FISHERIES.—In addition to the other eligible purposes and uses of direct loan obligations provided for in this chapter, the Secretary may issue direct loan obligations for the purpose of—

(A) financing the construction or reconstruction of a fishing vessel in a fishery managed under a limited access system; or

(B) financing the purchase of harvesting rights in a fishery that is federally managed under a limited access system.

(Pub. L. 109–304, §8(c), Oct. 6, 2006, 120 Stat. 1603; Pub. L. 109–163, div. C, title XXXV, §3507(a)(1)(C), (d), Jan. 6, 2006, 119 Stat. 3555, 3557; Pub. L. 110–181, div. C, title XXXV, §3522(a)(10)(B), (b), Jan. 28, 2008, 122 Stat. 598; Pub. L. 114–120, title III, §302(a)(2), Feb. 8, 2016, 130 Stat. 52; Pub. L. 116–92, div. C, title XXXV, §3506(b), Dec. 20, 2019, 133 Stat. 1971.)

§53703. APPLICATION AND ADMINISTRATION

(a) TIME FOR DECISION.—

(1) IN GENERAL.—The Secretary or Administrator shall approve or deny an application for a loan guarantee under this chapter within 270 days after the date on which the signed application is received by the Secretary or Administrator.

(2) EXTENSION.—On request by an applicant, the Secretary or Administrator may extend the 270-day period in paragraph (1) to a date not later than 2 years after the date on which the signed application was received by the Secretary or Administrator.

(b) CERTIFICATION OF REVIEW.—The Secretary or Administrator may not guarantee or make a commitment to guarantee an obligation under this chapter unless the Secretary or Administrator certifies that a full and fair consideration of all the regulatory requirements, including economic soundness and financial requirements applicable to the obligor and related parties, and a thorough assessment of the technical, economic, and financial aspects of the loan application, has been made.

(c) INDEPENDENT ANALYSIS.—

(1) IN GENERAL.—To assess and mitigate the risks due to factors associated with markets, technology, financial, or legal structures related to an application or guarantee under this chapter, the Secretary or Administrator may utilize third party experts, including legal counsel, to—

(A) process and review applications under this chapter, including conducting independent analysis and review of aspects of an application;

(B) represent the Secretary or Administrator in structuring and documenting the obligation guarantee;

(C) analyze and review aspects of, structure, and document the obligation guarantee during the term of the guarantee;

(D) recommend financial covenants or financial ratios to be met by the applicant during the time a guarantee under this chapter is outstanding that are—

(i) based on the financial covenants or financial ratios, if any, that are then applicable to the obligor under private sector credit agreements; and

(ii) in lieu of other financial covenants applicable to the obligor under this chapter with respect to requirements regarding long-term debt-to-equity, minimum working capital, or minimum amount of equity; and

(E) represent the Secretary or Administrator to protect the security interests of the Government relating to an obligation guarantee.

(2) PRIVATE SECTOR EXPERT.—Independent analysis, review, and representation conducted under this subsection shall be performed by a private sector expert in the applicable field who is selected by the Secretary or Administrator.

(d) VESSELS OF NATIONAL INTEREST.—

(1) NOTICE OF FUNDING.—The Secretary or Administrator may post a notice in the Federal Register regarding the availability of funding for obligation guarantees under this chapter for the construction, reconstruction, or reconditioning of a Vessel of National

Interest and include a timeline for the submission of applications for such vessels.

(2) VESSEL CHARACTERISTICS.—

(A) IN GENERAL.—The Secretary or Administrator, in consultation with the Secretary of Defense, the Secretary of the Department in which the Coast Guard is operating when it is not operating as service in the Department of the Navy, or the heads of other Federal agencies, shall develop and publish a list of vessel types that would be considered Vessels of National Interest.

(B) REVIEW.—Such list shall be reviewed and revised every four years or as necessary, as determined by the Administrator.

(Pub. L. 109–304, §8(c), Oct. 6, 2006, 120 Stat. 1604; Pub. L. 109–163, div. C, title XXXV, §3507(a)(1)(D), (2)(G), (b)(7), Jan. 6, 2006, 119 Stat. 3555, 3556; Pub. L. 110–181, div. C, title XXXV, §3522(a)(10)(B), (b), Jan. 28, 2008, 122 Stat. 598; Pub. L. 116–92, div. C, title XXXV, §3506(c), Dec. 20, 2019, 133 Stat. 1971.)

§53704. FUNDING LIMITS

(a) GENERAL LIMITATIONS.—The total unpaid principal amount of obligations guaranteed under this chapter and outstanding at one time may not exceed $12,000,000,000. Of that amount, $850,000,000 shall be limited to obligations related to fishing vessels and fishery facilities.

(b) ADDITIONAL LIMITATIONS.—Additional limitations may not be imposed on new commitments to guarantee loans for any fiscal year, except in amounts established in advance by annual authorization laws. A vessel eligible for a guarantee under this chapter may not be denied eligibility because of its type.

(c) LIMITS BASED ON RISK FACTORS.—

(1) DEFINITION.—In this subsection, the term "cost" has the meaning given that term in section 502 of the Federal Credit Reform Act of 1990 (2 U.S.C. 661a).

(2) SYSTEM OF RISK CATEGORIES.—The Secretary or Administrator shall—

(A) establish, and update annually, a system of risk categories for obligations guaranteed under this chapter that categorizes the relative risk of guarantees based on the risk factors set forth in paragraph (4);

(B) determine annually for each risk category a subsidy rate equivalent to the cost of obligations in the category, expressed as a percentage of the amount guaranteed for obligations in the category; and

(C) ensure that each risk category is comprised of loans that are relatively homogeneous in cost and share characteristics predictive of defaults and other costs, given the facts known at the time of obligation or commitment, using a risk category system that is based on historical analysis of program data and statistical evidence concerning the likely costs of defaults or other costs that are expected to be associated with the loans in the category.

(3) USE OF SYSTEM.—

(A) PLACING OBLIGATION IN CATEGORY.—Before making a guarantee under this chapter for an obligation, and annually for projects subject to a guarantee, the Secretary or Administrator shall apply the risk factors specified in paragraph (4) to place the obligation in a risk category established under paragraph (2).

(B) REDUCTION OF AVAILABLE AMOUNT.—The Secretary or Administrator shall consider the total amount available to the Secretary or Administrator for making guarantees under this chapter to be reduced by the amount determined by multiplying—

　(i) the amount guaranteed under this chapter for an obligation; by

　(ii) the subsidy rate for the category in which the obligation is placed under subparagraph (A).

(C) ESTIMATED COST.—The estimated cost to the United States Government of a guarantee under this chapter for an obligation is deemed to be the amount determined under subparagraph (B) for the obligation.

(D) RESTRICTION ON FURTHER GUARANTEES.—The Secretary or Administrator may not guarantee obligations under this chapter after the total amount available to the Secretary or Administrator under appropriations laws for the cost of loan guarantees is considered to be reduced to zero under subparagraph (B).

(4) RISK FACTORS.—The risk factors referred to in this subsection are—

　(A) the period for which an obligation is guaranteed or to be guaranteed;

　(B) the amount of an obligation guaranteed or to be guaranteed in relation to the total cost of the project financed or to be financed by the obligation;

　(C) the financial condition of an obligor or applicant for a guarantee;

　(D) if applicable, other guarantees related to the project;

　(E) if applicable, the projected employment of each vessel or equipment to be financed with an obligation;

　(F) if applicable, the projected market that will be served by each vessel or equipment to be financed with an obligation;

　(G) the collateral provided for a guarantee for an obligation;

　(H) the management and operating experience of an obligor or applicant for a guarantee;

　(I) whether a guarantee under this chapter is or will be in effect during the construction period of the project; and

　(J) the concentration risk presented by an unduly large percentage of loans outstanding by any one borrower or group of affiliated borrowers.

(Pub. L. 109–304, §8(c), Oct. 6, 2006, 120 Stat. 1604; Pub. L. 109–163, div. C, title XXXV, §3507(a)(1)(C), Jan. 6, 2006, 119 Stat. 3555; Pub. L. 110–181, div. C, title XXXV, §3522(a)(10)(B), (b), Jan. 28, 2008, 122 Stat. 598; Pub. L. 116–92, div. C, title XXXV, §3506(d), Dec. 20, 2019, 133 Stat. 1972.)

§53705. PLEDGE OF UNITED STATES GOVERNMENT

(a) FULL FAITH AND CREDIT.—The full faith and credit of the United States Government is pledged to the payment of a guarantee made under this chapter, for both principal and interest, including interest (as may be provided for in the guarantee) accruing between the date of default under a guaranteed obligation and the date of payment in full of the guarantee.

(b) INCONTESTABILITY.—A guarantee or commitment to guarantee made under this chapter is conclusive evidence of the eligibility of the obligation for the guarantee. The validity of a guarantee or commitment to guarantee made under this chapter is incontestable.

(Pub. L. 109–304, §8(c), Oct. 6, 2006, 120 Stat. 1606; Pub. L. 109–163, div. C, title XXXV, §3507(a)(1)(C), Jan. 6, 2006, 119 Stat. 3555; Pub. L. 110–181, div. C, title XXXV, §3522(b), Jan. 28, 2008, 122 Stat. 598.)

§53706. Eligible purposes of obligations

(a) IN GENERAL.—To be eligible for a guarantee under this chapter, an obligation must aid in any of the following:

(1)(A) Financing (including reimbursement of an obligor for expenditures previously made for) the construction, reconstruction, or reconditioning of a vessel designed principally for research, or for commercial use—

(i) in the coastwise or intercoastal trade;

(ii) on the Great Lakes, or on bays, sounds, rivers, harbors, or inland lakes of the United States;

(iii) in foreign trade as defined in section 109(b) of this title;

(iv) as an ocean thermal energy conversion facility or plantship; or

(v) as a floating drydock in the construction, reconstruction, reconditioning, or repair of vessels.

(B) A guarantee under subparagraph (A) may not be made more than one year after delivery of the vessel (or redelivery if the vessel was reconstructed or reconditioned) unless the proceeds of the obligation are used to finance the construction, reconstruction, or reconditioning of a vessel or of facilities or equipment related to marine operations.

(2) Financing (including reimbursement of an obligor for expenditures previously made for) the construction, reconstruction, reconditioning, or purchase of a vessel owned by citizens of the United States and designed principally for research, or for commercial use in the fishing industry.

(3) Financing the purchase, reconstruction, or reconditioning of a vessel or fishery facility—

(A) for which an obligation was guaranteed under this chapter; and

(B) that, under subchapter II of this chapter—

(i) is a vessel or fishery facility for which an obligation was accelerated and paid;

(ii) was acquired by the Federal Ship Financing Fund or successor account under section 53717 of this title; or

(iii) was sold at foreclosure begun or intervened in by the Secretary or Administrator.

(4) Financing any part of the repayment to the United States Government of any amount of a construction-differential subsidy paid for a vessel.

(5) Refinancing an existing obligation (regardless of whether guaranteed under this chapter) issued for a purpose described in paragraphs (1)–(4), including a short-term obligation incurred to obtain temporary funds with the intention of refinancing.

(6) Financing or refinancing (including reimbursement of an obligor for expenditures previously made for) the construction, reconstruction, reconditioning, or purchase of a fishery facility.

(7) Financing or refinancing—

(A) the purchase of individual fishing quotas in accordance with section 303(d)(4) of the Magnuson-Stevens Fishery Conservation and Management Act (including the reimbursement of obligors for expenditures previously made for such a purchase);

(B) activities that assist in the transition to reduced fishing capacity; or

(C) technologies or upgrades designed to improve collection and reporting of fishery-dependent data, to reduce bycatch, to improve selectivity or reduce adverse impacts of fishing gear, or to improve safety.

(8) Financing (including reimbursement of an obligor for expenditures previously made for) the reconstruction, reconditioning, retrofitting, repair, reconfiguration, or similar work in a shipyard located in the United States.

(b) NON-VESSELS TREATED AS VESSELS.—An obligation guaranteed under subsection (a)(6) or (7) shall be treated, for purposes of this chapter, in the same manner and to the same extent as an obligation that aids in financing the construction, reconstruction, reconditioning, or purchase of a vessel, except with respect to provisions that by their nature can only be applied to vessels.

(c) PRIORITIES FOR CERTAIN VESSELS.—

(1) VESSELS.—In guaranteeing or making a commitment to guarantee an obligation under this chapter, the Administrator shall give priority to—

(A) a vessel that is otherwise eligible for a guarantee and is constructed with assistance under subtitle D of the Maritime Security Act of 2003 (46 U.S.C. 53101 note);

(B) after applying subparagraph (A), a vessel that is otherwise eligible for a guarantee and that the Secretary of Defense determines—

(i) is suitable for service as a naval auxiliary in time of war or national emergency; and

(ii) meets a shortfall in sealift capacity or capability; and

(C) after applying subparagraphs (A) and (B), Vessels of National Interest.

(2) TIME FOR DETERMINATION.—The Secretary of Defense shall determine whether a vessel satisfies paragraph (1)(B) not later than 30 days after receipt of a request from the Administrator for such a determination.

(Pub. L. 109–304, §8(c), Oct. 6, 2006, 120 Stat. 1606; Pub. L. 109–163, div. C, title XXXV, §3507(a)(1)(D), (2)(A), (B), (b)(2), Jan. 6, 2006, 119 Stat. 3555, 3556; Pub. L. 109–479, title II, §209, Jan. 12, 2007, 120 Stat. 3617; Pub. L. 110–181, div. C, title XXXV, §3522(a)(2), (10)(B), (b), Jan. 28, 2008, 122 Stat. 596, 598; Pub. L. 116–92, div. C, title XXXV, §3506(e), Dec. 20, 2019, 133 Stat. 1972; Pub. L. 118–31, div. C, title XXXV, §3536(a), Dec. 22, 2023, 137 Stat. 835.)

§53707. FINDINGS RELATED TO OBLIGORS AND OPERATORS

(a) RESPONSIBLE OBLIGOR.—The Secretary or Administrator may not guarantee or make a commitment to guarantee an obligation under this chapter unless the Secretary or Administrator finds that the obligor is responsible and has the ability, experience, financial resources, and other qualifications necessary for the adequate operation and maintenance of each vessel that will serve as security for the guarantee.

(b) OPERATORS OF LINER VESSELS.—The Administrator may not guarantee or make a commitment to guarantee a loan for the construction, reconstruction, or reconditioning of a liner vessel under this chapter unless the Chairman of the Federal Maritime Commission certifies that the operator of the vessel has not been found by the Commission to have committed, within the previous 5 years—

(1) a violation of part A of subtitle IV of this title that involves unjust or unfair discriminatory treatment or undue or unreasonable prejudice or disadvantage with respect to a United States shipper, ocean transportation intermediary, ocean common carrier, or port; or

(2) a violation of part B of subtitle IV of this title.

(c) OPERATORS OF FISHING VESSELS.—The Secretary may not guarantee or make a commitment to guarantee a loan for the construction, reconstruction, or reconditioning of a fishing vessel under this chapter if the operator of the vessel has been—

(1) held liable, or the vessel has been held liable in rem, for a civil penalty under section 308 of the Magnuson-Stevens Fishery Conservation and Management Act (16 U.S.C. 1858) and the operator has not paid the penalty;

(2) found guilty of an offense under section 309 of the Magnuson-Stevens Fishery Conservation and Management Act (16 U.S.C. 1859) and not paid the assessed fine or served the assessed sentence;

(3) held liable for a civil or criminal penalty under section 105 of the Marine Mammal Protection Act of 1972 (16 U.S.C. 1375) and not paid the assessed fine or served the assessed sentence; or

(4) held liable for a civil penalty by the Coast Guard under this title or title 33 and not paid the assessed fine.

(d) WAIVERS CONCERNING FINANCIAL CONDITION.—The Secretary or Administrator shall prescribe regulations concerning circumstances under which waivers of, or exceptions to, otherwise applicable regulatory requirements concerning financial condition can be made. The regulations shall require that—

(1) the economic soundness requirements in section 53708(a) of this title are met after the waiver of the financial condition requirement; and

(2) if the Secretary or Administrator considers necessary, the waiver shall provide for the imposition of other requirements on the obligor designed to compensate for any significant increase in risk associated with the obligor's failure to meet regulatory requirements applicable to financial condition.

(Pub. L. 109–304, §8(c), Oct. 6, 2006, 120 Stat. 1607; Pub. L. 109–163, div. C, title XXXV, §3507(a)(1)(D), (b)(3)(B), (C), (c)(1), Jan. 6, 2006, 119 Stat. 3555, 3556; Pub. L. 110–181, div. C, title XXXV, §3522(a)(3), (b), Jan. 28, 2008, 122 Stat. 597, 598.)

§53708. FINDINGS RELATED TO ECONOMIC SOUNDNESS

(a) BY ADMINISTRATOR.—The Administrator may not guarantee or make a commitment to guarantee an obligation under this chapter unless the Administrator finds that the property or project for which the obligation will be executed will be economically sound. In making that finding, the Administrator shall consider—

(1) the need in the particular segment of the maritime industry for new or additional capacity, including any impact on existing equipment for which a guarantee under this chapter is in effect;

(2) the market potential for employment of the vessel over the life of the guarantee;

(3) projected revenues and expenses associated with employment of the vessel;

(4) any charter, contract of affreightment, transportation agreement, or similar agreement or undertaking relevant to the employment of the vessel;

(5) other relevant criteria; and

(6) for inland waterways, the need for technical improvements, including increased fuel efficiency or improved safety.

(b) BY SECRETARY.—The Secretary may not guarantee or make a commitment to guarantee an obligation under this chapter unless the Secretary finds, at or prior to the time the commitment is made or the guarantee becomes effective, that—

(1) the property or project for which the obligation will be executed will be economically sound; and

(2) for a fishing vessel, the purpose of the financing or refinancing is consistent with—

(A) the wise use of the fisheries resources and the development, advancement, management, conservation, and protection of the fisheries resources; or

(B) the need for technical improvements, including increased fuel efficiency or improved safety.

(c) USED FISHING VESSELS AND FACILITIES.—The Secretary may not guarantee or make a commitment to guarantee an obligation under this chapter for the purchase of a used fishing vessel or used fishery facility unless the vessel or facility will be—

(1) reconstructed or reconditioned in the United States and will contribute to the development of the United States fishing industry; or

(2) used—

(A) in the harvesting of fish from an underused fishery; or

(B) for a purpose described in the definition of "fishery facility" in section 53701 of this title with respect to an underused fishery.

(d) INDEPENDENT ANALYSIS.—The Secretary or Administrator may make a determination that aspects of an application under this chapter require independent analysis to be conducted by third party experts due to risk factors associated with markets, technology, or financial structures. A third party independent analysis conducted under this subsection shall be performed by a private sector expert in assessing such risk factors who is selected by the Secretary or Administrator.

(e) ADDITIONAL EQUITY BECAUSE OF INCREASED RISKS.—Notwithstanding any other provision of this chapter, the Secretary or Administrator may make a determination that an application under this title requires additional equity because of increased risk factors associated with markets, technology, or financial structures.

(Pub. L. 109–304, §8(c), Oct. 6, 2006, 120 Stat. 1608; Pub. L. 109–163, div. C, title XXXV, §3507(a)(1)(D),

(2)(D), (b)(3)(A), (4), Jan. 6, 2006, 119 Stat. 3555, 3556; Pub. L. 110–181, div. C, title XXXV, §3522(a)(4), (b), Jan. 28, 2008, 122 Stat. 597, 598.)

§53709. Amount of obligations

(a) In General.—The principal of an obligation may not be guaranteed in an amount greater than the amount determined by multiplying the percentage applicable under subsection (b) by—

(1) the amount paid by or for the account of the obligor (as determined by the Secretary or Administrator, which determination shall be conclusive) for the construction, reconstruction, or reconditioning of the vessel used as security for the guarantee; or

(2) if the obligor creates an escrow fund under section 53715 of this title, the actual cost of the vessel.

(b) Limitations on Amount Borrowed.—

(1) In general.—Except as otherwise provided, the principal amount of an obligation guaranteed under this chapter may not exceed 75 percent of the actual cost or depreciated actual cost, as determined by the Secretary or Administrator, of the vessel used as security for the guarantee.

(2) Certain approved vessels.—The principal amount may not exceed 87.5 percent of the actual cost or depreciated actual cost if—

(A) the size and speed of the vessel are approved by the Secretary or Administrator;

(B) the vessel is or would have been eligible for mortgage aid for construction under section 509 of the Merchant Marine Act, 1936, or would have been eligible except that the vessel was built with a construction-differential subsidy and the subsidy has been repaid; and

(C) the vessel is of a type described in that section for which the minimum down payment required by that section is 12.5 percent of the cost of the vessel.

(3) Fishing vessels and fishery facilities.—For a fishing vessel or fishery facility, the principal amount may not exceed 80 percent of the actual cost or depreciated actual cost. However, debt for the vessel or facility may not be placed through the Federal Financing Bank.

(4) OTEC.—For an ocean thermal energy conversion facility or plantship constructed without a construction-differential subsidy, the principal amount may not exceed 87.5 percent of the actual cost or depreciated actual cost of the facility or plantship.

(c) Security Involving Multiple Vessels.—The principal amount of an obligation having more than one vessel as security for the guarantee may not exceed the sum of the principal amounts allowable for all the vessels.

(d) Prohibition on Uniform Percentage Limitations.—The Secretary or Administrator may not establish a percentage under any provision of subsection (b) that is to be applied uniformly to all guarantees or commitments to guarantee made under that provision.

(e) Prohibition on Minimum Principal Amount.—The Secretary may not establish, as a condition of eligibility for a guarantee under this chapter, a minimum principal amount for an obligation covering the reconstruction or reconditioning of a fishing vessel or fishery facility. For purposes of this chapter, the reconstruction or reconditioning of a fishing vessel or fishery facility does not include the routine minor repair or maintenance of the vessel or facility.

(Pub. L. 109–304, §8(c), Oct. 6, 2006, 120 Stat. 1609; Pub. L. 109–163, div. C, title XXXV, §3507(a)(1)(C), (D), Jan. 6, 2006, 119 Stat. 3555; Pub. L. 110–181, div. C, title XXXV, §3522(a)(10)(B), (b), Jan. 28, 2008, 122 Stat. 598; Pub. L. 116–92, div. C, title XXXV, §3506(f), Dec. 20, 2019, 133 Stat. 1972.)

§53710. CONTENTS OF OBLIGATIONS

(a) IN GENERAL.—An obligation guaranteed under this chapter must—

(1) provide for payments by the obligor satisfactory to the Secretary or Administrator;

(2) provide for interest (exclusive of guarantee fees and other fees) at a rate not more than the annual rate on the unpaid principal that the Secretary or Administrator determines is reasonable, considering the range of interest rates prevailing in the private market for similar loans and the risks assumed by the Secretary or Administrator;

(3) have a maturity date satisfactory to the Secretary or Administrator, but—

(A) not more than 25 years after the date of delivery of the vessel used as security for the guarantee; or

(B) if the vessel has been reconstructed or reconditioned, not more than the later of—

(i) 25 years after the date of delivery of the vessel; or

(ii) the remaining years of useful life of the vessel as determined by the Secretary or Administrator; and

(4) provide, or a related agreement must provide, that if the vessel used as security for the guarantee is a delivered vessel, the vessel shall be—

(A) in class A–1, American Bureau of Shipping, or meet other standards acceptable to the Secretary or Administrator, with all required certificates, including marine inspection certificates of the Coast Guard, and with all outstanding requirements and recommendations necessary for class retention accomplished, unless the Secretary or Administrator permits a deferment of repairs necessary to meet these requirements;

(B) well equipped, in good repair, and in every respect seaworthy and fit for service; and

(C) documented under the laws of the United States for the term of the guarantee of the obligation or until the obligation is paid in full, whichever is sooner.

(b) PROVISIONS FOR CERTAIN PASSENGER VESSELS.—

(1) IN GENERAL.—With the Administrator's approval, if the vessel used as security for the guarantee is a passenger vessel having the tonnage, speed, passenger accommodations, and other characteristics described in section 503 of the Merchant Marine Act, 1936, an obligation guaranteed under this chapter or a related agreement may provide that—

(A) the only recourse by the United States Government against the obligor for payments under the guarantee will be repossession of the vessel and assignment of insurance claims; and

(B) the obligor's liability for payments under the guarantee will be satisfied and discharged by the surrender of the vessel and all interest in the vessel to the Government in the condition described in paragraph (2).

(2) SURRENDER OF VESSEL.—

(A) IN GENERAL.—On surrender, the vessel must be—

(i) free and clear of all liens and encumbrances except the security interest conveyed to the Administrator under this chapter;

(ii) in class; and

(iii) in as good order and condition (ordinary wear and tear excepted) as when acquired by the obligor.

(B) COVERING DEFICIENCIES BY INSURANCE.—To the extent covered by insurance, a deficiency related to a requirement in subparagraph (A) may be satisfied by assignment of the obligor's insurance claims to the Government.

(c) OTHER PROVISIONS TO PROTECT SECURITY INTERESTS AND PROVIDE FOR THE FINANCIAL STABILITY OF THE OBLIGOR.—An obligation guaranteed under this chapter and any related agreement must contain other provisions, which shall include—

(1) provisions for the protection of the security interests of the Government (including acceleration, assumption, and subrogation provisions and the issuance of notes by the obligor to the Secretary or Administrator), liens and releases of liens, payment of taxes; and

(2) any other provisions that the Secretary or Administrator may prescribe.

(Pub. L. 109–304, §8(c), Oct. 6, 2006, 120 Stat. 1610; Pub. L. 109–163, div. C, title XXXV, §3507(a)(1)(D), (2)(C), Jan. 6, 2006, 119 Stat. 3555; Pub. L. 110–181, div. C, title XXXV, §3522(a)(5), (9)(A), (10)(B), (b), Jan. 28, 2008, 122 Stat. 598; Pub. L. 116–92, div. C, title XXXV, §3506(g), Dec. 20, 2019, 133 Stat. 1972.)

§53711. SECURITY INTEREST

(a) IN GENERAL.—The Secretary or Administrator may guarantee an obligation under this chapter only if the obligor conveys or agrees to convey to the Secretary or Administrator a security interest the Secretary or Administrator considers necessary to protect the interest of the United States Government.

(b) MULTIPLE VESSELS AND TYPES OF SECURITY.—The security interest may relate to more than one vessel and may consist of more than one type of security. If the security interest relates to more than one vessel, the obligation may have the latest maturity date allowable under section 53710(a)(3) of this title for any of the vessels used as security for the guarantee. However, the Secretary or Administrator may require such payments of principal prior to maturity, with respect to all related obligations, as the Secretary or Administrator considers necessary to maintain adequate security for the guarantee.

(Pub. L. 109–304, §8(c), Oct. 6, 2006, 120 Stat. 1612; Pub. L. 109–163, div. C, title XXXV, §3507(a)(1)(C), (D), Jan. 6, 2006, 119 Stat. 3555; Pub. L. 110–181, div. C, title XXXV, §3522(a)(10)(B), (b), Jan. 28, 2008, 122 Stat. 598.)

§53712. Monitoring financial condition and operations of obligor

(a) IN GENERAL.—The Secretary or Administrator shall monitor the financial condition and operations of the obligor on a regular basis during the term of the guarantee. The Secretary or Administrator shall document the results of the monitoring on an annual or quarterly basis depending on the condition of the obligor. If the Secretary or Administrator determines that the financial condition of the obligor warrants additional protections to the Secretary or Administrator, the Secretary or Administrator shall take appropriate action under subsection (b). If the Secretary or Administrator determines that the financial condition of the obligor jeopardizes its continued ability to perform its responsibilities in connection with the guarantee of an obligation by the Secretary or Administrator, the Secretary or Administrator shall make an immediate determination whether default should take place and whether further measures described in subsection (b) should be taken to protect the interests of the Secretary or Administrator while ensuring that program objectives are met.

(b) CONTRACT PROVISIONS TO PROTECT SECRETARY OR ADMINISTRATOR.—The Secretary or Administrator shall include provisions in a loan agreement with an obligor that provides additional authority to the Secretary or Administrator to take action to limit potential losses in connection with a defaulted loan or a loan that is in jeopardy due to the deteriorating financial condition of the obligor. If the Secretary or Administrator has waived a requirement under section 53707(d) of this title, the loan agreement shall include requirements for additional payments, collateral, or equity contributions to meet the waived requirement upon the occurrence of verifiable conditions indicating that the obligor's financial condition enables the obligor to meet the waived requirement.

(Pub. L. 109–304, §8(c), Oct. 6, 2006, 120 Stat. 1612; Pub. L. 109–163, div. C, title XXXV, §3507(a)(1)(D), (b)(6), Jan. 6, 2006, 119 Stat. 3555, 3556; Pub. L. 110–181, div. C, title XXXV, §3522(a)(6), (10)(B), (b), Jan. 28, 2008, 122 Stat. 598.)

§53713. Administrative fees

(a) IN GENERAL.—The Secretary or Administrator shall charge and collect from the obligor fees the Secretary or Administrator considers reasonable for processing the application and monitoring the loan guarantee, including for—

(1) investigating an application for a guarantee;

(2) appraising property offered as security for a guarantee;

(3) issuing a commitment;

(4) providing services related to an escrow fund under section 53715 of this title or a deposit fund under section 53716 of this title;

(5) inspecting property during construction, reconstruction, or reconditioning; and

(6) monitoring and providing services related to the obligor's compliance with any terms related to the obligations, the guarantee, or maintenance of the Secretary or Administrator's security interests under this chapter.

(b) TOTAL FEE LIMITATION.—The total fees under subsection (a) may not exceed 0.5 percent of the original principal amount of the obligations to be guaranteed.

(c) FEES FOR INDEPENDENT ANALYSIS.—

(1) IN GENERAL.—The Secretary or Administrator may charge and collect fees to cover

the costs of independent analysis under section 53703(c) of this title. Notwithstanding section 3302 of title 31, any fee collected under this subsection shall—

(A) be credited as an offsetting collection to the account that finances the administration of the loan guarantee program;

(B) be available for expenditure only to pay the costs of activities and services for which the fee is imposed; and

(C) remain available until expended.

(2) FEE LIMITATION INAPPLICABLE.—Fees collected under this subsection are not subject to the limitation of subsection (b).

(Pub. L. 109–304, §8(c), Oct. 6, 2006, 120 Stat. 1612; Pub. L. 109–163, div. C, title XXXV, §3507(a)(1)(D), Jan. 6, 2006, 119 Stat. 3555; Pub. L. 110–181, div. C, title XXXV, §3522(a)(10)(B), (b), Jan. 28, 2008, 122 Stat. 598; Pub. L. 116–92, div. C, title XXXV, §3506(h), Dec. 20, 2019, 133 Stat. 1973.)

§53714. GUARANTEE FEES

(a) REGULATIONS.—Subject to this section, the Secretary or Administrator shall prescribe regulations to assess a fee for guaranteeing an obligation under this chapter.

(b) COMPUTATION OF FEE.—

(1) IN GENERAL.—The amount of the fee for a guarantee under this chapter shall be equal to the sum of the amounts determined under paragraph (2) for the years in which the guarantee is in effect.

(2) PRESENT VALUE FOR EACH YEAR.—The amount referred to in paragraph (1) for a year in which the guarantee is in effect is the present value of the amount calculated under paragraph (3). To determine the present value, the Secretary or Administrator shall apply a discount rate determined by the Secretary of the Treasury, considering current market yields on outstanding obligations of the United States Government having periods to maturity comparable to the period to maturity for the guaranteed obligation.

(3) CALCULATION OF AMOUNT.—The amount referred to in paragraph (2) shall be calculated by multiplying—

(A) the estimated average unpaid principal amount of the obligation that will be outstanding during the year (excluding the average amount, other than interest, on deposit during the year in an escrow fund under section 53715 of this title); by

(B) the fee rate set under paragraph (4).

(4) SETTING FEE RATES.—To set the fee rate referred to in paragraph (3)(B), the Secretary or Administrator shall establish a formula that—

(A) takes into account the security provided for the guaranteed obligation; and

(B) is a sliding scale based on the creditworthiness of the obligor, using—

(i) the lowest allowable rate under paragraph (5) for the most creditworthy obligors; and

(ii) the highest allowable rate under paragraph (5) for the least creditworthy obligors.

(5) PERMISSIBLE RANGE OF RATES.—The fee rate set under paragraph (4) shall be—

(A) for a delivered vessel or equipment, at least 0.5 percent and not more than 1 percent; and

(B) for a vessel to be constructed, reconstructed, or reconditioned or equipment to be delivered, at least 0.25 percent and not more than 0.5 percent.

(c) WHEN FEE COLLECTED.—A fee for the guarantee of an obligation under this chapter shall be collected not later than the date on which an amount is first paid on the obligation.

(d) FINANCING THE FEE.—A fee paid under this section is eligible to be financed under this chapter and shall be included in the actual cost of the obligation guaranteed.

(e) NOT REFUNDABLE.—A fee paid under this section is not refundable. However, an obligor shall receive credit for the amount paid for the remaining term of the obligation if the obligation is refinanced and guaranteed under this chapter after the refinancing.

(Pub. L. 109–304, §8(c), Oct. 6, 2006, 120 Stat. 1613; Pub. L. 109–163, div. C, title XXXV, §3507(a)(1)(D), Jan. 6, 2006, 119 Stat. 3555; Pub. L. 110–181, div. C, title XXXV, §3522(a)(10)(B), (b), Jan. 28, 2008, 122 Stat. 598.)

§53715. ESCROW FUND

(a) IN GENERAL.—If the proceeds of an obligation guaranteed under this chapter are to be used to finance the construction, reconstruction, or reconditioning of a vessel that will serve as security for a guarantee under this chapter, the Secretary or Administrator may accept and hold in escrow, under an escrow agreement with the obligor, a portion of the proceeds of all obligations guaranteed under this chapter whose proceeds are to be so used which is equal to—

(1) the excess of—

(A) the principal amount of all obligations whose proceeds are to be so used; over

(B) 75 percent or 87.5 percent, whichever is applicable under section 53709(b) of this title, of the amount paid by or for the account of the obligor for the construction, reconstruction, or reconditioning of the vessel; plus

(2) any interest the Secretary or Administrator may require on the amount described in paragraph (1).

(b) SECURITY INVOLVING BOTH UNCOMPLETED AND DELIVERED VESSELS.—If the security for the guarantee of an obligation relates both to a vessel to be constructed, reconstructed, or reconditioned and to a delivered vessel, the principal amount of the obligation shall be prorated for purposes of subsection (a) under regulations prescribed by the Secretary or Administrator.

(c) DISBURSEMENT BEFORE TERMINATION OF AGREEMENT.—

(1) PURPOSES.—The Secretary or Administrator shall disburse amounts in the escrow fund, as specified in the escrow agreement, to—

(A) pay amounts the obligor is obligated to pay for—

(i) the construction, reconstruction, or reconditioning of a vessel used as security for the guarantee; and

(ii) interest on the obligations;

(B) redeem the obligations under a refinancing guaranteed under this chapter; and

(C) pay any excess interest deposits to the obligor at times provided for in the escrow agreement.

(2) MANNER OF PAYMENT.—If a payment becomes due under the guarantee before the termination of the escrow agreement, the amount in the escrow fund at the time the payment becomes due, including realized income not yet paid to the obligor, shall be paid into the appropriate account under section 53717 of this title. The amount shall be credited against amounts due or to become due from the obligor to the Secretary or Administrator on the guaranteed obligations or, to the extent not so required, be paid to the obligor.

(d) PAYMENTS REQUIRED BEFORE DISBURSEMENT.—

(1) IN GENERAL.—No disbursement shall be made under subsection (c) to any person until the total amount paid by or for the account of the obligor from sources other than the proceeds of the obligation equals at least 25 percent or 12.5 percent, whichever is applicable under section 53709(b) of this title, of the aggregate actual cost of the vessel, as previously approved by the Secretary or Administrator. If the aggregate actual cost of the vessel has increased since the Secretary's or Administrator's initial approval or if it increases after the first disbursement is permitted under this subsection, then no further disbursements shall be made under subsection (c) until the total amount paid by or for the account of the obligor from sources other than the proceeds of the obligation equals at least 25 percent or 12.5 percent, as applicable, of the increase, as determined by the Secretary or Administrator, in the aggregate actual cost of the vessel. This paragraph does not require the Secretary or Administrator to consent to finance any increase in actual cost unless the Secretary or Administrator determines that such an increase in the obligation meets all the terms and conditions of this chapter or other applicable law.

(2) DOCUMENTED PROOF OF PROGRESS REQUIREMENT.—The Secretary or Administrator shall, by regulation, establish a transparent, independent, and risk-based process for verifying and documenting the progress of projects under construction before disbursing guaranteed loan funds. At a minimum, the process shall require documented proof of progress in connection with the construction, reconstruction, or reconditioning of a vessel or vessels before disbursements are made from the escrow fund. The Secretary or Administrator may require that the obligor provide a certificate from an independent party certifying that the requisite progress in construction, reconstruction, or reconditioning has taken place.

(e) DISBURSEMENT ON TERMINATION OF AGREEMENT.—

(1) IN GENERAL.—If a payment has not become due under the guarantee before the termination of the escrow agreement, the balance of the escrow fund at the time of termination shall be disbursed to—

(A) prepay the excess of—

(i) the principal amount of all obligations whose proceeds are to be used to finance the construction, reconstruction, or reconditioning of the vessel used or to be used as security for the guarantee; over

(ii) 75 percent or 87.5 percent, whichever is applicable under section 53709(b) of this title, of the actual cost of the vessel to the extent paid; and

(B) pay interest on that prepaid amount of principal.

(2) REMAINING BALANCE.—Any remaining balance of the escrow fund shall be paid to the obligor.

(f) INVESTMENT.—The Secretary or Administrator may invest and reinvest any part of an escrow fund in obligations of the United States Government with maturities such that the escrow fund will be available as required for purposes of the escrow agreement. Investment income shall be paid to the obligor when received.

(g) TERMS TO PROTECT GOVERNMENT.—The escrow agreement shall contain other terms the Secretary or Administrator considers necessary to protect fully the interests of the Government.

(Pub. L. 109–304, §8(c), Oct. 6, 2006, 120 Stat. 1614; Pub. L. 109–163, div. C, title XXXV, §3507(a)(1)(H), (3), Jan. 6, 2006, 119 Stat. 3555; Pub. L. 110–181, div. C, title XXXV, §3522(a)(10)(B), (11), (b), Jan. 28, 2008, 122 Stat. 598.)

§53716. DEPOSIT FUND

(a) IN GENERAL.—There is a deposit fund in the Treasury for purposes of this section. The Secretary or Administrator, in accordance with an agreement under subsection (b), may deposit into and hold in the fund cash belonging to an obligor to serve as collateral for a guarantee made under this chapter with respect to the obligor.

(b) AGREEMENT.—The Secretary or Administrator and an obligor shall make a reserve fund or other collateral account agreement to govern the deposit, withdrawal, retention, use, and reinvestment of cash of the obligor held in the fund. The agreement shall contain—

(1) terms and conditions required by this section;

(2) terms that grant to the United States Government a security interest in all amounts deposited into the fund; and

(3) any additional terms considered by the Secretary or Administrator to be necessary to protect fully the interests of the Government.

(c) INVESTMENT.—The Secretary or Administrator may invest and reinvest any part of the amounts in the fund in obligations of the Government with maturities such that amounts in the fund will be available as required for purposes of the agreement under subsection (b). Cash balances in the fund in excess of current requirements shall be maintained in a form of uninvested funds, and the Secretary of the Treasury shall pay interest on these funds.

(d) WITHDRAWALS.—

(1) IN GENERAL.—Cash deposited into the fund may not be withdrawn without the consent of the Secretary or Administrator.

(2) USE OF INCOME.—Subject to paragraph (3), the Secretary or Administrator may pay any income earned on cash of an obligor deposited into the fund in accordance with the agreement with the obligor under subsection (b).

(3) RETENTION AGAINST DEFAULT.—The Secretary or Administrator may retain and offset any or all of the cash of an obligor in the fund, and any income realized thereon, as

part of the Secretary's or Administrator's recovery against the obligor in case of a default by the obligor on an obligation.

(Pub. L. 109–304, §8(c), Oct. 6, 2006, 120 Stat. 1616; Pub. L. 109–163, div. C, title XXXV, §3507(a)(1)(H), (3), Jan. 6, 2006, 119 Stat. 3555; Pub. L. 110–181, div. C, title XXXV, §3522(a)(10)(B), (11), (b), Jan. 28, 2008, 122 Stat. 598.)

§53717. MANAGEMENT OF FUNDS IN THE TREASURY

(a) DEFINITION.—In this section, the term "FCRA" means the Federal Credit Reform Act of 1990 (2 U.S.C. 661 et seq.).

(b) LOAN GUARANTEES BY ADMINISTRATOR.—

(1) WHEN NOT SUBJECT TO FCRA.—The Administrator shall account for payments and disbursements involving obligations guaranteed under this chapter and not subject to FCRA in an account in the Treasury entitled the Federal Ship Financing Fund Liquidating Account (a liquidating account as defined in FCRA).

(2) WHEN SUBJECT TO FCRA.—The Administrator shall account for payments and disbursements involving obligations guaranteed under this chapter and subject to FCRA in a separate account in the Treasury entitled the Federal Ship Financing Guaranteed Loan Financing Account (a financing account as defined in FCRA).

(c) LOAN GUARANTEES BY SECRETARY.—

(1) WHEN NOT SUBJECT TO FCRA.—The Secretary shall account for payments and disbursements involving obligations guaranteed under this chapter and not subject to FCRA in a separate account in the Treasury established for this purpose.

(2) WHEN SUBJECT TO FCRA.—The Secretary shall account for payments and disbursements involving obligations guaranteed under this chapter and subject to FCRA in a separate account in the Treasury established for this purpose.

(d) DIRECT LOANS BY SECRETARY.—The Secretary shall account for payments and disbursements involving direct loans made under this chapter in a separate account in the Treasury established for this purpose.

(Pub. L. 109–304, §8(c), Oct. 6, 2006, 120 Stat. 1616; Pub. L. 109–163, div. C, title XXXV, §3507(a)(1)(B), (D), (c)(2), Jan. 6, 2006, 119 Stat. 3555, 3556; Pub. L. 110–181, div. C, title XXXV, §3522(a)(7), (9)(B), (b), Jan. 28, 2008, 122 Stat. 598.)

§53718. ANNUAL REPORT TO CONGRESS

The Administrator shall report to Congress annually on the loan guarantee program under this chapter. Each report shall include—

(1) the size, in dollars, of the portfolio of loans guaranteed;
(2) the size, in dollars, of projects in the portfolio facing financial difficulties;
(3) the number and type of projects covered;
(4) a profile of pending loan applications;
(5) the amount of appropriations available for new guarantees;
(6) a profile of each project approved since the last report; and
(7) a profile of any defaults since the last report.

(Pub. L. 109–304, §8(c), Oct. 6, 2006, 120 Stat. 1617; Pub. L. 109–163, div. C, title XXXV, §3507(c)(3),

Jan. 6, 2006, 119 Stat. 3556; Pub. L. 110–181, div. C, title XXXV, §3522(a)(9)(C), (b), Jan. 28, 2008, 122 Stat. 598.)

§53719. BEST PRACTICES

The Secretary or Administrator shall ensure that all standard documents and agreements that relate to loan guarantees made pursuant to this chapter are reviewed and updated every four years to ensure that such documents and agreements meet the current commercial best practices to the extent permitted by law.

(Added Pub. L. 116–92, div. C, title XXXV, §3506(i)(1), Dec. 20, 2019, 133 Stat. 1973.)

SUBCHAPTER II—DEFAULT PROVISIONS

§53721. RIGHTS OF OBLIGEE

(a) DEMANDS BY OBLIGEES.—Except as provided in subsection (c), if an obligor has continued in default for 30 days in the payment of principal or interest on an obligation guaranteed under this chapter, the obligee or the obligee's agent may demand that the Secretary or Administrator pay the unpaid principal amount of the obligation and the unpaid interest on the obligation to the date of payment. The demand must be made within the earlier of—

(1) a period that may be specified in the guarantee or a related agreement; or
(2) 90 days from the date of the default.

(b) PAYMENTS BY SECRETARY OR ADMINISTRATOR.—

(1) IN GENERAL.—If a demand is made under subsection (a), the Secretary or Administrator shall pay to the obligee or the obligee's agent the unpaid principal amount of the obligation and the unpaid interest on the obligation to the date of payment. Payment shall be made within the earlier of—

(A) a period that may be specified in the guarantee or a related agreement; or
(B) 30 days from the date of the demand.

(2) IF NO EXISTING DEFAULT.—The Secretary or Administrator is not required to make payment under this subsection if, within the appropriate period under paragraph (1), the Secretary or Administrator finds that the obligor was not in default or that the default was remedied before the demand.

(c) ASSUMPTION OF RIGHTS AND OBLIGATIONS BEFORE DEMAND.—An obligee or the obligee's agent may not demand payment under this section if the Secretary or Administrator, before the demand and on terms that may be provided in the obligation or a related agreement, has assumed the obligor's rights and duties under the obligation and any related agreement and made any payment in default. However, the guarantee of the obligation remains in effect after the Secretary's or Administrator's assumption.

(Pub. L. 109–304, §8(c), Oct. 6, 2006, 120 Stat. 1617; Pub. L. 109–163, div. C, title XXXV, §3507(a)(1)(C), (F), Jan. 6, 2006, 119 Stat. 3555; Pub. L. 110–181, div. C, title XXXV, §3522(a)(10)(B), (11), (b), Jan. 28, 2008, 122 Stat. 598.)

§53722. ACTIONS BY SECRETARY OR ADMINISTRATOR

(a) GENERAL AUTHORITY.—On default under an obligation or related agreement between the Secretary or Administrator and the obligor, the Secretary or Administrator, on terms that may be provided in the obligation or agreement, may—

(1) assume the obligor's rights and duties under the obligation or agreement, make any payment in default, and notify the obligee or the obligee's agent of the default and the Secretary's or Administrator's assumption; or

(2) notify the obligee or the obligee's agent of the default.

(b) DEMANDS BY OBLIGEES.—

(1) DEMAND.—If the Secretary or Administrator proceeds under subsection (a)(2), the obligee or the obligee's agent may demand that the Secretary or Administrator pay the unpaid principal amount of the obligation and the unpaid interest on the obligation. The demand must be made within the earlier of—

(A) a period that may be specified in the guarantee or a related agreement; or

(B) 60 days from the date of the Secretary's or Administrator's notice.

(2) PAYMENT.—If a demand is made under paragraph (1), the Secretary or Administrator shall pay to the obligee or the obligee's agent the unpaid principal amount of the obligation and the unpaid interest on the obligation to the date of payment. Payment shall be made within the earlier of—

(A) a period that may be specified in the guarantee or a related agreement; or

(B) 30 days from the date of the demand.

(c) CONTINUED EFFECT OF GUARANTEE.—A guarantee of an obligation remains in effect after an assumption of the obligation by the Secretary or Administrator.

(d) ADDITIONAL RESPONSES.—If there is a default on an obligation, the Secretary or Administrator shall conduct operations under this chapter in a manner that—

(1) maximizes the net present value return from the sale or disposition of assets associated with the obligation, including prompt referral to the Attorney General for collection as appropriate;

(2) minimizes the amount of any loss realized in the resolution of the guarantee;

(3) ensures adequate competition and fair and consistent treatment of offerors; and

(4) requires appraisal of assets by an independent appraiser.

(Pub. L. 109–304, §8(c), Oct. 6, 2006, 120 Stat. 1618; Pub. L. 109–163, div. C, title XXXV, §3507(a)(1)(C), (F), Jan. 6, 2006, 119 Stat. 3555; Pub. L. 110–181, div. C, title XXXV, §3522(a)(10)(B), (11), (b), Jan. 28, 2008, 122 Stat. 598.)

§53723. PAYMENTS BY SECRETARY OR ADMINISTRATOR AND ISSUANCE OF OBLIGATIONS

(a) CASH PAYMENT.—Amounts required to be paid by the Secretary or Administrator under section 53721 or 53722 of this title shall be paid in cash.

(b) ISSUANCE OF OBLIGATIONS.—If amounts in the appropriate account under section 53717 of this title are not sufficient to make a payment required under section 53721 or 53722 of this title, the Secretary or Administrator may issue obligations to the Secretary of the Treasury. The Secretary or Administrator, with the approval of the Secretary of the Treasury, shall prescribe the form, denomination, maturity, and other terms (except the interest rate) of the obligations. The Secretary of the Treasury shall set the interest rate for the obligations, considering the current average market yield on outstanding marketable obligations of the United States Government of comparable maturities during the month before the obligations are issued.

(c) PURCHASE OF OBLIGATIONS.—The Secretary of the Treasury shall purchase the obligations issued under this section. To purchase the obligations, the Secretary of the Treasury may use as a public debt transaction the proceeds from the sale of securities issued under chapter 31 of title 31. The purposes for which securities may be issued under that chapter are extended to include the purchase of obligations under this subsection. The Secretary of the Treasury may sell obligations purchased under this section. A redemption, purchase, or sale of the obligations by the Secretary of the Treasury is a public debt transaction of the Government.

(d) DEPOSITS AND REDEMPTIONS.—The Secretary or Administrator shall deposit amounts borrowed under this section in the appropriate account under section 53717 of this title and make redemptions of the obligations from that account.

(Pub. L. 109–304, §8(c), Oct. 6, 2006, 120 Stat. 1618; Pub. L. 109–163, div. C, title XXXV, §3507(a)(1)(G), Jan. 6, 2006, 119 Stat. 3555; Pub. L. 110–181, div. C, title XXXV, §3522(a)(10)(B), (b), Jan. 28, 2008, 122 Stat. 598.)

§53724. RIGHTS TO SECURED PROPERTY

(a) ACQUISITION OF SECURITY RIGHTS.—When the Secretary or Administrator makes a payment on, or assumes, an obligation under section 53721 or 53722 of this title, the Secretary or Administrator acquires the rights under the security agreement with the obligor in the security held by the Secretary or Administrator to guarantee the obligation.

(b) USE AND DISPOSITION OF SECURED PROPERTY.—Notwithstanding any other law relating to the acquisition, handling, or disposal of property by the United States Government, the Secretary or Administrator has the right, in the Secretary's or Administrator's discretion, to complete, reconstruct, recondition, renovate, repair, maintain, operate, charter, or sell any property acquired under a security agreement with an obligor, or to place a vessel so acquired in the National Defense Reserve Fleet. The terms of a sale under this subsection shall be as approved by the Secretary or Administrator.

(Pub. L. 109–304, §8(c), Oct. 6, 2006, 120 Stat. 1619; Pub. L. 109–163, div. C, title XXXV, §3507(a)(1)(F), Jan. 6, 2006, 119 Stat. 3555; Pub. L. 110–181, div. C, title XXXV, §3522(a)(10)(B), (11), (b), Jan. 28, 2008, 122 Stat. 598.)

§53725. ACTIONS AGAINST OBLIGOR

(a) IN GENERAL.—For a default under a guaranteed obligation or related agreement, the Secretary or Administrator may take any action against the obligor or another liable party that the Secretary or Administrator considers necessary to protect the interests of the United States Government. A civil action may be brought in the name of the United States or the obligee. The obligee shall make available to the Government all records and evidence necessary to prosecute the action.

(b) TITLE, POSSESSION, AND PURCHASE.—

(1) IN GENERAL.—The Secretary or Administrator may—

(A) accept a conveyance of title to and possession of property from the obligor or another party liable to the Secretary or Administrator; and

(B) purchase the property for an amount not greater than the unpaid principal amount of the obligation and interest thereon.

(2) PAYMENT OF EXCESS.—If, through the sale of property, the Secretary or Administrator receives an amount of cash greater than the unpaid principal amount of the obligation, the unpaid interest on the obligation, and the expenses of collecting those amounts, the Secretary or Administrator shall pay the excess to the obligor.

(Pub. L. 109–304, §8(c), Oct. 6, 2006, 120 Stat. 1619; Pub. L. 109–163, div. C, title XXXV, §3507(a)(1)(F), Jan. 6, 2006, 119 Stat. 3555; Pub. L. 110–181, div. C, title XXXV, §3522(a)(10)(B), (b), Jan. 28, 2008, 122 Stat. 598.)

SUBCHAPTER III—PARTICULAR PROJECTS

§53731. COMMERCIAL DEMONSTRATION OCEAN THERMAL ENERGY CONVERSION FACILITIES AND PLANTSHIPS

(a) IN GENERAL.—Under subchapter I of this chapter, the Administrator may guarantee or make a commitment to guarantee the payment of the principal of and interest on an obligation that aids in financing (including reimbursement of an obligor for expenditures previously made for) the construction, reconstruction, or reconditioning of a commercial demonstration ocean thermal energy conversion facility or plantship. This section may be used to guarantee obligations for a total of not more than 5 separate facilities and plantships or a demonstrated 400 megawatt capacity, whichever comes first.

(b) APPLICABILITY OF OTHER PROVISIONS.—Except as otherwise provided in this section, a guarantee or commitment to guarantee under this section is subject to all the provisions applicable to a guarantee or commitment to guarantee under subchapter I of this chapter.

(c) ECONOMIC SOUNDNESS.—The required determination of economic soundness under section 53708 of this title applies to a guarantee or commitment to guarantee for that portion of a facility or plantship not to be supported with appropriated Federal funds.

(d) REASONABLENESS OF RISK.—A guarantee or commitment to guarantee may not be made under this section unless the Secretary of Energy, in consultation with the Administrator, certifies to the Administrator that, for the facility or plantship for which the guarantee or commitment to guarantee is sought, there is sufficient guarantee of performance and payment to lower the risk to the United States Government to a reasonable level. In deciding whether to issue such a certification, the Secretary of Energy shall consider—

(1) the successful demonstration of the technology to be used in the facility at a scale sufficient to establish the likelihood of technical and economic viability in the proposed market; and

(2) the need of the United States to develop new and renewable sources of energy and the benefits to be realized from the construction and successful operation of the facility or plantship.

(e) AMOUNT OF OBLIGATION.—The total principal amount of an obligation guaranteed under this section may not exceed 87.5 percent of—

(1) the actual cost or depreciated actual cost of the facility or plantship; or

(2) if the facility or plantship is supported with appropriated Federal funds, the total principal amount of that portion of the actual cost or depreciated actual cost for which the obligor is obligated to secure financing under the agreement between the obligor and the Department of Energy or other Federal agency.

(f) OTEC DEMONSTRATION FUND.—

(1) IN GENERAL.—There is a special subaccount, known as the OTEC Demonstration Fund, in the account established under section 53717(b)(1) of this title.

(2) USE AND OPERATION.—The OTEC Demonstration Fund shall be used for obligation guarantees authorized under this section that do not qualify under subchapter I of this chapter. Except as otherwise provided in this section, the OTEC Demonstration Fund shall be operated in the same manner as the parent account. However—

(A) amounts received by the Administrator under subchapter I of this chapter related to guarantees or commitments to guarantee made under this section shall be deposited only in the OTEC Demonstration Fund; and

(B) when obligations issued by the Administrator under section 53723 of this title related to the OTEC Demonstration Fund are outstanding, any amount received by the Administrator under subchapter I of this chapter related to ocean thermal energy conversion facilities or plantships shall be deposited in the OTEC Demonstration Fund.

(3) TRANSFERS.—Assets in the OTEC Demonstration Fund may be transferred to the parent account when and to the extent the balance in the OTEC Demonstration Fund exceeds the total guarantees or commitments to guarantee made under this section then outstanding, plus obligations issued by the Administrator under section 53723 of this title related to the OTEC Demonstration Fund.

(4) LIABILITY.—The parent account is not liable for a guarantee or commitment to guarantee made under this section.

(5) MAXIMUM UNPAID PRINCIPAL AMOUNT.—The total unpaid principal amount of the obligations guaranteed with the backing of the OTEC Demonstration Fund and outstanding at any one time may not exceed $1,650,000,000.

(g) ISSUANCE AND PAYMENT OF OBLIGATIONS.—Section 53723 of this title applies to the OTEC Demonstration Fund. However, obligations issued by the Administrator under that section related to the OTEC Demonstration Fund shall be payable only from proceeds realized by the OTEC Demonstration Fund.

(h) TAXATION OF INTEREST.—Interest on an obligation guaranteed under this section shall be included in gross income under chapter 1 of the Internal Revenue Code of 1986 (26 U.S.C. ch. 1).

(Pub. L. 109–304, §8(c), Oct. 6, 2006, 120 Stat. 1620; Pub. L. 109–163, div. C, title XXXV, §3507(a)(2)(H), Jan. 6, 2006, 119 Stat. 3555; Pub. L. 110–181, div. C, title XXXV, §3522(a)(9)(D), (b), Jan. 28, 2008, 122 Stat. 598.)

[§53732. Repealed. Pub. L. 116–92, div. C, title XXXV, §3506(i)(2), Dec. 20, 2019, 133 Stat.

CHAPTER 537—LOANS AND GUARANTEES

[§53732. Repealed. Pub. L. 116–92, div. C, title XXXV, §3506(i)(2), Dec. 20, 2019, 133 Stat. 1974]

Section, Pub. L. 109–304, §8(c), Oct. 6, 2006, 120 Stat. 1621; Pub. L. 109–163, div. C, title XXXV, §3507(a)(1)(C), (D), (2)(E), (F), (I), (J), (b)(3)(A), (5), (8), Jan. 6, 2006, 119 Stat. 3555, 3556; Pub. L. 110–181, div. C, title XXXV, §3522(a)(8), (9)(E), (b), Jan. 28, 2008, 122 Stat. 598, authorized the Administrator to guarantee an obligation for an eligible export vessel in accordance with certain laws and terms and established an interagency council.

§53733. Shipyard modernization and improvement

(a) DEFINITIONS.—In this section:

(1) ADVANCED SHIPBUILDING TECHNOLOGY.—The term "advanced shipbuilding technology" includes—

(A) numerically controlled machine tools, robots, automated process control equipment, computerized flexible manufacturing systems, associated computer software, and other technology for improving shipbuilding and related industrial production that advance the state-of-the-art; and

(B) novel techniques and processes designed to improve shipbuilding quality, productivity, and practice, and to promote sustainable development, including engineering design, quality assurance, concurrent engineering, continuous process production technology, energy efficiency, waste minimization, design for recyclability or parts reuse, inventory management, upgraded worker skills, and communications with customers and suppliers.

(2) GENERAL SHIPYARD FACILITY.—The term "general shipyard facility" means—

(A) for operations on land—

(i) a structure or appurtenance thereto designed for the construction, reconstruction, repair, rehabilitation, or refurbishment of a vessel, including a graving dock, building way, ship lift, wharf, or pier crane;

(ii) the land necessary for the structure or appurtenance; and

(iii) equipment that is for use with the structure or appurtenance and that is necessary for performing a function referred to in clause (i); and

(B) for operations not on land, a vessel, floating drydock, or barge built in the United States and used for, equipped to be used for, or of a type normally used for, performing a function referred to in subparagraph (A)(i).

(3) MODERN SHIPBUILDING TECHNOLOGY.—The term "modern shipbuilding technology" means the best available proven technology, techniques, and processes appropriate to enhancing the productivity of shipyards.

(b) GENERAL AUTHORITY.—Under subchapter I of this chapter, the Administrator may guarantee or make a commitment to guarantee the payment of the principal of and interest on an obligation for advanced shipbuilding technology and modern shipbuilding technology of a general shipyard facility in the United States. Only a private shipyard is eligible to receive a guarantee.

(c) APPLICABILITY OF OTHER PROVISIONS.—Except as otherwise provided in this section, a guarantee or commitment to guarantee under this section is subject to all the provisions applicable to a guarantee or commitment to guarantee under subchapter I of this chapter.

(d) AMOUNT OF OBLIGATION.—The principal amount of an obligation guaranteed under this chapter may not exceed 87.5 percent of the actual cost of the advanced shipbuilding technology or modern shipbuilding technology.

(e) TRANSFER OF AMOUNTS.—The Administrator may accept the transfer of amounts from a department, agency, or instrumentality of the United States Government and may use those amounts to cover the cost (as defined in section 502 of the Federal Credit Reform Act of 1990 (2 U.S.C. 661a)) of making guarantees or commitments to guarantee under this section.

(Pub. L. 109–304, §8(c), Oct. 6, 2006, 120 Stat. 1623; Pub. L. 109–163, div. C, title XXXV, §3507(a)(2)(K), Jan. 6, 2006, 119 Stat. 3555; Pub. L. 110–181, div. C, title XXXV, §3522(a)(9)(F), (b), Jan. 28, 2008, 122 Stat. 598.)

§53734. REPLACEMENT OF VESSELS BECAUSE OF CHANGES IN OPERATING STANDARDS

(a) GENERAL AUTHORITY.—Notwithstanding any other provision of this chapter, the Secretary or Administrator, on terms the Secretary or Administrator may prescribe, may guarantee or make a commitment to guarantee the payment of the principal of and interest on an obligation that aids in financing or refinancing (including reimbursement of an obligor for expenditures previously made for) a contract for the construction or reconstruction of a vessel if—

(1) the vessel is designed and to be used for commercial use in coastwise, intercoastal, or foreign trade;

(2) the construction or reconstruction is necessary to replace a vessel that cannot continue to be operated because of a change required by law in the standards for the operation of vessels, and the applicant for the guarantee or commitment would not otherwise legally be able to continue operating vessels in the trades in which the applicant operated vessels before the change;

(3) the applicant is presently engaged in transporting cargoes in vessels of the type and class that will be constructed or reconstructed under this section and agrees to employ vessels constructed or reconstructed under this section as replacements only for vessels made obsolete by the change in operating standards;

(4) the capacity of the vessels to be constructed or reconstructed under this section will not increase the cargo carrying capacity of the vessels being replaced;

(5) the Secretary or Administrator has not determined that the market demand for the vessel over its useful life will diminish so as to make granting the guarantee fiduciarily imprudent;

(6) the vessel, if to be reconstructed, will have a useful life of at least 15 years after the reconstruction; and

(7) the Secretary or Administrator has considered the criteria specified in section 53708(a)(3)–(5) of this title.

(b) TERM AND AMOUNT OF OBLIGATION.—

(1) TERM.—The term of an obligation guaranteed under this section may not exceed 25 years.

(2) AMOUNT.—The amount of an obligation guaranteed under this section may not exceed 87.5 percent of the actual cost or depreciated actual cost to the applicant for the construction or reconstruction of the vessel. The Secretary or Administrator may not establish a percentage under this paragraph that is to be applied uniformly to all guarantees or commitments to guarantee made under this section.

(c) APPLICABILITY OF OTHER PROVISIONS.—A guarantee or commitment to guarantee under this section is also subject to sections 53701, 53702(a), 53704, 53705, 53707(a), 53708(d) and (e), 53709(a), 53710(a)(1), (2), and (4) and (c), 53711(a), 53713, 53714, 53717, and 53721–53725 of this title.

(d) SECURITY AGAINST DEFAULT.—The Secretary or Administrator shall require by regulation that an applicant under this section provide adequate security against default.

(e) GUARANTEE FEES.—The Secretary or Administrator may establish a fee for the guarantee of an obligation under this section that is in addition to the fee established under section 53714 of this title. The fee may be—

(1) an annual fee of not more than an additional 1 percent added to the fee established under section 53714 of this title; or

(2) a fee based on the amount of the obligation versus the percentage of the obligor's fleet being replaced by vessels constructed or reconstructed under this section.

(Pub. L. 109–304, §8(c), Oct. 6, 2006, 120 Stat. 1624; Pub. L. 109–163, div. C, title XXXV, §3507(a)(1)(E), Jan. 6, 2006, 119 Stat. 3555; Pub. L. 110–181, div. C, title XXXV, §3522(a)(10)(B), (b), Jan. 28, 2008, 122 Stat. 598.)

§53735. FISHERIES FINANCING AND CAPACITY REDUCTION

(a) DEFINITION.—In this section, the term "program" means a fishing capacity reduction program established under section 312 of the Magnuson-Stevens Fishery Conservation and Management Act (16 U.S.C. 1861a).

(b) GUARANTEE AUTHORITY.—The Secretary may guarantee the repayment of debt obligations issued by entities under this section. Debt obligations to be guaranteed may be issued by any entity that has been approved by the Secretary and has agreed with the Secretary to conditions the Secretary considers necessary for this section to achieve the objective of the program and to protect the interest of the United States.

(c) REQUIREMENTS OF OBLIGATIONS.—A debt obligation guaranteed under this section shall—

(1) be treated in the same manner and to the same extent as other obligations guaranteed under this chapter, except with respect to provisions of this chapter that by their nature cannot be applied to obligations guaranteed under this section;

(2) have the fishing fees established under the program paid into a separate subaccount of the fishing capacity reduction fund established under this section;

(3) not exceed $100,000,000 in an unpaid principal amount outstanding at any one time for a program;

(4) have such maturity (not to exceed 20 years), take such form, and contain such conditions as the Secretary determines necessary for the program to which they relate;

(5) have as the exclusive source of repayment (subject to the second sentence of subsection (d)(2)) and as the exclusive payment security, the fishing fees established under the program; and

(6) at the discretion of the Secretary be issued in the public market or sold to the Federal Financing Bank.

(d) FISHING CAPACITY REDUCTION FUND.—

(1) IN GENERAL.—There is a separate account in the Treasury, known as the Fishing Capacity Reduction Fund. Within the Fund, at least one subaccount shall be established for each program into which shall be paid all fishing fees established under the program and other amounts authorized for the program.

(2) AVAILABILITY OF AMOUNTS.—Amounts in the Fund shall be available, without appropriation or fiscal year limitation, to the Secretary to pay the cost of the program, including payments to financial institutions to pay debt obligations incurred by entities under this section. Funds available for this purpose from other amounts available for the program may also be used to pay those debt obligations.

(3) INVESTMENT.—Amounts in the Fund that are not currently needed for the purpose of this section shall be kept on deposit or invested in obligations of the United States Government.

(e) REGULATIONS.—The Secretary shall prescribe regulations the Secretary considers necessary to carry out this section.

(Pub. L. 109–304, §8(c), Oct. 6, 2006, 120 Stat. 1625; Pub. L. 109–163, div. C, title XXXV, §3507(a)(1)(H), (d), Jan. 6, 2006, 119 Stat. 3555, 3557; Pub. L. 110–181, div. C, title XXXV, §3522(b), Jan. 28, 2008, 122 Stat. 598.)

CHAPTER 539—WAR RISK INSURANCE

§53901. DEFINITIONS

In this chapter:

(1) AMERICAN VESSEL.—The term "American vessel" includes—

(A) a documented vessel with a registry or coastwise endorsement under chapter 121 of this title;

(B) an undocumented vessel owned or chartered by or made available to the United States Government; and

(C) a tug, barge, or other watercraft (whether or not documented) owned by a citizen of the United States and used in essential water transportation or in the fisheries, except only for sport fishing.

(2) CARGO.—The term "cargo" includes a loaded or empty container on a vessel.

(3) TRANSPORTATION IN THE WATERBORNE COMMERCE OF THE UNITED STATES.—The term "transportation in the waterborne commerce of the United States" includes the operation of a vessel in the fisheries, except only for sport fishing.

(4) WAR RISKS.—The term "war risks" includes, to the extent the Secretary of Transportation determines—

(A) any part of a loss excluded from marine insurance coverage under a "free of capture or seizure" clause or analogous clause; and

(B) any other loss from a hostile act, including confiscation, expropriation, nationalization, or deprivation.

(Pub. L. 109–304, §8(c), Oct. 6, 2006, 120 Stat. 1626.)

§53902. AUTHORITY TO PROVIDE INSURANCE

(a) IN GENERAL.—With the approval of the President, and after such consultation with interested agencies of United States Government as the President may require, the Secretary of Transportation may provide insurance and reinsurance against loss or damage from war risks as provided by this chapter whenever it appears to the Secretary that insurance adequate for the needs of the waterborne commerce of the United States cannot be obtained on reasonable terms and conditions from companies authorized to do insurance business in a State of the United States.

(b) CONSIDERATION OF RISK.—Insurance or reinsurance under this chapter shall be based, insofar as practicable, on consideration of the risk involved.

(c) AVAILABILITY OF VESSEL DURING WAR OR NATIONAL EMERGENCY.—Insurance or reinsurance for a vessel may be provided under this chapter only on the condition that the vessel will be available to the Government in time of war or national emergency.

(Pub. L. 109–304, §8(c), Oct. 6, 2006, 120 Stat. 1627.)

§53903. INSURABLE INTERESTS

(a) IN GENERAL.—The Secretary of Transportation may provide insurance and reinsurance under this chapter for—

(1) an American vessel, including a vessel under construction;

(2) a foreign vessel—

(A) owned by a citizen of the United States; or

(B) engaged in transportation in the waterborne commerce of the United States or in such other transportation by water or such other services as the Secretary considers to be in the interest of the national defense or national economy of the United States, when so engaged;

(3) cargo—
    (A) shipped or to be shipped on a vessel insurable under this section, including by express or registered mail;
    (B) owned by a citizen or resident of the United States;
    (C) imported to or exported from the United States, or sold or purchased by a citizen or resident of the United States, under a contract of sale or purchase the terms of which provide that the risk of loss by war risks or the obligation to provide insurance against war risks is on a citizen or resident of the United States; or
    (D) shipped between ports in the United States;

(4) disbursements, including advances to masters and general average disbursements, and freight and passage money of a vessel insurable under this section;
(5) personal effects of an individual on a vessel insurable under this section;
(6) loss of life, injury, or detention by an enemy of the United States after capture, with respect to an individual on a vessel insurable under this section; and
(7) statutory or contractual obligations or other liabilities of a vessel insurable under this section or of the owner or charterer of such a vessel, of a nature customarily covered by insurance.

(b) CONSIDERATIONS FOR FOREIGN VESSELS.—In determining whether to provide insurance or reinsurance for a foreign vessel, the Secretary shall consider the characteristics, employment, and general management of the vessel by the owner or charterer.

(c) NON-WAR RISKS.—Insurance of a risk under subsection (a)(5)–(7), insofar as it involves a liability related to an individual on the vessel, may include risks other than war risks to the extent the Secretary considers advisable.

(Pub. L. 109–304, §8(c), Oct. 6, 2006, 120 Stat. 1627.)

§53904. LIABILITY INSURANCE FOR PERSONS INVOLVED IN WAR OR DEFENSE EFFORTS

(a) IN GENERAL.—The Secretary of Transportation may provide insurance under this chapter against legal liability that a person may incur in providing services or facilities for a vessel if, in the opinion of the Secretary, the insurance—
    (1) is required in prosecuting a war or for national defense; and
    (2) cannot be obtained at reasonable rates or on reasonable terms and conditions from approved companies authorized to do insurance business in a State of the United States.

(b) LIMITATIONS.—Employer liability insurance and worker compensation insurance against legal liability to employees may not be provided under this section.

(Pub. L. 109–304, §8(c), Oct. 6, 2006, 120 Stat. 1628.)

§53905. AGENCY INSURANCE

(a) IN GENERAL.—With the approval of the President, an agency of the United States Government may obtain insurance provided for by this chapter from the Secretary of Transportation, except as provided in sections 17302 and 17303 of title 40.

(b) PREMIUM WAIVERS.—With the approval of the President, the Secretary of Transportation may provide insurance under this chapter at the request of the Secretary of Defense and other agencies the President may prescribe, without payment of an insurance premium if the Secretary of Defense or agency agrees to indemnify the Secretary of Transportation against loss covered by the insurance. The Secretary of Defense and agencies may make such an indemnity agreement.

(c) PRESIDENTIAL APPROVAL.—The signature of the President (or an official designated by the President) on the agreement shall be treated as the approval required by section 53902(a) of this title.

(Pub. L. 109–304, §8(c), Oct. 6, 2006, 120 Stat. 1628.)

§53906. HULL INSURANCE VALUATION

(a) STATED VALUATION.—The valuation in a hull insurance policy for actual or constructive total loss of the insured vessel shall be a stated valuation determined by the Secretary of Transportation. The stated valuation—

(1) shall exclude national defense features paid for by the United States Government; and

(2) may not exceed the amount that would be payable if the ownership of the vessel had been requisitioned under chapter 563 of this title at the time the insurance attached under the policy.

(b) REJECTING STATED VALUATION.—Within 60 days after the insurance attaches under a policy referred to in subsection (a) or within 60 days after the Secretary determines the valuation, whichever is later, the insured may reject the valuation and pay, at the rate provided in the policy, premiums based on the asserted valuation the insured specifies at the time of rejection. However, the asserted valuation is not binding on the Government in any subsequent action on the policy.

(c) AMOUNT OF CLAIM.—If a vessel is actually or constructively totally lost and the insured under a policy referred to in subsection (a) has not rejected the stated valuation determined by the Secretary, the amount of a claim adjusted, compromised, settled, adjudged, or paid may not exceed the stated valuation. However, if the insured has rejected the valuation, the insured—

(1) shall be paid, as a tentative advance only, 75 percent of the stated valuation; and

(2) may bring a civil action against the United States in a court having jurisdiction of the claim to recover a valuation equal to the just compensation the court determines would have been payable if the ownership of the vessel had been requisitioned under chapter 563 of this title at the time the insurance attached under the policy.

(d) ADJUSTING PREMIUMS.—If a court makes a determination as provided under subsection (c)(2), premiums paid under the policy shall be adjusted based on the court's determination and the rates provided for in the policy.

(Pub. L. 109–304, §8(c), Oct. 6, 2006, 120 Stat. 1629.)

§53907. REINSURANCE

(a) IN GENERAL.—To the extent the Secretary of Transportation is authorized to provide insurance under this chapter, the Secretary may provide reinsurance to a company authorized to do insurance business in a State of the United States. The Secretary may obtain reinsurance from such a company for any insurance provided by the Secretary under this chapter.

(b) RATES.—The Secretary may not provide reinsurance at rates less than, nor obtain reinsurance at rates more than, the rates established by the Secretary on the same or similar risks or the rates charged by the insurance company for the insurance reinsured, whichever is more advantageous to the Secretary. However, the Secretary may provide an allowance to the insurance company for the costs of services and facilities the company provides, in an amount the Secretary considers reasonable according to good business practice. The allowance to the company may not include any amount for soliciting or stimulating insurance business.

(Pub. L. 109–304, §8(c), Oct. 6, 2006, 120 Stat. 1629.)

§53908. ADDITIONAL INSURANCE PRIVATELY OBTAINED

With the approval of the Secretary of Transportation, a person having an insurable interest in a vessel may obtain insurance on the vessel with other underwriting agents in addition to the insurance with the Secretary. The Secretary is not entitled to the benefit of the additional insurance.

(Pub. L. 109–304, §8(c), Oct. 6, 2006, 120 Stat. 1630.)

§53909. WAR RISK INSURANCE REVOLVING FUND

(a) IN GENERAL.—There is a war risk insurance revolving fund in the Treasury.

(b) DEPOSITS.—There shall be deposited in the fund amounts appropriated to carry out this chapter and amounts received in carrying out this chapter.

(c) PAYMENTS.—There shall be paid from the fund amounts for return premiums, losses, settlements, judgments, and all liabilities incurred by the United States Government under this chapter.

(d) INVESTMENT.—The Secretary of Transportation may request the Secretary of the Treasury to invest such portion of the fund as is not, in the judgment of the Secretary of Transportation, required to meet the current needs of the fund. These investments shall be made by the Secretary of the Treasury in public debt securities of the Government, with maturities suitable to the needs of the fund, and bearing interest rates determined by the Secretary of the Treasury, taking into consideration current market yields on outstanding marketable obligations of the Government of comparable maturity. Interest and benefits from the securities shall be deposited in the fund.

(Pub. L. 109–304, §8(c), Oct. 6, 2006, 120 Stat. 1630; Pub. L. 109–364, div. C, title XXXV, §3510(a)(1), Oct. 17, 2006, 120 Stat. 2520; Pub. L. 110–181, div. C, title XXXV, §3526(g), Jan. 28, 2008, 122 Stat. 602.)

§53910. ADMINISTRATIVE

(a) ACCORDANCE WITH COMMERCIAL PRACTICE.—In carrying out this chapter, the Secretary of Transportation may act in accordance with commercial practice in the marine insurance business.

(b) REGULATIONS.—The Secretary may prescribe regulations the Secretary considers appropriate to carry out this chapter.

(c) POLICIES, RATES, AND ANNUAL FEES.—The Secretary may prescribe and change forms and policies, and fix and change the amounts insured and rates of premium, under this chapter.

(d) ANNUAL FEES.—The Secretary may charge and collect an annual fee in an amount calculated to cover the expenses of processing applications for insurance, employing underwriting agents, and appointing experts under this chapter.

(e) PAYMENT OF CLAIMS AND JUDGMENTS.—The Secretary may settle and pay claims, and pay judgments against the United States, related to insurance under this chapter.

(f) UNDERWRITING AGENTS.—

(1) IN GENERAL.—The Secretary may, and when the Secretary finds it practical to do so shall, employ a domestic company or group of domestic companies, authorized to do marine insurance business in a State of the United States, to act as underwriting agent for the Secretary. The services of an underwriting agent may be used in adjusting claims, but a claim may not be paid until approved by the Secretary.

(2) COMPENSATION.—The Secretary may allow the company or group of companies reasonable compensation for services as the underwriting agent. The compensation may include an allowance for expenses reasonably incurred by the agent, but may not include any amount for soliciting or stimulating business.

(g) FEES FOR ARRANGING INSURANCE.—Except as provided in subsection (f)(2), the Secretary may not pay an insurance broker or other person acting in a similar intermediary capacity a fee or other consideration for participating in arranging insurance when the Secretary directly insures any of the risk.

(h) EMPLOYMENT OF MARINE INSURANCE EXPERTS.—The Secretary, without regard to the laws and regulations on the employment of Federal employees, may appoint and prescribe the duties of experts in marine insurance as the Secretary considers necessary to carry out this chapter.

(i) SERVICES OF OTHER GOVERNMENT AGENCIES.—With the consent of another agency of the United States Government, the Secretary may use information, services, facilities, officers, and employees of the agency in carrying out this chapter.

(j) VESSEL LOCATION REPORTING.—The Secretary may prescribe by regulation vessel location reporting requirements for a vessel insured under this chapter.

(Pub. L. 109–304, §8(c), Oct. 6, 2006, 120 Stat. 1630.)

§53911. CIVIL ACTIONS FOR LOSSES

(a) IN GENERAL.—If there is a disagreement about a loss insured under this chapter, a civil action in admiralty may be brought against the United States in the district court of the United States for the district in which the plaintiff or the plaintiff's agent resides. If the

[§53912. Repealed. Pub. L. 115–232, div. C, title
XXXV, §3504(a), Aug. 13, 2018, 132 Stat. 2308]

CHAPTER 541—MISCELLANEOUS

plaintiff has no residence in the United States, the action may be brought in the United States District Court for the District of Columbia or in the district court for any district in which the Attorney General agrees to accept service. Any person who may have an interest in the insurance may be made a party, either initially or on the motion of either party.

(b) EXCLUSIVE REMEDY.—A civil action against the United States under this section is exclusive of any other action by reason of the same subject matter against an officer, employee, or agent employed or retained by the Government under this chapter.

(c) PROCEDURE.—A civil action under this section shall be heard and determined under chapter 309 of this title.

(d) TOLLING OF LIMITATIONS PERIOD.—If a claim is filed with the Secretary of Transportation, the running of the limitations period for bringing a civil action is suspended until the Secretary denies the claim, and for 60 days thereafter. The Secretary is deemed to have denied the claim if the Secretary does not act on the claim within 6 months after the claim is filed, unless the Secretary for good cause shown agrees with the claimant on a different period for the Secretary to act on the claim.

(e) INTERPLEADER.—If the Secretary acknowledges the indebtedness of the Government under the insurance and there is a dispute about the persons entitled to receive payment, the Government may bring a civil action interpleading those persons. The action shall be brought in the United States District Court for the District of Columbia or in the district court for the district in which any of those persons resides. A person not residing or found in the district may be made a party by service in any reasonable manner the court directs. If the court is satisfied that unknown persons might make a claim under the insurance, the court may direct service on those unknown persons by publication in the Federal Register. Judgment after service by publication in the Federal Register discharges the Government from further liability to all persons.

(Pub. L. 109–304, §8(c), Oct. 6, 2006, 120 Stat. 1631.)

[§53912. REPEALED. PUB. L. 115–232, DIV. C, TITLE XXXV, §3504(A), AUG. 13, 2018, 132 STAT. 2308]

Section, Pub. L. 109–304, §8(c), Oct. 6, 2006, 120 Stat. 1632; Pub. L. 110–417, div. C, title XXXV, §3509, Oct. 14, 2008, 122 Stat. 4769; Pub. L. 113–66, div. C, title XXXV, §3502, Dec. 26, 2013, 127 Stat. 1085, set an expiration date of authority to provide insurance and reinsurance under this chapter.

CHAPTER 541—MISCELLANEOUS

Sec.
54101.   Assistance for small shipyards.

§54101. ASSISTANCE FOR SMALL SHIPYARDS

(a) ESTABLISHMENT OF PROGRAM.—Subject to the availability of appropriations, the Administrator of the Maritime Administration shall execute agreements with shipyards to provide assistance—

(1) in the form of grants, loans, and loan guarantees to small shipyards for capital

improvements; and

(2) for maritime training programs to foster technical skills and operational productivity relating to shipbuilding, ship repair, and associated industries.

(b) AWARDS.—

(1) IN GENERAL.—In providing assistance under the program, the Administrator shall consider projects that foster—

(A) efficiency, competitive operations, and quality ship construction, repair, and reconfiguration; and

(B) employee skills and enhanced productivity related to shipbuilding, ship repair, and associated industries.

(2) TIMING OF GRANT NOTICE.—The Administrator shall post a Notice of Funding Opportunity regarding grants awarded under this section not more than 15 days after the date of enactment of the appropriations Act for the fiscal year concerned.

(3) TIMING OF GRANTS.—The Administrator shall award grants under this section not later than 120 days after the date of the enactment of the appropriations Act for the fiscal year concerned.

(4) REUSE OF UNEXPENDED GRANT FUNDS.—Notwithstanding paragraph (3), amounts awarded as a grant under this section that are not expended by the grantee shall remain available to the Administrator for use for grants under this section.

(c) USE OF FUNDS.—

(1) IN GENERAL.—Assistance provided under this section may be used to—

(A) make capital and related improvements in small shipyards; and

(B) provide training for workers in shipbuilding, ship repair, and associated industries.

(2) ADMINISTRATIVE COSTS.—Not more than 2 percent of amounts made available to carry out the program may be used for the necessary costs of grant administration.

(d) PROHIBITED USES.—

(1) IN GENERAL.—Grants awarded under this section may not be used to construct buildings or other physical facilities or to acquire land.

(2) BUY AMERICA.—

(A) IN GENERAL.—Subject to subparagraph (B), no funds may be obligated by the Administrator of the Maritime Administration under this section, unless each product and material purchased with those funds (including products and materials purchased by a grantee), and including any commercially available off-the-shelf item, is—

(i) an unmanufactured article, material, or supply that has been mined or produced in the United States; or

(ii) a manufactured article, material, or supply that has been manufactured in the United States substantially all from articles, materials, or supplies mined, produced, or manufactured in the United States.

(B) EXCEPTIONS.—

(i) IN GENERAL.—Notwithstanding subparagraph (A), the requirements of that subparagraph shall not apply with respect to a particular product or material if the Administrator determines—

(I) that the application of those requirements would be inconsistent with the public interest;

(II) that such product or material is not available in the United States in sufficient and reasonably available quantities, of a satisfactory quality, or on a timely basis; or

(III) that inclusion of a domestic product or material will increase the cost of that product or material by more than 25 percent, with respect to a certain contract between a grantee and that grantee's supplier.

(ii) FEDERAL REGISTER.—A determination made by the Administrator under this subparagraph shall be published in the Federal Register.

(C) DEFINITIONS.—In this paragraph:

(i) The term "commercially available off-the-shelf item" means—

(I) any item of supply (including construction material) that is—

(aa) a commercial item, as defined by section 2.101 of title 48, Code of Federal Regulations (as in effect on the date of the enactment of the National Defense Authorization Act for Fiscal Year 2020); and

(bb) sold in substantial quantities in the commercial marketplace; and

(II) does not include bulk cargo, as defined in section 40102(4) of this title, such as agricultural products and petroleum products.

(ii) The term "product or material" means an article, material, or supply brought to the site by the recipient for incorporation into the building, work, or project. The term also includes an item brought to the site preassembled from articles, materials, or supplies. However, emergency life safety systems, such as emergency lighting, fire alarm, and audio evacuation systems, that are discrete systems incorporated into a public building or work and that are produced as complete systems, are evaluated as a single and distinct construction material regardless of when or how the individual parts or components of those systems are delivered to the construction site.

(iii) The term "United States" includes the District of Columbia, the Commonwealth of Puerto Rico, the Northern Mariana Islands, Guam, American Samoa, and the Virgin Islands.

(e) MATCHING REQUIREMENTS; ALLOCATION.—

(1) FEDERAL FUNDING.—Federal funds for any eligible project under this section shall not exceed 75 percent of the total cost of such project.

(2) ALLOCATION OF FUNDS.—

(A) IN GENERAL.—The Administrator may not award more than 25 percent of the funds made available to carry out this section for any fiscal year to any small shipyard in one geographic location that has more than 600 employees.

(B) INELIGIBILITY.—A maritime training center that has received funds awarded under section 51706 of title 46, United States Code, shall not be eligible for grants under this subsection for training purposes in the same fiscal year.

(f) APPLICATIONS.—

(1) IN GENERAL.—To be eligible for assistance under this section, an applicant shall submit an application, in such form, and containing such information and assurances as the Administrator may require, within 60 days after the date of enactment of the appropriations Act for the fiscal year concerned.

(2) MINIMUM STANDARDS FOR PAYMENT OR REIMBURSEMENT.—Each application submitted under paragraph (1) shall include a comprehensive description of—

(A) the need for the project;

(B) the methodology for implementing the project; and

(C) any existing programs or arrangements that can be used to supplement or leverage assistance under the program.

(3) PROCEDURAL SAFEGUARDS.—The Administrator, in consultation with the Office of the Inspector General, shall issue guidelines to establish appropriate accounting, reporting, and review procedures to ensure that—

(A) grant funds are used for the purposes for which they were made available;

(B) grantees have properly accounted for all expenditures of grant funds; and

(C) grant funds not used for such purposes and amounts not obligated or expended are returned.

(4) PROJECT APPROVAL REQUIRED.—The Administrator may not award a grant under this section unless the Administrator determines that—

(A) sufficient funding is available to meet the matching requirements of subsection (e);

(B) the project will be completed without unreasonable delay; and

(C) the recipient has authority to carry out the proposed project.

(g) AUDITS AND EXAMINATIONS.—All grantees under this section shall maintain such records as the Administrator may require and make such records available for review and audit by the Administrator.

(h) SMALL SHIPYARD DEFINED.—In this section, the term "small shipyard" means a shipyard facility in one geographic location that does not have more than 1,200 employees.

(i) AUTHORIZATION OF APPROPRIATIONS.—There are authorized to be appropriated to the Administrator of the Maritime Administration for fiscal year 2021 to carry out this section $20,000,000.

(Added Pub. L. 110–417, div. C, title XXXV, §3508(a), Oct. 14, 2008, 122 Stat. 4767; amended Pub. L. 113–281, title III, §303, Dec. 18, 2014, 128 Stat. 3043; Pub. L. 115–91, div. C, title XXXV, §§3501(b), 3505(a), Dec. 12, 2017, 131 Stat. 1909, 1913; Pub. L. 115–232, div. C, title XXXV, §§3511, 3546(r), Aug. 13, 2018, 132 Stat. 2311, 2327; Pub. L. 116–92, div. C, title XXXV, §3507(a), (b), Dec. 20, 2019, 133 Stat. 1974, 1976; Pub. L. 116–283, div. C, title XXXV, §3501(c)(2), Jan. 1, 2021, 134 Stat. 4397; Pub. L.

117–263, div. C, title XXXV, §3532(d), Dec. 23, 2022, 136 Stat. 3092.)

[§54102. Renumbered §51706]

CHAPTER 543—PORT INFRASTRUCTURE DEVELOPMENT PROGRAM

Sec.
54301.   Port infrastructure development program.

§54301. Port infrastructure development program

(a) PORT AND INTERMODAL IMPROVEMENT PROGRAM.—

(1) GENERAL AUTHORITY.—Subject to the availability of appropriations, the Secretary of Transportation shall make grants, on a competitive basis, to eligible applicants to assist in funding eligible projects for the purpose of improving the safety, efficiency, or reliability of the movement of goods through ports and intermodal connections to ports.

(2) ELIGIBLE APPLICANT.—The Secretary may make a grant under this subsection or subsection (b) to the following:

(A) A State.

(B) A political subdivision of a State, or a local government.

(C) A public agency or publicly chartered authority established by 1 or more States.

(D) A special purpose district with a transportation function.

(E) An Indian Tribe (as defined in section 4 of the Indian Self-Determination and Education Assistance Act (25 U.S.C. 5304), without regard to capitalization), or a consortium of Indian Tribes.

(F) A multistate or multijurisdictional group of entities described in this paragraph.

(G) A lead entity described in subparagraph (A), (B), (C), (D), (E), or (F) jointly with a private entity or group of private entities, including the owners or operators of a facility, or collection of facilities at a port.

(3) ELIGIBLE PROJECTS.—The Secretary may make a grant under this subsection—

(A) for a project, or package of projects, that—

(i) is either—

(I) within the boundary of a port; or

(II) outside the boundary of a port, but is directly related to port operations or to an intermodal connection to a port; and

(ii) will be used to improve the safety, efficiency, or reliability of—

(I) the loading and unloading of goods at the port, such as for marine terminal equipment;

(II) the movement of goods into, out of, around, or within a port, such as for highway or rail infrastructure, intermodal facilities, freight intelligent transportation systems, and digital infrastructure systems;

(III) operational improvements, including projects to improve port resilience;

302

(IV) environmental and emission mitigation measures; including projects for—

(aa) port electrification or electrification master planning;

(bb) harbor craft or equipment replacements or retrofits;

(cc) development of port or terminal microgrids;

(dd) providing idling reduction infrastructure;

(ee) purchase of cargo handling equipment and related infrastructure;

(ff) worker training to support electrification technology;

(gg) installation of port bunkering facilities from oceangoing vessels for fuels;

(hh) electric vehicle charge or hydrogen refueling infrastructure for drayage and medium or heavy duty trucks and locomotives that service the port and related grid upgrades; or

(ii) other related port activities, including charging infrastructure, electric rubber-tired gantry cranes, and anti-idling technologies; or

(V) port and port-related infrastructure that supports seafood and seafood-related businesses, including the loading and unloading of commercially harvested fish and fish products, seafood processing, cold storage, and other related infrastructure.

(B) notwithstanding paragraph (6)(A)(v), to provide financial assistance to 1 or more projects under subparagraph (A) for development phase activities, including planning, feasibility analysis, revenue forecasting, environmental review, permitting, and preliminary engineering and design work.

(4) PROHIBITED USES.—A grant award under this subsection may not be used—

(A) to finance or refinance the construction, reconstruction, reconditioning, or purchase of a vessel that is eligible for such assistance under chapter 537, unless the Secretary determines such vessel—

(i) is necessary for a project described in paragraph (3)(A)(ii)(III) of this subsection; and

(ii) is not receiving assistance under chapter 537; or

(B) for any project within a small shipyard (as defined in section 54101).

(5) APPLICATIONS AND PROCESS.—

(A) APPLICATIONS.—To be eligible for a grant under this subsection or subsection (b), an eligible applicant shall submit to the Secretary an application in such form, at such time, and containing such information as the Secretary considers appropriate.

(B) SOLICITATION PROCESS.—Not later than 90 days after the date that amounts are made available for grants under this subsection or subsection (b) for a fiscal year, the Secretary shall solicit grant applications for eligible projects in accordance with this subsection.

(6) PROJECT SELECTION CRITERIA.—

(A) IN GENERAL.—The Secretary may select a project described in paragraph (3) for funding under this subsection if the Secretary determines that—

(i) the project improves the safety, efficiency, or reliability of the movement of goods through a port or intermodal connection to a port;

(ii) the project is cost effective (except in the case of a project described under subparagraph (C)); [1]

(iii) the eligible applicant has authority to carry out the project;

(iv) the eligible applicant has sufficient funding available to meet the matching requirements under paragraph (8);

(v) the project will be completed without unreasonable delay; and

(vi) the project cannot be easily and efficiently completed without Federal funding or financial assistance available to the project sponsor.

(B) ADDITIONAL CONSIDERATIONS.—In selecting projects described in paragraph (3) for funding under this subsection, the Secretary shall give substantial weight to—

(i) the utilization of non-Federal contributions;

(ii) the net benefits of the funds awarded under this subsection, considering the cost-benefit analysis of the project, as applicable (except in the case of a project described under subparagraph (C)); [1] and

(iii) a port's increased resilience as a result of the project.

(C) [2] IN GENERAL.—In selecting projects described in paragraph (3), the Maritime Administrator, in consultation with the Secretary of Defense, may give priority to providing funding to strategic seaports in support of national security requirements.

(C) [2] NONCONTIGUOUS STATES AND TERRITORIES.—The requirements under subparagraphs (A)(ii) and (B)(ii) shall not apply in the case of a project described in paragraph (3) in a noncontiguous State or territory.

(7) ALLOCATION OF FUNDS.—

(A) GEOGRAPHIC DISTRIBUTION.—Not more than 25 percent of the amounts made available for grants under this subsection for a fiscal year may be used to make grants for projects in any 1 State.

(B) SMALL PROJECTS.—The Secretary shall reserve 25 percent of the amounts made available for grants under this subsection each fiscal year to make grants for eligible projects described in subsection (b). The requirement under paragraph (6)(A)(ii) shall not apply to grants made under subsection (b).

(C) DEVELOPMENT PHASE ACTIVITIES.—Of the amounts made available for grants under this section for a fiscal year—

(i) not more than 10 percent may be used to make grants for development phase activities under paragraph (3)(B); and

(ii) not more than 10 percent may be used to make grants for development phase activities under subsection (b)(5)(A)(ii)(III).

(8) FEDERAL SHARE OF TOTAL PROJECT COSTS.—

(A) TOTAL PROJECT COSTS.—To be eligible for a grant under this subsection or subsection (b), an eligible applicant shall submit to the Secretary an estimate of the total costs of the project for which the grant is requested based on the best available information, including any available engineering studies, studies of economic feasibility, environmental analyses, and information on the expected use of equipment or facilities.

(B) FEDERAL SHARE.—

(i) IN GENERAL.—Except as provided in clause (ii), the Federal share of the total costs of a project under this subsection or subsection (b) shall not exceed 80 percent.

(ii) RURAL AREAS.—The Secretary may increase the Federal share of costs above 80 percent for a project for which a grant is awarded under subsection (b) or that is located in a rural area.

(9) PROCEDURAL SAFEGUARDS.—The Secretary shall issue guidelines to establish appropriate accounting, reporting, and review procedures for grants made under this subsection and subsection (b) to ensure that—

(A) grant funds are used for the purposes for which those funds were made available;

(B) each grantee properly accounts for all expenditures of grant funds; and

(C) grant funds not used for such purposes and amounts not obligated or expended are returned.

(10) GRANT CONDITIONS.—

(A) IN GENERAL.—The Secretary shall require as a condition of making a grant under this subsection or subsection (b) that a grantee—

(i) maintain such records as the Secretary considers necessary;

(ii) make the records described in clause (i) available for review and audit by the Secretary; and

(iii) periodically report to the Secretary such information as the Secretary considers necessary to assess progress.

(B) EFFICIENT USE OF NON-FEDERAL FUNDS.—

(i) IN GENERAL.—Notwithstanding any other provision of law ans [3] subject to approval by the Secretary, in the case of any grant for a project under this section, during the period beginning on the date on which the grant recipient is selected and ending on the date on which the grant agreement is signed—

(I) the grant recipient may obligate and expend non-Federal funds with respect to the project for which the grant is provided; and

(II) any non-Federal funds obligated or expended in accordance with subclause (I) shall be credited toward the non-Federal cost share for the project for which the grant is provided.

(ii) REQUIREMENTS.—

(I) APPLICATION.—In order to obligate and expend non-Federal funds under clause (i), the grant recipient shall submit to the Secretary a request to obligate and expend non-Federal funds under that clause, including—

(aa) a description of the activities the grant recipient intends to fund;

(bb) a justification for advancing the activities described in item (aa), including an assessment of the effects to the project scope, schedule, and budget if the request is not approved; and

(cc) the level of risk of the activities described in item (aa).

(II) APPROVAL.—The Secretary shall approve or disapprove each request submitted under subclause (I).

(III) COMPLIANCE WITH APPLICABLE REQUIREMENTS.—Any obligation or expenditure of non-Federal funds under clause (i) shall be in compliance with all applicable requirements, including any requirements included in the grant agreement.

(iii) EFFECT.—The obligation or expenditure of any non-Federal funds in accordance with this subparagraph shall not—

(I) affect the signing of a grant agreement or other applicable grant procedures with respect to the applicable grant;

(II) create an obligation on the part of the Federal Government to repay any non-Federal funds if the grant agreement is not signed; or

(III) affect the ability of the recipient of the grant to obligate or expend non-Federal funds to meet the non-Federal cost share for the project for which the grant is provided after the period described in clause (i).

(C) ADDITIONAL REQUIREMENT.—The Secretary shall apply the same requirements of section 117(k) of title 23, United States Code, to a port project assisted in whole or in part under this section as the Secretary does a port-related freight project under section 117 of title 23, United States Code.

(D) CONSTRUCTION, REPAIR, OR ALTERATION OF VESSELS.—With regard to the construction, repair, or alteration of vessels, the same requirements of section 117(k) of title 23, United States Code, shall apply regardless of whether the location of contract performance is known when bids for such work are solicited.

(11) ADMINISTRATION.—

(A) ADMINISTRATIVE AND OVERSIGHT COSTS.—The Secretary may retain not more than 2 percent of the amounts appropriated for each fiscal year to make grants for port development under this section for the administrative and oversight costs incurred by the Secretary to make grants for port development under this section.

(B) AVAILABILITY.—

(i) IN GENERAL.—Amounts appropriated to make grants for port development under this section shall remain available until expended.

(ii) UNEXPENDED FUNDS.—Amounts awarded as a grant for port development under this section that are not expended by the grantee during the 5-year period following the date of the award or that are returned under paragraph (9)(C) shall remain available to the Secretary for use for grants under this subsection in a subsequent fiscal year. Any such amount may only be expended to award a grant under the same subsection of this section under which the original grant was made.

(12) DEFINITIONS.—In this subsection and subsection (b):
(A) PORT.—The term "port" includes—
(i) any port on the navigable waters of the United States; and
(ii) any harbor, marine terminal, or other shore side facility used principally for the movement of goods on inland waters.

(B) PROJECT.—The term "project" includes construction, reconstruction, environmental rehabilitation, acquisition of property, including land related to the project and improvements to the land, equipment acquisition, and operational improvements.
(C) RURAL AREA.—The term "rural area" means an area that is outside an urbanized area.
(D) RESILIENCE.—The term "resilience" means the ability to anticipate, prepare for, adapt to, withstand, respond to, and recover from operational disruptions and sustain critical operations at ports, including disruptions caused by natural or manmade hazards, such as sea level rise, flooding, earthquakes, hurricanes, tsunami inundation or other extreme weather events.
(E) STRATEGIC SEAPORT DEFINED.—In this subsection the term "strategic seaport" means a military port or and [4] commercial port that is subject to a port planning order or Basic Ordering Agreement (or both) that is projected to be used for the deployment of forces and shipment of ammunition or sustainment supplies in support of military operations.

(b) ASSISTANCE FOR SMALL INLAND RIVER AND COASTAL PORTS AND TERMINALS.—
(1) IN GENERAL.—From amounts reserved under subsection (a)(7)(B), the Secretary, acting through the Administrator of the Maritime Administration, shall make grants under this subsection to eligible applicants for eligible projects at a port, to and from which the average annual tonnage of cargo for the immediately preceding 3 calendar years from the time an application is submitted is less than 8,000,000 short tons, as determined using United States Army Corps of Engineers data or data provided by an independent audit.
(2) INDEPENDENT AUDIT.—
(A) IN GENERAL.—If an eligible applicant provides data by an independent audit for purposes of paragraph (1), the Secretary shall use such data to make a tonnage determination if the Secretary determines that it is acceptable to use such data instead of using Corps of Engineers data.
(B) ACCEPTABLE USE OF DATA.—For purposes of subparagraph (A), an acceptable use of data means that the Secretary has determined such data is a reasonable substitute for Army Corps data.
(C) JUSTIFICATION.—If the Secretary makes a determination pursuant to subparagraph (A) that it is not acceptable to use independent audit data provided by an

eligible applicant, the Secretary shall provide the eligible applicant with notification of, and justification for, such determination.

(3) TONNAGE DETERMINATION.—In making a determination of the average annual tonnage of cargo using Corps of Engineers data for purposes of evaluating an application of an eligible applicant pursuant to paragraph (1), the Secretary shall use data that is specific to the eligible applicant.

(4) AWARDS.—In providing assistance under this subsection, the Secretary shall—

(A) take into account—

(i) the economic advantage and the contribution to freight transportation at a port; and

(ii) the competitive disadvantage of such a port;

(B) not make more than 1 award per applicant under this subsection for each fiscal year appropriation; and

(C) take into consideration the degree to which a project would promote the enhancement and efficiencies of a port.

(5) USE OF FUNDS.—

(A) IN GENERAL.—Assistance provided under this subsection may be used for a project that—

(i) is—

(I) within the boundary of a port; or

(II) outside the boundary of a port, but is directly related to port operations or to an intermodal connection to a port; and

(ii) for—

(I) making capital improvements, including to piers, wharves, docks, terminals, and similar structures used principally for the movement of goods;

(II) acquiring, improving, repairing, or maintaining transportation or physical infrastructure, buildings, or equipment;

(III) performing development phase activities described in subsection (a)(3)(B) related to carrying out an activity described in this clause; and

(IV) otherwise fulfilling the purposes for which such assistance is provided.

(B) ACQUISITION METHODS.—The Secretary may not require as a condition of issuing a grant under this subsection—

(i) direct ownership of either a facility or equipment to be procured using funds awarded under this subsection; or

(ii) that equipment procured using such funds be new.

(6) PROHIBITED USES.—Funds provided under this subsection may not be used for—

(A) projects conducted on property outside the boundary of a port unless such property is directly related to port operations or to an intermodal connection to a port;

(B) any single grant award more than 10 percent of total allocation of funds to carry out this subsection per fiscal year appropriation; or

(C) activities, including channel improvements or harbor deepening that is part of a Federal channel or an access channel associated with a Federal channel, authorized, as of the date of the application for assistance under this subsection, to be carried out by of the United States Army Corps of Engineers.

(7) MATCHING REQUIREMENTS.—

(A) IN GENERAL.—Any costs of the project to be paid by the recipient's matching share pursuant to subsection (a)(8)(B) may—

(i) be incurred prior to the date on which assistance is provided; and

(ii) include a loan agreement, a commitment from investors, cash on balance sheet, or other contributions determined acceptable by the Secretary.

(B) DETERMINATION OF EFFECTIVENESS.—In determining whether a project meets the criteria under clauses (i), (iii), (iv), (v), and (vi) of subsection (a)(6)(A), the Secretary shall accept documentation used to obtain a commitment of the matching funds covered by this paragraph, including feasibility studies, business plans, investor prospectuses, loan applications, or similar documentation.

(c) ADDITIONAL AUTHORITY OF THE SECRETARY.—In carrying out this section, the Secretary may—

(1) coordinate with other Federal agencies to expedite the process established under the National Environmental Policy Act of 1969 (42 U.S.C. 4321 et seq.) for the improvement of port facilities to improve the efficiency of the transportation system, to increase port security, or to provide greater access to port facilities;

(2) seek to coordinate all reviews or requirements with appropriate Federal, State, and local agencies; and

(3) in addition to any financial assistance provided under subsection (a) or subsection (b), provide such technical assistance to any eligible applicants as described in subsection (a)(2).

(Added and amended Pub. L. 117–81, div. C, title XXXV, §3513(a), (b), Dec. 27, 2021, 135 Stat. 2240; Pub. L. 118–31, div. C, title XXXV, §§3511, 3512, 3513(b), 3514(a), Dec. 22, 2023, 137 Stat. 808–810.)

[1] *Probably means the subpar. (C) relating to noncontiguous states and territories.*

[2] *So in original. There are two subpars. (C).*

[3] *So in original. Probably should be "and".*

[4] *So in original.*

PART D—PROMOTIONAL PROGRAMS

CHAPTER 551—COASTWISE TRADE

Sec.

§55101. APPLICATION OF COASTWISE LAWS

(a) IN GENERAL.—Except as provided in subsection (b), the coastwise laws apply to the United States, including the island territories and possessions of the United States.

(b) EXCEPTIONS.—The coastwise laws do not apply to—

(1) American Samoa;

(2) the Northern Mariana Islands, except as provided in section 502(b) of the Covenant To Establish a Commonwealth of the Northern Mariana Islands in Political Union With the United States of America (48 U.S.C. 1801 note); or

(3) the Virgin Islands until the President declares by proclamation that the coastwise laws apply to the Virgin Islands.

(Pub. L. 109–304, §8(c), Oct. 6, 2006, 120 Stat. 1632; Pub. L. 110–181, div. C, title XXXV, §3527(a), Jan. 28, 2008, 122 Stat. 602.)

§55102. TRANSPORTATION OF MERCHANDISE

(a) DEFINITION.—In this section, the term "merchandise" includes—

(1) merchandise owned by the United States Government, a State, or a subdivision of a State; and

(2) valueless material.

(b) REQUIREMENTS.—Except as otherwise provided in this chapter or chapter 121 of this title, a vessel may not provide any part of the transportation of merchandise by water, or by land and water, between points in the United States to which the coastwise laws apply, either directly or via a foreign port, unless the vessel—

(1) is wholly owned by citizens of the United States for purposes of engaging in the coastwise trade; and

(2) has been issued a certificate of documentation with a coastwise endorsement under chapter 121 or is exempt from documentation but would otherwise be eligible for such a certificate and endorsement.

(c) PENALTY.—Merchandise transported in violation of subsection (b) is liable to seizure by and forfeiture to the Government. Alternatively, an amount equal to the value of the merchandise (as determined by the Secretary of Homeland Security) or the actual cost of the transportation, whichever is greater, may be recovered from any person transporting the merchandise or causing the merchandise to be transported.

(Pub. L. 109–304, §8(c), Oct. 6, 2006, 120 Stat. 1632.)

§55103. TRANSPORTATION OF PASSENGERS

(a) IN GENERAL.—Except as otherwise provided in this chapter or chapter 121 of this title, a vessel may not transport passengers between ports or places in the United States to which the coastwise laws apply, either directly or via a foreign port, unless the vessel—

(1) is wholly owned by citizens of the United States for purposes of engaging in the coastwise trade; and

(2) has been issued a certificate of documentation with a coastwise endorsement under chapter 121 or is exempt from documentation but would otherwise be eligible for such a certificate and endorsement.

(b) PENALTY.—The penalty for violating subsection (a) is $300 for each passenger transported and landed.

(Pub. L. 109–304, §8(c), Oct. 6, 2006, 120 Stat. 1633.)

§55104. TRANSPORTATION OF PASSENGERS BETWEEN PUERTO RICO AND OTHER PORTS IN THE UNITED STATES

(a) DEFINITIONS.—In this section:

(1) CERTIFICATE.—The term "certificate" means a certificate of financial responsibility for indemnification of passengers for nonperformance of transportation issued by the Federal Maritime Commission under section 44102 of this title.

(2) PASSENGER VESSEL.—The term "passenger vessel" means a vessel of similar size, or offering similar service, as any other vessel transporting passengers under subsection (b).

(b) EXEMPTION.—Except as otherwise provided in this section, a vessel not qualified to engage in the coastwise trade may transport passengers between a port in Puerto Rico and another port in the United States.

(c) EXPIRATION OF EXEMPTION.—

(1) WHEN COASTWISE-QUALIFIED VESSEL OFFERING SERVICE.—On a showing to the Secretary of the department in which the Coast Guard is operating, by the vessel owner or charterer, that a United States passenger vessel qualified to engage in the coastwise trade is offering or advertising passenger service between a port in Puerto Rico and another port in the United States pursuant to a certificate, the Secretary shall notify the owner or operator of each vessel transporting passengers under subsection (b) to terminate that transportation within 270 days after the Secretary's notification. Except as provided in subsection (d), the authority to transport passengers under subsection (b) expires at the end of that 270-day period.

(2) WHEN NON-COASTWISE-QUALIFIED VESSEL OFFERING SERVICE.—On a showing to the Secretary, by the vessel owner or charterer, that a United States passenger vessel not qualified to engage in the coastwise trade is offering or advertising passenger service between a port in Puerto Rico and another port in the United States pursuant to a certificate, the Secretary shall notify the owner or operator of each foreign vessel transporting passengers under subsection (b) to terminate that transportation within 270 days after the Secretary's notification. Except as provided in subsection (d), the authority of a foreign vessel to transport passengers under subsection (b) expires at the end of that 270-day period.

(d) DELAYING EXPIRATION.—If the vessel offering or advertising the service described in subsection (c) has not begun that service within 270 days after the Secretary's notification, the expiration provided by subsection (c) is delayed until 90 days after the vessel offering or advertising the service begins that service.

(e) REINSTATEMENT OF EXEMPTION.—If the Secretary finds that the service on which an expiration was based is no longer available, the expired authority to transport passengers is reinstated.

(Pub. L. 109–304, §8(c), Oct. 6, 2006, 120 Stat. 1633.)

§55105. TRANSPORTATION OF HAZARDOUS WASTE

(a) IN GENERAL.—The transportation of hazardous waste, as defined in section 1004(5) of the Resource Conservation and Recovery Act of 1976 (42 U.S.C. 6903(5)), from a point in the United States to sea for incineration is deemed to be transportation of merchandise under section 55102 of this title.

(b) NONAPPLICATION TO CERTAIN FOREIGN VESSELS.—

(1) IN GENERAL.—Subsection (a) does not apply to transportation performed by a foreign ocean incineration vessel owned by or under construction on May 1, 1982, for a corporation wholly owned by citizens of the United States under section 50501(a)–(c) of this title.

(2) STANDARDS FOR INCINERATION EQUIPMENT.—Incineration equipment on a vessel described in paragraph (1) must meet standards of the Coast Guard and the Environmental Protection Agency.

(3) INSPECTION.—A vessel described in paragraph (1) shall be inspected by the Coast Guard, regardless of whether inspected by the nation in which it is registered. The inspection shall be the same as would be required of a vessel of the United States,

including drydock inspection and internal examination of tanks and void spaces. The inspection may be made concurrently with an inspection by that nation or within one year after the initial issuance or next scheduled issuance of the Safety of Life at Sea Safety Construction Certificate. In making the inspection, the Coast Guard shall refer to the condition of the hull and superstructure established by the initial foreign certification as the basis for evaluating the current condition of the hull and superstructure. The Coast Guard shall allow the substitution of fittings, material, apparatus, equipment, and appliances different from those required for vessels of the United States if satisfied they are equivalent and at least as effective as those required for vessels of the United States. A satisfactory inspection under this paragraph shall be certified in writing by the Secretary of Homeland Security.

(c) EFFECTIVE DATE.—Subsection (a) is not effective until an appropriate vessel has been built and documented under chapter 121 of this title.

(Pub. L. 109–304, §8(c), Oct. 6, 2006, 120 Stat. 1634; Pub. L. 109–241, title IX, §902(o), July 11, 2006, 120 Stat. 569; Pub. L. 110–181, div. C, title XXXV, §3525(a)(4), (b), Jan. 28, 2008, 122 Stat. 601.)

§55106. MERCHANDISE TRANSFERRED BETWEEN BARGES

(a) IN GENERAL.—On terms and conditions the Secretary of Homeland Security may prescribe by regulation, the Secretary may suspend the application of section 55102 of this title to the transportation of merchandise that is transferred, when moving in the foreign trade of the United States, from a barge certified by the owner or operator as designed specifically for carriage on a vessel and carried regularly on a vessel in foreign trade, to another such barge owned or leased by the same owner or operator. However, this subsection does not apply to transportation between the continental United States and noncontiguous States, territories, or possessions to which the coastwise laws apply.

(b) RECIPROCITY REQUIREMENT FOR FOREIGN VESSELS.—This section applies to a vessel of foreign registry only if the Secretary of Homeland Security finds, based on information from the Secretary of State, that the government of the nation of registry extends reciprocal privileges to vessels of the United States.

(Pub. L. 109–304, §8(c), Oct. 6, 2006, 120 Stat. 1635.)

§55107. EMPTY CARGO CONTAINERS AND BARGES

(a) IN GENERAL.—Subject to subsections (b) and (c), and on terms and conditions the Secretary of Homeland Security may prescribe by regulation, section 55102 of this title does not apply to the transportation of—

(1) empty cargo vans, empty lift vans, or empty shipping tanks;

(2) equipment for use with cargo vans, lift vans, or shipping tanks;

(3) empty barges specifically designed for carriage aboard a vessel and equipment (except propulsion equipment) for use with those barges;

(4) empty instruments for international traffic exempted from the customs laws under section 322(a) of the Tariff Act of 1930 (19 U.S.C. 1322(a)); or

(5) stevedoring equipment and material.

(b) CONDITIONS.—

(1) PARAGRAPHS (1)–(4).—Paragraphs (1)–(4) of subsection (a) apply only if the items named are owned or leased by the owner or operator of the vessel and transported for its use in handling its cargo in foreign trade.

(2) PARAGRAPH (5).—Paragraph (5) of subsection (a) applies only if the items named are—

(A) owned or leased by the owner or operator of the vessel or by the stevedoring company having the contract for the loading or unloading of the vessel; and

(B) transported without charge for use in the handling of cargo in foreign trade.

(c) RECIPROCITY REQUIREMENT FOR FOREIGN VESSELS.—This section applies to a vessel of foreign registry only if the Secretary of Homeland Security finds, based on information from the Secretary of State, that the government of the nation of registry extends reciprocal privileges to vessels of the United States.

(Pub. L. 109–304, §8(c), Oct. 6, 2006, 120 Stat. 1635.)

§55108. PLATFORM JACKETS

(a) DEFINITIONS.—In this section:

(1) COASTWISE QUALIFIED VESSEL.—The term "coastwise qualified vessel" means a vessel that has been issued a certificate of documentation with a coastwise endorsement under chapter 121 of this title.

(2) PLATFORM JACKET.—The term "platform jacket" refers to a single physical component and includes any type of offshore exploration, development, or production structure or component thereof, including—

(A) platform jackets;

(B) tension leg or SPAR platform superstructures (including the deck, drilling rig and support utilities, and supporting structure);

(C) hull (including vertical legs and connecting pontoons or vertical cylinder);

(D) tower and base sections of a platform jacket;

(E) jacket structures; and

(F) deck modules (known as "topsides").

(b) AUTHORIZED TRANSPORTATION.—Section 55102 of this title does not apply to the transportation of a platform jacket in or on a non-coastwise qualified launch barge between two points in the United States, at one of which there is an installation or other device within the meaning of section 4(a) of the Outer Continental Shelf Lands Act (43 U.S.C. 1333(a)), if—

(1) the launch barge was built before December 31, 2000, and has a launch capacity of at least 12,000 long tons; and

(2) the Secretary of Transportation makes a determination, in accordance with procedures established under subsection (c), that a suitable coastwise qualified vessel is not available for use in the transportation and, if needed, launch or installation of a platform jacket.

(c) PROCEDURES TO MAXIMIZE USE OF COASTWISE QUALIFIED VESSELS.—The Secretary of Transportation shall adopt procedures implementing this section that are reasonably designed to provide timely information so as to maximize the use of coastwise qualified vessels. The procedures shall, among other things, establish that for purposes of this section, a coastwise qualified vessel shall be deemed to be not available only if—

(1) on application by an owner or operator for the use of a non-coastwise qualified launch barge for transportation of a platform jacket under this section (which application shall include all relevant information, including engineering details and timing requirements), the Secretary promptly publishes a notice in the Federal Register—

(A) describing the project and the platform jacket involved;

(B) advising that all relevant information reasonably needed to assess the transportation requirements for the platform jacket will be made available to interested parties on request; and

(C) requesting that information on the availability of coastwise qualified vessels be submitted within 30 days after publication of that notice; and

(2)(A) no information is submitted to the Secretary within that 30 day period; or

(B) the owner or operator of a coastwise qualified vessel submits information to the Secretary asserting that the owner or operator has a suitable coastwise qualified vessel available for the transportation, but the Secretary determines, within 90 days after the notice is first published, that the coastwise qualified vessel is not suitable or reasonably available for the transportation.

(Pub. L. 109–304, §8(c), Oct. 6, 2006, 120 Stat. 1636.)

§55109. DREDGING

(a) IN GENERAL.—Except as provided in subsection (b), a vessel may engage in dredging in the navigable waters of the United States only if—

(1) the vessel is wholly owned by citizens of the United States for purposes of engaging in the coastwise trade;

(2) the charterer, if any, is a citizen of the United States for purposes of engaging in the coastwise trade; and

(3) the vessel has been issued a certificate of documentation with a coastwise endorsement under chapter 121 of this title or is exempt from documentation but would otherwise be eligible for such a certificate and endorsement.

(b) DREDGING OF GOLD IN ALASKA.—A documented vessel with a registry endorsement may engage in the dredging of gold in Alaska.

(c) PENALTY.—If a vessel is operated in knowing violation of this section, the vessel and its equipment are liable to seizure by and forfeiture to the United States Government.

(Pub. L. 109–304, §8(c), Oct. 6, 2006, 120 Stat. 1637.)

§55110. TRANSPORTATION OF VALUELESS MATERIAL OR DREDGED MATERIAL

Section 55102 of this title applies to the transportation of valueless material or dredged material, regardless of whether it has commercial value, from a point in the United States or on the high seas within the exclusive economic zone, to another point in the United States or on the high seas within the exclusive economic zone.

(Pub. L. 109–304, §8(c), Oct. 6, 2006, 120 Stat. 1637; Pub. L. 110–181, div. C, title XXXV, §3527(b)(1), Jan. 28, 2008, 122 Stat. 602.)

§55111. Towing

(a) In General.—Except when towing a vessel in distress, a vessel may not do any part of any towing described in subsection (b) unless the towing vessel—

(1) is wholly owned by citizens of the United States for purposes of engaging in the coastwise trade; and

(2) has been issued a certificate of documentation with a coastwise endorsement under chapter 121 of this title or is exempt from documentation but would otherwise be eligible for such a certificate and endorsement.

(b) Applicable Towing.—Subsection (a) applies to the towing of—

(1) a vessel between ports or places in the United States to which the coastwise laws apply, either directly or via a foreign port or place;

(2) a vessel from point to point within the harbors of ports or places to which the coastwise laws apply; or

(3) a vessel transporting valueless material or dredged material, regardless of whether it has commercial value, from a point in the United States or on the high seas within the exclusive economic zone, to another point in the United States or on the high seas within the exclusive economic zone.

(c) Penalties.—

(1) Owner and Master.—The owner and master of a vessel towing another vessel in violation of this section are each liable for a penalty of at least $350 but not more than $1,100. A penalty under this paragraph constitutes a lien on the vessel. The lien is enforceable in a district court of the United States for any district in which the vessel is found. Clearance may not be granted to the vessel until the penalties have been paid.

(2) Vessel.—In addition to the penalties under paragraph (1), the towing vessel is liable for a penalty of $60 per ton based on the tonnage of each towed vessel.

(Pub. L. 109–304, §8(c), Oct. 6, 2006, 120 Stat. 1637.)

§55112. Vessel escort operations and towing assistance

(a) In General.—Except in the case of a vessel in distress, only a vessel of the United States may perform the following escort vessel operations within the navigable waters of the United States:

(1) Operations that commence or terminate at a port or place in the United States.

(2) Operations required by United States law or regulation.

(3) Operations provided in whole or in part within or through navigation facilities owned, maintained, or operated by the United States Government or the approaches to those facilities, other than facilities operated by the Great Lakes St. Lawrence Seaway Development Corporation on the St. Lawrence River portion of the Seaway.

(b) Escort Vessels.—For purposes of this section, an escort vessel is—

(1) any vessel that is assigned and dedicated to assist another vessel, whether or not

tethered to that vessel, solely as a safety precaution to assist in controlling the speed or course of the assisted vessel in the event of a steering or propulsion equipment failure, or any other similar emergency circumstance, or in restricted waters where additional assistance in maneuvering the vessel is required to ensure its safe operation; and

(2) in the case of a vessel being towed under section 55111 of this title, any vessel that is assigned and dedicated to the vessel being towed in addition to any towing vessel required under that section.

(c) RELATIONSHIP TO OTHER LAW.—This section does not affect section 55111 of this title.

(d) PENALTY.—A person violating this section is liable to the Government for a civil penalty of not more than $10,000 for each day during which the violation occurs.

(Pub. L. 109–304, §8(c), Oct. 6, 2006, 120 Stat. 1638; Pub. L. 116–260, div. AA, title V, §512(c)(6)(D), Dec. 27, 2020, 134 Stat. 2757.)

§55113. USE OF FOREIGN DOCUMENTED OIL SPILL RESPONSE VESSELS

Notwithstanding any other provision of law, an oil spill response vessel documented under the laws of a foreign country may operate in waters of the United States on an emergency and temporary basis, for the purpose of recovering, transporting, and unloading in a United States port oil discharged as a result of an oil spill in or near those waters, if—

(1) an adequate number and type of oil spill response vessels documented under the laws of the United States cannot be engaged to recover oil from an oil spill in or near those waters in a timely manner, as determined by the Federal On-Scene Coordinator for a discharge or threat of a discharge of oil; and

(2) the foreign country has by its laws accorded to vessels of the United States the same privileges accorded to vessels of the foreign country under this section.

(Pub. L. 109–304, §8(c), Oct. 6, 2006, 120 Stat. 1638.)

§55114. UNLOADING FISH FROM FOREIGN VESSELS

(a) PROHIBITIONS.—Except as otherwise provided by this section or a treaty or convention to which the United States is a party, a foreign vessel may not unload, in a port of the United States—

(1) its catch of fish taken on board on the high seas or fish products processed from that catch of fish; or

(2) fish or fish products taken on board that vessel on the high seas from a vessel engaged in fishing operations or the processing of fish or fish products.

(b) REGULATIONS ON OBTAINING INFORMATION.—The Secretary of Commerce may prescribe regulations the Secretary considers necessary to obtain information on the transportation of fish products by vessels of the United States for foreign fish processing vessels to points in the United States.

(c) VIRGIN ISLANDS.—

(1) IN GENERAL.—A foreign vessel of not more than 50 feet overall in length may unload its catch of fresh fish (whole or with the heads, viscera, or fins removed, but not frozen, otherwise processed, or further advanced) in a port of the Virgin Islands

for immediate consumption in those islands. Fish unloaded under this paragraph may be sold or transferred only for immediate consumption. In the absence of satisfactory evidence that a sale or transfer to an agent, representative, or employee of a freezer or cannery is for immediate consumption, the sale or transfer is deemed not to be for immediate consumption. This paragraph does not prohibit the freezing, smoking, or other processing of fresh fish by the ultimate consumer of the fish.

(2) SEIZURE, FORFEITURE, AND PENALTY.—Fish unloaded in the Virgin Islands that are retained, sold, or transferred, except as allowed by paragraph (1), are liable to seizure by and forfeiture to the United States Government. A person retaining, selling, transferring, buying, or receiving the fish is liable to the Government for a civil penalty of not more than $1,000 for each violation. A penalty or forfeiture under this paragraph may be compromised, modified, or remitted under section 2107(b) of this title.

(d) NORTHERN MARIANA ISLANDS.—Subsection (a) does not apply to the Northern Mariana Islands.

(Pub. L. 109–304, §8(c), Oct. 6, 2006, 120 Stat. 1639.)

§55115. SUPPLIES ON FISH PROCESSING VESSELS

Section 55102 of this title does not apply to supplies aboard a United States documented fish processing vessel that are necessary and used for processing or assembling fishery products aboard such a vessel.

(Pub. L. 109–304, §8(c), Oct. 6, 2006, 120 Stat. 1640.)

§55116. CANADIAN RAIL LINES

Section 55102 of this title does not apply to the transportation of merchandise between points in the continental United States, including Alaska, over through routes in part over Canadian rail lines and connecting water facilities if the routes are recognized by the Surface Transportation Board and rate tariffs for the routes have been filed with the Board.

(Pub. L. 109–304, §8(c), Oct. 6, 2006, 120 Stat. 1640.)

§55117. GREAT LAKES RAIL ROUTE

Section 55102 of this title does not apply to the transportation of merchandise loaded on a railroad car or to a motor vehicle with or without a trailer, and with its passengers or contents when accompanied by the operator, when the railroad car or motor vehicle is transported in a railroad car ferry operated between fixed terminals on the Great Lakes as part of a rail route, if—

(1) the car ferry is owned by a common carrier by water and operated as part of a rail route with the approval of the Surface Transportation Board;

(2) the stock of the common carrier by water, or its predecessor, was owned or controlled by a common carrier by rail prior to June 5, 1920;

(3) the stock of the common carrier owning the car ferry is, with the approval of the Board, now owned or controlled by a common carrier by rail; and

(4) the car ferry is built in and documented under the laws of the United States.

(Pub. L. 109–304, §8(c), Oct. 6, 2006, 120 Stat. 1640.)

§55118. Foreign Railroads Whose Road Enters by Ferry, Tugboat, or Towboat

A foreign railroad, whose road enters the United States by ferry, tugboat, or towboat, may own and operate a vessel not having a coastwise endorsement in connection with the water transportation of the passenger, freight, express, baggage, and mail cars used by that road, together with the passengers, freight, express matter, baggage, and mails transported in those cars. However, the foreign railroad is subject to the same restrictions imposed by law on a vessel of the United States entering a port of the United States from the same foreign country. Except as otherwise authorized by this chapter, the ferry, tugboat, or towboat may not, under penalty of forfeiture, be used in the transportation of merchandise between ports or places in the United States to which the coastwise laws apply.

(Pub. L. 109–304, §8(c), Oct. 6, 2006, 120 Stat. 1640.)

§55119. Yukon River

Section 55102 of this title does not apply to the transportation of merchandise on the Yukon River until the Alaska Railroad is completed and the Secretary of Transportation finds that proper facilities will be available for transportation by citizens of the United States to properly handle the traffic.

(Pub. L. 109–304, §8(c), Oct. 6, 2006, 120 Stat. 1640.)

§55120. Transshipment of Imported Merchandise Intended for Immediate Exportation

The Secretary of Homeland Security may prescribe regulations for the transshipment and transportation of merchandise that is imported into the United States by sea for immediate exportation to a foreign port by sea, or by a river, the right to ascend or descend which for the purposes of commerce is secured by treaty to the citizens of the United States and the subjects of a foreign power.

(Pub. L. 109–304, §8(c), Oct. 6, 2006, 120 Stat. 1641.)

§55121. Transportation of Merchandise and Passengers on Canadian Vessels

(a) Between Rochester and Alexandria Bay.—Until passenger service is established by vessels of the United States between the port of Rochester, New York, and the port of Alexandria Bay, New York, the Secretary of Homeland Security may issue annually permits to Canadian passenger vessels to transport passengers between those ports. Canadian vessels holding such a permit are not subject to section 55103 of this title.

(b) Within Alaska or Between Alaska and Other Points in the United States.—Until the Secretary of Transportation determines that service by vessels of the United States is available to provide the transportation described in paragraph (1) or (2), sections 55102 and 55103 of this title do not apply to the transportation on Canadian vessels of—

(1) passengers between ports in southeastern Alaska; or

(2) passengers or merchandise between Hyder, Alaska, and other points in

southeastern Alaska or in the United States outside Alaska.

(Pub. L. 109–304, §8(c), Oct. 6, 2006, 120 Stat. 1641.)

§55122. FLOATING DRY DOCKS

(a) IN GENERAL.—Section 55102 of this title does not apply to the movement of a floating dry dock if—

(1) the floating dry dock—

(A) is being used to launch or raise a vessel in connection with the construction, maintenance, or repair of that vessel;

(B) is owned and operated by—

(i) a shipyard located in the United States that is an eligible owner specified under section 12103(b) of this title; or

(ii) an affiliate of such a shipyard; and

(C)(i) was owned or contracted for purchase by such shipyard or affiliate prior to the date of the enactment of the Carl Levin and Howard P. "Buck" McKeon National Defense Authorization Act for Fiscal Year 2015; or

(ii) had a letter of intent for purchase by such shipyard or affiliate signed prior to such date of enactment; and

(2) the movement occurs within 5 nautical miles of the shipyard or affiliate that owns and operates such floating dry dock or, in the case of a dry dock described in paragraph (1)(C)(ii), occurs between Honolulu, Hawaii, and Pearl Harbor, Hawaii.

(b) DRY DOCKS FOR CONSTRUCTION OF CERTAIN NAVAL VESSELS.—

(1) IN GENERAL.—In applying subsection (a) to a floating dry dock used for the construction of naval vessels in a shipyard located in the United States, the ownership and operation requirement in paragraph (1)(B) of that subsection shall be treated as satisfied and "December 19, 2017" shall be substituted for the date referred to in paragraph (1)(C) of that subsection if the Secretary of the Navy determines that—

(A) such dry dock is necessary for the timely completion of such construction; and

(B) such dry dock—

(i) is owned and operated by—

(I) a shipyard located in the United States that is an eligible owner specified under section 12103(b); or

(II) an affiliate of such a shipyard; or

(ii) is—

(I) owned by the State in which the shipyard is located or a political subdivision of that State; and

(II) operated by a shipyard located in the United States that is an eligible owner specified under section 12103(b).

(2) NOTICE TO CONGRESS.—Not later than 30 days after making a determination under paragraph (1), the Secretary of the Navy shall notify the Committee on Armed Services

and the Committee on Transportation and Infrastructure of the House of Representatives and the Committee on Armed Services and the Committee on Commerce, Science, and Transportation of the Senate of such determination.

(c) DEFINITION.—In this section, the term "floating dry dock" means equipment with wing walls and a fully submersible deck.

(Added Pub. L. 113–291, div. C, title XXXV, §3502(a), Dec. 19, 2014, 128 Stat. 3904; amended Pub. L. 114–328, div. C, title XXXV, §3508, Dec. 23, 2016, 130 Stat. 2780; Pub. L. 117–263, div. K, title CXV, §11525, Dec. 23, 2022, 136 Stat. 4145.)

§55123. PRIORITY LOADING FOR COAL

A vessel engaged in the coastwise transportation of coal produced in the United States, from a port in the United States to another port in the United States, shall be given priority in loading at any of those ports ahead of a waiting vessel engaged in the export transportation of coal produced in the United States. However, if the Secretary of Transportation finds that it is in the national interest, the Secretary may eliminate this priority loading at any port. The Secretary shall report to Congress within 30 days an action eliminating priority loading under this section.

(Pub. L. 109–304, §8(c), Oct. 6, 2006, 120 Stat. 1642, §55301; renumbered §55123, Pub. L. 116–283, div. A, title X, §1024(b)(1)(A), Jan. 1, 2021, 134 Stat. 3842.)

CHAPTER 553—PASSENGER AND CARGO PREFERENCES

SUBCHAPTER I—GENERAL [1]

SUBCHAPTER II—EXPORT TRANSPORTATION OF AGRICULTURAL COMMODITIES

SUBCHAPTER III—AMERICAN GREAT LAKES VESSELS

---

¹ So in original. Does not conform to subchapter heading.

SUBCHAPTER I—GOVERNMENT IMPELLED TRANSPORTATION

§55301. REPORT ON ADMINISTRATION OF PROGRAMS BY OTHER FEDERAL DEPARTMENTS AND AGENCIES

(a) IN GENERAL.—The Administrator of the Maritime Administration shall annually submit to Congress a report on the administration by—

(1) the Department of Defense of section 2631 of title 10; and

(2) other Federal departments and agencies of programs the Administrator determines are subject to section 55305 of this title.

(b) CONTENTS.—Each annual report required under subsection (a) shall include, for each Federal department or agency that administers a program covered by the report—

(1) the gross tonnage of cargo (equipment, materials, or agricultural products), expressed by type of cargo, transported on United States flag vessels as compared to on foreign vessels; and

(2) the total number of United States flag vessels and total number of foreign vessels contracted by each department or agency.

(c) AGENCY REPORTING REQUIREMENTS.—Not later than January 31 of each year, the head of each Federal department or agency that administers a program covered by a report required under subsection (a) shall submit to the Administrator of the Maritime Administration the information described in subsection (b) for that department or agency.

(Added Pub. L. 118–31, div. C, title XXXV, §3521(a)(1), Dec. 22, 2023, 137 Stat. 819.)

§55302. TRANSPORTATION OF UNITED STATES GOVERNMENT PERSONNEL

(a) IN GENERAL.—An officer or employee of the United States Government traveling by sea on official business overseas or to or from a territory or possession of the United States shall travel and transport personal effects on a vessel documented under the laws of the

United Sates if such a vessel is available, unless the necessity of the mission requires the use of a foreign vessel.

(b) REGULATIONS.—The Administrator of General Services shall prescribe regulations under which agencies may not pay for or reimburse an officer or employee for travel or transportation expenses incurred on a foreign vessel in the absence of satisfactory proof of the necessity of using the vessel.

(Pub. L. 109–304, §8(c), Oct. 6, 2006, 120 Stat. 1642.)

§55303. MOTOR VEHICLES OWNED BY UNITED STATES GOVERNMENT PERSONNEL

Notwithstanding any other law, privately-owned American shipping services may be used to transport motor vehicles owned by personnel of the United States Government whenever transportation of those vehicles at Government expense is otherwise authorized by law.

(Pub. L. 109–304, §8(c), Oct. 6, 2006, 120 Stat. 1642.)

§55304. EXPORTS FINANCED BY THE UNITED STATES GOVERNMENT

It is the sense of Congress that any loans made by an instrumentality of the United States Government to foster the exporting of agricultural or other products shall provide that the products may be transported only on vessels of the United States unless, as to any or all of those products, the Secretary of Transportation, after investigation, certifies to the instrumentality that vessels of the United States are not available in sufficient number, in sufficient tonnage capacity, on necessary schedules, or at reasonable rates.

(Pub. L. 109–304, §8(c), Oct. 6, 2006, 120 Stat. 1642.)

§55305. CARGOES PROCURED, FURNISHED, OR FINANCED BY THE UNITED STATES GOVERNMENT

(a) MINIMUM TONNAGE.—When the United States Government procures, contracts for, or otherwise obtains for its own account, or furnishes to or for the account of a foreign country, organization, or persons without provision for reimbursement, any equipment, materials, or commodities, or provides financing in any way with Federal funds for the account of any persons unless otherwise exempted, within or without the United States, or advances funds or credits, or guarantees the convertibility of foreign currencies in connection with the furnishing or obtaining of the equipment, materials, or commodities, the appropriate agencies shall take steps necessary and practicable to ensure that at least 50 percent of the gross tonnage of the equipment, materials, or commodities (computed separately for dry bulk carriers, dry cargo liners, and tankers) which may be transported on ocean vessels is transported on privately-owned commercial vessels of the United States, as provided under subsection (b), to the extent those vessels are available at fair and reasonable rates for commercial vessels of the United States, in a manner that will ensure a fair and reasonable participation of commercial vessels of the United States in those cargoes by geographic areas.

(b) ELIGIBLE VESSELS.—To be eligible to carry cargo as provided under subsection (a), a privately-owned commercial vessel shall be documented under the laws of the United

States—
(1) for not less than three years; or
(2) after January 1, 2030, for less than three years, if the vessel owner signs an agreement with the Secretary providing that—
(A) the vessel shall remain documented under the laws of the United States for not less than three years; and
(B) the vessel owner shall, upon request of the Secretary, agree to enroll the vessel in an emergency preparedness agreement or voluntary agreement authorized under section 708 of the Defense Production Act of 1950 (50 U.S.C. 4558) and shall ensure the vessel remains so enrolled until the vessel ceases to be documented under the laws of the United States.

(c) VIOLATION OF AGREEMENT.—A vessel under an agreement executed pursuant to subsection (b)(2) may be seized by, and forfeited to, the United States if, in violation of that agreement—
(1) the vessel owner places the vessel under foreign registry; or
(2) a person operates the vessel under the authority of a foreign country.

(d) WAIVERS.—(1) Notwithstanding any other provision of law, when the President, the Secretary of Defense, or the Secretary of Transportation declares the existence of an emergency justifying a temporary waiver of this section or section 55314 of this title, the President, the Secretary of Defense, or the Secretary of Transportation, following a determination by the Maritime Administrator, acting in the Administrator's capacity as Director, National Shipping Authority, of the non-availability of qualified United States flag capacity at fair and reasonable rates for commercial vessels of the United States to meet the requirements of this section or section 55314 of this title, may waive compliance with such section to the extent, in the manner, and on the terms the Maritime Administrator, acting in such capacity, prescribes, and no other waivers of the requirements of this section or section 55314 of this title shall be authorized.
(2)(A) Subject to subparagraphs (B) and (C), a waiver issued under this subsection shall be for a period of not more than 60 days.
(B) Upon termination of the period of a waiver issued under this subsection, the Maritime Administrator may extend the waiver for an additional period of not more than 30 days, if the Maritime Administrator makes the determinations described in paragraph (1).
(C) The aggregate duration of the period of all waivers and extensions of waivers under this subsection with respect to any one set of events shall not exceed three months in a fiscal year.
(3) The Maritime Administrator shall—
(A) for each determination referred to in paragraph (1), identify any actions that could be taken to enable qualified United States flag capacity to meet the requirements of this section or section 55314 at fair and reasonable rates for commercial vessels of the United States;
(B) provide notice of each determination referred to in paragraph (1) to the Secretary of Transportation and, as applicable, the President or the Secretary of Defense; and
(C) publish each determination referred to in paragraph (1)—

(i) on the website of the Maritime Administration not later than 24 hours after notice of the determination is provided to the Secretary of Transportation; and

(ii) in the Federal Register.

(4) The Maritime Administrator shall notify—

(A) the Committee on Commerce, Science, and Transportation of the Senate and the Committee on Transportation and Infrastructure of the House of Representatives of—

(i) any request for a waiver (or an extension thereof) made by the Secretary of Transportation of this section or section 55314(a) [1] of this title by not later than 72 hours after receiving such a request; and

(ii) the issuance of any such waiver (or an extension thereof), and why such waiver or extension was necessary, by not later than 72 hours after such issuance; and

(B) the Committee on Commerce, Science, and Transportation and the Committee on Armed Services of the Senate and the Committee on Transportation and Infrastructure and the Committee on Armed Services of the House of Representatives of—

(i) any request for a waiver (or an extension thereof) made by the Secretary of Defense of this section or section 55314(a) [1] of this title by not later than 72 hours after receiving such a request; and

(ii) the issuance of any such waiver (or an extension thereof), and why such waiver or extension was necessary, by not later than 72 hours after such issuance.

(e) PROGRAMS OF OTHER AGENCIES.—

(1) Each department or agency that has responsibility for a program under this section shall administer that program with respect to this section under regulations and guidance issued by the Secretary of Transportation. The Secretary, after consulting with the department or agency or organization or person involved, shall have the sole responsibility for determining if a program is subject to the requirements of this section.

(2) The Secretary—

(A) shall conduct an annual review of the administration of programs determined pursuant to paragraph (1) as subject to the requirements of this section and annually submit to the Committee on Transportation and Infrastructure of the House of Representatives and the Committee on Commerce, Science, and Transportation of the Senate a report on the administration of such programs;

(B) may direct agencies to require the transportation on United States-flagged vessels of cargo shipments not otherwise subject to this section in equivalent amounts to cargo determined to have been shipped on foreign carriers in violation of this section;

(C) may impose on any person that violates this section, or a regulation prescribed under this section, a civil penalty of not more than $25,000 for each violation willfully and knowingly committed, with each day of a continuing violation following the date of shipment to be a separate violation; and

(D) may take other measures as appropriate under the Federal Acquisition Regulations issued pursuant to section 25(c)(1) [1] of the Office of Federal Procurement

Policy Act (41 U.S.C. 1303(a)(1)) or contract with respect to each violation.

(f) SECURITY OF GOVERNMENT-IMPELLED CARGO.—

(1) In order to ensure the safety of vessels and crewmembers transporting equipment, materials, or commodities under this section, the Secretary of Transportation shall direct each department or agency (except the Department of Defense), when responsible for the carriage of such equipment, materials, or commodities, to reimburse, subject to the availability of appropriations, the owners or operators of vessels of the United States carrying such equipment, materials, or commodities for the cost of providing armed personnel aboard such vessels if the vessels are transiting high-risk waters.

(2) In this subsection, the term "high-risk waters" means waters so designated by the Commandant of the Coast Guard in the maritime security directive issued by the Commandant and in effect on the date on which an applicable voyage begins, if the Secretary of Transportation—

(A) determines that an act of piracy occurred in the 12-month period preceding the date the voyage begins; or

(B) in such period, issued an advisory warning that an act of piracy is possible in such waters.

(Pub. L. 109–304, §8(c), Oct. 6, 2006, 120 Stat. 1642; Pub. L. 110–417, div. C, title XXXV, §3511(a), (b), Oct. 14, 2008, 122 Stat. 4769; Pub. L. 112–213, title V, §503, Dec. 20, 2012, 126 Stat. 1575; Pub. L. 113–281, title III, §306, Dec. 18, 2014, 128 Stat. 3044; Pub. L. 115–232, div. C, title XXXV, §3546(s), Aug. 13, 2018, 132 Stat. 2327; Pub. L. 117–263, div. C, title XXXV, §3502(b), Dec. 23, 2022, 136 Stat. 3065; Pub. L. 118–31, div. C, title XXXV, §3531(a), Dec. 22, 2023, 137 Stat. 825.)

[1] See References in Text note below.

SUBCHAPTER II—EXPORT TRANSPORTATION OF AGRICULTURAL COMMODITIES

§55311. FINDINGS AND PURPOSES

(a) FINDINGS.—Congress finds that—

(1) a productive and healthy agricultural industry and a strong and active United States maritime industry are vitally important to the economic well-being and security of the United States;

(2) both industries must compete in international markets increasingly dominated by foreign trade barriers and the subsidization practices of foreign governments; and

(3) increased agricultural exports and the use of merchant vessels of the United States contribute positively to the United States balance of trade and generate employment opportunities in the United States.

(b) PURPOSES.—The purposes of this subchapter are to—

(1) enable the Secretary of Agriculture to plan export programs effectively, by clarifying the ocean transportation requirements applicable to those programs;

(2) take immediate and positive steps to promote the growth of the cargo-carrying capacity of the United States merchant marine;

(3) expand international trade in United States agricultural commodities and products

and develop, maintain, and expand markets for United States agricultural exports;

(4) improve the efficiency of administration of both the commodity purchasing and selling activities and the ocean transportation activities associated with export programs sponsored by the Secretary;

(5) stimulate and promote the agricultural and maritime industries of the United States and encourage cooperative efforts by both industries to address their common problems; and

(6) provide for the appropriate disposition of these findings and purposes.

(Pub. L. 109–304, §8(c), Oct. 6, 2006, 120 Stat. 1643.)

§55312. DETERMINING PREVAILING WORLD MARKET PRICE

(a) AGRICULTURAL COMMODITIES AND PRODUCTS.—The prevailing world market price for agricultural commodities or their products shall be determined under this subchapter under procedures prescribed by the Secretary of Agriculture. The Secretary shall prescribe the procedures by regulation, with notice and opportunity for public comment under section 553 of title 5.

(b) SERVICES AND NON-AGRICULTURAL COMMODITIES AND PRODUCTS.—If a determination of the prevailing world market price of any other type of materials, goods, equipment, or service is required to determine whether a barter or exchange transaction is subject to section 55314(b)(6) or (7) of this title, the determination shall be made by the Secretary of Agriculture in consultation with the heads of other appropriate agencies.

(Pub. L. 109–304, §8(c), Oct. 6, 2006, 120 Stat. 1644.)

§55313. EXEMPTION OF CERTAIN AGRICULTURAL EXPORTS FROM CARGO PREFERENCE PROVISIONS

Sections 55304 and 55305 of this title do not apply to export activities of the Secretary of Agriculture or the Commodity Credit Corporation under which—

(1) agricultural commodities or their products acquired by the Corporation are made available to United States exporters, users, processors, or foreign purchasers for the purpose of developing, maintaining, or expanding export markets for United States agricultural commodities or their products at prevailing world market prices;

(2) payments are made available to United States exporters, users, or processors or, except as provided in section 55314 of this title, cash grants are made available to foreign purchasers, for the purpose described in paragraph (1);

(3) commercial credit guarantees are blended with direct credits from the Corporation to reduce the effective rate of interest on export sales of United States agricultural commodities or their products;

(4) credit or credit guarantees for not more than 3 years are extended by the Corporation to finance or guarantee export sales of United States agricultural commodities or their products; or

(5) agricultural commodities or their products owned or controlled by or under loan from the Corporation are exchanged or bartered for materials, goods, equipment, or services at least equal in value to the agricultural commodities or their products for which they are exchanged or bartered (determined on the basis of prevailing world market

prices at the time of the exchange or barter), but this paragraph does not exempt from the cargo preference provisions referred to in section 55314(b) of this title any requirement otherwise applicable to the materials, goods, equipment, or services imported under the transaction.

(Pub. L. 109–304, §8(c), Oct. 6, 2006, 120 Stat. 1644.)

§55314. TRANSPORTATION REQUIREMENTS FOR CERTAIN EXPORTS SPONSORED BY THE SECRETARY OF AGRICULTURE

[(a) Repealed. Pub. L. 112–141, div. F, title I, §100124(a)(1), July 6, 2012, 126 Stat. 915.]

(b) APPLICABLE EXPORT ACTIVITY.—The activities specified in this subsection are export activities (except inspection or weighing activities, other activities carried out for health or safety, or technical assistance provided in the handling of commercial transactions) of the Secretary of Agriculture or the Commodity Credit Corporation—

(1) carried out under the Food for Peace Act (7 U.S.C. 1691 et seq.);

(2) carried out under section 416 of the Agricultural Act of 1949 (7 U.S.C. 1431);

(3) carried out under the Bill Emerson Humanitarian Trust Act (7 U.S.C. 1736f–1);

(4) under which agricultural commodities or their products are—

(A) donated through foreign governments or private or public agencies, including intergovernmental organizations; or

(B) sold for foreign currencies or for dollars on credit terms of more than 10 years;

(5) under which agricultural commodities or their products are made available for emergency food relief at less than prevailing world market prices;

(6) under which a cash grant is made directly or through an intermediary to a foreign purchaser to enable the purchaser to obtain United States agricultural commodities or their products in an amount greater than the difference between the prevailing world market price and the United States market price, free along side vessel at a United States port; or

(7) under which agricultural commodities owned or controlled by or under loan from the Corporation are exchanged or bartered for materials, goods, equipment, or services produced in foreign countries, except export activities described in section 55313(5) of this title.

[(c) Repealed. Pub. L. 112–141, div. F, title I, §100124(a)(1), July 6, 2012, 126 Stat. 915.]

(Pub. L. 109–304, §8(c), Oct. 6, 2006, 120 Stat. 1645; Pub. L. 110–246, title III, §3001(b)(1)(A), (2)(Y), June 18, 2008, 122 Stat. 1820, 1821; Pub. L. 110–417, div. C, title XXXV, §3511(d), Oct. 14, 2008, 122 Stat. 4770; Pub. L. 111–84, div. A, title X, §1073(c)(15), Oct. 28, 2009, 123 Stat. 2475; Pub. L. 112–141, div. F, title I, §100124(a), July 6, 2012, 126 Stat. 915.)

§55315. MINIMUM TONNAGE

(a) DEFINITION.—In this section, the term "base period" means the 5-year period running from the sixth through the second prior fiscal years.

(b) REQUIREMENT.—For each fiscal year, the minimum quantity of agricultural commodities to be exported under programs specified in section 55314(b) of this title is the average of the tonnage exported under those programs during the base period, discarding the high and low years.

(c) WAIVERS.—The President may waive the minimum quantity for a fiscal year under this section if the President determines and reports to Congress, together with reasons, that the quantity cannot be used effectively for the purposes of those programs or, based on a certification by the Secretary of Agriculture, that the commodities are not available for reasons that include the unavailability of funds.

(Pub. L. 109–304, §8(c), Oct. 6, 2006, 120 Stat. 1646; Pub. L. 112–141, div. F, title I, §100124(c)(1), July 6, 2012, 126 Stat. 915.)

[§§55316, 55317. REPEALED. PUB. L. 113–67, DIV. A, TITLE VI, §602(A), DEC. 26, 2013, 127 STAT. 1188]

Section 55316, Pub. L. 109–304, §8(c), Oct. 6, 2006, 120 Stat. 1647; Pub. L. 110–246, title III, §3001(b)(1)(A), (2)(Y), June 18, 2008, 122 Stat. 1820, 1821; Pub. L. 112–141, div. F, title I, §100124(b), (c)(2), July 6, 2012, 126 Stat. 915, related to financing the transportation of agricultural commodities.

Section 55317, Pub. L. 109–304, §8(c), Oct. 6, 2006, 120 Stat. 1648; Pub. L. 112–141, div. F, title I, §100124(c)(3), July 6, 2012, 126 Stat. 915, provided for the termination of this subchapter 90 days after the notification under section 55316(f) of this title is made, subject to certain exceptions.

§55318. EFFECT ON OTHER LAW

This subchapter does not affect chapter 5 of title 5.

(Pub. L. 109–304, §8(c), Oct. 6, 2006, 120 Stat. 1648.)

SUBCHAPTER III—AMERICAN GREAT LAKES VESSELS

§55331. DEFINITIONS

In this subchapter:

(1) AMERICAN GREAT LAKES VESSEL.—The term "American Great Lakes vessel" means a vessel so designated under section 55332 of this title, but only during the period the designation is in effect.

(2) GREAT LAKES.—The term "Great Lakes" means Lake Superior, Lake Michigan, Lake Huron, Lake Erie, Lake Ontario, the Saint Lawrence River west of Saint Regis, New York, and their connecting and tributary waters.

(3) GREAT LAKES SHIPPING SEASON.—The term "Great Lakes shipping season" means the period each year during which the Saint Lawrence Seaway is open for navigation by vessels, as declared by the Great Lakes St. Lawrence Seaway Development Corporation.

(Pub. L. 109–304, §8(c), Oct. 6, 2006, 120 Stat. 1648; Pub. L. 116–260, div. AA, title V, §512(c)(6)(E), Dec. 27, 2020, 134 Stat. 2757.)

§55332. DESIGNATING AMERICAN GREAT LAKES VESSELS

(a) DESIGNATIONS.—The Secretary of Transportation shall designate a vessel as an

American Great Lakes vessel if—

(1) an application for designation is submitted to the Secretary under regulations prescribed by the Secretary;

(2) the vessel is documented under the laws of the United States;

(3) the vessel, on the effective date of the designation, is—

(A) at least 1, but not more than 6, years old; or

(B) at least 1, but not more than 11, years old if the Secretary finds that suitable vessels are not available to provide the type of service for which the vessel will be used after the designation;

(4) the vessel has not previously been designated as an American Great Lakes vessel; and

(5) the owner makes an agreement as provided under subsection (b).

(b) AGREEMENTS.—A vessel may be designated as an American Great Lakes vessel only if the person that will be the owner of the vessel at the time of the designation makes an agreement with the Secretary providing that if the Secretary determines that the vessel is necessary to the defense of the United States, the United States Government will have an exclusive right, during the 120-day period following the date of a revocation of the designation under section 55335 of this title, to purchase the vessel for a price equal to the greater of—

(1) the approximate world market value of the vessel; or

(2) the cost of the vessel to the owner less a reasonable amount for depreciation.

(c) CERTAIN FOREIGN DOCUMENTATION AND SALE NOT PROHIBITED.—Notwithstanding any other law, if the Government does not exercise its right of purchase under an agreement under subsection (b), the owner of the vessel is not prohibited from—

(1) documenting the vessel under the laws of a foreign country; or

(2) selling the vessel to a person not a citizen of the United States.

(d) REGULATIONS.—The Secretary shall prescribe regulations establishing requirements for submitting applications under this section.

(Pub. L. 109–304, §8(c), Oct. 6, 2006, 120 Stat. 1649.)

§55333. EXEMPTION FROM RESTRICTION ON TRANSPORTING CERTAIN CARGO

The 3-year documentation requirement of section 55305(a) of this title does not apply to a vessel designated as an American Great Lakes vessel during the period of its designation.

(Pub. L. 109–304, §8(c), Oct. 6, 2006, 120 Stat. 1649.)

§55334. RESTRICTIONS ON OPERATIONS

(a) PROHIBITIONS.—Except as provided in subsection (b), an American Great Lakes vessel may not be used to—

(1) engage in trade—

(A) from a port in the United States that is not located on the Great Lakes; or

(B) between ports in the United States;

(2) transport bulk cargo (as defined in section 40102 of this title) that is subject to section 55305 or 55314 of this title or section 2631 of title 10; or
(3) provide a service (except ocean freight service) as—
(A) a contract carrier; or
(B) a common carrier on a fixed advertised schedule offering frequent sailings at regular intervals in the foreign trade of the United States.

(b) OFF-SEASON EXCEPTION.—An American Great Lakes vessel may be used for not more than 90 days during any 12-month period to engage in trade prohibited by subsection (a)(1)(A), except during the Great Lakes shipping season.

(Pub. L. 109–304, §8(c), Oct. 6, 2006, 120 Stat. 1649.)

§55335. REVOCATIONS AND TERMINATIONS OF DESIGNATIONS

(a) REVOCATIONS.—After notice and an opportunity for a hearing, the Secretary of Transportation may revoke a designation of a vessel as an American Great Lakes vessel if the Secretary finds that—
(1) the vessel does not meet a requirement for the designation;
(2) the vessel has been operated in violation of this subchapter; or
(3) the owner or operator of the vessel has violated an agreement made under section 55332(b) of this title.

(b) TERMINATIONS.—On petition and a showing of good cause by the owner of a vessel, the Secretary may terminate the designation of a vessel as an American Great Lakes vessel. The Secretary may impose conditions in a termination order to prevent significant adverse effects on other operators of vessels of the United States.

(Pub. L. 109–304, §8(c), Oct. 6, 2006, 120 Stat. 1650.)

§55336. CIVIL PENALTY

After notice and an opportunity for a hearing, the Secretary of Transportation may impose a civil penalty of not more than $1,000,000 on the owner of an American Great Lakes vessel for any act for which the designation may be revoked under section 55335 of this title.

(Pub. L. 109–304, §8(c), Oct. 6, 2006, 120 Stat. 1650.)

[CHAPTER 555—TRANSFERRED]

[§§55501, 55502. RENUMBERED §§50401, 50402]

CHAPTER 556—MARINE HIGHWAYS

Sec.

§55601. United States Marine Highway Program

(a) Establishment.—

(1) In general.—There is in the Department of Transportation a program, to be known as the "United States marine highway program".

(2) Additional program activities.—In carrying out the program established under this subsection, the Secretary of Transportation may—

(A) coordinate with ports, State departments of transportation, localities, other public agencies, and appropriate private sector entities on the development of landside facilities and infrastructure to support marine highway transportation; and

(B) develop performance measures for the program.

(b) Marine Highway Transportation Routes.—

(1) Designation.—The Secretary may designate a route as a marine highway transportation route, or modify such a designation, if—

(A) such route—

(i) provides a coordinated and capable alternative to landside transportation;

(ii) mitigates or relieves landside congestion;

(iii) promotes marine highway transportation; or

(iv) uses vessels documented under chapter 121; and

(B) such designation or modification is requested by—

(i) the government of a State or territory;

(ii) a metropolitan planning organization;

(iii) a port authority;

(iv) a non-Federal navigation district; or

(v) a Tribal government.

(2) Determination.—Not later than 180 days after the date on which the Maritime Administrator receives a request for the designation or modification of a marine highway route under paragraph (1), the Maritime Administrator shall make a determination of whether to make the requested designation or modification.

(3) Notification.—Not later than 14 days after the date on which the Maritime Administrator makes a determination under paragraph (2), the Maritime Administrator shall notify the requester of the determination.

(c) Map of Marine Highway Program Routes.—

(1) In general.—The Maritime Administrator shall make publicly available a map showing the location of marine highway routes, including such routes along the coasts,

in the inland waterways, and at sea and update that map when a marine highway route is designated or modified pursuant to subsection (b).

(2) COORDINATION.—The Maritime Administrator shall coordinate with the Administrator of the National Oceanic and Atmospheric Administration to incorporate the map referred to in paragraph (1) into the Marine Cadastre.

(d) ASSISTANCE.—

(1) IN GENERAL.—The Secretary may make grants to, or enter into contracts or cooperative agreements with, eligible entities to implement a marine highway transportation project or a component of such a project if the Secretary determines that the project or component—

    (A) meets the criteria referred to in subsection (b)(1)(A); and

    (B) develops, expands, or promotes—

        (i) marine highway transportation; or

        (ii) shipper use of marine highway transportation.

(2) APPLICATION.—

    (A) IN GENERAL.—To be eligible to receive a grant or to enter into a contract or cooperative agreement under this subsection, an eligible entity shall submit to the Secretary an application in such form and manner, and at such time, as the Secretary may require. Such an application shall include the following:

        (i) A comprehensive description of—

            (I) the marine highway route to be served by the marine highway transportation project;

            (II) the supporters of the marine highway transportation project, which may include business affiliations, private sector stakeholders, State departments of transportation, metropolitan planning organizations, municipalities, or other governmental entities (including Tribal governments), as applicable;

            (III) the need for such project; and

            (IV) the performance measure for the marine highway transportation project, such as volumes of cargo or passengers moved, or contribution to environmental mitigation, safety, reduced vehicle miles traveled, or reduced maintenance and repair costs.

        (ii) A demonstration, to the satisfaction of the Secretary, that—

            (I) the marine highway transportation project is financially viable; and

            (II) the funds or other assistance provided under this subsection will be spent or used efficiently and effectively.

        (iii) Such other information as the Secretary may require.

    (B) PRE-PROPOSAL.—

        (i) IN GENERAL.—Prior to accepting a full application under subparagraph (A), the Secretary may require that an eligible entity first submit a pre-proposal that contains a brief description of the item referred to in clauses (i) through (iii) of such subparagraph.

(ii) FEEDBACK.—Not later than 30 days after receiving a pre-proposal under clause (i) from an eligible entity, the Secretary shall provide to the eligible entity feedback to encourage or discourage the eligible entity from submitting a full application. An eligible entity may still submit a full application even if that eligible entity is not encouraged to do so after submitting a pre-proposal.

(C) PROHIBITION.—The Secretary may not require separate applications for project designation and for assistance under this section.

(D) GRANT APPLICATION FEEDBACK.—Following the award of assistance under this subsection for a particular fiscal year, the Secretary may provide feedback to an applicant to help such applicant improve future applications if the feedback is requested by that applicant.

(3) TIMING.—

(A) NOTICE OF FUNDING OPPORTUNITY.—The Secretary shall post a notice of funding opportunity regarding grants, contracts, or cooperative agreements under this subsection not more than 60 days after the date of the enactment of the appropriations Act for the fiscal year concerned.

(B) AWARDING OF ASSISTANCE.— The Secretary shall award grants, contracts, or cooperative agreements under this subsection not later than 270 days after the date of the enactment of the appropriations Act for the fiscal year concerned.

(4) NON-FEDERAL SHARE.—

(A) IN GENERAL.—Except as provided in subparagraph (B), not more than 80 percent of the funding for any project for which funding is provided under this subsection may come from Federal sources.

(B) TRIBAL GOVERNMENTS AND RURAL AREAS.—The Secretary may increase the Federal share of funding for the project to an amount above 80 percent in the case of an award of assistance under this subsection—

(i) to an eligible entity that is a Tribal government; or

(ii) for a project located in a rural area.

(5) PREFERENCE FOR FINANCIALLY VIABLE PROJECTS.— In awarding grants or entering into contracts or cooperative agreements under this subsection, the Secretary shall give a preference to a project or component of a project that presents the most financially viable transportation service and require the lowest percentage of Federal share of the funding.

(6) TREATMENT OF UNEXPENDED FUNDS.—Notwithstanding paragraph (3)(B), amounts awarded under this subsection that are not expended by the recipient within five years after obligation of funds or that are returned shall remain available to the Secretary to make grants and enter into contracts and cooperative agreements under this subsection.

(7) CONDITIONS ON PROVISION OF ASSISTANCE.—The Secretary may not provide assistance to an eligible entity under this subsection unless the Secretary determines that—

(A) sufficient funding is available to meet the non-Federal share requirement under paragraph (4);

(B) the marine highway project for which such assistance is provided will be completed without unreasonable delay; and

(C) the eligible entity has the authority to implement the proposed marine highway project.

(8) PROHIBITED USES.—Assistance provided under this subsection may not be used—

(A) to improve port or land-based infrastructure outside the United States; or

(B) unless the Secretary determines that such activities are necessary to carry out the marine highway project for which such assistance is provided, to raise sunken vessels, construct buildings or other physical facilities, or acquire land.

(9) GEOGRAPHIC DISTRIBUTION.—In making grants, contracts, and cooperative agreements under this section the Secretary shall take such measures so as to ensure an equitable geographic distribution of funds.

(10) ELIGIBLE ENTITY.—In this subsection, the term "eligible entity" means—

(A) a State, a political subdivision of a State, or a local government;

(B) a United States metropolitan planning organization;

(C) a United States port authority;

(D) a Tribal government; or

(E) a United States private sector operator of marine highway projects or private sector owners of facilities, including an Alaska Native Corporation, with an endorsement letter from the requester of a marine highway route designation or modification referred to in subsection (b)(1)(B).

(Added Pub. L. 110–140, title XI, §1121(a), Dec. 19, 2007, 121 Stat. 1760; amended Pub. L. 111–84, div. C, title XXXV, §3515, Oct. 28, 2009, 123 Stat. 2724; Pub. L. 112–213, title IV, §405(a), Dec. 20, 2012, 126 Stat. 1571; Pub. L. 116–283, div. G, title LVXXXIII [LXXXIII], §8332(d)(3), Jan. 1, 2021, 134 Stat. 4704; Pub. L. 117–263, div. C, title XXXV, §3521(a)(1), Dec. 23, 2022, 136 Stat. 3074.)

§55602. CARGO AND SHIPPERS

(a) MEMORANDUMS OF AGREEMENT.—The Secretary of Transportation shall enter into memorandums of understanding with the heads of other Federal entities to transport federally owned or generated cargo using a marine highway transportation project designated under section 55601 when practical or available.

(b) SHORT-TERM INCENTIVES.—The Secretary shall consult shippers and other participants in transportation logistics and develop proposals for short-term incentives to encourage the use of marine highway transportation.

(Added Pub. L. 110–140, title XI, §1121(a), Dec. 19, 2007, 121 Stat. 1761; amended Pub. L. 116–283, div. G, title LVXXXIII [LXXXIII], §8332(d)(4), Jan. 1, 2021, 134 Stat. 4705.)

§55603. MULTISTATE, STATE, TRIBAL, AND REGIONAL TRANSPORTATION PLANNING

(a) IN GENERAL.—The Secretary, in consultation with Federal entities, State and local governments, Tribal governments, and appropriate private sector entities, may develop strategies to encourage the use of marine highway transportation for transportation of passengers and cargo.

(b) STRATEGIES.—If the Secretary develops strategies under subsection (a), the Secretary may—

(1) assess the extent to which States, local governments, and Tribal governments include marine highway transportation and other marine transportation solutions in transportation planning;

(2) encourage State and Tribal departments of transportation to develop strategies, where appropriate, to incorporate marine highway transportation, ferries, and other marine transportation solutions for regional and interstate transport of freight and passengers in transportation planning; and

(3) encourage groups of States, Tribal governments, and multistate transportation entities to determine how marine highways can address congestion, bottlenecks, and other interstate transportation challenges.

(Added Pub. L. 117–263, div. C, title XXXV, §3521(b)(1), Dec. 23, 2022, 136 Stat. 3078.)

§55604. RESEARCH ON MARINE HIGHWAY TRANSPORTATION

The Secretary of Transportation, in consultation with the Administrator of the Environmental Protection Agency, may conduct research on marine highway transportation, regarding—

(1) the economic effects of marine highway transportation on the United States economy;

(2) the effects of marine highway transportation, including with respect to the provision of additional transportation options, on rural areas;

(3) the environmental and transportation benefits to be derived from marine highway transportation alternatives for other forms of transportation;

(4) technology, vessel design, and other improvements that would reduce emissions, increase fuel economy, and lower costs of marine highway transportation and increase the efficiency of intermodal transfers; and

(5) solutions to impediments to marine highway transportation projects designated under section 55601.

(Added Pub. L. 110–140, title XI, §1121(a), Dec. 19, 2007, 121 Stat. 1761; amended Pub. L. 116–283, div. G, title LVXXXIII [LXXXIII], §8332(d)(4), (5), Jan. 1, 2021, 134 Stat. 4705; Pub. L. 117–263, div. C, title XXXV, §3521(c), Dec. 23, 2022, 136 Stat. 3078.)

§55605. DEFINITIONS

In this chapter:

(1) The term "marine highway transportation" means the carriage by a documented vessel of cargo (including such carriage of cargo and passengers), if such cargo—

(A) is—

(i) contained in intermodal cargo containers and loaded by crane on the vessel;

(ii) loaded on the vessel by means of wheeled technology, including roll-on roll-off cargo;

(iii) shipped in discrete units or packages that are handled individually, palletized, or unitized for purposes of transportation;

(iv) bulk, liquid, or loose cargo loaded in tanks, holds, hoppers, or on deck; or

(v) freight vehicles carried aboard commuter ferry boats; and

(B) is—

(i) loaded at a port in the United States and unloaded either at another port in the United States or at a port in Canada or Mexico; or

(ii) loaded at a port in Canada or Mexico and unloaded at a port in the United States.

(2) The term "Tribal government" means the recognized governing body of any Indian or Alaska Native Tribe, band, nation, pueblo, village, community, component band, or component reservation, individually identified (including parenthetically) in the list published most recently, as of the date of enactment of the James M. Inhofe National Defense Authorization Act for Fiscal Year 2023, pursuant to section 104 of the Federally Recognized Indian Tribe List Act of 1994 (25 U.S.C. 5131).

(3) The term "Alaska Native Corporation" has the meaning given the term "Native Corporation" under section 3 of the Alaska Native Claims Settlement Act (43 U.S.C. 1602).

(Added Pub. L. 110–140, title XI, §1121(a), Dec. 19, 2007, 121 Stat. 1761; amended Pub. L. 112–213, title IV, §405(b), Dec. 20, 2012, 126 Stat. 1571; Pub. L. 114–92, div. C, title XXXV, §3508, Nov. 25, 2015, 129 Stat. 1223; Pub. L. 116–283, div. G, title LVXXXIII [LXXXIII], §8332(d)(6), Jan. 1, 2021, 134 Stat. 4705; Pub. L. 117–263, div. C, title XXXV, §3521(d)(1), Dec. 23, 2022, 136 Stat. 3079.)

PART E—CONTROL OF MERCHANT MARINE CAPABILITIES

CHAPTER 561—RESTRICTIONS ON TRANSFERS

§56101. APPROVAL REQUIRED TO TRANSFER VESSEL TO NONCITIZEN

(a) RESTRICTIONS.—

(1) IN GENERAL.—Except as otherwise provided in this section, section 12119 of this title, or section 611 of the Merchant Marine Act, 1936, a person may not, without the approval of the Secretary of Transportation—

(A) sell, lease, charter, deliver, or in any other manner transfer, or agree to sell, lease, charter, deliver, or in any other manner transfer, to a person not a citizen of the

United States, an interest in or control of—

    (i) a documented vessel owned by a citizen of the United States; or

    (ii) a vessel last documented under the laws of the United States; or

    (B) place under foreign registry, or operate under the authority of a foreign country, a documented vessel or a vessel last documented under the laws of the United States.

    (2) EXCEPTIONS.—Paragraph (1)(A) does not apply to a vessel that has been operated only for pleasure or only as a fishing vessel, fish processing vessel, or fish tender vessel (as defined in section 2101 of this title).

    (b) APPROVAL BEFORE DOCUMENTATION.—To promote financing with respect to a vessel to be documented under chapter 121 of this title, the Secretary may grant approval under subsection (a) before the vessel is documented.

    (c) EXCEPTIONS.—Notwithstanding any other provision of this subtitle, the Merchant Marine Act, 1936, or any contract with the Secretary made under this subtitle or that Act, a person may place a vessel under foreign registry without the approval of the Secretary if—

    (1)(A) the Secretary, in conjunction with the Secretary of Defense, determines that at least one replacement vessel of equal or greater military capability and of a capacity that is equivalent or greater, as measured by deadweight tons, gross tons, or container equivalent units, as appropriate, is documented under chapter 121 of this title by the owner of the vessel placed under foreign registry; and

    (B) the replacement vessel is not more than 10 years old on the date of that documentation; or

    (2) an operating agreement covering the vessel under chapter 531 of this title has expired.

    (d) STATUS OF PROHIBITED TRANSACTION.—A charter, sale, or transfer of a vessel, or of an interest in or control of a vessel, in violation of this section is void.

    (e) PENALTIES.—

    (1) CRIMINAL PENALTY.—A person that knowingly sells, charters, or transfers a vessel, or an interest in or control of a vessel, in violation of this section shall be fined under title 18, imprisoned for not more than 5 years, or both.

    (2) CIVIL PENALTY.—A person that sells, charters, or transfers a vessel, or an interest in or control of a vessel, in violation of this section is liable to the United States Government for a civil penalty of not more than $10,000 for each violation.

    (3) FORFEITURE.—A documented vessel may be seized by and forfeited to the Government if, in violation of this section, a person—

    (A) knowingly sells, charters, or transfers the vessel or an interest in or control of the vessel; or

    (B) places the vessel under foreign registry or operates the vessel under the authority of a foreign country.

    (f) FOREIGN VESSEL CHARTERS FOR PASSENGER VESSELS.—The Maritime Administrator shall make publicly available on an appropriate website of the Maritime Administration—

(1) a detailed summary of each request for a determination, approval, or confirmation that a vessel charter for a passenger vessel is encompassed by the general approval of time charters issued pursuant to this section or regulations prescribed pursuant to such section; and

(2) the final action of the Administration with respect to such request, after the provision of notice and opportunity for public comment.

(Pub. L. 109–304, §8(c), Oct. 6, 2006, 120 Stat. 1651; Pub. L. 118–31, div. C, title XXXV, §3514(b)(2), (3), Dec. 22, 2023, 137 Stat. 810.)

§56102. ADDITIONAL CONTROLS DURING WAR OR NATIONAL EMERGENCY

(a) IN GENERAL.—During war, or a national emergency declared by Presidential proclamation, a person may not, without the approval of the Secretary of Transportation—

(1) place under foreign registry a vessel owned in whole or in part by a citizen of the United States or a corporation incorporated under the laws of the United States or of a State;

(2) sell, mortgage, lease, charter, deliver, or in any other manner transfer, or agree to sell, mortgage, lease, charter, deliver, or in any other manner transfer, to a person not a citizen of the United States—

   (A) a vessel owned as described in paragraph (1), or an interest therein;

   (B) a vessel documented under the laws of the United States, or an interest therein; or

   (C) a facility for building or repairing vessels, or an interest therein;

(3) issue, assign, or transfer to a person not a citizen of the United States an instrument of indebtedness secured by a mortgage of a vessel to a trustee, by an assignment of an owner's interest in a vessel under construction to a trustee, or by a mortgage of a facility for building or repairing vessels to a trustee, unless the trustee or a substitute trustee is approved by the Secretary under subsection (b);

(4) enter into an agreement or understanding to construct a vessel in the United States for, or to be delivered to, a person not a citizen of the United States without expressly stipulating that construction will not begin until after the war or national emergency has ended;

(5) enter into an agreement or understanding whereby there is vested in, or for the benefit of, a person not a citizen of the United States the controlling interest in a corporation that is incorporated under the laws of the United States or a State and that owns a vessel or facility for building or repairing vessels; or

(6) cause or procure a vessel, constructed in whole or in part in the United States and never cleared for a foreign port, to depart from a port of the United States before it has been documented under the laws of the United States.

(b) TRUSTEES.—

(1) APPROVAL.—The Secretary shall approve a trustee or substitute trustee under subsection (a)(3) if and only if the trustee is a bank or trust company that—

   (A) is organized as a corporation, and is doing business, under the laws of the United States or a State;

(B) is authorized under those laws to exercise corporate trust powers;

(C) is a citizen of the United States;

(D) is subject to supervision or examination by Federal or State authority; and

(E) has a combined capital and surplus (as set forth in its most recent published report of condition) of at least $3,000,000.

(2) Disapproval.—If a trustee or substitute trustee ceases to meet the conditions in paragraph (1), the Secretary shall disapprove the trustee or substitute trustee. After the disapproval, the restrictions on transfer or assignment without the Secretary's approval in subsection (a)(3) apply.

(3) Operation of vessel.—During a period when subsection (a) applies, a trustee referred to in subsection (a)(3), even though approved as a trustee by the Secretary, may not operate the vessel under the mortgage or assignment without the Secretary's approval.

(c) Status of Prohibited Transaction.—A transaction in violation of this section is void.

(d) Recovery of Consideration.—

(1) In general.—A person that deposited or paid consideration in connection with a transaction prohibited by this section may recover the consideration after tender of the vessel, facility, stock, or other security, or interest therein, to the person entitled to it, or the forfeiture thereof to the United States Government.

(2) Exception.—Paragraph (1) does not apply if the person in whose interest the consideration was deposited, or to whom it was paid, entered into the transaction in the belief that the person depositing or paying the consideration was a citizen of the United States.

(e) Penalties.—

(1) Criminal penalty.—A person that violates, or attempts or conspires to violate, this section shall be fined under title 18, imprisoned for not more than 5 years, or both.

(2) Forfeiture.—The following shall be forfeited to the Government:

(A) A vessel, a facility for building or repairing vessels, or an interest in a vessel or such a facility, that is sold, mortgaged, leased, chartered, delivered, transferred, or documented, or agreed to be sold, mortgaged, leased, chartered, delivered, transferred, or documented, in violation of this section.

(B) Stock and other securities sold or transferred, or agreed to be sold or transferred, in violation of this section.

(C) A vessel departing in violation of subsection (a)(6).

(Pub. L. 109–304, §8(c), Oct. 6, 2006, 120 Stat. 1652.)

§56103. Conditional approvals

(a) In General.—In approving an act or transaction under section 56101 or 56102 of this title, the Secretary of Transportation may do so absolutely or upon conditions the Secretary considers advisable. The Secretary shall state the conditions in the notice of approval.

(b) VIOLATIONS.—A violation of a condition of approval is subject to the same penalties as a violation resulting from an act done without the required approval. The violation occurs at the time the condition is violated.

(Pub. L. 109–304, §8(c), Oct. 6, 2006, 120 Stat. 1654.)

§56104. PENALTY FOR FALSE STATEMENTS

A person that knowingly makes a false statement of a material fact to the Secretary of Transportation or another officer, employee, or agent of the Department of Transportation, to obtain the Secretary's approval under section 56101 or 56102 of this title, shall be fined under title 18, imprisoned for not more than 5 years, or both.

(Pub. L. 109–304, §8(c), Oct. 6, 2006, 120 Stat. 1654.)

§56105. FORFEITURE PROCEDURE

(a) IN GENERAL.—A forfeiture under this chapter may be enforced in the same way as a forfeiture under the laws on the collection of duties. However, such a forfeiture may be remitted without seizure of the vessel.

(b) PRIOR CONVICTIONS.—In a proceeding under this chapter to enforce a forfeiture, a prior criminal conviction of a person for a violation of this chapter with respect to the subject matter of the forfeiture is prima facie evidence of the violation against the person convicted.

(Pub. L. 109–304, §8(c), Oct. 6, 2006, 120 Stat. 1654.)

CHAPTER 563—EMERGENCY ACQUISITION OF VESSELS

[1] So in original. Probably should be followed by a period.

§56301. GENERAL AUTHORITY

During a national emergency declared by Presidential proclamation, or a period for which the President has proclaimed that the security of the national defense makes it advisable, the Secretary of Transportation may requisition or purchase, or requisition or charter the use of, a vessel owned by citizens of the United States, a documented vessel, or a vessel under construction in the United States.

(Pub. L. 109–304, §8(c), Oct. 6, 2006, 120 Stat. 1654.)

§56302. CHARTER TERMS

(a) IN GENERAL.—If a vessel is requisitioned for use but not ownership under this chapter, the Secretary of Transportation, at the time of requisition or as soon thereafter as the situation allows, shall offer the person entitled to possession of the vessel a charter containing—

(1) the terms the Secretary believes should govern the relationship between the United States Government and the person; and

(2) the rate of hire the Secretary considers just compensation for the use of the vessel and the services required under the charter.

(b) REFUSAL TO ACCEPT.—If the person does not accept the charter and rate of hire, the parties shall proceed as provided in section 56304 of this title.

(Pub. L. 109–304, §8(c), Oct. 6, 2006, 120 Stat. 1654.)

§56303. COMPENSATION

(a) IN GENERAL.—As soon as practicable, the Secretary of Transportation shall determine and pay just compensation for a vessel requisitioned under this chapter.

(b) FACTORS NOT AFFECTING VALUE.—The value of a vessel may not be considered enhanced by the circumstances requiring its requisition. Consequential damages arising from the requisition may not be paid.

(c) EFFECT OF CONSTRUCTION-DIFFERENTIAL SUBSIDY.—

(1) IF PAID.—If a construction-differential subsidy has been paid for the vessel, the value of the vessel at the time of requisition shall be determined under section 802 of the Merchant Marine Act, 1936.

(2) IF NOT PAID.—If a construction-differential subsidy has not been paid for the vessel, the value of any national defense features previously paid for by the United States Government shall be excluded.

(d) LOSS OR DAMAGE DURING CHARTER.—If a vessel is lost or damaged by a risk assumed by the Government under the charter, but a valuation for the vessel or a means of compensation has not been agreed to, the Secretary shall pay just compensation for the loss or damage, to the extent the person is not reimbursed through insurance.

(Pub. L. 109–304, §8(c), Oct. 6, 2006, 120 Stat. 1655.)

§56304. DISPUTED COMPENSATION

If the person entitled to compensation disputes the amount of just compensation determined by the Secretary of Transportation under this chapter, the Secretary shall pay the person, as a tentative advance, 75 percent of the amount determined. The person may bring a civil action against the United States to recover just compensation. If the tentative advance paid under this section is greater than the amount of the court's judgment, the person shall refund the difference.

(Pub. L. 109–304, §8(c), Oct. 6, 2006, 120 Stat. 1655.)

§56305. VESSEL ENCUMBRANCES

(a) IN GENERAL.—The existence of an encumbrance on a vessel does not prevent the requisition of the vessel under this chapter.

(b) DEPOSIT IN TREASURY.—

(1) IN GENERAL.—If an encumbrance exists, the Secretary of Transportation may deposit part of the compensation or advance of compensation to be paid under this chapter (but not more than the total amount of all encumbrances) in a fund in the Treasury. The Secretary shall publish notice of the creation of the fund in the Federal Register.

(2) AVAILABILITY OF AMOUNTS DEPOSITED.—Amounts deposited in the fund shall be available to pay the compensation or any of the encumbrances (including encumbrances stipulated to in a court of the United States or a State) existing at the time the vessel was requisitioned.

(c) CIVIL ACTION.—

(1) IN GENERAL.—Within 6 months after publication of notice under subsection (b), the holder of an encumbrance may bring a civil action in admiralty, according to the principles of libels in rem, against the fund.

(2) VENUE.—The action must be brought in the district court of the United States—

(A) from whose custody the vessel was or may be requisitioned; or

(B) in whose district the vessel was located when it was requisitioned.

(3) SERVICE OF PROCESS.—Service of process shall be made on the appropriate United States Attorney, the Attorney General, and the Secretary, in the manner provided by the Federal Rules of Civil Procedure (28 App. U.S.C.). Notice of the action shall be given to all interested persons as ordered by the court.

(4) AS BETWEEN PRIVATE PARTIES.—The action shall proceed and be determined according to the principles of law and the rules of practice applicable in like cases between private parties.

(Pub. L. 109–304, §8(c), Oct. 6, 2006, 120 Stat. 1655.)

§56306. USE AND TRANSFER OF VESSELS

(a) IN GENERAL.—The Secretary of Transportation may repair, recondition, reconstruct, operate, or charter for operation, a vessel acquired under this chapter.

(b) TRANSFER TO OTHER AGENCIES.—The Secretary may transfer the possession or control of a vessel acquired under this chapter to another department or agency of the United States Government on terms and conditions approved by the President. The department or agency shall promptly reimburse the Secretary for expenditures for just compensation, purchase price, charter hire, repairs, reconditioning, or reconstruction.

(Pub. L. 109–304, §8(c), Oct. 6, 2006, 120 Stat. 1656.)

§56307. RETURN OF VESSELS

When a vessel requisitioned for use but not ownership is returned to the owner, the Secretary of Transportation shall—

(1) return the vessel in a condition at least as good as when taken, less ordinary wear and tear; or

(2) pay the owner an amount sufficient to recondition the vessel to that condition, less ordinary wear and tear.

(Pub. L. 109–304, §8(c), Oct. 6, 2006, 120 Stat. 1656.)

§56308. TRANSFER OF SUBSTITUTE VESSELS

In the case of any vessel constructed in the United States after January 1, 1937, which has been taken by the United States for use in any manner, the Secretary of Transportation, if in his opinion the transfer would aid in carrying out the policies of this Act,[1] is authorized to transfer to the owner of such vessel another vessel which is deemed by the Secretary to be of comparable type with adjustments for depreciation and difference in design or speed, and to the extent applicable, such other adjustments and terms and conditions, including transfer of mortgage obligations in favor of the United States binding upon the old vessel, as the Secretary may prescribe.

(Added and amended Pub. L. 115–91, div. C, title XXXV, §3502(a)(2), (b)(5), Dec. 12, 2017, 131 Stat. 1910.)

[1] See References in Text note below.

§56309. EMERGENCY FOREIGN VESSEL ACQUISITION; PURCHASE OR REQUISITION OF VESSELS LYING IDLE IN UNITED STATES WATERS

During any period in which vessels may be requisitioned under this chapter, the President is authorized and empowered through the Secretary of Transportation to purchase, or to requisition, or for any part of such period to charter or requisition the use of, or to take over the title to or possession of, for such use or disposition as he shall direct, any merchant vessel not owned by citizens of the United States which is lying idle in waters within the jurisdiction of the United States and which the President finds to be necessary to the national defense. Just compensation shall be determined and made to the owner or owners of any such vessel in accordance with the applicable provisions of this chapter. Such compensation hereunder, or advances on account thereof, shall be deposited with the Treasurer of the United States in a separate deposit fund. Payments for such compensation and also for payment of any valid claim upon such vessel in accord with the provisions of section 56305, shall be made from such fund upon the certificate of the Secretary of Transportation.

(Added and amended Pub. L. 115–91, div. C, title XXXV, §3504(a), Dec. 12, 2017, 131 Stat. 1911.)

§56310. Voluntary purchase or charter agreements

During any period in which vessels may be requisitioned under this chapter as amended,[1] the President is authorized through the Secretary of Transportation to acquire by voluntary agreement of purchase or charter the ownership or use of any merchant vessel not owned by citizens of the United States.

(Added and amended Pub. L. 115–91, div. C, title XXXV, §3504(b), Dec. 12, 2017, 131 Stat. 1912.)

---

[1] *So in original.*

§56311. Requisitioned vessels

(a) Any vessel not documented under the laws of the United States, acquired by or made available to the Secretary of Transportation under section 56309 or 56310, as applicable, or otherwise, may, notwithstanding any other provision of law, in the discretion of the Secretary of the department in which the Coast Guard is operating be documented as a vessel of the United States under such rules and regulations or orders, and with such limitations, as the Secretary of the department in which the Coast Guard is operating may prescribe or issue as necessary or appropriate to carry out the purposes and provisions of section 56309 or 56310, as applicable, and in accordance with the provisions of subsection (c), engage in the coastwise trade when so documented. Any document issued to a vessel under the provisions of this subsection shall be surrendered at any time that such surrender may be ordered by the Secretary of the department in which the Coast Guard is operating. No vessel, the surrender of the documents of which has been so ordered, shall, after the effective date of such order, have the status of a vessel of the United States unless documented anew.

(b) The President may, notwithstanding any other provisions of law, by rules and regulations or orders, waive compliance with any provision of law relating to masters, officers, members of the crew, or crew accommodations on any vessel documented under authority of this section to such extent and upon such terms as he finds necessary because of the lack of physical facilities on such vessels, and because of the need to employ aliens for their operation. No vessel shall cease to enjoy the benefits and privileges of a vessel of the United States by reason of the employment of any person in accordance with the provisions of this subsection.

(c) Any vessel while documented under the provisions of this section, when chartered under section 56309 or 56310, as applicable, by the Secretary of Transportation to Government agencies or departments or to private operators, may engage in the coastwise trade under permits issued by the Secretary of Transportation, who is authorized to issue permits for such purpose pursuant to such rules and regulations as he may prescribe. The Secretary of Transportation is authorized to prescribe such rules and regulations as he may deem necessary or appropriate to carry out the purposes and provisions of this section. Section 57109 shall not apply with respect to vessels chartered to Government agencies or departments or to private operators or otherwise used or disposed of under section 56309 or 56310, as applicable. Existing laws covering the inspection of steam vessels are made applicable to vessels documented under this section only to such extent and upon such conditions as may be required by regulations of the Secretary of the department in which the Coast Guard is operating: *Provided,* That in determining to what extent those laws should be made applicable, due consideration shall be given to the primary purpose of transporting commodities essential to the national defense.

(d) The Secretary of Transportation without regard to the [1] section 6101 of title 41 may repair, reconstruct, or recondition any vessels to be utilized under section 56309 or 56310, as applicable. The Secretary of Transportation and any other Government department or agency by which any vessel is acquired or chartered, or to which any vessel is transferred or made available under section 56309 or 56310, as applicable, may, with the aid of any funds available and without regard to the provisions of section 6101 of title 41, repair, reconstruct, or recondition any such vessels to meet the needs of the services intended, or provide facilities for such repair, reconstruction, or reconditioning. The Secretary of Transportation may operate or charter for operation any vessel to be utilized under section 56309 or 56310, as applicable [2] to private operators, citizens of the United States, or to any department or agency of the United States Government, without regard to the provisions of chapter 575, and any department or agency of the United States Government is authorized to enter into such charters.

(e) In case of any voyage of a vessel documented under the provisions of this section begun before the date of termination of an effective period of section 196 of this title, but is completed after such date, the provisions of this section shall continue in effect with respect to such vessel until such voyage is completed.

(Added and amended Pub. L. 115–91, div. C, title XXXV, §3504(c), Dec. 12, 2017, 131 Stat. 1912.)

[1] So in original. The word "the" probably should not appear.

[2] So in original. Probably should be followed by a comma.

§56312. DOCUMENTED DEFINED

In sections 56309 through 56311, the term "documented" means, with respect to a vessel, that a certificate of documentation has been issued for the vessel under chapter 121.

(Added Pub. L. 115–91, div. C, title XXXV, §3504(d), Dec. 12, 2017, 131 Stat. 1913.)

CHAPTER 565—ESSENTIAL VESSELS AFFECTED BY NEUTRALITY ACT

§56501. Definition

In this chapter, the term "essential vessel" means a vessel that is—

(1)(A) security for a mortgage indebtedness to the United States Government; or

(B) constructed under this subtitle or required by a contract under this subtitle to be operated on a certain essential foreign trade route; and

(2) necessary in the interests of commerce and national defense to be maintained in condition for prompt use.

(Pub. L. 109–304, §8(c), Oct. 6, 2006, 120 Stat. 1656.)

§56502. Adjusting obligations and arranging maintenance

(a) General Authority.—On written application, the Secretary of Transportation may adjust obligations and arrange for maintenance of an essential vessel as provided in this chapter if the Secretary determines, after any investigation or proceeding the Secretary considers desirable, that—

(1) the operation of the vessel in the service, route, or line to which it is assigned under this subtitle, or in which it otherwise would be operated, is not—

(A) lawful under the Neutrality Act of 1939 (22 U.S.C. 441 et seq.) or a proclamation issued under that Act; or

(B) compatible with maintaining the availability of the vessel for national defense and commerce;

(2) it is not feasible under existing law to employ the vessel in any other service or operation in foreign or domestic trade (except temporary or emergency operation under section 56503(b)(5) of this title); and

(3) the applicant, because of the restrictions of the Neutrality Act of 1939 (22 U.S.C. 441 et seq.) or the withdrawal of vessels for national defense under paragraph (1), is not earning or will not earn a reasonable return on the capital necessarily employed in its business.

(b) Effective Period.—Adjustments and arrangements under subsection (a) shall continue in effect only as long as the circumstances described in subsection (a) continue to exist.

(Pub. L. 109–304, §8(c), Oct. 6, 2006, 120 Stat. 1657.)

§56503. Types of adjustments and arrangements

(a) Suspension Requirements.—An adjustment or arrangement under this chapter shall include suspension of—

(1) the requirement to operate the vessel in foreign trade under the applicable operating-differential or construction-differential subsidy contract or mortgage or other agreement; and

(2) the right to operating-differential subsidy for the vessel.

(b) Discretionary Adjustments and Arrangements.—To the extent the Secretary of Transportation considers appropriate to carry out the purposes of this subtitle, an adjustment or arrangement under this chapter may include any of the following:

(1) Lay-up of the vessel by the owner or in the custody of the Secretary, with payment or reimbursement by the Secretary of necessary and proper expenses (including reasonable overhead and insurance) or a fixed periodic allowance instead of payment or reimbursement.

(2) Postponement, for not more than the total period of the lay-up, of the maturity date of each installment of the principal of obligations to the United States Government for the vessel (regardless of whether the maturity date is during a lay-up period), or rearrangement of those maturities.

(3) Postponement or cancellation of interest accruing on the obligations during a lay-up period.

(4) Extension, for not more than the total period of the lay-up, of the 20-year life limitation for the vessel and other limitations and provisions of this subtitle based on a 20-year life.

(5) Provision for temporary or emergency employment of the vessel (instead of lay-up) as may be practicable, with such arrangements for management of the vessel, payment of expenses, and application of the proceeds of the employment, as the Secretary may approve, with any period of operation being included as part of the lay-up period.

(6) Payment to the Secretary, on termination of the arrangements with the applicant, of the applicant's net profits (earned while the arrangements were in effect) in excess of 10 percent a year on the capital necessarily employed in the applicant's business, as reimbursement for obligations postponed or canceled and expenses incurred or paid by the Secretary under this section.

(c) LAID-UP VESSELS.—Under subsection (b)(6), capital of the applicant represented by a vessel of the applicant laid-up or operated under this section shall be included in capital necessarily employed in the applicant's business. The Secretary may require a vessel laid-up or operated under this section to be security for reimbursement.

(Pub. L. 109–304, §8(c), Oct. 6, 2006, 120 Stat. 1657.)

§56504. CHANGES IN ADJUSTMENTS AND ARRANGEMENTS

The Secretary of Transportation may change an adjustment or arrangement made under this chapter as the Secretary considers necessary to carry out this chapter.

(Pub. L. 109–304, §8(c), Oct. 6, 2006, 120 Stat. 1658.)

PART F—GOVERNMENT-OWNED MERCHANT VESSELS

CHAPTER 571—GENERAL AUTHORITY

§57100. NATIONAL DEFENSE RESERVE FLEET

(a) FLEET COMPONENTS.—The Secretary of Transportation shall maintain a National Defense Reserve Fleet, including any vessel assigned by the Secretary to the Ready Reserve Force component of the fleet, consisting of those vessels owned or acquired by the United States Government that the Secretary of Transportation, after consultation with the Secretary of the Navy, determines are of value for national defense purposes and that the Secretary of Transportation decides to place and maintain in the fleet. Vessels in the National Defense Reserve Fleet, including vessels loaned to State maritime academies, shall be considered public vessels of the United States.

(b) PERMITTED USES.—Except as otherwise provided by law, a vessel in the fleet may be used—

(1) for an account of an agency of the United States Government in a period during which vessels may be requisitioned under section 902 of the Merchant Marine Act, 1936 (46 App. U.S.C. 1242); [1] or

(2) on the request of the Secretary of Defense, and in accordance with memoranda of agreement between the Secretary of Transportation and the Secretary of Defense, for—

(A) testing for readiness and suitability for mission performance;

(B) defense sealift functions for which other sealift assets are not reasonably available; and

(C) support of the deployment of the United States armed forces in a military contingency, for military contingency operations, or for civil contingency operations upon orders from the National Command Authority;

(3) for otherwise lawfully permitted storage or transportation of non-defense-related cargo as directed by the Secretary of Transportation with the concurrence of the Secretary of Defense;

(4) for training purposes to the extent authorized by the Secretary of Transportation with the concurrence of the Secretary of Defense;

(5) on a reimbursable basis, for charter to the government of any State, locality, or Territory of the United States, except that the prior consent of the Secretary of Defense for such use shall be required with respect to any vessel in the Ready Reserve Force or in the National Defense Reserve Fleet which is maintained in a retention status for the Department of Defense; or

(6) for civil contingency operations and Maritime Administration promotional and

media events, in accordance with subsection (f).

(c) READY RESERVE FORCE MANAGEMENT.—

(1) MINIMUM REQUIREMENTS.—To ensure the readiness of vessels in the Ready Reserve Force component of the National Defense Reserve Fleet, the Secretary of Transportation shall, at a minimum—

(A) maintain all of the vessels in a manner that will enable each vessel to be activated within a period specified in plans for mobilization of the vessels;

(B) activate and conduct sea trials on each vessel at a frequency that is considered by the Secretary to be necessary;

(C) maintain and adequately crew, as necessary, in an enhanced readiness status those vessels that are scheduled to be activated in 5 or less days;

(D) locate those vessels that are scheduled to be activated near embarkation ports specified for those vessels; and

(E) notwithstanding section 2109 of title 46, United States Code, have each vessel inspected by the Secretary of the department in which the Coast Guard is operating to determine if the vessel meets the safety standards that would apply under part B of subtitle II of that title if the vessel were not a public vessel.

(2) VESSEL MANAGERS.—

(A) ELIGIBILITY FOR CONTRACT.—A person, including a shipyard, is eligible for a contract for the management of a vessel in the Ready Reserve Force if the Secretary determines, at a minimum, that the person has—

(i) experience in the operation of commercial-type vessels or public vessels owned by the United States Government; and

(ii) the management capability necessary to operate, maintain, and activate the vessel at a reasonable price.

(B) CONTRACT REQUIREMENT.—The Secretary of Transportation shall include in each contract for the management of a vessel in the Ready Reserve Force a requirement that each seaman who performs services on any vessel covered by the contract hold the license or merchant mariner's document that would be required under chapter 71 or chapter 73 of title 46, United States Code, for a seaman performing that service while operating the vessel if the vessel were not a public vessel.

(d) APPLICABILITY OF LIMITATIONS ON OVERHAUL, REPAIR, AND MAINTENANCE IN FOREIGN SHIPYARDS.—

(1) APPLICATION OF LIMITATION.—The provisions of section 8680 of title 10 shall apply to vessels specified in subsection (b), and to the Secretary of Transportation with respect to those vessels, in the same manner as those provisions apply to vessels specified in subsection (b) of such section, and to the Secretary of the Navy, respectively.

(2) COVERED VESSELS.—Vessels specified in this paragraph are vessels maintained by the Secretary of Transportation in support of the Department of Defense, including any vessel assigned by the Secretary of Transportation to the Ready Reserve Force that is owned by the United States.

(e) EXEMPTION FROM TANK VESSEL CONSTRUCTION STANDARDS.—Vessels in the National Defense Reserve Fleet are exempt from the provisions of section 3703a.

(f) USE OF NDRF VESSELS FOR CIVIL CONTINGENCY OPERATIONS AND PROMOTIONAL AND MEDIA EVENTS.—With the concurrence of the Secretary of Defense, the Secretary of Transportation may allow the use of vessels in the National Defense Reserve Fleet (NDRF) for civil contingency operations requested by another Federal agency, and for Maritime Administration promotional and media events relating to demonstration projects and research and development supporting the Administration's mission, if the Secretary of Transportation determines such use is in the best interest of the Government after considering the following factors:

(1) AVAILABILITY.—The availability of NDRF or Ready Reserve Force (RRF) resources and the impact of such use on NDRF and RRF mission support to the defense and homeland security requirements of the Government.

(2) INTERFERENCE.—Whether the such [2] use of vessels will support the mission of the Maritime Administration and not significantly interfere with NDRF vessel maintenance, repair, safety, readiness, and resource availability.

(3) SAFETY.—Whether safety precautions will be taken, including indemnification of liability when applicable.

(4) COST.—Whether any costs incurred by such use will be funded as a reimbursable transaction between Federal agencies, as applicable.

(5) OTHER MATTERS.—Any other matters the Maritime Administrator considers appropriate.

(g) VESSEL STATUS.—A vessel in the National Defense Reserve Fleet determined by the Maritime Administration to be an obsolete vessel shall remain a vessel within the meaning of that term in section 3 of title 1, United States Code, and subject to the rights and responsibilities of a vessel under admiralty law at least until such time as the vessel is delivered to a dismantling facility or is disposed of otherwise from the National Defense Reserve Fleet.

(Added and amended Pub. L. 115–91, div. C, title XXXV, §3502(a)(3), (b)(6), Dec. 12, 2017, 131 Stat. 1910; Pub. L. 115–232, div. A, title VIII, §809(q), Aug. 13, 2018, 132 Stat. 1844; Pub. L. 118–31, div. C, title XXXV, §3514(j)(2), Dec. 22, 2023, 137 Stat. 811.)

[1] See References in Text note below.

[2] So in original.

§57101. PLACEMENT OF VESSELS IN NATIONAL DEFENSE RESERVE FLEET

(a) IN GENERAL.—Any vessel acquired by the Maritime Administration of 1,500 gross tons or more or such other vessels as the Secretary of Transportation determines are appropriate shall be placed in the National Defense Reserve Fleet.

(b) REMOVAL FROM FLEET.—A vessel placed in the Fleet under subsection (a) may not be traded out or sold from the Fleet, except as provided in section 57102, 57103, or 57104 or chapter 533, 537, 573, or 575 of this title, or section 308704 of title 54.

(c) AUTHORITY OF FEDERAL ENTITIES TO TRANSFER VESSELS.—All Federal entities are authorized to transfer vessels to the National Defense Reserve Fleet without reimbursement subject to the approval of the Secretary of Transportation and the Secretary of the Navy with respect to Ready Reserve Force vessels and the Secretary of Transportation with respect to all other vessels.

(Pub. L. 109–304, §8(c), Oct. 6, 2006, 120 Stat. 1658; Pub. L. 112–213, title IV, §§406, 407, Dec. 20, 2012, 126 Stat. 1571; Pub. L. 115–91, div. C, title XXXV, §3502(b)(7), Dec. 12, 2017, 131 Stat. 1911; Pub. L. 118–31, div. C, title XXXV, §3514(j)(3), Dec. 22, 2023, 137 Stat. 811.)

§57102. DISPOSITION OF VESSELS

(a) IN GENERAL.—If the Secretary of Transportation determines that a vessel is an obsolete vessel, the Secretary may dispose of such vessel (by sale or by purchase of disposal services).

(b) SELLING PROCEDURE.—The sale of a vessel under subsection (a) shall be made on a best value basis. The purchaser does not have to be a citizen of the United States. The purchaser shall provide a surety bond, with a surety approved by the Secretary, to ensure that the vessel will not be operated in the foreign trade of the United States at any time within 10 years after the sale, in competition with a vessel owned by a citizen of the United States and documented under the laws of the United States.

(Pub. L. 109–304, §8(c), Oct. 6, 2006, 120 Stat. 1658; Pub. L. 118–31, div. C, title XXXV, §3514(j)(4), Dec. 22, 2023, 137 Stat. 811.)

§57103. DONATION OF VESSELS IN THE NATIONAL DEFENSE RESERVE FLEET

(a) IN GENERAL.—The Secretary of Transportation may convey the right, title, and interest of the United States Government in any vessel of the National Defense Reserve Fleet that has been identified by the Secretary as an obsolete vessel, if the recipient—

(1) is a non-profit organization, a State, or a municipal corporation or political subdivision of a State;

(2) agrees not to use, or allow others to use, the vessel for commercial transportation purposes;

(3) agrees to make the vessel available to the Government whenever the Secretary indicates that it is needed by the Government;

(4) agrees to hold the Government harmless for any claims arising from exposure to asbestos, polychlorinated biphenyls, lead paint, or other hazardous substances after conveyance of the vessel, except for claims arising from use of the vessel by the Government;

(5) has a conveyance plan and a business plan that describes the intended use of the vessel, each of which has been submitted to and approved by the Secretary;

(6) has provided proof, as determined by the Secretary, of resources sufficient to accomplish the transfer, necessary repairs and modifications, and initiation of the intended use of the vessel; and

(7) agrees that when the recipient no longer requires the vessel for use as described in the business plan required under paragraph (5)—

(A) the recipient will, at the discretion of the Secretary, reconvey the vessel to the

Government in good condition except for ordinary wear and tear; or

(B) if the Board of Trustees of the recipient has decided to dissolve the recipient according to the laws of the State in which the recipient is incorporated, then—

(i) the recipient shall distribute the vessel, as an asset of the recipient, to a person that has been determined exempt from taxation under section 501(c)(3) of the Internal Revenue Code of 1986 (26 U.S.C. 501(c)(3)), or to the Federal Government or a State or local government for a public purpose; and

(ii) the vessel shall be disposed of by a court of competent jurisdiction of the county in which the principal office of the recipient is located, for such purposes as the court shall determine, or to such organizations as the court shall determine are organized exclusively for public purposes.

(b) OTHER EQUIPMENT.—At the Secretary's discretion, additional equipment from other obsolete vessels of the Fleet may be conveyed to assist the recipient with maintenance, repairs, or modifications.

(c) ADDITIONAL TERMS.—The Secretary may require any additional terms the Secretary considers appropriate.

(d) DELIVERY OF VESSEL.—If conveyance is made under this section, the vessel shall be delivered to the recipient at a time and place to be determined by the Secretary. The vessel shall be conveyed in an "as is" condition.

(e) LIMITATIONS.—If at any time prior to delivery of the vessel to the recipient, the Secretary determines that a different disposition of the vessel would better serve the interests of the Government, the Secretary shall pursue the more favorable disposition of the obsolete vessel and shall not be liable for any damages that may result from an intended recipient's reliance upon a proposed transfer.

(f) REVERSION.—The Secretary shall include in any conveyance under this section terms under which all right, title, and interest conveyed by the Secretary shall revert to the Government if the Secretary determines the vessel has been used other than as described in the business plan required under subsection (a)(5).

(Pub. L. 109–304, §8(c), Oct. 6, 2006, 120 Stat. 1659; Pub. L. 112–213, title IV, §408(a), Dec. 20, 2012, 126 Stat. 1571; Pub. L. 118–31, div. C, title XXXV, §3514(j)(5), Dec. 22, 2023, 137 Stat. 812.)

§57104. ACQUISITION OF VESSELS FROM SALE OF OBSOLETE VESSELS

(a) IN GENERAL.—The Secretary of Transportation may acquire suitable documented vessels with amounts in the Vessel Operations Revolving Fund derived from the sale of obsolete vessels in the National Defense Reserve Fleet.

(b) VALUATION.—The acquired and obsolete vessels shall be valued at their scrap value in domestic or foreign markets as of the date of the acquisition for or sale from the Fleet. However, the value assigned to those vessels shall be determined on the same basis, with consideration given to the fair value of the cost of moving the vessel sold from the Fleet to the place of scrapping.

(c) COSTS INCIDENT TO LAY-UP.—Costs incident to the lay-up of the vessel acquired under this section may be paid from amounts in the Fund.

(d) TRANSFERS TO NON-CITIZENS.—A vessel sold from the Fleet under this section may be scrapped in an approved foreign market without obtaining additional separate approval from the Secretary to transfer the vessel to a person not a citizen of the United States.

(Pub. L. 109–304, §8(c), Oct. 6, 2006, 120 Stat. 1660.)

§57105. ACQUISITION OF VESSELS FOR ESSENTIAL SERVICES, ROUTES, OR LINES

(a) IN GENERAL.—The Secretary of Transportation may acquire a vessel, by purchase or otherwise, if—

(1) the Secretary considers the vessel necessary to establish, maintain, improve, or serve as a replacement on an essential service, route, or line in the foreign commerce of the United States, as determined under section 50103 of this title;

(2) the vessel was constructed in the United States; and

(3) the Secretary of the Navy has certified to the Secretary of Transportation that the vessel is suitable for economical and speedy conversion into a naval or military auxiliary or otherwise suitable for use by the United States Government in time of war or national emergency.

(b) PRICE.—The price paid for the vessel shall be based on a fair and reasonable valuation. However, the price may not exceed by more than 5 percent the cost of the vessel to the owner (excluding any construction-differential subsidy and the cost of national defense features paid by the Secretary of Transportation) plus the actual cost previously expended for reconditioning, less depreciation based on a 25-year life for a dry-cargo or passenger vessel and a 20-year life for a tanker or other liquid bulk carrier vessel.

(c) DOCUMENTATION.—A vessel acquired under this section that is not documented under the laws of the United States at the time of acquisition shall be so documented as soon as practicable.

(Pub. L. 109–304, §8(c), Oct. 6, 2006, 120 Stat. 1660.)

§57106. MAINTENANCE, IMPROVEMENT, AND OPERATION OF VESSELS

(a) IN GENERAL.—The Secretary of Transportation may maintain, repair, recondition, remodel, and improve vessels owned by the United States Government and in the possession or under the control of the Secretary, to equip them adequately for competition in the foreign trade of the United States. The Secretary may operate such a vessel or charter the vessel on terms and conditions the Secretary considers appropriate to carry out the purposes of this subtitle.

(b) DOCUMENTATION AND RESTRICTIONS ON OPERATION.—A vessel reconditioned, remodeled, or improved under subsection (a) shall be documented under the laws of the United States and remain so documented for at least 5 years after completion of the reconditioning, remodeling, or improvement. During that period, it shall be operated on voyages that are not exclusively coastwise.

(Pub. L. 109–304, §8(c), Oct. 6, 2006, 120 Stat. 1661.)

§57107. VESSELS FOR OTHER AGENCIES

(a) IN GENERAL.—The Secretary of Transportation may construct, reconstruct, repair, equip, and outfit, by contract or otherwise, vessels or parts thereof, for any other department or agency of the United States Government to the extent the other department or agency is authorized by law to do so for its own account.

(b) EFFECT ON CONTRACT AUTHORIZATION.—An obligation incurred or expenditure made by the Secretary under this section does not affect any contract authorization of the Secretary, but instead shall be charged against the existing appropriation or contract authorization of the department or agency.

(c) SALVAGING CARGOES.—

(1) REIMBURSABLE AGREEMENTS.—The Secretary of Transportation, acting through the Administrator of the Maritime Administration, may enter into reimbursable agreements with other Federal entities to provide legal services to such entities relating to the salvaging of cargoes for which such entities have custody, or control, or for which for such entities have trustee responsibilities from vessels in the custody or control of the Maritime Administration or its predecessor agencies. The Secretary may receive and retain reimbursement from such entities for all costs incurred related to the provision of such services.

(2) AMOUNTS RECEIVED.—Amounts received as reimbursements under this subsection shall be credited to the fund or account that was used to cover the costs incurred by the Secretary or, if the period of availability of obligations for that appropriation has expired, to the appropriation of funds that is currently available to the Secretary for substantially the same purpose. Amounts so credited shall be merged with amounts in such fund or account and shall be available for the same purposes, and subject to the same conditions and limitations, as amounts in such fund or account.

(3) ADVANCE PAYMENTS.—Payments made in advance shall be for any part of the estimated cost as determined by the Secretary of Transportation. Adjustments to the amounts paid in advance shall be made as agreed to by the Secretary of Transportation and the head of the ordering agency or unit based on the actual cost of goods or services provided.

(Pub. L. 109–304, §8(c), Oct. 6, 2006, 120 Stat. 1661; Pub. L. 116–92, div. C, title XXXV, §3508, Dec. 20, 2019, 133 Stat. 1976.)

§57108. CONSIDERATION OF BALLAST AND EQUIPMENT IN DETERMINING SELLING PRICE

The Maritime Administration may not sell a vessel until its ballast and equipment have been inventoried and their value considered in determining the selling price of the vessel.

(Pub. L. 109–304, §8(c), Oct. 6, 2006, 120 Stat. 1661.)

§57109. OPERATION OF VESSELS PURCHASED, CHARTERED, OR LEASED FROM SECRETARY OF TRANSPORTATION

Unless otherwise authorized by the Secretary of Transportation, a vessel purchased, chartered, or leased from the Secretary may be operated only under a certificate of documentation with a registry or coastwise endorsement. Such a vessel, while employed solely as a merchant vessel, is subject to the laws, regulations, and liabilities governing merchant vessels, whether the United States Government has an interest in the vessel as an owner or holds a mortgage, lien, or other interest.

(Pub. L. 109–304, §8(c), Oct. 6, 2006, 120 Stat. 1661.)

§57110. SALVAGE RECOVERIES FOR SUBROGATED OWNERSHIP OF VESSELS AND CARGOES

(a) SALVAGE AGREEMENTS.—The Secretary of Transportation is authorized to enter into marine salvage agreements for the recoveries, sale, and disposal of sunken or damaged vessels, cargoes, or properties owned or insured by or on behalf of the Maritime Administration, the United States Shipping Board, the U.S. Shipping Bureau, the United States Maritime Commission, or the War Shipping Administration.

(b) MILITARY CRAFT.—The Secretary of Transportation shall consult with the Secretary of the military department concerned prior to engaging in or authorizing any activity under subsection (a) that will disturb sunken military craft, as such term is defined in section 1408(3) of the Ronald W. Reagan National Defense Authorization Act for Fiscal Year 2005 (Public Law 108–375; 10 U.S.C. 113 note).

(c) RECOVERIES.—Notwithstanding any other provision of law, the net proceeds from salvage agreements entered into as authorized in subsection (a) shall remain available until expended and be distributed as follows:

(1) Fifty percent shall be available to the Administrator of the Maritime Administration for the payment or reimbursement of expenses incurred by or on behalf of State maritime academies or the United States Merchant Marine Academy for facility and training ship maintenance, repair, and modernization, and for the purchase of simulators and fuel.

(2) The remainder shall be distributed for maritime heritage preservation to the Department of the Interior for grants as authorized by section 308703 of title 54.

(Added Pub. L. 116–92, div. C, title XXXV, §3509(a), Dec. 20, 2019, 133 Stat. 1977, §57111; renumbered §57110, Pub. L. 118–31, div. C, title XXXV, §3514(j)(1)(A), Dec. 22, 2023, 137 Stat. 811.)

§57111. DEFINITION OF OBSOLETE VESSEL

In this chapter, the term "obsolete vessel" means a vessel that—

(1) is or will be in the custody and control of the Maritime Administration for purposes of disposing of the vessel; and

(2) has been determined by the Secretary of Transportation to be of insufficient value, with respect to the programs of the Maritime Administration, to warrant—

(A) preserving for future use or spare parts harvesting; or

(B) retaining in the National Defense Reserve Fleet.

(Added Pub. L. 118–31, div. C, title XXXV, §3514(j)(1)(B), Dec. 22, 2023, 137 Stat. 811.)

CHAPTER 573—VESSEL TRADE-IN PROGRAM

§57301. DEFINITIONS

In this chapter:

(1) NEW VESSEL.—The term "new vessel" means a vessel—

(A) constructed under this subtitle and acquired within 2 years after the date of completion; or

(B) constructed in a domestic shipyard on private account and not under this subtitle, and documented under the laws of the United States.

(2) OBSOLETE VESSEL.—The term "obsolete vessel" means a vessel that—

(A) is of at least 1,350 gross tons;

(B) the Secretary of Transportation believes should, because of its age, obsolescence, or other reasons, be replaced in the public interest; and

(C) has been owned by a citizen of the United States for at least 3 years immediately before its acquisition under this chapter.

(Pub. L. 109–304, §8(c), Oct. 6, 2006, 120 Stat. 1662.)

§57302. AUTHORITY TO ACQUIRE VESSELS

To promote the construction of new, safe, and efficient vessels to carry the domestic and foreign waterborne commerce of the United States, the Secretary of Transportation may acquire an obsolete vessel in exchange for an allowance of credit toward the cost of construction or purchase of a new vessel as provided in this chapter.

(Pub. L. 109–304, §8(c), Oct. 6, 2006, 120 Stat. 1662.)

§57303. UTILITY VALUE AND TONNAGE REQUIREMENTS

(a) UTILITY VALUE.—The utility value of a new vessel to be acquired under this chapter for operation in the domestic or foreign commerce of the United States may not be substantially less than that of the obsolete vessel acquired in exchange under this chapter.

(b) TONNAGE.—If the Secretary of Transportation finds that the new vessel will have a utility value at least equal to that of the obsolete vessel, the new vessel may be of lesser gross tonnage than the obsolete vessel. However, the gross tonnage of the new vessel must be at least one-third the gross tonnage of the obsolete vessel.

(Pub. L. 109–304, §8(c), Oct. 6, 2006, 120 Stat. 1662.)

§57304. ELIGIBLE ACQUISITION DATES

At the option of the owner, the acquisition of an obsolete vessel under this chapter shall occur—

(1) when the owner contracts for the construction or purchase of a new vessel; or

(2) within 5 days of the actual date of delivery of the new vessel to the owner.

(Pub. L. 109–304, §8(c), Oct. 6, 2006, 120 Stat. 1662.)

§57305. DETERMINATION OF TRADE-IN ALLOWANCE

(a) IN GENERAL.—The Secretary of Transportation shall determine the trade-in allowance for an obsolete vessel at the time of acquisition of the vessel. The allowance shall be the fair value of the vessel. In determining the value, the Secretary shall consider—

(1) the scrap value of the obsolete vessel in American and foreign markets;

(2) the depreciated value based on a 20-year or 25-year life, whichever applies to the obsolete vessel; and

(3) the market value of the obsolete vessel for operation in world commerce or in the domestic or foreign commerce of the United States.

(b) USE OF OBSOLETE VESSELS.—If acquisition of the obsolete vessel occurs when the owner contracts for the construction of the new vessel, and the owner uses the obsolete vessel during the period of construction of the new vessel, the Secretary shall reduce the trade-in allowance by an amount representing the fair value of that use. The Secretary shall establish the rate for use of the obsolete vessel when the contract for construction of the new vessel is made.

(Pub. L. 109–304, §8(c), Oct. 6, 2006, 120 Stat. 1663.)

§57306. PAYMENT OF TRADE-IN ALLOWANCE

(a) ACQUISITION AT TIME OF CONTRACT.—If acquisition of an obsolete vessel under this chapter occurs when the owner contracts for the construction or purchase of the new vessel, the Secretary of Transportation shall apply the trade-in allowance to the purchase price of the new vessel rather than paying it to the owner. If the new vessel is constructed under this subtitle, the Secretary may apply the trade-in allowance to the required cash payments on terms and conditions the Secretary may prescribe. If the new vessel is not constructed under this subtitle, the Secretary shall pay the trade-in allowance to the builder of the vessel for the account of the owner when the Secretary acquires the obsolete vessel.

(b) ACQUISITION AT TIME OF DELIVERY.—If acquisition of the obsolete vessel occurs when the new vessel is delivered to the owner, the Secretary shall deposit the trade-in allowance in the owner's capital construction fund.

(Pub. L. 109–304, §8(c), Oct. 6, 2006, 120 Stat. 1663.)

§57307. RECOGNITION OF GAIN FOR TAX PURPOSES

The owner of an obsolete vessel does not recognize a gain under the Federal income tax laws when the vessel is transferred to the Secretary of Transportation in exchange for a trade-in allowance under this chapter. The basis of the new vessel acquired with the allowance is the same as the basis of the obsolete vessel—

(1) increased by the difference between the cost of the new vessel and the trade-in allowance of the obsolete vessel; and

(2) decreased by the amount of loss recognized on the transfer.

(Pub. L. 109–304, §8(c), Oct. 6, 2006, 120 Stat. 1663.)

§57308. Use of vessels at least 25 years old

An obsolete vessel acquired under this chapter that is or becomes at least 25 years old may not be used for commercial operation. However, the vessel may be used—

(1) during a period in which vessels may be requisitioned under chapter 563 of this title; or

(2) except as otherwise provided in this subtitle, on trade routes serving only the foreign trade of the United States.

(Pub. L. 109–304, §8(c), Oct. 6, 2006, 120 Stat. 1664.)

CHAPTER 575—CONSTRUCTION, CHARTER, AND SALE OF VESSELS

SUBCHAPTER I—GENERAL

SUBCHAPTER II—CHARTERS

SUBCHAPTER III—MISCELLANEOUS

SUBCHAPTER I—GENERAL

§57501. COMPLETION OF LONG-RANGE PROGRAM

Whenever the Secretary of Transportation determines that the objectives and policies declared in sections 50101 and 50102 of this title cannot be fully realized within a reasonable time under title V of the Merchant Marine Act, 1936, and the President approves the determination, the Secretary, in accordance with this chapter, shall complete the long-range program described in section 50102 of this title.

(Pub. L. 109–304, §8(c), Oct. 6, 2006, 120 Stat. 1664; Pub. L. 114–120, title III, §313(b)(1), Feb. 8, 2016, 130 Stat. 58.)

§57502. CONSTRUCTION, RECONDITIONING, AND REMODELING OF VESSELS

(a) IN GENERAL.—The Secretary of Transportation may have new vessels constructed, and have old vessels reconditioned or remodeled, as the Secretary determines necessary to carry out the objectives of this subtitle.

(b) PLACE OF WORK.—Construction, reconditioning, and remodeling of vessels under subsection (a) shall take place in shipyards in the continental United States (including Alaska and Hawaii). However, if satisfactory contracts cannot be obtained from private shipbuilders, the Secretary may have the work done in navy yards.

(c) APPLICABILITY OF CONSTRUCTION-DIFFERENTIAL SUBSIDY PROVISIONS.—Contracts for the construction, reconstruction, or reconditioning of a vessel by a private shipbuilder under this chapter are subject to the provisions of title V of the Merchant Marine Act, 1936, applicable to a contract with a private shipbuilder for the construction of a vessel under title V of that Act.

(Pub. L. 109–304, §8(c), Oct. 6, 2006, 120 Stat. 1664.)

§57503. COMPETITIVE BIDDING

(a) ADVERTISEMENT AND BIDDING.—The Secretary of Transportation may make a contract with a private shipbuilder for the construction of a new vessel, or for the reconstruction or reconditioning of an existing vessel, only after due advertisement and upon sealed competitive bids.

(b) OPENING OF BIDS.—Bids required under this section shall be opened at the time and place stated in the advertisement for bids. All interested persons, including representatives of the press, shall be permitted to attend. The results of the bidding shall be publicly announced.

(Pub. L. 109–304, §8(c), Oct. 6, 2006, 120 Stat. 1665.)

§57504. CHARTER OR SALE OF VESSELS ACQUIRED BY DEPARTMENT OF TRANSPORTATION

Vessels transferred to or otherwise acquired by the Department of Transportation in any manner may be chartered or sold by the Secretary of Transportation as provided in this chapter.

(Pub. L. 109–304, §8(c), Oct. 6, 2006, 120 Stat. 1665.)

§57505. EMPLOYMENT OF VESSELS ON FOREIGN TRADE ROUTES

(a) IN GENERAL.—The Secretary of Transportation shall arrange for the employment of the Department of Transportation's vessels in steamship lines on such trade routes, exclusively serving the foreign trade of the United States, as the Secretary determines are essential for the development and maintenance of the commerce of the United States and the national defense. However, the Secretary shall first determine that those routes are not being adequately served by existing steamship lines privately owned and operated by citizens of the United States and documented under the laws of the United States.

(b) POLICY TO ENCOURAGE PRIVATE OPERATION.—The Secretary shall have a policy of encouraging private operation of each essential steamship line now owned by the United States Government by—

(1) selling the line to a citizen of the United States; or

(2) demising the Secretary's vessels on bareboat charter to citizens of the United States who agree to maintain the line in the manner provided in this chapter.

(Pub. L. 109–304, §8(c), Oct. 6, 2006, 120 Stat. 1665.)

§57506. MINIMUM SELLING PRICE OF VESSELS

(a) IN GENERAL.—A vessel constructed under this subtitle or the Merchant Marine Act, 1936, may not be sold by the Secretary of Transportation for less than the price specified in this section.

(b) OPERATION IN FOREIGN TRADE.—If the vessel is to be operated in foreign trade, the minimum price is the estimated foreign construction cost (exclusive of national defense features) determined as of the date the construction contract is executed, less depreciation under subsection (d).

(c) OPERATION IN DOMESTIC TRADE.—If the vessel is to be operated in domestic trade, the minimum price is the cost of construction in the United States (exclusive of national defense features), less depreciation under subsection (d).

(d) DEPRECIATION.—Depreciation under subsections (b) and (c) shall be based on—

(1) a 25-year life for dry-cargo and passenger vessels; and

(2) a 20-year life for tankers and other bulk liquid carrier vessels.

(Pub. L. 109–304, §8(c), Oct. 6, 2006, 120 Stat. 1665.)

SUBCHAPTER II—CHARTERS

§57511. DEMISE CHARTERS

A charter by the Secretary of Transportation under this chapter shall demise the vessel to the charterer subject to all usual conditions contained in a bareboat charter. The charter shall be for a term the Secretary considers to be in the best interest of the United States Government and the merchant marine.

(Pub. L. 109–304, §8(c), Oct. 6, 2006, 120 Stat. 1666.)

§57512. COMPETITIVE BIDDING

(a) IN GENERAL.—The Secretary of Transportation may charter a vessel of the Department of Transportation to a private operator only on the basis of competitive sealed bidding. The bids must be submitted in strict compliance with the terms and conditions of a public advertisement soliciting the bids.

(b) ADVERTISEMENT FOR BIDS.—An advertisement for bids shall state—

(1) the number, type, and tonnage of the vessels being offered for bareboat charter for operation as a steamship line on a designated trade route;

(2) the minimum number of sailings required;

(3) the length of time of the charter;

(4) the right of the Secretary to reject all bids; and

(5) other information the Secretary considers necessary for the information of prospective bidders.

(c) OPENING OF BIDS.—Bids required under this section shall be opened at the time and place stated in the advertisement for bids. All interested persons, including representatives of the press, shall be permitted to attend. The results of the bidding shall be publicly announced.

(Pub. L. 109–304, §8(c), Oct. 6, 2006, 120 Stat. 1666.)

§57513. MINIMUM BID

The Secretary of Transportation shall reject any bid for the charter under this subchapter of a vessel constructed under this subtitle or the Merchant Marine Act, 1936, if the charter hire offered is lower than the minimum charter hire would be if the vessel were chartered under section 57531 of this title.

(Pub. L. 109–304, §8(c), Oct. 6, 2006, 120 Stat. 1666.)

§57514. QUALIFICATIONS OF BIDDERS

(a) CONSIDERATIONS.—In deciding whether to award a charter to a bidder, the Secretary of Transportation shall consider—

(1) the bidder's financial resources, credit standing, and practical experience in operating vessels; and

(2) other factors a prudent business person would consider in entering into a transaction involving a large capital investment.

(b) DISQUALIFICATIONS.—The Secretary may not charter a vessel to a person appearing to lack sufficient capital, credit, and experience to operate the vessel successfully over the period covered by the charter.

(Pub. L. 109–304, §8(c), Oct. 6, 2006, 120 Stat. 1666.)

§57515. AWARDING OF CHARTERS

(a) IN GENERAL.—The Secretary of Transportation shall award the charter to the bidder proposing to pay the highest monthly charter hire. However, the Secretary may reject the highest or most advantageous or any other bid if the Secretary considers the charter hire offered too low or determines that the bidder lacks the qualifications required by section 57514 of this title.

(b) HIGHEST BID REJECTED.—If the Secretary rejects the highest bid, the Secretary

may—
(1) award the charter to the next highest bidder; or
(2) reject all bids and either readvertise the line or operate the line until conditions appear more favorable to reoffer the line for private charter.

(c) REASON FOR REJECTION.—On request of a bidder, the reason for rejection shall be stated in writing to the bidder.

(Pub. L. 109–304, §8(c), Oct. 6, 2006, 120 Stat. 1667.)

§57516. OPERATING-DIFFERENTIAL SUBSIDIES

If the Secretary of Transportation considers it necessary, the Secretary may make a contract with a charterer of a vessel owned by the Secretary for payment of an operating-differential subsidy, on the same terms and conditions, and subject to the same limitations and restrictions, as otherwise provided with respect to payment of operating-differential subsidies to operators of privately-owned vessels.

(Pub. L. 109–304, §8(c), Oct. 6, 2006, 120 Stat. 1667.)

§57517. RECOVERY OF EXCESS PROFITS

(a) IN GENERAL.—A charter under this chapter shall provide that if, at the end of a calendar year subsequent to the execution of the charter, the cumulative net voyage profit (after payment of the charter hire reserved in the charter and payment of the charterer's fair and reasonable overhead expenses applicable to operation of the chartered vessel) exceeds 10 percent a year of the charterer's capital necessarily employed in the business of the chartered vessel, the charterer shall pay to the Secretary of Transportation, as additional charter hire, half the cumulative net voyage profit in excess of 10 percent a year. However, any cumulative net voyage profit accounted for under this subsection is not to be included in the calculation of cumulative net voyage profit in any subsequent year.

(b) TERMS TO BE DEFINED AND USED.—The Secretary shall define the terms "net voyage profit", "fair and reasonable overhead expenses", and "capital necessarily employed" for this section. Each advertisement for bids and each charter shall contain these definitions, stating the formula for determining each of these three amounts.

(Pub. L. 109–304, §8(c), Oct. 6, 2006, 120 Stat. 1667.)

§57518. PERFORMANCE BOND

The Secretary of Transportation shall require a charterer of a vessel of the Secretary to deposit with the Secretary an undertaking, with approved sureties, in such amount as the Secretary may require as security for the faithful performance of the terms of the charter, including indemnity against liens on the chartered vessel.

(Pub. L. 109–304, §8(c), Oct. 6, 2006, 120 Stat. 1667.)

§57519. INSURANCE

A charter under this chapter shall require the charterer to carry, at the charterer's expense, insurance on the chartered vessel covering all marine and port risks, protection and indemnity risks, and all other hazards and liabilities, adequate to cover damages claimed against and losses sustained by the chartered vessel arising during the term of the charter. The insurance shall be in such form, in such amount, and with such companies as the Secretary of Transportation may require. In accordance with law, any of the insurance risks may be underwritten by the Secretary.

(Pub. L. 109–304, §8(c), Oct. 6, 2006, 120 Stat. 1667.)

§57520. VESSEL MAINTENANCE

(a) IN GENERAL.—A charter under this chapter shall require the charterer, at the charterer's expense, to—

(1) keep the chartered vessel in good repair and efficient operating condition; and

(2) make any repairs required by the Secretary of Transportation.

(b) INSPECTION.—The charter shall provide that the Secretary has the right to inspect the vessel at any time to ascertain its condition.

(Pub. L. 109–304, §8(c), Oct. 6, 2006, 120 Stat. 1668.)

§57521. TERMINATION OF CHARTER DURING NATIONAL EMERGENCY

A charter under this chapter shall provide that during a national emergency proclaimed by the President or a period for which the President has proclaimed that the security of the national defense makes it advisable, the Secretary of Transportation may terminate the charter without cost to the United States Government on such notice to the charterer as the President determines.

(Pub. L. 109–304, §8(c), Oct. 6, 2006, 120 Stat. 1668.)

§57522. BOOKS AND RECORDS, BALANCE SHEETS, AND INSPECTION AND AUDITING

Every contract executed by the Secretary of Transportation under this chapter shall contain provisions requiring (1) that, the contractor and every affiliate, domestic agent, subsidiary, or holding company connected with, or directly or indirectly controlling or controlled by, the contractor, to keep its books, records, and accounts, relating to the maintenance, operation, and servicing of the vessels, services, routes, and lines covered by the contract, in such form and under such regulations as may be prescribed by the Secretary of Transportation; (2) that the contractor and every affiliate, domestic agent, subsidiary, or holding company connected with, or directly or indirectly controlling or controlled by, the contractor, to file, upon notice from the Secretary of Transportation, balance sheets, profit and loss statements, and such other statements of financial operations, special report, memoranda of any facts and transactions, which in the opinion of the Secretary of Transportation affect the financial results in, the performance of, or transactions or operations under, such contract; (3) that the Secretary of Transportation shall be authorized to examine and audit the books, records, and accounts of all persons referred to in this section whenever he may deem it necessary or desirable; and (4) that upon the willful failure or refusal of any person described in this section to comply with the contract provisions required by this section, the Secretary of Transportation shall have the right to rescind the contract, and upon such rescission, the United States shall be relieved of all further liability on such contract.

(Added and amended Pub. L. 114–120, title III, §313(c)(1), Feb. 8, 2016, 130 Stat. 58.)

SUBCHAPTER III—MISCELLANEOUS

§57531. CONSTRUCTION AND CHARTER OF VESSELS FOR UNSUCCESSFUL ROUTES

(a) IN GENERAL.—If the Secretary of Transportation finds that a trade route determined to be essential under section 50103 of this title cannot be successfully developed and maintained and the Secretary's replacement program cannot be achieved under private operation of the trade route by a citizen of the United States with vessels documented under chapter 121 of this title, without further aid by the United States Government in addition to the financial aid authorized under title V of the Merchant Marine Act, 1936, the Secretary, without advertisement or competition, may—

(1) have constructed, in private shipyards or in navy yards, vessels of the types necessary for the trade route; and

(2) demise charter those new vessels to the operator of vessels of the United States established on the trade route.

(b) AMOUNT OF CHARTER HIRE.—

(1) IN GENERAL.—The annual charter hire under subsection (a) shall be at least 4 percent of the price (referred to in this section as the "foreign cost") at which the vessel would be sold if constructed under title V of the Merchant Marine Act, 1936, plus—

(A) a percentage of the depreciated foreign cost computed annually determined by the Secretary of the Treasury, taking into consideration the current average market yield on outstanding marketable obligations of the Government with remaining periods to maturity comparable to the term of the charter, adjusted to the nearest one-eighth percent; and

(B) an allowance adequate in the judgment of the Secretary of Transportation to cover administrative costs.

(2) DEPRECIATION.—Depreciation under paragraph (1)(A) shall be based on—

(A) a 25-year life for dry-cargo and passenger vessels; and

(B) a 20-year life for tankers and other bulk liquid carrier vessels.

(c) OPTION TO PURCHASE.—The charter may contain an option to the charterer to purchase the vessels from the Secretary of Transportation within 5 years after delivery under the charter, on the same terms and conditions as provided in title V of the Merchant Marine Act, 1936, for the purchase of new vessels from the Secretary. However—

(1) the purchase price shall be the foreign cost less depreciation to the date of purchase based on the useful life specified in subsection (b)(2);

(2) the required cash payment payable at the time of the purchase shall be 25 percent of the purchase price;

(3) the charter may provide that any part of the charter hire paid in excess of the

minimum charter hire provided for in this section may be credited against the cash payment payable at the time of the purchase;

(4) the balance of the purchase price shall be paid within the remaining years of useful life (as specified in subsection (b)(2)) after the date of delivery of the vessel under the charter and in approximately equal annual installments, except that the first installment, which shall be payable on the next ensuing anniversary date of the delivery under the charter, shall be a proportionate part of the annual installment; and

(5) interest shall be payable on the unpaid balances from the date of purchase, at a rate not less than—

(A) a rate determined by the Secretary of the Treasury, taking into consideration the current average market yield on outstanding marketable obligations of the Government with remaining periods to maturity comparable to the average maturities of the loans, adjusted to the nearest one-eighth percent; plus

(B) an allowance adequate in the judgment of the Secretary of Transportation to cover administrative costs.

(d) OPERATION OF VESSEL.—

(1) PERMISSIBLE VOYAGES.—The charter shall provide for operation of the vessel exclusively—

(A) in foreign trade;

(B) on a round-the-world voyage;

(C) on a round voyage from the west coast of the United States to a European port that includes an intercoastal port of the United States;

(D) on a round voyage from the Atlantic coast of the United States to the Orient that includes an intercoastal port of the United States; or

(E) on a voyage in foreign trade on which the vessel may stop at Hawaii or an island territory or possession of the United States.

(2) DOMESTIC TRADE.—The charter shall provide if the vessel is operated in domestic trade on any of the services specified in paragraph (1), the charterer will pay annually to the Secretary of Transportation that proportion of 1/25 of the difference between the domestic and foreign cost of the vessel as the gross revenue derived from the domestic trade bears to the gross revenue derived from the entire voyages completed during the preceding year.

(Pub. L. 109–304, §8(c), Oct. 6, 2006, 120 Stat. 1668; Pub. L. 114–120, title III, §313(b)(2), Feb. 8, 2016, 130 Stat. 58.)

§57532. OPERATION OF EXPERIMENTAL VESSELS

(a) DEFINITION.—In this section, the term "experimental vessel" means a vessel owned by the United States Government (including a vessel in the National Defense Reserve Fleet) that has been constructed, reconditioned, or remodeled for experimental or testing purposes.

(b) AUTHORITY TO OPERATE.—The Secretary of Transportation, for the purpose of practical development, trial, and testing, may operate an experimental vessel under a bareboat charter or general agency agreement in the foreign or domestic trade of the United

States or for use for the account of a department or agency of the Government, without regard to other provisions of this subtitle and other laws related to chartering and general agency operations. Not more than 10 vessels may be operated and tested under this section in any one year.

(c) TERMS OF OPERATION.—Operation of a vessel under this section shall be on terms the Secretary considers appropriate to carry out the purposes of this subtitle. A bareboat charter under this section shall be at reasonable rates and include restrictions the Secretary considers appropriate to protect the public interest, including provisions for recapture of profits under section 57517 of this title. A charter or general agency agreement under this section shall be reviewed annually to determine whether conditions exist to justify continuance of the charter or agreement.

(d) RIGHTS OF SEAMEN.—A seaman engaged in vessel operations of the Secretary under this section and employed through a general agent in connection with a charter or agreement under this section is entitled to all the rights and remedies provided in sections 1(a) and (c), 3(c), and 4 of the Act of March 24, 1943 (50 U.S.C. 4701(a), (c), 4703(c), and 4704).

(Pub. L. 109–304, §8(c), Oct. 6, 2006, 120 Stat. 1670; Pub. L. 115–232, div. C, title XXXV, §3546(u), Aug. 13, 2018, 132 Stat. 2327.)

§57533. VESSEL CHARTERING AUTHORITY

The Secretary of Transportation may enter into contracts or other agreements on behalf of the United States to purchase, charter, operate, or otherwise acquire the use of any vessels documented under chapter 121 of this title and any other related real or personal property. The Secretary is authorized to use this authority as the Secretary deems appropriate.

(Added Pub. L. 110–181, div. C, title XXXV, §3511(a), Jan. 28, 2008, 122 Stat. 593.)

PART G—RESTRICTIONS AND PENALTIES

CHAPTER 581—RESTRICTIONS AND PENALTIES

§58101. OPERATING IN DOMESTIC INTERCOASTAL OR COASTWISE SERVICE

(a) PROHIBITION.—A subsidy may not be awarded or paid to a contractor under the operating-differential subsidy program, and a vessel may not be chartered to a person under chapter 575 of this title, if the contractor or charterer, or a holding company, subsidiary, affiliate, or associate of the contractor or charterer, or an officer, director, agent, or executive thereof, directly or indirectly—

(1) owns, charters, or operates a vessel engaged in the domestic intercoastal or coastwise service; or

(2) owns a pecuniary interest in a person that owns, charters, or operates a vessel in the domestic intercoastal or coastwise service.

(b) WAIVER.—A person may apply to the Secretary of Transportation for a waiver of subsection (a). Before deciding on the waiver, the Secretary shall give the applicant and other interested persons an opportunity for a hearing. The Secretary may not grant the waiver if the Secretary finds it would—

(1) result in unfair competition to a person operating exclusively in the domestic intercoastal or coastwise service; or

(2) be prejudicial to the objectives and policy of this subtitle.

(c) CONTINUOUS OPERATION SINCE 1935.—The Secretary shall grant an application under subsection (b) without requiring further proof that the public interest and convenience will be served and without further proceedings as to the competition in the route or trade, if the contractor or other person, or a predecessor in interest, was in bona-fide operation as a common carrier by water in the domestic intercoastal or coastwise trade in 1935 over the route or in the trade for which the application is made and has so operated since that time or, if engaged in furnishing seasonal service only, was in bona-fide operation in 1935 during the season ordinarily covered by its operation, except in either event as to interruptions of service over which the applicant or its predecessor in interest had no control.

(d) DIVERSION INTO INTERCOASTAL OR COASTWISE OPERATIONS.—If an application under subsection (b) is approved, a person referred to in this section may not divert, directly or indirectly, money, property, or any other thing of value, used in a foreign-trade operation for which a subsidy is paid by the United States Government, into intercoastal or coastwise operations.

(Pub. L. 109–304, §8(c), Oct. 6, 2006, 120 Stat. 1670.)

§58102. DEFAULT ON PAYMENT OR MAINTENANCE OF RESERVES

The Secretary of Transportation may supervise the number and compensation of all officers and employees of a contractor under the operating-differential subsidy program or a charterer under chapter 575 of this title, receiving an operating-differential subsidy, if the contractor or charterer—

(1) is in default on a mortgage, note, purchase contract, or other obligation to the Secretary; or

(2) has not maintained, in a manner satisfactory to the Secretary, all of the reserves provided for in this subtitle.

(Pub. L. 109–304, §8(c), Oct. 6, 2006, 120 Stat. 1671.)

§58103. Employing another person as managing or operating agent

(a) Prohibition.—Except with the written consent of the Secretary of Transportation, a contractor holding a contract under the operating-differential subsidy program or under chapter 575 of this title may not—

(1) employ another person as the managing or operating agent of the operator; or

(2) charter a vessel, on which an operating-differential subsidy is to be paid, for operation by another person.

(b) Applicability of Provisions to Charterer.—If a charter prohibited by this section is made, the person operating the chartered vessel is subject to all the provisions of this subtitle and the operating-differential subsidy program, including limitations of profits and salaries.

(Pub. L. 109–304, §8(c), Oct. 6, 2006, 120 Stat. 1671.)

§58104. Willful violation constitutes breach of contract or charter

A willful violation of any provision of sections 58101–58103 of this title constitutes a breach of the contract or charter. On determining that a violation has occurred, the Secretary of Transportation may declare the contract or charter rescinded.

(Pub. L. 109–304, §8(c), Oct. 6, 2006, 120 Stat. 1672.)

§58105. Preferences for cargo in which charterer has interest

A contractor receiving an operating-differential subsidy, or a charterer under chapter 575 of this title, may not unjustly discriminate in any manner so as to give preference, directly or indirectly, to cargo in which the contractor or charterer has a direct or indirect ownership, purchase, or vending interest.

(Pub. L. 109–304, §8(c), Oct. 6, 2006, 120 Stat. 1672.)

§58106. Concerted discriminatory activities

(a) Prohibition.—A contractor receiving an operating-differential subsidy, or a charterer under chapter 575 of this title, may not continue as a party to or conform to an agreement with another carrier by water, or engage in a practice in concert with another carrier by water, that is unjustly discriminatory or unfair to any other citizen of the United States operating a common carrier by water employing only vessels documented under the laws of the United States on an established trade route from and to a United States port.

(b) Government Payment Prohibited.—No payment or subsidy of any kind may be paid, directly or indirectly, out of funds of the United States Government to a contractor or charterer that has violated subsection (a).

(c) Civil Action.—A person whose business or property is injured by a violation of subsection (a) may bring a civil action in the district court of the United States for the district in which the defendant resides, is found, or has an agent. If the person prevails, the person shall be awarded—

(1) 3 times the damages; and

(2) costs, including reasonable attorney fees.

(Pub. L. 109–304, §8(c), Oct. 6, 2006, 120 Stat. 1672.)

§58107. DISCRIMINATION AT PORTS BY WATER COMMON CARRIERS

(a) PROHIBITION.—A common carrier by water may not, directly or indirectly, through an agreement, conference, association, understanding, or otherwise, prevent or attempt to prevent any other common carrier by water from serving any port described in subsection (b) at the same rates the first carrier charges at the nearest port already regularly served by it.

(b) PORTS.—A port referred to in subsection (a) is one that is—
(1) designed for the accommodation of ocean-going vessels;
(2) located on an improvement project authorized by law or by a Federal agency; and
(3) located within the continental limits of the United States.

(c) OTHER AUTHORITY NOT LIMITED.—This section does not limit the authority otherwise vested in the Secretary of Transportation and the Federal Maritime Commission.

(Pub. L. 109–304, §8(c), Oct. 6, 2006, 120 Stat. 1672.)

§58108. CHARGES FOR TRANSPORTATION SUBJECT TO SUBTITLE IV OF TITLE 49

(a) PROHIBITION.—A carrier may not charge, collect, or receive for transportation subject to subtitle IV of title 49 of persons or property, under any joint rate, fare, or charge, or under any export, import, or other proportional rate, fare, or charge, that is based in whole or in part on the fact that the persons or property affected are to be transported to, or have been transported from, a port in a territory or possession of the United States or in a foreign country, by a carrier by water in foreign commerce, any lower rate, fare, or charge than the carrier charges, collects, or receives for the transportation of persons or similar property for the same distance, in the same direction, and over the same route, in commerce wholly within the United States, unless the vessel used for the transportation is or was at the time of the transportation documented under the laws of the United States.

(b) SUSPENSION OF PROHIBITION.—Whenever the Secretary of Transportation believes that adequate shipping facilities to or from any port in a territory or possession of the United States or a foreign country are not being provided by vessels documented under the laws of the United States, the Secretary shall certify this fact to the Surface Transportation Board. On receiving the certification, the Board may by order suspend the operation of subsection (a) with respect to the rates, fares, and charges for the transportation by rail of persons and property transported from or to be transported to those ports, for such time and under such terms and conditions as the Secretary may specify in the order or in any supplemental order.

(c) TERMINATION OF SUSPENSION.—Whenever the Secretary believes that adequate shipping facilities are being provided to those ports by vessels documented under the laws of the United States, and certifies that fact to the Board, the Board may order the termination of the suspension.

(Pub. L. 109–304, §8(c), Oct. 6, 2006, 120 Stat. 1673.)

§58109. PENALTIES

(a) INDIVIDUALS.—An individual convicted of violating section 58101(d), 58103, or 58105 of this title shall be fined under title 18, imprisoned for at least one year but not more than 5 years, or both.

(b) ORGANIZATIONS.—An organization convicted of committing an act prohibited by this subtitle shall be fined under title 18.

(c) INELIGIBILITY TO RECEIVE BENEFITS.—An individual or organization convicted of violating a section referred to in subsection (a) is ineligible, at the discretion of the Secretary of Transportation, to receive any benefit under the construction-differential subsidy or operating-differential subsidy programs, or a charter under chapter 575 of this title, for 5 years after the conviction.

(Pub. L. 109–304, §8(c), Oct. 6, 2006, 120 Stat. 1673.)

SUBTITLE VI
CLEARANCE, TONNAGE TAXES, AND DUTIES

Subtitle VI—Clearance, Tonnage Taxes, and Duties

CHAPTER 601—ARRIVAL AND DEPARTURE REQUIREMENTS

§60101. BOARDING ARRIVING VESSELS BEFORE INSPECTION

(a) REGULATIONS.—The Secretary of Homeland Security shall prescribe and enforce regulations on the boarding of a vessel arriving at a port of the United States before the vessel has been inspected and secured.

(b) CRIMINAL PENALTY.—A person violating a regulation prescribed under this section shall be fined under title 18, imprisoned for not more than 6 months, or both.

(c) RELATIONSHIP TO OTHER LAW.—This section shall be construed as supplementary to section 2279 of title 18.

(Pub. L. 109–304, §9(b), Oct. 6, 2006, 120 Stat. 1674.)

§60102. PRODUCTION OF CERTIFICATE ON ENTRY

On entry of a vessel documented under chapter 121 of this title, the master or other individual in charge of the vessel shall produce the certificate of documentation to the customs officer at the place where the vessel is entered. If the certificate is not produced, the vessel is not entitled to the privileges of a documented vessel.

(Pub. L. 109–304, §9(b), Oct. 6, 2006, 120 Stat. 1674.)

§60103. OATH OF OWNERSHIP ON ENTRY

(a) REQUIRED STATEMENT.—On entry of a vessel of the United States from a foreign port, the individual designated under subsection (b) shall state under oath that—

(1) the vessel's certificate of documentation contains the names of all the owners of the vessel; or

(2) part of the ownership has been transferred since the certificate was issued and, to the best of the individual's knowledge and belief, the vessel is still owned only by citizens of the United States.

(b) PERSON TO MAKE STATEMENT.—The statement under subsection (a) shall be made by—

(1) an owner if one resides at the port of entry; or

(2) the master if an owner does not reside at the port of entry.

(c) CONSEQUENCE OF NOT MAKING STATEMENT.—If the appropriate individual does not make the statement required by this section, the vessel is not entitled to the privileges of a vessel of the United States.

(Pub. L. 109–304, §9(b), Oct. 6, 2006, 120 Stat. 1674.)

§60104. DEPOSITING CERTIFICATES OF DOCUMENTATION WITH CONSULAR OFFICERS

(a) REQUIREMENT OF MASTER.—When a vessel owned by citizens of the United States, on a voyage from a port in the United States, arrives at a foreign port, the master of the vessel shall deposit the vessel's certificate of documentation with a consular officer at the foreign port if there is a consular officer at that port.

(b) RETURN OF CERTIFICATE.—When the master produces a clearance from the appropriate officer of the foreign port, the consular officer shall return the certificate of documentation to the master if the master has complied with the provisions of law related to the discharge of seamen in a foreign country and the payment of fees of consular officers.

(c) CIVIL PENALTY AND COLLECTION.—The master of a vessel failing to deposit the certificate of documentation as required by subsection (a) is liable to the United States Government for a civil penalty of $500. The consular officer shall bring an action to recover the penalty in any court of competent jurisdiction. The action shall be brought in the name of the consular officer for the benefit of the United States.

(Pub. L. 109–304, §9(b), Oct. 6, 2006, 120 Stat. 1675.)

§60105. CLEARANCE OF VESSELS

(a) VESSELS OF THE UNITED STATES.—Except as otherwise provided by law, a vessel of the United States shall obtain clearance from the Secretary of Homeland Security before proceeding from a port or place in the United States—

(1) for a foreign port or place;

(2) for another port or place in the United States if the vessel has on board foreign merchandise for which entry has not been made; or

(3) outside the territorial sea to visit a hovering vessel or to receive merchandise while outside the territorial sea.

(b) OTHER VESSELS.—Except as otherwise provided by law, a vessel that is not a vessel of the United States shall obtain clearance from the Secretary before proceeding from a port or place in the United States—

(1) for a foreign port or place;

(2) for another port or place in the United States; or

(3) outside the territorial sea to visit a hovering vessel or to receive or deliver merchandise while outside the territorial sea.

(c) REGULATIONS.—The Secretary may by regulation—

(1) prescribe the manner in which clearance under this section is to be obtained, including the documents, data, or information which shall be submitted or transmitted, pursuant to an authorized data interchange system, to obtain the clearance;

(2) permit clearance to be obtained before all requirements for clearance are complied with, but only if the owner or operator of the vessel files a bond in an amount set by the Secretary conditioned on the compliance by the owner or operator with all specified requirements for clearance within a time period (not exceeding 4 business days) established by the Secretary; and

(3) permit clearance to be obtained at a place other than a designated port of entry, under conditions the Secretary may prescribe.

(Pub. L. 109–304, §9(b), Oct. 6, 2006, 120 Stat. 1675.)

§60106. STATE INSPECTION LAWS

When State law requires a certificate of inspection for goods carried on a vessel, a vessel transporting the goods may not be cleared until the certificate is produced.

(Pub. L. 109–304, §9(b), Oct. 6, 2006, 120 Stat. 1676.)

§60107. PAYMENT OF FEES ON DEPARTING VESSEL

A departing vessel may be cleared only when all legal fees that have accrued on the vessel are paid and proof of payment is presented to the individual granting the clearance.

(Pub. L. 109–304, §9(b), Oct. 6, 2006, 120 Stat. 1676.)

§60108. DUTY TO TRANSPORT TENDERED CARGO

Clearance may be refused to a vessel or vehicle transporting cargo destined for a domestic or foreign port when the owner, master, or other individual in charge refuses to accept cargo tendered in good condition, with proper charges, for the same or an intermediate port by a citizen of the United States. This section does not apply if the vessel or vehicle is already fully loaded (giving appropriate consideration to its proper loading) or is not adaptable to transport the tendered cargo.

(Pub. L. 109–304, §9(b), Oct. 6, 2006, 120 Stat. 1676.)

§60109. DUTY TO TRANSPORT MONEY AND SECURITIES OF THE UNITED STATES GOVERNMENT

Before being given clearance, a vessel owned by a citizen of the United States and bound on a voyage from a port in the United States to another port in the United States or in a foreign country, or on a voyage from a port in a foreign country to a port in the United States, shall receive on board any bullion, coin, notes, bonds, or other securities of the United States Government that an agency, consular officer, or other agent of the

Government offers. The vessel shall transport the items securely and deliver them promptly to the proper authorities or consignees on arriving at the port of destination. Compensation shall be paid for services provided under this section that is equal to compensation paid to other carriers in the ordinary transaction of business.

(Pub. L. 109–304, §9(b), Oct. 6, 2006, 120 Stat. 1676.)

CHAPTER 603—TONNAGE TAXES AND LIGHT MONEY

§60301. REGULAR TONNAGE TAXES

(a) LOWER RATE.—A tax is imposed at the rate of 4.5 cents per ton, not to exceed a total of 22.5 cents per ton per year, for fiscal years 2006 through 2010, and 2 cents per ton, not to exceed a total of 10 cents per ton per year, for each fiscal year thereafter, at each entry in a port of the United States of—

(1) a vessel entering from a foreign port or place in North America, Central America, the West Indies Islands, the Bahama Islands, the Bermuda Islands, or the coast of South America bordering the Caribbean Sea; or

(2) a vessel returning to the same port or place in the United States from which it departed, and not entering the United States from another port or place, except—

(A) a vessel of the United States;

(B) a recreational vessel (as defined in section 2101 of this title); or

(C) a barge.

(b) HIGHER RATE.—A tax is imposed at the rate of 13.5 cents per ton, not to exceed a total of 67.5 cents per ton per year, for fiscal years 2006 through 2010, and 6 cents per ton, not to exceed a total of 30 cents per ton per year, for each fiscal year thereafter, on a vessel at each entry in a port of the United States from a foreign port or place not named in subsection (a)(1).

(c) EXCEPTION FOR VESSELS ENTERING OTHER THAN BY SEA.—Subsection (a) does not apply to a vessel entering other than by sea from a foreign port or place at which tonnage, lighthouse, or other equivalent taxes are not imposed on vessels of the United States.

(Pub. L. 109–304, §9(b), Oct. 6, 2006, 120 Stat. 1677; Pub. L. 109–171, title IV, §4001, Feb. 8, 2006, 120 Stat. 27; Pub. L. 110–181, div. C, title XXXV, §3524, Jan. 28, 2008, 122 Stat. 600.)

§60302. SPECIAL TONNAGE TAXES

(a) ENTRY FROM FOREIGN PORT OR PLACE.—Regardless of whether a tax is imposed under section 60301 of this title, a tax is imposed on a vessel at each entry in a port of the United States from a foreign port or place at the following rates:

(1) 30 cents per ton on a vessel built in the United States but owned in any part by a subject of a foreign country.

(2) 50 cents per ton on other vessels not of the United States.

(3) 50 cents per ton on a vessel of the United States having an officer who is not a citizen of the United States.

(4) $2 per ton on a foreign vessel entering from a foreign port or place at which vessels of the United States are not ordinarily allowed to enter and trade.

(b) VESSELS NOT OF THE UNITED STATES TRANSPORTING PROPERTY BETWEEN DISTRICTS.—Regardless of whether a tax is imposed under section 60301 of this title, a tax of 50 cents per ton is imposed on a vessel not of the United States at each entry in one customs district from another district when transporting goods loaded in one district to be delivered in another district.

(c) EXCEPTION FOR VESSELS BECOMING DOCUMENTED.—The tax of 50 cents per ton under this section does not apply to a vessel that—

(1) is owned only by citizens of the United States; and

(2) after entering a port of the United States, becomes documented as a vessel of the United States before leaving that port.

(Pub. L. 109–304, §9(b), Oct. 6, 2006, 120 Stat. 1677.)

§60303. LIGHT MONEY

(a) IMPOSITION OF TAX.—A tax of 50 cents per ton, to be called "light money", is imposed on a vessel not of the United States at each entry in a port of the United States. This tax shall be imposed and collected under the same regulations that apply to tonnage taxes.

(b) EXCEPTION FOR VESSELS OWNED BY CITIZENS.—

(1) IN GENERAL.—Subsection (a) does not apply to a vessel owned only by citizens of the United States if—

(A) the vessel is carrying a regular document issued by a customhouse of the United States proving the vessel to be owned only by citizens of the United States; and

(B) on entry of the vessel from a foreign port, the individual designated under paragraph (2) states under oath that—

(i) the document contains the names of all the owners of the vessel; or

(ii) part of the ownership has been transferred since the document was issued and, to the best of that individual's knowledge and belief, the vessel is still owned only by citizens of the United States.

(2) PERSON TO MAKE STATEMENT.—The statement under paragraph (1)(B) shall be made by—

(A) an owner if one resides at the port of entry; or

(B) the master if an owner does not reside at the port of entry.

(c) EXCEPTION FOR VESSELS BECOMING DOCUMENTED.—Subsection (a) does not apply to a vessel that—

(1) is owned only by citizens of the United States; and

(2) after entering a port of the United States, becomes documented as a vessel of the United States before leaving that port.

(Pub. L. 109–304, §9(b), Oct. 6, 2006, 120 Stat. 1678; Pub. L. 115–232, div. C, title XXXV, §3546(v), Aug. 13, 2018, 132 Stat. 2327.)

§60304. PRESIDENTIAL SUSPENSION OF TONNAGE TAXES AND LIGHT MONEY

If the President is satisfied that the government of a foreign country does not impose discriminating or countervailing duties to the disadvantage of the United States, the President shall suspend the imposition of special tonnage taxes and light money under sections 60302 and 60303 of this title on vessels of that country.

(Pub. L. 109–304, §9(b), Oct. 6, 2006, 120 Stat. 1678.)

§60305. VESSELS IN DISTRESS

A vessel is exempt from tonnage taxes and light money when it enters because it is in distress.

(Pub. L. 109–304, §9(b), Oct. 6, 2006, 120 Stat. 1678.)

§60306. VESSELS NOT ENGAGED IN TRADE

A vessel is exempt from tonnage taxes and light money when not engaged in trade.

(Pub. L. 109–304, §9(b), Oct. 6, 2006, 120 Stat. 1678.)

§60307. VESSELS ENGAGED IN COASTWISE TRADE OR THE FISHERIES

A vessel with a registry endorsement or a coastwise endorsement, trading from one port in the United States to another port in the United States or employed in the bank, whale, or other fisheries, is exempt from tonnage taxes and light money.

(Pub. L. 109–304, §9(b), Oct. 6, 2006, 120 Stat. 1678.)

§60308. VESSELS ENGAGED IN GREAT LAKES TRADE

A documented vessel with a registry endorsement, engaged in foreign trade on the Great Lakes or their tributary or connecting waters in trade with Canada, does not become subject to tonnage taxes or light money because of that trade.

(Pub. L. 109–304, §9(b), Oct. 6, 2006, 120 Stat. 1679.)

§60309. PASSENGER VESSELS MAKING TRIPS BETWEEN PORTS OF THE UNITED STATES AND FOREIGN PORTS

A passenger vessel making at least 3 trips per week between a port of the United States and a foreign port is exempt from tonnage taxes and light money.

(Pub. L. 109–304, §9(b), Oct. 6, 2006, 120 Stat. 1679.)

§60310. Vessels making daily trips on interior waters

A vessel making regular daily trips between a port of the United States and a port of Canada only on interior waters not navigable to the ocean is exempt from tonnage taxes and light money, except on its first clearing each year.

(Pub. L. 109–304, §9(b), Oct. 6, 2006, 120 Stat. 1679.)

§60311. Hospital vessels in time of war

In time of war, a hospital vessel is exempt from tonnage taxes, light money, and pilotage charges in the ports of the United States if the vessel is one for which the conditions of the international convention for the exemption of hospital ships from taxation in time of war, concluded at The Hague on December 21, 1904, are satisfied. The President by proclamation shall name the vessels for which the conditions are satisfied and state when the exemption begins and ends.

(Pub. L. 109–304, §9(b), Oct. 6, 2006, 120 Stat. 1679.)

§60312. Rights under treaties preserved

This chapter and chapter 605 of this title do not affect a right or privilege of a foreign country relating to tonnage taxes or other duties on vessels under a law or treaty of the United States.

(Pub. L. 109–304, §9(b), Oct. 6, 2006, 120 Stat. 1679.)

CHAPTER 605—DISCRIMINATING DUTIES AND RECIPROCAL PRIVILEGES

§60501. Vessels allowed to import

(a) In General.—Except as otherwise provided by treaty, goods may be imported into the United States from a foreign port or place only in—

(1) a vessel of the United States; or

(2) a foreign vessel owned only by citizens or subjects of the country—

(A) in which the goods are grown, produced, or manufactured; or

(B) from which the goods can only be, or most usually are, first shipped for transportation.

(b) EXCEPTION FOR VESSELS OF COUNTRIES NOT MAINTAINING SIMILAR RESTRICTIONS.—Subsection (a) does not apply to a vessel of a foreign country that does not maintain a similar restriction against United States documented vessels.

(c) EXCEPTION FOR VESSELS BECOMING DOCUMENTED.—Subsection (a) does not apply to a vessel that—

(1) is owned only by citizens of the United States; and

(2) after entering a port of the United States, becomes documented as a vessel of the United States before leaving that port.

(d) SEIZURE AND FORFEITURE.—If goods are imported in violation of this section, the goods and the vessel in which they are imported, along with its equipment and other cargo, may be seized by and forfeited to the United States Government.

(Pub. L. 109–304, §9(b), Oct. 6, 2006, 120 Stat. 1679.)

§60502. DISCRIMINATING DUTY ON GOODS IMPORTED IN FOREIGN VESSELS OR FROM CONTIGUOUS COUNTRIES

(a) IMPOSITION OF DUTY.—A discriminating duty of 10 percent ad valorem (in addition to other duties imposed by law) is imposed on goods—

(1) imported in a vessel not of the United States unless the vessel—

(A) is entitled by law or treaty to enter the ports of the United States on payment of the same duties as are payable on goods imported in a vessel of the United States; or

(B)(i) is owned only by citizens of the United States; and

(ii) after entering a port of the United States, becomes documented as a vessel of the United States before leaving that port; or

(2) produced or manufactured in a foreign country not contiguous to the United States and imported from a country contiguous to the United States, unless imported in the usual course of strictly retail trade.

(b) SEIZURE AND FORFEITURE.—If goods are imported without payment of the duty required by this section, the goods and the vessel in which they are imported may be seized by, and forfeited to, the United States Government.

(Pub. L. 109–304, §9(b), Oct. 6, 2006, 120 Stat. 1680.)

§60503. RECIPROCAL SUSPENSION OF DISCRIMINATING DUTIES

(a) GENERAL AUTHORITY.—On receiving satisfactory proof from the government of a foreign country that it has suspended, in any part, the imposition of discriminating duties for any class of vessels owned by citizens of the United States or goods imported in those vessels, the President may proclaim a reciprocal suspension of discriminating duties for the same class of vessels owned by citizens of that country or goods imported in those vessels.

(b) EFFECTIVE AND EXPIRATION DATES.—A suspension under this section takes effect retroactively from the date the President received the proof from the foreign government, and expires when that government stops granting the reciprocal suspension.

(Pub. L. 109–304, §9(b), Oct. 6, 2006, 120 Stat. 1680.)

§60504. Reciprocal privileges for recreational vessels

When the President is satisfied that yachts owned by residents of the United States and used only for pleasure are allowed to arrive at, depart from, and cruise in the waters of a foreign port without entering, clearing, or paying any duties or fees (including cruising license fees), the Secretary of Homeland Security may allow yachts from that foreign port used only for pleasure to arrive at and depart from the ports of the United States and to cruise in the waters of the United States without paying any duties or fees. However, the Secretary may require foreign yachts to obtain a license to cruise in the waters of the United States. The license shall be in the form prescribed by the Secretary and contain limitations about length of time, direction, place of cruising and action, and other matters the Secretary considers appropriate. The license shall be issued without cost to the yacht.

(Pub. L. 109–304, §9(b), Oct. 6, 2006, 120 Stat. 1680.)

§60505. Retaliatory suspension of commercial privileges

(a) General Authority.—The President may proclaim a suspension of commercial privileges to vessels of a foreign country when—

(1) vessels of that country have been given the same commercial privileges in the ports and waters of the United States given to vessels of the United States (except the privilege of engaging in coastwise commerce); and

(2) vessels of the United States are denied commercial privileges in the ports or waters of that country given to vessels of that country.

(b) Application.—A suspension under this section shall apply to the same commercial privileges denied to vessels of the United States in the ports or waters of the foreign country, and to the same class of vessels of that country as the class of vessels of the United States denied the privileges.

(c) Effective Date.—The President shall designate the effective date of the suspension in the proclamation.

(d) Penalties.—

(1) Seizure and forfeiture.—If the master, officer, or agent of a vessel of a foreign country does an act for the vessel in the ports or waters of the United States in violation of a proclamation issued under this section, the vessel and the goods on the vessel may be seized by, and forfeited to, the United States Government.

(2) Fine or imprisonment.—A person opposing an official of the Government enforcing this section shall be fined under title 18, imprisoned for not more than 2 years, or both.

(Pub. L. 109–304, §9(b), Oct. 6, 2006, 120 Stat. 1681.)

§60506. Retaliation against British dominions of North America

(a) General Authority.—The President by proclamation may prohibit vessels of the British dominions of North America, their masters and crews, and products of or coming from those dominions, from entering waters, ports, or places of the United States when the

President is satisfied that—

(1) fishermen or fishing vessels of the United States in waters, ports, or places of the British dominions of North America are being or recently have been—

(A) denied rights provided by law or treaty;

(B) subjected to unreasonable restrictions in the exercise of those rights; or

(C) otherwise harassed;

(2) fishermen or fishing vessels of the United States, having a permit under the laws of the United States to dock or trade at a port or place in the British dominions of North America, are being or recently have been—

(A) denied the privilege of entering the port or place in the same manner and under the same regulations applicable to trading vessels of the most-favored-nation;

(B) prevented from buying supplies allowed to be sold to trading vessels of the most-favored-nation; or

(C) otherwise harassed; or

(3) other vessels of the United States or their masters or crews in waters, ports, or places of the British dominions of North America are being or recently have been—

(A) denied privileges given to vessels of the most-favored-nation or their masters or crews; or

(B) otherwise harassed.

(b) COVERAGE AND EXCEPTIONS.—The President may apply a proclamation under this section to any of the subjects named, and may include exceptions for vessels in distress or need of supplies. The President may change, revoke, and renew the proclamation.

(c) PENALTIES.—A person violating a proclamation issued under this section shall be fined under title 18, imprisoned for not more than 2 years, or both. A vessel or goods found in waters, ports, or places of the United States in violation of the proclamation may be seized by, and forfeited to, the United States Government.

(Pub. L. 109–304, §9(b), Oct. 6, 2006, 120 Stat. 1681.)

§60507. SUSPENSION OF FREE PASSAGE THROUGH SAINT MARYS FALLS CANAL

(a) PURPOSE.—The purpose of this section is to secure reciprocal advantages for the citizens, ports, and vessels of the United States.

(b) GENERAL AUTHORITY.—When the President is satisfied that vessels of the United States, or passengers or cargo being transported to a port of the United States, are prohibited from passing through a canal or lock connected with the navigation of the Saint Lawrence River, the Great Lakes, or their connecting waterways, or burdened in that passage by tolls or other means that are unreasonable in view of the free passage through the Saint Marys Falls Canal allowed to vessels of all countries, the President by proclamation may suspend the right of free passage through the Saint Marys Falls Canal for vessels owned by subjects of the country imposing the prohibition, tolls, or other burdens and for passengers and cargo being transported to the ports of that country, even when carried in vessels of the United States. The suspension shall apply to the extent and for the time the President considers appropriate.

(c) IMPOSITION OF TOLL.—

(1) IN GENERAL.—During a suspension under this section, the President shall impose a toll of not more than $2 per ton on cargo and not more than $5 on each passenger.

(2) EXCEPTIONS.—Notwithstanding paragraph (1), a toll may not be imposed on passengers or cargo landed at Ogdensburg, New York, or any port west of Ogdensburg and south of a line drawn from the northern boundary of New York through the Saint Lawrence River, the Great Lakes, and their connecting channels to the northern boundary of Minnesota.

(d) COLLECTION OF TOLL.—

(1) IN GENERAL.—A toll imposed under this section shall be collected under regulations prescribed by the Secretary of Homeland Security. The Secretary may require the master of a vessel to provide a sworn statement of the amount and kind of cargo, the number of passengers, and the destination of the passengers and cargo.

(2) PROOF OF LANDING.—When applicable, the Secretary also may require satisfactory proof that the passengers and cargo were landed at a port described in subsection (c)(2). Until that proof is provided, the Secretary may assume the passengers and cargo were not landed at such a port, and the amount of a toll that otherwise would be imposed is a lien enforceable against the vessel when found in the waters of the United States.

(Pub. L. 109–304, §9(b), Oct. 6, 2006, 120 Stat. 1682.)

SUBTITLE VII
SECURITY AND DRUG ENFORCEMENT

Subtitle VII—Security and Drug Enforcement

[1] *So in original. The period probably should not appear.*

CHAPTER 700—PORTS AND WATERWAYS SAFETY

SUBCHAPTER I—VESSEL OPERATIONS

SUBCHAPTER II—PORTS AND WATERWAYS SAFETY

SUBCHAPTER III—CONDITIONS FOR ENTRY INTO PORTS IN THE UNITED STATES

SUBCHAPTER IV—DEFINITIONS REGULATIONS, ENFORCEMENT, INVESTIGATORY POWERS,

APPLICABILITY [2]

SUBCHAPTER V—REGATTAS AND MARINE PARADES

SUBCHAPTER VI—REGULATION OF VESSELS IN TERRITORIAL WATERS OF THE UNITED STATES [2]

[1] So in original. Does not conform to section catchline.

[2] So in original. Does not conform to subchapter heading.

SUBCHAPTER I—VESSEL OPERATIONS

§70001. VESSEL TRAFFIC SERVICES

(a) IN GENERAL.—Subject to the requirements of section 70004, the Secretary—

(1) in any port or place under the jurisdiction of the United States, in the navigable waters of the United States, or in any area covered by an international agreement negotiated pursuant to section 70005, may construct, operate, maintain, improve, or expand vessel traffic services, that consist of measures for controlling or supervising vessel traffic or for protecting navigation and the marine environment and that may include one or more of reporting and operating requirements, surveillance and communications systems, routing systems, and fairways;

(2) shall require appropriate vessels that operate in an area of a vessel traffic service to utilize or comply with that service;

(3) may require vessels to install and use specified navigation equipment, communications equipment, electronic relative motion analyzer equipment, or any electronic or other device necessary to comply with a vessel traffic service or that is necessary in the interests of vessel safety, except that the Secretary shall not require fishing vessels under 300 gross tons as measured under section 14502, or an alternate tonnage measured under section 14302 as prescribed by the Secretary under section

14104, or recreational vessels 65 feet or less to possess or use the equipment or devices required by this subsection solely under the authority of this chapter;

(4) may control vessel traffic in areas subject to the jurisdiction of the United States that the Secretary determines to be hazardous, or under conditions of reduced visibility, adverse weather, vessel congestion, or other hazardous circumstances, by—

(A) specifying times of entry, movement, or departure;

(B) establishing vessel traffic routing schemes;

(C) establishing vessel size, speed, or draft limitations and vessel operating conditions; and

(D) restricting operation, in any hazardous area or under hazardous conditions, to vessels that have particular operating characteristics or capabilities that the Secretary considers necessary for safe operation under the circumstances;

(5) may require the receipt of prearrival messages from any vessel, destined for a port or place subject to the jurisdiction of the United States, in sufficient time to permit advance vessel traffic planning before port entry, which shall include any information that is not already a matter of record and that the Secretary determines necessary for the control of the vessel and the safety of the port or the marine environment; and

(6) may prohibit the use on vessels of electronic or other devices that interfere with communication and navigation equipment, except that such authority shall not apply to electronic or other devices certified to transmit in the maritime services by the Federal Communications Commission and used within the frequency bands 157.1875–157.4375 MHz and 161.7875–162.0375 MHz.

(b) NATIONAL POLICY.—

(1) ESTABLISHMENT AND UPDATE OF NATIONAL POLICY.—

(A) ESTABLISHMENT OF POLICY.—Not later than one year after the date of enactment of this section, the Secretary shall establish a national policy which is inclusive of local variances permitted under subsection (c), to be applied to all vessel traffic service centers and publish such policy in the Federal Register.

(B) UPDATE.—The Secretary shall periodically update the national policy established under subparagraph (A) and shall publish such update in the Federal Register or on a publicly available website.

(2) ELEMENTS.—The national policy established and updated under paragraph (1) shall include, at a minimum, the following:

(A) Standardization of titles, roles, and responsibilities for all personnel assigned, working, or employed in a vessel traffic service center.

(B) Standardization of organizational structure within vessel traffic service centers, to include supervisory and reporting chain and processes.

(C) Establishment of directives for the application of authority provided to each vessel traffic service center, specifically with respect to directing or controlling vessel movement when such action is justified in the interest of safety.

(D) Establishment of thresholds and measures for monitoring, informing, recommending, and directing vessel traffic.

(E) Establishment of national procedures and protocols for vessel traffic management.

(F) Standardization of training for all vessel traffic service directors, operators, and watchstanders.

(G) Establishment of certification and competency evaluation for all vessel traffic service directors, operators, and watchstanders.

(H) Establishment of standard operating language when communicating with vessel traffic users.

(I) Establishment of data collection, storage, management, archiving, and dissemination policies and procedures for vessel incidents and near-miss incidents.

(c) LOCAL VARIANCES.—

(1) DEVELOPMENT.—In this section, the Secretary may provide for such local variances as the Secretary considers appropriate to account for the unique vessel traffic, waterway characteristics, and any additional factors that are appropriate to enhance navigational safety in any area where vessel traffic services are provided.

(2) REVIEW AND APPROVAL BY SECRETARY.—The Captain of the Port covered by a vessel traffic service center may develop and submit to the Secretary regional policies in addition to the national policy established and updated under subsection (b) to account for variances from that national policy with respect to local vessel traffic conditions and volume, geography, water body characteristics, waterway usage, and any additional factors that the Captain considers appropriate.

(3) REVIEW AND IMPLEMENTATION.—Not later than 180 days after receiving regional policies under paragraph (2)—

(A) the Secretary shall review such regional policies; and

(B) the Captain of the port concerned shall implement the policies that the Secretary approves.

(4) MAINTENANCE.—The Secretary shall maintain a central depository for all local variances approved under this section.

(d) COOPERATIVE AGREEMENTS.—

(1) IN GENERAL.—The Secretary may enter into cooperative agreements with public or private agencies, authorities, associations, institutions, corporations, organizations, or other persons to carry out the functions under subsection (a)(1).

(2) INTERNATIONAL COORDINATION.—With respect to vessel traffic service areas that cross international boundaries, the Secretary may enter into bilateral or cooperative agreements with international partners to jointly carry out the functions under subsection (a)(1) and to jointly manage such areas to collect, share, assess, and analyze information in the possession or control of the international partner.

(3) LIMITATION.—

(A) INHERENTLY GOVERNMENTAL FUNCTION.—A nongovernmental entity may not under this subsection carry out an inherently governmental function.

(B) DEFINITION OF INHERENTLY GOVERNMENTAL FUNCTION.—In this paragraph, the term "inherently governmental function" means any activity that is so intimately related to the public interest as to mandate performance by an officer or employee of the Federal Government, including an activity that requires either the exercise of discretion in applying the authority of the Government or the use of judgment in making a decision for the Government.

(4) DISCLOSURE.—The Commandant of the Coast Guard shall de-identify information prior to release to the public, including near miss incidents.

(e) PERFORMANCE EVALUATION.—
(1) IN GENERAL.—The Secretary shall develop and implement a standard method for evaluating the performance of vessel traffic service centers.
(2) ELEMENTS.—The standard method developed and implemented under paragraph (1) shall include, at a minimum, analysis and collection of data with respect to the following within a vessel traffic service area covered by each vessel traffic service center:
(A) Volume of vessel traffic, categorized by type of vessel.
(B) Total volume of flammable, combustible, or hazardous liquid cargo transported, categorized by vessel type as provided in the Notice of Arrival, if applicable, or as determined by other means.
(C) Data on near-miss incidents.
(D) Data on marine casualties.
(E) Application by vessel traffic operators of traffic management authority during near-miss incidents and marine casualties.
(F) Other additional methods as the Secretary considers appropriate.

(3) REPORT.—Not later than 1 year after the date of the enactment of this paragraph, and biennially thereafter, the Secretary shall submit to the Committee on Commerce, Science, and Transportation of the Senate and the Committee on Transportation and Infrastructure of the House of Representatives a report on the evaluation conducted under paragraph (1) of the performance of vessel traffic service centers, including—
(A) recommendations to improve safety and performance; and
(B) data regarding marine casualties and near-miss incidents that have occurred during the period covered by the report.

(f) RISK ASSESSMENT PROGRAM.—
(1) IN GENERAL.—The Secretary shall develop a continuous risk assessment program to evaluate and mitigate safety risks for each vessel traffic service area to improve safety and reduce the risks of oil and hazardous material discharge in navigable waters.
(2) METHOD FOR ASSESSMENT.—The Secretary, in coordination with stakeholders and the public, shall develop a standard method for conducting risk assessments under paragraph (1) that includes the collection and management of all information necessary to identify and analyze potential hazardous navigational trends within a vessel traffic service area.
(3) INFORMATION TO BE ASSESSED.—
(A) IN GENERAL.—The Secretary shall ensure that a risk assessment conducted

under paragraph (1) includes an assessment of the following:

(i) Volume of vessel traffic, categorized by type of vessel.

(ii) Total volume of flammable, combustible, or hazardous liquid cargo transported, categorized by vessel type as provided in the Notice of Arrival, if applicable, or as determined by other means.

(iii) Data on near-miss events incidents.

(iv) Data on marine casualties.

(v) Geographic locations for near-miss events incidents and marine casualties, including latitude and longitude.

(vi) Cyclical risk factors such as weather, seasonal water body currents, tides, bathymetry, and topography.

(vii) Weather data, in coordination with the National Oceanic and Atmospheric Administration.

(B) INFORMATION STORAGE AND MANAGEMENT POLICIES.—The Secretary shall retain all information collected under subparagraph (A) and ensure policies and procedures are in place to standardize the format in which that information is retained to facilitate statistical analysis of that information to calculate within a vessel traffic service area, at a minimum, the incident rate, intervention rate, and casualty prevention rate.

(4) PUBLIC AVAILABILITY.—

(A) ASSESSMENTS AND INFORMATION.—In accordance with section 552 of title 5, the Secretary shall make any risk assessments conducted under paragraph (1) and any information collected under paragraph (3)(A) available to the public.

(B) INFORMATION IN POSSESSION OR CONTROL OF INTERNATIONAL PARTNERS.—The Secretary shall endeavor to coordinate with international partners as described in subsection (d)(2) to enter into agreements to make information collected, shared, and analyzed under that paragraph available to the public.

(C) DISCLOSURE.—The Commandant of the Coast Guard shall de-identify information prior to release to the public, including near-miss incidents.

(g) VESSEL TRAFFIC SERVICE TRAINING.—

(1) TRAINING PROGRAM.—

(A) IN GENERAL.—The Secretary shall develop a comprehensive nationwide training program for all vessel traffic service directors, operators, and watchstanders.

(B) ELEMENTS.—The comprehensive nationwide training program under subparagraph (A) and any variances to that program under subsection (c) shall include, at a minimum, the following:

(i) Realistic vessel traffic scenarios to the maximum extent practicable that integrate—

(I) the national policy developed under subsection (b);

(II) international rules under the International Navigational Rules Act of 1977 (33 U.S.C. 1601 et seq.);

(III) inland navigation rules under part 83 of title 33, Code of Federal Regulations;

(IV) the application of vessel traffic authority; and

(V) communication with vessel traffic service users.

(ii) Proficiency training with respect to use, interpretation, and integration of available data on vessel traffic service display systems such as radar, and vessel automatic identification system feeds.

(iii) Practical application of—

(I) the international rules under the International Navigational Rules Act of 1977 (33 U.S.C. 1601 et seq.); and

(II) the inland navigation rules under part 83 of title 33, Code of Federal Regulations.

(iv) Proficiency training with respect to the operation of radio communications equipment and any other applicable systems necessary to execute vessel traffic service authorities.

(v) Incorporation of the Standard Marine Communication Phrases adopted by the International Maritime Organization by resolution on April 4, 2000, as amended and consolidated, or any successor resolution.

(vi) Incorporation to the maximum extent possible of guidance and recommendations contained in vessel traffic services operator training, vessel traffic services supervisor training, or other relevant training set forth by the International Association of Marine Aids to Navigation and Lighthouse Authorities.

(vii) A minimum number of hours of training for an individual to complete before the individual is qualified to fill a vessel traffic services position without supervision.

(viii) Local area geographic and operational familiarization.

(ix) Such additional components as the Secretary considers appropriate.

(2) STANDARD COMPETENCY QUALIFICATION PROCESS.—

(A) IN GENERAL.—The Secretary shall develop a standard competency qualification process to be applied to all personnel assigned, employed, or working in a vessel traffic service center.

(B) APPLICATION OF PROCESS.—The competency qualification process developed under subparagraph (A) shall include measurable thresholds for determining proficiency.

(3) INTERNATIONAL AND INLAND NAVIGATION RULES TEST.—

(A) IN GENERAL.—All personnel assigned, employed, or working in a vessel traffic service center with responsibilities that include communicating, interacting, or directing vessels within a vessel traffic service area, as determined under the national policy developed under subsection (b), shall be required to pass a United States international and inland navigation rules test developed by the Secretary.

(B) ELEMENTS OF TEST.—The Secretary shall determine the content and passing standard for the rules test developed under subparagraph (A).

(C) TESTING FREQUENCY.—The Secretary shall establish a frequency, not to exceed once every 5 years, for personnel described in subparagraph (A) to be required to pass the rules test developed under such subparagraph.

(h) RESEARCH ON VESSEL TRAFFIC.—

(1) VESSEL COMMUNICATION.—The Secretary shall conduct research, in consultation with subject matter experts identified by the Secretary, to develop more effective procedures for monitoring vessel communications on radio frequencies to identify and address unsafe situations in a vessel traffic service area. The Secretary shall consider data collected under subparagraph (A) of subsection (f)(3).

(2) PROFESSIONAL MARINER REPRESENTATION.—

(A) IN GENERAL.—The Secretary shall conduct research, in consultation with local stakeholders and subject matter experts identified by the Secretary, to evaluate and determine the feasibility, costs and benefits of representation by professional mariners on the vessel traffic service watchfloor at each vessel traffic service center.

(B) IMPLEMENTATION.—The Secretary shall implement representation by professional mariners on the vessel traffic service watchfloor at those vessel traffic service centers for which it is determined feasible and beneficial pursuant to research conducted under subparagraph (A).

(i) INCLUSION OF IDENTIFICATION SYSTEM ON CERTAIN VESSELS.—

(1) IN GENERAL.—The National Navigation Safety Advisory Committee shall advise and provide recommendations to the Secretary on matters relating to the practicability, economic costs, regulatory burden, and navigational impact of outfitting vessels lacking independent means of propulsion that carry flammable, combustible, or hazardous liquid cargo with vessel automatic identification systems.

(2) REGULATIONS.—Based on the evaluation under paragraph (1), the Secretary shall prescribe such regulations as the Secretary considers appropriate to establish requirements relating to the outfitting of vessels described in such subparagraph with vessel automatic identification systems.

(j) PERIODIC REVIEW OF VESSEL TRAFFIC SERVICE NEEDS.—

(1) IN GENERAL.—Based on the performance evaluation conducted under subsection (e) and the risk assessment conducted under subsection (f), the Secretary shall periodically review vessel traffic service areas to determine—

(A) if there are any additional vessel traffic service needs in those areas; and

(B) if a vessel traffic service area should be moved or modified.

(2) INFORMATION TO BE ASSESSED.—

(A) IN GENERAL.—The Secretary shall ensure that a review conducted under paragraph (1) includes an assessment of the following:

(i) Volume of vessel traffic, categorized by type of vessel.

(ii) Total volume of flammable, combustible, or hazardous liquid cargo transported, categorized by vessel type as provided in the Notice of Arrival, if applicable, or as determined by other means.

(iii) Data on near miss incidents.

(iv) Data on marine casualties.

(v) Geographic locations for near-miss incidents and marine casualties, including latitude and longitude.

(vi) Cyclical risk factors such as weather, seasonal water body currents, tides, bathymetry, and topography.

(vii) Weather data, in coordination with the National Oceanic and Atmospheric Administration.

(3) STAKEHOLDER INPUT.—In conducting the periodic reviews under paragraph (1), the Secretary shall seek input from port and waterway stakeholders to identify areas of increased vessel conflicts or marine casualties that could benefit from the use of routing measures or vessel traffic service special areas to improve safety, port security, and environmental protection.

(4) DISCLOSURE.—The Commandant of the Coast Guard shall de-identify information prior to release to the public, including near miss incidents.

(k) LIMITATION OF LIABILITY FOR COAST GUARD VESSEL TRAFFIC SERVICE PILOTS AND NON-FEDERAL VESSEL TRAFFIC SERVICE OPERATORS.—

(1) COAST GUARD VESSEL TRAFFIC SERVICE PILOTS.—Any pilot, acting in the course and scope of his or her duties while at a Coast Guard Vessel Traffic Service Center, who provides information, advice, or communication assistance while under the supervision of a Coast Guard officer, member, or employee shall not be liable for damages caused by or related to such assistance unless the acts or omissions of such pilot constitute gross negligence or willful misconduct.

(2) NON-FEDERAL VESSEL TRAFFIC SERVICE OPERATORS.—An entity operating a non-Federal vessel traffic information service or advisory service pursuant to a duly executed written agreement with the Coast Guard, and any pilot acting on behalf of such entity, is not liable for damages caused by or related to information, advice, or communication assistance provided by such entity or pilot while so operating or acting unless the acts or omissions of such entity or pilot constitute gross negligence or willful misconduct.

(l) EXISTING AUTHORITY.—Nothing in this section shall be construed to alter the existing authorities of the Secretary to enhance navigation, vessel safety, marine environmental protection, and to ensure safety and preservation of life and property at sea.

(m) DEFINITIONS.—In this section:

(1) HAZARDOUS LIQUID CARGO.—The term "hazardous liquid cargo" has the meaning given that term in regulations prescribed under section 5103 of title 49.

(2) MARINE CASUALTY.—The term "marine casualty" has the meaning given that term in regulations prescribed under section 6101(a).

(3) VESSEL TRAFFIC SERVICE AREA.—The term "vessel traffic service area" means an area specified in subpart C of part 161 of title 33, Code of Federal Regulations, or any successor regulation.

(4) VESSEL TRAFFIC SERVICE CENTER.—The term "vessel traffic service center" means a center for the provision of vessel traffic services in a vessel traffic service area.

(5) NEAR MISS INCIDENT.—The term "near miss incident" means any occurrence or

series of occurrences having the same origin, involving one or more vessels, facilities, or any combination thereof, resulting in the substantial threat of a marine casualty.

(6) DE-IDENTIFIED.—The term "de-identified" means the process by which all information that is likely to establish the identity of the specific persons or entities noted in the reports, data, or other information is removed from the reports, data, or other information.

(Added Pub. L. 115–282, title IV, §401(a), Dec. 4, 2018, 132 Stat. 4253; amended Pub. L. 116–283, div. G, title LVXXXIII [LXXXIII], §8345, Jan. 1, 2021, 134 Stat. 4711.)

§70002. SPECIAL POWERS

The Secretary may order any vessel, in a port or place subject to the jurisdiction of the United States or in the navigable waters of the United States, to operate or anchor in a manner the Secretary directs if—

(1) the Secretary has reasonable cause to believe such vessel does not comply with any regulation issued under section 70034 or any other applicable law or treaty;

(2) the Secretary determines such vessel does not satisfy the conditions for port entry set forth in section 70021 or 70022 of this title; or

(3) by reason of weather, visibility, sea conditions, port congestion, other hazardous circumstances, or the condition of such vessel, the Secretary is satisfied such direction is justified in the interest of safety.

(Added Pub. L. 115–282, title IV, §401(a), Dec. 4, 2018, 132 Stat. 4255; amended Pub. L. 116–283, div. G, title LVXXXV [LXXXV], §8508(2)(A), Jan. 1, 2021, 134 Stat. 4755.)

§70003. PORT ACCESS ROUTES

(a) AUTHORITY TO DESIGNATE.—Except as provided in subsection (b) and subject to the requirements of subsection (c), in order to provide safe access routes for the movement of vessel traffic proceeding to or from ports or places subject to the jurisdiction of the United States, the Secretary shall designate necessary fairways and traffic separation schemes for vessels operating in the territorial sea of the United States and in high seas approaches, outside the territorial sea, to such ports or places. Such a designation shall recognize, within the designated area, the paramount right of navigation over all other uses.

(b) LIMITATION.—

(1) IN GENERAL.—No designation may be made by the Secretary under this section if—

(A) the Secretary determines such a designation, as implemented, would deprive any person of the effective exercise of a right granted by a lease or permit executed or issued under other applicable provisions of law; and

(B) such right has become vested before the time of publication of the notice required by paragraph (1) of subsection (c).

(2) CONSULTATION REQUIRED.—The Secretary shall make the determination under paragraph (1)(A) after consultation with the head of the agency responsible for executing the lease or issuing the permit.

(c) Consideration of Other Uses.—Before making a designation under subsection (a), and in accordance with the requirements of section 70004, the Secretary shall—

(1) undertake a study of the potential traffic density and the need for safe access routes for vessels in any area for which fairways or traffic separation schemes are proposed or that may otherwise be considered and publish notice of such undertaking in the Federal Register;

(2) in consultation with the Secretary of State, the Secretary of the Interior, the Secretary of Commerce, the Secretary of the Army, and the Governors of affected States, as their responsibilities may require, take into account all other uses of the area under consideration, including, as appropriate, the exploration for, or exploitation of, oil, gas, or other mineral resources, the construction or operation of deepwater ports or other structures on or above the seabed or subsoil of the submerged lands or the Outer Continental Shelf of the United States, the establishment or operation of marine or estuarine sanctuaries, and activities involving recreational or commercial fishing; and

(3) to the extent practicable, reconcile the need for safe access routes with the needs of all other reasonable uses of the area involved.

(d) Study.—In carrying out the Secretary's responsibilities under subsection (c), the Secretary shall—

(1) proceed expeditiously to complete any study undertaken; and

(2) after completion of such a study, promptly—

(A) issue a notice of proposed rulemaking for the designation contemplated; or

(B) publish in the Federal Register a notice that no designation is contemplated as a result of the study and the reason for such determination.

(e) Implementation of Designation.—In connection with a designation made under this section, the Secretary—

(1) shall issue reasonable rules and regulations governing the use of such designated areas, including rules and regulations regarding the applicability of rules 9 and 10 of the International Regulations for Preventing Collisions at Sea, 1972, relating to narrow channels and traffic separation schemes, respectively, in waters where such regulations apply;

(2) to the extent that the Secretary finds reasonable and necessary to effectuate the purposes of the designation, make the use of designated fairways and traffic separation schemes mandatory for specific types and sizes of vessels, foreign and domestic, operating in the territorial sea of the United States and for specific types and sizes of vessels of the United States operating on the high seas beyond the territorial sea of the United States;

(3) may, from time to time, as necessary, adjust the location or limits of designated fairways or traffic separation schemes in order to accommodate the needs of other uses that cannot be reasonably accommodated otherwise, except that such an adjustment may not, in the judgment of the Secretary, unacceptably adversely affect the purpose for which the existing designation was made and the need for which continues; and

(4) shall, through appropriate channels—

(A) notify cognizant international organizations of any designation, or adjustment thereof; and

(B) take action to seek the cooperation of foreign States in making it mandatory for vessels under their control to use, to the same extent as required by the Secretary for vessels of the United States, any fairway or traffic separation scheme designated under this section in any area of the high seas.

(Added Pub. L. 115–282, title IV, §401(a), Dec. 4, 2018, 132 Stat. 4255.)

§70004. CONSIDERATIONS BY SECRETARY

In carrying out the duties of the Secretary under sections 70001, 70002, and 70003, the Secretary shall—

(1) take into account all relevant factors concerning navigation and vessel safety, protection of the marine environment, and the safety and security of United States ports and waterways, including—

(A) the scope and degree of the risk or hazard involved;

(B) vessel traffic characteristics and trends, including traffic volume, the sizes and types of vessels involved, potential interference with the flow of commercial traffic, the presence of any unusual cargoes, and other similar factors;

(C) port and waterway configurations and variations in local conditions of geography, climate, and other similar factors;

(D) the need for granting exemptions for the installation and use of equipment or devices for use with vessel traffic services for certain classes of small vessels, such as self-propelled fishing vessels and recreational vessels;

(E) the proximity of fishing grounds, oil and gas drilling and production operations, or any other potential or actual conflicting activity;

(F) environmental factors;

(G) economic impact and effects;

(H) existing vessel traffic services; and

(I) local practices and customs, including voluntary arrangements and agreements within the maritime community; and

(2) at the earliest possible time, consult with and receive and consider the views of representatives of the maritime community, ports and harbor authorities or associations, environmental groups, and other persons who may be affected by the proposed actions.

(Added Pub. L. 115–282, title IV, §401(a), Dec. 4, 2018, 132 Stat. 4257.)

§70005. INTERNATIONAL AGREEMENTS

(a) TRANSMITTAL OF REGULATIONS.—The Secretary shall transmit, via the Secretary of State, to appropriate international bodies or forums, any regulations issued under this subchapter, for consideration as international standards.

(b) AGREEMENTS.—The President is authorized and encouraged to—

(1) enter into negotiations and conclude and execute agreements with neighboring nations, to establish compatible vessel standards and vessel traffic services, and to

establish, operate, and maintain international vessel traffic services, in areas and under circumstances of mutual concern; and

(2) enter into negotiations, through appropriate international bodies, and conclude and execute agreements to establish vessel traffic services in appropriate areas of the high seas.

(c) OPERATIONS.—The Secretary, pursuant to any agreement negotiated under subsection (b) that is binding upon the United States in accordance with constitutional requirements, may—

(1) require vessels operating in an area of a vessel traffic service to utilize or to comply with the vessel traffic service, including the carrying or installation of equipment and devices as necessary for the use of the service; and

(2) waive, by order or regulation, the application of any United States law or regulation concerning the design, construction, operation, equipment, personnel qualifications, and manning standards for vessels operating in waters over which the United States exercises jurisdiction if such vessel is not en route to or from a United States port or place, and if vessels en route to or from a United States port or place are accorded equivalent waivers of laws and regulations of the neighboring nation, when operating in waters over which that nation exercises jurisdiction.

(d) SHIP REPORTING SYSTEMS.—The Secretary, in cooperation with the International Maritime Organization, may implement and enforce two mandatory ship reporting systems, consistent with international law, with respect to vessels subject to such reporting systems entering the following areas of the Atlantic Ocean:

(1) Cape Cod Bay, Massachusetts Bay, and Great South Channel (in the area generally bounded by a line starting from a point on Cape Ann, Massachusetts at 42 deg. 39' N., 70 deg. 37' W; then northeast to 42 deg. 45' N., 70 deg. 13' W; then southeast to 42 deg. 10' N., 68 deg. 31' W, then south to 41 deg. 00' N., 68 deg. 31' W; then west to 41 deg. 00' N., 69 deg. 17' W; then northeast to 42 deg. 05' N., 70 deg. 02' W, then west to 42 deg. 04' N., 70 deg. 10' W; and then along the Massachusetts shoreline of Cape Cod Bay and Massachusetts Bay back to the point on Cape Ann at 42 deg. 39' N., 70 deg. 37' W).

(2) In the coastal waters of the Southeastern United States within about 25 nm along a 90 nm stretch of the Atlantic seaboard (in an area generally extending from the shoreline east to longitude 80 deg. 51.6' W with the southern and northern boundary at latitudes 30 deg. 00' N., 31 deg. 27' N., respectively).

(Added Pub. L. 115–282, title IV, §401(a), Dec. 4, 2018, 132 Stat. 4257.)

§70006. ESTABLISHMENT BY SECRETARY OF THE DEPARTMENT IN WHICH THE COAST GUARD IS OPERATING OF ANCHORAGE GROUNDS AND REGULATIONS GENERALLY

(a) IN GENERAL.—The Secretary of Homeland Security is authorized, empowered, and directed to define and establish anchorage grounds for vessels in all harbors, rivers, bays, and other navigable waters of the United States whenever it is manifest to the said Secretary that the maritime or commercial interests of the United States require such anchorage grounds for safe navigation and the establishment of such anchorage grounds shall have been recommended by the Chief of Engineers, and to adopt suitable rules and regulations in relation thereto; and such rules and regulations shall be enforced by the Coast Guard under the direction of the Secretary of Transportation: *Provided,* That at ports or places where there is no Coast Guard vessel available such rules and regulations may be enforced by the Chief of Engineers under the direction of the Secretary of Homeland Security. In the event of the violation of any such rules and regulations by the owner, master, or person in charge of any vessel, such owner, master, or person in charge of such vessel shall be liable to a penalty of up to $10,000. Each day during which a violation continues shall constitute a separate violation. The said vessel may be holden for the payment of such penalty, and may be seized and proceeded against summarily by libel for the recovery of the same in any United States district court for the district within which such vessel may be and in the name of the officer designated by the Secretary of Homeland Security.

(b) DEFINITION.—As used in this section "navigable waters of the United States" includes all waters of the territorial sea of the United States as described in Presidential Proclamation No. 5928 of December 27, 1988.

(Added Pub. L. 116–283, div. G, title LVXXXV [LXXXV], §8501(a)(6), Jan. 1, 2021, 134 Stat. 4745.)

§70007. ANCHORAGE GROUNDS

(a) ANCHORAGE GROUNDS.—

(1) ESTABLISHMENT.—The Secretary of the department in which the Coast Guard is operating shall define and establish anchorage grounds in the navigable waters of the United States for vessels operating in such waters.

(2) RELEVANT FACTORS FOR ESTABLISHMENT.—In carrying out paragraph (1), the Secretary shall take into account all relevant factors concerning navigational safety, protection of the marine environment, proximity to undersea pipelines and cables, safe and efficient use of Marine Transportation System, and national security.

(b) VESSEL REQUIREMENTS.—Vessels, of certain sizes or type determined by the Secretary, shall—

(1) set and maintain an anchor alarm for the duration of an anchorage;

(2) comply with any directions or orders issued by the Captain of the Port; and

(3) comply with any applicable anchorage regulations.

(c) PROHIBITIONS.—A vessel may not—

(1) anchor in any Federal navigation channel unless authorized or directed to by the Captain of the Port;

(2) anchor in near proximity, within distances determined by the Coast Guard, to an undersea pipeline or cable, unless authorized or directed to by the Captain of the Port; and

(3) anchor or remain anchored in an anchorage ground during any period in which the Captain of the Port orders closure of the anchorage ground due to inclement weather, navigational hazard, a threat to the environment, or other safety or security concern.

(d) SAFETY EXCEPTION.—Nothing in this section shall be construed to prevent a vessel from taking actions necessary to maintain the safety of the vessel or to prevent the loss of life or property.

(Added Pub. L. 117–263, div. K, title CXIII, §11318(a), Dec. 23, 2022, 136 Stat. 4090.)

SUBCHAPTER II—PORTS AND WATERWAYS SAFETY

§70011. WATERFRONT SAFETY

(a) IN GENERAL.—The Secretary may take such action as is necessary to—

(1) prevent damage to, or the destruction of, any bridge or other structure on or in the navigable waters of the United States, or any land structure or shore area immediately adjacent to such waters; and

(2) protect the navigable waters and the resources therein from harm resulting from vessel or structure damage, destruction, or loss.

(b) ACTIONS AUTHORIZED.—Actions authorized by subsection (a) include—

(1) establishing procedures, measures, and standards for the handling, loading, unloading, storage, stowage, and movement on a structure (including the emergency removal, control, and disposition) of explosives or other dangerous articles and substances, including oil or hazardous material as those terms are defined in section 2101;

(2) prescribing minimum safety equipment requirements for a structure to assure adequate protection from fire, explosion, natural disaster, and other serious accidents or casualties;

(3) establishing water or waterfront safety zones, or other measures, for limited, controlled, or conditional access and activity when necessary for the protection of any vessel, structure, waters, or shore area; and

(4) establishing procedures for examination to assure compliance with the requirements prescribed under this section.

(c) STATE LAW.—Nothing in this section, with respect to structures, prohibits a State or political subdivision thereof from prescribing higher safety equipment requirements or safety standards than those that may be prescribed by regulations under this section.

(Added Pub. L. 115–282, title IV, §401(a), Dec. 4, 2018, 132 Stat. 4258.)

§70012. NAVIGATIONAL HAZARDS

(a) REPORTING PROCEDURE.—The Secretary shall establish a program to encourage fishermen and other vessel operators to report potential or existing navigational hazards involving pipelines to the Secretary through Coast Guard field offices.

(b) SECRETARY'S RESPONSE.—

(1) NOTIFICATION BY THE OPERATOR OF A PIPELINE.—Upon notification by the operator of a pipeline of a hazard to navigation with respect to that pipeline, the Secretary shall immediately notify Coast Guard headquarters, the Pipeline and Hazardous Materials Safety Administration, other affected Federal and State agencies, and vessel owners and operators in the pipeline's vicinity.

(2) NOTIFICATION BY OTHER PERSONS.—Upon notification by any other person of a hazard or potential hazard to navigation with respect to a pipeline, the Secretary shall promptly determine whether a hazard exists, and if so shall immediately notify Coast Guard headquarters, the Pipeline and Hazardous Materials Safety Administration, other affected Federal and State agencies, vessel owners and operators in the pipeline's vicinity, and the owner and operator of the pipeline.

(c) PIPELINE DEFINED.—For purposes of this section, the term "pipeline" has the meaning given the term "pipeline facility" in section 60101(a)(18) of title 49.

(Added Pub. L. 115–282, title IV, §401(a), Dec. 4, 2018, 132 Stat. 4259.)

§70013. REQUIREMENT TO NOTIFY COAST GUARD OF RELEASE OF OBJECTS INTO THE NAVIGABLE WATERS OF THE UNITED STATES

(a) REQUIREMENT.—As soon as a person has knowledge of any release from a vessel or facility into the navigable waters of the United States of any object that creates an obstruction prohibited under section 10 of the Act of March 3, 1899, popularly known as the Rivers and Harbors Appropriations Act of 1899 (33 U.S.C. 403), such person shall notify the Secretary and the Secretary of the Army of such release.

(b) RESTRICTION ON USE OF NOTIFICATION.—Any notification provided by an individual in accordance with subsection (a) may not be used against such individual in any criminal case, except a prosecution for perjury or for giving a false statement.

(Added Pub. L. 115–282, title IV, §401(a), Dec. 4, 2018, 132 Stat. 4259.)

§70014. AIMING LASER POINTER AT VESSEL

(a) PROHIBITION.—It shall be unlawful to cause the beam of a laser pointer to strike a vessel operating on the navigable waters of the United States.

(b) EXCEPTIONS.—This section shall not apply to a member or element of the Department of Defense or Department of Homeland Security acting in an official capacity for the purpose of research, development, operations, testing, or training.

(c) LASER POINTER DEFINED.—In this section the term "laser pointer" means any device designed or used to amplify electromagnetic radiation by stimulated emission that emits a beam designed to be used by the operator as a pointer or highlighter to indicate, mark, or identify a specific position, place, item, or object.

(Added Pub. L. 116–283, div. G, title LVXXXIII, §8342(a), Jan. 1, 2021, 134 Stat. 4709.)

SUBCHAPTER III—CONDITION FOR ENTRY INTO PORTS IN THE UNITED STATES

§70021. CONDITIONS FOR ENTRY TO PORTS IN THE UNITED STATES

(a) IN GENERAL.—No vessel that is subject to chapter 37 shall operate in the navigable waters of the United States or transfer cargo or residue in any port or place under the jurisdiction of the United States, if such vessel—

(1) has a history of accidents, pollution incidents, or serious repair problems that, as

determined by the Secretary, creates reason to believe that such vessel may be unsafe or may create a threat to the marine environment;

(2) fails to comply with any applicable regulation issued under section 70034, chapter 37, or any other applicable law or treaty;

(3) discharges oil or hazardous material in violation of any law of the United States or in a manner or quantities inconsistent with any treaty to which the United States is a party;

(4) does not comply with any applicable vessel traffic service requirements;

(5) is manned by one or more officers who are licensed by a certificating State that the Secretary has determined, pursuant to section 9101 of title 46, does not have standards for licensing and certification of seafarers that are comparable to or more stringent than United States standards or international standards that are accepted by the United States;

(6) is not manned in compliance with manning levels as determined by the Secretary to be necessary to insure the safe navigation of the vessel; or

(7) while underway, does not have at least one licensed deck officer on the navigation bridge who is capable of clearly understanding English.

(b) Exceptions.—

(1) In general.—The Secretary may allow provisional entry of a vessel that is not in compliance with subsection (a), if the owner or operator of such vessel proves, to the satisfaction of the Secretary, that such vessel is not unsafe or a threat to the marine environment, and if such entry is necessary for the safety of the vessel or persons aboard.

(2) Provisions not applicable.—Paragraphs (1), (2), (3), and (4) of subsection (a) of this section shall not apply to a vessel allowed provisional entry under paragraph (1) if the owner or operator of such vessel proves, to the satisfaction of the Secretary, that such vessel is no longer unsafe or a threat to the marine environment, and is no longer in violation of any applicable law, treaty, regulation, or condition, as appropriate.

(Added Pub. L. 115–282, title IV, §401(a), Dec. 4, 2018, 132 Stat. 4260.)

§70022. Prohibition on entry and operation

(a) Prohibition.—

(1) In general.—Except as otherwise provided in this section, no vessel described in subsection (b) may enter or operate in the navigable waters of the United States or transfer cargo in any port or place under the jurisdiction of the United States.

(2) Limitations on application.—

(A) In general.—The prohibition under paragraph (1) shall not apply with respect to—

(i) a vessel described in subsection (b)(1), if the Secretary of State determines that—

(I) the vessel is owned or operated by or on behalf of a country the government of which the Secretary of State determines is closely cooperating with the United States with respect to implementing the applicable United Nations Security Council resolutions (as such term is defined in section 3 of the North Korea Sanctions and Policy Enhancement Act of 2016); or

(II) it is in the national security interest not to apply the prohibition to such vessel; or

(ii) a vessel described in subsection (b)(2), if the Secretary of State determines that the vessel is no longer registered as described in that subsection.

(B) NOTICE.—Not later than 15 days after making a determination under subparagraph (A), the Secretary of State shall submit to the Committee on Foreign Affairs and the Committee on Transportation and Infrastructure of the House of Representatives and the Committee on Foreign Relations and the Committee on Commerce, Science, and Transportation of the Senate written notice of the determination and the basis upon which the determination was made.

(C) PUBLICATION.—The Secretary of State shall publish a notice in the Federal Register of each determination made under subparagraph (A).

(b) VESSELS DESCRIBED.—A vessel referred to in subsection (a) is a foreign vessel for which a notice of arrival is required to be filed under section 70001(a)(5), and that—

(1) is on the most recent list of vessels published in Federal [1] Register under subsection (c)(2); or

(2) more than 180 days after the publication of such list, is knowingly registered, pursuant to the 1958 Convention on the High Seas entered into force on September 30, 1962, by a government the agents or instrumentalities of which are maintaining a registration of a vessel that is included on such list.

(c) INFORMATION AND PUBLICATION.—The Secretary of the department in which the Coast Guard is operating, with the concurrence of the Secretary of State, shall—

(1) maintain timely information on the registrations of all foreign vessels over 300 gross tons that are known to be—

(A) owned or operated by or on behalf of the Government of North Korea or a North Korean person;

(B) owned or operated by or on behalf of any country in which a sea port is located, the operator of which the President has identified in the most recent report submitted under section 205(a)(1)(A) of the North Korea Sanctions and Policy Enhancement Act of 2016; or

(C) owned or operated by or on behalf of any country identified by the President as a country that has not complied with the applicable United Nations Security Council resolutions (as such term is defined in section 3 of such Act); and

(2) periodically publish in the Federal Register a list of the vessels described in paragraph (1).

(d) NOTIFICATION OF GOVERNMENTS.—

(1) IN GENERAL.—The Secretary of State shall notify each government, the agents or instrumentalities of which are maintaining a registration of a foreign vessel that is included on a list published under subsection (c)(2), not later than 30 days after such publication, that all vessels registered under such government's authority are subject to

subsection (a).

(2) ADDITIONAL NOTIFICATION.—In the case of a government that continues to maintain a registration for a vessel that is included on such list after receiving an initial notification under paragraph (1), the Secretary shall issue an additional notification to such government not later than 120 days after the publication of a list under subsection (c)(2).

(e) NOTIFICATION OF VESSELS.—Upon receiving a notice of arrival under section 70001(a)(5) from a vessel described in subsection (b), the Secretary of the department in which the Coast Guard is operating shall notify the master of such vessel that the vessel may not enter or operate in the navigable waters of the United States or transfer cargo in any port or place under the jurisdiction of the United States, unless—

(1) the Secretary of State has made a determination under subsection (a)(2); or

(2) the Secretary of the department in which the Coast Guard is operating allows provisional entry of the vessel, or transfer of cargo from the vessel, under subsection (f).

(f) PROVISIONAL ENTRY OR CARGO TRANSFER.—Notwithstanding any other provision of this section, the Secretary of the department in which the Coast Guard is operating may allow provisional entry of, or transfer of cargo from, a vessel, if such entry or transfer is necessary for the safety of the vessel or persons aboard.

(g) RIGHT OF INNOCENT PASSAGE AND RIGHT OF TRANSIT PASSAGE.—This section shall not be construed as authority to restrict the right of innocent passage or the right of transit passage as recognized under international law.

(Added and amended Pub. L. 116–283, div. G, title LVXXXV [LXXXV], §8508(1), Jan. 1, 2021, 134 Stat. 4755.)

---

[1] *So in original. Probably should be preceded by "the".*

SUBCHAPTER IV—DEFINITIONS, REGULATIONS, ENFORCEMENT, INVESTIGATORY POWERS, APPLICABILITY

§70031. DEFINITIONS

As used in subchapters I through III and this subchapter, unless the context otherwise requires:

(1) The term "marine environment" means—

(A) the navigable waters of the United States and the land and resources therein and thereunder;

(B) the waters and fishery resources of any area over which the United States asserts exclusive fishery management authority;

(C) the seabed and subsoil of the Outer Continental Shelf of the United States, the resources thereof, and the waters superjacent thereto; and

(D) the recreational, economic, and scenic values of such waters and resources.

(2) The term "Secretary" means the Secretary of the department in which the Coast Guard is operating, except that such term means the Secretary of Transportation with respect to the application of this chapter to the Saint Lawrence Seaway.

(3) The term "navigable waters of the United States" includes all waters of the territorial sea of the United States as described in Presidential Proclamation No. 5928 of December 27, 1988.

(Added Pub. L. 115–282, title IV, §401(a), Dec. 4, 2018, 132 Stat. 4261; amended Pub. L. 116–283, div. G, title LVXXXV [LXXXV], §8507(a)(4), Jan. 1, 2021, 134 Stat. 4753.)

§70032. SAINT LAWRENCE SEAWAY

The authority granted to the Secretary under sections 70001, 70002, 70003, 70004, and 70011 may not be delegated with respect to the Saint Lawrence Seaway to any agency other than the Great Lakes St. Lawrence Seaway Development Corporation. Any other authority granted the Secretary under subchapters I through III and this subchapter shall be delegated by the Secretary to the Great Lakes St. Lawrence Seaway Development Corporation to the extent the Secretary determines such delegation is necessary for the proper operation of the Saint Lawrence Seaway.

(Added Pub. L. 115–282, title IV, §401(a), Dec. 4, 2018, 132 Stat. 4261; amended Pub. L. 116–260, div. AA, title V, §512(c)(6)(F), Dec. 27, 2020, 134 Stat. 2757; Pub. L. 116–283, div. G, title LVXXXV [LXXXV], §8507(a)(5), Jan. 1, 2021, 134 Stat. 4753.)

§70033. LIMITATION ON APPLICATION TO FOREIGN VESSELS

Except pursuant to international treaty, convention, or agreement, to which the United States is a party, subchapters I through III and this subchapter shall not apply to any foreign vessel that is not destined for, or departing from, a port or place subject to the jurisdiction of the United States and that is in—

(1) innocent passage through the territorial sea of the United States; or

(2) transit through the navigable waters of the United States that form a part of an international strait.

(Added Pub. L. 115–282, title IV, §401(a), Dec. 4, 2018, 132 Stat. 4261; amended Pub. L. 116–283, div. G, title LVXXXV [LXXXV], §8507(a)(6), Jan. 1, 2021, 134 Stat. 4753.)

§70034. REGULATIONS

(a) IN GENERAL.—In accordance with section 553 of title 5, the Secretary shall issue, and may from time to time amend or repeal, regulations necessary to implement subchapters I through III and this subchapter.

(b) CONSULTATION.—In the exercise of the regulatory authority under subchapters I through III and this subchapter, the Secretary shall consult with, and receive and consider the views of all interested persons, including—

(1) interested Federal departments and agencies;

(2) officials of State and local governments;

(3) representatives of the maritime community;

(4) representatives of port and harbor authorities or associations;

(5) representatives of environmental groups;

(6) any other interested persons who are knowledgeable or experienced in dealing with problems involving vessel safety, port and waterways safety, and protection of the marine environment; and

(7) advisory committees consisting of all interested segments of the public when the establishment of such committees is considered necessary because the issues involved are highly complex or controversial.

(Added Pub. L. 115–282, title IV, §401(a), Dec. 4, 2018, 132 Stat. 4261; amended Pub. L. 116–283, div. G, title LVXXXV [LXXXV], §8507(a)(7), Jan. 1, 2021, 134 Stat. 4753.)

§70035. Investigatory Powers

(a) SECRETARY.—The Secretary may investigate any incident, accident, or act involving the loss or destruction of, or damage to, any structure subject to subchapters I through III and this subchapter, or that affects or may affect the safety or environmental quality of the ports, harbors, or navigable waters of the United States.

(b) POWERS.—In an investigation under this section, the Secretary may issue subpoenas to require the attendance of witnesses and the production of documents or other evidence relating to such incident, accident, or act. If any person refuses to obey a subpoena, the Secretary may request the Attorney General to invoke the aid of the appropriate district court of the United States to compel compliance with the subpoena. Any district court of the United States may, in the case of refusal to obey a subpoena, issue an order requiring compliance with the subpoena, and failure to obey the order may be punished by the court as contempt. Witnesses may be paid fees for travel and attendance at rates not exceeding those allowed in a district court of the United States.

(Added Pub. L. 115–282, title IV, §401(a), Dec. 4, 2018, 132 Stat. 4262; amended Pub. L. 116–283, div. G, title LVXXXV [LXXXV], §8507(a)(8), Jan. 1, 2021, 134 Stat. 4753.)

§70036. Enforcement

(a) CIVIL PENALTY.—

(1) IN GENERAL.—Any person who is found by the Secretary, after notice and an opportunity for a hearing, to have violated subchapters I through III or this subchapter or a regulation issued under subchapters I through III or this subchapter shall be liable to the United States for a civil penalty, not to exceed $25,000 for each violation. Each day of a continuing violation shall constitute a separate violation. The amount of such civil penalty shall be assessed by the Secretary, or the Secretary's designee, by written notice. In determining the amount of such penalty, the Secretary shall take into account the nature, circumstances, extent, and gravity of the prohibited acts committed and, with respect to the violator, the degree of culpability, any history of prior offenses, ability to pay, and such other matters as justice may require.

(2) COMPROMISE, MODIFICATION, OR REMISSION.—The Secretary may compromise, modify, or remit, with or without conditions, any civil penalty that is subject to imposition or that has been imposed under this section.

(3) FAILURE TO PAY PENALTY.—If any person fails to pay an assessment of a civil penalty after it has become final, the Secretary may refer the matter to the Attorney General of the United States, for collection in any appropriate district court of the United States.

(b) CRIMINAL PENALTY.—

(1) CLASS D FELONY.—Any person who willfully and knowingly violates subchapters I through III or this subchapter or any regulation issued thereunder commits a class D felony.

(2) CLASS C FELONY.—Any person who, in the willful and knowing violation of subchapters I through III or this subchapter or of any regulation issued thereunder, uses a dangerous weapon, or engages in conduct that causes bodily injury or fear of imminent bodily injury to any officer authorized to enforce the provisions of such a subchapter or the regulations issued under such subchapter, commits a class C felony.

(c) IN REM LIABILITY.—Any vessel that is used in violation of subchapters I, II, or III or this subchapter, or any regulations issued under such subchapter, shall be liable in rem for any civil penalty assessed pursuant to subsection (a) and may be proceeded against in the United States district court for any district in which such vessel may be found.

(d) INJUNCTION.—The United States district courts shall have jurisdiction to restrain violations of subchapter I, II, or III or this subchapter or of regulations issued under such subchapter, for cause shown.

(e) DENIAL OF ENTRY.—Except as provided in section 70021 or 70022, the Secretary may, subject to recognized principles of international law, deny entry by any vessel that is not in compliance with subchapter I, II, or III or this subchapter or the regulations issued under such subchapter—

(1) into the navigable waters of the United States; or

(2) to any port or place under the jurisdiction of the United States.

(f) WITHHOLDING OF CLEARANCE.—

(1) IN GENERAL.—If any owner, operator, or individual in charge of a vessel is liable for a penalty or fine under this section, or if reasonable cause exists to believe that the owner, operator, or individual in charge may be subject to a penalty or fine under this section, the Secretary of the Treasury, upon the request of the Secretary, shall with respect to such vessel refuse or revoke any clearance required by section 60105 of title 46.

(2) GRANTING CLEARANCE REFUSED OR REVOKED.—Clearance refused or revoked under this subsection may be granted upon filing of a bond or other surety satisfactory to the Secretary.

(Added Pub. L. 115–282, title IV, §401(a), Dec. 4, 2018, 132 Stat. 4262; amended Pub. L. 116–283, div. G, title LVXXXV [LXXXV], §§8507(a)(9), 8508(2)(B), Jan. 1, 2021, 134 Stat. 4753, 4755.)

SUBCHAPTER V—REGATTAS AND MARINE PARADES

§70041. REGATTAS AND MARINE PARADES

(a) IN GENERAL.—The Commandant of the Coast Guard may issue regulations to promote the safety of life on navigable waters during regattas or marine parades.

(b) DETAIL AND USE OF VESSELS.—To enforce regulations issued under this section—

(1) the Commandant may detail any public vessel in the service of the Coast Guard and make use of any private vessel tendered gratuitously for that purpose; and

(2) upon the request of the Commandant, the head of any other Federal department or agency may enforce the regulations by means of any public vessel of such department and any private vessel tendered gratuitously for that purpose.

(c) TRANSFER OF AUTHORITY.—The authority of the Commandant under this section may be transferred by the President for any special occasion to the head of another Federal department or agency whenever in the President's judgment such transfer is desirable.

(d) PENALTIES.—

(1) IN GENERAL.—For any violation of regulations issued pursuant to this section the following penalties shall be incurred:

(A) A licensed officer shall be liable to suspension or revocation of license in the manner prescribed by law for incompetency or misconduct.

(B) Any person in charge of the navigation of a vessel other than a licensed officer shall be liable to a penalty of $5,000.

(C) The owner of a vessel (including any corporate officer of a corporation owning the vessel) actually on board shall be liable to a penalty of $5,000, unless the violation of regulations occurred without the owner's knowledge.

(D) Any other person shall be liable to a penalty of $2,500.

(2) MITIGATION OR REMISSION.—The Commandant may mitigate or remit any penalty provided for in this subsection in the manner prescribed by law for the mitigation or remission of penalties for violation of the navigation laws.

(Added Pub. L. 115–282, title IV, §406(a), Dec. 4, 2018, 132 Stat. 4265.)

SUBCHAPTER VI—REGULATION OF VESSELS IN TERRITORIAL WATERS OF UNITED STATES

§70051. REGULATION OF ANCHORAGE AND MOVEMENT OF VESSELS DURING NATIONAL EMERGENCY

Whenever the President by proclamation or Executive order declares a national emergency to exist by reason of actual or threatened war, insurrection, or invasion, or disturbance or threatened disturbance of the international relations of the United States, or whenever the Attorney General determines that an actual or anticipated mass migration of aliens en route to, or arriving off the coast of, the United States presents urgent circumstances requiring an immediate Federal response, the Secretary of the department in which the Coast Guard is operating may make, subject to the approval of the President, rules and regulations governing the anchorage and movement of any vessel, foreign or domestic, in the territorial waters of the United States, may inspect such vessel at any time, place guards thereon, and, if necessary in his opinion in order to secure such vessels from damage or injury, or to prevent damage or injury to any harbor or waters of the United States, or to secure the observance of the rights and obligations of the United States, may take, by and with the consent of the President, for such purposes, full possession and control of such vessel and remove therefrom the officers and crew thereof and all other persons not specially authorized by him to go or remain on board thereof.

Whenever the President finds that the security of the United States is endangered by reason of actual or threatened war, or invasion, or insurrection, or subversive activity, or of disturbances or threatened disturbances of the international relations of the United States, the President is authorized to institute such measures and issue such rules and regulations—

(a) to govern the anchorage and movement of any foreign-flag vessels in the territorial waters of the United States, to inspect such vessels at any time, to place guards thereon, and, if necessary in his opinion in order to secure such vessels from damage or injury, or to prevent damage or injury to any harbor or waters of the United States, or to secure the observance of rights and obligations of the United States, may take for such purposes full possession and control of such vessels and remove therefrom the officers and crew thereof, and all other persons not especially authorized by him to go or remain on board thereof;

(b) to safeguard against destruction, loss, or injury from sabotage or other subversive acts, accidents, or other causes of similar nature, vessels, harbors, ports, and waterfront facilities in the United States and all territory and water, continental or insular, subject to the jurisdiction of the United States.

The President may delegate the authority to issue such rules and regulations to the Secretary of the department in which the Coast Guard is operating. Any appropriation available to any of the Executive Departments shall be available to carry out the provisions of this subchapter.

(Added Pub. L. 115–282, title IV, §407(b)(5), Dec. 4, 2018, 132 Stat. 4267; amended Pub. L. 116–283, div. G, title LVXXXV [LXXXV], §8507(a)(10), Jan. 1, 2021, 134 Stat. 4753.)

§70052. SEIZURE AND FORFEITURE OF VESSEL; FINE AND IMPRISONMENT

(a) IN GENERAL.—If any owner, agent, master, officer, or person in charge, or any member of the crew of any such vessel fails to comply with any regulation or rule issued or order given under the provisions of this subchapter, or obstructs or interferes with the exercise of any power conferred by this subchapter, the vessel, together with her tackle, apparel, furniture, and equipment, shall be subject to seizure and forfeiture to the United States in the same manner as merchandise is forfeited for violation of the customs revenue laws; and the person guilty of such failure, obstruction, or interference shall be punished by imprisonment for not more than ten years and may, in the discretion of the court, be fined not more than $10,000.

(b) APPLICATION TO OTHERS.—If any other person knowingly fails to comply with any regulation or rule issued or order given under the provisions of this subchapter, or knowingly obstructs or interferes with the exercise of any power conferred by this subchapter, he shall be punished by imprisonment for not more than ten years and may, at the discretion of the court, be fined not more than $10,000.

(c) Civil Penalty.—A person violating this subchapter, or a regulation prescribed under this subchapter, shall be liable to the United States Government for a civil penalty of not more than $25,000 for each violation. Each day of a continuing violation shall constitute a separate violation.

(d) In Rem Liability.—Any vessel that is used in violation of this subchapter, or of any regulation issued under this subchapter, shall be liable in rem for any civil penalty assessed pursuant to subsection (c) and may be proceeded against in the United States district court for any district in which such vessel may be found.

(e) Withholding of Clearance.—

(1) In general.—If any owner, agent, master, officer, or person in charge of a vessel is liable for a penalty or fine under subsection (c), or if reasonable cause exists to believe that the owner, agent, master, officer, or person in charge may be subject to a penalty or fine under this section, the Secretary of the department in which the Coast Guard is operating may, with respect to such vessel, refuse or revoke any clearance required by section 4197 [1] of the Revised Statutes of the United States (46 U.S.C. App. 91).

(2) Clearance upon filing of bond or other surety.—The Secretary of the department in which the Coast Guard is operating may require the filing of a bond or other surety as a condition of granting clearance refused or revoked under this subsection.

(Added Pub. L. 115–282, title IV, §407(c)(3), Dec. 4, 2018, 132 Stat. 4267; amended Pub. L. 116–283, div. G, title LVXXXV [LXXXV], §8507(a)(11), Jan. 1, 2021, 134 Stat. 4754.)

[1] *See References in Text note below.*

§70053. Enforcement provisions

The President may employ such departments, agencies, officers, or instrumentalities of the United States as he may deem necessary to carry out this subchapter.

(Added Pub. L. 115–282, title IV, §407(d)(3), Dec. 4, 2018, 132 Stat. 4267.)

§70054. Definitions

In this subchapter:

(1) United states.—The term "United States" includes all territory and waters, continental or insular, subject to the jurisdiction of the United States.

(2) Territorial waters.—The term "territorial waters of the United States" includes all waters of the territorial sea of the United States as described in Presidential Proclamation 5928 of December 27, 1988.

(Added Pub. L. 115–282, title IV, §407(a), Dec. 4, 2018, 132 Stat. 4266.)

CHAPTER 701—PORT SECURITY

SUBCHAPTER I—GENERAL

SUBCHAPTER II—PORT SECURITY ZONES

SUBCHAPTER I—GENERAL

415

§70101. Definitions

For the purpose of this chapter:

(1) The term "Area Maritime Transportation Security Plan" means an Area Maritime Transportation Security Plan prepared under section 70103(b).

(2) The term "cybersecurity risk" has the meaning given the term in section 2200 of the Homeland Security Act of 2002.

(3) The term "facility" means any structure or facility of any kind located in, on, under, or adjacent to any waters subject to the jurisdiction of the United States.

(4) The term "National Maritime Transportation Security Plan" means the National Maritime Transportation Security Plan prepared and published under section 70103(a).

(5) The term "owner or operator" means—

(A) in the case of a vessel, any person owning, operating, or chartering by demise, such vessel; and

(B) in the case of a facility, any person owning, leasing, or operating such facility.

(6) The term "Secretary" means the Secretary of the department in which the Coast Guard is operating.

(7) The term "transportation security incident" means a security incident resulting in a significant loss of life, environmental damage, transportation system disruption, or economic disruption in a particular area. In this paragraph, the term "economic disruption" does not include a work stoppage or other employee-related action not related to terrorism and resulting from an employee-employer dispute.

(Added Pub. L. 107–295, title I, §102(a), Nov. 25, 2002, 116 Stat. 2068; amended Pub. L. 109–347, title I, §124, Oct. 13, 2006, 120 Stat. 1900; Pub. L. 115–254, div. J, §1805(b), Oct. 5, 2018, 132 Stat. 3534; Pub. L. 117–263, div. G, title LXXI, §7143(d)(10), Dec. 23, 2022, 136 Stat. 3664.)

§70102. United States facility and vessel vulnerability assessments

(a) Initial Assessments.—The Secretary shall conduct an assessment of vessel types and United States facilities on or adjacent to the waters subject to the jurisdiction of the United States to identify those vessel types and United States facilities that pose a high risk of being involved in a transportation security incident.

(b) Facility and Vessel Assessments.—(1) Based on the information gathered under subsection (a) of this section, the Secretary shall conduct a detailed vulnerability assessment of the facilities and vessels that may be involved in a transportation security incident. The vulnerability assessment shall include the following:

(A) Identification and evaluation of critical assets and infrastructures.

(B) Identification of the threats to those assets and infrastructures.

(C) Identification of weaknesses in physical security, security against cybersecurity risks, passenger and cargo security, structural integrity, protection systems, procedural policies, communications systems, transportation infrastructure, utilities, contingency response, and other areas as determined by the Secretary.

(2) Upon completion of an assessment under this subsection for a facility or vessel, the Secretary shall provide the owner or operator with a copy of the vulnerability assessment

for that facility or vessel.

(3) The Secretary shall update each vulnerability assessment conducted under this section at least every 5 years.

(4) In lieu of conducting a facility or vessel vulnerability assessment under paragraph (1), the Secretary may accept an alternative assessment conducted by or on behalf of the owner or operator of the facility or vessel if the Secretary determines that the alternative assessment includes the matters required under paragraph (1).

(c) SHARING OF ASSESSMENT INTEGRATION OF PLANS AND EQUIPMENT.—The owner or operator of a facility, consistent with any Federal security restrictions, shall—

(1) make a current copy of the vulnerability assessment conducted under subsection (b) available to the port authority with jurisdiction of the facility and appropriate State or local law enforcement agencies; and

(2) integrate, to the maximum extent practical, any security system for the facility with compatible systems operated or maintained by the appropriate State, law enforcement agencies, and the Coast Guard.

(Added Pub. L. 107–295, title I, §102(a), Nov. 25, 2002, 116 Stat. 2068; amended Pub. L. 108–458, title IV, §4072(b), Dec. 17, 2004, 118 Stat. 3730; Pub. L. 111–281, title VIII, §822, Oct. 15, 2010, 124 Stat. 3003; Pub. L. 115–254, div. J, §1805(d)(1), Oct. 5, 2018, 132 Stat. 3535.)

[§70102A. REPEALED. PUB. L. 116–283, DIV. G, TITLE LVXXXV [LXXXV], §8507(D)(1), JAN. 1, 2021, 134 STAT. 4754]

Section, as added and amended Pub. L. 115–282, title IV, §408(a), (b), Dec. 4, 2018, 132 Stat. 4268, related to port, harbor, and coastal facility security.

§70103. MARITIME TRANSPORTATION SECURITY PLANS

(a) NATIONAL MARITIME TRANSPORTATION SECURITY PLAN.—(1) The Secretary shall prepare a National Maritime Transportation Security Plan for deterring and responding to a transportation security incident.

(2) The National Maritime Transportation Security Plan shall provide for efficient, coordinated, and effective action to deter and minimize damage from a transportation security incident, and shall include the following:

(A) Assignment of duties and responsibilities among Federal departments and agencies and coordination with State and local governmental agencies.

(B) Identification of security resources.

(C) Procedures and techniques to be employed in deterring a national transportation security incident.

(D) Establishment of procedures for the coordination of activities of—

(i) Coast Guard maritime security teams established under this chapter; and

(ii) Federal Maritime Security Coordinators required under this chapter.

(E) A system of surveillance and notice designed to safeguard against as well as ensure earliest possible notice of a transportation security incident and imminent threats of such a security incident to the appropriate State and Federal agencies.

(F) Establishment of criteria and procedures to ensure immediate and effective Federal identification of a transportation security incident, or the substantial threat of such a security incident.

(G) Designation of—

(i) areas for which Area Maritime Transportation Security Plans are required to be prepared under subsection (b); and

(ii) a Coast Guard official who shall be the Federal Maritime Security Coordinator for each such area.

(H) A risk-based system for evaluating the potential for violations of security zones designated by the Secretary on the waters subject to the jurisdiction of the United States.

(I) A recognition of certified systems of intermodal transportation.

(J) A plan for ensuring that the flow of cargo through United States ports is reestablished as efficiently and quickly as possible after a transportation security incident.

(K) A plan to detect, respond to, and recover from cybersecurity risks that may cause transportation security incidents.

(3) The Secretary shall, as the Secretary considers advisable, revise or otherwise amend the National Maritime Transportation Security Plan.

(4) Actions by Federal agencies to deter and minimize damage from a transportation security incident shall, to the greatest extent possible, be in accordance with the National Maritime Transportation Security Plan.

(5) The Secretary shall inform vessel and facility owners or operators of the provisions in the National Transportation Security Plan that the Secretary considers necessary for security purposes.

(b) AREA MARITIME TRANSPORTATION SECURITY PLANS.—(1) The Federal Maritime Security Coordinator designated under subsection (a)(2)(G) for an area shall—

(A) submit to the Secretary an Area Maritime Transportation Security Plan for the area; and

(B) solicit advice from the Area Security Advisory Committee required under this chapter, for the area to assure preplanning of joint deterrence efforts, including appropriate procedures for deterrence of a transportation security incident.

(2) The Area Maritime Transportation Security Plan for an area shall—

(A) when implemented in conjunction with the National Maritime Transportation Security Plan, be adequate to deter a transportation security incident in or near the area to the maximum extent practicable;

(B) describe the area and infrastructure covered by the plan, including the areas of population or special economic, environmental, or national security importance that might be damaged by a transportation security incident;

(C) describe in detail how the plan is integrated with other Area Maritime Transportation Security Plans, and with facility security plans and vessel security plans under this section;

(D) include consultation and coordination with the Department of Defense on matters relating to Department of Defense facilities and vessels;

(E) establish area response and recovery protocols to prepare for, respond to, mitigate against, and recover from a transportation security incident consistent with section 202 of the SAFE Port Act of 2006 (6 U.S.C. 942) and subsection (a) of this section;

(F) include any other information the Secretary requires;

(G) include a salvage response plan—

(i) to identify salvage equipment capable of restoring operational trade capacity; and

(ii) to ensure that the waterways are cleared and the flow of commerce through United States ports is reestablished as efficiently and quickly as possible after a maritime transportation security incident;

(H) include a plan for detecting, responding to, and recovering from cybersecurity risks that may cause transportation security incidents; and

(I) be updated at least every 5 years by the Federal Maritime Security Coordinator.

(3) The Secretary shall review and approve Area Maritime Transportation Security Plans and updates under this subsection.

(4) In security zones designated by the Secretary in each Area Maritime Transportation Security Plan, the Secretary shall consider—

(A) the use of public/private partnerships to enforce security within the security zones, shoreside protection alternatives, and the environmental, public safety, and relative effectiveness of such alternatives; and

(B) technological means of enhancing the security zones of port, territorial waters, and waterways of the United States.

(c) VESSEL AND FACILITY SECURITY PLANS.—(1) Within 6 months after the prescription of interim final regulations on vessel and facility security plans, an owner or operator of a vessel or facility described in paragraph (2) shall prepare and submit to the Secretary a security plan for the vessel or facility, for deterring a transportation security incident to the maximum extent practicable.

(2) The vessels and facilities referred to in paragraph (1)—

(A) except as provided in subparagraph (B), are vessels and facilities that the Secretary believes may be involved in a transportation security incident; and

(B) do not include any vessel or facility owned or operated by the Department of Defense.

(3) A security plan required under this subsection shall—

(A) be consistent with the requirements of the National Maritime Transportation Security Plan and Area Maritime Transportation Security Plans;

(B) identify the qualified individual having full authority to implement security actions, and require immediate communications between that individual and the appropriate Federal official and the persons providing personnel and equipment pursuant to subparagraph (C);

(C) include provisions for—

(i) establishing and maintaining physical security, passenger and cargo security, and personnel security;

(ii) establishing and controlling access to secure areas of the vessel or facility, including access by persons engaged in the surface transportation of intermodal containers in or out of a port facility;

(iii) procedural security policies;

(iv) communications systems;

(v) detecting, responding to, and recovering from cybersecurity risks that may cause transportation security incidents; and

(vi) other security systems;

(D) identify, and ensure by contract or other means approved by the Secretary, the availability of security measures necessary to deter to the maximum extent practicable a transportation security incident or a substantial threat of such a security incident;

(E) describe the training, periodic unannounced drills, and security actions of persons on the vessel or at the facility, to be carried out under the plan to deter to the maximum extent practicable a transportation security incident, or a substantial threat of such a security incident;

(F) provide a strategy and timeline for conducting training and periodic unannounced drills;

(G) be updated at least every 5 years;

(H) be resubmitted for approval of each change to the vessel or facility that may substantially affect the security of the vessel or facility; and

(I) in the case of a security plan for a facility, be resubmitted for approval of each change in the ownership or operator of the facility that may substantially affect the security of the facility.

(4) The Secretary shall—

(A) promptly review each such plan or update;

(B) require amendments to any plan or update that does not meet the requirements of this subsection;

(C) approve any plan or update that meets the requirements of this subsection; and

(D) subject to the availability of appropriations, periodically, but not less than one time per year, conduct a risk-based, no notice facility inspection to verify the effectiveness of each such facility security plan or update.

(5) A vessel or facility for which a plan is required to be submitted under this subsection may not operate after the end of the 12-month period beginning on the date of the prescription of interim final regulations on vessel and facility security plans, unless—

(A) the plan has been approved by the Secretary; and

(B) the vessel or facility is operating in compliance with the plan.

(6) Notwithstanding paragraph (5), the Secretary may authorize a vessel or facility to operate without a security plan approved under this subsection, until not later than 1 year after the date of the submission to the Secretary of a plan for the vessel or facility, if

the owner or operator of the vessel or facility certifies that the owner or operator has ensured by contract or other means approved by the Secretary to deter to the maximum extent practicable a transportation security incident or a substantial threat of such a security incident.

(7) The Secretary shall require each owner or operator of a vessel or facility located within or adjacent to waters subject to the jurisdiction of the United States to implement any necessary interim security measures, including cargo security programs, to deter to the maximum extent practicable a transportation security incident until the security plan for that vessel or facility operator is approved.

(8)(A) The Secretary shall require that the qualified individual having full authority to implement security actions for a facility described in paragraph (2) shall be a citizen of the United States.

(B) The Secretary may waive the requirement of subparagraph (A) with respect to an individual if the Secretary determines that it is appropriate to do so based on a complete background check of the individual and a review of all terrorist watch lists to ensure that the individual is not identified on any such terrorist watch list.

(d) NONDISCLOSURE OF INFORMATION.—

(1) IN GENERAL.—Information developed under this section or sections 70102, 70104, and 70108 is not required to be disclosed to the public, including—

(A) facility security plans, vessel security plans, and port vulnerability assessments; and

(B) other information related to security plans, procedures, or programs for vessels or facilities authorized under this section or sections 70102, 70104, and 70108.

(2) LIMITATIONS.—Nothing in paragraph (1) shall be construed to authorize the designation of information as sensitive security information (as defined in section 1520.5 of title 49, Code of Federal Regulations)—

(A) to conceal a violation of law, inefficiency, or administrative error;

(B) to prevent embarrassment to a person, organization, or agency;

(C) to restrain competition; or

(D) to prevent or delay the release of information that does not require protection in the interest of transportation security, including basic scientific research information not clearly related to transportation security.

(e) ESPECIALLY HAZARDOUS CARGO.—

(1) ENFORCEMENT OF SECURITY ZONES.—Consistent with other provisions of Federal law, the Coast Guard shall coordinate and be responsible for the enforcement of any Federal security zone established by the Coast Guard around a vessel containing especially hazardous cargo. The Coast Guard shall allocate available resources so as to deter and respond to a transportation security incident, to the maximum extent practicable, and to protect lives or protect property in danger.

(2) ESPECIALLY HAZARDOUS CARGO DEFINED.—In this subsection, the term "especially hazardous cargo" means anhydrous ammonia, ammonium nitrate, chlorine, liquefied natural gas, liquefied petroleum gas, and any other substance, material, or group or class of material, in a particular amount and form that the Secretary determines by

regulation poses a significant risk of creating a transportation security incident while being transported in maritime commerce.

(f) Nondisclosure of Port Security Plans.—Notwithstanding any other provision of law, information related to security plans, procedures, or programs for passenger vessels or passenger terminals authorized under this chapter is not required to be disclosed to the public.

(Added Pub. L. 107–295, title I, §102(a), Nov. 25, 2002, 116 Stat. 2069; amended Pub. L. 108–458, title IV, §4072(a), Dec. 17, 2004, 118 Stat. 3730; Pub. L. 109–347, title I, §§101–103, 113(c), Oct. 13, 2006, 120 Stat. 1887, 1888, 1896; Pub. L. 111–83, title V, §561(b), Oct. 28, 2009, 123 Stat. 2182; Pub. L. 111–281, title VIII, §§812(c), 826, Oct. 15, 2010, 124 Stat. 2997, 3004; Pub. L. 115–254, div. J, §§1805(d)(2), 1806, Oct. 5, 2018, 132 Stat. 3535, 3536; Pub. L. 115–282, title IV, §§402(c), 408(d), Dec. 4, 2018, 132 Stat. 4264, 4268; Pub. L. 116–283, div. G, title LVXXXII [LXXXII], §8240(a), title LVXXXIII [LXXXIII], §8344, title LVXXXV [LXXXV], §8507(d)(1), Jan. 1, 2021, 134 Stat. 4666, 4710, 4754.)

§70104. Transportation security incident response

(a) Facility and Vessel Response Plans.—The Secretary shall—

(1) establish security incident response plans for vessels and facilities that may be involved in a transportation security incident; and

(2) make those plans available to the Administrator of the Federal Emergency Management Agency for inclusion in the Administrator's response plan for United States ports and waterways.

(b) Contents.—Response plans developed under subsection (a) shall provide a comprehensive response to an emergency, including notifying and coordinating with local, State, and Federal authorities, including the Administrator of the Federal Emergency Management Agency, securing the facility or vessel, and evacuating facility and vessel personnel.

(c) Inclusion in Security Plan.—A response plan required under this subsection for a vessel or facility may be included in the security plan prepared under section 70103(c).

(Added Pub. L. 107–295, title I, §102(a), Nov. 25, 2002, 116 Stat. 2072; amended Pub. L. 109–295, title VI, §612(c), Oct. 4, 2006, 120 Stat. 1410.)

§70105. Transportation worker identification credentials

(a) Prohibition.—(1) The Secretary shall prescribe regulations to prevent an individual from entering an area of a vessel or facility that is designated as a secure area by the Secretary for purposes of a security plan for the vessel or facility that is approved by the Secretary under section 70103 of this title unless the individual—

(A) holds a transportation worker identification credential issued under this section and is authorized to be in the area in accordance with the plan; or

(B) is accompanied by another individual who holds a transportation worker identification credential issued under this section and is authorized to be in the area in accordance with the plan.

(2) A person shall not admit an individual into such a secure area unless the entry of the

individual into the area is in compliance with paragraph (1).

(b) ISSUANCE OF CREDENTIALS.—(1) The Secretary shall issue a biometric transportation worker identification credential to an individual specified in paragraph (2), unless the Secretary determines under subsection (c) that the individual poses a security risk warranting denial of the credential.

(2) This subsection applies to—

(A) an individual allowed unescorted access to a secure area designated in a vessel or facility security plan approved under section 70103 of this title;

(B) an individual issued a license, certificate of registry, or merchant mariners document under part E of subtitle II of this title allowed unescorted access to a secure area designated in a vessel security plan approved under section 70103 of this title;

(C) a vessel pilot;

(D) an individual engaged on a towing vessel that pushes, pulls, or hauls alongside a tank vessel allowed unescorted access to a secure area designated in a vessel security plan approved under section 70103 of this title;

(E) an individual with access to security sensitive information as determined by the Secretary;

(F) other individuals engaged in port security activities as determined by the Secretary;

(G) a member of the Armed Forces who—

(i) is undergoing separation, discharge, or release from the Armed Forces under honorable conditions;

(ii) applies for a transportation worker identification credential; and

(iii) is otherwise eligible for such a credential; and

(H) other individuals as determined appropriate by the Secretary including individuals employed at a port not otherwise covered by this subsection.

(3) The Secretary may extend for up to one year the expiration of a biometric transportation worker identification credential required by this section to align the expiration with the expiration of a license, certificate of registry, or merchant mariner document required under chapter 71 or 73.

(c) DETERMINATION OF TERRORISM SECURITY RISK.—

(1) DISQUALIFICATIONS.—

(A) PERMANENT DISQUALIFYING CRIMINAL OFFENSES.—Except as provided under paragraph (2), an individual is permanently disqualified from being issued a biometric transportation worker identification credential under subsection (b) if the individual has been convicted, or found not guilty by reason of insanity, in a civilian or military jurisdiction of any of the following felonies:

(i) Espionage or conspiracy to commit espionage.

(ii) Sedition or conspiracy to commit sedition.

(iii) Treason or conspiracy to commit treason.

(iv) A Federal crime of terrorism (as defined in section 2332b(g) of title 18), a crime under a comparable State law, or conspiracy to commit such crime.

(v) A crime involving a transportation security incident.

(vi) Improper transportation of a hazardous material in violation of section

5104(b) of title 49, or a comparable State law.

(vii) Unlawful possession, use, sale, distribution, manufacture, purchase, receipt, transfer, shipment, transportation, delivery, import, export, or storage of, or dealing in, an explosive or explosive device. In this clause, an explosive or explosive device includes—

(I) an explosive (as defined in sections 232(5) and 844(j) of title 18);

(II) explosive materials (as defined in subsections (c) through (f) of section 841 of title 18); and

(III) a destructive device (as defined in 921(a)(4) of title 18 or section 5845(f) of the Internal Revenue Code of 1986).

(viii) Murder.

(ix) Making any threat, or maliciously conveying false information knowing the same to be false, concerning the deliverance, placement, or detonation of an explosive or other lethal device in or against a place of public use, a State or other government facility, a public transportation system, or an infrastructure facility.

(x) A violation of chapter 96 of title 18, popularly known as the Racketeer Influenced and Corrupt Organizations Act, or a comparable State law, if one of the predicate acts found by a jury or admitted by the defendant consists of one of the crimes listed in this subparagraph.

(xi) Attempt to commit any of the crimes listed in clauses (i) through (iv).

(xii) Conspiracy or attempt to commit any of the crimes described in clauses (v) through (x).

(B) INTERIM DISQUALIFYING CRIMINAL OFFENSES.—Except as provided under paragraph (2), an individual is disqualified from being issued a biometric transportation worker identification credential under subsection (b) if the individual has been convicted, or found not guilty by reason of insanity, during the 7-year period ending on the date on which the individual applies for such credential, or was released from incarceration during the 5-year period ending on the date on which the individual applies for such credential, of any of the following felonies:

(i) Unlawful possession, use, sale, manufacture, purchase, distribution, receipt, transfer, shipment, transportation, delivery, import, export, or storage of, or dealing in, a firearm or other weapon. In this clause, a firearm or other weapon includes—

(I) firearms (as defined in section 921(a)(3) of title 18 or section 5845(a) of the Internal Revenue Code of 1986); and

(II) items contained on the U.S. Munitions Import List under section 447.21 of title 27, Code of Federal Regulations.

(ii) Extortion.

(iii) Dishonesty, fraud, or misrepresentation, including identity fraud and money laundering if the money laundering is related to a crime described in this subparagraph or subparagraph (A). In this clause, welfare fraud and passing bad checks do not constitute dishonesty, fraud, or misrepresentation.

(iv) Bribery.

(v) Smuggling.

(vi) Immigration violations.

(vii) Distribution of, possession with intent to distribute, or importation of a controlled substance.

(viii) Arson.

(ix) Kidnaping or hostage taking.

(x) Rape or aggravated sexual abuse.

(xi) Assault with intent to kill.

(xii) Robbery.

(xiii) Conspiracy or attempt to commit any of the crimes listed in this subparagraph.

(xiv) Fraudulent entry into a seaport in violation of section 1036 of title 18, or a comparable State law.

(xv) A violation of the chapter 96 of title 18 (popularly known as the Racketeer Influenced and Corrupt Organizations Act) or a comparable State law, other than any of the violations listed in subparagraph (A)(x).

(C) UNDER WANT, WARRANT, OR INDICTMENT.—An applicant who is wanted, or under indictment, in any civilian or military jurisdiction for a felony listed in paragraph (1)(A), is disqualified from being issued a biometric transportation worker identification credential under subsection (b) until the want or warrant is released or the indictment is dismissed.

(D) OTHER POTENTIAL DISQUALIFICATIONS.—Except as provided under subparagraphs (A) through (C), an individual may not be denied a transportation worker identification credential under subsection (b) unless the Secretary determines that individual—

(i) has been convicted within the preceding 7-year period of a felony or found not guilty by reason of insanity of a felony—

(I) that the Secretary believes could cause the individual to be a terrorism security risk to the United States; or

(II) for causing a severe transportation security incident;

(ii) has been released from incarceration within the preceding 5-year period for committing a felony described in clause (i);

(iii) may be denied admission to the United States or removed from the United States under the Immigration and Nationality Act (8 U.S.C. 1101 et seq.); or

(iv) otherwise poses a terrorism security risk to the United States.

(E) MODIFICATION OF LISTED OFFENSES.—The Secretary may, by rulemaking, add to or modify the list of disqualifying crimes described in paragraph (1)(B).

(2) The Secretary shall prescribe regulations that establish a waiver process for issuing a transportation worker identification credential to an individual found to be otherwise ineligible for such a credential under subparagraph (A), (B), or (D) of paragraph (1). In deciding to issue a credential to such an individual, the Secretary shall—

(A) give consideration to the circumstances of any disqualifying act or offense, restitution made by the individual, Federal and State mitigation remedies, and other factors from which it may be concluded that the individual does not pose a terrorism risk warranting denial of the credential; and

(B) issue a waiver to an individual without regard to whether that individual would otherwise be disqualified if the individual's employer establishes alternate security arrangements acceptable to the Secretary.

(3) DENIAL OF WAIVER REVIEW.—

(A) IN GENERAL.—The Secretary shall establish a review process before an administrative law judge for individuals denied a waiver under paragraph (2).

(B) SCOPE OF REVIEW.—In conducting a review under the process established pursuant to subparagraph (A), the administrative law judge shall be governed by the standards of section 706 of title 5. The substantial evidence standard in section 706(2)(E) of title 5 shall apply whether or not there has been an agency hearing. The judge shall review all facts on the record of the agency.

(C) CLASSIFIED EVIDENCE.—The Secretary, in consultation with the Director of National Intelligence, shall issue regulations to establish procedures by which the Secretary, as part of a review conducted under this paragraph, may provide to the individual adversely affected by the determination an unclassified summary of classified evidence upon which the denial of a waiver by the Secretary was based.

(D) REVIEW OF CLASSIFIED EVIDENCE BY ADMINISTRATIVE LAW JUDGE.—

(i) REVIEW.—As part of a review conducted under this section, if the decision of the Secretary was based on classified information (as defined in section 1(a) of the Classified Information Procedures Act (18 U.S.C. App.)), such information may be submitted by the Secretary to the reviewing administrative law judge, pursuant to appropriate security procedures, and shall be reviewed by the administrative law judge ex parte and in camera.

(ii) SECURITY CLEARANCES.—Pursuant to existing procedures and requirements, the Secretary, in coordination (as necessary) with the heads of other affected departments or agencies, shall ensure that administrative law judges reviewing negative waiver decisions of the Secretary under this paragraph possess security clearances appropriate for such review.

(iii) UNCLASSIFIED SUMMARIES OF CLASSIFIED EVIDENCE.—As part of a review conducted under this paragraph and upon the request of the individual adversely affected by the decision of the Secretary not to grant a waiver, the Secretary shall provide to the individual and reviewing administrative law judge, consistent with the procedures established under clause (i), an unclassified summary of any classified information upon which the decision of the Secretary was based.

(E) NEW EVIDENCE.—The Secretary shall establish a process under which an individual may submit a new request for a waiver, notwithstanding confirmation by the administrative law judge of the Secretary's initial denial of the waiver, if the request is supported by substantial evidence that was not available to the Secretary at the time the initial waiver request was denied.

(4) The Secretary shall establish an appeals process under this section for individuals found to be ineligible for a transportation worker identification credential that includes notice and an opportunity for a hearing.

(5) Upon application, the Secretary may issue a transportation worker identification credential to an individual if the Secretary has previously determined, under section 5103a of title 49, that the individual does not pose a security risk.

(d) BACKGROUND RECORDS CHECK.—(1) On request of the Secretary, the Attorney General shall—

(A) conduct a background records check regarding the individual; and

(B) upon completing the background records check, notify the Secretary of the completion and results of the background records check.

(2) A background records check regarding an individual under this subsection shall consist of the following:

(A) A check of the relevant criminal history databases.

(B) In the case of an alien, a check of the relevant databases to determine the status of the alien under the immigration laws of the United States.

(C) As appropriate, a check of the relevant international databases or other appropriate means.

(D) Review of any other national security-related information or database identified by the Attorney General for purposes of such a background records check.

(e) RESTRICTIONS ON USE AND MAINTENANCE OF INFORMATION.—(1) Information obtained by the Attorney General or the Secretary under this section may not be made available to the public, including the individual's employer.

(2) Any information constituting grounds for denial of a transportation worker identification credential under this section shall be maintained confidentially by the Secretary and may be used only for making determinations under this section. The Secretary may share any such information with other Federal law enforcement agencies. An individual's employer may only be informed of whether or not the individual has been issued the credential under this section.

(f) DEFINITION.—In this section, the term "alien" has the meaning given the term in section 101(a)(3) of the Immigration and Nationality Act (8 U.S.C. 1101(a)(3)).

(g) APPLICATIONS FOR MERCHANT MARINERS' DOCUMENTS.—The Administrator of the Transportation Security Administration and the Commandant of the Coast Guard shall—

(1) develop and, no later than 2 years after the date of enactment of the Elijah E. Cummings Coast Guard Authorization Act of 2020, implement a joint application for merchant mariner's documents under chapter 73 and for a transportation worker identification credential issued under this section; and

(2) upon receipt of a joint application developed under paragraph (1) concurrently process an application from an individual for merchant mariner's documents under chapter 73 and an application from such individual for a transportation worker identification credential under this section.

(h) FEES.—The Secretary shall ensure that the fees charged each individual applying for a transportation worker identification credential under this section who has passed a background check under section 5103a(d) of title 49, United States Code, and who has a current hazardous materials endorsement in accordance with section 1572 of title 49, Code of Federal Regulations, and each individual with a current merchant mariners' document who has passed a criminal background check under section 7302(d)—

(1) are for costs associated with the issuance, production, and management of the transportation worker identification credential, as determined by the Secretary; and

(2) do not include costs associated with performing a background check for that individual, except for any incremental costs in the event that the scope of such background checks diverge.

(i) PRIORITY PROCESSING FOR SEPARATING SERVICE MEMBERS.—(1) The Secretary and the Secretary of Defense shall enter into a memorandum of understanding regarding the submission and processing of applications for transportation worker identification credentials under subsection (b)(2)(G).

(2) Not later than 30 days after the submission of such an application by an individual who is eligible to submit such an application, the Secretary shall process and approve or deny the application unless an appeal or waiver applies or further application documentation is necessary.

(j) DEPLOYMENT OF TRANSPORTATION WORKER IDENTIFICATION CREDENTIAL READERS.—

(1) PILOT PROGRAM.—

(A) IN GENERAL.—The Secretary shall conduct a pilot program to test the business processes, technology, and operational impacts required to deploy transportation worker identification credential readers at secure areas of the marine transportation system.

(B) GEOGRAPHIC LOCATIONS.—The pilot program shall take place at not fewer than 5 distinct geographic locations, to include vessels and facilities in a variety of environmental settings.

(C) COMMENCEMENT.—The pilot program shall commence not later than 180 days after the date of the enactment of the SAFE Port Act.

(2) CORRELATION WITH WORKER IDENTIFICATION CREDENTIAL.—

(A) IN GENERAL.—The pilot program described in paragraph (1) shall be conducted concurrently with the issuance of the transportation worker identification credentials described in subsection (b) to ensure credential and credential reader interoperability.

(B) FEE.—An individual charged a fee for a transportation worker identification credential issued under this section may not be charged an additional fee if the Secretary determines different transportation worker identification credentials are needed based on the results of the pilot program described in paragraph (1) or for other reasons related to the technology requirements for the transportation worker identification credential program.

(3) REGULATIONS.—Not later than 2 years after the commencement of the pilot

program under paragraph (1)(C), the Secretary, after a notice and comment period that includes at least 1 public hearing, shall promulgate final regulations that require the deployment of transportation worker identification credential readers that are consistent with the findings of the pilot program and build upon the regulations prescribed under subsection (a).

(k) LIMITATION.—The Secretary may not require the placement of an electronic reader for transportation worker identification credentials on a vessel unless—

(1) the vessel has more individuals on the crew that are required to have a transportation worker identification credential than the number the Secretary determines, by regulation issued under subsection (j)(3), warrants such a reader; or

(2) the Secretary determines that the vessel is at risk of a severe transportation security incident.

(l) The Secretary may use a secondary authentication system to verify the identification of individuals using transportation worker identification credentials when the individual's fingerprints are not able to be taken or read.

(m) ESCORTING.—The Secretary shall coordinate with owners and operators subject to this section to allow any individual who has a pending application for a transportation worker identification credential under this section or is waiting for reissuance of such credential, including any individual whose credential has been lost or stolen, and who needs to perform work in a secure or restricted area to have access to such area for that purpose through escorting of such individual in accordance with subsection (a)(1)(B) by another individual who holds a transportation worker identification credential. Nothing in this subsection shall be construed as requiring or compelling an owner or operator to provide escorted access.

(n) PROCESSING TIME.—The Secretary shall review an initial transportation worker identification credential application and respond to the applicant, as appropriate, including the mailing of an Initial Determination of Threat Assessment letter, within 30 days after receipt of the initial application. The Secretary shall, to the greatest extent practicable, review appeal and waiver requests submitted by a transportation worker identification credential applicant, and send a written decision or request for additional information required for the appeal or waiver determination, within 30 days after receipt of the applicant's appeal or waiver written request. For an applicant that is required to submit additional information for an appeal or waiver determination, the Secretary shall send a written decision, to the greatest extent practicable, within 30 days after receipt of all requested information.

(o) RECEIPT AND ACTIVATION OF TRANSPORTATION WORKER IDENTIFICATION CREDENTIAL.—

(1) IN GENERAL.—Not later than one year after the date of publication of final regulations required by subsection (j)(3) of this section the Secretary shall develop a plan to permit the receipt and activation of transportation worker identification credentials at any vessel or facility described in subsection (a) of this section that desires to implement this capability. Such receipt and activation shall comply, to the extent possible, with all appropriate requirements of Federal standards for personal identity verification and

credential.

(2) LIMITATION.—The Secretary may not require any such vessel or facility to provide on-site receipt and activation of transportation worker identification credentials.

(Added Pub. L. 107–295, title I, §102(a), Nov. 25, 2002, 116 Stat. 2073; amended Pub. L. 109–241, title III, §309, July 11, 2006, 120 Stat. 528; Pub. L. 109–347, title I, §104(a), (b), Oct. 13, 2006, 120 Stat. 1888, 1890; Pub. L. 110–53, title XIII, §1309(a), Aug. 3, 2007, 121 Stat. 397; Pub. L. 111–281, title VIII, §§809, 814, 818(a), 819, 823, title IX, §903(c)(2), Oct. 15, 2010, 124 Stat. 2995, 2999–3001, 3003, 3011; Pub. L. 111–330, §1(13), Dec. 22, 2010, 124 Stat. 3570; Pub. L. 114–120, title III, §306(a)(9), Feb. 8, 2016, 130 Stat. 54; Pub. L. 114–328, div. C, title XXXV, §3509(a), Dec. 23, 2016, 130 Stat. 2780; Pub. L. 116–283, div. G, title LVXXXIII [LXXXIII], §8346, Jan. 1, 2021, 134 Stat. 4718; Pub. L. 117–263, div. K, title CXVIII, §11804(a), Dec. 23, 2022, 136 Stat. 4163.)

§70106. DEPLOYABLE, SPECIALIZED FORCES

(a) ESTABLISHMENT.—

(1) IN GENERAL.—To enhance the domestic maritime security capability of the United States, the Secretary shall establish deployable specialized forces of varying capabilities as are needed to safeguard the public and protect vessels, harbors, ports, facilities, and cargo in waters subject to the jurisdiction of the United States from destruction, loss or injury from crime, or sabotage due to terrorist activity, and to respond to such activity in accordance with the transportation security plans developed under section 70103.

(2) ENHANCED TEAMS.—Such specialized forces shall include no less than two enhanced teams to serve as deployable forces capable of combating terrorism, engaging in interdiction, law enforcement, and advanced tactical maritime security operations to address known or potentially armed security threats (including non-compliant actors at sea), and participating in homeland security, homeland defense, and counterterrorism exercises in the maritime environment.

(b) MISSION.—The combined force of the specialized forces established under subsection (a) shall be trained, equipped, and capable of being deployed to—

(1) deter, protect against, and rapidly respond to threats of maritime terrorism;

(2) conduct maritime operations to protect against and disrupt illegal use, access to, or proliferation of weapons of mass destruction;

(3) enforce moving or fixed safety or security zones established pursuant to law;

(4) conduct high speed intercepts;

(5) board, search, and seize any article or thing on or at, respectively, a vessel or facility found to present a risk to the vessel or facility, or to a port;

(6) rapidly deploy to supplement United States armed forces domestically or overseas;

(7) respond to criminal or terrorist acts so as to minimize, insofar as possible, the disruption caused by such acts;

(8) assist with facility vulnerability assessments required under this chapter; and

(9) carry out any other missions of the Coast Guard as are assigned to it by the Secretary.

(c) MINIMIZATION OF RESPONSE TIMES.—The enhanced teams established under subsection (a)(2) shall, to the extent practicable, be stationed in such a way so as to minimize the response time to maritime terrorist threats and potential or actual transportation security incidents.

(d) COORDINATION WITH OTHER AGENCIES.—To the maximum extent feasible, the combined force of the specialized forces established under subsection (a) shall coordinate their activities with other Federal, State, and local law enforcement and emergency response agencies.

(Added Pub. L. 107–295, title I, §102(a), Nov. 25, 2002, 116 Stat. 2074; amended Pub. L. 109–241, title III, §305, July 11, 2006, 120 Stat. 528; Pub. L. 111–281, title VIII, §804(a), Oct. 15, 2010, 124 Stat. 2990.)

§70107. GRANTS

(a) IN GENERAL.—The Secretary shall establish a grant program for the allocation of funds based on risk to implement Area Maritime Transportation Security Plans and facility security plans among port authorities, facility operators, and State and local government agencies required to provide port security services and to train public safety personnel under section 70132 of this title. Before awarding a grant under the program, the Secretary shall provide for review and comment by the appropriate Federal Maritime Security Coordinators and the Maritime Administrator. In administering the grant program, the Secretary shall take into account national economic, energy, and strategic defense concerns based upon the most current risk assessments available.

(b) ELIGIBLE COSTS.—The following costs of funding the correction of Coast Guard identified vulnerabilities in port security and ensuring compliance with Area Maritime Transportation Security Plans and facility security plans are eligible to be funded:

(1) Salary, benefits, overtime compensation, retirement contributions, and other costs of additional Coast Guard mandated security personnel.

(2) The cost of acquisition, operation, and maintenance of security equipment or facilities to be used for security monitoring and recording, security gates and fencing, marine barriers for designated security zones, security-related lighting systems, remote surveillance, concealed video systems, security vessels, and other security-related infrastructure or equipment that contributes to the overall security of passengers, cargo, or crewmembers. Grants awarded under this section may not be used to construct buildings or other physical facilities, except those which are constructed under terms and conditions consistent with the requirements under section 611(j)(8) of the Robert T. Stafford Disaster Relief and Emergency Assistance Act (42 U.S.C. 5196(j)(8)), including those facilities in support of this paragraph, and specifically approved by the Secretary. Costs eligible for funding under this paragraph may not exceed the greater of—

(A) $1,000,000 per project; or

(B) such greater amount as may be approved by the Secretary, which may not exceed 10 percent of the total amount of the grant.

(3) The cost of screening equipment, including equipment that detects weapons of mass destruction and conventional explosives, and of testing and evaluating such equipment, to certify secure systems of transportation.

(4) The cost of conducting vulnerability assessments to evaluate and make recommendations with respect to security.

(5) The cost of conducting exercises or training for prevention and detection of, preparedness for, response to, or recovery from terrorist attacks.

(6) The cost of establishing or enhancing mechanisms for sharing terrorism threat information and ensuring that the mechanisms are interoperable with Federal, State, and local agencies.

(7) The cost of equipment (including software) required to receive, transmit, handle, and store classified information.

(8) The cost of training public safety personnel—

    (A) to enforce a security zone under section 70132 of this title; or

    (B) assist in the enforcement of a security zone.

(c) MATCHING REQUIREMENTS.—

(1) 75-PERCENT FEDERAL FUNDING.—Except as provided in paragraph (2), Federal funds for any eligible project under this section shall not exceed 75 percent of the total cost of such project.

(2) EXCEPTIONS.—

    (A) SMALL PROJECTS.—There are no matching requirements for grants under subsection (a) for projects costing not more than $25,000.

    (B) HIGHER LEVEL OF SUPPORT REQUIRED.—If the Secretary determines that a proposed project merits support and cannot be undertaken without a higher rate of Federal support, then the Secretary may approve grants under this section with a matching requirement other than that specified in paragraph (1).

    (C) TRAINING.—There are no matching requirements for grants under subsection (a) to train public safety personnel in the enforcement of security zones under section 70132 of this title or in assisting in the enforcement of such security zones.

(d) COORDINATION AND COOPERATION AGREEMENTS.—The Secretary shall ensure that projects paid for, or the costs of which are reimbursed, under this section within any area or port are coordinated with other projects, and may require cooperative agreements among users of the port and port facilities with respect to projects funded under this section.

(e) MULTIPLE-YEAR PROJECTS.—

(1) LETTERS OF INTENT.—The Secretary may execute letters of intent to commit funding to such authorities, operators, and agencies.

(2) LIMITATION.—Not more than 20 percent of the grant funds awarded under this subsection in any fiscal year may be awarded for projects that span multiple years.

(f) CONSISTENCY WITH PLANS.—The Secretary shall ensure that each grant awarded under subsection (e)—

(1) is used to supplement and support, in a consistent and coordinated manner, the applicable Area Maritime Transportation Security Plan; and

(2) is coordinated with any applicable State or Urban Area Homeland Security Plan.

(g) APPLICATIONS.—Any entity subject to an Area Maritime Transportation Security Plan may submit an application for a grant under this section, at such time, in such form, and containing such information and assurances as the Secretary may require.

(h) REPORTS.—Not later than 180 days after the date of the enactment of the SAFE Port Act, the Secretary, acting through the Commandant of the Coast Guard, shall submit a report to Congress, in a secure format, describing the methodology used to allocate port security grant funds on the basis of risk.

(i) ADMINISTRATION.—

(1) IN GENERAL.—The Secretary shall require eligible port authorities, facility operators, and State and local agencies required to provide security services, to submit an application, at such time, in such form, and containing such information and assurances as the Secretary may require, and shall include appropriate application, review, and delivery mechanisms.

(2) MINIMUM STANDARDS FOR PAYMENT OR REIMBURSEMENT.—Each application for payment or reimbursement of eligible costs shall include, at a minimum, the following:

(A) A copy of the applicable Area Maritime Transportation Security Plan or facility security plan.

(B) A comprehensive description of the need for the project, and a statement of the project's relationship to the applicable Area Maritime Transportation Security Plan or facility security plan.

(C) A determination by the Captain of the Port that the security project addresses or corrects Coast Guard identified vulnerabilities in security and ensures compliance with Area Maritime Transportation Security Plans and facility security plans.

(3) PROCEDURAL SAFEGUARDS.—The Secretary shall by regulation establish appropriate accounting, reporting, and review procedures to ensure that amounts paid or reimbursed under this section are used for the purposes for which they were made available, all expenditures are properly accounted for, and amounts not used for such purposes and amounts not obligated or expended are recovered.

(4) PROJECT APPROVAL REQUIRED.—The Secretary may approve an application for the payment or reimbursement of costs under this section only if the Secretary is satisfied that—

(A) the project is consistent with Coast Guard vulnerability assessments and ensures compliance with Area Maritime Transportation Security Plans and facility security plans;

(B) enough money is available to pay the project costs that will not be reimbursed by the United States Government under this section;

(C) the project will be completed without unreasonable delay; and

(D) the recipient has authority to carry out the project as proposed.

(j) AUDITS AND EXAMINATIONS.—A recipient of amounts made available under this section shall keep such records as the Secretary may require, and make them available for review and audit by the Secretary, the Comptroller General of the United States, or the Inspector General of the department in which the Coast Guard is operating.

(k) REPORTS ON SECURITY FUNDING AND COMPLIANCE.—

(1) INITIAL REPORT.—Within 6 months after the date of enactment of this Act, the Secretary shall transmit an unclassified report to the Senate Committee on Commerce, Science, and Transportation and the House of Representatives Committee on

Transportation and Infrastructure, that—

(A) includes a funding proposal and rationale to fund the correction of Coast Guard identified vulnerabilities in port security and to help ensure compliance with Area Maritime Transportation Security Plans and facility security plans for fiscal years 2003 through 2008; and

(B) includes projected funding proposals for fiscal years 2003 through 2008 for the following security programs:

(i) The Sea Marshall program.

(ii) The Automated Identification System and a system of polling vessels on entry into United States waters.

(iii) The maritime intelligence requirements in this Act.

(iv) The issuance of transportation security cards required by section 70105.

(v) The program of certifying secure systems of transportation.

(2) OTHER EXPENDITURES.—The Secretary shall, as part of the report required by paragraph (1) report, in coordination with the Commissioner of Customs, on projected expenditures of screening and detection equipment and on cargo security programs over fiscal years 2003 through 2008.

(3) ANNUAL REPORTS.—Annually, beginning 1 year after transmittal of the report required by paragraph (1) until October 1, 2009, the Secretary shall transmit an unclassified annual report to the Senate Committee on Commerce, Science, and Transportation and the House of Representatives Committee on Transportation and Infrastructure, on progress in achieving compliance with the correction of Coast Guard identified vulnerabilities in port security and compliance with Area Maritime Transportation Security Plans and facility security plans that—

(A) identifies any modifications necessary in funding to ensure the correction of Coast Guard identified vulnerabilities and ensure compliance with Area Maritime Transportation Security Plans and facility security plans;

(B) includes an assessment of progress in implementing the grant program established by subsection (a);

(C) includes any recommendations the Secretary may make to improve these programs; and

(D) with respect to a port selected by the Secretary, describes progress and enhancements of applicable Area Maritime Transportation Security Plans and facility security plans and how the Maritime Transportation Security Act of 2002 has improved security at that port.

(l) AUTHORIZATION OF APPROPRIATIONS.—There are authorized to be appropriated $400,000,000 for each of the fiscal years 2007 through 2013 to carry out this section.

(m) INVESTIGATIONS.—

(1) IN GENERAL.—The Secretary shall conduct investigations, fund pilot programs, and award grants, to examine or develop—

(A) methods or programs to increase the ability to target for inspection vessels, cargo, crewmembers, or passengers that will arrive or have arrived at any port or place in the United States;

(B) equipment to detect accurately explosives, chemical, or biological agents that could be used in a transportation security incident against the United States;

(C) equipment to detect accurately nuclear or radiological materials, including scintillation-based detection equipment capable of signalling the presence of nuclear or radiological materials;

(D) improved tags and seals designed for use on shipping containers to track the transportation of the merchandise in such containers, including sensors that are able to track a container throughout its entire supply chain, detect hazardous and radioactive materials within that container, and transmit that information to the appropriate law enforcement authorities;

(E) tools, including the use of satellite tracking systems, to increase the awareness of maritime areas and to identify potential transportation security incidents that could have an impact on facilities, vessels, and infrastructure on or adjacent to navigable waterways, including underwater access;

(F) tools to mitigate the consequences of a transportation security incident on, adjacent to, or under navigable waters of the United States, including sensor equipment, and other tools to help coordinate effective response to a transportation security incident;

(G) applications to apply existing technologies from other areas or industries to increase overall port security;

(H) improved container design, including blast-resistant containers; and

(I) methods to improve security and sustainability of port facilities in the event of a maritime transportation security incident, including specialized inspection facilities.

(2) IMPLEMENTATION OF TECHNOLOGY.—

(A) IN GENERAL.—In conjunction with ongoing efforts to improve security at United States ports, the Secretary may conduct pilot projects at United States ports to test the effectiveness and applicability of new port security projects, including—

(i) testing of new detection and screening technologies;

(ii) projects to protect United States ports and infrastructure on or adjacent to the navigable waters of the United States, including underwater access; and

(iii) tools for responding to a transportation security incident at United States ports and infrastructure on or adjacent to the navigable waters of the United States, including underwater access.

(B) AUTHORIZATION OF APPROPRIATIONS.—There is authorized to be appropriated to the Secretary $35,000,000 for each of fiscal years 2005 through 2009 to carry out this subsection.

(3) NATIONAL PORT SECURITY CENTERS.—

(A) IN GENERAL.—The Secretary may make grants or enter into cooperative agreements with eligible nonprofit institutions of higher learning to conduct investigations in collaboration with ports and the maritime transportation industry focused on enhancing security of the Nation's ports in accordance with this subsection through National Port Security Centers.

(B) APPLICATIONS.—To be eligible to receive a grant under this paragraph, a nonprofit institution of higher learning, or a consortium of such institutions, shall submit an application to the Secretary in such form and containing such information as the Secretary may require.

(C) COMPETITIVE SELECTION PROCESS.—The Secretary shall select grant recipients under this paragraph through a competitive process on the basis of the following criteria:

(i) Whether the applicant can demonstrate that personnel, laboratory, and organizational resources will be available to the applicant to carry out the investigations authorized in this paragraph.

(ii) The applicant's capability to provide leadership in making national and regional contributions to the solution of immediate and long-range port and maritime transportation security and risk mitigation problems.

(iii) Whether the applicant can demonstrate that the applicant has an established, nationally recognized program in disciplines that contribute directly to maritime transportation safety and education.

(iv) Whether the applicant's investigations will involve major United States ports on the East Coast, the Gulf Coast, and the West Coast, and Federal agencies and other entities with expertise in port and maritime transportation.

(v) Whether the applicant has a strategic plan for carrying out the proposed investigations under the grant.

(4) ADMINISTRATIVE PROVISIONS.—

(A) NO DUPLICATION OF EFFORT.—Before making any grant, the Secretary shall coordinate with other Federal agencies to ensure the grant will not duplicate work already being conducted with Federal funding.

(B) ACCOUNTING.—The Secretary shall by regulation establish accounting, reporting, and review procedures to ensure that funds made available under paragraph (1) are used for the purpose for which they were made available, that all expenditures are properly accounted for, and that amounts not used for such purposes and amounts not expended are recovered.

(C) RECORDKEEPING.—Recipients of grants shall keep all records related to expenditures and obligations of funds provided under paragraph (1) and make them available upon request to the Inspector General of the department in which the Coast Guard is operating and the Secretary for audit and examination.

(5) ANNUAL REVIEW AND REPORT.—The Inspector General of the department in which the Coast Guard is operating shall annually review the programs established under this subsection to ensure that the expenditures and obligations of funds are consistent with the purposes for which they are provided, and report the findings to the Committee on Commerce, Science, and Transportation of the Senate and the Committee on Transportation and Infrastructure of the House of Representatives.

(Added Pub. L. 107–295, title I, §102(a), Nov. 25, 2002, 116 Stat. 2075; amended Pub. L. 108–293, title VIII, §§804(a), (b), 808(a), Aug. 9, 2004, 118 Stat. 1081, 1083; Pub. L. 109–347, title I, §112, Oct. 13, 2006, 120 Stat. 1894; Pub. L. 111–281, title VIII, §828(b), Oct. 15, 2010, 124 Stat. 3007; Pub. L. 114–120, title

[§70107A. Repealed. Pub. L. 115–254, div. J,
§1809(a)(1), Oct. 5, 2018, 132 Stat. 3537]

CHAPTER 701—PORT SECURITY

III, §306(a)(10), Feb. 8, 2016, 130 Stat. 54; Pub. L. 116–283, div. G, title LVXXXIII [LXXXIII], §8314(1), Jan. 1, 2021, 134 Stat. 4699.)

[§70107A. Repealed. Pub. L. 115–254, div. J, §1809(a)(1), Oct. 5, 2018, 132 Stat. 3537]

Section, added Pub. L. 109–347, title I, §108(a), Oct. 13, 2006, 120 Stat. 1892; amended Pub. L. 111–281, title VIII, §§803, 824, Oct. 15, 2010, 124 Stat. 2990, 3003, related to interagency operational centers for port security.

§70108. Foreign port assessment

(a) In General.—The Secretary shall assess the effectiveness of the antiterrorism measures maintained at—

(1) a foreign port—

(A) served by vessels documented under chapter 121 of this title; or

(B) from which foreign vessels depart on a voyage to the United States; and

(2) any other foreign port the Secretary believes poses a security risk to international maritime commerce.

(b) Procedures.—In conducting an assessment under subsection (a), the Secretary shall assess the effectiveness of—

(1) screening of containerized and other cargo and baggage;

(2) security measures to restrict access to cargo, vessels, and dockside property to authorized personnel only;

(3) additional security on board vessels;

(4) licensing or certification of compliance with appropriate security standards;

(5) the security management program of the foreign port; and

(6) other appropriate measures to deter terrorism against the United States.

(c) Consultation.—In carrying out this section, the Secretary shall consult with—

(1) the Secretary of Defense and the Secretary of State—

(A) on the terrorist threat that exists in each country involved; and

(B) to identify foreign ports that pose a high risk of introducing terrorism to international maritime commerce;

(2) appropriate authorities of foreign governments; and

(3) operators of vessels.

(d) Periodic Reassessment.—The Secretary, acting through the Commandant of the Coast Guard, shall reassess the effectiveness of antiterrorism measures maintained at ports as described under subsection (a) and of procedures described in subsection (b) not less than once every 3 years.

(e) Limitation on Statutory Construction.—The absence of an inspection of a foreign port shall not bar the Secretary from making a finding that a port in a foreign country does not maintain effective antiterrorism measures.

(f) RECOGNITION OF ASSESSMENT CONDUCTED BY OTHER ENTITIES.—

(1) CERTIFICATION AND TREATMENT OF ASSESSMENTS.—For the purposes of this section and section 70109, the Secretary may treat an assessment that a foreign government (including, for the purposes of this subsection, an entity of or operating under the auspices of the European Union) or international organization has conducted as an assessment that the Secretary has conducted for the purposes of subsection (a), if—

(A) the Secretary certifies that the foreign government or international organization—

(i) has conducted the assessment in accordance with subsection (b); and

(ii) has provided the Secretary with sufficient information pertaining to its assessment (including information regarding the outcome of the assessment); and

(B) the foreign government that conducted the assessment is not a state sponsor of terrorism (as defined in section 3316(h)).

(2) AUTHORIZATION TO ENTER INTO AN AGREEMENT.—For the purposes of this section and section 70109, the Secretary, in consultation with the Secretary of State, may enter into an agreement with a foreign government (including, for the purposes of this subsection, an entity of or operating under the auspices of the European Union) or international organization, under which parties to the agreement—

(A) conduct an assessment, required under subsection (a);

(B) share information pertaining to such assessment (including, but not limited to, information on the outcome of the assessment); or

(C) both.

(3) LIMITATIONS.—Nothing in this section may be construed—

(A) to require the Secretary to treat an assessment conducted by a foreign government or an international organization as an assessment that satisfies the requirement under subsection (a);

(B) to limit the discretion or ability of the Secretary to conduct an assessment under this section;

(C) to limit the authority of the Secretary to repatriate aliens to their respective countries of origin; or

(D) to prevent the Secretary from requesting security and safety measures that the Secretary considers necessary to safeguard Coast Guard personnel during the repatriation of aliens to their respective countries of origin.

(4) NOTIFICATION TO CONGRESS.—Not later than 30 days before entering into an agreement or arrangement with a foreign government under paragraph (2), the Secretary shall notify the Committee on Homeland Security and the Committee on Transportation and Infrastructure of the House of Representatives and the Committee on Commerce, Science, and Transportation of the Senate of the proposed terms of such agreement or arrangement.

(g) STATE SPONSORS OF TERRORISM AND INTERNATIONAL TERRORIST ORGANIZATIONS.—The Secretary—

(1) may not enter into an agreement under subsection (f)(2) with—

(A) a foreign government that is a state sponsor of terrorism (as defined in section 3316(h)); or

(B) an entity designated by the Secretary of State as a foreign terrorist organization pursuant to section 219 of the Immigration and Nationality Act (8 U.S.C. 1189); and

(2) shall—

(A) deem any port that is under the jurisdiction of a foreign government that is a state sponsor of terrorism as not having effective antiterrorism measures for purposes of this section and section 70109; and

(B) immediately apply the sanctions described in section 70110(a) to such port.

(Added Pub. L. 107–295, title I, §102(a), Nov. 25, 2002, 116 Stat. 2079; amended Pub. L. 109–347, title II, §234, Oct. 13, 2006, 120 Stat. 1918; Pub. L. 111–281, title VIII, §806(a)(1), (c)(2)(B), Oct. 15, 2010, 124 Stat. 2992, 2993; Pub. L. 114–120, title III, §317, Feb. 8, 2016, 130 Stat. 62; Pub. L. 118–31, div. E, title LVI, §5603, Dec. 22, 2023, 137 Stat. 959.)

§70109. NOTIFYING FOREIGN AUTHORITIES

(a) IN GENERAL.—Unless the Secretary finds that a port in a foreign country maintains effective antiterrorism measures, the Secretary shall notify the appropriate authorities of the government of the foreign country of the finding and recommend the steps necessary to improve the antiterrorism measures in use at the port.

(b) TRAINING PROGRAM.—The Secretary, in cooperation with the Secretary of State, shall operate a port security training program for ports in foreign countries that are found under section 70108 to lack effective antiterrorism measures.

(Added Pub. L. 107–295, title I, §102(a), Nov. 25, 2002, 116 Stat. 2080; amended Pub. L. 111–281, title VIII, §806(a)(2), Oct. 15, 2010, 124 Stat. 2992.)

§70110. ACTIONS AND ASSISTANCE FOR FOREIGN PORTS OR FACILITIES AND UNITED STATES TERRITORIES

(a) IN GENERAL.—Unless the Secretary finds that a foreign port or facility maintains effective antiterrorism measures, the Secretary—

(1) may prescribe conditions of entry into the United States for any vessel arriving from that port or facility, or any vessel carrying cargo or passengers originating from or transshipped through that port or facility;

(2) may deny entry into the United States to any vessel that does not meet such conditions; and

(3) shall provide public notice for passengers of the ineffective antiterrorism measures.

(b) EFFECTIVE DATE FOR SANCTIONS.—Any action taken by the Secretary under subsection (a) for a particular port or facility shall take effect—

(1) 90 days after the government of the foreign country with jurisdiction over or control of that port or facility is notified under section 70109 unless the Secretary finds that the government has brought the antiterrorism measures at the port or facility up to the security level the Secretary used in making an assessment under section 70108 before the end of that 90-day period; or

(2) immediately upon the finding of the Secretary under subsection (a) if the Secretary finds, after consulting with the Secretary of State, that a condition exists that threatens the safety or security of passengers, vessels, or crew traveling to or from the port or facility.

(c) STATE DEPARTMENT TO BE NOTIFIED.—The Secretary immediately shall notify the Secretary of State of a finding that a port or facility does not maintain effective antiterrorism measures.

(d) ACTION CANCELED.—An action required under this section is no longer required if the Secretary decides that effective antiterrorism measures are maintained at the port or facility.

(e) ASSISTANCE FOR FOREIGN PORTS, FACILITIES, AND UNITED STATES TERRITORIES.—

(1) IN GENERAL.—The Secretary, in consultation with the Secretary of Transportation, the Secretary of State, and the Secretary of Energy, shall identify assistance programs that could facilitate implementation of port or facility security antiterrorism measures in foreign countries and territories of the United States. The Secretary shall establish a strategic plan to utilize those assistance programs to assist ports and facilities that are found by the Secretary under subsection (a) not to maintain effective antiterrorism measures in the implementation of port or facility security antiterrorism measures.

(2) CARIBBEAN BASIN.—The Secretary, in coordination with the Secretary of State and in consultation with the Organization of American States and the Commandant of the Coast Guard, shall place particular emphasis on utilizing programs to facilitate the implementation of port or facility security antiterrorism measures at the ports located in the Caribbean Basin, as such ports pose unique security and safety threats to the United States due to—

(A) the strategic location of such ports between South America and the United States;

(B) the relative openness of such ports; and

(C) the significant number of shipments of narcotics to the United States that are moved through such ports.

(f) COAST GUARD ASSISTANCE PROGRAM.—

(1) IN GENERAL.—The Secretary may lend, lease, donate, or otherwise provide equipment, and provide technical training and support, to the owner or operator of a foreign port or facility—

(A) to assist in bringing the port or facility into compliance with applicable International Ship and Port Facility Code standards; and

(B) to assist the port or facility in correcting deficiencies identified in periodic port assessments and reassessments required under section 70108 of this title.

(2) CONDITIONS.—The Secretary—

(A) may provide such assistance based upon an assessment of the risks to the security of the United States and the inability of the owner or operator of the port or facility to bring the port or facility into compliance with those standards and to maintain compliance with, or exceed, such standards;

(B) may not provide such assistance unless the port or facility has been subjected to a comprehensive port security assessment by the Coast Guard; and

(C) may only lend, lease, or otherwise provide equipment that the Secretary has first determined is not required by the Coast Guard for the performance of its missions.

(Added Pub. L. 107–295, title I, §102(a), Nov. 25, 2002, 116 Stat. 2080; amended Pub. L. 109–347, title II, §233(b), Oct. 13, 2006, 120 Stat. 1917; Pub. L. 111–281, title VIII, §806(a)(3)–(c)(2)(A), Oct. 15, 2010, 124 Stat. 2992, 2993; Pub. L. 111–330, §1(12), Dec. 22, 2010, 124 Stat. 3570.)

§70111. ENHANCED CREWMEMBER IDENTIFICATION

(a) REQUIREMENT.—Not later than 1 year after the date of enactment of the SAFE Port Act, the Secretary, in consultation with the Attorney General and the Secretary of State, shall require crewmembers on vessels calling at United States ports to carry and present on demand any identification that the Secretary decides is necessary.

(b) FORMS AND PROCESS.—Not later than 1 year after the date of enactment of the SAFE Port Act, the Secretary, in consultation with the Attorney General and the Secretary of State, shall establish the proper forms and process that shall be used for identification and verification of crewmembers.

(Added Pub. L. 107–295, title I, §102(a), Nov. 25, 2002, 116 Stat. 2080; amended Pub. L. 109–347, title I, §110, Oct. 13, 2006, 120 Stat. 1893.)

§70112. MARITIME SECURITY ADVISORY COMMITTEES

(a) NATIONAL MARITIME SECURITY ADVISORY COMMITTEE.—

(1) ESTABLISHMENT.—There is established a National Maritime Security Advisory Committee (in this subsection referred to as the "Committee").

(2) FUNCTION.—The Committee shall advise the Secretary on matters relating to national maritime security, including on enhancing the sharing of information related to cybersecurity risks that may cause a transportation security incident, between relevant Federal agencies and—

(A) State, local, and tribal governments;

(B) relevant public safety and emergency response agencies;

(C) relevant law enforcement and security organizations;

(D) maritime industry;

(E) port owners and operators; and

(F) terminal owners and operators.

(3) MEMBERSHIP.—

(A) IN GENERAL.—The Committee shall consist of at least 8 members, but not more than 21 members, appointed by the Secretary in accordance with this subsection and

441

section 15109 of this title.

(B) EXPERTISE.—Each member of the Committee shall have particular expertise, knowledge, and experience in matters relating to the function of the Committee.

(C) REPRESENTATION.—Each of the following shall be represented by at least 1 member of the Committee:

(i) Port authorities.

(ii) Facilities owners and operators.

(iii) Terminal owners and operators.

(iv) Vessel owners and operators.

(v) Maritime labor organizations.

(vi) The academic community.

(vii) State and local governments.

(viii) The maritime industry.

(D) DISTRIBUTION.—If the Committee consists of at least 8 members who, together, satisfy the minimum representation requirements of subparagraph (C), the Secretary shall, based on the needs of the Coast Guard, determine the number of additional members of the Committee who represent each entity specified in that subparagraph. Neither this subparagraph nor any other provision of law shall be construed to require an equal distribution of members representing each entity specified in subparagraph (C).

(4) ADMINISTRATION.—For purposes of section 15109 of this title, the Committee shall be treated as a committee established under chapter 151 of such title.

(b) AREA MARITIME SECURITY ADVISORY COMMITTEES.—

(1) IN GENERAL.—

(A) ESTABLISHMENT.—The Secretary may—

(i) establish an Area Maritime Security Advisory Committee for any port area of the United States; and

(ii) request such a committee to review the proposed Area Maritime Transportation Security Plan developed under section 70103(b) and make recommendations to the Secretary that the committee considers appropriate.

(B) ADDITIONAL FUNCTIONS AND MEETINGS.—A committee established under this subsection for an area—

(i) may advise, consult with, report to, and make recommendations to the Secretary on matters relating to maritime security in that area;

(ii) may make available to the Congress recommendations that the committee makes to the Secretary; and

(iii) shall meet at the call of—

(I) the Secretary, who shall call such a meeting at least once during each calendar year; or

(II) a majority of the committee.

(2) MEMBERSHIP.—

(A) IN GENERAL.—Each committee established under this subsection shall consist of at least 7 members appointed by the Secretary, each of whom has at least 5 years practical experience in maritime security operations.

(B) TERMS.—The term of each member of a committee established under this subsection shall be for a period of not more than 5 years, specified by the Secretary.

(C) NOTICE.—Before appointing an individual to a position on a committee established under this subsection, the Secretary shall publish a notice in the Federal Register soliciting nominations for membership on the committee.

(D) BACKGROUND EXAMINATIONS.—The Secretary may require an individual to have passed an appropriate security background examination before appointment to a committee established under this subsection.

(E) REPRESENTATION.—Each committee established under this subsection shall be composed of individuals who represent the interests of the port industry, terminal operators, port labor organizations, and other users of the port areas.

(3) CHAIRPERSON AND VICE CHAIRPERSON.—

(A) IN GENERAL.—Each committee established under this subsection shall elect 1 of the committee's members as the Chairperson and 1 of the committee's members as the Vice Chairperson.

(B) VICE CHAIRPERSON ACTING AS CHAIRPERSON.—The Vice Chairperson shall act as Chairperson in the absence or incapacity of the Chairperson, or in the event of a vacancy in the office of the Chairperson.

(4) OBSERVERS.—

(A) IN GENERAL.—The Secretary shall, and the head of any other interested Federal agency may, designate a representative to participate as an observer with a committee established under this subsection.

(B) ROLE.—The Secretary's designated representative to a committee established under this subsection shall act as the executive secretary of the committee and shall perform the duties set forth in section 1009(c) of title 5.

(5) CONSIDERATION OF VIEWS.—The Secretary shall consider the information, advice, and recommendations of each committee established under this subsection in formulating policy regarding matters affecting maritime security.

(6) COMPENSATION AND EXPENSES.—

(A) IN GENERAL.—A member of a committee established under this subsection, when attending meetings of the committee or when otherwise engaged in the business of the committee, is entitled to receive—

(i) compensation at a rate fixed by the Secretary, not exceeding the daily equivalent of the current rate of basic pay in effect for GS–15 of the General Schedule under section 5332 of title 5 including travel time; and

(ii) travel or transportation expenses under section 5703 of title 5.

(B) STATUS.—A member of a committee established under this subsection shall not be considered to be an officer or employee of the United States for any purpose based on the receipt of any payment under this paragraph.

(7) CHAPTER 10 OF TITLE 5.—Chapter 10 of title 5 does not apply to a committee established under this subsection.

(Added Pub. L. 107–295, title I, §102(a), Nov. 25, 2002, 116 Stat. 2081; amended Pub. L. 108–293, title VIII, §806, Aug. 9, 2004, 118 Stat. 1082; Pub. L. 109–241, title IX, §901(m), July 11, 2006, 120 Stat. 565; Pub. L. 111–281, title VIII, §810, Oct. 15, 2010, 124 Stat. 2995; Pub. L. 115–254, div. J, §1805(c)(1), Oct. 5, 2018, 132 Stat. 3534; Pub. L. 115–282, title VI, §602(a), Dec. 4, 2018, 132 Stat. 4290; Pub. L. 117–286, §4(a)(294), (295), Dec. 27, 2022, 136 Stat. 4338.)

§70113. MARITIME INTELLIGENCE

(a) IN GENERAL.—The Secretary shall implement a system to collect, integrate, and analyze information concerning vessels operating on or bound for waters subject to the jurisdiction of the United States, including information related to crew, passengers, cargo, and intermodal shipments. The system may include a vessel risk profiling component that assigns incoming vessels a terrorism risk rating.

(b) CONSULTATION.—In developing the information system under subsection (a), the Secretary shall consult with the Transportation Security Oversight Board and other departments and agencies, as appropriate.

(c) INFORMATION INTEGRATION.—To deter a transportation security incident, the Secretary may collect information from public and private entities to the extent that the information is not provided by other Federal departments and agencies.

(Added Pub. L. 107–295, title I, §102(a), Nov. 25, 2002, 116 Stat. 2082; amended Pub. L. 108–293, title VIII, §803(a), Aug. 9, 2004, 118 Stat. 1080.)

§70114. AUTOMATIC IDENTIFICATION SYSTEMS

(a) SYSTEM REQUIREMENTS.—(1) Subject to paragraph (2), the following vessels, while operating on the navigable waters of the United States, shall be equipped with and operate an automatic identification system under regulations prescribed by the Secretary:

(A) A self-propelled commercial vessel of at least 65 feet overall in length.

(B) A vessel carrying more than a number of passengers for hire determined by the Secretary.

(C) A towing vessel of more than 26 feet overall in length and 600 horsepower.

(D) Any other vessel for which the Secretary decides that an automatic identification system is necessary for the safe navigation of the vessel.

(2) The Secretary may—

(A) exempt a vessel from paragraph (1) if the Secretary finds that an automatic identification system is not necessary for the safe navigation of the vessel on the waters on which the vessel operates; and

(B) waive the application of paragraph (1) with respect to operation of vessels on navigable waters of the United States specified by the Secretary if the Secretary finds that automatic identification systems are not needed for safe navigation on those waters.

(b) REGULATIONS.—The Secretary shall prescribe regulations implementing subsection (a), including requirements for the operation and maintenance of the automatic identification systems required under subsection (a).

(Added Pub. L. 107–295, title I, §102(a), Nov. 25, 2002, 116 Stat. 2082.)

§70115. LONG-RANGE VESSEL TRACKING SYSTEM

Not later than April 1, 2007, the Secretary shall, consistent with international treaties, conventions, and agreements to which the United States is a party, develop and implement a long-range automated vessel tracking system for all vessels in United States waters that are equipped with the Global Maritime Distress and Safety System or equivalent satellite technology. The system shall be designed to provide the Secretary the capability of receiving information on vessel positions at interval positions appropriate to deter transportation security incidents. The Secretary may use existing maritime organizations to collect and monitor tracking information under the system.

(Added Pub. L. 107–295, title I, §102(a), Nov. 25, 2002, 116 Stat. 2083; amended Pub. L. 108–293, title VIII, §803(b), Aug. 9, 2004, 118 Stat. 1080; Pub. L. 109–347, title I, §107(a), Oct. 13, 2006, 120 Stat. 1891.)

§70116. PORT, HARBOR, AND COASTAL FACILITY SECURITY

(a) GENERAL AUTHORITY.—The Secretary may take actions described in subsection (b) to prevent or respond to an act of terrorism, cyber incidents, transnational organized crime, and foreign state threats against—

    (1) an individual, vessel, or public or commercial structure, that is—

        (A) subject to the jurisdiction of the United States; and

        (B) located within or adjacent to the marine environment; or

    (2) a vessel of the United States or an individual on board that vessel.

(b) SPECIFIC AUTHORITY.—Under subsection (a), the Secretary may—

    (1) carry out or require measures, including inspections, port and harbor patrols, the establishment of security and safety zones, and the development of contingency plans and procedures, to prevent or respond to acts of terrorism cyber [1] incidents, transnational organized crime, and foreign state threats;

    (2) recruit members of the Regular Coast Guard and the Coast Guard Reserve and train members of the Regular Coast Guard and the Coast Guard Reserve in the techniques of preventing and responding to acts of terrorism cyber [1] incidents, transnational organized crime, and foreign state threats; and

    (3) dispatch properly trained and qualified, armed (as needed), Coast Guard personnel on vessels and public or commercial structures on or adjacent to waters subject to United States jurisdiction to deter or respond to acts of terrorism, cyber incidents, transnational organized crime, foreign state threats, or transportation security incidents, as defined in

[§70117. Repealed. Pub. L. 111–281, title II,
§208(b), Oct. 15, 2010, 124 Stat. 2912]

CHAPTER 701—PORT SECURITY

section 70101 of title 46, United States Code.

(c) DEFINITIONS, ADMINISTRATION, AND ENFORCEMENT.—This section shall be treated as part of chapter 700 for purposes of sections 70031, 70032, 70033, 70035, and 70036. When preventing or responding to acts of terrorism, cyber incidents, transnational organized crime, or foreign state threats, the Secretary may carry out this section without regard to chapters 5 and 6 of title 5 or Executive Order Nos. 12866 and 13563.

(Added and amended Pub. L. 115–282, title IV, §402(b)(1), (2), Dec. 4, 2018, 132 Stat. 4264; Pub. L. 116–283, div. G, title LVXXXIII [LXXXIII], §8341, Jan. 1, 2021, 134 Stat. 4709.)

---

1 *So in original. Probably should be preceded by a comma.*

[§70117. REPEALED. PUB. L. 111–281, TITLE II, §208(B), OCT. 15, 2010, 124 STAT. 2912]

Section, added Pub. L. 108–293, title VIII, §801(a), Aug. 9, 2004, 118 Stat. 1078, §70118; renumbered §70117, Pub. L. 109–241, title IX, §901(l)(1), July 11, 2006, 120 Stat. 565; Pub. L. 109–304, §15(33)(A), Oct. 6, 2006, 120 Stat. 1705; Pub. L. 110–181, div. C, title XXXV, §3529(c)(1), Jan. 28, 2008, 122 Stat. 603, related to firearms, arrests, and seizure of property.

§70118. ENFORCEMENT BY STATE AND LOCAL OFFICERS

(a) IN GENERAL.—Any State or local government law enforcement officer who has authority to enforce State criminal laws may make an arrest for violation of a security zone regulation prescribed under section 1 *1* of title II of the Act of June 15, 1917 (chapter 30; 50 U.S.C. 191) or security or safety zone regulation under section 7(b) *1* of the Ports and Waterways Safety Act (33 U.S.C. 1226(b)) or a safety zone regulation prescribed under section 10(d) of the Deepwater Port Act of 1974 (33 U.S.C. 1509(d)) by a Coast Guard official authorized by law to prescribe such regulations, if—

(1) such violation is a felony; and

(2) the officer has reasonable grounds to believe that the person to be arrested has committed or is committing such violation.

(b) OTHER POWERS NOT AFFECTED.—The provisions of this section are in addition to any power conferred by law to such officers. This section shall not be construed as a limitation of any power conferred by law to such officers, or any other officer of the United States or any State. This section does not grant to such officers any powers not authorized by the law of the State in which those officers are employed.

(Added Pub. L. 108–293, title VIII, §801(a), Aug. 9, 2004, 118 Stat. 1078, §70119; renumbered §70118, Pub. L. 109–241, title IX, §901(l)(1), July 11, 2006, 120 Stat. 565; Pub. L. 109–304, §15(33)(A), Oct. 6, 2006, 120 Stat. 1705; Pub. L. 110–181, div. C, title XXXV, §3529(c)(1), Jan. 28, 2008, 122 Stat. 603.)

---

1 *See References in Text note below.*

§70119. CIVIL PENALTY

(a) IN GENERAL.—Any person that violates this chapter or any regulation under this chapter shall be liable to the United States for a civil penalty of not more than $25,000 for each day during which the violation continues.

(b) CONTINUING VIOLATIONS.—The maximum amount of a civil penalty for a violation under this section shall not exceed $50,000.

(Added Pub. L. 107–295, title I, §102(a), Nov. 25, 2002, 116 Stat. 2084, §70117; renumbered §70119, Pub. L. 108–293, title VIII, §802(a)(1), Aug. 9, 2004, 118 Stat. 1078; amended Pub. L. 109–241, title III, §306(a), July 11, 2006, 120 Stat. 528.)

§70120. IN REM LIABILITY FOR CIVIL PENALTIES AND CERTAIN COSTS

(a) CIVIL PENALTIES.—Any vessel operated in violation of this chapter or any regulations prescribed under this chapter shall be liable in rem for any civil penalty assessed pursuant to section 70119 for such violation, and may be proceeded against for such liability in the United States district court for any district in which the vessel may be found.

(b) REIMBURSABLE COSTS OF SERVICE PROVIDERS.—A vessel shall be liable in rem for the reimbursable costs incurred by any service provider related to implementation and enforcement of this chapter and arising from a violation by the operator of the vessel of this chapter or any regulations prescribed under this chapter, and may be proceeded against for such liability in the United States district court for any district in which such vessel may be found.

(c) DEFINITIONS.—In this subsection—

(1) the term "reimbursable costs" means costs incurred by any service provider acting in conformity with a lawful order of the Federal government or in conformity with the instructions of the vessel operator; and

(2) the term "service provider" means any port authority, facility or terminal operator, shipping agent, Federal, State, or local government agency, or other person to whom the management of the vessel at the port of supply is entrusted, for—

(A) services rendered to or in relation to vessel crew on board the vessel, or in transit to or from the vessel, including accommodation, detention, transportation, and medical expenses; and

(B) required handling of cargo or other items on board the vessel.

(Added Pub. L. 108–293, title VIII, §802(a)(2), Aug. 9, 2004, 118 Stat. 1078, §70117; renumbered §70120 and amended Pub. L. 109–241, title IX, §901(l)(2), (3), July 11, 2006, 120 Stat. 565; Pub. L. 109–304, §15(33)(B), (C), Oct. 6, 2006, 120 Stat. 1705; Pub. L. 110–181, div. C, title XXXV, §3529(c)(1), Jan. 28, 2008, 122 Stat. 603.)

§70121. WITHHOLDING OF CLEARANCE

(a) REFUSAL OR REVOCATION OF CLEARANCE.—If any owner, agent, master, officer, or person in charge of a vessel is liable for a penalty under section 70119, or if reasonable cause exists to believe that the owner, agent, master, officer, or person in charge may be subject to a penalty under section 70119, the Secretary may, with respect to such vessel, refuse or revoke any clearance required by section 60105 of this title.

(b) CLEARANCE UPON FILING OF BOND OR OTHER SURETY.—The Secretary may require the filing of a bond or other surety as a condition of granting clearance refused or revoked under this subsection.

(Added Pub. L. 108–293, title VIII, §802(a)(2), Aug. 9, 2004, 118 Stat. 1079, §70118; renumbered §70121 and amended Pub. L. 109–241, title IX, §901(l)(2), (4), July 11, 2006, 120 Stat. 565; Pub. L. 109–304, §15(33)(B), (D), Oct. 6, 2006, 120 Stat. 1705; Pub. L. 110–181, div. C, title XXXV, §3529(c)(1), Jan. 28, 2008, 122 Stat. 603.)

§70122. WATERWAY WATCH PROGRAM

(a) PROGRAM ESTABLISHED.—There is hereby established, within the Coast Guard, the America's Waterway Watch Program.

(b) PURPOSE.—The Secretary shall administer the Program in a manner that promotes voluntary reporting of activities that may indicate that a person or persons may be preparing to engage or engaging in a violation of law relating to a threat or an act of terrorism (as that term is defined in section 3077 of title 18) against a vessel, facility, port, or waterway.

(c) INFORMATION; TRAINING.—

(1) INFORMATION.—The Secretary may establish, as an element of the Program, a network of individuals and community-based organizations that encourage the public and industry to recognize activities referred to in subsection (b), promote voluntary reporting of such activity, and enhance the situational awareness within the Nation's ports and waterways. Such network shall, to the extent practicable, be conducted in cooperation with Federal, State, and local law enforcement agencies.

(2) TRAINING.—The Secretary may provide training in—

(A) observing and reporting on covered activities; and

(B) sharing such reports and coordinating the response by Federal, State, and local law enforcement agencies.

(d) VOLUNTARY PARTICIPATION.—Participation in the Program—

(1) shall be wholly voluntary;

(2) shall not be a prerequisite to eligibility for, or receipt of, any other service or assistance from, or to participation in, any other program of any kind; and

(3) shall not require disclosure of information regarding the individual reporting covered activities or, for proprietary purposes, the location of such individual.

(e) COORDINATION.—The Secretary shall coordinate the Program with other like watch programs. The Secretary shall submit, concurrent with the President's budget submission for each fiscal year, a report on coordination of the Program and like watch programs within the Department of Homeland Security to the Committee on Commerce, Science, and Transportation of the Senate and the Committee on Homeland Security of the House of Representatives.

(f) AUTHORIZATION OF APPROPRIATIONS.—There are authorized to be appropriated for the purposes of this section $3,000,000 for each of fiscal years 2011 through 2016. Such funds shall remain available until expended.

(Added Pub. L. 111–281, title VIII, §801(a), Oct. 15, 2010, 124 Stat. 2988; amended Pub. L. 114–120, title

III, §306(a)(11), Feb. 8, 2016, 130 Stat. 55.)

§70123. MOBILE BIOMETRIC IDENTIFICATION

(a) IN GENERAL.—Within one year after the date of the enactment of the Coast Guard Authorization Act of 2010, the Secretary shall conduct, in the maritime environment, a program for the mobile biometric identification of suspected individuals, including terrorists, to enhance border security and for other purposes.

(b) REQUIREMENTS.—The Secretary shall ensure the program required in this section is coordinated with other biometric identification programs within the Department of Homeland Security.

(c) DEFINITION.—For the purposes of this section, the term "biometric identification" means use of fingerprint and digital photography images and facial and iris scan technology and any other technology considered applicable by the Department of Homeland Security.

(Added Pub. L. 111–281, title VIII, §807(a), Oct. 15, 2010, 124 Stat. 2993.)

§70124. REGULATIONS

Unless otherwise provided, the Secretary may issue regulations necessary to implement this chapter.

(Added Pub. L. 111–281, title VIII, §820(a), Oct. 15, 2010, 124 Stat. 3001.)

§70125. PORT SECURITY TRAINING FOR FACILITY SECURITY OFFICERS

(a) FACILITY SECURITY OFFICERS.—The Secretary shall establish comprehensive facility security officer training requirements designed to provide full security training that would lead to certification of such officers. In establishing the requirements, the Secretary shall—

(1) work with affected industry stakeholders; and

(2) evaluate—

(A) the requirements of subsection (b);

(B) existing security training programs employed at marine terminal facilities; and

(C) existing port security training programs developed by the Federal Government.

(b) REQUIREMENTS.—The training program shall provide validated training that—

(1) provides training at the awareness, performance, management, and planning levels;

(2) utilizes multiple training mediums and methods;

(3) establishes a validated provisional on-line certification methodology;

(4) provide for continuing education and training for facility security officers beyond certification requirements, including a program to educate on the dangers and issues associated with the shipment of hazardous and especially hazardous cargo;

(5) addresses port security topics, including—

(A) facility security plans and procedures, including how to develop security plans and security procedure requirements when threat levels are elevated;

(B) facility security force operations and management;

(C) physical security and access control at facilities;

(D) methods of security for preventing and countering cargo theft;

(E) container security;

(F) recognition and detection of weapons, dangerous substances, and devices;

(G) operation and maintenance of security equipment and systems;

(H) security threats and patterns;

(I) security incident procedures, including procedures for communicating with governmental and nongovernmental emergency response providers; and

(J) evacuation procedures;

(6) is consistent with, and supports implementation of, the National Incident Management System, the National Response Plan, the National Infrastructure Protection Plan, the National Preparedness Guidance, the National Preparedness Goal, the National Maritime Transportation Security Plan, and other such national initiatives;

(7) is evaluated against clear and consistent performance measures;

(8) addresses security requirements under facility security plans;

(9) addresses requirements under the International Code for the Security of Ships and Port Facilities to address shore leave for mariners and access to visitors, representatives of seafarers' welfare organizations, and labor organizations; and

(10) such other subject matters as may be prescribed by the Secretary.

(c) CONTINUING SECURITY TRAINING.—The Secretary, in coordination with the Secretary of Transportation, shall work with State and local law enforcement agencies and industry stakeholders to develop and certify the following additional security training requirements for Federal, State, and local officials with security responsibilities at United States seaports:

(1) A program to familiarize them with port and shipping operations, requirements of the Maritime Transportation Security Act of 2002 (Public Law 107–295), and other port and cargo security programs that educates and trains them with respect to their roles and responsibilities.

(2) A program to familiarize them with dangers and potential issues with respect to shipments of hazardous and especially hazardous cargoes.

(3) A program of continuing education as deemed necessary by the Secretary.

(d) TRAINING PARTNERS.—In developing curriculum and delivering training established pursuant to subsections (a) and (c), the Secretary, in coordination with the Maritime Administrator of the Department of Transportation and consistent with section 109 of the Maritime Transportation Security Act of 2002 (46 U.S.C. 70101 note), shall work with institutions with maritime expertise and with industry stakeholders with security expertise to develop appropriate training capacity to ensure that training can be provided in a geographically balanced manner to personnel seeking certification under subsection (a) or education and training under subsection (c).

(e) ESTABLISHED GRANT PROGRAM.—The Secretary shall issue regulations or grant solicitations for grants for homeland security or port security to ensure that activities surrounding the development of curriculum and the provision of training and these activities are eligible grant activities under both grant programs.

(Added Pub. L. 111–281, title VIII, §821(a), Oct. 15, 2010, 124 Stat. 3001; amended Pub. L. 111–330,

§1(14), Dec. 22, 2010, 124 Stat. 3570.)

SUBCHAPTER II—PORT SECURITY ZONES

§70131. Definitions

In this subchapter:

(1) Law enforcement agency.—The term "law enforcement agency" means an agency of a State, a political subdivision of a State, or a Federally recognized tribe that is authorized by law to supervise the prevention, detection, investigation, or prosecution of any violation of criminal law.

(2) Security zone.—The term "security zone" means a security zone, established by the Commandant of the Coast Guard or the Commandant's designee pursuant to section 1 [1] of title II of the Act of June 15, 1917 (50 U.S.C. 191) or section 7(b) [1] of the Ports and Waterways Safety Act (33 U.S.C. 1226(b)), for a vessel carrying especially hazardous cargo when such vessel—

(A) enters, or operates within, the internal waters of the United States and the territorial sea of the United States; or

(B) transfers such cargo or residue in any port or place, under the jurisdiction of the United States, within the territorial sea of the United States or the internal waters of the United States.

(Added Pub. L. 111–281, title VIII, §828(a), Oct. 15, 2010, 124 Stat. 3005; amended Pub. L. 111–330, §1(16), Dec. 22, 2010, 124 Stat. 3570.)

[1] *See References in Text note below.*

§70132. Credentialing standards, training, and certification for State and local support for the enforcement of security zones for the transportation of especially hazardous cargo

(a) Standard.—The Commandant of the Coast Guard shall establish, by regulation, national standards for training and credentialing of public safety personnel—

(1) to enforce a security zone; or

(2) to assist in the enforcement of a security zone.

(b) Training.—

(1) The Commandant of the Coast Guard—

(A) shall develop and publish a training curriculum for—

(i) public safety personnel to enforce a security zone;

(ii) public safety personnel to enforce or assist in the enforcement of a security zone; and

(iii) personnel who are employed or retained by a facility or vessel owner to assist in the enforcement of a security zone; and

(B) may—

(i) test and deliver such training, the curriculum for which is developed pursuant to subparagraph (A);

(ii) enter into an agreement under which a public entity (including a Federal agency) or private entity may test and deliver such training, the curriculum for which has been developed pursuant to subparagraph (A); and

(iii) may accept a program, conducted by a public entity (including a Federal agency) or private entity, through which such training is delivered the curriculum for which is developed pursuant to subparagraph (A).

(2) Any Federal agency that provides such training, and any public or private entity that receives moneys, pursuant to section 70107(b)(8) of this title, to provide such training, shall provide such training—

(A) to public safety personnel who enforce or assist in the enforcement of a security zone; and

(B) on an availability basis to—

(i) public safety personnel who assist in the enforcement of a security zone; and

(ii) personnel who are employed or retained by a facility or vessel owner or operator to assist in the enforcement of a security zone.

(3) If a Federal agency provides the training, the head of such agency may, notwithstanding any other provision of law, accept payment from any source for such training, and any amount received as payment shall be credited to the appropriation, current at the time of collection, charged with the cost thereof and shall be merged with, and available for, the same purposes of such appropriation.

(4) Notwithstanding any other provision of law, any moneys, awarded by the Department of Homeland Security in the form of awards or grants, may be used by the recipient to pay for training of personnel to assist in the enforcement of security zones and limited access areas.

(c) CERTIFICATION; TRAINING PARTNERS.—In developing and delivering training under the training program, the Secretary, in coordination with the Maritime Administrator of the Department of Transportation, and consistent with section 109 of the Maritime Transportation Security Act of 2002 (46 U.S.C. 70101 note), shall—

(1) work with government training facilities, academic institutions, private organizations, employee organizations, and other entities that provide specialized, state-of-the-art training for governmental and nongovernmental emergency responder providers or commercial seaport personnel and management;

(2) utilize, as appropriate, government training facilities, courses provided by community colleges, public safety academies, State and private universities, and other facilities; and

(3) certify organizations that offer the curriculum for training and certification.

(d) PUBLIC SAFETY PERSONNEL DEFINED.—For the purposes of this section, the term "public safety personnel" includes any Federal, State (or political subdivision thereof), territorial, or Tribal law enforcement officer, firefighter, or emergency response provider.

(Added Pub. L. 111–281, title VIII, §828(a), Oct. 15, 2010, 124 Stat. 3005; amended Pub. L. 111–330, §1(16), Dec. 22, 2010, 124 Stat. 3570; Pub. L. 116–283, div. G, title LVXXXIII [LXXXIII], §8314(2), Jan. 1, 2021, 134 Stat. 4699.)

CHAPTER 703—MARITIME SECURITY

§70301. DEFINITIONS

In this chapter:

(1) COMMON CARRIER.—The term "common carrier" has the meaning given that term in section 40102 of this title.

(2) PASSENGER VESSEL.—The term "passenger vessel" has the meaning given that term in section 2101 of this title.

(3) SECRETARY.—The term "Secretary" means the Secretary of the department in which the Coast Guard is operating.

(Pub. L. 109–304, §10(2), Oct. 6, 2006, 120 Stat. 1683.)

§70302. INTERNATIONAL MEASURES FOR SEAPORT AND VESSEL SECURITY

Congress encourages the President to continue to seek agreement on international seaport and vessel security through the International Maritime Organization. In developing an agreement, each member country of the International Maritime Organization should consult with appropriate private sector interests in that country. The agreement would establish seaport and vessel security measures and could include—

(1) seaport screening of cargo and baggage similar to that done at airports;

(2) security measures to restrict access to cargo, vessels, and dockside property to authorized personnel only;

(3) additional security on board vessels;

(4) licensing or certification of compliance with appropriate security standards; and

(5) other appropriate measures to prevent unlawful acts against passengers and crews on vessels.

(Pub. L. 109–304, §10(2), Oct. 6, 2006, 120 Stat. 1683.)

§70303. SECURITY STANDARDS AT FOREIGN PORTS

(a) GENERAL REQUIREMENTS.—The Secretary shall develop and implement a plan to assess the effectiveness of the security measures maintained at foreign ports that the

Secretary, in consultation with the Secretary of State, determines pose a high risk of acts of terrorism against passenger vessels. In carrying out this subsection, the Secretary shall consult with the Secretary of State about the terrorist threat that exists in each country and poses a high risk of acts of terrorism against passenger vessels.

(b) NOTICE AND RECOMMENDATIONS TO OTHER COUNTRIES.—If the Secretary, after implementing the plan under subsection (a), determines that a port does not maintain and administer effective security measures, the Secretary of State (after being informed by the Secretary) shall—

(1) notify the appropriate government authorities of the country in which the port is located of the determination; and

(2) recommend steps necessary to bring the security measures at that port up to the standard used by the Secretary in making the assessment under subsection (a).

(c) ANTITERRORISM ASSISTANCE.—The President is encouraged to provide antiterrorism assistance related to maritime security under chapter 8 of part II of the Foreign Assistance Act of 1961 (22 U.S.C. 2349aa et seq.) to foreign countries, especially for a port that the Secretary determines under subsection (b) does not maintain and administer effective security measures.

(Pub. L. 109–304, §10(2), Oct. 6, 2006, 120 Stat. 1684.)

§70304. TRAVEL ADVISORIES ON SECURITY AT FOREIGN PORTS

(a) GENERAL REQUIREMENTS.—On being notified by the Secretary that the Secretary has determined that a condition exists that threatens the safety or security of passengers, passenger vessels, or crew traveling to or from a foreign port that the Secretary has determined under section 70303(b) of this title does not maintain and administer effective security measures, the Secretary of State immediately shall issue a travel advisory for that port. The Secretary of State shall take the necessary steps to widely publicize the travel advisory.

(b) LIFTING ADVISORIES.—A travel advisory issued under subsection (a) may be lifted only if the Secretary, in consultation with the Secretary of State, has determined that effective security measures are maintained and administered at the port.

(c) NOTICE TO CONGRESS.—The Secretary of State shall notify Congress immediately of any change in the status of a travel advisory issued under this section.

(Pub. L. 109–304, §10(2), Oct. 6, 2006, 120 Stat. 1684.)

§70305. SUSPENSION OF PASSENGER SERVICES

(a) GENERAL AUTHORITY.—Whenever the President determines that a foreign nation permits the use of territory under its jurisdiction as a base of operations or training for, or as a sanctuary for, or in any way arms, aids, or abets, a terrorist or terrorist group that knowingly uses the illegal seizure of passenger vessels or the threat thereof as an instrument of policy, the President may suspend the right of any passenger vessel common carrier to operate to or from, and the right of any passenger vessel of the United States to use, a port in that foreign nation for passenger service. The suspension may be without notice or hearing and for as long as the President determines is necessary to ensure the security of passenger vessels against unlawful seizure.

(b) PROHIBITION.—A passenger vessel common carrier, or a passenger vessel of the United States, may not operate in violation of a suspension under this section.

(c) PENALTIES.—

(1) DENIAL OF ENTRY.—If a person operates a vessel in violation of this section, the Secretary may deny the vessels of that person entry to ports of the United States.

(2) CIVIL PENALTY.—A person violating this section is liable to the United States Government for a civil penalty of not more than $50,000. Each day a vessel uses a prohibited port is a separate violation.

(Pub. L. 109–304, §10(2), Oct. 6, 2006, 120 Stat. 1684.)

§70306. REPORT ON TERRORIST THREATS

(a) CONTENT.—The Secretary shall submit an annual report to Congress on the threat from acts of terrorism to United States ports and vessels operating from those ports. The Secretary shall include a description of activities undertaken under title I of the Maritime Transportation Security Act of 2002 (Public Law 107–295, 116 Stat. 2066) and an analysis of the effect of those activities on port security against acts of terrorism.

(b) SUBMISSION.—The report shall be submitted to the Committee on International Relations and the Committee on Transportation and Infrastructure of the House of Representatives and the Committee on Foreign Relations and the Committee on Commerce, Science, and Transportation of the Senate. Any classified information in the report shall be submitted separately as an addendum.

(Pub. L. 109–304, §10(2), Oct. 6, 2006, 120 Stat. 1685; Pub. L. 109–241, title IX, §901(q), July 11, 2006, 120 Stat. 566; Pub. L. 110–181, div. C, title XXXV, §3525(a)(5), (b), Jan. 28, 2008, 122 Stat. 601.)

CHAPTER 705—MARITIME DRUG LAW ENFORCEMENT

Sec.

§70501. FINDINGS AND DECLARATIONS

Congress finds and declares that (1) trafficking in controlled substances aboard vessels is a serious international problem, is universally condemned, and presents a specific threat to the security and societal well-being of the United States and (2) operating or embarking in a submersible vessel or semi-submersible vessel without nationality and on an international voyage is a serious international problem, facilitates transnational crime, including drug

455

trafficking, and terrorism, and presents a specific threat to the safety of maritime navigation and the security of the United States.

(Pub. L. 109–304, §10(2), Oct. 6, 2006, 120 Stat. 1685; Pub. L. 110–407, title II, §201, Oct. 13, 2008, 122 Stat. 4299.)

§70502. Definitions

(a) Application of Other Definitions.—The definitions in section 102 of the Comprehensive Drug Abuse Prevention and Control Act of 1970 (21 U.S.C. 802) apply to this chapter.

(b) Vessel of the United States.—In this chapter, the term "vessel of the United States" means—

(1) a vessel documented under chapter 121 of this title or numbered as provided in chapter 123 of this title;

(2) a vessel owned in any part by an individual who is a citizen of the United States, the United States Government, the government of a State or political subdivision of a State, or a corporation incorporated under the laws of the United States or of a State, unless—

(A) the vessel has been granted the nationality of a foreign nation under article 5 of the 1958 Convention on the High Seas; and

(B) a claim of nationality or registry for the vessel is made by the master or individual in charge at the time of the enforcement action by an officer or employee of the United States who is authorized to enforce applicable provisions of United States law; and

(3) a vessel that was once documented under the laws of the United States and, in violation of the laws of the United States, was sold to a person not a citizen of the United States, placed under foreign registry, or operated under the authority of a foreign nation, whether or not the vessel has been granted the nationality of a foreign nation.

(c) Vessel Subject to the Jurisdiction of the United States.—

(1) In general.—In this chapter, the term "vessel subject to the jurisdiction of the United States" includes—

(A) a vessel without nationality;

(B) a vessel assimilated to a vessel without nationality under paragraph (2) of article 6 of the 1958 Convention on the High Seas;

(C) a vessel registered in a foreign nation if that nation has consented or waived objection to the enforcement of United States law by the United States;

(D) a vessel in the customs waters of the United States;

(E) a vessel in the territorial waters of a foreign nation if the nation consents to the enforcement of United States law by the United States; and

(F) a vessel in the contiguous zone of the United States, as defined in Presidential Proclamation 7219 of September 2, 1999 (43 U.S.C. 1331 note), that—

(i) is entering the United States;

(ii) has departed the United States; or

(iii) is a hovering vessel as defined in section 401 of the Tariff Act of 1930 (19

U.S.C. 1401).

(2) CONSENT OR WAIVER OF OBJECTION.—Consent or waiver of objection by a foreign nation to the enforcement of United States law by the United States under paragraph (1)(C) or (E)—

(A) may be obtained by radio, telephone, or similar oral or electronic means; and

(B) is proved conclusively by certification of the Secretary of State or the Secretary's designee.

(d) VESSEL WITHOUT NATIONALITY.—

(1) IN GENERAL.—In this chapter, the term "vessel without nationality" includes—

(A) a vessel aboard which the master or individual in charge makes a claim of registry that is denied by the nation whose registry is claimed;

(B) a vessel aboard which the master or individual in charge fails, on request of an officer of the United States authorized to enforce applicable provisions of United States law, to make a claim of nationality or registry for that vessel;

(C) a vessel aboard which the master or individual in charge makes a claim of registry and for which the claimed nation of registry does not affirmatively and unequivocally assert that the vessel is of its nationality; and

(D) a vessel aboard which no individual, on request of an officer of the United States authorized to enforce applicable provisions of United States law, claims to be the master or is identified as the individual in charge, and that has no other claim of nationality or registry under paragraph (1) or (2) of subsection (e).

(2) RESPONSE TO CLAIM OF REGISTRY.—The response of a foreign nation to a claim of registry under paragraph (1)(A) or (C) may be made by radio, telephone, or similar oral or electronic means, and is proved conclusively by certification of the Secretary of State or the Secretary's designee.

(e) CLAIM OF NATIONALITY OR REGISTRY.—A claim of nationality or registry under this section includes only—

(1) possession on board the vessel and production of documents evidencing the vessel's nationality as provided in article 5 of the 1958 Convention on the High Seas;

(2) flying its nation's ensign or flag; or

(3) a verbal claim of nationality or registry by the master or individual in charge of the vessel.

(f) SEMI-SUBMERSIBLE VESSEL; SUBMERSIBLE VESSEL.—In this chapter:

(1) SEMI-SUBMERSIBLE VESSEL.—The term "semi-submersible vessel" means any watercraft constructed or adapted to be capable of operating with most of its hull and bulk under the surface of the water, including both manned and unmanned watercraft.

(2) SUBMERSIBLE VESSEL.—The term "submersible vessel" means a vessel that is capable of operating completely below the surface of the water, including both manned and unmanned watercraft.

(Pub. L. 109–304, §10(2), Oct. 6, 2006, 120 Stat. 1685; Pub. L. 109–241, title III, §303, July 11, 2006,

120 Stat. 527; Pub. L. 110–181, div. C, title XXXV, §3525(a)(6), (b), Jan. 28, 2008, 122 Stat. 601; Pub. L. 110–407, title II, §203, Oct. 13, 2008, 122 Stat. 4300; Pub. L. 117–263, div. K, title CXV, §11519, Dec. 23, 2022, 136 Stat. 4142.)

§70503. PROHIBITED ACTS

(a) PROHIBITIONS.—While on board a covered vessel, an individual may not knowingly or intentionally—

(1) manufacture or distribute, or possess with intent to manufacture or distribute, a controlled substance;

(2) destroy (including jettisoning any item or scuttling, burning, or hastily cleaning a vessel), or attempt or conspire to destroy, property that is subject to forfeiture under section 511(a) of the Comprehensive Drug Abuse Prevention and Control Act of 1970 (21 U.S.C. 881(a)); or

(3) conceal, or attempt or conspire to conceal, more than $100,000 in currency or other monetary instruments on the person of such individual or in any conveyance, article of luggage, merchandise, or other container, or compartment of or aboard the covered vessel if that vessel is outfitted for smuggling.

(b) EXTENSION BEYOND TERRITORIAL JURISDICTION.—Subsection (a) applies even though the act is committed outside the territorial jurisdiction of the United States.

(c) NONAPPLICATION.—

(1) IN GENERAL.—Subject to paragraph (2), subsection (a) does not apply to—

(A) a common or contract carrier or an employee of the carrier who possesses or distributes a controlled substance in the lawful and usual course of the carrier's business; or

(B) a public vessel of the United States or an individual on board the vessel who possesses or distributes a controlled substance in the lawful course of the individual's duties.

(2) ENTERED IN MANIFEST.—Paragraph (1) applies only if the controlled substance is part of the cargo entered in the vessel's manifest and is intended to be imported lawfully into the country of destination for scientific, medical, or other lawful purposes.

(d) BURDEN OF PROOF.—The United States Government is not required to negative a defense provided by subsection (c) in a complaint, information, indictment, or other pleading or in a trial or other proceeding. The burden of going forward with the evidence supporting the defense is on the person claiming its benefit.

(e) COVERED VESSEL DEFINED.—In this section the term "covered vessel" means—

(1) a vessel of the United States or a vessel subject to the jurisdiction of the United States; or

(2) any other vessel if the individual is a citizen of the United States or a resident alien of the United States.

(Pub. L. 109–304, §10(2), Oct. 6, 2006, 120 Stat. 1687; Pub. L. 114–120, title III, §314(a), (b), (e)(1), Feb. 8, 2016, 130 Stat. 59.)

§70504. JURISDICTION AND VENUE

(a) JURISDICTION.—Jurisdiction of the United States with respect to a vessel subject to this chapter is not an element of an offense. Jurisdictional issues arising under this chapter are preliminary questions of law to be determined solely by the trial judge.

(b) VENUE.—A person violating section 70503 or 70508—

(1) shall be tried in the district in which such offense was committed; or

(2) if the offense was begun or committed upon the high seas, or elsewhere outside the jurisdiction of any particular State or district, may be tried in any district.

(Pub. L. 109–304, §10(2), Oct. 6, 2006, 120 Stat. 1688; Pub. L. 110–407, title II, §202(b)(2), Oct. 13, 2008, 122 Stat. 4300; Pub. L. 115–91, div. A, title X, §1012(a), Dec. 12, 2017, 131 Stat. 1546.)

§70505. FAILURE TO COMPLY WITH INTERNATIONAL LAW AS A DEFENSE

A person charged with violating section 70503 of this title, or against whom a civil enforcement proceeding is brought under section 70508, does not have standing to raise a claim of failure to comply with international law as a basis for a defense. A claim of failure to comply with international law in the enforcement of this chapter may be made only by a foreign nation. A failure to comply with international law does not divest a court of jurisdiction and is not a defense to a proceeding under this chapter.

(Pub. L. 109–304, §10(2), Oct. 6, 2006, 120 Stat. 1688; Pub. L. 110–407, title II, §202(b)(3), Oct. 13, 2008, 122 Stat. 4300.)

§70506. PENALTIES

(a) VIOLATIONS.—A person violating paragraph (1) of section 70503(a) of this title shall be punished as provided in section 1010 of the Comprehensive Drug Abuse Prevention and Control Act of 1970 (21 U.S.C. 960). However, if the offense is a second or subsequent offense as provided in section 1012(b) of that Act (21 U.S.C. 962(b)), the person shall be punished as provided in section 1012 of that Act (21 U.S.C. 962).

(b) ATTEMPTS AND CONSPIRACIES.—A person attempting or conspiring to violate section 70503 of this title is subject to the same penalties as provided for violating section 70503.

(c) SIMPLE POSSESSION.—

(1) IN GENERAL.—Any individual on a vessel subject to the jurisdiction of the United States who is found by the Secretary, after notice and an opportunity for a hearing, to have knowingly or intentionally possessed a controlled substance within the meaning of the Controlled Substances Act (21 U.S.C. 812) shall be liable to the United States for a civil penalty of not to exceed $5,000 for each violation. The Secretary shall notify the individual in writing of the amount of the civil penalty.

(2) DETERMINATION OF AMOUNT.—In determining the amount of the penalty, the Secretary shall consider the nature, circumstances, extent, and gravity of the prohibited acts committed and, with respect to the violator, the degree of culpability, any history of prior offenses, ability to pay, and other matters that justice requires.

(3) TREATMENT OF CIVIL PENALTY ASSESSMENT.—Assessment of a civil penalty under this subsection shall not be considered a conviction for purposes of State or Federal law but may be considered proof of possession if such a determination is relevant.

(d) PENALTY.—A person violating paragraph (2) or (3) of section 70503(a) shall be fined in accordance with section 3571 of title 18, imprisoned not more than 15 years, or both.

(Pub. L. 109–304, §10(2), Oct. 6, 2006, 120 Stat. 1688; Pub. L. 111–281, title III, §302, Oct. 15, 2010, 124 Stat. 2923; Pub. L. 114–120, title III, §314(c), Feb. 8, 2016, 130 Stat. 59.)

§70507. FORFEITURES

(a) IN GENERAL.—Property described in section 511(a) of the Comprehensive Drug Abuse Prevention and Control Act of 1970 (21 U.S.C. 881(a)) that is used or intended for use to commit, or to facilitate the commission of, an offense under section 70503 or 70508 of this title may be seized and forfeited in the same manner that similar property may be seized and forfeited under section 511 of that Act (21 U.S.C. 881).

(b) PRIMA FACIE EVIDENCE OF VIOLATION.—Practices commonly recognized as smuggling tactics may provide prima facie evidence of intent to use a vessel to commit, or to facilitate the commission of, an offense under section 70503 of this title, and may support seizure and forfeiture of the vessel, even in the absence of controlled substances aboard the vessel. The following indicia, among others, may be considered, in the totality of the circumstances, to be prima facie evidence that a vessel is intended to be used to commit, or to facilitate the commission of, such an offense:

(1) The construction or adaptation of the vessel in a manner that facilitates smuggling, including—

(A) the configuration of the vessel to ride low in the water or present a low hull profile to avoid being detected visually or by radar;

(B) the presence of any compartment or equipment that is built or fitted out for smuggling, not including items such as a safe or lock-box reasonably used for the storage of personal valuables;

(C) the presence of an auxiliary tank not installed in accordance with applicable law or installed in such a manner as to enhance the vessel's smuggling capability;

(D) the presence of engines that are excessively over-powered in relation to the design and size of the vessel;

(E) the presence of materials used to reduce or alter the heat or radar signature of the vessel and avoid detection;

(F) the presence of a camouflaging paint scheme, or of materials used to camouflage the vessel, to avoid detection; or

(G) the display of false vessel registration numbers, false indicia of vessel nationality, false vessel name, or false vessel homeport.

(2) The presence or absence of equipment, personnel, or cargo inconsistent with the type or declared purpose of the vessel.

(3) The presence of excessive fuel, lube oil, food, water, or spare parts, inconsistent with legitimate vessel operation, inconsistent with the construction or equipment of the vessel, or inconsistent with the character of the vessel's stated purpose.

(4) The operation of the vessel without lights during times lights are required to be displayed under applicable law or regulation and in a manner of navigation consistent with smuggling tactics used to avoid detection by law enforcement authorities.

(5) The failure of the vessel to stop or respond or heave to when hailed by government

authority, especially where the vessel conducts evasive maneuvering when hailed.

(6) The declaration to government authority of apparently false information about the vessel, crew, or voyage or the failure to identify the vessel by name or country of registration when requested to do so by government authority.

(7) The presence of controlled substance residue on the vessel, on an item aboard the vessel, or on an individual aboard the vessel, of a quantity or other nature that reasonably indicates manufacturing or distribution activity.

(8) The use of petroleum products or other substances on the vessel to foil the detection of controlled substance residue.

(9) The presence of a controlled substance in the water in the vicinity of the vessel, where given the currents, weather conditions, and course and speed of the vessel, the quantity or other nature is such that it reasonably indicates manufacturing or distribution activity.

(Pub. L. 109–304, §10(2), Oct. 6, 2006, 120 Stat. 1688; Pub. L. 114–120, title III, §314(d), Feb. 8, 2016, 130 Stat. 59.)

§70508. Operation of submersible vessel or semi-submersible vessel without nationality

(a) In General.—An individual may not operate by any means or embark in any submersible vessel or semi-submersible vessel that is without nationality and that is navigating or has navigated into, through, or from waters beyond the outer limit of the territorial sea of a single country or a lateral limit of that country's territorial sea with an adjacent country, with the intent to evade detection.

(b) Evidence of Intent To Evade Detection.—In any civil enforcement proceeding for a violation of subsection (a), the presence of any of the indicia described in paragraph (1)(A), (E), (F), or (G), or in paragraph (4), (5), or (6), of section 70507(b) may be considered, in the totality of the circumstances, to be prima facie evidence of intent to evade detection.

(c) Defenses.—

(1) In general.—It is a defense in any civil enforcement proceeding for a violation of subsection (a) that the submersible vessel or semi-submersible vessel involved was, at the time of the violation—

(A) a vessel of the United States or lawfully registered in a foreign nation as claimed by the master or individual in charge of the vessel when requested to make a claim by an officer of the United States authorized to enforce applicable provisions of United States law;

(B) classed by and designed in accordance with the rules of a classification society;

(C) lawfully operated in government-regulated or licensed activity, including commerce, research, or exploration; or

(D) equipped with and using an operable automatic identification system, vessel monitoring system, or long range identification and tracking system.

(2) Production of documents.—The defenses provided by this subsection are proved conclusively by the production of—

(A) government documents evidencing the vessel's nationality at the time of the offense, as provided in article 5 of the 1958 Convention on the High Seas;

(B) a certificate of classification issued by the vessel's classification society upon completion of relevant classification surveys and valid at the time of the offense; or

(C) government documents evidencing licensure, regulation, or registration for research or exploration.

(d) CIVIL PENALTY.—A person violating this section shall be liable to the United States for a civil penalty of not more than $1,000,000.

(Added Pub. L. 110–407, title II, §202(a), Oct. 13, 2008, 122 Stat. 4299.)

SUBTITLE VIII
MISCELLANEOUS

Subtitle VIII—Miscellaneous

CHAPTER 801—WRECKS AND SALVAGE

§80101. VESSEL STRANDED ON FOREIGN COAST

(a) DUTIES OF CONSULAR OFFICER.—When a vessel of the United States is stranded on a coast of a foreign country, the consular officer in that country shall take proper measures, to the extent the laws of that country allow, to—

(1) save and secure the vessel and property on the vessel; and

(2) prepare an inventory of the property that is saved.

(b) DELIVERY TO OWNER.—After deducting the expenses, the consular officer shall deliver the property, with an inventory, to the owner of the property.

(c) LIMITATION ON TAKING POSSESSION.—A consular officer may not take possession of property under this section when the owner, master, or consignee is present or able to take possession of the property.

(Pub. L. 109–304, §11, Oct. 6, 2006, 120 Stat. 1690.)

[§80102. REPEALED. PUB. L. 110–375, §1(1), OCT. 8, 2008, 122 STAT. 4055]

Section, Pub. L. 109–304, §11, Oct. 6, 2006, 120 Stat. 1690, related to license to salvage on Florida coast.

§80103. PROPERTY ON FLORIDA COAST TO BE TAKEN TO PORT OF ENTRY

(a) IN GENERAL.—Property taken from a wreck, the sea, or a key or shoal, on the coast of Florida and within the jurisdiction of the United States, shall be brought to a port of entry of the United States.

(b) SEIZURE AND FORFEITURE.—A vessel transporting property described in subsection (a) to a foreign port may be seized by, and forfeited to, the United States Government. A

forfeiture under this subsection accrues half to the informer and half to the Government.
(Pub. L. 109–304, §11, Oct. 6, 2006, 120 Stat. 1690.)

§80104. SALVAGING OPERATIONS BY FOREIGN VESSELS

(a) PROHIBITION.—Except as provided in this section or section 80105 of this title, a foreign vessel may not, under penalty of forfeiture, engage in salvaging operations on the Atlantic or Pacific coast of the United States, in any portion of the Great Lakes or their connecting or tributary waters, including any portion of the Saint Lawrence River through which the international boundary line extends, or in territorial waters of the United States on the Gulf of Mexico.

(b) WHEN SUITABLE VESSEL NOT AVAILABLE.—The Secretary of Homeland Security may authorize a foreign vessel to engage in salvaging operations in a particular locality if, on investigation, the Secretary is satisfied that there is not available in that locality a suitable vessel that is—

(1) owned only by citizens of the United States (including a Bowaters corporation under section 12118 of this title); and

(2) documented under chapter 121 of this title or numbered under chapter 123 of this title.

(c) OPERATIONS AUTHORIZED BY TREATY.—This section does not prohibit or restrict assistance to vessels or salvaging operations authorized by treaty, including—

(1) article II of the Treaty between the United States and Great Britain concerning reciprocal rights for United States and Canada in the conveyance of prisoners and wrecking and salvage, signed at Washington, May 18, 1908 (35 Stat. 2036); or

(2) the Treaty between the United States of America and Mexico to facilitate assistance to and salvage of vessels in territorial waters, signed at Mexico City, June 13, 1935 (49 Stat. 3359).

(Pub. L. 109–304, §11, Oct. 6, 2006, 120 Stat. 1691.)

§80105. CANADIAN VESSELS AIDING VESSELS IN UNITED STATES WATERS

(a) IN GENERAL.—Canadian vessels and wrecking equipment may give aid to Canadian or other vessels and property wrecked, disabled, or in distress in the waters of the United States contiguous to Canada, including—

(1) the canal and improvement of the waters between Lake Erie and Lake Huron; and

(2) the Saint Marys River and canal.

(b) RECIPROCITY.—This section does not apply after the President proclaims that privileges reciprocal to those under subsection (a) have been withdrawn or rendered inoperative by the Government of Canada.

(Pub. L. 109–304, §11, Oct. 6, 2006, 120 Stat. 1691.)

§80106. INTERNATIONAL AGREEMENT ON DERELICTS

The President may make an international agreement with other governments interested in the navigation of the North Atlantic Ocean, providing for the reporting, marking, and removal of dangerous wrecks, derelicts, and other menaces to navigation outside the coast waters of the countries bordering the North Atlantic Ocean.

(Pub. L. 109–304, §11, Oct. 6, 2006, 120 Stat. 1691.)

§80107. Salvors of life to share in remuneration

(a) Entitlement of Salvors.—A salvor of human life, who gave aid following an accident giving rise to salvage, is entitled to a fair share of the payment awarded to the salvor for salvaging the vessel or other property or preventing or minimizing damage to the environment.

(b) Common Ownership of Vessels.—The right to remuneration for aid or salvage services is not affected by common ownership of the vessels giving and receiving the aid or salvage services.

(c) Time Limit on Bringing Actions.—A civil action to recover remuneration for giving aid or salvage services must be brought within 2 years after the date the aid or salvage services were given, unless the court in which the action is brought is satisfied that during that 2-year period there had not been a reasonable opportunity to seize the aided or salvaged vessel within the jurisdiction of the court or within the territorial waters of the country of the plaintiff's residence or principal place of business.

(d) Nonapplication.—This section does not apply to a vessel of war or a vessel owned by the United States Government appropriated only to a public service.

(Pub. L. 109–304, §11, Oct. 6, 2006, 120 Stat. 1691.)

CHAPTER 803—ICE AND DERELICTS

§80301. International agreements

(a) General Authority.—The President may make agreements with interested maritime countries to—

(1) maintain in the North Atlantic Ocean a service of ice patrol, of study and observation of ice and current conditions, and of assistance to vessels and their crews requiring assistance within the limits of the patrol;

(2) maintain a service of study and observation of ice and current conditions in the waters affecting the set and drift of ice in the North Atlantic Ocean; and

(3) take all practicable steps to ensure the destruction or removal of derelicts in the northern part of the Atlantic Ocean, east of the line drawn from Cape Sable to a point in latitude 34 degrees north, longitude 70 degrees west, if the destruction or removal is necessary.

(b) Payment Between Countries.—The President may include in an agreement under subsection (a) a provision for—

(1) payment to the United States Government by other countries for their proportionate share of the expense of maintaining the services; or

(2) contribution by the Government for its proportionate share if the agreement provides for another country to maintain the services.

(c) PAYMENTS.—Payments received pursuant to subsection (b)(1) shall be credited to the appropriation for operations and support of the Coast Guard.

(Pub. L. 109–304, §11, Oct. 6, 2006, 120 Stat. 1692; Pub. L. 113–281, title III, §314(a)(1), Dec. 18, 2014, 128 Stat. 3049; Pub. L. 116–283, div. G, title LVXXXV [LXXXV], §8513(b), Jan. 1, 2021, 134 Stat. 4761.)

§80302. PATROL SERVICES

(a) GENERAL REQUIREMENTS.—Unless the agreements made under section 80301 of this title provide otherwise, an ice patrol shall be maintained during the entire ice season in guarding the southeastern, southern, and southwestern limits of the region of icebergs in the vicinity of the Grand Banks of Newfoundland. The patrol shall inform trans-Atlantic and other passing vessels by radio and other available means of the ice conditions and the extent of the dangerous region. During the ice season, there shall be maintained a service of study of ice and current conditions, a service of providing assistance to vessels and crews requiring assistance, and a service of removing and destroying derelicts. Any of these services may be maintained during the remainder of the year as may be advisable.

(b) WARNINGS TO VESSELS.—The ice patrol shall warn any vessel known to be approaching a dangerous area and recommend safe routes.

(c) RECORDING AND REPORTING INCIDENTS.—

(1) RECORDING.—The ice patrol shall record the name of a vessel and the facts of the case when the patrol observes or knows that the vessel—

(A) is on other than a regular recognized or advertised route crossing the North Atlantic Ocean;

(B) has crossed the fishing banks of Newfoundland north of latitude 43 degrees north during the fishing season; or

(C) has passed through regions known or believed to be endangered by ice when proceeding to and from ports of North America.

(2) REPORTING.—The name of the vessel and all pertinent information about the incident shall be reported to the government of the country to which the vessel belongs if that government requests.

(d) ADMINISTRATION.—The Commandant, under the direction of the Secretary of the department in which the Coast Guard is operating, shall carry out the services provided for in this section and shall assign necessary aircraft, material, and personnel of the Coast Guard. On request of such Secretary, the head of an agency may detail personnel, lend or contribute material or equipment, or otherwise assist in carrying out the services provided for in this section.

(e) ANNUAL REPORT.—The Commandant shall publish an annual report of the activities of the services provided for in this section. A copy of the report shall be provided to each interested foreign government and to each agency assisting in the work.

(Pub. L. 109–304, §11, Oct. 6, 2006, 120 Stat. 1692; Pub. L. 113–281, title III, §314(a)(2), Dec. 18, 2014, 128 Stat. 3049; Pub. L. 115–232, div. C, title XXXV, §3541(b)(16), Aug. 13, 2018, 132 Stat. 2324.)

§80303. SPEED OF VESSEL IN ICE REGION

(a) REQUIREMENT.—The master of a vessel of the United States, when ice is reported on or near the vessel's course, shall proceed at a moderate speed or change the course of the vessel to go well clear of the danger zone.

(b) CIVIL PENALTY.—A master violating this section is liable to the United States Government for a civil penalty of not more than $500.

(Pub. L. 109–304, §11, Oct. 6, 2006, 120 Stat. 1693.)

§80304. LIMITATION ON ICE PATROL DATA

Notwithstanding sections 80301 and 80302, data collected by an ice patrol conducted by the Coast Guard under this chapter may not be disseminated to a vessel unless such vessel is—

(1) documented under the laws of the United States; or

(2) documented under the laws of a foreign country that made the payment or contribution required under section 80301(b) for the year preceding the year in which the data is collected.

(Added Pub. L. 113–281, title III, §314(a)(3), Dec. 18, 2014, 128 Stat. 3049.)

CHAPTER 805—SAFE CONTAINERS FOR INTERNATIONAL CARGO

§80501. DEFINITIONS

In this chapter:

(1) CONTAINER.—The term "container" has the meaning given that term in the Convention.

(2) CONVENTION.—The term "Convention" means the International Convention for Safe Containers, and its annexes, done at Geneva, Switzerland, December 2, 1972.

(3) INTERNATIONAL TRANSPORT.—The term "international transport" means the

transportation of a container between—

    (A) a place in a foreign country and a place in the jurisdiction of the United States; or

    (B) two places outside the United States by United States carriers.

    (4) OWNER.—The term "owner" includes the lessee or bailee of a container if a written lease or bailment provides for the lessee or bailee to exercise the owner's responsibility for maintaining and examining the container.

    (5) SAFETY APPROVAL PLATE.—The term "safety approval plate" has the meaning given that term in annex I of the Convention.

(Pub. L. 109–304, §11, Oct. 6, 2006, 120 Stat. 1694.)

§80502. APPLICATION OF CONVENTION

The Convention applies to an owner of a container used in international transport if the owner is domiciled or has its principal office in the United States.

(Pub. L. 109–304, §11, Oct. 6, 2006, 120 Stat. 1694.)

§80503. GENERAL AUTHORITY OF THE SECRETARY

(a) IN GENERAL.—The Secretary of the department in which the Coast Guard is operating shall carry out the Convention and this chapter in the United States.

(b) REGULATIONS.—The Secretary shall prescribe regulations to carry out this chapter. The regulations shall—

    (1) establish procedures for testing, inspecting, and initially approving containers and designs for containers, including procedures for attaching, invalidating, and removing safety approval plates for containers;

    (2) establish procedures to be followed by the owners of containers for the periodic examination of containers as provided in the Convention; and

    (3) provide a method for developing, collecting, and disseminating information about container safety and the international transport of containers.

(c) SAFETY APPROVAL PLATES.—If the owner of a container without a safety approval plate establishes that the container satisfies the standards of the Convention, the Secretary may authorize a safety approval plate to be attached to the container.

(d) SCHEDULE OF FEES.—The Secretary may prescribe a schedule of fees for services performed by the Secretary, or by a person delegated authority under section 80506 of this title, for the testing, inspection, and initial approval of containers and container designs.

(e) ENCOURAGING INTERMODAL TRANSPORT.—To the maximum extent possible, the Secretary shall encourage the development and use of intermodal transport, using containers built to facilitate economical, safe, and expeditious handling of containerized cargo without intermediate reloading when it is being transported over land, air, and sea areas.

(Pub. L. 109–304, §11, Oct. 6, 2006, 120 Stat. 1694.)

§80504. APPROVAL AND EXAMINATION

(a) DOMICILE AND PRINCIPAL OFFICE IN UNITED STATES.—A container owner domiciled and having its principal office in the United States shall have the container—

(1) approved initially under procedures prescribed by the Secretary of the department in which the Coast Guard is operating or by the government of another country that is a party to the Convention; and

(2) examined periodically as provided in the Convention under procedures prescribed by the Secretary.

(b) DOMICILE OR PRINCIPAL OFFICE IN UNITED STATES.—A container owner domiciled or having its principal office in the United States shall have the container—

(1) approved initially under procedures prescribed by the Secretary or by the government of another country that is a party to the Convention; and

(2) examined periodically as provided in the Convention, under procedures prescribed by the government of the country in which the owner is domiciled or has its principal office, as long as that country is a party to the Convention.

(c) NEITHER DOMICILE NOR PRINCIPAL OFFICE IN UNITED STATES.—A container owner neither domiciled nor having its principal office in the United States or another country that is a party to the Convention may submit a container for initial approval and periodic examination under procedures prescribed by the Secretary.

(Pub. L. 109–304, §11, Oct. 6, 2006, 120 Stat. 1695.)

§80505. ENFORCEMENT

(a) IN GENERAL.—To enforce the Convention, this chapter, and regulations prescribed under this chapter, the Secretary of the department in which the Coast Guard is operating may—

(1) examine, or require to be examined, containers in international transport;

(2) approve designs for containers;

(3) inspect and test containers being manufactured;

(4) issue a detention order removing or excluding a container from service until the container owner satisfies the Secretary that the container meets the standards of the Convention, if the container—

(A) does not have a safety approval plate attached to it; or

(B) has a safety approval plate attached but there is significant evidence that the container is in a condition that creates an obvious risk to safety;

(5) take other appropriate action, including issuing necessary orders, to remove a container from service or restrict its use if the container is not in compliance with the Convention, this chapter, or regulations prescribed under this chapter, but does not present an obvious risk to safety; and

(6) allow a container found to be unsafe or without a safety approval plate to be moved to another location for repair or other disposition, under restrictions consistent with the intent of the Convention.

(b) Payment of Expenses.—

(1) Examination.—The owner of a container involved in an action by the Secretary under this section related to an examination of the container shall pay or reimburse the Secretary for the expenses arising from that action, except for the costs of routine examinations of the container or a safety approval plate.

(2) Testing, inspection, and initial approval.—The owner of a container submitted to the procedure established by the Secretary for testing, inspection, and initial approval, and the manufacturer of a container that submits a design to the procedure established by the Secretary for testing, inspection, and initial approval, shall pay or reimburse the Secretary for the expenses arising from the testing, inspection, or approval.

(3) Credit to appropriation.—Amounts received by the Secretary as reimbursement shall be credited to the appropriation for operations and support of the Coast Guard.

(c) Presumption Based on Safety Approval Plate.—A container bearing a safety approval plate authorized by a country that is a party to the Convention is presumed to be in a safe condition unless there is significant evidence that the container is in a condition that creates an obvious risk to safety.

(d) Notice of Orders.—

(1) In general.—When the Secretary issues a detention or other order under this section, the Secretary promptly shall notify in writing—

(A) the owner of the container;

(B) the owner's agent; or

(C) if the identity of the owner is not apparent from the container or shipping documents, the custodian.

(2) Information to include.—The notification shall identify the container involved, give the location of the container, and describe the condition or situation giving rise to the order.

(e) Duration of Orders.—An order issued by the Secretary under this section remains in effect until—

(1) the Secretary declares the container to be in compliance with the standards of the Convention; or

(2) the container is removed permanently from service.

(f) Notice of Defective Container to Country Issuing Safety Approval Plate.—If the Secretary has reason to believe that a container bearing a safety approval plate issued by another country was defective at the time of approval, the Secretary shall notify that country.

(Pub. L. 109–304, §11, Oct. 6, 2006, 120 Stat. 1695; Pub. L. 116–283, div. G, title LVXXXV [LXXXV], §8513(b), Jan. 1, 2021, 134 Stat. 4761.)

§80506. Delegation of authority

(a) In General.—The Secretary of the department in which the Coast Guard is operating may delegate to any person, including a public or private agency or nonprofit organization, authority to grant initial approval for containers and designs and to attach safety approval plates.

(b) REGULATIONS.—Before making a delegation under this section, the Secretary shall prescribe regulations establishing—

(1) criteria to be followed in selecting a person to whom authority is to be delegated;

(2) a detailed description of the duties and powers to be carried out by the person to whom authority is delegated, including the records the person shall keep; and

(3) the review the Secretary will conduct to decide whether the person is carrying out the delegated duties and powers properly.

(c) INSPECTION OF RECORDS.—A person delegated authority under this section shall make available to the Secretary for inspection, on request, records the person is required to keep.

(d) PENALTIES AND ORDERS.—A person delegated authority under this section may not—

(1) assess or collect, or attempt to assess or collect, a penalty for violation of the Convention, this chapter, or an order issued by the Secretary under this chapter; or

(2) issue or attempt to issue a detention or other order.

(e) PUBLICATION.—The Secretary shall publish in the Federal Register or other appropriate publication—

(1) the name and address of each person to whom authority is delegated;

(2) the duties and powers delegated; and

(3) the period of the delegation.

(f) REVOCATION.—The Secretary may revoke a delegation of authority under this section at any time.

(Pub. L. 109–304, §11, Oct. 6, 2006, 120 Stat. 1696.)

§80507. EMPLOYEE PROTECTION

(a) PROHIBITION.—A person may not discharge or discriminate against an employee because the employee has reported the existence of an unsafe container or a violation of this chapter or a regulation prescribed under this chapter.

(b) COMPLAINTS.—An employee alleging to have been discharged or discriminated against in violation of subsection (a) may file a complaint with the Secretary of Labor. The complaint must be filed within 60 days after the violation.

(c) ENFORCEMENT.—The Secretary of Labor may investigate the complaint. If the Secretary of Labor finds there has been a violation, the Secretary of Labor may bring a civil action in an appropriate district court of the United States. The court has jurisdiction to restrain violations of subsection (a) and order appropriate relief, including reinstatement of the employee to the employee's former position with back pay.

(d) NOTICE TO COMPLAINANT.—Within 30 days after receiving a complaint under this section, the Secretary of Labor shall notify the complainant of the intended action on the complaint.

(Pub. L. 109–304, §11, Oct. 6, 2006, 120 Stat. 1697.)

§80508. AMENDMENTS TO CONVENTION

(a) PROPOSALS BY UNITED STATES.—The Secretary of State, with the concurrence of the Secretary of the department in which the Coast Guard is operating, may propose amendments to the Convention or request a conference for amending the Convention as provided in article IX of the Convention.

(b) PROPOSALS BY OTHER COUNTRIES.—An amendment communicated to the United States under article IX(2) of the Convention may be accepted for the United States by the President, with the advice and consent of the Senate. The President may declare that the United States does not accept an amendment.

(c) AMENDMENTS TO ANNEXES.—

(1) IN GENERAL.—The Secretary of State, with the concurrence of the Secretary of the department in which the Coast Guard is operating—

(A) may propose amendments to the annexes to the Convention;

(B) may propose a conference for amending annexes to the Convention; and

(C) shall consider and act on amendments to the annexes to the Convention adopted by the Maritime Safety Committee of the International Maritime Organization and communicated to the United States under article X(2) of the Convention.

(2) ACTION FOLLOWING APPROVAL OR OBJECTION.—If a proposed amendment to an annex is approved by the United States, the amendment shall enter into force as provided in article X of the Convention. If a proposed amendment is objected to, the Secretary of State promptly shall communicate the objection as provided in article X(3) of the Convention.

(d) APPOINTMENT OF ARBITRATOR.—The Secretary of State, with the concurrence of the Secretary of the department in which the Coast Guard is operating, shall appoint an arbitrator when one is required to resolve a dispute within the meaning of article XIII of the Convention.

(Pub. L. 109–304, §11, Oct. 6, 2006, 120 Stat. 1697.)

§80509. CIVIL PENALTY

(a) IN GENERAL.—An owner, agent, or custodian who has been notified of an order issued under section 80505 of this title and fails to take reasonable and prompt action to prevent or stop a container subject to the order from being moved in violation of the order is liable to the United States Government for a civil penalty of not more than $5,000 for each container moved. Each day the container remains in service while the order is in effect is a separate violation.

(b) ASSESSMENT AND COLLECTION.—

(1) IN GENERAL.—After notice and an opportunity for a hearing, the Secretary of the department in which the Coast Guard is operating shall assess and collect any penalty under this section.

(2) FACTORS TO CONSIDER.—In determining the amount of the penalty, the Secretary shall consider the gravity of the violation, the hazards involved, and the record of the person charged with respect to violations of the Convention, this chapter, or regulations

prescribed under this chapter.

(3) REMISSION, MITIGATION, OR COMPROMISE.—The Secretary may remit, mitigate, or compromise a penalty under this section.

(4) ENFORCEMENT.—If a person fails to pay a penalty under this section, the Secretary shall refer the matter to the Attorney General for collection in an appropriate district court of the United States.

(Pub. L. 109–304, §11, Oct. 6, 2006, 120 Stat. 1698.)

SECTIONS 123(A), (B)1, AND 124 OF THE FRANK LOBIONDO COAST GUARD AUTHORIZATION ACT OF 2018

PUBLIC LAW 115-282

Frank LoBiondo Coast Guard Authorization Act of 2018

[(Public Law 115–282)]

[As Amended Through P.L. 117–263, Enacted December 23, 2022]

AN ACT To authorize appropriations for the Coast Guard, and for other purposes.

Be it enacted by the Senate and House of Representatives of the United States of America in Congress assembled,

SECTION 1. SHORT TITLE.

This Act may be cited as the "Frank LoBiondo Coast Guard Authorization Act of 2018".

SEC. 2. TABLE OF CONTENTS.

The table of contents of this Act is as follows:

* * * * * * *

TITLE I—REORGANIZATION OF TITLE 14, UNITED STATES CODE

* * * * * * *

SEC. 123. REFERENCES.

(a) **[14 U.S.C. 101 note]** DEFINITIONS.—In this section, the following definitions apply:

(1) REDESIGNATED SECTION.—The term "redesignated section" means a section of title 14, United States Code, that is redesignated by this title, as that section is so redesignated.

(2) SOURCE SECTION.—The term "source section" means a section of title 14, United States Code, that is redesignated by this title, as that section was in effect before the redesignation.

(b) REFERENCE TO SOURCE SECTION.—

(1) [14 U.S.C. 101 note] TREATMENT OF REFERENCE.—A reference to a source section, including a reference in a regulation, order, or other law, is deemed to refer to the corresponding redesignated section.

(2) [49 U.S.C. 303-305] TITLE 14.—In title 14, United States Code, each reference in the text of such title to a source section is amended by striking such reference and inserting a reference to the appropriate, as determined using the tables located in this title, redesignated section.

(c) OTHER CONFORMING AMENDMENTS.—

(1) REFERENCE TO SECTION 182.—Section 1923(c) of title 14, United States Code, as so redesignated by this title, is further amended by striking "section 182" and inserting "section 1922".

(2) REFERENCES TO CHAPTER 11.—Title 14, United States Code, is further amended—

(A) in section 2146(d), as so redesignated by this title, by striking "chapter 11 of this title" and inserting "this chapter"; and

(B) in section 3739, as so redesignated by this title, by striking "chapter 11" each place that it appears and inserting "chapter 21".

(3) REFERENCE TO CHAPTER 13.—Section 3705(b) of title 14, United States Code, as so redesignated by this title, is further amended by striking "chapter 13" and inserting "chapter 27".

(4) REFERENCE TO CHAPTER 15.—Section 308(b)(3) of title 14, United States Code, as so redesignated by this title, is further amended by striking "chapter 15" and inserting "chapter 11".

(5) REFERENCES TO CHAPTER 19.—Title 14, United States Code, is further amended—

  (A) in section 4901(4), as so redesignated by this title, by striking "chapter 19" and inserting "section 318"; and

  (B) in section 4902(4), as so redesignated by this title, by striking "chapter 19" and inserting "section 318".

  (6) REFERENCE TO CHAPTER 23.—Section 701(a) of title 14, United States Code, as so redesignated by this title, is further amended by striking "chapter 23" and inserting "chapter 39".

SEC. 124. [14 U.S.C. 101 note] RULE OF CONSTRUCTION.

This title, including the amendments made by this title, is intended only to reorganize title 14, United States Code, and may not be construed to alter—

  (1) the effect of a provision of title 14, United States Code, including any authority or requirement therein;

  (2) a department or agency interpretation with respect to title 14, United States Code; or

  (3) a judicial interpretation with respect to title 14, United States Code.

* * * * * * *